Christians in Asia
before 1500

Christians in Asia
before 1500

Ian Gillman
and
Hans-Joachim Klimkeit

Ann Arbor

THE UNIVERSITY OF MICHIGAN PRESS

© 1999 Ian Gillman and Hans-Joachim Klimkeit

Published in the United States of America by
The University of Michigan Press

2001 2000 1999 1998   4 3 2 1

Library of Congress Cataloging-in-Publication Data

Gillman, Ian.
    Christians in Asia before 1500 / Ian Gillman and Hans-Joachim
Klimkeit.
      p. cm.
    Includes bibliographical references and index.
    ISBN 0-472-11040-3 (alk. paper)
    1. Asia—Church history.   2. Church history—Primitive and early
church, ca. 30–600.   3. Church history—Middle Ages, 600–1500.
    I. Klimkeit, Hans-Joachim.   II. Title.
    BR1065.G55   1999
    275—dc21
                                                       98-47118
                                                        CIP

Contents

Maps and Plates

MAPS

PLATES
(between folios 186 & 187)

Foreword

From June 15 to 27, 1980, a conference gathered in Honolulu under the theme 'East-West Religions in Encounter: Buddhist-Christian Renewal and the Future of Humanity'. We two met at that conference, and common interests and ready personal rapport led to the conclusion that a book on this topic was overdue. So we resolved to attempt it together – and like many resolutions the fulfillment was long in appearing. The teaching and existing research commitments of each of us imposed their inevitable delays, and it was not until 1987 that it was possible to begin to give the task the attention it deserved.

Along the way we had decided on the division of labours, to make the most of the information to which we had access. It was determined, inter alia, that the overall editorial responsibility would be borne by Ian Gillman, if only because we decided that the volume should appear at first in English. So such responsibility rests with him, as does that for the chapters apart from those focussing on Central Asia and China, where Hans-Joachim Klimkeit has primary responsibility.

We had each been convinced for some years that there was a widespread ignorance primarily among Western Christians, but to some degree also among Asian Christians, about the history of Christianity in Asia prior to the arrival in AD 1498 of Vasco da Gama in Calicut. There was keen interest in a paper on the complex religious situation in medieval Central Asia, given by Professor Klimkeit, at that conference in Honolulu. In fact it was this paper which drew us together. The interest shown revealed that this lack of knowledge was not confined to general readers but was to be found also among scholars. Certainly it was a topic left untouched in the curriculum of church history courses undertaken by theological students. So, few, if any, ministers, pastors or priests were acquainted with it to any appreciable degree from their years of pre-ordination study.

Our purpose is to produce a work which would increase awareness of the history of Christianity in Asia from New Testament times to around AD 1500. Primarily it is aimed at general readers, theological students and those with an interest in missiology and the ways in which Christianity has related itself to various cultures. At the same time scholars may welcome a volume which brings together the results of research by many, results which are otherwise to be found in a multitude of monographs and periodicals.

In addition, in some particular areas, such as Central and South-East Asia, virtually new ground is broken or results made more generally known for what may well be the first time. It is no claim of ours to have been pioneers in all the areas covered. But we hope that we may fairly lay claim to having provided accounts which will enable a wide range of readers to enter into a new, and perhaps first, appreciation of a period in the history of Christianity which included remarkable achievements across vast distances, as well as some sad declines and tragic disasters.

An enterprise of this kind is only possible because of the labours of others upon whose specialist studies and publications we have drawn. It has also been dependent on library collections to be found in Germany, England, India, China and Australia, as well as to the art collection of the Oriental Department of the State Hermitage Museum (St. Petersburg, Russia), and our thanks are due to those who collect and care for such resources. So to all of those into whose labours we have entered and whose names appear in bibliographies and footnotes – as to librarians at large – we express our thanks.

Gratitude is due also to our two universities and to the departments within which each of us works:

- Frau Liesel Werner (of Bonn) and Mrs. Margaret Lewis (of St. Lucia) for their care with the typing of the manuscript and to Frau Claudia Seele as well as Frau Carmen Holzer (of Bonn), Mrs. Michelle Weil (of St. Lucia) and Ulrich Vollmer (of Bonn) for their editorial skills in the final stages;
- Suzanne Gray of the Graphic Art Unit of The University of Queensland for the preparation of the maps;
- the General Photographic Unit of The University of Queensland for the reproduction of the photographs and drawings.

It is extended also to our publishers and particularly to the 'German Academic Exchange Service' which supported Ian Gillman's stay in Germany in 1987, 1991 and 1995, as well as the German Research Society, the Klopstock Foundation, Hamburg, the Gerda Henkel Foundation, Düsseldorf, and the 'German Missiological Society' which gave means for procuring necessary literature. Thanks are also due to UNESCO, Paris, and especially to Mr. Doudou Diène of UNESCO's scheme 'Integral Study of the Silk Roads: Roads of Dialogue', for their interest in our work which led to the inclusion of this volume in the series of publications of that scheme. The authors are responsible for the choice and the presentation of the facts contained in this book and for the opinions expressed therein, which are not necessarily those of the 'Integral Study of the Silk Roads: Roads of Dialogue' Project and do not commit UNESCO.

That June 1980 conference, at the University of Hawaii, initiated not only this project but also the warm friendship within which it has proceeded – a friendship intensified by shared experiences, albeit brief, in Queensland and Germany.

Ian Gillman
Department of Studies in Religion
The University of Queensland
St Lucia/Australia

Hans-Joachim Klimkeit
Department of Religious Studies
The University of Bonn
Bonn/Germany

Abbreviations

AA	Acta Antiqua Academiae Scientiarum Hungaricae
ANFa	The Ante-Nicene Fathers
AoF	Altorientlische Forschungen
AOH	Acta Orientalia Academiae Scientiarum Hungaricae
APAW	Abhandlungen der Preussischen Akademie der Wissenschaften
AR	Arbeitsmaterialien zur Religionsgeschichte
ARWAW	Abhandlungen der Rheinisch-Westfälischen Akademie der Wissenschaften
AsF	Asiatische Forschungen
BJRL	Bulletin of the John Rylands Library
BSOAS	Bulletin of the School of Oriental and African Studies
BT	Berliner Turfantexte
CAJ	Central Asiatic Journal
ChH	Church History
ChinRec	Chinese Recorder
CleM	The Clergy Monthly
CSCO.Sub	Corpus Scriptorum Christianorum Orientalium. Subsidia
CStS	Collected Studies Series
IndAnt	The Indian Antiquary
JAC	Jahrbuch für Antike und Christentum
JAH	Journal of Asian History
JAOS	Journal of the American Oriental Society
JNCB	Journal of the North China Branch of the Royal Asiatic Society
JRAS	Journal of the Royal Asiatic Society
JRCAS	Journal of the Royal Central Asian Society
JRH	Journal of Religious History
JSFO	Journal de la Société Finno-Ougrienne
MAIS	Mémoirs de l'Académie Impériale des Sciences de St. Pétersbourg
MIO	Mitteilungen des Instituts für Orientforschung, Berlin
MSer	Monumenta Serica

NEMBN	Notices et extraits des manuscrits de la Bibliothèque Nationale et autres bibliothèques
NPNF	A Select Library of the Nicene and Post-Nicene Fathers of the Christian Church
OCA	Orientalia Christiana Analecta
OCP	Orientalia Christiana Periodica
OLA	Orientalia Lovanensia Analecta
PETSE	Papers of the Estonian Theological Society in Exile
RhWAW.G	Rheinisch-Westfälische Akademie der Wissenschaften, Düsseldorf. – Vorträge G, Geisteswissenschaften
RM	Die Religionen der Menschheit
SGKAO	Schriften zur Geschichte und Kultur des Alten Orients
SHR	Studies in the History of Religions
SPAW	Sitzungsberichte der Preussischen Akademie der Wissenschaften
StOR	Studies in Oriental Religions
TP	T'oung Pao
TRE	Theologische Realenzyklopädie
UAJb	Ural-Altaische Jahrbücher
VigChr	Vigiliae Christianae
WHS	Works Issued by the Hakluyt Society
ZAS	Zentralasiatische Studien
ZDMG	Zeitschrift der Deutschen Morgenländischen Gesellschaft
ZKG	Zeitschrift für Kirchengeschichte
ZMR	Zeitschrift für Missionskunde und Religionswissenschaft
ZRGG	Zeitschrift für Religions- und Geistesgeschichte

Chapter 1

Introduction

'Christians in Asia *before* 1500!?' This is likely to be the response of most people in the countries long occupied and more recently settled by Europeans. Such a response is not limited to those who have at best a marginal interest in the history of Christianity. It will be found also among many devout Christians and even among those who have undergone some systematic theological education. In part this response has its roots in ignorance – and that is forgivable to a degree. Less open to forgiveness are the various 'imperialisms' which undergird that ignorance. These are of three major types – political, intellectual and Scriptural.

The age of 'Western' imperialism, in terms of colonial empires, has almost passed, whatever may be said about it having been succeeded by forms of economic and ideological colonialism. The vestiges of 'Western' political colonialism to be found in such places as the South Pacific are under close scrutiny by the world community. But the ways of thinking built up over 400 years, since the Portuguese and Spanish began to build such empires in Africa, Asia and the Americas, have not passed out of currency among Europeans and their descendants elsewhere.

There remains ingrained within the consciousness and subconsciousness of such peoples a sense of superiority in things political, moral and technological. As Christianity has been intertwined with European history for well over 1600 years it is not unnatural, although it may be illogical, to extend that sense of primacy for things European to the area of Christianity also. It is assumed that Christianity is as 'Western' in its origins and its normative expressions as is 'Coca-Cola', regardless of where in the world it is found today.

There exists also in the minds of 'Westerners' a form of intellectual imperialism. It is rooted in the dramatic achievements of ancient Graeco-Roman civilization, and in the development of 'Western' scholarship since the Renaissance (14th–16th centuries) and the Enlightenment (17th–18th centuries). There is much here to explain the assumption of the superiority, as well as the distinctiveness of 'Western' intellectual processes and achievements. The legacies of Francis Bacon (1561–1626), René

1

Descartes (1596–1650), Immanuel Kant (1724–1804), Isaac Newton (1642–1727) and Albert Einstein (1879–1955) have included also, for Westerners today, an assumption that their ways of arriving at the truth of a matter are the only valid ways. Businessmen who enter negotiations with the Japanese or Chinese have learned to modify any such assumptions they bring to trade negotiations, if they are to attain their commercial objectives. Western scholars have not yet shown the same readiness to accept the possibility that there may be ways to the truth other than those to which they are accustomed. There is still much to be learned from such a book as that of Hajime Nakamura, entitled *Ways of Thinking of Eastern Peoples: India, China, Tibet, Japan,* first published by East West Center Press in 1964.

Not to be prepared to learn and not uncritically to understand, is to cut oneself off from alternative, and by no means inappropriate ways of arriving at valid conclusions. And it is to subject such Asian peoples to a form of imperialism no less arrogantly presumptuous than was that of the Conquistadors.

If a number of these assumptions lie deep, and are but rarely if ever recognized by 'Westerners' and those who have absorbed such 'Western' attitudes, there is another imperialism that has a particular effect on Christians from such lands. It is not only that, on the whole, they have tended to focus attention on the development of Latin Christianity, in both its Catholic and Protestant expressions, in their awareness of church history. This has been tragic enough in that it has resulted in their being largely ignorant of the great tradition represented by Eastern Orthodoxy, and those age-old Churches which developed outside the boundaries of the ancient Roman Empire.

It goes deeper than that, for it is grounded in, and given normalcy by, the very shape of the New Testament. The list of books accepted as authoritative and which make up the New Testament today (i.e. the canon) was determined in the West over a number of centuries. While the gospels and much of the Acts of the Apostles concern people and events in Palestine, Egypt and Syria and have one reference to Arabia, the bulk of the epistles and the Revelation of St. John are applied primarily to areas west of the 'Middle East' (itself a European convention, as an Australian knows full well, for he must regard the so-called 'Middle East' as the 'Middle North-West', and the 'Far East' as the 'Middle and Far North'). That, and the primacies of the Bishops of Rome in the Latin 'West' and of the Bishops of Constantinople in the Greek 'East', have conspired to give to 'Western' presumptions something of the sanctity of Holy Writ itself. Nothing in the New Testament readings, heard Sunday by Sunday for centuries, has spurred Western Christians to think further east than the River Jordan and the Gadarene area of the Decapolis in their environing of Christianity in the first few centuries of this era.

Of course, when pressed, such Christians will admit quite readily that their religion had its beginnings in Asia among Asians, and this despite the fact that some artists in the West have depicted Jesus as if he were of Nordic origins. They may even admit that Christianity has its roots in Asia as much as does Islam, Hinduism, Buddhism and Zoroastrianism – not to mention Judaism. Not one of the great world religions had its origin in Europe – whatever the influence of European thought and categories etc. upon them. This very fact, in a somewhat paradoxical fashion may help to explain why Westerners want to think that Christianity is in some way 'European' – a sort of religious gamesmanship not unrelated to the desire to have an apostle as the founder of your particular Church.

Linked to the above 'imperialisms' is a consequence of them and the historical development of those forms of Christianity with which Westerners are familiar. There can be no doubt that contemporary expressions of Christianity, Catholic, Protestant and Eastern Orthodox, show not only traces of the religion's roots in Judaism but also the strong influence of Platonic, Aristotelian, Stoic and neo-Platonic thought – and one might add Manichaeism also in the case of that great formative thinker, Augustine of Hippo (d. AD 430). Prime examples of such influ-ences, familiar to all, are the widespread belief of many Christians in the 'immortality of the soul', a belief most commonly associated with Plato, which stands in contrast to the Christian doctrine of the 'resurrection of the body'; the extolling of Stoic virtues as if, per se, they were Christian; the tendency to regard 'ignorance' as a sin more dangerous than 'wilful autonomy'; and the denigration of the 'material world' and the exaltation of 'things spiritual'. Amongst those of the Catholic and Protestant traditions there is evident also the influence of the Roman legal cast of mind. Perhaps this is most obvious in such phenomena as the belief that every 'mystery' of the faith can be and should be defined, even those of the 'how' of the Eucharist, and the ways in which God's grace and human response are related to each other. It appears also in those theories of the atonement which are dependent on the work of Anselm of Canterbury (d. AD 1109) with the consequent difficulty experienced in relating such legalistic theories to the essential 'union symbolism' of the two great sacraments of Baptism and Holy Communion.

That all this has led to a form of syncretism, to varying degrees, in Latin and Greek Christianity is as undeniable as it is inevitable. What is unjustifiable is the conviction held by many from those same traditions that, while their forms of syncretism are not only permissible but also divinely approved, the syncretisms of others put the 'faith once delivered to the saints' in jeopardy. This attitude set at nought the valiant attempts of Matteo Ricci S.J. (d. AD 1610) in China and of Roberto di Nobili S.J. (d. AD 1656) in South India, to provide expressions of Christianity less dependent on the Graeco-Roman heritage and more attuned to those of

Confucianism and of Hinduism respectively. Such efforts were condemned by the Vatican and discontinued at its insistent direction, until greater wisdom prevailed in the latter half of this century.

The fear of non-European syncretism, thus implanted, has been for generations an unwarranted hindrance to the development of valid expressions of Christianity in Asia and elsewhere, expressions which relate more closely to the cultures involved. While it may be superficially comforting for the Western visitor to find Protestants in Japan worshipping and theologizing in ways distinctively European and North American, it is at depth disturbing. Western attitudes and demands have combined with local fears of wandering back into old attitudes from which they have been delivered, to make it difficult to be both authentically Christian and authentically Japanese – a problem with which Japanese Christians are by no means unfamiliar.

Last, in this catalogue of Western 'failures' is the heritage of text-books and teachers who have encouraged generations of children to believe that Vasco da Gama (d. AD 1524) 'discovered' India in 1498. That he found a new way to India via the Cape of Good Hope, and had the help of an Indian pilot for the last leg from the east coast of Africa tends to be glossed over. That India was long known in and traded with by ancient Europe, and that it had a succession of visitors from Europe who wrote of their experiences there up until several decades before da Gama's arrival in 1498 is either unknown or ignored. Yet who has not heard of Marco Polo (d. AD 1324) at least? Such facts have been obscured as thoroughly as has knowledge of the epic Chinese voyages to Africa, and possibly to Australia, in the 14th century. The European sense of supremacy is made uncomfortable by such facts.

No less discomforting is the 'news' that Christianity had reached and been founded in China within a generation of the death of Augustine of Canterbury in AD 604. It seems hard for many to credit that missionaries were on their way east to China at the same time as Augustine was travelling north-west from Rome, passing a number of Irish-founded monasteries, on his way to England; – and all of this some 120 years before Boniface began the evangelisation of Germany. Likewise it is 'news' to most that the first country to adopt Christianity on a national basis was Armenia, about a decade before the religion was granted toleration in the Roman Empire, and almost eighty years before it was established as the official religion of that Empire. As a final straw there may come the shattering revelation that Christians in South India have a long-held claim to the foundation of their Church by the Apostle Thomas, a claim virtually as old and as strong as that of Rome to St. Peter and far better substantiated than those of Scotland and Russia to St. Andrew.

Perhaps the strangeness of all this is best captured by the following passage from D. F. Lach and C. Flaumenhaft, a description which applies

4

strictly not to the arrival of the first Portuguese fleet under da Gama, but to that of the second fleet in 1500 under Pedro Cabral (d. AD 1526). Nevertheless, its impact and 'the turning on the head' of our usual presuppositions are salutary:

> 'How would Portugal and Europe have reacted in 1498 if they had been "discovered" by Asians? Suppose several strange ships manned by odd-looking foreigners had dropped anchor at Lisbon, and, after a friendly reception by the King, had suddenly bombarded some ships in Lisbon harbour before sailing off with a trio of hostages to some unknown destination.'[1]

Numbers of Western and Asian scholars have been aware for generations that such presumptions as those outlined here are invalid despite the breadth of their currency. Detailed studies of the history, growth and decline, literature and art of Christians across Asia before 1500, have appeared in both scholarly journals and in books which have had limited circulations. The most complete treatment, together with a survey of literature, is to be found in P. Kawerau, *Ostkirchengeschichte*, I: *Das Christentum in Asien und Afrika bis zum Auftreten der Portugiesen im Indischen Ozean*, Louvain 1983 (CSCO.Sub 70). Readers are referred also to a work published in the final stage af the preparation of this volume, viz. S. H. Moffett, *A History of Christianity in Asia*, vol. 1: *Beginnings to 1500*, San Francisco 1992. The authors of this volume are convinced that the time has long since come when Christians outside Asia were made aware of the long history and achievements of those of their faith in that continent before the arrival of da Gama. Equally they are convinced that Christians in Asia today should be aware and proud of the heritage that is theirs, and so be able to cast off once and for all, any necessity to be regarded as 'younger Churches' – a title which carried with it echoes of the paternalism of the 'West'.

But what is meant by 'Asia' in this context? For our purposes it is that land mass and the islands off shore, to the east of the coastline of modern Israel, Lebanon and Syria, and the eastern shores of the Black Sea, to Japan; and south of the 60° N parallel of latitude to include modern Indonesia. The major areas which will concern us will be ancient and medieval Syria and Arabia, Armenia, Georgia, Mesopotamia, Iran, Afghanistan, India, Sri Lanka, Central Asia, Mongolia and China; with some reference to Tibet, South-East Asia, Indonesia and Japan. Within this are to be found today the world's two most populous nations and by far most of the world's Hindus, Buddhists, and Muslims. For all that, it is an area all too easily by-passed by Europeans and North Americans in their apprehensions of the world.

It is our hope that this survey will increase awareness among Christians at least, and promote greater understanding.

5

FURTHER READING

Nakamura, H.: *Ways of Thinking of Eastern Peoples. India, China, Tibet, Japan*, Honolulu 1964 – To read the Introduction would provide useful insights on its own.

Lach, D. F. & Flaumenhaft, C. (eds.): *Asia on the Eve of Europe's Expansion*, Englewood Cliffs, N.J. 1965.

Panikkar, K. M.: *Asia and Western Dominance*, 5th impr., London 1959.

Lach, D. F.: *Asia in the Making of Europe*, vol. 1, 2nd ed., Chicago 1971.

Chapter 2

Apostolic Times and Apostolic Traditions

If you were to walk down the Strand in London, leaving Trafalgar Square behind you, until you reached the famed 'oranges and lemons' church of St. Clement's Dane you would have passed Somerset House on your right and be within a few paces of St. Catherine's House. If then you proceeded to Chancery Lane you would find the census records room in the Public Records Office. In any one of these places, the census records office, St. Catherine's House or Somerset House, you will encounter on any week day, dozens of people intent on a quest. In the census records office they stare at the screens of microfilm readers, in a room filled with rows of these machines. At St. Catherine's House they will be poring over large volumes listing births, deaths and marriages. In Somerset House they will be searching for and examining wills and other legal documents related to the estates of those long dead.

You will hear, also, a babel of accents and the ages of the researchers will range from those in the late teens to those of advanced years. There will be cries of exaltation and groans of despair. Some will leave with an air of pleasure and achievement; others will wear looks of frustration and disappointment. All of them are about the task of unearthing their 'roots', by tracing ancestors – *if* they can find them in the records.

Such an interest has increased among many in the West in recent years and genealogy is a growth area, as publishers can testify. Yet it is not something entirely new, for knowing a family tree has been of significance to many, in so far as it applies not only to humans, but also to such as horses, cats and dogs, for example. Nor is it a matter of common concern only for colleges of heralds or family or clan societies in Europe, North America and elsewhere. In a society as different from these as was that of the Pacific Islanders, being able to recite accurately the names of one's ancestors for a large number of generations was commonplace, and this long before that society had committed its languages to writing. The same could be said for non-literate societies elsewhere.

While this activity remains important for a range of people from royalty to greyhound breeders, it has had, also, a deep significance for the

Church. For centuries lists have been kept of the names of bishops of dioceses and of ministers of parishes. If these lists have about them, in earliest times, more of an air of hopeful imagination than of hard fact, this seems to cause little concern despite the fact that much hangs on such succession lists. While on one hand the Roman claim to primacy in the Church rests on the contention that the Bishop of Rome is the successor today of Simon Peter, the chief apostle, others go back one step further and claim to be in 'succession from Christ'. So the secular genealogists have parallels in the ecclesiastical realm.

One of the boons for those who research their own family is that they may find that they have one or more distinguished ancestors. Human nature is such that it finds it as difficult to keep such a distinction quiet as it finds it easy to forget an ancestor whose life or death was one of shame. (The luminosity of the distinguished one is usually enough to put several of the shady ones well into the shadow of oblivion.)

So it should not be difficult for us to understand that an early congregation of Christians revelled in the fact, if it was such, that it had an apostle as the founder of its community. It was on a par with being one of the congregations like Philippi, Thessalonica, Rome, and even Corinth, who had received letters directly from St. Paul. The next best thing was to come from an area like Galatia, or, if such specificity failed, to surround an epistle with no stated address with the tradition that it was directed to the 'Ephesians'. On the other hand there was little to provide comfort if you were one of six out of the seven churches mentioned in Revelation 1–3 – as was Ephesus itself (see Revelation 2:1–7).

Of course your cup would be full to overflowing if you had more than one apostle associated with your Church and an apostolic letter directed to you as well – as was the case with Rome. That would allow you to take in your stride the claim of Antioch to Peter as its founder before he ever went to Rome and its claim also to associations with St. Paul. There is no apostolic letter addressed to the Church of Jesus Christ at Antioch, and not one of the apostles is reported to have died there. Jerusalem of course was a special case, but after Jewish revolts it virtually ceased to exist, being replaced by the Roman colony of Aelia, until its fortunes were revived by the interest of Helena, the mother of Constantine the Great, early in the 4th century. By that time other claims to primacy had been staked and registered, if not always universally accepted.

The matter of apostolic succession assumed greater significance, both ecclesiastical and political, among those cities which had claims to leadership in the ancient world. The Church in Antioch and that in Rome could each point to St. Peter as its founder. The Alexandrian Church had to be content to claim Mark, an evangelist and close confidant of St. Peter, if only an erstwhile one of St. Paul (Acts 15:37–41). A new necessity arose when in AD 330 Constantine set up a new capital for the Roman Empire on the site of the ancient town of Byzantium. It was to be 'New' or 'Second' Rome, or, as it was more widely known, Constantinople.

For perfectly understandable reasons old Rome and its bishops were suspicious of this new capital and the ambitions of its bishops. Attempts were made by the rulings of ecumenical councils to bolster the claims of the Bishops of Constantinople to virtual parity with the Bishops of Rome – not that the latter would ever accept and promulgate such rulings in the areas under their direct jurisdiction. While Rome may refuse to accept and so ignore the canons which sought to give Constantinople virtual parity with it, it was not possible to ignore the claim to apostolic foundation of 'New Rome' by St. Andrew, anymore than it would resile from its claim to foundation by St. Peter. (Although Andrew never had the status accorded to his brother, Peter, his membership with James and John and Peter of the inner circle of disciples notwithstanding.)

This case illustrates the power of necessity, as this was understood at the time. Of course it continued to make its impact later and elsewhere, as we find with both the Scots and the Russians claiming associations with the same St. Andrew, the English with St. George of Asia Minor, and the French attempt in the 9th century to associate its patron saint, Denis, with the reputedly apostolic Dionysius (or Denis) the Areopagite. As the last case shows, if the cold hard facts of history were in short supply, much of any deficiency could be made up with a little imagination. The odd vision or two and the writings of later enthusiasts, not unwilling to embroider existing legends or to add one or two of their own – all with the best of intentions of course did the rest. One of the results of such activity was that some apostles seem to have been as omnipresent as was George Washington, to judge from the number of places in which he is supposed to have slept in the United States.

Most of us are well aware of the journeys of St. *Paul* outlined as they are in the Acts of the Apostles. Scripture leaves him in Rome, where tradition has it that, with St. *Peter*, he was executed by Nero in AD 64. The details of Peter's journeys are not as clear, but obviously he covered much of Palestine and Syria, visited Galatia, and by tradition was in Rome. *James*, one of the sons of Zebedee, died a martyr in Jerusalem, although some traditions would have us believe that he preached in Spain, prior to his death. *John*, his brother, spent his later years in Ephesus, and died there, once again according to later tradition, while *Andrew* is said to have preached in Greece and to have been martyred there. (At least that gave some regional association with Constantinople.) It is reported that *Matthew* preached and died in Ethiopia, although some traditions locate his ministry and death in Persia. *Philip* is reputed to have preached in Phrygia and to have died at Herapolis, near Laodicea and Colossae in Asia Minor while nothing is known of the ministries of *James the Less* or of *Matthias* (who replaced Judas Iscariot as one of the twelve, in Acts 1:15–26).

Apart from the rather remote possibility that Matthew had some associations with Persia, none of the above apostles of whom scripture and tradition records anything, ministered in the Asia which concerns us – apart i.e. from Syria itself.

But we are left with four apostles for whom we have not accounted. The two most shadowy of these are *Jude* (or *Thaddeus*) and *Simon the Zealot*. They are linked together in a number of ancient traditions. Simon is said to have first gone to Egypt and Jude to Mesopotamia, but together they are reported to have ministered in Edessa and in Persia. Some accounts say that they were martyred at Sufian in Persia while others point to Edessa as the place of death. Their deaths are remembered on the same day in the calendar within the Roman Catholic Church. At least with these two apostles we have traditions which point strongly to Mesopotamia and to Persia.

Points further east are associated with both the remaining apostles, Bartholomew (or Nathanael) and Thomas. *Bartholomew* is associated in tradition with a number of countries in Asia, most notably with Armenia where he is said to have been flayed alive at Derbend on the Caspian Sea. But there is too an earlier tradition, reported by the 4th century bishop-historian Eusebius of Caesarea and echoed by Jerome, that Bartholomew ministered also in India. To that possibility we shall have to return.

Thomas was reputedly the most travelled of all the apostles for not only are there traditional associations with Edessa, where reputedly his relics were interred until transferred to the West, but also with Parthia, according to the report of Eusebius of Caesarea. However, another tradition linking him both to Edessa and to India and even to China, begins with the so-called *Acts of Thomas*, seen by some as a Gnostic document dating from the 3rd century. Certainly by the 4th century there is a strong tradition that he ministered to both North-West and South India, and that he was martyred at Mylapore near present day Madras. A 7th century source brings much of this traditional material together, but locates the place of death in India at Calamine. While Western scholarship has serious reservations about the substance of these Indian claims, they are not only accepted but are defended fiercely by Christians in South India to this day. To this matter we have to return also in subsequent pages.

We have just referred to the questioning attitude of Western scholarship towards many of these traditional claims. Given the modern canons of historiography which are accepted and used throughout the world today, and given also the lack of contemporary documentary, epigraphical and archaeological evidence to confirm in detail the traditional claims about the apostles, such scholarly doubts are both understandable and defensible. However, they may carry no more ultimate disturbance of those who cling to these ancient traditions than could the doubts and questions of the Pharisees the convictions of the man born blind but given his sight by Jesus in John 9. Apostolic convictions seem not to be open to demolition by such scholarly scepticism. This raises the interesting question as to which has the greater long term importance – clearly established historical veracity or an ongoing enlivening tradition which has given and continues to give purpose, dignity and significance to the lives of thousands? The authors of this book belong to a scholarly tradition which would incline them to stress historical veracity – but they are aware also of that dynamic inherent in the traditions with which we have been dealing. It may be that for overlong we in the West have given overmuch importance to the conviction that in uncovering the origins of something we reveal also the heart of its significance. Perhaps the ongoing and ever changing influence of a belief outweighs the importance of its origins. This is a tension we will carry with us as we turn to explore the particular areas of Asia and the lives of early Christians there.

FURTHER READING

Consult articles about the 'apostles' in religious encyclopedias such as Cross, F. L. & Livingstone, E. A. (eds.): *The Oxford Dictionary of the Christian Church*, 2nd ed., London 1974, or any dictionary of the saints and Browning, R.: *The Twelve Apostles*, New York 1974.

'The Acts of Thomas' is available in any edition of the New Testament Apocrypha, e.g. that of M. R. James, Oxford 1924, or E. Hennecke and W. Schneemelcher, vol. 2, London 1965.

Note also the comments on historicity's limits by Williams, H. A.: *Some Day I'll Find You. An Autobiography*, London 1984, pp. 367–371.

Chapter 3

A Necessary Excursus into Theology

This work cannot unfold without reference to the various 'Christianities' which bear such titles as 'Catholic' or 'Orthodox', 'Nestorian', and 'Monophysite' or 'Jacobite'. Then too we have that self-declared form of purified and enlightened Christianity known as '*Manichaeism*' as well as the widely-held understanding of the world and of human existence called '*Gnosticism*'. While it may not be necessary to spell out the details of Hindu, Buddhist, Zoroastrian and Muslim beliefs, it is important that we grasp the essentials of the forms of Christianity or quasi-Christianity which we shall meet. This we will attempt to do as painlessly and clearly as possible.

The earliest Christians faced the problem of holding together the monotheism they inherited from Judaism, the revelation they had in Jesus of Nazareth, and the continuing experience of the presence, guidance and empowerment of the Holy Spirit. On one hand there was a necessary and fundamental stress on the oneness of God. On the other hand an inescapable emphasis on the threeness involved in that revelation.

Various proposals were advanced to overcome this dilemma in the first three centuries of the Christian era, but, on the whole they fell into two classes. Some ascribed the fulness of divinity to God the Father alone, and lesser qualities of divinity to the Son and to the Holy Spirit. This approach was called 'subordinationism' or 'dynamic monarchianism', the latter name referring to the fact that the full power (Greek: *dynamis*) of God was reserved to the one ruler-monarch – God the Father. Foremost among proponents of this approach was Paul of Samosata, who was, until deposed in the mid-third century, Bishop of Antioch, a centre which has importance for our later concerns.

The other class of proposals argued that the one God revealed himself in three distinct forms or 'modes', and from the last term this was called 'modalistic monarchianism'. At no one time was God to be thought of as simultaneously being Father, Son and Spirit under this approach, which was seen to preserve the fulness of the divinity of both the Son and the Spirit. The leading proponent of this view was Sabellius, in the opening

13

decades of the 3rd century. After gaining early support it was rejected vehemently as being false to the data of revelation.

Matters came to a head early in the 4th century with the subordinationist views of Arius of Alexandria (d. AD 336). The first ecumenical council of the Church, planned initially for Ancyra (Ankara) and eventually held at *Nicea in AD 325* had to add this issue to its agenda. The creeds, referred to as 'ecumenical' were drafted originally in the Greek language and adopted in their Greek forms. Translations into Latin and Syriac, e.g., would work their own subtle changes on the original text, as of course would later translations into English, German, French etc. The resultant Creed of Nicea came out against the Arian view that the Son of God was to be numbered with the creatures, albeit the 'first-born', and described him as 'of the substance of the Father, God of God, Light of Light, very God of very God, begotten not made'. There was no doubt from this about the full divinity of the Son. Nor was there doubt about his essential humanity, for the creed declared also that he 'was incarnate and was made man'.

The Creed of Nicea did not receive whole-hearted support from most in the Greek East at first, because of suspicions that it was tainted with Sabellianism, and also because of the political wheeling and dealing of the followers of Arius, who included, eventually, several of the emperors. However, by the time of the second ecumenical council at *Constantinople in AD 381*, the declarations of Nicea had taken root. Later generations regarded that second council as having expanded the document from Nicea to deal equally with the divinity of the Holy Spirit. He had rated a mere mention in AD 325, but thereafter was described as 'the Lord, and Giver of Life . . . who with the Father and the Son together is worshipped and glorified'. This creed also set out to exclude the late 4th century heresy of Apollinarius of Laodicea (d. ca. AD 390), who had held that in Jesus Christ we are met by one with a fully divine soul/mind and a human body (see also p. 40). In the eyes of his critics this left the human soul outside the redemption wrought by the Christ. Despite it having been an early attempt to avoid sundering the divine and the human in Jesus Christ, the view was condemned.

Indeed note must be taken of the fact that the key concern in all these debates was to ensure the redeeming work of Jesus Christ. As was said, in criticism of Apollinarius' view, 'a half human Saviour is only useful for a half-fallen humanity' – and – 'what he did not take he did not redeem'. Whatever the form of words used the ability of Jesus Christ to redeem was tied to the fulness of his divinity, and our involvement in redemption tied to the fulness of his humanity.

The expansion of the creed of Nicea, traced to Constantinople (AD 381) is what is known today as the '*Nicene Creed*'.

So by AD 381 the vast majority of Christians within the Roman Empire, and some outside its boundaries (like those in Persia and India – but not the Goths who remained committed to Arianism) had accepted the declaration that the Son of God, who took flesh in Jesus the Christ, was truly God, and that the incarnate one was also truly man.

This set up the agenda for the next debate as the Nicene declaration required you to ascribe simultaneously to the one logical subject, Jesus Christ, two natures, one divine and the other human.[1] But this broke the current assumptions of logic in that it was required that for any one logical subject there could be only one nature. This would indicate that if you began with two natures, one divine and the other human, you would need two logical subjects, one for each nature – the Christ for the divine nature and Jesus of Nazareth for the human nature. Alternatively, if you began with Jesus Christ as the one logical subject, logically you could have but one nature. In less precise language something of the same approach could be expressed if you were to affirm that in the incarnate one there was to be found one logical subject '*out of*' two 'natures' rather than '*in*' two 'natures'.

The debate raged for some 70 years before there was an official, but not universally accepted, resolution of it. The controversy was shot through with personal and regional rivalries, not least that between the two great cities of Antioch and Alexandria. The discussions were complicated by the fact that while Antioch's presuppositions were Aristotelian, historical and exegetical, those of Alexandria were Platonic, philosophical and theological, not that such distinctions would have been clearly recognized at the time. With such differences in presuppositions it was inevitable that one would misunderstand the statements of the other, given the political fact that each was anxious to put the other in the worst possible light.

A number of paradoxes resulted. A leader of the Antiochene school, Nestorius (d. AD 451), was dethroned from his bishopric of Constantinople by the third ecumenical council at *Ephesus in AD 431* for supposedly holding to a two nature/two subject view of Christ, a view which was given the name of 'Nestorianism'. (However, it is almost certain that he did not hold to such a view himself.) On the other hand, the views of his main antagonist, Cyril of Alexandria (d. AD 444), were seen as providing the basis for a one subject/one nature view, although again it is more than doubtful that he himself was a 'mono-physite'. Such facts did not prevent the ensuing Nestorian and Monophysite schools from claiming to be following respectively the 'blessed Nestorius' or the 'blessed Cyril'.

Most of this debate was centered in the Greek speaking, eastern half of the Empire, as was most theological formulation for the first five centuries. But by AD 449, as the Alexandrians continued to pursue their Antiochene rivals, the Bishop of Rome, Leo I (d. ca. AD 461), entered the lists with his *Tome*, a theological statement which gave due weight to the two natures without departing from the affirmation of but one logical subject. Such a view triumphed at the fourth ecumenical council at *Chalcedon in AD 451*, and was expressed in the 'Chalcedonian formula'. This not only re-affirmed what had been said previously (up to Ephesus AD 431) but declared that Jesus Christ was to be acknowledged in two natures, without the natures being fused together or undergoing change into one nature and without them being separated or divided between two logical subjects, i.e. it denied both the so-called Monophysite and Nestorian positions. The council drove home the point by declaring that:

> 'The distinction of the natures, being by no means taken away by the union (in the one subject), but rather the property of each nature being preserved, and concurring in one subject and one subsistence, not parted or divided into two subjects.'

The council had made a declaration which violated common logical assumptions, but, as it saw it, was faithful to the data of the revelation. And it was this declaration which was regarded as the test of orthodoxy by both Rome and Constantinople. But Chalcedon was paradoxical in that while it praised Cyril of Alexandria it denounced the one-nature Christology which many saw as essential to his position; and while it condemned Nestorius it espoused a two-nature Christology.

For reasons to do with differing theologies, but also with national and cultural antipathies to the Graeco-Roman establishment, two major dissident groups emerged. The vast majority of those who had admired Nestorius and his predecessors at the Antioch school, Diodore of Tarsus (d. ca. AD 394) and Theodore of Mopsuestia (d. AD 428), moved out of Syria into Mesopotamia and Persia. They propounded the views ascribed to Nestorius and were called '*Nestorians*' by their adversaries. By the end of the 5th century they had come to dominate the Church in Persia and became thereafter the great missionaries of their form of Christianity across Asia.

In the Egyptian and Syrian countrysides the viewpoint ascribed to Cyril of Alexandria became known as *Monophysitism.* Spreading south from Egypt into Ethiopia and to points east of Syria in Persia where it competed with Nestorianism for the hearts of the inhabitants, it remained a thorn in the side of the imperial authorities. Fruitlessly they tried both persecution and compromise to overcome such dissidence in one sensitive area on the border with Persia and in the other which was one of the main granaries of the Empire. The Monophysites of Syria and points east took the name of *Jacobites*, from Jacob Baradai (d. AD 578), one of their chief leaders and organizers. Those in Egypt were known in the main, as *Copts* and their form of Church and theology as *Coptic*, this latter name coming from the Greek word for an Egyptian. While the two groups of Monophysites had much in common, they were not without schisms between them from time to time.

Each of the three parties, Orthodox-Catholic-Chalcedonian; Nestorian; and Monophysite-Jacobite-Coptic, accused the others of heresy, despite

16

the undoubted fact that all three held with enthusiasm to the 'Nicene Creed'. The affirmations of this creed were to be found in widespread areas of Asia, including a 7th–8th-century Sogdian Nestorian version from Central Asia. Similarly there is a Chinese version of the 'Gloria Patri' which comes from 7th–10th century Tunhuang on the eastern end of the famous 'Silk Road' and it too reflects faithfully the form used in the West.

Throughout we should remember that, with the Nestorians (and the Monophysites) rejecting Chalcedon's formulation, we would not expect to see reflections of it in any of their creeds. One might as well try to measure metre distances with an imperial measure ruler! As they all held to the 'Nicene Creed' that is the measure to be used. Indeed is there any Nestorian Creed which spells out an alternative to Chalcedon in explicit terms? Another parallel would be that one will be disappointed if looking for the canon of Chalcedon which raises Constantinople to virtual parity with Rome in any Latin version of the canons authorised by the papacy.

However, the names of the key leaders in their respective traditions were included in liturgies, and traditional opponents were denounced vigorously. In this way, at least, if not in continuing debate among all Church members, the issues were perpetuated. But we may be forgiven for wondering what such references meant to devout worshippers within decades of the schisms, apart from symbols of identification. This the Portuguese discovered when they encountered the Thomas Christians on the Malabar coast of South India in the 16th century.

Christianity, of whatever form did not have a monopoly in the area of offers of eternal salvation, in what was very much a buyers' market. Across Asia Christianity was in competition with ancient faiths such as Hinduism, Buddhism, Zoroastrianism, and occasionally Judaism, each with its distinctive understanding of the ultimate(s) and each with its own way to peace in this world and in any hereafter. In due time it was also to meet the challenge of Islam, the creed which in the end, largely by force of arms under Timur the Lame (d. AD 1405), obliterated it in those areas of Asia in which it was once at its strongest.

However, two other competitors shared not a little with Christianity at least in terminology, but ante-dated Islam. Consequently these two offered challenges of particular power, both inside and outside the Roman Empire.

Gnosticism was the older of these two rivals and there is much debate among scholars as to the time and place of its origins, but Jewish and Jewish-Christian roots are by no means excluded. Certainly the forms considered most dangerous by Christians post-dated the 1st century AD and reached their peaks of influence in the 2nd century. Gnosticism was an eclectic understanding of existence which combined Persian, Egyptian, Stoic, Platonic and Pythagorean emphases with some drawn from Christianity. It included a dualism of spirit and matter, with the former exalted and the latter decried. One consequence of this was the claim by the Gnostics that Jesus only seemed to be human – a view called 'Docetism' from the Greek word 'to seem'. Salvation from this world and its woes, and the recovery of one's temporarily lost divinity was available through secret knowledge (Greek: *gnosis*). This *gnosis* was only available to initiates, and such initiates were a select band, for not all humans were considered as suitable for salvation or capable or receiving the secret *gnosis*. So to be a Gnostic was to be one of the elite who possessed secrets of eternal value, and to be one who, after passing through a number of stages each with its secret password, would finally reach union with the ultimate. In the overtly Christian forms of this system Jesus has a key role as the divine revealer of the secret *gnosis* but his essential humanity and death on the cross are denied.

Sharing in the spiritual and docetic emphasis of Gnosticism, but not in its cosmological speculation and highly allegorical exegesis was *Marcion* (d. ca. AD 165). The son of a bishop from Asia Minor he saw himself as a reformer, using his understandings of St. Paul to counter growing legalism in 2nd century Christianity. Concern with the problem of evil led him to a dualistic view, in which the Jewish god and the Old Testament itself were regarded as evil. He put forward his own list of authoritative New Testament books, purged of the influence of Judaism. He was a genuine ascetic, and gathered around himself a counter-Church which persisted for some 500 years.

With a willingness even more explicitly to claim to be 'Christianity' in its most refined form, was *Manichaeism*. This movement had as its founder, Mani or Manes, who was born in Babylonia in AD 216. Eventually he died in chains, at the insistence of the Zoroastrian priesthood in AD 277, following a period of some support from the Persian King, Shapur I. Coming out of a Jewish-Christian sect, Mani stressed the sort of dualism of spirit and matter to be found among Gnostics and denied in Christianity, and saw in his own life parallels to that of Jesus. His followers tended to regard him as the promised Holy Spirit, or if they came from a Buddhist background, as Maitreya, the promised Buddha of the future. Avowedly syncretistic his aim was to bring together the valid insights of Buddha, Zoroaster, Jesus and the former prophets, and with his followers, to liberate the divine light which is imprisoned in matter.

No religion was as adept as this one at adapting itself and its vocabulary to the peoples it met from North-West Africa to China. It used art, fables, parables, hymnody, folklore and science as well as magic and astrology – all with great skill – to present its answers to the problems of existence. Like Gnosticism it had about it an air of elitism in its leadership, but was more open than its predecessor to membership by the masses. It also resembled Gnosticism in its attitude to Jesus whom it honoured as the great healer of mankind, but not as fully human nor as the one who suffered and died. Interested foremost in the divine message more than in the historical life of Jesus, Mani saw him as 'the Splendour', and the divine light bearer, in whose teaching is to be found redeeming wisdom and knowledge. Yet like Christianity, Manichaeism took sin with great seriousness for to sin against the divine light was to blaspheme. The possibility of external damnation was ever present at every level of the Manichaean community. Persecuted out of overt existence within the Roman Empire, it persisted in Asia, not least in Central Asia, where it was at its peak of influence from the 8th to the 13th centuries, and in South-East China up until the 16th century, when it too suffered eclipse at the hands of the Timurids in Central Asia and at the hands of the Confucians in South China.

FURTHER READING

Wand, J. W. C.: *The Four Great Heresies*, London 1955.
Sellers, R. V.: *Two Ancient Christologies*, London 1954.
Jonas, H.: *The Gnostic Religion. The Message of the Alien God and the Beginnings of Christianity*, 2nd ed., Boston 1963.
Wilson, R. McL.: 'Gnosis, Gnosticism and the New Testament', in: Bianchi, U. (ed.), *Le origini dello gnosticismo [. . .]*, Leiden 1967 (SHR 12), pp. 511–527.
Asmussen, J. P. (ed.): *Manichaean Literature. Representative Texts Chiefly from Middle Persian and Parthian Writings*, Delmar, N. Y. 1975 (Persian Heritage Series 22).
Widengren, G.: *Mani and Manichaeism*, trans. by Ch. Kessler, London 1965.
Lieu, S. N. C.: *Manichaeism in the Later Roman Empire and Medieval China. A Historical Survey*, 2nd ed., Tübingen 1992 (Wissenschaftliche Untersuchungen zum Neuen Testament 63).
Klimkeit, H.-J.: *Gnosis on the Silk Road. Gnostic Texts from Central Asia*, San Francisco 1993.

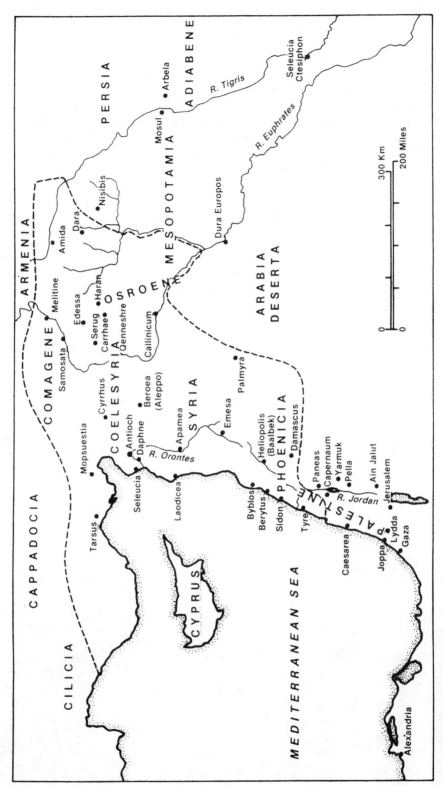

Map 1 Syria, Palestine and Mesopotamia

Chapter 4

Christians in Syria and Palestine

INTRODUCTION

Jerusalem, Bethlehem, Jericho, Nazareth, Capernaum, Caesarea, Joppa, Antioch and Damascus – all are familiar names to Christians of all traditions, even if many may have problems in locating them accurately on a map. Even without the background of the Old Testament record, the New Testament itself is replete with references to these and other locations in Palestine and Syria. We are equally familiar with the fact that organized Christianity had its origins in this area, as Jesus' followers 'filled with power' became his witnesses 'in Jerusalem, in all Judea and Samaria, and to the ends of the earth' (Acts 1:8).

It is also apparent to all that the nucleus of the Church consisted at first of Jews who accepted Jesus as the promised Messiah, despite his crucifixion and the seeming impossibility of his resurrection. That some of these Jewish Christians were conservative Aramaic and Hebrew speakers is as clear as is the fact that some of them were more at home with Greek and Hellenistic culture – the so-called 'Hebrews' and 'Hellenists' of Acts 6:1. The Jerusalem circle remained a focus of authority and leadership for these early Christians, led for a time by relatives of Jesus, the first being his brother James (see Mark 6:3, Gals. 1:19; 1 Cors. 15:7 and Acts 12:17, 15:13 and 21:18). That the spread of the faith was in part the result of persecution of a perceived fractious, heterodox group at the hands of the Jewish authorities is clear from Acts 8:1–4, although an apostolic core remained at Jerusalem, not always themselves safe from persecution (e.g. Acts 12:1–5). James himself was to be stoned to death in AD 62 during an inter-regnum between two Roman procurators. This prompted the Jerusalem congregation to desert Jerusalem, soon to be stormed by Titus to quell a rebellion in AD 70, and they found refuge in the Gentile city of Pella, across the Jordan River from Samaria. There they were led for some 40 years by a cousin of Jesus and James, named Simeon, and they came into contact with various Jewish sects who also had sought refuge in such areas from orthodox Judaism. Interchange of views resulted, some of which strengthened the Jewishness of these Jewish Christians, to whose distinctive emphases we must now turn.

THE ROLE OF JEWISH CHRISTIANITY

The dependence of both Western Catholic and Eastern Orthodox Christianity upon the traditions represented by the Pauline, Johannine and Petrine writings in the New Testament has been heavy indeed. So dominant has this been that there was long a tendency to disregard any other tradition as being significant. This has been corrected somewhat of late, not least through the work of the French historian Jean Daniélou and others. What is to be remembered is that what concerns us here are the forms of Jewish or Semitic Christianity found in Asia, and not whether such expressions have validity in the West. From such research has come the realisation that the Jewish Christianity to be found in Palestine, Syria and Mesopotamia formed a source of Christianity 'independent of and of equal importance with Latin and Greek Christianity.'[1] Whatever the distinctions that may be made quite rightly in terms of aspects of their literary and intellectual traditions, it is very doubtful that such distinctions would have bulked large, or even small, in the minds of ordinary believers. Along with Rome and Ephesus, Antioch and Edessa are seen to be main centres of the early Church.

It has also become clear that

> 'Christianity has been interpreted in several ways, according to the genius of the peoples to whom it was entrusted: if Rome stressed the legal aspects of the new religion, and the Greeks developed an ontological interpretation of God and Christ, the Syrians were not very interested in dogmatic strife, at least until Ephrem Syrus in the fourth century, and conceived their faith rather as a Way, a way of life.'[2]

Jewish Christianity would be conceived by many Jews as less iconoclastic with respect to the Law than was the approach of Paul. They were enabled by it to bring with them into Christianity rather more of what was to them a richly meaningful heritage, however little it may have mattered to Gentile Christians. While Jewish Christians may have had initially a greater interest in orthopraxy than in doctrinal orthodoxy, as interpreted by Paul, this is not to say that they did not have their own theological emphases and concerns.

Daniélou saw these Jewish Christians as falling into three major groups –

1 those who accepted Jesus as a prophet or as a messiah, but not as the Son of God, used only the Gospel of Matthew, rejected the letters of Paul and the virginal conception of Jesus, and were called the Ebionites;

2 those at Jerusalem and after, led at first by James, who favoured Jewish ways for themselves, but were not out to impose these comprehensively on Gentile converts. They were to be called 'Nazarenes' (as in Acts 24:5) or 'Nazorees' if they were East Syrian in location and Aramaic speakers,[3] and

3 those who drew on the late Judaic thought forms of the Pharisees, Essenes and Zealots rather than on those of rabbinic Judaism.

The last of these three groups was the one with lasting influence, and among their concerns were:

- a deep interest in cosmic history, from the very beginning of all things to their end in time and across all the dimensions of sub-terrestrial, terrestrial and supra-terrestrial space,[4]
- close consequent dependence on revelation, so that the mysteries of the created order and its purpose and goal may be perceived through all the richness of apocalyptic imagery,[5]
- a resulting *gnosis*, that 'saving knowledge of what the divine action proclaimed in the Gospel message has effected for all men and all creatures for all time, and of the divinely appointed means of arriving at this knowledge in the esoteric exegesis of the Scriptures.'[6]

The whole of human existence was set within the context of God's providential design, prefigured in the Genesis accounts of creation, which creation is inaugurated afresh in the Incarnation. Much exegesis was focussed on Genesis, in which it was believed were to be discerned the foundations of the doctrine of the Trinity, and the establishment of the Church. The beginning and the end of all things were bound together by Jesus and his cross. Indeed:

> 'For them redemption was a cosmic matter; the action of the Word extended through every region of the spiritual universe, from Sheol to the seventh heaven, and touched every creature. The Cross, the instrument of redemption, is not merely the historical and material gibbet used by God as the creative pivot of history, marvellous though that may be; it is also the double axis of the universe, transcending space by stretching out its arms to unite all nations of men and by reaching up its head to join heaven and earth, the angelic hierarchies and the spirits of them that sleep, and transcending Time by descending as a living being into the lower parts of the earth to preach salvation to the righteous who died before Christ, and by coming in the East as the glorious herald of the Saviour's final Return.'[7]

Related closely to the rite of initiation was

> 'the teachings of the Two Ways, . . . the Angel of Light and the Prince of Darkness, the spirits of the virtues and the demons of the vices, and the exhortations to steadfast singleness of mind

confronted the baptizand before admitting him to the sacramental world where the fire of Christ descended into the waters to destroy the demon, and the grains of God's wheat gathered from the mountains to await the Coming of the Lord.'[8]

Throughout all of this is a strong theme of continuity between the new covenant in Christ and the old covenant in Abraham, so that all the major features of Christianity are shown to have roots in the very beginnings of all things. From this could be drawn comprehensive assurance that, despite appearances to the contrary, all was secure in God's hands. Alongside this was to stand

- a distinctive approach to the doctrine of the Trinity, in which God was seen to have a form which may be intrinsically visible and where a female identity was assigned to the Holy Ghost, in ways virtually unknown in Hellenistic Christianity, and
- a deep interest in asceticism and the virtues of poverty and celibacy which had parallels among the Essenes and which were to have long standing influence in Aramaean Christianity, and clearly antedate any moves towards monasticism.

THE SPREAD OF CHRISTIANITY IN THE REGION

We have already noted some of the ways in which Christianity spread from Jerusalem to the north east via Pella. The Acts of the Apostles recounts the establishment of the faith among the Samaritans (8:4–25), at Caesarea (8:40 & 10:24 & 44–48) and Damascus (9:10 & 19), Lydda (9:32), Joppa (9:36–43 & 10:5 & 23), Tyre (21:4), Ptolemais (21:7) and Sidon (27:3) and Antioch (11:19–30) as well as in Cyprus (11:19).

Now while an evangelist like Philip was ready to preach to the Samaritans (Acts 8:5) and to an Ethiopean eunuch (Acts 8:26–39), it would seem that in Phoenicia, Cyprus and Antioch he restricted his preaching to Jews (Acts 11:19). Such a restriction was ignored by those who came from Cyprus and Cyrene and spoke to the Greeks (Acts 11:20). At very least they had the precedent of Peter's ministry to the Gentile 'God-fearer' Cornelius. Indeed what happened at Antioch in this regard became a pattern among the coastal towns and commercial centres of the region where Greek-speaking Christians predominated over those of Jewish extraction. So much was this the case that Jewish Christians at Antioch found it as much more comfortable to move to Beroea, as had those in Jerusalem found it to move to Pella – albeit for different reasons. As one author puts it,

'it seems that Christianity remained Greek so long as it centred in the commercial towns: the vernacular churches arose as Christianity spread outwards from the Levant among the inland population.'[9]

In such inland areas traditional pagan centres such as Emesa and Heliopolis resisted Christians to the point where some of those in the former had at first to live in neighbouring villages rather than in the town itself. They were less likely to meet obdurate opposition at Paneas and Palmyra, the royal house of the latter having within it Greek as well as Syrian blood. In due course Edessa was to become a key centre for the spread of Christianity among the Syriac-speaking population in the countryside and villages as was Antioch for those who were Greek-speaking in the towns.

As a result by the time of the Council of Nicea in AD 325 considerable headway had been made for Christianity in Coele-Syria, rather more than appears to have occurred in Phoenicia. In the process a not inconsiderable role was played by monks, who chose to settle among pagan populations and used patience, humility and perseverance as their evangelistic means. In addition it also appears that those 'God-fearers' associated with the Jewish communities in this region were no less significant than they were in centres in the Graeco-Roman world.

That there were in play cultural differences of significance is clear, and to a review of these we must turn.

CULTURAL TENSIONS

Passing reference has been made already to the fact that there were tensions between those whose cultural and racial background was Hellenistic and those whose backgrounds were Semitic. So e.g. Antioch had been founded in 300 BC as a colony, with a population drawn predominantly from displaced Athenians and Macedonians. While in due course there were attracted to it further 2nd century BC Greek refugees from Roman rule and considerable numbers of Jews and others, keen to share in its cultural and economic opportunities, it had about it always something of the air of an exotic Hellenistic island in a Syriac sea. Its famous theological school was Hellenistic rather than Oriental, and its great thinkers, from Ignatius through Theodore of Mopsuestia to Theodoret of Cyrrhus, were Greek-speaking and thinking Antiochenes, rather than offspring of the native Syrian soil. There were few traces in the city of indigenous Syrian cults and deities, attention being focussed rather on Zeus, Athene and Apollo. In due course these too gave way to the Christian God, whose devotees, to judge from their ridiculing of the Emperor Julian's attempts to re-establish pagan deities in AD 363, dominated the city.

In one significant area, however, the Hellenistic heritage left a lasting mark on Antiochene Christianity. In general terms, more than in detail, the approach adopted was Aristotelian rather than Platonic. This was one of the ways in which it differed from its great rival city of Alexandria, with its Platonic air and approach. It was also one of the causes of disagreement between the two centres on Christological doctrine in the 5th and later centuries. It accounts, in part, also for the Antiochene concern for the observable, concrete, and historical in the earthly life of Jesus of Nazareth, as mentor and saviour. This is not to say that Antioch was averse to many of the approaches, categories etc. of Platonism, or to deny that eventually full-blooded Aristotelianism was adopted by the Syriac-speaking Christians of East Syria, once Antioch's star had faded.

So the syndrome of a Hellenistic city set over against the indigenous population of the countryside was to be found in Antioch and Syria, as it was also to be seen in Alexandria and Egypt. It was to provide the soil in which indigenous Monophysite Churches in both areas would rise in opposition to the Chalcedonian orthodoxy of the city centres themselves.

Symptomatic of and contributing to such differences was the emergence of Syriac, as a dialect of Aramaic, in the 2nd century AD focussed on Edessa, where the Old Testament itself was translated into Syriac by Jews before the time of Tatian (late 2nd century). Syriac became the language in which Christianity was promulgated in Eastern Syria and points further east. It became the liturgical language in India and China as much as in Mesopotamia. By AD 160 there were Syriac, and Latin-speaking Christians as well as the predominantly Greek speakers. Syriac literature itself began to grow as more and more Christian writings were translated into this tongue, including the originally Greek harmony of the four gospels prepared by Tatian and entitled the *Diatessaron*. By the middle of the 4th century it was already an extensive corpus of literature, the value and quality of which was to be defended strongly by authors such as Severus of Nisibis (d. AD 667) over against attempts to denigrate it in favour of Greek. Its status as a language had been built up from ca. AD 200 by such writers as Bardaisan, Mani, Aphrahat (d. AD 345) and Ephrem Syrus (d. AD 373), notwithstanding the doubts about the Christian orthodoxy of the first two listed. What emerged from Aphrahat and Ephrem was a 'Christianity expressed in a relatively pure Semitic, and as yet unhellenized form.'[10] 'Indeed the Greek theology does not sit well on the Syriac mind, nor does it sound well in the Syriac language.'[11]

One interesting example of this is to be found in the word used as the equivalent of the Greek *soter* or saviour, with respect to Jesus. Although Syriac had several words which carried the meanings of 'to deliver', 'to protect' and 'to be made safe and sound', they chose to identify salvation with 'life'.

The 'saviour' is the 'life-giver' (Syriac *Maḥyānā*) which is reminiscent of one of the titles ascribed to the Holy Spirit in the Niceno-Constantinopolitan Creed.[12]

As F.C. Burkitt argued

'May we not therefore believe that this identification of "salvation" and "life" is the genuine Aramaic usage, and that the Greek Gospels have in this instance introduced a distinction which was not made by Christ and his Aramaic speaking disciples.'[13]

The Syriac language became the medium not only for transmitting the Greek Christian corpus to eastern Christians, but also that of secular Greek philosophy, and particularly that of Aristotle, to them, and later to the Arabs. It was able to provide the transition stage for technical terms which were not easily rendered directly from Greek into Arabic. Some monasteries, like that at Qenneshre on the Euphrates, specialised in such work, which also saw some reverse translation of hymns, hagiography and such a work as the *Acts of Thomas* into Greek, and later into Slavonic and Latin.

In terms of theology, the translation into Syriac of the works of the great exegete Theodore of Mopsuestia (d. AD 420), led to his interpretations becoming largely normative among many East Syrians, and to their adoption of Nestorianism. Such a move was furthered by the cultural antipathies felt towards Constantinople's attempted imposition of Graeco-Latin Chalcedonian orthodoxy, and equally against the tendency of Antioch to support a Monophysite view. Such developments are clear from the time of Severus (d. AD 538) at Antioch, where

'while one line looked westward to Byzantium, the other looked eastward in search of independence from the Greeks.'[14]

Indeed, nationalism, in Syria as in Egypt, expressed itself most vehemently under religious banners, not unlike the phenomena we associate today with Ulster and the Caucasus. Such banners had about them all the theological respectability of an endeavour to guarantee the divinity of Christ against perceived attempts to undermine this. An undergirding of East Syrian attitudes was provided by Aristotelian philosophy, which was taught widely at Edessa in the second quarter of the 5th century AD. Indeed, Aristotelianism, modified somewhat by neo-Platonism, provided the weapons for doctrinal disputations between Nestorians, Monophysites and Chalcedonians alike. The Nestorians in particular, centered as they came to be further east at Nisibis, depended on Aristotle's *Metaphysics*. To this they added elements of Pythagoreanism, Stoicism and Platonism.

'They absorbed what Greek had to give, because they needed it, and it became integrated into the older structure of their religion.'[15]

THREE KEY CENTRES: JERUSALEM, ANTIOCH, EDESSA

This chapter began with a list of place names made familiar to most by biblical references. But what of other centres of formative influence for Christians in Asia? We have noted already the role of *Jerusalem* in the earliest days of the Church. However, the departure of most Christians after AD 62, and the storming of the city in AD 70, was followed in AD 135 by its complete destruction and the expulsion of all Jews from Judea. A new Roman colony of Aelia Capitolina replaced Jerusalem, whose name no longer appeared on the maps of the day. As far as Christians were concerned, oversight of those at Aelia passed to the Metropolitan of Palestine, the Bishop of Caesarea. Following the victory of Constantine over the eastern Emperor Licinius in AD 324, the fortunes of Jerusalem revived, not least because of the interest of Constantine and his mother Helena in the restoration of sites holy to Christians, and the encouragement of pilgrimage.

At the Council of Nicea in AD 325, canon 7 made special provision for dignifying the Bishop of Aelia, while respecting the rights of the Metropolitan at Caesarea. Lustre was added to the reputation of Jerusalem by a Bishop such as Cyril (d. AD 386), while political manoeuvering for ecclesiastical status marked some other holders of the bishopric, not least Juvenal (d. AD 458). At the Council of Chalcedon in AD 451 the jurisdictions of the Bishops of Antioch and Jerusalem in the area were adjusted and fixed, and Jerusalem became the 5th and final patriarchate in the Church, but a patriarchate of honorific status rather than of effective power.

Whatever the somewhat contested rise to patriarchal status of Jerusalem, there was never doubt about the significance of *Antioch* (modern Antakya, cf. pl. 1). Probably the source from which came the Gospel of Matthew, its role in the New Testament period is apparent, and its associations with both Peter and Paul, if not as significant as those of Rome, are not to be denied. To such apostles it could add the name of its early Bishop Ignatius (d. AD 117) whose martyrdom sealed the influence of his advocacy of episcopacy and opposition to Docetism and Gnosticism in the Church. So significant was he that later Monophysite/Jacobite patriarchs of Antioch always included his name in their titles. Next in significance and reputation for sanctity stood the ascetic Simeon Stylites (d. AD 459), who took up his pillar-dwelling near Antioch, and was buried in that city. Near in wide repute throughout the Church was the famed preacher John Chrysostom (d. AD 407), while Theodoret of Cyrrhus (d. AD 457) was regarded as the outstanding Antiochene theologian of the mid-5th century. Of considerable renown throughout the middle ages was the Syrian mystic known as pseudo-Dionysius the Areopagite, who wrote at the turn of the 5th into the 6th century. His expression of Christianity in terms of neo-Platonism had far-reaching effects. Less conspicuous, but remembered for their apologetic works, were the Bishops Theophilus (d. ca. AD 190?) and Serapion (d. AD 211), the former being the first writer to use the term 'triad' or 'trinity' in reference to the Christian godhead.

Less acceptable to what came to be seen as orthodoxy were leaders such as Paul of Samosata (d. AD 272?); Lucian the Martyr (d. AD 312), the mentor of Arius; Apollinarius of Laodicea (d. AD 390); the exegetes Diodore of Tarsus (d. AD 394) and Theodore of Mopsuestia (d. AD 428); and the controversial Nestorius (d. AD 452). Antioch was also the home of the influential Monophysite theologian, Severus (d. AD 538).

So whether from the perspective of orthodoxy or heterodoxy, Antioch's place in Christian awareness was bound to be well to the fore. It remained for some six centuries at the forefront with Alexandria and Constantinople in the east, and with Rome overall.[16] The area over which it exercised patriarchial responsibility included Syria, Palestine, Cyprus, Arabia, Mesopotamia – and to a lesser degree Persia and India. Such oversight took in 11 metropolitan provinces and 127 episcopal dioceses.

While its significance as a Christian centre was apparent it was also highly significant in the socio-econo-political and military spheres. While not founded originally as a capital for the Seleucid dynasty it soon became just that, and down until its fall to the Arabs in AD 638 it continued to exercise an important role both prior to and within the Roman Empire. Subject to natural earthquakes and to social upheaval and riot, its history was by no means a consistently peaceful one. The city had a reputation for anti-Jewish riots, in protest against the privileges they were deemed to have been granted. The first such riot on record dates back to the reign of Antiochus Epiphanes (175–163 BC), while others occurred in Nero's reign (AD 54–68) and as late as the reign of Anastasius (AD 491–518). Taxation, famine, army numbers and ecclesiastical disputes all precipitated riots, until after AD 500 they became almost endemic, and as late as AD 610 had to be suppressed with severity. As a consequence Antioch's status as a metropolis was removed on at least three occasions, but its strategic importance was such that eventually such status had to be restored. Again and again it became the headquarters of Roman emperors intent on securing the borders with Persia and maintaining fruitful relations with Armenia to the north-east and with tributory states to the south. Small wonder that the fourth century AD pagan historian Ammianus Marcellinus called Antioch 'the fair crown of the Orient'.

If the Roman authorities found the population of Antioch less than tractable at times, they also found themselves at odds with Christians there, both before and after the conversion of Constantine. In AD 114–115, while Trajan was using Antioch as his base for his occupation of Mesopotamia and Armenia, the city was rocked by earthquakes. The population fixed on

Christians as scapegoats, for what was seen as retribution by the pagan gods. Numbers of Christians died and their Bishop, Ignatius, was despatched to Rome for execution, while Bishop Babylas (AD 240–250) died under the Decian persecution.

Within a few years Persian invaders had removed Bishop Demetrius to Persia, along with members of the city's citizens in AD 253, 254, and 260. This followed the defeat of the Emperor Valerian by Shapur I in AD 260, following which Roman control over Armenia and Mesopotamia also relaxed. Odeinath, Prince of Palmyra, seized the opportunity to demonstrate the aspirations of less Hellenized Syrians, asserted his independence and exercised rule over considerable parts of Syria. To do so he used Roman and Palmyrene forces intended for use against Persia but fell a victim to assassination in AD 266/267, being succeeded by his widow, Zenobia. With the support of the rulers of Palmyra, Paul of Samosata became both Bishop and self-styled chief fiscal officer in AD 260/261. He was deposed on a charge of heretical subordinationism with respect to the Trinity and the person of Christ by councils in AD 264 and 269, and ostensibly was replaced by Domnus. But Paul clung to his episcopal claims until after the Emperor Aurelian had defeated Zenobia of Palmyra in AD 272 and re-established Roman control. Paul was then evicted. Antioch had experienced contemporaneous rival claims to the episcopal office, not for the last time by any means.

During the last great persecution (AD 303–311) the distinguished teacher Lucian was martyred, his death adding further lustre to his reputation among former students like Arius (d. AD 336) and Eusebius of Nicomedia (d. AD 342). There was a civil disturbance in AD 330 when the anti-Arian Bishop Eustathius (d. AD 337) was deposed, and the Emperor Julian had little difficulty in keeping Nicene and Arian Antiochenes in fierce opposition to each other during his stay in Antioch in AD 361–362. The Emperor Valens (AD 364–378) persecuted Nicene Antiochenes, until dissuaded by the pagan scholar Themistius. Throughout this period from AD 360–370, there were at times no less than four bishops all vying for episcopal authority over the city and its area of jurisdiction. One of these schisms was associated with the attempts of Apollinarius of Laodicea (d. AD 390) to secure the acceptance of a bishop who was opposed to what was seen later as emerging Nestorianism under Diodore of Tarsus (d. AD 394).[17]

The Emperor Theodosius I (AD 379–395) restored support for Nicene Christianity, but was scandalised in AD 387 when Antiochenes, rioting against heavier taxation, destroyed imperial statues and busts, an act regarded as lese-majesty. Even the pleas of the aged bishop, Flavian, who hurried to Constantinople to beg clemency, could not avert all penalties. No more effective were the prayers of the monks who flocked to the city in considerable numbers at the time. This was one of the occasions when the city lost its civil and military status within the empire. Then from AD 404–413 Antioch was out of communion with Rome, during the days in which Chrysostom was out of favour at Constantinople.

The support of Antioch for Nestorius, against the charges of Cyril of Alexandria (d. AD 444) at the Council of Ephesus in AD 431, proved to be fruitless. A serious schism was only settled by the Formula of Reunion in AD 433, when, with papal support, Cyril of Alexandria and Theodoret of Cyrrhus were able to reach common ground. Some of the East Syrians, however, reacted against what they saw as overmuch concession to Nestorianism in the formula, foreshadowing later developments. Antioch itself felt that its views were given due weight at Chalcedon in AD 451, at which council its arch-enemy, Dioscurus of Alexandria (d. AD 454), was deposed. This was an occasion on which the Bishops of Rome and Antioch were at one in their opposition to the Bishop of Alexandria, foreshadowing an 'alliance' which was to have moderate longevity.

However, the same Chalcedonian 'solution' left a legacy of outraged supporters of the views they ascribed to Cyril of Alexandria, suspicious that Chalcedon had ceded ground to Nestorianism, and resentful of imperial rule and Hellenistic suzerainty. Those with Monophysite sympathies were encouraged in these during the reign of the Emperor Zeno (d. AD 491). This emperor, in a bid to secure his throne, in AD 482 promoted the *Henoticon*,[18] which was mildly critical of Chalcedon and allowed greater scope for Monophysite views, but led to a schism with Rome. Instrumental in its preparation was Peter (the Fuller) of Antioch (d. AD 488), who became bishop there. This allowed Monophysite views to gain ground, but not without opposition from those who adhered to Chalcedon. The orthodox bishop, Stephen, was murdered in AD 479 and during the reign of the pro-Monophysite Emperor Anastasius (d. AD 518), Monophysite monks invaded the city in a bid to unseat Bishop Flavian II, only to be expelled by citizens and orthodox monks. With Nestorians finding acceptance in Persia there were strategic reasons also for supporting Monophysite expressions in Syria, with refugees from Persia adding their weight to such developments.

Bishop Flavian was exiled to Petra in AD 512, and the patriarchate of Antioch came into the hands of the great Monophysite theologian Severus (d. AD 538), who condemned both the Council of Chalcedon and the *Tome* of Leo. Severus himself was forced to flee the city in AD 518 and a reaction against Monophysites set in until the mid-520's. By the end of that decade Persian forces were beginning a series of raids to the very outskirts of Antioch and in AD 540 the city, after reneging on a proposal to buy off the Persians, was assaulted and sacked by them. Captives were removed to Persia, after Edessa was refused permission to ransom them. Meanwhile in this period Jacob Baradai (d. AD 578) was busy laying foundations for the Monophysite Church which, from his name, was and is known as Jacobite.

Antioch's fortunes continued to decline throughout the 6th century, and the refusal of Emperor Justin II (d. AD 570) to pay due annual tribute led to further punitive raids from Persia. During AD 606–607 Persia occupied much of Syria, not without local acceptance because of resentment against the tyrannical brutalities of Phocas (d. AD 610) who had deposed the Emperor Maurice (d. AD 602) and persecuted both Monophysites and Jews. Riots in Antioch in AD 610 were suppressed savagely and both Antioch and Edessa fell once again to the Persians in AD 611–612. They remained in charge until AD 628 and endeavoured to compel adherence to the Nestorianism favoured in Persia itself.

The Emperor Heraclius (d. AD 641) tried to reconcile Monophysites to Constantinople, via the one-will doctrine of Monotheletism in the *Ecthesis* of AD 638.[19] Propounded by the Syrian born Sergius of Constantinople (d. AD 638), it gained some support from Pope Honorius I (d. AD 638) and was advocated during concurrent episcopal vacancies in both Antioch and Alexandria. But by then a new force was on the scene, for in AD 636 the Arabs had pushed northwards and defeated the Romans at Yarmuk. Heraclius was compelled to give up Syria and with it Jerusalem and Antioch, which passed into Arab hands in AD 638, and remained therein for three centuries. The city's leadership role had been in question since AD 500, and overall decline had been evident also since then. That the Monophysites of Syria should have preferred Muslim rule to that of Constantinople is evidence of feelings engendered earlier and deepened in that same period. While Antioch remained one of the five patriarchal sees, its influence was never again to be what it had been in the period up to AD 500, and its associations tended to be predominantly with Monophysitism, notwithstanding the fact there were, in later centuries, also a Chalcedonian Patriarch, a Catholic Melkite Patriarch and claimed associations by the Maronite Patriarchs – sometimes contemporaneously.

While Antioch was predominantly Hellenistic, the centre of *Edessa* (modern Urfa), some 260 kilometres to the east-north-east, was and remained predominantly Syrian in both speech and culture (cf. pls. 2 and 3). As alluded to already, Edessa played a major role in the evangelisation of Syriac-speaking areas and was a key link in the chain towards the east from Syria, being a meeting point for roads north and south, as well as east and west.

Unable to match Antioch in its associations with Peter and Paul, the necessities of the situation led to the claim that in ca. AD 35, King Abgar of Edessa had written to Jesus himself and had a reply. (The story is recounted in the *Doctrine of Addai* which dates from ca. AD 300 but contains also older material.) The origins of the Church were claimed to lie with Jesus' 'twin brother', Judas Thomas,[20] and with his disciple Addai, whom Eusebius of Caesarea suggested was one of the seventy described in Luke 10:1 & 17. However, there seems to be no historical substance for such claims, beyond the fact that the names Abgar and Addai both refer to historical figures, and that there was considerable reading back from the late 2nd century, when it is possible to see the Church in being in Edessa. If apostolic foundation is highly improbable, Edessa had other substantial claims to fame in early Christianity. From it are reputed to have come the manuscripts which lie behind the important biblical codices Syrus Sinaiticus and Syrus Curetonianus. In addition it is associated with formative figures such as Tatian (late 2nd century), a disciple of Justin Martyr; Aphrahat (d. AD 345) and Ephrem Syrus (d. AD 373), the latter two being widely regarded in the West for their devotional writing. To them, less acceptable as far as orthodoxy was concerned, was the distinguished Bardaisan (d. AD 222), and the fact that Lucian the Martyr was a student in Edessa until he left for Antioch in AD 260. Such names, together with its history as a centre of learning, missionary endeavour and asceticism guaranteed Edessa a place among the leading centres of Christianity, east of Jordan.

The weight of scholarly opinion favours the case that Christianity reached Edessa not from Antioch in the west but from the region of Adiabene, with its centre at Arbela (modern Erbil), to the east. This was an area with a considerable Jewish population, and from AD 40, with its ruling house converts to Judaism. These Jews were largely outside rabbinic influence but open to those pious Jews, and Jewish-Christians who came from Palestine, with which good links were maintained. It would appear that Christianity took root among such Jews and associated god-fearers at Arbela towards the end of the 1st century AD. The first Bishop of Arbela reputedly dated from about AD 100 and he and his immediate successors had Jewish names, while the first martyrs there are recorded in AD 123.

From Arbela Christianity may well have travelled west to Edessa, with a Jewish-Christian called Addai, in the first decade of the 2nd century. Both cities shared trading links and the Syriac language, as well as considerable numbers of Jewish residents as the seed plots for Christian planting.

This is not to say that Christians were the only planters in the area. Local cults associated with the worship of the planets persisted down to the 4th century. Judaism maintained its hold, related somewhat to a strong and early Jewish academy at Nisibis. It would seem that Christianity at Edessa was beset with the possibilities of syncretism with native cults, with the challenges offered by followers of Marcion for decades after AD 140. Out of such challenges could emerge also a group called the Quqites, propounding a type of Samaritan-Iranian Gnosticism, and other expressions of Gnosticism, Christian and non-Christian. In many ways this situation epitomised a syncretistic age which spread as far east as China under the Han dynasty. This came to something of a halt by the beginning of the 3rd century, signified in part by the Sasanian dynasty's assumption of power in Persia.

However, within this syncretistic milieu can be placed such works as the *Gospel of Thomas*, the *Odes of Solomon* and the *Psalms* and the *Acts of Thomas*. Also germane to the syncretistic 'Gnostic' context is the fact that the Nag-Hammadi works, the *Gospel of Philip* and the *Gospel of Truth*, were also known at Edessa. Something of a climax in this situation is reached with Bardaisan to whom reference will be made below. Of a decidedly different nature, being a harmony of the four canonical gospels, is the *Diatessaron* of Tatian, dating to ca. AD 170 in Edessa. This harmony had wide recognition and use across Syriac-speaking areas, and its replacement by the canonical gospels in the fifth century was resisted strenuously.

Not only was Edessa subject to various religious influences. Its geographical and strategic location on the border lands between the empires of Rome and Persia made it politically significant, and subject to political change. Early in the Christian era its sympathies lay with the Persians, and the Jewish population resisted Trajan's invasion in AD 114–115 to their cost – as also did their religious compatriots at the Emperor's rear in Cyprus, Egypt and Cyrenaica. Roman might was demonstrated again by Marcus Aurelius in the war of AD 161–166, out of which the western areas of Mesopotamia passed under Roman rule. The city of Edessa was surrounded by Roman territory after AD 164, with Nisibis developed as a provincial capital, and the princes of Edessa and of Osrhoene became Roman vassals. The major Edessene ruler concerned was Abgar IX, the Great, who ruled from AD 177–212, and saw Roman sovereignty asserted afresh over against Persia by Septimius Severus in AD 198. Edessa itself was declared a Roman *colonia* in AD 213–214 and it was regarded as securely within the Roman sphere, the local dynasty retiring to Rome in AD 243.

There was something of a change in fortunes in AD 260 when Valerian was defeated by the Sasanian Shapur I not far from Edessa. This left Persia supreme as far west as Antioch for some years, but in AD 297 Rome re-took Nisibis and retained it until Julian's defeat in AD 363. Thereafter it remained in Persian hands for some 120 years and left Edessa very much a frontier city. This meant that not only was the Jewish minority in Edessa cut off from their cultural support base in Nisibis, but that the distinguished Christian school in the latter city moved to Edessa. There its presence shed further lustre on the city which became the centre of theological instruction and of Western culture for all the Christians of the east. Indeed Edessa, for all its vaunting of Syriac had never been entirely isolated from Western culture, and in upper circles was bilingual, so that Christian writings appeared also in Greek. Wealthy families sent their sons to be educated in Antioch, Alexandria or in Greece itself, so that, at least among a significant minority, Greek learning was no stranger to Edessa.

Christianity at Edessa entered a new phase with the conversion to it of Abgar IX (AD 177–212),[21] which made of the city the first Christian city-state in the world. The king apparently maintained altars to the planet deities, but his acceptance of Christianity gave it enhanced status among his subjects. It was at about this time that the Church in Edessa also came under the aegis of that at Antioch – i.e. to say those who belonged to the congregation(s) so minded, for the Christians continued to have their sectarian disputes among themselves. This reached the level where the members of the Antioch-related group(s) took the name of the first Bishop, Palut, who was consecrated by Serapion of Antioch (d. AD 211) and were known as 'Palutians' in distinction from other Christians. Of this practice and of 'heretical' divisions Ephrem Syrus was complaining as late as the second half of the 4th century, and this may be evidence that divisions were not yet healed at Edessa – nor were they to be. However, we can see that whereas Christianity was probably a minority movement at Edessa early in the 3rd century, by the outset of the 4th century in one form or another it had captured the loyalty of most of the population.

This support was shown in striking fashion during the Diocletian persecution of the Church. Beginning in AD 303 the persecution did not touch Edessa for six years and only then over the misgivings of local Roman authorities and at the insistence of those at Antioch. Two martyrs, Shmona and Gurya, were executed secretly so as not to arouse the anger of the Edessenes, while a third

> 'Habbib was escorted to his death by a crowd of Christians, and after his death he was buried with honour and even with the participation of Jews and pagans. The Christians showed no hesitation in declaring their faith, "because those who were persecuted were more numerous than those who were persecuting." Edessa was now a Christian city.'[22]

It would appear that Bishop Iona began to build the cathedral some four years after these martyrdoms, a cathedral famed in the middle ages as one of the wonders of the world and admired by Christians and Muslims alike. He began also a line of bishops which continued unbroken for 1000 years. Nor was Edessa left out of key conciliar determinations, for from Nicea (AD 325) onwards it was represented at all such assemblies. The churches and religious institutions, relating to health and the needy, grew in number, and the responsibilities of the bishops multiplied, including some for the administration of justice in secular as well as ecclesiastical cases.

Edessa became renowned not only for asceticism, piety and learning, and the numbers of monks and anchorites in and near it, but also as a pilgrimage centre. It had its own famed stylite,[23] Theodoulos, in the late 4th century.

> 'From all Christendom, pilgrims flocked to visit the shrines of Edessa with their holy relics of Addai and Abgar, of the martyrs Shmona, Gurya, and Habbib, and the bodies of St. Thomas and St. Damian.'[24]

Associated with its reputation were copies of the letter reputedly sent from Jesus to *Abgar*, and a portrait of Jesus himself. Such relics were so important that each contending party among the Christians of Edessa needed their own 'authentic originals' until the 'genuine' articles were transferred to Constantinople in AD 994.

As a Christian city Edessa had not only a wondrous cathedral but also become a significant centre of Christian learning. While the great theological school at Edessa, 'led' at first by Ephrem Syrus, was sensitive to both Greek and Syriac traditions and emphases, there was always a strain of Syrian independence evident. This latter strain came under stress in the bishopric of Rabbula (d. AD 435) who after the condemnation of Nestorianism by the Council of Ephesus in AD 431, set about bringing Edessa into conformity with the Church at large and its predominantly Graeco-Latin approach. Rabbula's love of order and uniformity threatened the distinctive Syrian tradition, but there was a sustained endeavour to impose Greek theology, despite the fact that this did 'not fit easily with the exuberant, non-dogmatic Syriac outlook.'[25] Somewhat symbolic of this 'Hellenizing' approach was the deliberate ousting of Tatian's *Diatessaron* in favour of the canonical four gospels in the Syriac Church.

The anti-Nestorian stance and the determination of the Council of Chalcedon in AD 451 led to two reactions in Edessa. Those imbued with the approach of Theodore of Mopsuestia (d. AD 428), and what they saw as the emphases of Nestorius led by Hiba (d. AD 451), opposed Rabbula until in AD 489 their school was closed and they departed eastwards into Persia. Their history we shall follow later. At Edessa itself two major groups remained – that which was committed to Chalcedon and became known as the Melkites; and that which adopted Syrian Monophysitism, expressed this through the Jacobite Church, and had majority support. It is of some interest to note that the most prized relic of the latter group was 'Jesus' letter to Abgar', while the former group prized above all else the 'portrait of Jesus', the preferences themselves being reflections of the respective theologies espoused. It may be that Monophysite preferences were also behind the refusal of Edessa to support rebellion against the Emperor Zeno in the last quarter of the 5th century.

To the city's later history we shall return below.

SOME MAJOR FIGURES AND THEIR INFLUENCE

Reference has been made to already a number of those whose impact on Christianity in this overall area was significant. Like the writer to the Hebrews in chapter 11 verse 32, time forbids discussing all the leaders of thought and practice. So the focus falls on those less known to most Christians of today, without in any way wishing thereby to denigrate the contributions of such men as Ignatius (d. AD 117) and Theophilus

(d. ca. AD 200) and Serapion of Antioch (d. AD 211), Eusebius of Caesarea (d. AD 339), Cyril of Jerusalem (d. AD 386), Apollinarius of Laodicea (d. AD 390), Eusebius of Emesa (d. AD 360), John Chrysostom (d. AD 407), Theodoret of Cyrrhus (d. AD 457) and John of Damascus (d. ca. AD 754). Their contributions, positive and negative, are taken up within the forms of the faith familiar to Christians of the Catholic/ Orthodox tradition. Concern here is rather with those whose influence led to forms of Christianity more familiar in Asia before 1500.

Among those whose impact was felt initially in western Syria, and associated with Antioch, were Paul of Samosata, Lucian the Martyr, Diodore of Tarsus and Theodore of Mopsuestia. We have met *Paul of Samosata* already, when he emerged as Bishop of Antioch in AD 260–261, under the aegis of the rulers of Palmyra. He accrued a reputation not only for flamboyance, vanity, and extravagance, but also for dubious morality. While our knowledge of him is limited to the comments of his critics, it is clear seven decades after his lifetime that he was regarded as the father of heresies. Nevertheless, it is clear from what we know of the events of his own period that he was

> 'a man of undoubted ability and of sufficient personal power to attract and hold widespread support including that of a number of bishops, especially in the less Hellenized areas.'[26]

The attempts of a synod in AD 264 to convince Paul to change his views on the godhead and Christology failed to produce results, and he was excommunicated for heresy by another synod in AD 268. He had enough support, from anti-Roman elements in and around Antioch to cling to his bishopric, even as a declared heretic and schismatic, until AD 272.

It would seem that Paul rejected the Origenist approach to the godhead by refusing to see the Word as anything more than an impersonal force. As he saw it:

> 'God possesses an immanent power or quality which emerges before creation into some kind of manifestation of divinity and that this manifestation was in some way effective in the act of creation which followed, and later in Jesus Christ.'[27]

This was extended to the point of denying any real divinity to the Son of Mary. Leontius of Byzantium quotes Paul as claiming:

> 'The man Jesus is anointed, the Word is not. . . . Mary did not give birth to the Word since she is not before all ages. Mary received the Word. She gave birth to a man like ourselves, though better in all respects since the grace which is in him is of the Holy Spirit.'[28]

The Word was to take possession of Jesus at his birth without substantially altering his essential humanity. In place of a substantial unity, which Paul saw as compromising the dignity of the Word, there is simply a 'coming together', 'participation' or 'communion'. While condemned, his views reveal a desire to guarantee that such experiences of Jesus as temptation, hunger, pain and grief were truly human and not charades. Despite the condemnation of such views in AD 268 by no means did they disappear then, or even with the eventual ejection of Paul from Antioch.

Arriving in Antioch from Edessa during Paul of Samosata's episcopate was *Lucian*, who died under the persecutor Maximin Daia in AD 312. Regarded as the founder of the historical exegetical school of Antioch, Lucian eschewed the allegorical exegesis of Origen and made a careful recension of the Septuagint, comparing Greek and Hebrew texts, and of the gospels. His text became the standard version for Greek-speaking Christians and he won the praise of the scholar Eusebius of Caesarea and of the famed preacher John Chrysostom. In his exegetical and textual work he aimed at clarity of detail and account, at intelligibility combined with facility of expression. The accuracy of the historical account bulked larger than some hidden spiritual significance, as with the exegesis of Origen. This placed a distinctive stamp on the Antiochene school, which he led.

While rejecting Origenist exegesis it appears that Lucian did adopt the subordinationist theology of the Alexandrian master in one of his modes. In part this, and the support of some of his pupils for a fellow-pupil Arius of Alexandria (d. AD 336) has led to Lucian being seen as the father of Arianism. This would seem to be an over-simplification of the position, for his followers, the 'Collucianists', do not seem to have given Arius support comprehensively or consistently. Indeed the name of Lucian is associated with definitely anti-Arian statements in an AD 341 creed from Antioch. What is clear is that Lucian espoused a theology with a clear subordination in the relationship of the three personae of the godhead. He had such a theology in common with many others, and his name may well have been used posthumously by extremists with whom he would have disagreed.

Nor do later Syrian writers, for all their predilection with the probing of historical roots, associate Lucian with Arianism, as they do Eusebius of Caesarea. Indeed he is commonly praised:

> 'So strong an opponent of Arianism as Severus of Antioch (see under) writes of him as "Lucian the martyr, the blessed friend to labour", and cites his authority as equal to that of "our blessed Syrian doctors, Mar Ephrem and Mar Jacob and Mar Isaac and Mar Akhsenaya".'[29]

Despite the persecution by Arians of the Church in East Syria, the outrage of the latter is not directed at Lucian, but at the 'Eusebians'. If indeed no proto-Arian but a convinced subordinationist Origenist, Lucian's claim to fame and to influence in the exegetical school at Antioch is beyond dispute.

Significant later for his apologetic, doctrinal and exegetical writings was *Diodore of Tarsus* (d. AD 394), an Antiochene by birth, who lived an ascetic monastic life near that town until exiled by the Arian Emperor Valens in AD 372. Lauded by the Emperor Theodosius, but condemned by Apollinarius in ca. AD 375 and by Cyril of Alexandria in AD 438, Diodore was to be condemned also at Constantinople in AD 499.

While not in detailed agreement with Paul of Samosata, the fragments we have of Diodore's teaching indicate that he set out to separate the divine from the human in Christ, the two qualities co-existing in harmony. He traced moral progress in Christ, reaching perfection at his baptism by John. In no sense would he tolerate a confusion of the human Jesus and the divine Word. While holding to an essential distinction between the human and the divine, he argued for no two-fold activity in the one person, Jesus Christ – but at times distinguished sharply between the 'impassible' Word and the suffering human Jesus. At the same time he held that the indwelling of the divine Word makes Jesus necessarily different from the rest of mankind.

Repudiating accusations that he advocated two deities, one coming into existence when the Word entered the human Jesus, Diodore held that

> 'the divine Word . . . took possession of the human body and operated through it. Human occupation of a house, to use Diodore's own analogy, does not render the house human, a divine occupation of a temple does not render the temple divine. It may well be said . . . that he offers us two persons, one divine and one human, but hardly two Gods, one eternal and one temporal.'[30]

While Diodore's theology so far as we are able to reconstruct it from fragmentary remains, is hardly comprehensive or fully-rounded, we are in a better position when it comes to the most distinguished of the Antiochene exegetes, *Theodore of Mopsuestia* (d. AD 428). Like his predecessors he was given to work from a firm historical basis in his exegesis, and he is opposed to Christian exegesis of Old Testament passages, and very circumspect in the use of typology even with respect to Christ. So firm is he against allegorical exegesis that he does not hesitate to attack even St. Paul's use of it, with reference to Sarah and Hagar in Galatians 4:21–31. 'In short, typology based upon historical fact is permitted, allegory is not.'[31] In due course he suffered the wrath of the Church in AD 553, when it was clear that he had denied that the suffering servant passage of Isaiah 53 referred to Christ. He held that the prophet, in using the past tense throughout must have been referring to a past event, not one to come.

Like Diodore, Theodore opposed adamantly any confusion of the two natures of Christ, which would lead to 'one naturism' (or Monophysitism). In part this was due to his conviction that in no way must human freedom be imperilled, not least in Jesus. So firm was he on this, and on the consequent separation of the two natures that it seemed to his critics that he was in fact proposing two distinct logical subjects or 'personae' – a human Jesus and a divine Christ – or two sons. This, Theodore denied explicitly, but his use of words like 'conjunction' and 'indwelling' (cf. Diodore above) only seemed to confirm the suspicions of his critics. Indeed many of the fragments of Theodore's works which have survived indicate that the critics were not without justification for their views.

He emphasised consistently that the humanity of Jesus Christ was involved in moral struggle, analogous to our own. While it is the Word which initiates such moral effort, it is the thoroughly human will which responds and grows in wisdom. It was in part for this reason that he was adamantly opposed to Apollinarius' proposal that in Jesus Christ we have no human soul-mind, but a human body enlivened and directed by a fully divine soul-mind, that of the Word. The relationship of the two natures, one to the other, was described in terms of 'inhabitation', but Theodore always contended that the observed expression of this is *one* person. That adoration is offered to the man Jesus is justifiable only because of this indwelling Word, the qualities of which do affect the essentially human.

Theodore had difficulties with the title *Theotokos* (literally 'God-bearer' but usually rendered 'mother of God') ascribed to the Virgin Mary. As the following quotation makes clear much in the way of qualification and explanation was seen as necessary if the term was to be used validly.

> 'The Word plainly did not have his origin in Mary's womb, for he was begotten before all ages, but since the Word was already inhabiting the infant who was born, the term theotokos is not inappropriate. Then they ask whether Mary was the mother of man or the mother of God. Let us answer that she was both, the first by nature of the fact, the second [by the relationship of the Word to the humanity which he had assumed].'[32]

His problems were shared by his student Nestorius, who preferred the, for him, less ambiguous title *Christotokos* or 'Christ-bearer'.

In the process of human salvation, for Theodore, due regard must be kept for the deliberate moral action of humans. Along with other Antiochenes, he started his thinking from the humanity of Jesus and worked towards an understanding of christology which would not put in hazard human responsibility.

He framed his thought in biblical categories rather than philosophical, unlike most of those who followed him, and this was partly what led his opponents into finding difficulties in his christology. They linked him with Nestorius in one direction and with Paul of Samosata in the other direction, despite his own rejection of Paul as 'an angel of Satan' in company with Arius.[33]

If the reputation of Theodore suffered at the hands of Monophysites and many Chalcedonians, it was enhanced as the years passed, among the East Syrians and Nestorians. There he was known as 'the Interpreter', following the translation of his works into Syriac, during his own lifetime.

Post-Chalcedon tensions in Antioch between those who favoured the council's determinations and those who, out of Monophysite sympathies, regarded it as too concessive to Nestorianism led to a double episcopate from the time of *Severus* (d. AD 538). This great Monophysite theologian was consecrated as bishop in AD 512, after some 3 years spent in Constantinople. His first act as bishop was to condemn both Chalcedon and the *Tome* of Leo, to the embarrassment of the Emperor Anastasius I and the outrage of the Pope. The situation remained volatile, and in AD 518 Severus was forced to flee secretly to Alexandria, but was able to resume a significant role in Constantinople between AD 531–532 and 536, in the reign of Justinian and Theodora.

During his exile he had developed a philosophically grounded defence of Monophysitism, depending not a little on others' tendencies to confuse the *ousia* (universal generic essence) with the *hypostasis* (single entity or specific subject) in which the *ousia* is encountered. By his careful definition of terms Severus showed his awareness that the Monophysite position had philosophical roots and was to be defended with philosophical argument. Against both 'Nestorians' and 'Chalcedonians' he argued that the union of the natures in Christ is closer than the sort of partnership which Peter and Paul have in their both being apostles. For Severus the humanity and divinity in Christ cannot be regarded as having distinct individual existence after the union. It is impossible to regard the human will as functioning apart from the divine will, or as being free to reject God's demands.

So the constituent elements of Christ are regarded as one, not two, and the sort of union which Severus envisaged meant that Christ could not have been ignorant in any way. While he claimed that the essential humanity of Christ was not lost in his divinity, as a drop of water is in the sea, the humanity for which he argued was radically different from that argued for by Theodore of Mopsuestia or the Chalcedonians. However, he won the support of the Empress Theodora, and throughout his life he

> 'not only restored the situation of his party thanks to his energetic action in Syria; he likewise gave it doctrinal equipment and determined its theology: we can say that the Monophysitism of history, the doctrine which has lasted until modern times is Severian Monophysitism.'[34]

While it was Severus who played the key intellectual role for Monophysitism, the key organisational task fell to *Jacob Baradai* (d. AD 578). Inveigled from east of Edessa to Constantinople by Theodora, he was confronted with dispirited, harried and somewhat divided Monophysites, when he was consecrated as one of two new metropolitans in AD 542. (The consecration took place at the express requests of the Empress and of the ruler of the Ghassanid Arabs, who occupied the border area between the Roman and Persian Empires.) While technically set apart as Bishop of Edessa, he travelled widely, frequently disguised as a beggar, and via ordinations and consecrations kept the Monophysite cause alive. He did so not only within the Roman Empire, but also within Persia, travelling to Seleucia to gain tolerance for them and to consecrate their own Catholicos in AD 559. Fluent in Greek, Syriac and Arabic he was one of the great figures of his day, and gave his name to the Jacobite (Syrian) Church which resulted. His work took in not only Syria and Persia, but also mediating in divisions among the Monophysites of Egypt. He consecrated succeeding Monophysite patriarchs in Antioch, some 27 bishops, and, reputedly, 100,000 priests (!). While not successful in all his efforts to build Monophysite unity, he nevertheless put that Church on a firm footing.

When the focus shifts eastward it lights first on *Tatian*, who seems to have returned from Rome to Mesopotamia under something of a cloud after the death of his teacher Justin Martyr in AD 165. From the four canonical gospels and the AD 140 *Gospel of Thomas* Tatian produced the harmony called the *Diatessaron*. This remained virtually the only version of the gospels in use among Syriac-speaking Christians for nearly 250 years, being replaced only in the 5th and 6th centuries. It also existed in other translations, thus spreading widely the influence of Tatian. He seems to have fitted readily into the predominantly Jewish-Christian groups at Edessa and from the east, not least because his ascetic and near-encratite emphases matched theirs.

Believing that humanity had lost its true spirituality and immortality, Tatian held that it now sought out the inferior, and that all forms of human life and activity are corrupt as a consequence. So he inveighed against procreation as a sure way to perdition.

'In Tatian's understanding the people of this world marry, but Christians do not: "the people of this world take a wife and make marriages; but they who shall be worthy of the life of that other world and of the resurrection of the blessed, will neither take wives nor make wedding feasts".'[35]

In this he was expressing views common among his East Syrian contemporaries, to be found also in the *Acts of Thomas* and given further affirmation in the writings of Aphrahat. He called on all Christians to imitate Christ, who

'as God's only-begotten son . . . lived a single life, asexual, demonstrating man's original unity and immortality. . . . Man becomes an immortal son of God when he is united to God's beloved Son, who is represented as the Spirit of the Lord.'[36]

In Judas Thomas, the one identified with the heavenly brother, Jesus, we see the example *non pareil* for us.

Tatian saw the Holy Spirit dwelling in us as in a temple, and in this and in the emphasis which separates what Christ did as a human being from what he did as God, he prefigures what was going to emerge in Diodore of Tarsus and Theodore of Mopsuestia. His emphases were also to be exploited by Mani, especially those which focussed on the activity of the divine Spirit, which was seen to have found an ultimate dwelling place in Mani himself, the promised Paraclete.

Overlapping in time with Tatian was the eclectic philosopher *Bardaisan* (d. AD 222), who came of noble, possibly Parthian, stock in Edessa. Raised in the royal court and subject to the various Jewish-Christian and Iranian-Zoroastrian influences abroad in Edessa, he became a Christian in the last quarter of the second century. As a scholar he sought to reconcile Christian beliefs with the Hellenized astrology of Babylonia, within his own philosophical system, a system with much in common with the concerns of contemporary fellow philosophers of the second century, as e.g. in the *Hermetica* of Hermes Trismegistos.

It is clear that he gathered a number of disciples, possibly from the upper social classes, and was strongly opposed to the Marcionite group, which with his own group, probably represented 'Christianity' in its earliest days in Edessa. Bardaisan seems to have left Edessa after the intervention there of the Emperor Caracalla in AD 216. For the rest of his life it appears that he lived in Armenia, continuing his study and, inter alia, meeting in AD 218 members of an Indian embassy sent to the Emperor Elagabalus.

From the most interesting of his extant works, the *Book of the Laws of the Lands*, we learn of Christians in India, Persia, Media and Parthia, and of laws which apply from India to Germany and Britain. Such laws are depicted as ways in which human free will has set limits to the ways in which astrological fate determines the destinies of men and women. We learn also of the ethic which distinguished Christians from their heathen neighbours, and accounted for at least some of the attraction of Christianity for not a few.

Much given to a love of liberty, Bardaisan set out upon his own distinctive path, drawing the teeth of astrological determinism and yet making room for astral influence in his system, an inclusion rejected by later critics. Indeed, it was virtually inevitable that he would run foul of later orthodoxy, and indeed among the Greek fathers, he is seen as an arch-heretic and a Valentinian Gnostic. Not a little of the condemnation lacked basis in fact, but even his compatriot Ephrem Syrus was strongly critical of a number of the aspects of his teaching.

As for his theology he held to one God, described in terms of Father, Mother and Son, with the former two probably not unrelated to sun and moon deities, and the Mother being related also to the Holy Spirit and to wisdom. In his emphasis upon one God he was clearly different from Marcion, as Ephrem admitted. The Son is identified with Jesus who comes less as a saviour than as an enlightener, or giver of wisdom. Bardaisan was docetic in that he did not hold that Jesus had a truly human body, for the latter was regarded as inherently impure. So he denied the resurrection of the body while holding to that of the soul.

His cosmology combined Jewish-Christian and Zoroastrian concepts, with the light set over against the darkness, but in no way is God responsible for evil or for matter. The four elements of earth, water, fire and light, through contact with darkness, emerge as created matter. A time of the cleansing from darkness is anticipated, so there is an eschatological emphasis in Bardaisan's approach.

As to humanity he held that the soul descends to the body through the spheres of the planets, each of which affects the soul and thus helps determine human weal and woe in the world. Adam made wrong use of the gift of the spirit, and, consequently, the soul is prevented from donning again its primal celestial robe in the 'Bridal-chamber of Light'. Evil is present in the body through mixing with darkness in creation, but that evil can generate no activity of its own. The impetus for this must come from human free will which Bardaisan held as captive ultimately neither to nature (or law) nor to fate (or chance). Given knowledge and faith, humans were challenged to strive after good in this world. The knowledge is brought into the world by Jesus, and this via human reason (or *nous*) delivers us from the impediments to our returning to the intended celestial state.

This view of cosmology is different in important aspects from 2nd century Gnosticism, like that of Valentinus. There are a number of similarities with the systems of Poimandres and the Hermetic *gnosis*, but it is not just to class Bardaisan with the Gnostics against whom Irenaeus and Hippolytus contended. His *gnosis* is acquired not by revelation but by intellectual insight. He has no tradition of secret *gnosis* of his own, and matter is not evil in its own right. There is no place for the 'Demiurge Creator', nor are humans divided into the spiritual, psychic and carnal categories of Gnosticism.

Nor as we have seen, may he be identified with Marcion, against whom he wrote. Instead of ascribing evil to creation, itself an accident, as did Marcion, for Bardaisan it is the substructure of salvation. Less pessimistic about humanity than was Marcion, he places more reliance on human endeavour.

Rather it is closer to the mark to realise that Bardaisan's system provided an avenue of thought which Mani exploited. The latter was a passive ascetic, but Bardaisan was an active combatant against evil. Each of them cast the struggle in terms of the liberation of particles of light (Mani) or the expulsion of darkness (Bardaisan). As Ephrem Syrus summed it up:

'Because Mani was unable to find another way out, he entered, though unwillingly by the door which Bardaisan opened.'[37]

Or as F.C. Burkitt put it

'. . . the religion of Mani becomes more comprehensible if the ideas of Bardaisan are recognized as one of its formative elements.'[38]

He was a groundbreaker, whom Mani was to follow, and left behind him a school which revived Syriac literature and philosophy. Some of these moved on into Manichaeism, while others joined the more Gnostically and astrologically-shaped 4th century Audians. However, some Bardaisanites remained in the time of Jacob of Edessa (d. AD 708), retained their interest in 'science' and played a part in conveying the sciences of antiquity to Islam. By then Muslims and Christians alike detected in them a dualism akin to that of the Manichaeans and the Gnostics, a dualism acceptable to neither Islam nor Christianity.

Working some 400 kilometres east-south-east of Edessa was the 'Syrian sage' *Aphrahat* (d. AD 345). Described as a monk and the Bishop of the convent at Mar Mattai, near Mosul, Aphrahat was born of pagan Persian parents ca. AD 280, and became a convert to Christianity in adulthood. He lived under Sasanid rule in Persia and witnessed Shapur II's persecution of Christians. At the same time he lived in an area which had become a focal point for Judaism, and it is clear that he was influenced by Jewish ideas far more than by those associated with Greece.

Because Jews seemed to have been treated less harshly than were Christians in Persia, doubtless in part because of the favour shown to the latter by the Roman emperors, apart from Julian, later Aphrahat was stridently critical of the Jews. However, a Jewish scholar, Jacob Neusner, absolves him from vilification of the Jews and regards him as a well-informed critic who used the scriptures in a rational, historical and mainly non-allegorical way to make his points.[39] Nevertheless, he used every text he could press into service to demonstrate that the old chosen people had been replaced by the new Israel, the Church of the Gentiles. He departs into allegory, when in discussing the woman in the parable in Luke 15:8, who lost one of ten pieces of silver, he claimed that she

'represents the house of Israel, who had lost the first of the ten commandments on which the remaining nine depend, and so in effect has lost all.'[40]

We know that between AD 336 and 345 he wrote some 22 *'Demonstrations'* or *'Homilies'* or *'Treatises'*, in which he displayed a profound knowledge of

Scripture – and of Christian theology, as interpreted through Syrian eyes. He contends against Marcionites, the Valentinian Gnostics and Manichaeans, but is strangely silent about Arius and Sabellius. It may be that he found the Greek approaches of Athanasius and Basil, e.g., uncongenial to his Syrian outlook. To him Christianity was not so much about speculations concerning divinity as about the revelation that the divine spirit was ready to indwell humanity and enable it in its struggle against moral evil.

Unlike Marcion or Theodore of Mopsuestia, Aphrahat was ready to see prophecies of Christ in the Old Testament. So he was given to see Old Testament 'types' pointing forward to Christ, and was ready to press some references into service in a way which seems forced to later readers. So e.g., he linked the reference to Zechariah 3:9 to 'a single stone with seven facets, or eyes' to the reference in Isaiah 11:2 to the seven aspects of the spirit of the Lord, of wisdom, understanding, counsel, might, knowledge and fear of the Lord. He went on and

> 'interprets the seven eyes (facets) as the seven gifts of the Spirit [as in Isaiah 11:2] . . . and goes further to interpret these as the seven eyes of the Lord which look upon the whole earth.'[41]

At the same time, possibly within a tradition established by Theophilus of Antioch (d. ca. AD 190), a Syrian by birth, he kept a strong emphasis on historicity, and that historical event provided the links between the Old and New Testaments. This approach has caused Neusner to comment that

> 'from the Apostolic Fathers to Nicea, Aphrahat remains very much by himself in his concentration on Scriptures as fundamentally historical documents.'[42]

Within the ascetic tradition we met in Tatian, Aphrahat plays a significant role. If humanity is to be a fit dwelling-place for the divine spirit, then celibacy is a prerequisite. He himself was a member of the group called the 'Sons of the Covenant', which he regarded as the backbone of the Church, a Church faced with persecution by a world for which he had but little regard. 'Virginity' is made virtually synonymous with 'holiness', and eremitic monks set out to live this out, in company with the animals, in what was seen as a return to primal Eden. To this were added mortifications and even the casting of oneself into fire or the jaws of wild animals, as a sort of martyrdom.

Baptism was not the common seal of the faith of every Christian but was reserved for celibates or those prepared to embrace celibacy for the rest of their lives. They thus made themselves 'single' for the Lord, or thus accepted 'circumcision of the heart'. It was in this way that you joined the 'community of the Covenant', or 'holy war'. As Aphrahat put it:

'He whose heart is set on the state of matrimony, let him marry
before baptism, lest he fall in the spiritual contest and be slain. He
also that loveth his possessions, let him turn back from the army, lest
when the battle wax too fierce for him he remembereth his property
and turn back and he that turneth back then is covered with
disgrace.'[43]

Those who were unprepared for this life, remained as unbaptised
'hearers', while those who were baptised lived as ascetic celibates in their
own homes, or accepted lives as hermits, anchorites or coenobitic monks.

Such stringency may not sit easily with us today, but it would be unfair to
leave the reader with the impression that Aphrahat is an unattractive
fanatic. As, e.g., the references from Neusner illustrate, even those whose
sympathies lie with the targets of Aphrahat's criticisms find much to
admire in the man, not least the love he has for the Church and his
opposition to arrogance and abuse of authority.[44]

If Aphrahat represents a Syriac approach with little sympathy with that
of the west, in *Ephrem Syrus* (d. AD 373) we meet someone who from
Edessa exercised much more of a mediating role, even between Antioch
and Alexandria. Through quite early translations into Greek his works,
poetry and hymnody in particular, became quite well known in the west.[45]

Most probably born in Nisibis, Ephrem came under the influence of
leaders such as the Bishop Jacob of Nisibis who attended the Council of
Nicea in AD 325. He appears to have been baptised and to have embraced
the solitary life at the age of 18 years and to have been ordained as a
deacon. Opposed to the emphases of the Emperor Julian, who visited
Nisibis in AD 362–363, Ephrem was caught up in the upshot of Julian's
defeat and death in AD 363, in that Nisibis was ceded to the Persians. After
a relatively short time there following this change in the city's status, he
joined others in exile. He settled on the outskirts of Edessa, lived in a
mountain cave and became a 'Son of the Covenant'.

While remaining interested in developments in Edessa and in particular
in the foundation there of a theological school among the refugees, the
so-called 'School of the Persians', it seems doubtful that he was the
school's founder or its first principal. If literary work took up most of his
time he still gained and retained the confidence of the Edessenes, to the
point where, not long before his death he was asked to superintend the
relief of the needy following a famine.

He was appalled at the minority status accorded to what he saw as
orthodox Christianity on his arrival and took up his pen to attack the
heretics in both prose and verse, most prominently in a work entitled, like
that of Irenaeus, *Against the Heresies.*[46] Not only did he oppose those
heresies which were the objects of Aphrahat's polemic, but he also sought
to combat Arianism, which had strong support from the Emperor Valens,

47

who visited Edessa in AD 372. One is tempted to believe that Ephrem played a part in so influencing the Edessenes that when Valens is said to have

> 'threatened the orthodox Christians there with a choice between death and apostasy to Arianism ... the people went out in multitudes to await martyrdom at the "famous splendid shrine" of St. Thomas, outside the city.'[47]

Only then could the Emperor be induced to revoke his order, but some three months after Ephrem's death in June AD 373, the bishop, Barsai and a number of others were expelled from Edessa, only to return after the death of Valens in AD 378 to regain their churches from Arian control.

Ephrem, while probably bi-lingual, was clearly acquainted with classical Greek philosophers. But he does not appear to have been ready to follow some Greek theologians in their attempts to use logic beyond what was, in his view, the reach of the human intellect in theology. In many ways he reflected earlier Syrian theological emphases on the free will and on a view of salvation in terms of 'recapitulation' (cf. Irenaeus) and the recovery of 'paradise lost'.

He was firmly opposed to syncretisms, of the type he detected in Bardaisan and his followers. To condemnations of magic and a reliance in astrology, he linked denunciation of shameful sexual conduct.

> 'When Ephrem, in his *Hymns contra Haereses* warns against the Books of the Chaldeans, because they make people err (V:14), or against sorcery that turns us into pagans (V:19), or against the cult of the Venus star in whose honour lewdness is committed (VIII:IX:8), these are exactly the same objections that the Church fathers formulate against the Bardaisanites and the Manichees.'[48]

More specifically Bardaisan was attacked for denying true monotheism, creatio ex nihilo, the resurrection of the body and for the subjection of God to planetary powers. Strongly monist in his approach, he condemned the elaborate cosmologies of the heretics. In many ways he marked the close of an early stage in Syrian theology and the opening of a new one.

Continuity with predecessors is seen in his approach to exegesis, in which he resembles Aphrahat. He is ready to find prophecies of Christ and of the Acts of the Apostles in the Old Testament, but is restrained in his use of typology, and even more restrained in his use of allegory. However, like Aphrahat, he is ready to apply allegory in instances where the obtuseness of the Jews is under focus. Thus, e.g. the blind and dumb man in Matthew 12:22 is said to represent the Israel depicted in Isaiah 6:10, while his healing points to those who believe. On the other hand he explicitly rejects Paul's allegorization of Sarah and Hagar, as was Theodore to do, or the allegorization of the six days of creation. In the usual Syrian tradition, even before Theodore of Mopsuestia's approach became normative after AD 428, Ephrem set out to apply historical common sense as a guiding principle.

Linked to this is his concern, along with Aphrahat once more, with those in the Old Testament who prefigure the sufferings of Jesus, from Moses, through Elijah and Elisha to Samuel, David, and Jeremiah. For him suffering was at the heart of the Christian life, as he saw it reflected in Colossians 1:24. So in his commentary on the *Diatessaron* he wrote:

'Jesus died to the world in order that no one should live to the world, and He existed in a crucified body in order that no one should walk sensually by it. He died to our world in His body in order that He may make (us) alive by His body to His world. And He mortified the life of the body in order that we may not live carnally by flesh. He is made the Master, a teacher not in tribulations of others but by his own suffering. And He Himself first tasted bitterness and (thereby) He showed us that no one can become His disciple by name but through suffering.'[49]

This he links with the condemnation of all that is flippant, especially laughter, which he calls

'the beginning of destruction of soul . . . laughter expels the virtues and pushes aside the thoughts on death and meditation on the punishment. O, Lord, banish from me laughter and give me weeping and lamenting, which Thou demandest from me.'[50]

Here we meet a typical Syrian stress on asceticism, linked to the ideal of the life of the anchorite, a life which parallels that of Jesus, not least in mountainous and desert areas. Christ dwells wholly in his disciples, and most particularly is this so among the anchorites in the wilderness. The elite of such anchorites are those

'who lived as though they were children of nature without a dwelling-place, and who used only grass, roots and fruits.'[51]

Ephrem provided great advocacy for the solitary monastic life, perhaps in the face of criticism of it. While he allowed for the fact that two or three monks may wish to live in community, it was no norm for monastic life in his view. This was in spite of the fact that the coenobitic or communal type of monasticism was growing in popularity towards the end of the 4th century. At most, Ephrem would see such a form as but an initiation into a monastic life which could only be realised in its fulness in solitude. However, he did stress the importance of study for the monk, as one of the ways towards spiritual maturity. Study and ascetic rigour combined to enrich the monastic ideal which he held up for others.

49

The rigour of Ephrem's approach may not appeal to many today, any more than does that of Aphrahat. However, there is no denying his achievements or the fact that translations of his works introduced Western Christians to the poetry and hymnody of the Syrian Church. He remains the most celebrated Father of that Church, a scientist as well as a theologian, with a regard for learning wherever he found it. He combined awareness of the importance of pastoral duties with a mastery of Syriac style. One scholar sums him up thus:

> 'I do not hesitate to evaluate Ephrem . . . as the greatest poet of the patristic age and, perhaps the only theologian-poet to rank beside Dante.'[52]

The new age heralded by Ephrem is clearly in evidence in the work of *Rabbula* (d. AD 435). Born of wealthy parents near Aleppo he travelled to Jerusalem and at his conversion, was baptised in the Jordan. He foreswore his wealth and family, and embraced the life of a recluse, until chosen as Bishop of Edessa in AD 411.

In Edessa itself Rabbula found much to which to bring his passion for order. The nobility in fact had clung to the old 'pagan' ideas associated with Bardaisan and had even been granted some tolerance for assembly, but not for sacrifices, by the Emperor Theodosius in AD 382. Rabbula set to work to demolish pagan shrines and to replace them with churches and infirmaries for the sick and needy. While Bardaisanites were still to be found at Edessa as late as AD 700, such moves, along with action against remaining Arians and Marcionites, brought greater attachment to Christianity amongst the population.

As to the Church itself, Rabbula, a great lover of order and conformity, set out to bring the Church at Edessa more into line with other major centres of the Church. Himself an austere man with a simple life style, he demanded the same from his clergy and the monks – the 'Sons and Daughters of the Covenant'. He promulgated canons to govern the lives of both groups – failure to conform entailed exile from his diocese.[53]

In his quest for conformity with Christianity at large, Rabbula at first was prepared to back John of Antioch (d. AD 441) and those favourably inclined towards Nestorius. However, the fact that Theodoret of Cyrrhus was able to show that the *Diatessaron* was open to a Nestorian interpretation, was enough to spur on Rabbula in his efforts to have it replaced by the latest Antiochene version of the four gospels. In the 'School of the Persians' at Edessa a leading figure was Hiba (d. AD 457), who was to succeed Rabbula eventually and who was the major translator into Syriac of the works of Diodore of Tarsus and Theodore of Mopsuestia. Hiba and his bishop came into conflict with each other, as Rabbula more and more distanced himself from the pro-Nestorius camp and allied himself with that camp's chief enemy, Cyril of Alexandria (d. AD 444). The die against Nestorianism was clearly cast at the Council of Ephesus in AD 431, the same year in which Rabbula summoned a council in Edessa, which consigned the writings of Theodore to the flames and expelled Hiba from the city. Cyril sent one of his works to Rabbula for translation into Syriac, thus beginning the corpus of 'Monophysite' writings in that language, referred to by the Jacobite Church. Rabbula himself spent considerable periods of time in these last years of his life promulgating anti-Nestorian ideas in the area around Edessa. This campaign set the Nestorians against him, not least because they regarded his attitude towards Theodore as persecution of the dead. At the bishop's death there was considerable bitterness among his opponents and foreboding about the future among his supporters.

Such foreboding was justified, for Rabbula was succeeded by Hiba, who was suspended for his pro-Nestorian views at the 'council' of Ephesus (AD 449) and reinstated conditionally at the Council of Chalcedon (AD 451). His death in AD 457 saw the Monophysites, who were rising to power in Antioch also, regain the bishopric at Edessa via the moderate Cyrillian, Nuna. The leading Nestorian scholar Bar Sauma (d. AD 490) was expelled from Edessa and went to Nisibis where he founded a school and eventually became bishop. The 'School of the Persians' at Edessa was closed in AD 489 and the staff and students, along with craftsmen and merchants who sympathised with them, migrated east to Nisibis.

The upshot of this was that Rabbula had succeeded in bringing Edessa more into line with the Western Church, albeit eventually into its Monophysite expression of Christology. No longer was it cut off from the other Churches of the Roman Empire by its gospel version, its liturgy and its doctrine. But this was at the cost of the loss of individual identity of life and thought. After Rabbula the theology of Edessa and East Syria became derivative from Greek theology, despite clashes in both cultural background and linguistic formation. And:

> 'While Monophysites looked to Antioch with the empire, the Nestorians segregated themselves in Kurdistan and Upper Mesopotamia, within the orbit of Persian domination.'[54]

And as for Edessa itself, it never again reached the status it had during the time of Ephrem, even with its association with the polymath *Jacob of Edessa* (d. AD 708) whose scientific, theological and philosophical interests showed increasing dependence on those of Greek thinkers. However, it was Jacob, after the decisions of the third Council of Constantinople in AD 681 to reaffirm Chalcedon and denounce the attempts to reach out to Monophysites through Monotheletism (i.e. that the Christ had only one will) who set about consolidating Monophysite doctrine. Lost to the Roman Empire by Arab triumphs in Egypt and Syria, the Monophysites felt free to be even more open in the condemnation of Chalcedon. There it was claimed, using the pretext of the madness of Eutyches, the 'Nestorian worship of a man' had been brought into the Church. Jacob claimed that the unity of the nature of the Trinity depended on the unity of the nature of Christ. In addition, in explicit opposition to Chalcedon, he held that the incarnation 'from two natures' rather than 'in two natures' was the crucial anchor of all true Christology. In addition he reminded all that the humanity, or as it was commonly called 'the flesh of Christ', had no existence of its own prior to the incarnation, and therefore that only the divine nature was a true hypostasis or logical subject of the Logos. So it was held that the person of Jesus Christ was of 'one incarnate nature of God the Logos', which Jacob saw as prefigured in the creation of 'man' as body and soul. In consequence Jacob's confession held that

> 'the holy, almighty, immortal God was crucified for us and died. Nor do we maintain, as do the Nestorians, those man-worshippers, that a mortal man died for us.'[55]

In such ways Jacob consolidated the earlier work of Severus of Antioch, and the lines between Monophysites, and Chalcedonians and Nestorians became clear to all concerned, despite reminders that they dealt with mysteries which were beyond adequate formulation.

THE ASCETIC SPIRIT OF SYRIAN CHRISTIANITY

Doubtless enough has been said already to alert the reader to the peculiarly ascetical tone of Christianity in Syria and Palestine. As one author summed up the situation:

> 'Early Syriac Christianity is permeated with asceticism.'[56]

It would seem probable that much of this had its roots in various Jewish groups like the Essenes, but there does seem to have been something of a propensity for mortification and fasting within the Syrian spirit long before the appearance of Christianity

> 'The same psyche which was formerly devoted to pre-Christian deities, was now placed at the disposal of the aims of Christian asceticism.'[57]

So the soil itself, within the Syrian countryside, was receptive to such seed.

The seed itself may be seen within Jewish Christianity in Jerusalem, in its first leader James. According to Hegesippus, as reported by Eusebius of Caesarea, James

> 'drank no wine nor strong drink nor did he eat flesh. No razor came upon his head; he did not anoint himself with oil, and he did not use the bath.'[58]

There are echoes here of the attitude of the Nazarenes, and at very least James ensured that the determinations of the council of Jerusalem, in Acts 15:29, included provisions concerning types of meat which could be eaten. Out of such a source could emerge, amongst those influenced by Jewish Christianity, features such as abstention from meat and wine, and various sorts of purification.

To the figure and influence of James could be added that of John the Baptist, whom Tatian, in the *Diatessaron* had on a diet of milk and honey, which was reputedly the food of heaven. It was clearly more difficult to make an ascetic of Jesus, who, it seems, was accused of being 'a glutton, and a drunkard, a friend of tax collectors and sinners' (Luke 7:34; cf. also 7:31–50). However, that did not prevent particular use being made of other references in the same gospel, as well as of such passages as 1 Corinthians 12 and 2 Corinthians 11:2 and Matthew 19:12. So Luke 6:20 & 21 were taken literally to exalt actual physical poverty and hunger, devoid of the references in the parallel Matthew 5:3 & 6 to the spiritual dimension of each. Such an approach was bolstered by reference to Luke 6:24 & 25. Along with these went the references in Luke 20:34–36 which favour celibacy as being 'angelic', and becomes even more explicitly so in the Old Syriac version. (Here we are reminded of what was said above about the emphases of Tatian and Aphrahat.) In similar vein, as far as the Syrian Church was concerned, the women in the parable of the bridesmaids (Matthew 25:1–13) are 'virgins', not just young girls, as in some modern English translations (e.g. R.S.V. and N.R.S.V.), and the virginity could be applied to men as well as to women. James of Jerusalem was cited as favouring virginity and, along with Essene influence this seems to have been sufficient to ease aside Judaism's support for marriage.[59]

We have met already a number of the later key contributors to the stress on asceticism. That the ascetic was regarded with the same respect as the martyr is clear, and even in the time of Ignatius of Antioch asceticism was an option for devoted Christians. A contemporary of the bishop at Antioch was Saturninus (d. AD 135) who, as a pupil in the school of Simon Magus and Menander, advocated celibacy and the rejection of animal food in his form of Gnosticism. Another Syrian Gnostic teacher of that period was Cerdo of whom it was reported that Marcion was a pupil, and who pushed Syrian dualism. Even when such 'Gnosticisms' were rejected by Christians, the ascetic stress remained and gained a sympathetic response from those who favoured rescuing the baby from the bathwater – to use a somewhat unfortunate figure.

A major influence was exerted by Tatian, who was subsequently regarded as the main protagonist of encratism, a system which places severe restrictions on the use of material good things along the lines represented already in James, but carried to extremes. As we lack a copy of

Tatian's *Diatessaron* in the original Syriac it is difficult to determine just how encratite it was. However, the views of Tatian are reported by Jerome, inter alia, to have been that he used the statement that

> "'if one seeds on flesh, he will reap perdition from the flesh" as an argument and interpreted it as meaning that he who seeds in flesh is none else than a person who enters into union with a woman, and that whoever has intercourse with his wife will reap perdition from the flesh.'[60]

> 'The people of this world take a wife and make marriages; but they who shall be worthy of the life of that other world and of the resurrection of the blessed, will neither take wives nor make wedding feasts.'[61]

Vööbus sums up thus:

> 'All the available sources are unanimous in their testimony that the fundamental conception around which the Christian belief was centered was the doctrine that the Christian life is unthinkable outside the bounds of virginity.'[62]

While the *Doctrine of Addai* depicts asceticism, including poverty, as a feature of the early Edessene Church, such an approach is very obvious in the *Acts of Thomas*, which was written at Edessa in all likelihood before AD 250. So in section 12 of this work the readers are reminded thus:

> '. . . know this, that if you abandon this filthy intercourse you become holy temples, pure and free from afflictions and pains both manifest and hidden, and you will not be girt about with cares for life and for children, *the end of which is destruction.* . . . But if you obey, and keep your souls pure unto God, you shall have living children whom these hurts do not touch, and shall be without care, leading an undisturbed life without grief or anxiety, waiting to receive that incorruptible and true marriage (as befitting for you), and in it you shall be groomsmen entering into that bridal chamber <which is full of> immortality and light.'[63]

The symbol of the 'bridal chamber', but not that of the Church as the bride of Christ, was much beloved of Aphrahat, who clearly preferred virginity to marriage. Ephrem was to make more of the latter image and so to develop it that Mary and the Church have the status of a 'second Eve', to parallel that of Jesus as the 'second Adam'. However, as A. Baker points out, the Syrians did grasp the gospel principle that it is

> 'not physical continence that avails anything but the single-minded dedication to Christ.'[64]

Undergirding all of this were convictions such as:

- the possession of anything is itself tantamount to sin
- the cross of suffering is to be borne by every Christian
- the sins of mankind are to be mourned
- all are called to mortification, to the point of virtual suicide.

Solitary ascetics were known in Syria from the mid-third century, and the eremitic form of monasticism was obvious also from early in the fourth century led by Hilarion (d. AD 371). The ascetics included women, as Eusebius reported, and they gathered others who would share in lives of meditation and service to others, with the aim of attaining a vision of God. Some of the more extreme ascetics adopted what appear to later generations as somewhat bizarre life styles, including those who ate only grass, herbs and roots, and exposed themselves naked to the bitter cold of winter and the searing heat of summer.

Doubtless the most famous of such ascetics were the stylites, who made their solitary homes atop stone pillars. The most celebrated of such was *Simeon Stylites*, who in AD 410–412 located himself some 50 kilometres east of Antioch and from AD 417–459 lived on top of a pillar (see pl. 4). Theodore reported that Christians came to consult the Stylite from as far away as Britain and Spain. Clearly he was regarded as someone who continued the office of 'prophet' in the Church and provided the model of the 'holy man' of later generations, down to and including the *startsi* of Russia.

Early in that same 5th century we have references aplenty to the 'Sons and Daughters of the Covenant', whom we have encountered already, when reviewing the lives of Aphrahat and Ephrem.

> 'They were neither hermits nor monks, and yet they are distinct from the common people, and belonged in a broad sense to the clergy . . . Virgins, dwelling apart from their families, would choose as their protectors ascetics of the opposite sex, travelling about with them, and even living in the same house with them. Such virgins were known as *syneisaktoi*. The practice of continents living together in this state of so-called "spiritual marriage" was vigorously opposed by the authorities of the Church.'[65]

Constituting an elite group, they were allowed to have modest possessions, and were forbidden to engage in any money making activity. At baptism, it was required that 'the heart be circumcised' and that a life of continence be embraced. Very much second best was the life which was governed precisely by the Ten Commandments. What had developed was a form of monasticism quite independent of that which appeared in Egypt under Antony. Equally second best in the eyes of this group were forms of coenobitic or communal monasticism, but these grew in popularity, along the model established by St. Basil the Great (d. AD 379) in the 6th century. Such a growth was against the condemnations of such as Isaac of Antioch (ca. AD 500), who regarded such coenobites as 'monks who had turned into merchants.'[66]

The ascetics' role was not entirely one of self-concern. Simeon Stylites, as well as being the spiritual mentor of many, was regarded virtually as the patron and protector of Antioch. His death, so soon after a particularly destructive earthquake at Antioch, was seen as a double penalty on the inhabitants of the city. The ascetics took up causes of social justice on behalf of the homeless, the needy, and poor and the powerless. Seeing themselves as outcastes, they campaigned for the suppressed and the powerless. In this they undertook roles quite different from those of the elite among the Manichaeans, even to the point of praying for barren women and for the restitution of marriages facing disruption – despite their own preferences for celibacy. It appears also that they opposed the institution of slavery as a denial of human dignity, and were ready to offer refuge, food, clothing and consolation to those in need. In all, asceticism was joined to concern for others in their attempts to imitate Christ and be joined with him.

SYRIAN MYSTICISM AND MONASTICISM

There was a close synergistic relationship between asceticism and mysticism as means towards the ultimate goal of vision of and union with God. The mystical emphasis was highly developed on Hellenistic and Jewish sources by *Dionysius the 'Areopagite'* in Syria in the 5th–6th centuries. While his influence was to be widespread in the West, after John Scotus Eriugena (d. ca. AD 877) had translated him, it was also significant for his influence among his Syrian countrymen.

Influences were not only homegrown for it is clear that the Egyptian *John of Lycopolis* (d. AD 394) was widely read in the Syriac translation, in which only are his works extant today. His treatise *The Spiritual State of the Soul* lays great stress on the ascetic preparation of the soul that seeks perfection, i.e. the life lived in conscious union with its Lord. John kept the focus on Christ for

> 'it is the "light of Christ" which dawns upon the soul, the "love of Christ" which cleanses it from sin, and the Path is the "way of Christ". It is through Christ . . . that the soul of the mystic comes to look upon the very essence of God, to be changed into his likeness and is made Godlike.'[67]

That renunciation of the material world is an integral part of the Way is made clear by John in many places, e.g.:

'Everything which is of this world is opposed to that which belongs to the Way of Christ. . . . As long as the mind is a captive to, and dominated by, the things of this world, whether they be great or small, so long will the light of the truth of the Way of Christ be hidden from it. . . . If a man does not, as far as is possible, keep his soul apart from the world, and renounce all that is in the world, both manifest and hidden, he cannot attain to the perfection of Christ Our Lord, to Whom be glory, and on us His mercy, for ever and ever. Amen.'[68]

Used as a guide to mystical doctrine and practice for more than 1300 years was the *Book of the Holy Hierotheos,* ascribed to the monk *Stephen Bar Sudayli* of Jerusalem ca. AD 500. With neo-Platonic and Alexandrian Christian emphases, the work set out 'to teach the Way of Perfection which leads to Heaven.'[69] It became the main source of western Syrian mysticism, as *Isaac of Nineveh* (d. ca. AD 700) became the chief representative of eastern Syriac mysticism. A bishop for only five months, Isaac became a mountain solitary, and sometime after AD 650 wrote his *Mystical Treatises* to guide other solitaries on the mystical path. In doing so he made use of Hierotheos, and of the 6th century solitary *Dorotheos* who established a laura near Gaza and stressed humility as the chief virtue in his *Instructions.* Also drawn upon were the Life of Anthony, St. Basil, Dionysius and Evagrius Ponticus (d. AD 399), the last being the first monk to write extensively.

Isaac was less concerned with the nature of the Godhead and with the final goal of union with God than with the Way of purification and illumination. His whole approach was eirenical, and once his particular references to Nestorian mentors were removed, his works had wide use among Monophysites and considerable influence on Muslim mysticism, being translated into both Greek and Arabic. This is not in anyway to gainsay his influence on Chalcedonian mysticism, but it was the Jacobites who preserved his writings, Nestorian as he was, for later generations. Isaac held that

'God is the only real Being; that man is made in the Divine image, and by purification can cleanse the soul from the defilements of sin, so that the image of God within it will once more be revealed. The soul, thus purified, can look upon God in all His Beauty, and once again be joined to That from Which it first came forth. He was plainly influenced by the teachings of the Alexandrian Hellenists and the Stoics – who taught that God was with man and within him – and to some extent by Philo, who also regarded man as the reflection of the Divine, and whose description of the soul rapt away from consciousness of itself when it has penetrated into the Holy of

Holies, is very like Isaac's description of the Vision. From Plato, no
doubt through the writings of Plotinus, he has taken the idea of the
ascent of the soul.'[70]

One 7th century Nestorian withstood all the blandishments of Alexandrian mysticism. He was *Sahdona* first of Nisibis and then of Edessa. In his *Book of Perfection* we see a restrained, deeply human spirituality, contrasting sharply with the ecstatic visionariness and esoteric intellectualism of his contemporary mystics.[71] In due course his Nestorian orthodoxy came under question and Sahdona found refuge in Edessa, where, in all probability the above work was written.

Such writings set a strong mystical mark alongside that of asceticism on Syrian monasticism. In contrast to the emphases on manual labour to be found in Benedictine, and also in Basilian, monasticism, the Syrian monks saw such labour as something fit only for weaker brethren. The emphasis was heavily on contemplation and no work was regarded as being more profitable than 'vigils'.

Monasticism itself, in its various forms, i.e. that of the solitary anchorites, that of those who pursued the solitary life in proximity to others in lauras or groups of dwellings, and that lived communally in the coenobitic fashion, grew in Palestine, Syria and Mesopotamia along organized lines from ca. AD 306. It was in that year that *Hilarion* (d. AD 371) began a solitary life near Gaza, and continued it until the crowds of people wishing to consult him caused him to leave for Egypt in AD 353. In Palestine itself in and around Gaza and Jerusalem monasticism flourished under the guidance of leaders and teachers such as *Euthymius* (d. AD 473) who established a laura at Khan-el-Ahmar in AD 426 and taught *Sabas* (d. AD 532). The latter founded a laura between Jerusalem and the Dead Sea and in AD 492 was made superior of all the monks in Palestine, being throughout a strong opponent of Origenism and Monophysitism. Leadership continued to be exercised by such as Dorotheos (6th cent.) who headed a monastery at Gaza.

While Palestine was thus a great centre of monasticism, much the same could be said for Syria. By AD 380 monks were settled in large numbers in the deserts, just beyond the limits of settlement in Syria and within the next 100 years Syria was dotted with monasteries and was to remain so up to the 11th century. As such, from the middle of the 4th century the monks exercised considerable influence in the countryside, not least in the displacement of paganism.

'At all times the monks, either as solitary holy men, or gathered in large communities, were in a position to influence people in all classes of society. In other words they could assist or harm in the same way as patrons whose influence was purely secular.'[72]

While further east such a figure as Ephrem seems to have had an anti-coenobitic approach, East Syrian anchorites often chose to live in proximity to each other in lauras. Some see *Jacob of Nisibis* (d. ca. AD 338) as having introduced monasticism into Mesopotamia by the end of the 3rd century. Located at first in the mountains near Nisibis the movement was marked always by that asceticism which abhorred death by natural means, and preferred to be destroyed through sufferings and torments which would fill up the sufferings of Christ (Colossians 1:24 and Hebrews 11:37). Be that as it may, the growth in numbers and in establishments caused Isaac of Antioch (4th cent.) to comment that the primitive housing stage had been left behind. Further consolidation occurred under the leadership of Abraham of Kushkan (d. AD 586), but the movement from eremitic to coenobitic monasticism was no easy one, nor was it welcomed by all monks. Indeed some opposed what they regarded as a retrograde development, and uniformity was impossible to effect, meaning that Syrian monasticism had to be marked by compromise.

The propensity towards asceticism or whatever the form of monasticism, was an emphasis shared by the Manichaeans, and may have been confirmed in Mani himself by experiences in India.

Indeed:

'Reports of the primitive monks give us a picture which is astonishingly congruous with the familiar portrait of the monks in India.'[73]

This led to strong condemnation from Ephrem who wrote:

'In Mani the lie from India has again come to domination.'[74]

That this had to be said is a measure of the fact that Manichaean emphases were all too obvious in Syrian monasticism. After all the Manichaeans claimed to be true Christians and many of their emphases were congenial to Syrian Christians. So widespread did the influence, and even the intermingling, become that when Manichaeism came under persecution in Persia ca. AD 275 Christian leaders were hard put but anxious to distinguish their faith from that of Mani. The same tactic had to be repeated in AD 410–415.

One group closely related to the Christians and marked by Mystical asceticism were the 4th to 7th century Messalians, who were accused by Theodoret of suffering from Manichaeism. Having varying relationships with the institutional Church

'common to the whole movement, in its various shades and ramifications, is a deep and determined discontent with the ordinary attainments in the outward forms and in the mechanization of the religious and ascetic life. It is the conviction of the Messalians, that the outward turning of the back upon the world and the reliance on external asceticism, does not automatically result in a turn into the inner world. Their emphasis is laid on an awareness of the all-pervading power of the Evil One and on longing for the coming of grace and mystical illumination, as a source of renewal.'[75]

Nevertheless, we must not forget the social concerns shown by the Syrian monks, who were admired for more than their famous ascetical devotion, as we have seen above. Syrian Christian schools, whether attached to monasteries or located within town bounds, were active as centres for the promotion of learning. At the more popular level they reached out to the boys of the urban communities. As one account has it of a school at Amid:

'The blessed [monks] . . . chose for themselves to teach boys. This they did out of the window since a seat was placed inside the window and hours were fixed for the boys to come, that is, in the morning and in the evening; and when they had taught one class to read the Psalms and the Scriptures, and these had withdrawn, another came in of little infants, thirty of them; and they would learn and go to their homes, for it was a populous village. And so the old men continued to do until the time of their end; and the boy pupils supplied their needs.'[76]

At a deeper level the scholars of the Syrian monasteries kept Greek learning alive during the 7th and 8th centuries, when it was at a low ebb in both the Latin West and the Greek East. A monastery like that at Qenneshre in North Syria produced a number of boy scholars and must have been one of the main centres of Greek learning at the time. Key figures produced by such schools were Severus of Nisibis and Jacob of Edessa. Probably the first among such distinguished schools was that at Nisibis, which we have met already and will meet again later. There the tutors were monks,

'and the students underwent a three years course, mainly theological, though Greek philosophy was studied as the foundation of Christian theology.'[77]

While Greek learning was thus preserved, it had a greater and seemingly more inhibiting influence on Syrian culture than on that of the Arabs. The native Syrian creative spark seemed to have dimmed, not least in the field in which it had shown exceptional skill, that of religious poetry. However, the reputation of the Syrian schools stood high and they were envied elsewhere. For example, Cassiodorus (d. AD 580) set up a theological college in the monasteries he founded at Vivarium, along the lines of those at Nisibis and Edessa, but they did not survive his death.

Overall, the Syrian monks were the sources of much learning and instruction not least on those things which belong to eternal peace. Increasingly the guidance of the religious and moral life of many people moved into their hands. They promoted the publication of key works, provided leaders for the Church and after AD 450 were instrumental in shaping the monasticism and religious life of Ethiopia. In addition they made an impact on the lives of the Arabs in the border lands and to the south.[78]

Very clearly the Syrian monks were imbued also with a strong missionary zeal, which we shall follow in some detail in later sections. Here we need note further only two examples, their impact on Armenia and Georgia to the north.

> 'What we have of the Armenian sources testifies to how deeply Christianity in this area became the operation field for Syrian monasticism. This is mirrored in many-sided activities in all the fields of Christian life and work. The Syrians created the tradition, ecclesiastical discipline, architecture and the beginnings of a religious literature before the rise of the indigenous literature – this for the purpose of instruction and worship. Syriac, too, became the language of liturgy and worship.'[79]

Pre-Christian inscriptions found in Georgia add their testimony also from the 4th century, and these inscriptions are of official character, but they are not written in Georgian, as we might expect, but in an Aramaic dialect. The inference is that the official language of the country was not Georgian at that time but an Aramaic dialect. If so this would have been a factor which must have facilitated the missionary enterprise of the Syrians in such a way that it would have been incredible had the Syrian monks stayed in Armenia, and not entered Georgia.[80]

COMMON RELIGIOSITY AND DISTINCTIVE COMMUNIONS

References have been made already to those religious approaches which made Syrian Christianity distinctive. The capacity of the Syriac language to absorb other dialects fostered the belief that the language itself smacked of heaven. Partly in reaction against what was regarded as Graeco-Roman presumption and arrogance, and partly via translations and other contributions of monasteries and schools, a distinctive Syrian approach was hammered out. Decades after Nicea it had a fierce advocate in Aphrahat (d. AD 345). That the approach could find its expression via asceticism and mysticism we have seen already.

It also produced its own emphases re symbols favoured in reference to the Church. While relatively little seems to be drawn explicitly from the Apostle Paul, under such as Aphrahat and Ephrem there are stresses laid on:

- Christians as the 'Church of the Gentiles', the 'new people' who have replaced the Old Testament 'chosen people'
- the physical body of Christ, not least via the sacrament of the Eucharist, probably to counter the anti-material views of the Gnostics, Marcion and Mani
- references to the body of Christ as temple or church
- Christ as the 'second Adam', a figure treated as a corporate personality, as was the first Adam
- images such as the vine, the vineyard, the tree of life and the rock, the last having considerably greater prominence in the Syriac Peshitta than in the Greek New Testament
- spiritual marriage, with the early stress on the Holy Spirit as 'mother' being replaced later by the Church having a maternal role – indeed relatively little is recorded about the role of the Holy Spirit
- the Church as a pilgrim group on the way to the fulfilment of the kingdom, along with an expression of the Church as both 'visible' and 'invisible'.

Following the condemnation of Nestorius at the Council of Ephesus in AD 431 life became less and less attractive for those who adopted Theodore of Mopsuestia as their great mentor. The efforts of Bishop Rabbula at Edessa to bring that Church more into line with the Church in the West, and subsequent events, saw the Nestorians begin to move east, their leader Bar Sauma doing so in ca. AD 460 after expulsion from Edessa. The Nestorian chapter at Edessa effectively concluded in AD 489 with the closure there of their school, which transferred to Nisibis within Persian territory. Consequently, Nestorians ceased to be a major concern for the Roman Imperial authorities.

While decisions of the Council of Chalcedon in AD 451 were regarded by its supporters as against Apollinarianism, Nestorianism and Eutychianism, those whose sympathies lay with what they took Cyril of Alexandria to have been arguing regarded Chalcedon's decisions as pro-Nestorian. Those who had shaped the council's declarations were not attuned to the ethos of either the Egyptian or the Syrian countrysides. To the populations of both areas most of Chalcedon was anathema, and increasingly a Monophysitism, attributed falsely to Cyril, was advanced.

At first, some effort was made to accommodate Monophysite concerns, as, e.g. in the *Henoticon*, proposed by the Emperor Zeno in AD 482. Its implied criticism of Chalcedon led to strong reactions from Rome, and eventually to the excommunication by the Bishop of Rome of the patriarchs of Alexandria and Constantinople and the Emperor. The resulting schism lasted until AD 518, when Justin I succeeded as Emperor and set about re-affirming Chalcedon. As part of such policy military and bureaucratic pressure was brought on the population of Syria, futher hardening it in its opposition to things Chalcedonian and Graeco-Roman both. Liturgically, this was expressed by the addition by Bishop Peter the Fuller (d. AD 488), of Antioch, to the *Trisagion* of the Monophysite clause 'who was cruficied for us', so that it read:

'Holy God, Holy Almighty, Holy Immortal, who was crucified for us, have mercy on us.'

Fifty-four Monophysite bishops were removed from their sees, and monks and priests pressured to conform to Chalcedon between AD 521 and 525. To preserve a Monophysite clergy one bishop, John of Tella (d. AD 538), engaged in clandestine ordinations as far as was practicable. In so doing he provided a model for similar activity later by Jacob Baradai. Out of this persecution there came renewed devotion to the Monophysite cause.

The persecution eased somewhat with Justinian's accession in AD 527, although the continued activities of John of Tella did not go unnoticed or approved. In effect he was building up an alternative communion with its own canons and structures for the future. Nevertheless, exiles were allowed to return, and with the support of the Empress Theodora some talks aimed at reconciliation occurred at Constantinople in AD 533. (Those involved include Severus, and John of Tella himself.) Papal opposition and the misgivings of Justinian led to the failure of these attempts by AD 535.

In AD 536, under the advocacy of Pope Agapetus I, the persecution of Monophysites was renewed. Their leaders were anathematised, Severus was gaoled, supporters were replaced in positions of leadership, and Monophysites were banished from Constantinople. Severus' works were burned and copying of them made a punishable offence. John of Tella was unable to ordain within the Empire and eventually he was caught and executed in February AD 538. Reliance for ordination came to rest on only one bishop who resided in Persia, but in AD 544–545 the borders were sealed due to war. Monophysite prospects seemed very dim indeed in Syria.

However, the strategically important Ghassanid Arab tribes on the borders between Persia and the Roman Empire, under their leader Harith bar Gabala, favoured Monophysitism. In AD 542–543 he asked the Empress Theodora to find two Monophysite bishops for his people, and she was ready to assist. Two monks at Constantinople were found and consecrated. One was Theodorus who became Bishop of Arabia, an area peopled by nomadic Arabs which reached almost to Jerusalem and an area in which Monophysite refugees found haven. The other was Jacob Baradai who was ostensibly Bishop of Edessa and whose work we have outlined already. Suffice it to record here that by AD 566 the Monophysite hierarchy in Syria seemed secure with a patriarch and two metropolitans.

This is not to imply that persecution from Constantinople ceased. The later years of Justinian and those of Justin II (AD 565–578) saw it ease and there were further attempts at reconciliation. These attempts had the support of the 'Green' faction in Constantinople, which faction maintained its sympathy for Monophysitism. However, with Maurice (AD 582–602) persecution was renewed, and at Edessa itself no less than 400 monks who refused to forswear Monophysite views were executed outside a city gate. The city's churches were handed over to the Chalcedonian Melkites, and the persecutions eased only when a number of natural calamities caused the persecutors to have second thoughts.

Phocas removed Maurice and ruled until AD 610, somewhat to the relief of the persecuted, not that he was any less anti-Monophysite. But in AD 610 he was replaced by Heraclius who was to reign until AD 641. Heraclius inherited considerable chaos throughout the Empire, with the Slavs and Avars in control of the Balkans and the Persians encamped in Asia Minor, somewhat to the relief of the Monophysites. It was not until AD 622 that Asia Minor was recovered, and after a series of setbacks and partial victories the lost Near East was recovered, and Persia humbled by AD 628. Throughout these vicissitudes the leaders of the Orthodox Church had been staunch allies of the Emperor who in AD 630 restored to Jerusalem the holy cross removed by the Persians seventeen years earlier.

Heraclius had visited Edessa in AD 628 and was impressed by its monastic piety and scholarship. The Bishop, Isaiah, refused him a role in the service in the cathedral unless the Emperor condemned both Chalcedon and the theological opinions expressed by Pope Leo the Great in AD 449, in what is called his *Tome*. This led to exile for the bishop, and a number of his aristocratic supporters, and to the Monophysite churches there being delivered into Melkite hands. However, Heraclius was convinced of the need to somehow reconcile Monophysites and Chalcedonians, not least in key areas such as Syria and Egypt. So he supported the monergism (single activity of Christ) attempts of Patriarch Sergius of Constantinople (d. AD 638) and gained support from Pope Honorius I of Rome (d. AD 638) and Cyrus, the Patriarch of Alexandria. But strong Chalcedonian condemnation of the approach came from the Patriarch of Jerusalem, Sophronius (d. AD 638). This led Sergius to amend his approach to monotheletism (one will in Christ) in AD 636, and Heraclius promulgated this in his *Ecthesis* of that year. However, it failed to gain support from the Monophysites and Honorius' successors in Rome were also opposed. So the final effort to find a formula under which Chalcedonians and Monophysites might find unity proved futile.

But in any case other factors intervened, for the Arab expansion overtook all these efforts, and by AD 639 Edessa was in Arab hands. The conquerors maintained the status quo concerning property, but at least the Monophysites were now removed from Byzantine attempts to enforce conformity with Chalcedon. So, as one Monophysite historian commented ruefully, but gratefully 'at this time the Great Church of Edessa . . . had passed from us. Nevertheless, the advantage to us was not small, in that we were delivered from the cruelty of the Byzantines and from their evil and their wrath and their bitter zeal against us, and we had rest.'[81]

In Edessa the Monophysites were represented by both Syrian Jacobites and Armenians, each of which maintained their own school in the city.

Throughout these upheavals there had been Monophysite expansion into northern Mesopotamia, at the expense of the Nestorians who had found a haven there. Such incursions had been sufficient to cause the Nestorian Patriarch, Ishu-Yab (d. AD 658), to upbraid the local Nestorians for their laxity. The momentous events in themselves encouraged belief that the last days were present and apocalyptic writing abounded, with persecutions and disasters seen as harbingers of the End of all things. So, e.g., Monophysites saw the Arab victories as divine punishment for Byzantine arrogance and persecution.

While after AD 450 Nestorian thought does not appear to have had the same flowering as that of the Monophysites, its stress on the essential humanity of Jesus said much to the harsh desert life experience of many solitary monks. Inspired by the 'companionship' of Jesus, as described in Hebrews 4:15, and also by the conviction that his obedience had rectified the disobedience of Adam, the Nestorian monks saw themselves as continuing this process. As the approach has been described:

'Through Christ's real humanity he is united to man and has thus renewed human life, indeed all material creation, just as he has renewed the spiritual realm through the union of that realm with his spiritual reality.'

This process is

'to be continued voluntarily by his church and initiating the church into the life of heaven in which man is freed from indigence and becomes immortal and immutable.'[82]

So while Syria, occupied by the Muslim Arabs after AD 638, had both adamant Chalcedonian Melkites and equally adamant Monophysites, it was the latter along with Nestorians who predominated in northern Mesopotamia. If the extremes were represented by the Monophysites and the Nestorians, they had in common their rejection and abhorrence of Chalcedon. To this must be added the fact that there is no surviving Syriac reference to the succession of Petrine primacy at Rome. In fact such primacy as there was was related to the Catholicos among Nestorians and to the Patriarch among Jacobites, or to the whole episcopal college in each group.

'At the same time, apart from the animus of the Jacobites against Pope Leo and of the "Nestorians" against Pope Celestine, they have nothing to say for good or ill about the Roman primacy; their isolation prevented irritations and embitterment, and often in the future was to make friendly relations, and even partial reunions, possible.'[83]

UNDER MUSLIMS AND CRUSADERS TO AD 1510

Reference has been made several times to the fact that some Christians, particularly the harried Monophysites, were ready to welcome the triumphs of the Muslim Arabs over the arrogant, persecuting Roman Empire. Naturally those Christians who supported Chalcedon, i.e. the Melkites, were appalled. So, Sophronius of Jerusalem (d. AD 638) called for repentance that they might all be freed from the Muslim yoke, and Maximus the Confessor (d. AD 662), in correspondence between AD 634 and 640, wrote of a 'barbaric nation from the desert' as having temporarily overrun lands not their own, a sign that the Anti-Christ was at hand.

While all Christians saw the Arabs as a scourge on others' heresies, it was not until around AD 700 that Islam assumed the place once assigned to Rome as the fourth member of the bestiary of Daniel 7. The *Apocalypse* of about AD 690 attributed to Methodius, for all its acceptance by Monophysite circles, regarded the Roman Empire as certain to be restored to control after some 70 years. The Arab triumph was seen as a temporary one, to punish the Empire for such faults as sexual licence, and while Arabic and Jewish eyes saw the capture of Constantinople as the ultimate goal, Christian hopes were focussed on the recapture of Jerusalem.

Once it was accepted that Arab rule was likely to be of long duration there was considerable emphasis on Muslim monotheism as a belief held in common with Christians. However, very little in the way of detail was known about Islam. When taken up in some detail by John of Damascus (d. AD 749), who served within the Umayyad bureaucracy, as had his father before him, Islam was depicted as itself a Christian heresy. Within a Christian ghetto, John prayed for the victory of the Byzantine emperor over 'the people of the Ishmaelites, who . . . as blasphemous enemies . . . are fighting against us.'[84] At the same time John seems more concerned over the iconoclasm of the Syrian born Emperor Leo III (d. AD 741) than he was over Islam, his iconoclast critics regarding him as 'pro-Saracen'. He opposed Islam on theological rather than political grounds, and: 'His aim was to inform the Christian community of the faith and practice of the Muslims with whom they shared their communal life, rather than to inflame hatred.'[85]

All too readily Constantinople's attitudes were based on hearsay and there was ready recourse to ad hominem attacks on Muhammad as an 'Arian', a 'liar', 'hypocrite', 'pseudo prophet' and 'adulterer', and on reputed Arab lechery. Far better informed on Islam was the Arabic-speaking Bishop Theodore Abu-Qurra in the latter half of the 8th century in Syria. In some 17 out of 52 short treatises, Theodore used but little abuse, relying more on dialogue and discussion. He attempted to expound the doctrine of the trinity to deal with Muslim charges of tri-theism, and dealt also with other main points of the critique directed against Christianity. A somewhat similar approach was taken by Nicetas Byzantios, in the 9th century. He covered similar areas, and despite his lack of knowledge of Arabic, he used several translated versions to refute the claims of the Qur'an. Clearly by the middle of the 9th century, with Dionysus of Tellmahre (d. AD 845) we have clear recognition that Islam was less of a Christian heresy than a distinctive new religion.

The dialogue approach is most obvious and detailed in the supposed correspondence between Caliph 'Umar II (d. AD 720) and the Emperor Leo III (d. AD 741). On what is argued to be a Greek original, followed by a Latin abridgement, and then an expanded Armenian form by Ghevond in the 9th–10th century,[86] a detailed dialogue is developed which revealed wide knowledge of respective Christian and Muslim emphases. In what may only be described as a good spirit one chided the other over such issues as the falsification of Scripture, the role and status of Jesus and of Muhammad, the divisions among both Christians and Muslims, the replacement of Saturday by Sunday or Friday and the veneration of relics and pictures on one hand and of the Ka'bah at Mecca on the other. Overall the consensus of opinion on the correspondence is that there was an authentic original, and if this is so, it reveals a considerable advance in understanding, even when we discount a good deal of the detailed contents as having been expanded over the years since the original.

With the further passage of the years, knowledge of the other faith increased, and with it understanding, not that Christians gave up hopes for the conversion of Muslims or vice-versa. So by the 12th century Byzantine views of Islam reflected some attitudes that were negative to the extreme, but also some that looked for agreement on a monotheistic basis. And in the later writings of the retired Emperor, John Cantacuzenos (d. AD 1383), there is informed discussion of Islam coupled with hopes for its conversion, hopes echoed by the theologian Gregory Palamas (d. AD 1358). It should be noted, in this connection, that Muslims who converted to Christianity were required still to anathematise Muhammad and all his relatives.

As we have seen with John of Damascus, Christians of whatever persuasion, including Melkites like John, were not averse to co-operating with and serving their new rulers. The Arabs were quick to recognize their need of help in the professional, educational and bureaucratic tasks associated with their new empire. Experienced Christian bureaucrats were widely employed, not least in the area of financial management. As Smith put it:

'Under the Umayad caliphs, Syrian Christians frequently held high office at Court, and in the reign of Mu'awiya, the governor of Medina employed Christians from Ayla to police the sacred city.'[87]

That this was not restricted to Syria or Arabia is clear from a report of Mukaddasi that in the 10th century

'the clerks in Syria and Egypt were Christians, as were most of the doctors in Syria. In 369 [AH, i.e. AD 991] the vizier in Baghdad was a Christian, Nasr ben Harun.'[88]

At a somewhat lesser, but still observable level were the contributions of Byzantine architects and craftsmen to the buildings and mosaic decorations of Damascus and Jerusalem, not least being the latter's famous Dome of the Rock.

Such contributions eased the path of conversion to Islam for not a few, as also did contributions from Christians towards the development of Islamic thought and institutions. Not least did these come from the fact that between AD 750 and 950 Jacobites and Nestorians, transmitted to the Muslims virtually all the knowledge enshrined in the Syriac language, and what was known of pagan Greek thought. In addition the Christian mysticism of the region played a role in the development of Sufism among Muslims.

From the Muslim side there was not only the acceptance of Christian contributions as a matter of expediency. While they looked for and encouraged the conversion of Christians to Islam, they saw them, along with the Jews, as 'people of the Book' because they shared with Muslims the heritage of the Hebrew scriptures. The Qur'an itself supported dialogue with non-believers, and Muslims, for all their enmity with the Roman Empire, were not universally hostile to Christians or their faith. Nor was any distinction made between the various Christian groups, except to have some special care with respect to the Melkites, whose attitude towards Constantinople was clearly more positive than that of the Jacobites. It was usual to leave Christian churches untouched, or at most to take over some in a town, or to share with Christians portions of the buildings concerned. The most renowned of such cases was the fact that

'the cathedral of St. John the Baptist in Damascus was shared by Muslims and Christians until the reign of al-Walid (AD 705–715), when on some pretext the whole was transformed into a mosque.'[89]

There are cases recorded also in which Muslims and Christians shared in ceremonies associated with the nativity of Christ.[90]

On a more individual level, a Muslim leader like 'Umar

'when he visited Syria in AD 639, stayed with the Bishop of Ayla, and he showed friendliness towards the Christians of the town. Elsewhere, many of those forming the agricultural population of Syria, while remaining Christian, settled down peacefully under Muslim rule.'[91]

Likewise many Christian Arabs, particularly the famous tribe of Banu Taghlib in Central Mesopotamia, while ready to ally themselves with Islam in war, retained their Christian faith, under both the Umayyad and Abbasid caliphates.

'The same was the case with the Beni Tanukh who remained Christian up to the reign of the Caliph al-Mahdi.'[92]

On the other hand the Banu Ghassan, like many other Christians, yielded to persuasion of argument and opportunity and became Muslim.

This leads us from the area of overall attitudes to that of official arrangements. What sort of modus vivendi was developed for Christians within Islamic society? In general the Christians were regarded as a *milla*, or religious sect, and were required to pay special tribute taxes, not least in lieu of military service. They were given the right to keep (most of) their churches, but, ostensibly, were not permitted to build new ones. Tax reforms instituted by 'Umar II (AD 717–720) encouraged conversions to Islam, but churches and monasteries remained exempt from such taxation. However, he insisted that Christians and Jews wear distinctive garb, and he excluded them from public office. Nevertheless, his reign was a brief one, and again we know but little as to how widely and strictly his measures were enforced. Even when the Caliph Mansur (AD 754–775) ordered the branding of all Christians, the execution of the decree varied from place to place, as had Roman persecutions of Christians before AD 311.

The best known detailed statement of the official situation is that in the so-called *Covenant of 'Umar.* Drawn up in the schools of law it came to be ascribed, like much else, to the famous caliph, 'Umar I (d. AD 644). Somewhat curiously couched in language which is that of the vanquished towards the victors, the text, in a letter of the chief commander in Syria, Abu 'Ubaida, runs as follows:

'When thou camest into our land we asked of thee safety for our lives and the people of our religion, and we imposed these terms on ourselves; not to build in Damascus and its environs church, convent, chapel, monk's hermitage, not to repair what is dilapidated of our churches nor any of them that are in Muslim quarters; not to withhold our churches from Muslims stopping there by night or day; to open their doors to the traveller and wayfarer; not to shelter there nor in our houses a spy, not to hide one who is a traitor to the Muslims; to beat the nakus [i.e. bell] only gently in our churches, not to display a cross on them, not to raise our voices in prayer or chanting in our churches, not to carry in procession a cross or our book, not to take out Easter or Palm Sunday processions; not to raise our voices over our dead, nor to show fires with them in the markets of the Muslims, nor bring our funerals near them; not to sell wine nor parade idolatry in companies of Muslims; not to entice a Muslim to our religion nor invite him to it; not to keep slaves who have been the property of Muslims; not to prevent any relative from entering Islam if he wish it; to keep our religion wherever we are; not to resemble the Muslims in wearing the kalansuwa, the turban, shoes, nor in the parting of the hair, nor in their way of riding; not to use their language nor be called by their names; to cut the hair in front and divide our forelocks; to tie the sunnar round our waists; not to engrave Arabic on our seals; not to ride on saddles; not to keep arms nor put them in our houses nor wear swords; to honour Muslims in their gatherings, to guide them on the road, to stand up in public meetings when they wish it; not to make our houses higher than theirs; not to teach our children the Koran; not to be partners with a Muslim except in business; to entertain every Muslim traveller in our customary style and feed him in it three days. We will not abuse a Muslim, and he who strikes a Muslim has forfeited his rights.'[93]

A briefer version, with some features distinctive to it, runs thus:

'These are the terms imposed on the Christians. The rich are to pay forty-eight dirhams, the middle class twenty-four, and the poor twelve. They are not to build churches, not to lift up a cross in the presence of Muslims, and to beat the nakus inside the churches only. They are to share their houses that the Muslims may dwell in them, otherwise I ['Umar] shall not be easy about you. They are to give that part of the churches towards Mecca as mosques for the Muslims, for they are in the middle of the towns. They are not to drive pigs into the presence of Muslims. They are to entertain them as guests three days and nights. They are to provide mounts, for those on foot, from village to village. They are to help them and not to betray them. They are not to make agreements with their enemies. He who breaks these conditions may be slain and his women and children made slaves.'[94]

It would appear that some of these provisions were first effected under 'Umar II, which doubtless helped the ascription of the document(s) to his illustrious predecessor and namesake. However, references to the *Covenant* are not common until later.

> 'In the first century (AH) it is ignored; in the second some of its provisions are sometimes observed. By 200 AH (i.e. AD 815/816) it existed in the traditional form, but with many minor variations.'[95]

So a continued Christian existence, within certain limitations, was quite possible, under Muslim rulers. Pressures to convert came via financial decrees on one hand and from perceived opportunities for advancement on the other. Sectarian divisions among Christians was another factor which promoted conversion to Islam. But even some who accepted Islam did so nominally rather than with conviction beyond such perceived opportunity. So many

> 'who formed an important part of the Umayyad armies, cared little for Islam, and were described as "Arabs" like strangers and Muslims with the characteristics of Christians.'[96]

The Jacobites, as the majority group of Christians in Syria and as far east as Nisibis, held their ground overall for some centuries. The monastery of Mar Barsauma, between Samosata and Melitene, was the seat of Jacobite patriarchs in the 8th and 9th centuries, and another important centre was Haran. Some Jacobite monasteries had as many as 1000 monks, mainly living in coenobitic fashion with associated hermits. Under the united Arab rule of Syria and Persia Jacobites had missionary opportunities further east, but were not in a position to seriously challenge Nestorian efforts in these areas. Nevertheless by AD 1280 Barhebraeus (d. AD 1286) reported that the Jacobite patriarch oversaw 20 metropolitans and about 100 bishops from Anatolia and Syria to lower Mesopotamia and Persia. Relations with Muslims continued along constructive lines up until the era of the crusades, but Jacobite numbers declined greatly late in the Middle Ages.

The 10th century saw a resurgence of Byzantine power under Emperor Nicephorus Phocas (d. AD 969). In AD 965 he had recaptured Tarsus, Mopsuestia and Cyprus. Antioch held out against the Byzantines until AD 969, and Aleppo fell to them in AD 970. Consolidation of gains, against the Fatimid reaction from Egypt ensued under the Emperor John Tzimisces (d. AD 976), and gains were made as far south as Caesarea, but caution dictated against over-extension of the lines of supply and communication. Fatimid reaction continued until the end of the century and reached its most extreme form under the caliphate of al-Hakim (AD 1009–1020), when

> 'the Christians of Egypt and Syria were persecuted, and the churches of Jerusalem were destroyed, and the furniture of the churches was

spoiled, and the Christians were made to wear a wooden cross of five pounds weight round their necks, and a large number became Muslims; and hearts were torn with pity. . . . And the bishop in Egypt related that in the western districts the number of churches destroyed reached about 40,000 churches and monasteries, and that only a few persons [Christians] remained.

The general accuracy of this brief statement is borne out by other authorities. It appears that the motive of Hakim was zeal for Islam, and he was particularly angered against the Christians and Jews because of the important positions they held in the state and their insolent bearing towards the Muslims.'[97]

Under the Emperor Basil II (d. AD 1025), Antioch was secured, and in the year of this Emperor's death Edessa was regained by the Byzantines.

A new power arose on the scene some 40 years later in the Seljuk Turks, who by AD 1067 had invaded Cilicia and had captured its capital Caesarea. Three years later the Byzantines took, but then lost Jerusalem to the Seljuks, to be followed that same year by the loss of Antioch. A major defeat for the Byzantines at Manzikert in Armenia in AD 1071 meant the loss of Asia Minor and a threat to Constantinople itself, while Syria and Palestine seemed secure in Seljuk hands. In Edessa there was a period of instability as between AD 1077 and 1086 the Armenian Philaretos ruled. Then the Seljuk Turks took control until AD 1095, when for the next three years the ruler was Thoros, a lieutenant of Philaretos. The crusades were to lead to further changes up until AD 1144.

The crusade period from AD 1095 to 1291 had long reaching effects on Christians in Syria and Palestine, as elsewhere. Byzantine requests for aid from the West led to a series of crusades which paid little if any attention to the claims of Constantinople to suzerainty. Indeed the crusade preached by Pope Urban II, and taken up by European princes, nobles and their followers, envisaged something far different from helping a fellow Christian ruler to regain his lost territories. The crusaders captured Antioch in AD 1098 and Jerusalem in AD 1099, crowning Baldwin as King of Jerusalem in 1100. In AD 1098 the Armenian ruler Thoros of Edessa was persuaded to name Baldwin as his successor in return for aid against the Seljuks. Thoros was murdered by the populace, but the city still came under crusader rule, with Joscelyn I as Count of Edessa from AD 1119–1131, and under Joscelyn II until AD 1144 when the Seljuks captured the city and rebuffed the count's attempt to retake it in AD 1146. He was forced to flee and the Turks set about ridding the city of its Christian population, by such measures as banishing many of the Armenians and replacing them with collaborating Jews. In addition marriage with the Turks by more than 100 Christian women within one year, further weakened the Christian position in the city.

The loss of Edessa precipitated the second crusade in AD 1147, but it proved to be fruitless and Jerusalem was lost to Saladin in AD 1187. The third crusade AD 1189–1192 regained some coastal areas but failed to take Jerusalem and the fourth crusade was diverted to and captured Constantinople, setting up a Latin kingdom (and patriarchate) which lasted from AD 1204 to 1261. Jerusalem was regained for some 15 years, AD 1229–1244, but by negotiation, not by force of arms. The failure of the crusaders was exacerbated when they failed to make common cause with the anti-Muslim Mongols, sometimes led by Nestorian generals and with pro-Christian khans, like Argun (d. AD 1291). This failure contributed to the Mamluk defeat of the Mongols at Ain Jalut in AD 1260, after Damascus and Aleppo had both fallen to the Mongols earlier that year. The remaining history of crusading efforts in Syria, Palestine and Egypt was one of failure, not least in the face of Mamluk power from Egypt. The Mamluks took Jaffa and Antioch in AD 1268, and took Acre, the last crusader possession on the mainland, in AD 1291.

The consequences of the crusades were many. The Latins introduced a new focus of loyalty for Christians. In both Edessa and Jerusalem in AD 1099 a Latin archbishop and a Latin patriarch respectively, were consecrated, to be followed in AD 1100 by a Latin patriarch at Antioch and in AD 1310 one was named for Alexandria.[98] Melkite Christians were challenged to give their obedience to Rome rather than to Constantinople, while the presence of Latin patriarchs virtually unchurched the Melkites. Loyalty to their patriarch was even strained among the Jacobites, with little courtesy extended to him, or to their own bishop at Edessa in AD 1100. It even came to schism between the patriarch and the Edessans.

Mamluk pressure made life difficult for both Melkites and Maronites, the latter group being made up of a nucleus of a small monastic group of Monothelites whose numbers were swelled by refugees in the mountains. The Maronites gave their ecclesiastical loyalty to Rome under Uniate arrangements from AD 1182,[99] while the Melkites still looked to Constantinople. Together the two groups made up about 30% of the population of Syria. Jacobites were to be found in the main in rural areas and Melkites in the cities, but overall Christians had lost majority status after AD 1200. The legacy of bitterness from the crusades soured relations between Christians and Muslims, which previously had been those of tolerance coupled with subtle pressures for conversion by the latter. The results could be seen in a report of a Western visitor, Varthema, who, in AD 1510, could report on the beauties of Damascus; populated by 'Moors', Mamluks and Greek Christians, most of the last being wealthy merchants, 'but they are ill-treated.'[100] No less must it be remembered that Greek Christians in these lands had suffered deeply under the crusaders who ostensibly had come to help, and, in fact, came to dominate and to exploit.

It remains to review briefly the fate of Syrian Christian culture and creativity over this whole period. In the time of the Umayyad caliphate, i.e. to AD 750, it made very significant contributions to Muslim culture and learning. So successful were they in this that the passage of the Umayyads saw consolidation of Islamic theocracy, and a concurrent decline in Syrian creativity. Indeed as the former grew the Syrian Christians, like Christians elsewhere under Muslim rule, were forced increasingly on to the defensive in order to preserve their heritage against an increasingly confident challenger.

The intellectual edge of this challenge had been honed by the Islamic philosopher al-Ghazzali (d. AD 1111), not least in his great work *The Revival of Religious Sciences*; by a somewhat intuitive blend of traditionalism and intellectualism he so systematised and explained Muslim thought and teaching that it marked a watershed for Muslims, which may be compared to that provided for Christans by Thomas Aquinas (d. AD 1274) in his *Summa Theologica*. Early in the 14th century, the Syriac literary tradition was replaced by that of Arabic, with only the Church liturgies retained in Syriac. The use of the Arabic vernacular over many generations had prepared the way for this shift. In many ways the work of the polymath Jacobite Bishop Barhebraeus (d. AD 1286) represents the height of Syriac achievement, after which decline set in. As for Greek, its use was preserved among the Melkites, with their relationship to Constantinople, but it too ceased to be used generally in the population at large by AD 900. That Syrian Christianity persisted is a tribute to the fidelity of many over the centuries. That it made a distinctive contribution to Christianity is as undeniable as it is little recognized among Western Christians. That it was a vehicle by which Islam was influenced constructively in its early years, and somewhat destructively via modern secularism in later centuries is also clear. And, finally, we need to recognize and pursue the influence of Syrian Christianity in areas to the south, north and east.

Map 2 Arabia

Chapter 5

Christians in 'Arabia'

Already we have had occasion to review some of the contacts of Syrian Christians with Arabs, all of the latter living north of that line between Aqabah and Basra which tends to mark the northern limit of what we now understand as Arabia. Such an understanding sells far short what was accepted as 'Arabia' in the time span which concerns us in this volume. Arabs lived in those border areas almost to Damascus in the west and as far north as Kurdistan and Nisibis in the east, as well as south to Yemen. Indeed the chief city of northern Mesopotamia, Nisibis, lay in an area referred to as 'the land of the Arabs'. And when we are told that after his conversion St. Paul went to 'Arabia' (see Galatians 1:17) it was probably to a district south of Damascus where he was unlikely to meet Jews.

As middle men in the caravan trade, the Arabs were also the border dwellers between the empires of Rome and Persia. The more settled among them in small kingdoms, played essential roles as border police who limited the depredations of their more nomadic cousins. Both empires made use of them from time to time, those used as mercenaries by later Roman rulers often being Monophysites (Jacobites), and those by the Sasanid Persians being Nestorians. The larger areas of land involved, technically within the bounds of the Roman Empire, were never subdued by the Romans beyond the country which lay east of the Jordan and several areas south of the Dead Sea.

CHRISTIAN BEGINNINGS AMONG ARABS

While Antioch had a highly credible claim to apostolic associations with Peter and Paul, and Edessa a less likely claim to such an association with the Apostle Thomas, Arabia was supposed to have been an area of concern for Bartholomew. This depends, however, on the claim that the 'India' referred to in connection with this last apostle was actually South Arabia. Even if this were so we lack any evidence beyond that created by wishful thinking.

The same 'association' of 'India' and South Arabia arises in connection with Pantaenus (d. AD 190), the founding teacher of the famous catechetical school at Alexandria.[1] He is reported as having visited the area in ca. AD 180, but it is more than likely that if this was so it was en route elsewhere. It is clear that again we have no hard evidence, and certainly there is no clue as to any large scale organized Christian community in Yemen, although it is clear that there were numbers of Jews there. Overall, there is no firm indication of Christians in appreciable numbers on the Arabian peninsula before the 4th century.

On the other hand by the mid-3rd century there were bishoprics among the Arabs south of Haran. And there was reported to be a bishopric from AD 225 at Baith Qatraye in Central-East Arabia.[2] Given the usefulness of the Arabian vastnesses as havens for those under persecution it is not surprising that Christians under threat in Persia or Syria should seek refuge there. Equally, Christian hermits found solitude in such desert areas, and those whose asceticism and wonder working powers impressed, had considerable influence on the Arabs among whom they lived. One such figure, enshrined in legend as the founder of Christianity in Najran, was the Syrian ascetic, Phemion, who was captured by Arabs and sold as a slave in that town. There his piety and wonder-working was said to have led to the conversion of much of the population. To such influences must be added those of Christian merchants who plied their trade and promoted their faith along the caravan routes which criss-crossed the area.

Then in the reign of the Emperor Constantius II (d. AD 361) an ambassador named Theophilus was sent to seek an alliance with the Himyarites and to foster the work of the Church in the Yemen. Permission was given to build churches and it was reported that the local king was converted. In any case we read of four bishoprics being established there, among converts who were at first Arian in theology but later embraced Nicene orthodoxy.

At the other end of 'Arabia' we have Christians established in Hira and Kufa by AD 380. Equally significant are references in Nestorian sources to the work of a trader called Hayyan or Hannan, who was converted at Hira during the reign of Yazdgard I (AD 399–420) and took his new faith back to Najran and points south. (Perhaps here we have substance for the earlier accounts related to Phemion.) Clearly by the end of the 4th century the Christian Church existed in a number of centres in southern Arabia. Indeed Najran became the major centre for Christians, situated as it was on the trade route from South Arabia to Syria, via Mecca. It was also a centre for growing Jewish power from AD 350 and the two faiths were destined to come into violent collision. Across the land mass Persian Christians had so established themselves in Qatar that their bishop was present at a council for the Persian Church in AD 410, while a monastery there is dated from the end of the previous century.

By AD 500 there was a bishop located in Najran, and a number of authorities including the Byzantine historian Theodore Anagnostes and the *Book of the Himyarites* (which dates from ca. AD 525) all agree that Christianity is clearly established in southern Arabia by that time, although the region known as Hadramaut saw but few Christians. While this was the case in this area, evidence from elsewhere indicates that Persian Nestorians had made inroads along the coast of the Persian Gulf by AD 500. As to the Arab tribes to the north we have encountered them already in their contacts with the Syrian Church. Those who had come to accept Christianity in the second half of the 4th century were represented by a 'bishop of the Arabs' at a synod at Antioch in AD 363–364. By AD 410 Hira had a bishop and it is claimed that the king of that centre himself became a Christian in AD 512.

By the latter date, of course, Christians in other areas were divided between Chalcedonians, Monophysites and Nestorians. Those who pressed upon Arabia from the north tended to be Monophysites, as were those Arab tribes in the north more closely related to the Roman Empire. Those who felt pressure along the Persian Gulf and to the south east came under Nestorian influence. The existence of a number of Chalcedonian (Melkite) monasteries in the Sinaitic peninsula was evidence of the third major group.

In the area of the Yemen it was the Monophysite form of Christianity which commanded most loyalty. This group began to look across the Red Sea to the Coptic Christian kingdom of Ethiopia for support, so that this African kingdom became another source from which Christianity was encouraged within Arabia. This became particularly important when, from AD 519 the Christians at Najran, not a few of them wealthy and not overly popular with non-Christian neighbours for their provocative arrogance, came under pressure from Jewish forces. Ethiopian forces intervened and limited the depredations of the Jews until AD 523. Then Najran itself was captured and plundered, churches burnt and many Christians were killed by the forces of Dhu Nuwas, the Jewish Sabaen king of the Himyarites since AD 518. Churches were also destroyed in other Christian centres at Sana, Marib, and Zufar. Pleas for aid in two directions led to another Ethiopian intervention, aided by Byzantine naval units, which led to the overthrow of the Jewish state and the installation of an Ethiopian governor in AD 525.

CONFLICTS WITHOUT AND WITHIN

The Jewish moves against Christians in southern Arabia and the intervention of the Ethiopians were both part of world-wide political moves. In the reign of Shapur II (d. AD 379) the Persians had stationed soldiers and officials in the eastern Arabian peninsula in part to enforce customs dues on the trade which flowed. Then Persia sought to counter Byzantine and Syrian influence in Arabia by its own efforts to establish a 'frontier' along a line from Hira to Mecca. It attempted also to include Medina in its sphere of influence through the Jewish tribes of al-Nadir and Turiaza. So it is probable that the Jewish campaigns against Christians in AD 519 and 523 had the tacit support of the Persians, the Zoroastrians for political and strategic reasons and the Nestorians for theological ones. On the other hand Constantinople had reached agreement with Ethiopia that it should act to support its Monophysite cousins. Constantinople's interest may well have been to find ways of keeping outflanking pressure on Persia, and such moves may date back to the mid-4th century and the embassy of Theophilus to South Arabia. This latter area was particularly important if there was ever to be a resumption of the once extensive Roman trade with South India, which trade had been disrupted during the disorders in the Empire of the third century. The Ethiopian presence in South Arabia continued for some 50 years, not without resentment from the Jews and the local non-Christian population. Yemeni nationalists revolted in AD 570 and received help from Sasanid cavalry. When the latter withdrew the Ethiopians re-established themselves. In AD 576 the Ethiopian-backed Himyarite king Abraha, built a new commodious church at Sana and made an unsuccessful bid to take Mecca, only three years before Muhammad's birth there. This was the last effort of the Christian-Ethiopian alliance, for the Persians returned, evicted the Ethiopians and remained as a garrison until the rise of Islam. Then

> 'Muhammad came to an agreement with Badhan, the Persian governor of that time', cut off from all aid from Persia itself, and 'the colony of Persian officials and soldiers in the Yemen seems to have gone over to the new faith and to have helped the Muslim commanders suppress the revolt of the local prophet al-Aswad.'[3]

Within those conflicts the three major expressions of Christianity took up various positions. Nestorians gave tacit support to Persian moves against those of Ethiopia, and the reverse applied to the Monophysites, with the Melkites caught between and favoured by very few of the Arabians.

The Christianity which reached the Arabs did so with the flavour of Aramaic culture and via the Syriac language. It continued to do so whether it came from Nestorian, Monophysite or Chalcedonian sources. While the hymns of Ephrem Syrus (d. AD 373) and of Jacob of Sarug (d. AD 521) would have been well known,

> 'there seems to be no evidence of a pre-Muslim translation of the Bible into Arabic, or of a Christian Church at that time using an Arabic service. It is probable that the Christian Bible in use in Arabia at this time was in Syriac.'[4]

To add to that, it appears probable that the knowledge of the gospels was confined to that within Tatian's *Diatessaron*, through which knowledge was also gleaned of Old Testament figures and events. Trade links between Christians from Najran to Zufar were predominantly with Syria, and this would have led to strong Monophysite (later Jacobite) influence there which would be consistent with the Monophysite leanings of the Ghassanid Arabs. It also helps to explain the relationship which developed with the Monophysite Christians of Ethiopia. That Jacobite Christianity remained strong at Najran, e.g., is clear from the fact that 20 years after the Hegira (i.e. AD 642) most of the Christians encountered there by Muslims were of that group. It is even believed that, while Mecca and Medina had relatively few Christians, the holy pictures on the Ka'bah were probably the work of a Coptic monk.[5]

As for the Nestorians, they became strongly missionary in the late 5th century, as they came to dominate the Christian Church in Persia. While at first they had concentrated their efforts along the areas bordering on the western shore of the Persian Gulf, including Bahrain, they made their presence felt also in Yemen once it became a Persian province in AD 597. Prior to that there had been a Nestorian synod at Qatar in AD 505 and there was to be another in the see of Darm in AD 676, attended by six bishops and one metropolitan, and presided over by the Patriarch George I (d. AD 680). That Nestorians saw themselves as having a continuing interest at least on paper is apparent from the appointment of a titular bishop for Yemen and Sana by the Catholicos Timothy I at the end of the 8th century. This was followed in AD 901 by correspondence between the Catholicos of the day and a priest in Yemen.

A further example of Nestorian expansion is provided by the church on the island of Socotra, which dates from the 6th century and was to continue its life down until destruction by the Muslims after the period which concerns us here. The traveller Cosmas Indicopleustes found Christians there in the 6th century and we have records of consecrations of bishops for the island under the Patriarch Enush in AD 880 and Sabrishu III (d. AD 1072). Marco Polo (d. AD 1324) reported on a bishop there who owed allegiance not to the Pope in Rome but to a patriarch at Baghdad,[6] and the Bishop of Socotra was present at the consecration of Yaballaha III as Patriarch in AD 1282.

Whatever their differences over Christology the Nestorians and Jacobites were one in their antipathy to Constantinople and 'the Greeks'. This antipathy was found among the tribes between the two great empires, and also within the Arabian peninsula. Along with this common influence, even on non-Christian Arabians, went that of the examples of piety and hospitality which they set before the Arabs. Veiled women, hospitality for travellers from monasteries, set hours for chanted prayers and offices, and a prostrate posture, facing east, for prayer were all features to be found among such Christians before the time of

Muhammad. Along with this went the general Christian contention (to be found, e.g., in the pre-Jacobite Syriac writings of Aphrahat) that the Jews had misinterpreted the Old Testament, a charge which Muslims were later to level also against Christians.

Important in the whole history of Christians in 'Arabia' were those tribes of borderland areas, which we have met, albeit briefly, on a number of occasions already. Both Persia and Rome used such Arab tribes as they could influence to act as police units against bedouin raiders and as screens against imperial expansion. Named in Acts 2:11, these Arabs were open to proselytising initially by Jewish Christians, and over succeeding generations most of them had some familiarity with Christianity. Origen was aware of heresies among the Christian Arabs, and the Emperor Philip the Arab (d. AD 249) knew of Christianity at Philopolis. An Arab Bishop of Bostra was present at the trials of Paul of Samosata in Antioch in AD 264 and 268. The fall of Palmyran power in AD 273 left such Arab tribes to their own devices, which included control of the overland trade routes until the 7th century.

After Constantine's accession to power throughout the Empire in AD 324, there were increased efforts to convert such Arabs. Julian sought to use them in his ill-fated campaign against Persia in AD 361–363. Impressed by Syrian asceticism numbers of Arabs embraced Christianity in the 4th century and, under pressure from a doughty dowager warrior queen, Mavia, one named Moses was consecrated as a bishop in ca. AD 373, a fact reported by the historians Socrates, Sozomen, and Theodoret.[7] It is from that date that the Christianization of the border land Arabs proceeded apace. Antioch had two Arab bishops under its oversight in AD 350 and by AD 451 there were 18 Arab metropolitans and bishops at the Council of Chalcedon. In this expansion a number of monasteries played important roles, not least of which was that at Hira, which was founded in the 5th century and became an important centre for advancing Nestorianism among the Arabs of the east.

Among those of the west, Monophysite views made gains and indeed it was the request of the Ghassanid king, Harith bar Gabala, in AD 542/543 which led to the appointment of two Monophysite bishops, one of which was the famous Jacob Baradai.

As cited by L. E. Browne, the writer Ibn Hauqal described the ensuing situation thus:

> 'They [the Arabs] settled down for the protection of Persia and Rome, so that some of them became Christians and embraced the religion of the Christians, such as Taghlib from Rabi'a in the land of al-Jazirah [Mesopotamia], and Ghassan and Bahra and Tanukh from Yaman in the land of Syria.'[8]

Browne adds:

> 'The two tribes which were of the greatest importance as protecting the frontiers just before the time of Muhammad were the Banu Ghassan on the Syrian frontier, and the Banu Hira on the Persian frontier. Of these the Banu Ghassan were all Monophysite Christians. . . . The Banu Hira were not all Christian, but among them were certain clans called 'Ibad who were Christians, mostly Nestorian, though some were Monophysite, for Monophysite bishops are recorded in the 6th and 7th centuries. The Banu Taghlib, who lived near the frontier of Mesopotamia, were entirely Christian.
>
> The tribe of Tai is interesting: originally coming from Yaman they migrated to Taima in Northern Hijaz, a town so closely in touch with Syria that it is mentioned several times in the Old Testament (Tema, Gen. 25:15, Isai. 21:14, Jer. 25:23). Here some of the tribe of Tai became Christians and others Jews, while the rest remained heathen. Owing to their proximity to Syria their name of Tai was often used by Syrian writers for Arabs in general.'[9]

Other tribes who were Christian were the Banu Tanukh near Aleppo, the Banu Salih, the Jurajima near Antioch and those of Bahra, Lakhan, and Judham. And to the eastern list we must add the Banu 'Abd-al-Qays in Bahrain.

Without the scriptures in their own language, and thus perhaps regarded as fringe dwellers of Christianity, these Arabs grew to stress orthopraxy more than orthodoxy (another foreshadowing of a feature of Islam, as it had been of Judaism). A further foreshadowing is to be seen in the contentions of Harith bar Gabala at Constantinople in AD 563, which included the claim that:

> 'The Trinity is one Divinity, one Nature, one Essence; those who will not accept this doctrine are to be anathematised.'[10]

Two bishops immediately found themselves under such an anathema and Harith added:

> 'Now I know that you are heretics. We and our armies accept this doctrine, as do the orientals.'[11]

While this may at first be seen as a simplistic Monophysitism, notice must be taken of two other factors. In Byzantine persecutions of Monophysites, Arab Christians had suffered along with non-Arabs, and loyalty to Constantinople was under considerable strain. The other factor was what was discerned by all Arab tribes as duplicity and treachery from their Roman and Persian 'allies'. Promised payment of the Ghassanids failed to materialise, and Harith's son Mundhir learned fortuitously of a Greek plot to assassinate him. While he continued to humble those Arab tribes who favoured Persia, and thus rendered service to Constantinople, his pleas there for a peaceful solution of problems were unproductive. In the end he was treacherously taken as a prisoner to the capital, and his people, outraged, rose in revolt, with deep hatred of Constantinople and all it represented. His son, Verman, also fell into Greek hands and joined his father in exile in Syria.

At the Persian end of the border lands things were not dissimilar. While Muhammad was a young man, the king of Hira, another Numan, was converted to Christianity. The Persians, like the Romans withdrew promised subsidies and engaged in what the Arabs saw as treachery. Khosrau II (d. AD 628) had the first and last Christian king of Hira murdered. As King Numan had aided the shah it is not clear why he was murdered. However,

> 'it is possible that his leanings towards Nestorianism, whose adherents had promoted a conspiracy against the shah, might have motivated Khosrau against him, especially since the shah had every reason to fear the influence of the Christians in his own court.'[12]

So Numan's people, the Lakhmids, rose in revolt, destroyed a Persian force, and constantly raided Persian territory in the years which led up to the appearance of Islam.

All of this unhappy story is summarised by one ancient writer thus:

> 'The kingdom of the Arabs was divided among fifteen princes; most of them joined forces with the Persians, and from this time onwards the rule of the Christian Arabs came to an end because of the treachery of the Greeks, and heresy was widespread amongst the Arabs.'[13]

In so far as Christianity was epitomised by Constantinople, the Greeks

> 'stood for tyranny and injustice in the eyes of the Arabs, and through them, Christianity was associated with perfidy.'[14]

What is remarkable is that loyalty to Christianity was to continue for so long among not a few of these Arab tribes, once Islam was present.

INTERACTION WITH ISLAM

As a trader Muhammad himself would have been aware of a Christian presence in Arabia and in Syria. While perhaps never one to sit at the feet of those learned in Christian doctrine, there is a tradition that one of his mentors was a monk, named Sarjis (Sergius), who was nicknamed Babira (the Experienced).[15] Certainly Muhammed numbered among his early associates a number of Christians, and his adopted son, Zaid, was of Christian parentage. Without a comprehensive grasp of Christian scripture, of which possibly he knew most via the *Diatessaron*, Muhammad was ready to interpret the Old Testament even more radically than did the Christians. This brought him into conflict with Jews at Medina, and helped alienate him from them, to a greater extent than from Christians at first.

Indeed the Qur'an contains a number of passages in which a warm respect is shown for Christians, not least for those whose sincerity is obvious, as priests and monks. So, e.g., there is Sura 5:82, which includes the words:

> '. . . And thou wilt find the nearest of them in affection to those who believe (to be) those who say: 'Lo! We are Christians! That is because there are among them priests and monks, and because they are not proud.'[16]

Of course this is not to imply that Muhammad and the Qur'an were not critical of aspects of Christian belief and practice. So, e.g. Sura 9:30 runs:

> '. . . and the Christians say: The Messiah is the son of Allah. . . . They imitate the saying of those who disbelieved of old. Allah (Himself) fighteth against them. How perverse are they!'[17]

If, as seems most probable, most of Muhammad's contacts were with Monophysite Christians, he was not likely to have heard as much stress on Jesus' humanity as on his divinity. However, it seems unlikely that greater contact with Nestorians would have produced a different attitude in Muhammad towards Christology. While no Docetist, in the strict sense, Muhammad did deny the death of Jesus on the cross.[18] In doing so, he did away altogether with the point at issue between Nestorians and Monophysites as to which nature suffered. At the same time he retained a deep reverence for the Virgin Mary, whose immaculate conception he supported some 1200 years before it became a dogma in the Roman Catholic Church.[19] And it is reported that of the pictures painted on the Ka'bah only that of the Virgin and child was retained after Muhammad.[20]

While he turned against the Jews and had them evicted from Medina, Muhammad continued to have a more positive attitude towards Christians, feeling that he had more in common with them, grave differences notwithstanding. So Christians at Najran were granted a wider measure of religious liberty, on condition that they paid a special tax, which in their case was levied in cloth. As one ancient Muslim writer, Yahya ben Adam, put it:

> 'Najran shall have the patronage of God and the protection of Muhammad the Prophet, the Apostle of God, for their goods and their lives, their lands and their religion, their absent ones, their present ones, and their relatives, their churches, and all that is in their hands whether small or great. A bishop shall not be moved

from his bishopric, nor a monk from his monastic life, nor a priest from his priesthood.'[21]

However, before the end of his life in AD 632 Muhammed was in conflict with Christians over his and their interpretations of the Old Testament, the Trinity and the Incarnation. It was understood that on his deathbed he decreed that there should be only one religion in Arabia, and this was the reason given for the eviction by 'Umar I of Christians from Najran in AD 635. They were moved to the region near Kufa and by AD 717 their numbers were said to have dropped from 40,000 to 4,000.[22] On the other hand those Christians more remote from Mecca in the South Yemen seem to have been allowed to remain and there is evidence of a Christian community there in the 8th century at least. At best these were vestiges which do not seem to have seen much of the succeeding century, so that 'Umar's policy effectively extinguished Christianity in the Arabian peninsula.

But what of those Arab Christians of the borderlands, among whom those evicted from Najran found refuge – albeit as Jacobites among those who were in the main Nestorians? Several significant factors must be kept in mind immediately. Some of the borderland Arab tribes had been largely Christian for over 200 years by the death of Muhammad. But their recent experience with the Byzantine Christians had led to deep convictions about duplicity and treachery to add to all too vivid acquaintance with persecution of Monophysites such as themselves. For a people given more to orthopraxy than to doctrinal orthodoxy these were serious marks against Chalcedonian Christianity. (That Islam was likewise given to orthopraxy rather than orthodoxy was not to be counted against it by such Christian Arabs.) In addition to resentment on that score, there was accrued rancour over their perception that, lacking the scriptures in their own tongue, they were regarded as peripheral Christians by Jacobites and Chalcedonians alike.

By a combination of ideology and conquest Muhammad and his close followers had created an Arabian nation out of the tribes of the peninsula. Not only that, but this new nation had humbled the power of the Roman Empire at Yarmuk in AD 636, and two years later had taken both Jerusalem and Antioch, and in the following year, Edessa. Sasanid Persia fell by AD 642, and by AD 649 had been joined by Egypt. The Arabs had come on to the world stage, no longer as somewhat despised mercenary auxiliaries, but as a great power to be reckoned with and respected for military prowess, if not yet for cultural achievement. It was then a matter of pride, freshly and irrefutably demonstrated to be an Arab, and to share in what had been achieved. To belong along with one's kinsfolk, to this world-changing movement was, understandably, a great attraction.

If disillusion with the old faith and its orthodox exponents went deep enough, the faith of some two centuries might be exchanged for what was not regarded as all that different at least in its practice. Where disillusion did not run so deep, and where the faith of the previous exploiting power was itself anathema because of its inherent dualism (as with the Zoroastrianism of Sasanid Persia) adherence to Christianity may continue – along with military alliance with Muslim cousins against Persia. Among such Christian Arabs pressures to conform to Islam would continue in various ways, but there was initially among eastern Arabs less inherent incentive to convert than was the case with their western kinsfolk.

Given all of this it is not surprising that the Banu Ghassan fairly quickly abjured Christianity and became Muslim. But other Christian Arabs retained their Christian faith for some time. So:

> 'The Jurajima made peace on condition of helping the Muslims in time of war, but they themselves remained Christian. The same was the case with the Beni Tanukh, who remained Christian up to the reign of the Caliph al-Mahdi.'[23]

As we move towards the east:

> 'In the Euphrates district a number of the nomad tribes remained Christian, including the Beni Taghlib, who refused to abjure their faith and imposed conditions, insisting on the free exercise of their faith, and on being excepted from the *jizya*, in lieu of which they paid a double alms. 'Umar would not bring pressure to bear upon them, but forbade them to teach Christianity to their children, a prohibition which they ignored. We hear of George, Bishop of the Arab tribes (d. ca. AD 724), whose diocese included the Arabs of al-Kufa, Tanukh, the Tha'labites, the Taghlibites, and other nomad Arabs of Mesopotamia. Christianity remained the religion of the Beni Taghlib under the rule of the Umayads and the 'Abbasides.'[24]

That Taghlib fidelity was at times costly is shown from some examples which come from the period between AD 683 and 710, to cover the three caliphs mentioned. The first example concerns the oldest of the three greatest Arab poets of the period, who was

> 'al-Akhtal (d. ca. AD 710) who, though a Christian from the Christian tribe of the Taghlib, became acquainted with the Umayyad family during the reign of Mu'awiya I and was official court poet for 'Abd-al-Malik. Despite some gentle pressure from his patrons he refused to become a Muslim, saying he could not give up the use of wine, and he ostentatiously went about the Umayyad court with a cross round his neck. Besides singing the praises of the Umayyads, he engaged in the usual boasting of the glories of his own tribe and the satirizing of

the shameful and dishonourable features in the lives of other tribes, either enemies of his own tribe or the tribes of rival poets.'[25]

The second example is related to the same poet, at least in its origins:

'In the reign of 'Abd ul Malik a lampoon of al Akhtal's was the cause of an attack on Taghlib, in which many men and women were killed. There is nothing to show that religion had anything to do with this, it may have been ordinary tribal warfare. At this time, however, persecution began. Muhammad, the governor of Mesopotamia, sent for Mu'adh, the chief of Taghlib, and persecuted him to make him turn Muslim. As he refused, he cast him into a pit of mud. Then he brought him out and flogged him, and, as he would not be persuaded, he had him killed. It continued in the next reign. Walid, the caliph, said to Sham'ala, the chief of Taghlib, "As you are a chief of the Arabs you shame them all by worshipping the cross; obey my wish and turn Muslim." He replied, "How so? I am chief of Taghlib and I fear lest I become a cause of destruction to them all, if I and they cease to believe in Christ." When Walid heard this he gave an order, and they dragged him away on his face. The caliph swore to him that if he did not turn Muslim he would make him eat his own flesh. This did not move him. Flesh was cut from his bones, roasted, and thrust into his mouth. As he endured this he was blinded. He lived, and the wounds could be seen on his body.'[26]

Such staunchness may not always have been present, but that it was among some is evidence of a depth of conviction which commands respect. That the Taghlib may have found allies and support among non-Arab Nestorians with whom to share the experience of pressure to convert is likely. That not a few Christians were their own worst enemies among Christian Arabs is a certainty. The example of the Taghlib is a lasting reminder of what might have been.

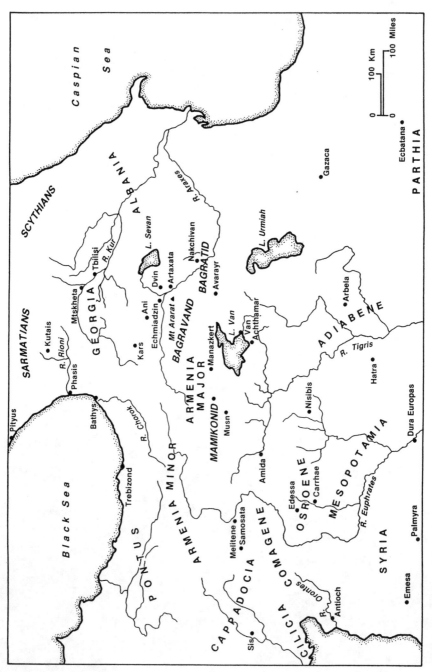

Map 3 Armenia and Georgia

Chapter 6

Christians in Armenia and Georgia

INTRODUCTION

To the north-east of Edessa lay the lands of the Armenians and the Georgians, the latter being sometimes referred to as Iberians. As described by S. C. Malan:

'The ancient land of Armenia . . . was bounded on the east by the lake of Urmiya and the courses of the rivers Kur and Araxes; on the west by the sources of the classic Halys; on the north by the upper courses of the Kur and Chorok; on the south by the high chain of the Kurdish Taurus, divided asunder by the rivers Euphrates and Tigris.'[1]

To the north of Armenia between Colchis which bordered the Black Sea and Albania to the east on the Caspian Sea, lay Georgia.

Armenia has a special place in the history of Christianity in that it was the first state of significance to declare itself Christian in the first decade of the 4th century AD. Georgia was to follow its southern neighbour by AD 330.

The discernible history of Armenia as a nation runs back to the days of Darius of Persia in 520 BC. From 149 BC to AD 428 it was ruled by the Arsacid dynasty, reaching its widest extent under Tigranes the Great (d. 55 BC). Along the way the Armenians, always more closely related in terms of culture, language, dress etc. to Persia than to the Graeco-Roman world, were at various times a Roman province and a Roman vassal state, or in the same sort of relationships to Persian rulers. Complete autonomy was more the exception than the norm. The succeeding dynasties were the Bagratides to AD 1045 and then the Rubenian from AD 1080–1375. However, from close to the end of the 4th century AD Armenian independence was more often a hope than an actuality, caught as the area was between the pretensions of Persians, Byzantines, Arabs, Mongols, Turks, crusaders and Mamluks.

CHRISTIAN BEGINNINGS AND ESTABLISHMENT

(a) Armenia

As Christians at Antioch and Rome could and did point to foundation associations with two apostles, so too did those in Armenia. In their case it was not with Peter and Paul, but with Bartholomew and Thaddeus. There is some debate whether the latter was one of the twelve or one of the seventy, but they were regarded as the first two 'Illuminators of Armenia'. In such traditions Bartholomew was associated with the north of the country and reputedly was martyred at Ardaze or at Derbend in AD 50. Thaddeus was seen as the 'illuminator' of the south and died at Albacus in AD 68, according to Armenian tradition. These 'apostolic' associations became significant when the Armenian Church wished to establish its autonomy against the claims of Antioch or Caesarea in Cappadocia to ecclesiastical suzerainty. The Antiochenes were prone to dismiss such apostolic claims and to point instead only to the work of the famous *Gregory the Illuminator* (d. AD 332). To him we shall return, noting only here that the Armenians were prone to refer to Gregory as the 'Second Illuminator', so as to maintain their claim to Bartholomew's and Thaddeus' primacy re foundation work.

That Christians existed in Armenia before the time of Gregory as is claimed is clear from persecution of them by Axidares (d. AD 113) and Khusrau I (d. AD 217). The eventual convert to Christianity, Tiridates III, launched a final persecution in AD 287. Reference is made to Christians in Armenia by Tertullian (d. AD 220), and Eusebius refers to a letter to Merozanes, Bishop of the Armenians, from Dionysius of Alexandria (d. AD 264).[2] But under pressure from Persia and Sarmatian invasions it was probably in a somewhat parlous condition by the second half of the third century. While the seeming rapid acceptance of Christianity in the 4th century would support some long standing foundations, hard evidence is scarce.

The situation becomes much clearer with Gregory, the son of a regicide who had been exiled to Cappadocia. There he was converted to Christianity, and he returned to Armenia in AD 288, to be gaoled for some 13 years. Release from prison followed his curing of the king's insanity, and the conversion of the king, Tiridates III (d. AD 314), ensued. (Some see this conversion as motivated in part by opposition to what was seen as the usurping Sasanian dynasty in Persia.) The nation followed suit, at least nominally, and Gregory was consecrated as Bishop, or Catholicos, by the Archbishop Leontius of Caesarea in Cappadocia. While some debate surrounds the actual date of the conversion of the king, Eusebius referred to the fact that the Roman Emperor Maximin Daia campaigned against the Armenians in AD 311 'as they also were Christians.'[3]

Gregory made Echmiadzin[4] the seat of his metropolis, substituted Armenian for Greek and Syriac as the liturgical language, and set up twelve episcopal sees each headed by a former pagan priest. He kept the metropolitan see (that of the Catholicos) in his own family and was succeeded by his son Aristakes, who was one of two Armenian bishops at the Council of Nicea (AD 325).

In a manner made familiar among Syrian Christians, Gregory

> 'established orders of anchorites, himself from time to time retiring from active life to mountain solitudes. . . . accompanied by a few of his hermits, dwelling in caves, subsisting on wild herbs, and devoting his time to study, meditation and prayer from which, periodically, he returned to his people to preach.'[5]

While the country was declared to be Christian the roots of conviction were shallow. On one hand traditional pagan ways remained, on the other the acceptance of Christianity was seen by not a few as a political move which would bolster resistance to Persian Mazdaism. The superintending catholicoi had no guarantee of tenure, nor even of life and limb. Uncertainty was increased by Persian invasions and the capture of the Armenian king in AD 367. Attempts to impose Mazdaism followed, along with martyrdoms and exiles, until, with the help of the Emperor Theodosius, the Persians were expelled in AD 371. By AD 385 the country was divided with the smaller western portion coming under Roman rule and the larger eastern section going to Persia, under tributary kings until AD 428. Consolidation of the Christian cause had to await granting of ecclesiastical independence from Caesarea in AD 375. Then the Catholicos became a patriarch more than the senior bishop and the Catholicos Norseses I was present at the Council of Constantinople in AD 381. The divisions of the country in AD 385 sealed the autonomy of the Armenian Church. The invention of the Armenian alphabet followed in AD 387 and Armenian scriptures appeared first in AD 443.

(b) Georgia

While located close to Armenia the rather more carefree Georgians saw themselves as a people apart from their neighbours, whom they regarded as dour, self-pitying, quarrelsome, and fanatical. Whatever the debt Christians in both countries had to Syrian monks, the Georgians were keen to distinguish themselves from the Armenians.

They had but little tradition of an apostolic founder, and in that they had one difference from the Armenians. (Some traditions point to roles for the Virgin Mary, for St. Andrew and for Simon the Canaanite, along with the relic of the supposed seamless robe of Jesus,[6] but these are the materials of which legends are made.) Instead, in due course they were to make much of an identification of the Cappadocian St. George with an old solar-lunar deity, to the point where later peasants ranked the saint above Jesus himself. The roles of horse and dragon also had old parallels in an ancient pagan past.

It appears that Christianity began to enter the region from the Black Sea Ports and Armenia, beginning in the area known as Colchis. Indeed, Irenaeus reported that Clement of Rome had been exiled to the Black Sea by Trajan ca. AD 100, and

> 'not long after . . . appeared in the Church of Colchis, Palm, himself a Colchian and Bishop of Pontus, together with his son, the heretic Marcion.'[7]

Both Clement and Palm are credited with extending the influence of Christianity in Georgia, not least in Colchis. In due course from Pitijus in the northern coastal area a bishop came to attend the Council of Nicea. Tradition has it that the key 'missionary' was a slave woman from Cappadocia, whose name was Nino, or some variant thereof. Possessed of healing powers, she cured the Georgian queen Nana of some complaint and the name of the Christian god delivered the king, Mirian (d. AD 342), from darkness during a hunting trip. The whole country followed the royal family into Christianity. This was believed to have occurred in AD 330, i.e. one generation after the conversion of Armenia. As in the latter case, political considerations played a role, in that Georgia too was as a result clearly differentiated from Persia and its national religion.

In eastern Georgia, or Albania, the initial work in the 4th century appears to have been that of a grandson of Gregory the Illuminator, who bore the same Christian name. While the first bishop probably came from Constantinople, there were relationships also with the Christians in Persia, as Georgian bishops participated in a synod of that Church which met in Seleucia in AD 419. Georgia received its own catholicate in the second half of the 5th century and by about AD 556 was ecclesiastically autonomous. Along the way a special alphabet was developed in AD 410, and a national Christian literature created, beginning with the scriptures and the liturgy.

For the Churches in both Armenia and Georgia a key role was played by the scholar *Mesrop* (d. AD 440). The Catholicos Sahak I (d. AD 439) sought someone who could make of Armenian a written language, while the king, Archil, was interested in the project as a means towards the conversion of his queen from paganism.[8] The bulk of the Armenians understood neither the Greek used in western regions nor the Syriac used elsewhere. Interpreters had to be used in Church services. So he supported the efforts of Mesrop who produced an efficient Armenian alphabet in AD 405. Thereafter work proceeded on the translations of the scriptures and the Liturgy of St. Basil, plus other liturgical, philosophical and historical works. This countered Syrian influence in eastern Armenia, which had Persian support in that it was related to the Christians within Persia itself.

'Mesrop sought to do the same sort of work for his people in Roman Armenia, but the Empire at first was not friendly to his project. He met with better success in the north, where he gave the Georgians and the Albanians each a national alphabet, the first in AD 410, the second in AD 423.'[9]

UNDER POLITICAL PRESSURES PRIOR TO ISLAM

By their very geographical locations both these countries were of considerable interest to the rulers of the Roman and Persian Empires. In fact, the two countries

'owed the survival of their cultural and political individuality to the equipoise of the two rivals.'[10]

Persian claims to overlordship went back to the Achaemenids, while Rome's dated to its defeat of the Caucasian allies of Mithridates by 64 BC.

'Neither power could acquiesce in the other's hegemony in Caucasia, which was of supreme strategic importance to both: it controlled the frontier between them as well as the passes protecting the civilized world from hyperborian barbarians beyond the mountains; thence the heart of Iran could be struck at, and the Roman lake reached through the Euxine.'[11]

An easy compromise was reached in a treaty in 63 BC and in theory at least, this held sway until the rise of the Sasanian dynasty after AD 224 which saw it as an affront to their imperial rights.

The conversion of both Armenia and Georgia to Christianity in the same decades as that religion received imperial acceptance in the Roman Empire set the stage for further confrontation. Then in AD 363 Julian was defeated and slain in his campaign against Sasanian Persia, and his successor Jovian was forced to cede Armenia, Georgia and Albania to Shapur II. However, within the decade Valens had recovered Armenia, but was able to regain only the western half of Georgia. Each side made power plays from time to time, including one venture in which Theodosius (d. AD 395) laid waste much of Georgia and took hostages.

'In AD 385 Persia and the Empire arrived at a compromise whereby Armenia was divided between them . . . the Empire gained . . . the strategic western portion of the country, while Persia acquired the lion's share, the greater eastern half, which until . . . AD 428, was permitted to be governed by tributary kings.'[12]

It was in such circumstances that Mesrop, in providing alphabets for both Armenians and Georgians, provided them with tools for distinct cultural and ecclesiastical identities.

A new phase opened with the accession in AD 438 of Yazdgard II to the Persian throne. He set out further to separate the Armenian Christians from those in the Roman Empire, not least in encouraging them to gain ecclesiastical autonomy. This he followed with a policy through which he aimed to make all of Caucasia Zoroastrian; and persecution of Christians ensued in Armenia.[13] This led after some vacillation to a revolt led by Vardan II, Prince of the Mamikonids. Rome, under the Emperor Marcian, was unable to help, and after the defection of some of his allies, Vardan and his forces were crushed by the Persians at Avarayr in June AD 451.

Some reconciliation ensued and Yazdgard agreed to suspend his policy of enforcing conversions to Zoroastrianism, although the Arsacid dynasty came to an end in AD 484. The Armenian dynasty had claimed that it represented the legitimate Iranian ruling house over against Sasanian usurpation, a further factor in exacerbating opposition between Armenia and Persia. By AD 552 the Catholicos Nerses II (d. AD 557) had gained agreement from Khosrau Anoshirvan that proselytising should cease. This was followed by an agreement of AD 556 between Justinian and Khosrau along religious toleration lines, linked to a 50 year political truce.[14] However, persecution of Christians resumed in AD 564 and continued on and off, depending on the extent of Roman intervention, until Maurice's decisive defeat of the Persians in AD 582. In the ensuing settlement Maurice endeavoured to secure the division and deportation of the whole Armenian population, but Persian lack of co-operation destroyed the scheme. Nevertheless many Armenians took refuge in Persian territory from what they saw as the cruel Byzantine harassment of them for their Monophysite beliefs.

The enforced conversion to Zoroastrianism policy of Yazdgard was employed also in Georgia, about one generation later than in Armenia. It led to a Georgian revolt in AD 460, and to the dispossession of the Arsacids there in AD 461. However, the pressure exerted against Christians in Georgia was less extreme than in Armenia. In the second half of the fifth century, the king Vakhtarg I (d. AD 499) was able to rid Georgia of the Zoroastrian fire cult and he built many churches and established a number of bishoprics. Attempts were made to play Persians off against Romans, with Georgia alternately a province of the Persian state in AD 510, and some local leadership in the hands of the kings of West Georgia and Lazica.

It was in this period that the Georgian Church came out from under 'Greek' authority in AD 556, and also that 13 Syrian fathers arrived to preach, establish monasteries and eventually to become bishops.

The triumph of Maurice encouraged Georgians to assert their independence, not only of Persia but also of Armenia. They were led in this between AD 580 and 610 by Guaram and the Stephens I & II. As both a political and a religious act the Georgians replaced the Persian fire on their coins with the Christian cross.

'It was in Duke Stephen I's time also that the Georgian Church finally broke with the Gregorian Church of Armenia, and was reunited with that of orthodox Byzantium.'[15]

But for both Armenia and Georgia, there was soon to be a new challenge to be met, for within a generation they were to be faced with Muslim Arab expansion. As it happened the commander of the Roman army defeated by the Arabs at Yarmuk in AD 636 was an Armenian, Vahan or Barnes who retired to a monastery in Sinai. The same resort was not open to the masses in the two regions which concern us here. However, this is not to say that considerable numbers of Armenians did not migrate into Asia Minor and to Constantinople. Indeed, they constituted a major 'foreign' element within the Byzantine Empire and many held important economic, administrative and military posts, as we have just noted. Two Armenians became emperors, viz. Leo V (AD 813–820) and Basil I (AD 867–886). They also became a commercially significant commercial minority in India and South East Asia prior to the arrival of the Portuguese at the end of the 15th century (see below in the chapters on those two regions).

THEOLOGICAL STANCES

(a) Armenia

Geopolitical forces were bound to be of considerable importance in the development of theology in Armenia. In as far as Armenians were concerned with their autonomy, in the area of theology they no more wanted to be dominated by Christians in Persia than by those in Constantinople or Rome.

However, before we review the major expressions of this issue we should note that among Armenian Christians there were to be found representatives of a number of 'heterodox' schools. The fifth century work of Bishop Eznik of Bagravand, entitled *The Sects Refuted* draws attention to Marcionites, as well as to pagans, Zoroastrians (Parsees) and 'philosophers'. By the latter he may well have meant Gnostics like the Archontics and Borborites, and to them we must add Manichaeans. Of more immediate concern for some time was the ascetical group known as the *Messalians*. Given to much prayer in an effort to dislodge Satan from the soul, they were condemned at the Council of Ephesus in AD 431 and came under close attention at a synod of the Armenian Church in AD 447. Special measures were enacted against any clergy involved, or those who failed to act against them. Despite such measures they persisted to the 7th century.

The most significant group, however, was that which had an adoptionist Christology, along the lines developed by Paul of Samosata. Such an Adoptionist was Archelaus, Bishop of Karkhar, who debated with Mani (d. AD 277) himself. Adoptionist ideas seem to have persisted in the general population, outside the monasteries, and in the 8th century, following the rise of Islam, to have reappeared as part of a quest for a simplified somewhat puritanical expression of Christianity. The impact was such that at a synod at Dvin in AD 719, the last canon focussed on this group, to include:

> 'No one ought to be found in the places of that most wicked sect of obscene men who are called Paulicians . . . but one ought to retreat from them in every way, to curse them and pursue them with hatred. For they are the sons of Satan, fuel for the eternal fires and alienated from the love of the Creator's will.'[16]

The *Paulicians* whose name is said by some to honour Paul the Apostle, by others Paul of Samosata, held that

> 'the Baptism of Jesus was necessarily the chief of all Christian feasts; and the Fish was the favourite symbol of Jesus Christ, because he, like it, was born in the waters.'[17]

As detailed in their work the *Key of Truth*, they held to three sacraments – believer's Baptism, Repentance and the Eucharist; they regarded Jesus Christ as a creature, but free of original sin; they made no use of the term 'trinity'; the Holy Spirit enters at Baptism; the Virgin Mary is not ever-virgin; they made no provision for the intercession of the saints, nor for the veneration of images or crosses. But there is debate as to whether or not they were dualists or Manichaeans at that stage.[18] Among them the 'elect' or 'perfect' were seen as virtual reincarnations of Jesus, and they held themselves to be the true Armenian Church. It is claimed that they had support from the Bagratuni clan, but with the defeat of the iconoclastic movement in Constantinople considerable numbers of the Paulicians were deported to Thrace in the 8th to 10th centuries after fierce armed resistance. There they formed some of the basic material out of which appeared the Bogomils, and later the Cathari or Albigensians of the 12th and 13th centuries in Provence, Lombardy and Bosnia.

When we return to the mainstream of Armenian Christianity we find that it is orthodox in every way up to and including the declarations of the Council of Ephesus in AD 431. An Armenian synod in AD 432 confirmed the findings of Ephesus AD 431, and in AD 435, a synod condemned the writings of Theodore of Mopsuestia, the mentor of Nestorius, but lately translated into Armenian. At the same time they espoused the theology of

Cyril of Alexandria (d. AD 444) with his emphasis on the unity of the natures in Christ. By that time Armenian attention was focussed, not on the Christological debates represented by Dioscurus of Alexandria (d. AD 454), Theodoret of Cyrrhus (d. AD 466) and Leo I of Rome (d. AD 461), but on survival in the face of the pressure of Yazdgard II. Pleas for assistance directed to the Emperor Marcian produced no aid, and the Armenians' main army was defeated in June AD 451, as we have seen above. Marcian was far more concerned with the projected Council of Chalcedon which was held in October AD 451.

The sharpness of the defeat by the Persians and the failure of Constantinople to help fellow Christians, together produced an antagonistic attitude which focussed on the Creed of Chalcedon. But no direct attention was given to it and the Christology it espoused until AD 491. By then Syrian Monophysites were hoping that the pro-Cyril of Alexandria Armenians would support them against both Constantinople and the Nestorians who were centred on and operating from their school at Nisibis within Persia. The Armenians had as little love for Nestorians from Persia as for Chalcedonians from Constantinople. During the 5th century distinctive Armenian views on the trinity and on Christian doctrine in general had been expressed respectively in two works, *The Teaching of St. Gregory*, and *The Discourse of St. Gregory*.

As expressed by Sirarpie Der Nersessian:

> 'The Armenian Church recognized the divine and human natures in Christ, a complete humanity animated by a rational soul. She violently rejected the mingling or confusion of the natures, taught by Eutyches . . . [and] maintained . . . that to speak of two natures after the union, as did the Chalcedonians, was to revert to the Nestorian heresy . . . As the Godhead was present in Christ's incarnation it was legitimate to say that God has been crucified for us.'[19]

So in AD 491 the Armenians expressed their suspicions of Chalcedon's Nestorianism, and in AD 506, at Dvin, this opinion was confirmed by a council of Armenian, Georgian and Albanian bishops, opting for the positions and condemnations adopted by the Dioscurus-dominated 'Council' of Ephesus in AD 449. At the same time the bishops were explicit in the condemnations of Arius and Eutyches, as well as of Nestorius, and they accepted the *Henoticon* of the Emperor Zeno, which sought to placate the Monophysites. Fear of both Persia and Constantinople was evident when in AD 519 the Emperor Justin moved to heal the rift between Constantinople and Rome over the *Henoticon*. So by AD 555 the Armenian bishops met again at Dvin and officially adopted a Monophysite Christology. As Toumanoff put it succinctly:

> 'With this the national Armenian Church was born.'[20]

Within Roman Armenia the Emperor Maurice (d. AD 602) maintained Chalcedonian orthodoxy by force of arms, and between AD 591 and 611 there were two Armenian Catholicoi – one in the Roman zone and another among the Monophysites. While Heraclius, with his army on hand in AD 632, received acceptance of his Monothelite compromise from the Armenians, it was rejected in AD 645 once the Byzantines had departed following Arab victories. Links were built up with the Jacobites of Edessa, and at an Armenian council of AD 728, the Metropolitan of Edessa was present. Once again

> 'the Council of Chalcedon was repudiated, union was established between the Armenians and the Jacobites, and certain ritual practices were instituted.'[21]

Later attempts like that of the scholarly Photius (d. AD 895), twice the Patriarch of Constantinople (AD 858–861 and 878–886), to persuade the Armenians that Chalcedon was not Nestorian failed, and one of their councils, in AD 862, reasserted the Cyrillian position against that of Chalcedon.

Throughout all of this the Armenian Church remained the principal source of national unity and autonomy. This was clear to the Byzantines, who realised that to force the Church to comply with their orthodoxy would be to humble Armenia as a whole, and tie it to the chariot of Constantinople. This was equally clear to the Armenians, who were driven by more than theological conviction in their refusal to accept Chalcedon. So while consistently avowing their rejection of Nestorians, Apollinarius and Eutyches, all condemned at Chalcedon – they rejected the conciliar formula itself. In AD 1165–1170, under the Catholicos Nerses IV, the Armenians were prepared to admit that Chalcedon was no more Nestorian than they were Eutychian, but Constantinople was not satisfied with this, and pressured a new Catholicos, Gregory, for fuller compliance up to AD 1177. The opposition of clergy and populace at large was as firm as that of similar groups in Constantinople to attempts to enforce the compromise *filioque*[22] formula of the Council of Florence in AD 1439. A change of emperor led to renewed attempts to pressure compliance in AD 1196. But by then the crusades were a major factor and in particular the Fourth Crusade's sack of Constantinople in AD 1204. Direct relationships with Byzantine rulers and the possibility of union of Churches were put to one side.

(b) Georgia

Up until the end of the 6th century the Church in Georgia followed very much the line advanced in Armenia. But as we have seen in the period from AD 580–610 the Georgians asserted their independence of their southern neighbour. In that same period under a series of strong thinkers the Georgians were prepared for a break with Armenia on one hand, and showed their maturity in a series of

> 'remarkable missions to the Huns undertaken by Aghovanian monks.'[23]

At the same time Armenia wanted to continue its ecclesiastical suzerainty over Georgia, which increasingly related itself to Constantinople. The Catholicos of Georgia, Cyrion I, and Catholicos Abraham of Armenia clashed in AD 607. As a consequence Cyrion was excommunicated by a council at Dvin in AD 608, and while Armenia remained tied to its anti-Chalcedonian stance Georgia was accepted back into the Chalcedonian fold. The whole context of such a move was to change dramatically with the Arab victory at Yarmuk in AD 636.

THE IMPACT OF ISLAM

Arabs inroads into Armenia began in AD 640 and in Georgia in AD 643. The situation remained somewhat fluid for a time, and in AD 647 the Emperor Constans II (d. AD 668) tried to regain Armenia. However, most Armenian leaders turned towards the Arabs rather than the Byzantines in the hope of retaining some measure of political autonomy and full ecclesiastical independence for their own form of Christianity.

A peace treaty was devised in AD 683–684 between the Armenian leader, Theodore Rshtuni, and the future caliph Mu'awiya. This recognized Armenia as an autonomous tributary state. At the same time Stephen II of Georgia accepted Arab suzerainty over his country, and two Arab-enclaves were established at Tbilisi (Tiflis) and at Juansher in Albania. The three Caucasian states

> 'formed one viceroyalty of the Caliphate (designated as Arminiya), Dvin being the seat of the viceroys.'[24]

Overall the Arabs were prepared to make use of Armenians and Georgians in administrative tasks, and they had no special quarrel with these groups, as long as they kept themselves away from entanglements with the Byzantines. This was not easy, but was assisted, among the Armenians, by the realisation that the Byzantines were always out to pressure conformity on doctrinal and liturgical matters. Despite occasional acts of Arab violence, like the sacking of the ecclesiastical capital, Dvin, in the Catholicate of Hovhannes V (AD 898–929), the Church was able to continue its life and act as the symbol of unity and national identity. So, e.g., a synod in AD 768 fixed the Armenian canon of the Old Testament along lines which differed from that employed by the Latin and Greek Churches, and also from that used by the Jews. This added further weight to that renewed repudiation of Chalcedon at the synod at Manzikert in AD 728. Such repudiation of things Byzantine was shown also, when,

'in the 9th century the Armenians joined forces with the Arabs to oppose the armies of the Emperor Theophilus (d. AD 842). They helped the emir of Tiflis to repulse the Greeks who had advanced as far as Kars; in the south the princes of Vaspurakan and Taron also fought on the side of the Arabs and expelled the Byzantine troops from the region of Melitene. Nor did the Armenians give any assistance to Basil I (d. AD 886) in his wars against the Arabs'[25],

Armenian though he was. Clearly, most of the Armenians had decided that their identity was under greater threat from the Byzantines than from the Arabs, whatever the common ground on Christianity they shared with the former. In AD 806 Ashot I had been recognized by the Abbasids as 'prince of Armenia', and his grandson, Ashot III was, in AD 860, entitled 'prince of princes' of Armenia, Georgia and the Caucasus. In AD 886 he was elected as King of Armenia, and during his reign Armenia reached from the Caspian Sea to the Euphrates and the economy and culture flourished. By the 10th century, however, the nobility acted to curtail royal power, to the point where the country split into six petty kingdoms, and its overall power and ability to resist invaders was seriously weakened.

By the 11th century Byzantine pressure was reasserting itself. In part it was by direct military actions, such as that of Constantine IX (d. AD 1055), who in AD 1045 annexed the country as a whole. In other ways they set out to destabilise the country and its Church, regarding the population en masse as untrustworthy and the Church as heretical. The Armenian clergy were harassed and the catholicate kept vacant for as long as possible – or alternatively the Catholicos might be kept within a monastery, as was Vkayaser (d. AD 1071) until after the Seljuks' victory at Manzikert. As a consequence ecclesiastical authority became divided and weakened and

'in AD 1100 we find no less than four prelates in different parts of the country, each claiming to be the representative of St. Gregory, and each condemning the others as rebels against his authority, and usurpers of the Patriarchal throne.'[26]

The 10th century had seen the Bagration family, ex Armenia, rise to leadership of Georgia. Under its leadership the country was united and the medieval system organized. A new capital was chosen by Bagrat III (d. AD 1014) at Kutais, and the Georgian language was revised to lay the foundations for a golden age of Georgian literature in the 12th and 13th centuries. Throughout the 9th to the 11th centuries, Georgian civilization was influenced also by the Byzantines through Georgian monasteries on Mt Sinai and Mt Athos, and later in Jerusalem.

The appearance of the Seljuk Turks heralded another era. Their utter defeat of the Byzantines, under Romanus IV, at Manzikert in Armenia in AD 1071, left Armenia exposed to a ruthless enemy. Catholicoi had to keep on the move, petty principalities emerged and numbers emigrated. Some went to Edessa and its environs which eventually they came to rule until AD 1098. Others, more significantly went to an area in Cilicia and Cappadocia made available by the Byzantines. In this area they came to dominate the passes between Syria and Asia Minor through the Taurus Mountains, and under the Bagratid prince, Rupen, there was established the Kingdom of *Lesser Armenia*, which existed from AD 1070–1375. To it we shall return as we consider the crusader period, within which it was to pay a significant role.

By AD 1072 the Seljuk Turks had turned the Kingdom of Georgia into anarchy, until the reign of David III (d. AD 1125). Under him independence was restored following a series of defeats of the Seljuks by the Georgians, with some outside help, between AD 1110–1121. In the course of this struggle the Georgians accrued a great reputation for valour and were described by the Saracens as 'the kernel of the religion of the cross.'[27] So in due time the Georgians were ready to assist the crusaders in their campaigns against the Saracens.

Led by David III and his descendants down to Queen Thamar (d. AD 1212) and her son, George IV (d. AD 1223), a golden age ensued for culture and civilization in Georgia. By the death of George IV Mongol invaders, not yet Muslim and sometimes under Nestorian leaders, were menacing Georgia. Somewhat in desperation the reigning queen, Rusudana, turned to Western Christians for the first time and appealed to Pope Gregory IX for help in AD 1239. In lieu of the requested military assistance the pope despatched Dominican friars, whose errand, in the opinion of a Russian historian, was 'to promote in Georgia the arrogant intentions of the court of Rome.'[28] Eventually a Latin episcopate was established in Tiflis, with the Dominican, Johannes Florentius, as the Latin bishop.[29] In conflicts between AD 1234 and 1242, independence was lost again, and the monarchy weakened as great landowners gained power. After AD 1258 the Georgians supported the Mongols in their campaigns against the Assassins, the radical sect among the Ismaili Shi'ite Muslims. They participated also in the Mongol sack of Baghdad in AD 1258. Then under George VI (d. AD 1346) independence for Georgia was regained but was to be lost yet again in the face of the fierce onslaughts of Timur Leng (Tamerlane – d. AD 1405). Thereafter it was weakened and divided between Persian and Ottoman interests. As for the Orthodox Church of Georgia, it

'bulked large in the country's life, and battling bishops led their troops into the fray alongside the armies of the king. The Church had wide powers of jurisdiction in the field of morals and private conduct, a monopoly of education, as well as enormous economic privileges, grants of land, and valuable immunities and benefactions.'[30]

Throughout this period the Armenians and the Georgians remained, on the whole, both faithful to their respective understandings of Christianity, and subject to the conditions imposed by Muslim rulers. That from time to time they were able to sample an independence which was related to and expressed through their faith further attached them to that faith when independence was lost or threatened.

THE ERA OF THE CRUSADERS AND THEREAFTER

When Cappadocia fell to the Seljuk Turks in AD 1074 numbers of Armenians who had found refuge there looked elsewhere for a home. So they moved to the south-east corner of Asia-Minor and to North Syria, where they found earlier Armenian migrants already residing in appreciable numbers. With them came their Catholicos and many of his clergy and out of this was to emerge the kingdom of Lesser Armenia.

Other displaced Armenians focussed their efforts in and around Edessa, which had a considerable Armenian population for centuries. There, with backing from Armenian nobles in the region Philaretos became ruler of the city in AD 1083, and the following year was invited also to rule Antioch. But in AD 1085 that city fell to the Seljuk Turks, and in the next year so did Edessa. In AD 1095 the Turks were evicted, and the Armenian Thoros ruled until AD 1098, when the crusader Baldwin I ousted him by subterfuge. This was followed by the action of Baldwin II in AD 1115 in displacing Armenian landowners around Edessa with Frankish nobles. This removed the Raban state of Armenians-in-exile, but, by intermarriage and via measures of autonomy, the Armenians remaining were reconciled somewhat to the Franks, who continued to recognize and respect the Catholicos. So early in the 12th century Syria was in Frankish hands and Cilicia was left as the land of Lesser Armenia.

Those in Lesser Armenia had been aware of their desperate situation vis-a-vis the Seljuks before the crusades began. Indeed, in AD 1084,

> 'the Armenians had sent a bishop to Gregory VII (1073–1085) to court his sympathy for the holy war, and to secure his support for the Armenians and their Church.'[31]

Rome saw the approach as one of unilateral submission to it. The Armenians had no such view and this led to a schism in the catholicate. That group favouring union with Rome was centred in the Lesser Armenian capital of Sis. Those Armenians who were prepared to honour, but not to submit to the pope came under the leadership of a group called 'The Band of Eastern Divines', and, located largely in what was once Greater Armenia, followed a Catholicos whose seat was at Achthamar.

With the arrival of the crusaders the Lesser Armenians gave them every assistance, even though it meant the loss of northern Syria and Edessa. The Armenians needed the crusaders, and such necessity, more than theological conviction, guided their policy. Intermarriages also helped to bind one group to the other. A council at Jerusalem in AD 1140 kept relations between Armenians and crusaders cordial, but, in an effort to spread their reliance the Armenians hoped also for some reconciliation with Constantinople, while the Emperor Manuel Comnenus lived. His death in AD 1180 put an end to these hopes, so again close relations with Rome were explored when an Armenian bishop took a profession of faith thither in AD 1184. The hope here was renewed help against the revived Muslim power of the Ayyubids led by Saladin (d. AD 1193). Once again Rome fumbled somewhat, by seeing this as an attempt to follow the precedent set by the Maronites' acceptance of Uniate status in AD 1082. The Armenians sought a pact between equals, not submission to Rome.

The height of the power of Lesser Armenia, still related ecclesiastically to Rome, came with the reigns of Leo II (d. AD 1219) and Hetum I (d. AD 1269). The chief protagonist of union with Rome was Nerses of Lampron (d. AD 1198), but his endeavours and concessions did not win universal support among Armenian monks, to say the least. (It was here too that we see the succession of the Hetumid dynasty to that of the Rubenids.) The kingdom played a significant military, diplomatic and economic role, not that Muslim pressure against it ceased. Leo failed to secure Antioch in AD 1194, when rejected by its populace, and in the face of Saladin's successes he pursued closer alliance with the west. He gave support to the Holy Roman Emperor, Frederick Barbarossa (d. AD 1190) and Henry VI (d. AD 1197).

> 'Pursuing his policy, Leo gave wholehearted support to Frederick's ill-starred crusade and worked for a reunion with Rome. His negotiations with Pope Celestine III and the Emperor Henry VI, began in 1195, were culminated in 1198/1199, when recognised by both as King of Armenia and recognising, together with the Catholicos Gregory VI Pahlavuni, the supremacy of the Holy See, Leo was solemnly crowned at Tarsus by Cardinal Conrad of Wittelsbach and by the Catholicos.'[32]

Leo's eventual successor was his son-in-law Hetum I, and reconciliation with Antioch was sealed by the marriage of his daughter to Bohemund VI in AD 1254. When Louis IX's crusade ended in failure in AD 1250, Hetum had taken due account of the appearance and successes of the non-Muslim Mongols, with their Nestorian advisors and, sometimes, generals.

So to balance the failing power of the crusaders he visited the Mongol court in AD 1253 and became a vassal ally. He, along with Georgians and others assisted the Mongols to capture and sack Baghdad in AD 1258, and to secure North Syria by the capture of Damascus and Aleppo early in AD 1260. Hetum also waged an economic war with Egypt in connection with the spice trade, thus foreshadowing the Portuguese efforts initiated by Vasco da Gama at the end of the 15th century.

Papal rejection of the proffered Mongol alliance, and of the Mongol request to restore a Greek patriarch to Antioch, contributed to the action of the crusaders in permitting unimpeded passage to Mamluk forces to confront the Mongols. Somewhat weakened by turmoil in the 'homeland', the Mongols were defeated at Ain Jalut in September AD 1260. Mamluk pressure came directly on the Armenians as Mongol allies, as far as Cilicia itself, now that the Il-Khans were removed from Syria. In the meantime Mongol rule in Greater Armenia was established by AD 1261. With some improvement in relations between the Mongols and Rome, Franciscans and Dominicans began to work among the Greater Armenians. Certainly there was greater contact with Latin Christianity, which contact followed contacts with the Mongols, especially the Il-Khans of Persia. Catholic work in Armenia had its base in Nakhchivan, and its main task force came from a Uniate Order of Armenian monks, the brothers of St. Gregory the Illuminator. So, a western visitor reported in ca. AD 1330 that Greater Armenia was

> 'inhabited chiefly by schismatic Armenians, but the Preaching and Minor friars have converted a good 4000 of them, and more . . . and we trust in the Lord that in a short time the whole residue shall be converted also if only the good friars go on so.'[33]

However, Armenian ecclesiastical autonomy was not so easily surrendered, and the proselytising of the friars angered the Armenian clergy.

Between AD 1275 and 1305 Lesser Armenia was constantly invaded and pillaged by Seljuks from the north and Mamluks from the south. Only by the payment of tribute and the cession of territory were the vestiges of independence retained. Hetum II offered submission to Rome in AD 1289, but this was highly unpopular with his people, despite the quest of the Il-Khan Abaqa for an alliance with the west. This Khan had a Christian wife, a daughter of the Emperor Michael Palaeologus (d. AD 1282), and with some of his successors pursued this aim via such endeavours as the embassy of the Nestorian monk, Rabban Sauma (d. AD 1294) in AD 1286–1288. All of these attempts failed, and Il-Khan interest ceased with the accession of Gazan as Il-Khan in AD 1295, and the adoption of Islam by the Mongols in AD 1304.

By that time also the last crusader outpost on the mainland had fallen and Lesser Armenia, gravely weakened both militarily and economically, was open to final destruction. This came at the hands of the Mamluks, in AD 1375 when the last Armenian king, Leo VI, and his capital, Sis, fell. Leo refused the chance to embrace Islam, and so with his wife, Margaret of Soissons, and their two children, he was imprisoned in Cairo. When freed in AD 1382, Leo had lost wife and children and he himself was to die in Paris in AD 1393. With him the political history of an independent Armenia ceased for centuries.

While the political independence of Armenia and Georgia disappeared their religious loyalty remained. Georgia continued to see itself as part of Eastern Orthodoxy, and Armenia, while firmly rejecting the 'Monophysite' label, walked its own distinctive path. In one way it returned to its origins in the year AD 1441, when for the first time since AD 454, the Catholicos Kiriak took up his residence again at Echmiadzin, associated as this had been with Gregory the Illuminator.

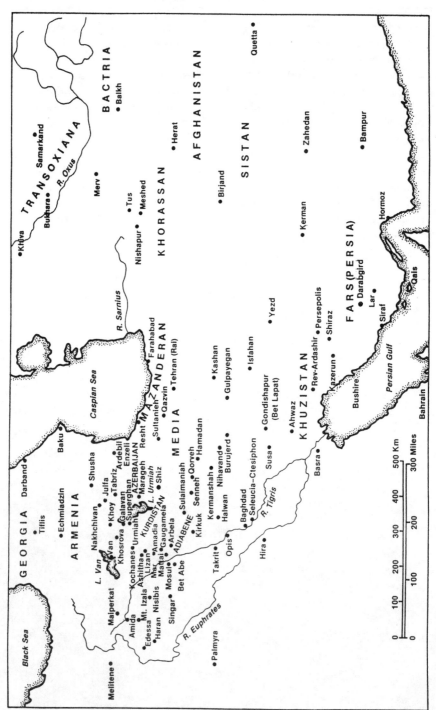

Map 4 Persia (Iran)

Chapter 7

Christians in Persia (Iran)[1]

FOUNDATIONS LAID

While 'apostolic' traditions link Matthew, Jude, Simon the Zealot and Thomas all with 'Persia', two of these reputedly being martyred at Sufian, we lack any firm evidence of apostolic foundation for the Christian Church in Persia. However, it is hardly insignificant that the first of the nations (of expatriate Jews?) to respond to the miracle of Pentecost were 'Parthians and Medes and Elamites and residents of Mesopotamia' (Acts 2:9). From other evidence, like that provided by Josephus[2], it seems that there was a considerable number of Jews living in the Adiabene area of Persia, which community some have wanted to identify with the 'lost tribes' of Israel.[3] As we have seen already it would seem that such a community, focussed on Arbela, was the source from which Christianity reached Edessa.

Such circumstantial evidence from apostolic times lends some credibility to the contentions of those who argue for Addai, identified with Thaddeus, as the founder of the Church in Persia.[4] Others dismiss this claim, along with its dependence on the 6th century *Chronicle of Arbela* and argue for a founding role for Tatian, a native of Adiabene, in the late second century.[5] So while Young tends to make much of the *Chronicle's* report of Paqida as first Bishop of Arbela (Arbil) from AD 104–114, and of the number of early bishops with Jewish names, there is firm evidence for the existence of Christians in the area by AD 170 and indeed as far afield as Bactria.[6]

With Adiabene as a possible refuge for Christians under persecution in the Roman Empire, their numbers grew markedly from AD 190–250, with the building of many churches, so that by AD 235 they had more than 20 bishops and some 18 dioceses.[7] By that time the Arsacid dynasty had been replaced by that of the Sasanians who were more firmly devoted to the Zoroastrian cause. In the latter they believed that they had a genuine Iranian answer to the intransigent religious dogmatism of both the Christians and the Manichaeans. However, that ancient Zoroastrian faith

109

was more prominent in the 'Persian' provinces than in Mesopotamia, where the Christians tended to congregate and flourish. Their numbers were supplemented significantly, including those of the clergy, by the captives brought from Antioch and other areas by Shapur I in his campaigns of AD 256 and 260. These captives included the Bishop of Antioch, Demetrius, and other high Church officials all of whom added their contributions to the developing organisation of the Church in Persia, especially in the second half of the 3rd century. In particular these captives were set to work to build the new town of Gondishapur, which in due time became a seat of learning, not least in medicine. It provided also another area of Christian strength outside of Adiabene and Nisibis, the latter being within the Roman Empire until AD 363.

While the Christians remained out of favour in the Roman Empire Sasanian rulers followed no particular course of antagonism towards these in their realm, whatever the urging of the Zoroastrian clergy. So the Church had time to organize and grow, not that tensions were always avoided between Greek speakers and Syriac speakers, or between Nisibis and the twin capital cities of Seleucia-Ctesiphon. Indeed just before AD 300 the Bishop of Seleucia-Ctesiphon made claim to primacy in the Persian Church, which claim by Papa bar Aggai, despite opposition from a number of quarters including Susa, seems to have been recognized by the powers that be, or were. As to lines of ecclesiastical authority, the Persian Church remained under the overall authority of Antioch.

Near the outset of the long reign of Shapur II (AD 309–379) two events, significant for Christians in the Sasanian Empire, occurred. In AD 311 Galerius (d. AD 311) promulgated an edict which put an end to the persecution of Christians by the Roman Empire. In AD 312 Constantine (d. AD 337) declared himself to be a Christian just before the battle which made him Emperor of the West. By AD 324 he was sole emperor and was showing consistent favour towards Christianity.

Eusebius records subsequent events and actions of Constantine, which latter may be characterised as enthusiasm outrunning sagacity, thus:

'The king of the Persians also having testified a desire to form an alliance with Constantine, by sending an embassy and presents as assurances of peace and friendship, the emperor, in negotiating this treaty, far surpassed the monarch who had first done him honour, in the magnificence with which he acknowledged his gifts. Having heard, too, that there were many churches of God in Persia, and that large numbers there were gathered into the fold of Christ, full of joy at this intelligence, he resolved to extend his anxiety for the general welfare to that country also, as one whose aim it was to care for all alike in every nation.'

The letter from Constantine to Shapur II is reproduced by Eusebius, and after declaring his faith in the Christian God he added:

> 'I cannot, then, my brother, believe that I err in acknowledging this one God, the author and parent of all things: whom many of my predecessors in power, led astray by the madness of error, have ventured to deny, but who were all visited with a retribution so terrible and so destructive, that all succeeding generations have held up their calamities as the most effectual warning to any who desire to follow in their steps. Of the number of these I believe him (Valerian) to have been, whom the lighting-stroke of Divine vengeance drove forth from hence, and banished to your dominions, and whose disgrace contributed to the fame of your celebrated triumph.'

Constantine concluded:

> 'Imagine, then, with what joy I heard tidings so accordant with my desire, that the fairest districts of Persia are filled with those men on whose behalf alone I am at present speaking, I mean the Christians. I pray, therefore, that both you and they may enjoy abundant prosperity, and that your blessings and theirs may be in equal measure; for thus you will experience the mercy and favour of that God who is the Lord and Father of all. And now, because your power is great, I commend these persons to your protection; because your piety is eminent, I commit them to your care. Cherish them with your wonted humanity and kindness; for by this proof of faith you will secure an immeasurable benefit both to yourself and us.'[8]

While Eusebius went on to see Constantine as the 'single pilot' of 'the nations of the world', such words as those in the letter were not likely to create equanimity in the heart of Shapur II, or to remove suspicions about the loyalty of his Christian subjects. There were some examples of localised persecution in AD 318, 327 and 339, and this was to become general from AD 340–379, after the death of Constantine.

THROUGH PERSECUTION TO AUTONOMY

The persecution, which was over almost 40 years, was the first major and known persecution of Christians in a spirit of orthodox Zoroastrianism. For reasons to do with strategic, political and economic considerations Shapur II gave the Zoroastrian clergy their opportunity to pursue their ideological aims. It is something of a paradox that throughout this period there was no absolute ban on Christianity, Christians continuing to carry their share of war service in the army. One of their number even commanded against the Romans on at least one occasion.[9]

111

Nevertheless what was referred to as 'the religion of Caesar' was clearly under heavy pressure. On one hand Shapur demanded a double poll tax from the 'Nazarenes', a demand which the Metropolitan, Shimun, refused. His arrest and execution followed, along with 100 other members of the clergy, largely on the grounds of suspicions about Christian loyalty in a war with the Romans which began in AD 337.[10]

On the side of religious belief the accusations against the Christians were explicit in a decree of Shapur, thus:

> 'These Christians destroy our holy Teaching, and teach men to serve one God, and not to honour the Sun, or Fire. They defile Water by their ablutions, they refrain from marriage and the propagation of children, and refuse to go to war with the King of Kings. They have no rules about the slaughter and eating of animals; they bury the corpses of men in the earth. They attribute the origin of snakes and creeping things to a good God. They despise many servants of the King, and teach witchcraft.'[11]

The persecution was reported to be very fierce between AD 344 and 367 in Susiana and Adiabene, with some 16,000 names listed as martyrs, which points to an even larger number of victims. No small part was played in promoting antagonism towards Christianity by the action of Theodosius I (d. AD 395) in AD 380 in declaring it the official religion of his Empire. Some Christians found refuge at Nisibis, which was within the Roman Empire until AD 363. The future of Christianity was bleak indeed while Shapur II lived, but, with his death in AD 379, the persecution ceased under Bahram IV (d. AD 399). Then when Yazdgard I (d. AD 420) succeeded in AD 399 a period of toleration ensued as the new emperor set about curbing the power of the nobles and of the Magians (late Zoroastrian clergy), incurring in so doing, the hatred and obloquy of the latter group.

Zoroastrian antipathy towards Yazdgard was not lessened when following a peace treaty with Constantinople in AD 410, the Christians convened in their first major synod at which the Roman ambassador, Bishop Marut of Maipherqat, was present. A skilled physician, Marut had rendered medical service to both Shapur II and Yazdgard I and was persona grata in both empires, and so able to assist the Christian cause in a way acceptable to the Sasanian ruler.

Under the presidency of its primate, Izhaq, the synod adopted the creeds and canons of Nicea (AD 325) and Constantinople (AD 381). The Persians had played no role in the Arian controversy, which raged while they were under persecution, and this brought them into line with the Church at large. At this synod some six provinces, each with its own metropolitan, and 26 bishops were recognized, 10 of the bishops being in areas outside metropolitan oversight. Some of these last ten were the far-flung dioceses of Qatar, the Islands and Rai. In addition a number of practices, concerning e.g. one bishop per diocese and liturgical seasonal observances, were brought into line with those of the Churches of the Roman Empire. Among such measures taken were some to prevent male and female clerical ascetics from living together in community:

'. . . that from now on no bishop, priest, deacon, sub-deacon or bar queiama, who lives together with woman, and not chastely and with holy awe along, as is fitting in the service of the Church, men alone with men will be received into the service of the Church.'[12]

The legitimacy of the Christian Church was further recognized by Yazdgard I with a decree of toleration, and its recognition as a legitimate minority group, or *millet*. Under this arrangement the Church was

'like a little state within the state, the Catholicos being responsible to the government for the behaviour of his people and for such things as collecting taxes from them.'[13]

So, e.g., Izhaq I was confirmed in office as Catholicos by the king, who offered to act against any schismatics, thus showing how intertwined Church and state had become, for good or evil. From the side of the Church a synod in AD 576 determined that:

'It is right that in all the churches of this exalted and glorious kingdom that our lord the victorious Chosroes [Khosrau I], king of kings, be named in the litanies during the liturgy. No metropolitan or bishop has any authority to waive this canon in any of the churches of his diocese and jurisdiction.'[14]

It was, however, something of a two edged sword to have royal approval for the appointment of the Catholicos, or later the patriarch. Royal disfavour could keep the post unfilled in a vacancy, such as that for 20 years from AD 600.

That the days of persecution were not entirely past, was clear from the fact that around the time of Yazdgard's death and Bahram V's accession, Magian clergy instigated attacks on Christians for the destruction of some Zoroastrian fire-temples. Christians had to learn not to be over-presumptuous about their status as a tolerated group. Also in AD 420 the orthodoxy of Persian Christians was further confirmed during the Catholicos Yaballaha's visit to the Emperor Theodosius II (d. AD 450). And in AD 422 a new treaty was signed between Persia and the Roman Empire which guaranteed freedom of worship to Christians in Persia.

Another synod convened in AD 424 and took crucial steps towards autonomy for the Church in Persia. Significant in this process was the decision as under:

'We have accepted and we accept the divine precepts and fatherly laws, which at various times have been transmitted to this Eastern land where we live, and lay down that the Father cannot be driven from his inheritance by his children, and the Head and Commander cannot be ordered about and dominated by those who are under him.

WHEREAS it has been decreed by the Western Fathers that our bishops are not allowed to hold an assembly against the will of their Head, nor to prepare in writing heads of accusation and reproach; but if they have any complaint to make, and obtain no satisfaction at the Assembly in presence of the Patriarch, they may appeal to his colleagues (the Patriarchs of Antioch, etc.), who shall examine the matter and decide between him and them;

And WHEREAS we have often experienced the fact that those who complain against the Catholicos have been condemned, punished for their folly by deprivation and deposition, and stripped of the title of their order and the vestment which they wore;

NOW, by the Word of God, WE DECREE that the Easterns shall not be permitted to carry complaints against their Patriarch before the Western Patriarchs, and that every case which cannot be determined in the presence of their Patriarch shall be left to the judgement of Christ. . . . No one for any reason shall be allowed to think or say that the Catholicos of the East can be judged by those under him, or by a patriarch like him. His own judgement is reserved for the Christ who has chosen him, raised him up, and placed him at the head of His Church.'[15]

While it may be that in this version the title 'Patriarch' is prematurely given to the Catholicos, the title being assumed officially in AD 498, it is clear that from this time onwards the Church in Persia saw no need to refer matters to the Patriarch of Antioch – nor to any other of the patriarchs in the Roman Empire. At the same time the jurisdiction of the Persian Church continued to expand, for at the synod were 36 bishops, including those of Merv and Herat, key centres for future expansion to the East. At the same time internal peace in the Church was promoted, while fellowship with Christians elsewhere was maintained, not least by the education in Greek of the clergy. In addition, it is clear from the names of those attending that some were Iranians, rather than all being of Syrian extraction.

That a peaceful coexistence with Zoroastrianism was not to be taken for granted was made painfully obvious in AD 446 when Yazdgard II (d. AD 457) began to persecute Christians and an infamous massacre occurred at Kirkuk. This was followed by attention to Christians in Assyria and Armenia. As a royal minister put it to the Christians of Armenia in AD 449:

'Know ye that every man who dwells under heaven and does not follow the religion of Mazdaism is deaf, blind, and deceived by the devil of Ahriman. Ahura-Mazda created men; and Ahriman pain, sickness and death. . . . Men who say that God is the author of death, and that good and evil come from him, are in error; in particular the Christians, who affirm that God is jealous, and that, just for a fig picked from a tree, he created death, and condemned men to undergo it. . . . The Christians also profess another error. They say that God, who created heaven and earth, was born of a virgin named Mary, whose husband was called Joseph. . . . Why do you share in the errors of the Roman Empire? What is more serious than anything else, they preach that God has been crucified by men; that he died and was buried; that he rose again and ascended into heaven. The evil spirits are not imprisoned and tormented by men, much less God, the Creator of all things.'[16]

Incomplete records indicate that 10 bishops and 153,000 clergy and laity died as martyrs.

By that time the impact of Nestorianism was beginning to be felt in Persia, and to that we shall turn below. In AD 498 the Catholicos became 'Patriarch of the East' and his headquarters were settled at Seleucia-Ctesiphon, which twin cities

'formed the centre of trade and travel between Europe and West Asia on one side, and India and China on the other.'[17]

It was strategically placed for overseeing extensive missionary work, to which we will give attention later. Suffice it to note here, that in the remaining years of the Sasanian dynasty, i.e. up to AD 651, Christian evangelism efforts continued. In AD 549 a bishop was consecrated for the Huns and Turks along the Oxus River, and before the time of Muhammad a bishop was to be found also in Samarkand, with an archbishop in Herat. Efforts were made also as we have seen in Arabia, and on both sides of the Persian Gulf by AD 650 there were 10 provinces and 96 bishops serving the Christians of Persia, and with the Jews, they numbered some 1.5 million. So Barthold notes:

'The exceptional success of Christianity in the western frontier districts of the Sasanian Empire from the estuary of the Euphrates and Tigris up to Armenia and the Caucasus. . . . By the time of the Muslim conquest, these districts, with the exception of a few Jewish colonies, became purely Christian.'[18]

BOTH AUTONOMOUS AND PREDOMINANTLY NESTORIAN

When the synod of AD 424 met and established the autonomy of the Church in Persia, Theodore of Mopsuestia had but four years to live, and also in AD 428 Nestorius (d. AD 451), his pupil and disciple, became the Bishop of Constantinople. Within a further three years the Council of Ephesus, largely driven by the advocacy of Cyril of Alexandria (d. AD 444), who held also the proxy power of the Bishop of Rome, had deposed Nestorius and declared heretical the Christology which came to be called 'Nestorianism'. The Church within the Roman Empire was thrown into serious division, represented by the respective and apparently irreconcilable views of those who spoke for Antioch and those who spoke for Alexandria. The attempt to settle matters, once and for all, at Chalcedon in AD 451, following the compromise Formula of Reunion in AD 433 and the tumultuous 'council' at Ephesus in AD 449, only led in the end to further division within the Empire, between Monophysites and Chalcedonians. As for the Nestorians, their presence, as well as their views, had been declared unacceptable within the Empire, so they had migrated east.

As we have seen already the so-called 'Persian school' at Edessa had been founded by some who had fled Nisibis when it fell to the Persians following the defeat of Julian in AD 363. It had a stress on diophysite Christology, made much of the exegesis of Theodore of Mopsuestia, and was frankly ready to propound Nestorian ideas. However, with the policy adopted by Rabbula, Bishop of Edessa, after the Council of Ephesus (AD 431), tensions ran high in the city. Unwelcome in the Empire at large, and in Edessa in particular after the death of their champion, the Bishop Hiba in AD 457, Nestorians began to leave for Nisibis within the Sasanian realm. In doing so they reconstituted at Nisibis what had been a school of long standing, tracing its lineage back to an early Jewish academy there. As for the Christian community itself, its history was intertwined with that of Arbela in Adiabene, and its Bishop Jacob had attended the Council of Nicea in AD 325. Given its varied history of Roman and Persian jurisdiction, and its location in the borderlands between the two empires, it is not surprising that it has been compared to the province of Alsace-Lorraine in Western Europe.[19]

Within the 'Persian school' at Edessa there had been strong reaction against both the decisions of the Council of Ephesus in AD 431 and what it saw as the compromising Formula of Reunion in AD 433. While some left for Nisibis in AD 457, its major early principal, *Narsai* (d. ca. AD 503), did not join them until ca. AD 471. It appears that he may well have been recruited by the Bishop, Bar Sauma (d. ca. AD 490), whose role in the Persian Church and state affairs we must survey below, and to have built on foundations laid by one Simon.[20] With the support of Bar Sauma, with whom Narsai did not always agree, and with the model of Edessa as an

116

institutional guide, the school at Nisibis grew. Strategically located for continuing to maintain a Nestorian witness in the Roman Empire, it was to be the prime early source of leaders and missionaries for the Church in Persia. Exegetically and theologically it followed the approach of Theodore of Mopsuestia, whose works had been translated into Syriac at Edessa after AD 450. Under pressure from the Emperor Zeno (d. AD 491), the school at Edessa was forced to shut its doors in AD 489, so that all its endeavours were focussed on Nisibis. With the support of the bishop's authority and the canons which he prepared, the school was run on strict coenobitic lines and prospered.

Narsai himself had a reputation for learning, piety, asceticism and poverty and a gift for poetry. So well developed was the latter that he won from the Nestorians the title of 'the harp of the Holy Spirit', while the Jacobites loathed him, and referred to him as 'the Leper'. Given to practical rather than speculative concerns, his literary remains focus on the 'mysteries' (or sacraments) and the liturgies associated with them, and have a clear didactic concern.[21]

Theological reflection, speculation and finesse of dogmatic definition play an insignificant part in the body of Narsai's literary creation.[22]

His great mentor was Theodore of Mopsuestia, of whom he wrote:

'It is proper to call him the doctor of the doctors, the agility of the spirit without which there would be no doctor who could give good instruction; through the treasury of his writings they have enriched all they have gained; and through his commentaries they have acquired the ability to interpret; from him I have learned, I also, to stutter; and in his conversation I have obtained the habit of meditation of the (divine) words; his meditation became for me as a guide towards the Scriptures; and he has elevated me towards the understanding of the books of the Spirit.'[23]

Able to combine the Hellenistic scholarship of the Antiochene school with the indigenous Syrian theology Narsai's learning was regarded by his contemporaries as unique. His reputation for sanctity did not save him from a falling out with Bar Sauma, although some believe that the disagreement may have had its roots in episcopal jealousy about just that reputation. The rift was serious enough to cause Narsai to seek monastic refuge for some six years, but in AD 496, six years after the death of the bishop, he is listed as the school's principal. He weathered accusations of collaboration with the Romans and died much honoured, while maintaining a strict discipline over his students and their predispositions to earn money or to slip across into Byzantine territory or to yield to sexual desire.[24] As far as can be ascertained there were no tuition fees and 'the School of Nisibis provided for the young Nestorian Church the systematic training of its ministry by a fixed program in an institution exclusively devoted to theological study. For several generations the School of Nisibis remained the principal institution for the education of the clergy, the missionaries, monks and teachers.'[25]

As for the Bishop of Nisibis, *Bar Sauma*[26], his name was systematically blackened by Jacobite authors, while even such an authority as J.P. Asmussen confused him with the Syrian archimandrite Barsumas who headed up his company of violent monks at the 'council' of Ephesus in AD 449.[27] Born between AD 400 and 405 not far from Nisibis, his native language was Syriac, but at Edessa, as a very good student, he mastered Greek, and later added Pahlavi. While he supported Hiba at Edessa he returned to Nisibis and was elected as bishop there in AD 457, the same year in which Babowai (d. AD 484), a convert from Zoroastrianism, became the Catholicos at Seleucia-Ctesiphon.

Bar Sauma was, from all accounts, an ecclesiastical politician of the first rank, and was given the sobriquet of 'the wild boar'. He was eager to make the most of the strategic location of Nisibis to the advantage of the Persian king against the Romans, and eager also to limit the autocratic tendencies of the Catholicos. In the latter cause he was aided by other bishops with similar concerns. For all that, he retained the loyalty of most of his people throughout his life. Accusations that he was anti-monastic were levelled at him by Jacobite critics, but

> '"Nestorian" monasticism continued to flourish in Bar Sauma's own bishopric of Nesibit'

and,

> 'there is no evidence that [he] persecuted monks in the area under his immediate jurisdiction.'[28]

While he acted as a mediator in treaty negotiations between Persians and Romans, his loyalty to the former was never questioned. Loyalty to the Catholicos was another matter altogether. Not only was he opposed to Babowai's monarchical approach, but he was antagonistic to the Catholicos' support for the dogmatic declaration of the Council of Chalcedon and its condemnation of Nestorius. While hardly a favourite courtier of Peroz (d. AD 484), Bar Sauma seems to have encouraged the Shah's suspicions of non-Nestorian Christians, as potential, if not actual, allies of the Hephthalite Huns who were allied to Rome. Persecution of such Christians ensued in AD 465, and Chalcedonians and Monophysites alike suffered. Clashing with the Catholicos also over the issue of clerical celibacy, which he opposed, Bar Sauma waited his opportunity to deal with one who had made the forbidden step of leaving Zoroastrianism to accept Christianity.

118

The *Henoticon* of Zeno in AD 482 was seen as a clear espousal of a
position more favourable to Monophysitism than to Chalcedon in the
Roman Empire, and it may have been this which caused Bar Sauma to
marshal his episcopal allies against Babowai. Among those allies was the
Bishop of Gondishapur, who traced his episcopal lineage back to the
exiled Demetrius[29] of Antioch (ca. AD 260). It was not surprising then
that, under Bar Sauma's leadership, a synod convened at Gondishapur (or
Bet Lapat) in AD 484, the same year in which Babowai was to be executed
for engaging in seditious correspondence with Byzantium. (It is possible
that Babowai was already in difficulties through promoting a festival to
commemorate those martyred by earlier Persian rulers.) While Bar Sauma
does not appear to have had any direct hand in seeing that this
correspondence reached official Persian hands,[30] it is most unlikely that
he regretted the outcome.

As for the AD 484 synod itself, it passed a number of canons aimed at
maintaining monogamy and lessening sexual licence, but authorities are
divided about whether it actually advocated clerical marriage in response
to Zoroastrian criticism.[31] However, it is clear that a synod in AD 486 did
do so, to the point of accepting it as a norm. But in AD 484 the synod did
condemn Babowai for simony, consequent action against him being
forestalled by his execution. So, the thirteenth canon of the council, on
simoniacal ordinations, though only in part extant, was clearly directed
against Babowai's practice of selling ecclesiastical offices:

"'Truly, upon one who gives money for, and buys an ecclesiastical
office, we impose the same censure, that he should not exercise his
ministry at all, as we remember the word of the blessed Peter, who
also excluded from the communion of faith an insolent one who
attempted to buy a spiritual gift for money saying to him: May your
money go with you to perdition. Since you thought that the gift of
God can be had for worldly goods, there will not be for you a part or
even a lot in this faith. Therefore he who gives and he who receives
money for one of the ecclesiastical orders, let him be excommunicated by Christ, the Lord of the Church." The extant part of the
eighteenth canon, concerned with unworthy ordinations, again must
have been closely connected with the irregular practices that
prevailed in such matters during Babowai's reign: He who gives
away one of the priestly orders because of covetousness or respect of
persons, even if to one of his own, not because of any need but because of the standing of the person who is ordained, let him be
accursed by the Lord of the priesthood. And if any of the bishops,
whose duty it is to take from him his dignity, is insolent, guilty, and
negligent, may Christ also take vengeance upon both of them,
because of their insolence.'[32]

Bar Sauma was able also to have the AD 484 synod declare itself in support of the approach of Theodore of Mopsuestia, thus:

'Nobody among us should have doubt concerning this holy man because of the evil rumors which the heretics have spread about him. For he was reputed during his lifetime to be illustrious and eminent among the teachers of the true faith, and after his death all the books of his commentaries and his homilies [were] approved and clear to those who understand the wise meaning of the divine Scriptures, and who honor the orthodox faith. For his books and his commentaries preserve the unblemished faith, as the meaning which befits the divine teaching in the New Testament. [His works] destroy and reject all of the teachings which strive against the guidance given by the prophets and against the good tidings coming from the apostles. If anyone therefore dares, secretly or openly, to traduce or to revile this teacher of truth and his holy writings, let him be accursed by the Truth [itself].'[33]

So with the removal of a Chalcedonian Catholicos, the espousal of Theodore and the products of the school at Nisibis the way was prepared for a Nestorian takeover of the Church in Persia.

Any hopes of Bar Sauma that he would succeed to the catholicate disappeared with the death of Peroz in the same year as Babowai, and the waning of support for Bar Sauma among the bishops who had opposed the former Catholicos. Instead, Aqaq (d. AD 496), an old Edessa classmate of Bar Sauma, was appointed in AD 485, and he played down any autocratic tendencies in the role of the Catholicos. While their theological differences were not great the new Catholicos and the Bishop of Nisibis did not see eye to eye, and the latter declined to attend the synod of AD 486, having pledged his loyalty to Aqaq late in AD 485. The synod of AD 486 spelled out a creed along clear Antiochene diophysite lines, without being anymore outspokenly Nestorian than was the Christological declaration of Chalcedon. This did not prevent growing animosity between the Catholicos and the Bishop of Nisibis, which led to mutual anathemas and interdicts, which ceased only with the death of the bishop in AD 490 or 491.

Over this same period the Catholicos, Aqaq, had been sent as an ambassador to Constantinople in AD 485 and in 491, where the Patriarch, Acacius, regarded the Persian Church as an ally against Monophysitism and as not blatantly Nestorian. It may have been, however, that Acacius pressured Aqaq to act against Bar Sauma for his treatment of Babowai. So links with the Church within the Roman Empire were not broken at this time.

Under the tolerant rule of the Shah Kavadh (d. AD 531), churches and monasteries were constructed, and the Church continued to grow. Babai (d. AD 502) succeeded as Catholicos in AD 497, and a crucial synod convened in AD 498 at Seleucia-Ctesiphon. Supported by Narsai, and the school of Nisibis, Babai moved to espouse that outright Nestorianism which Bar Sauma had supported. This involved, inter alia, the adoption of the formula 'two natures, two persons, and one presence'.[34] This move, in addition to that which changed the 'Catholicos' title to 'Patriarch' as a symbol of the complete autonomy of the Church in Persia, was aimed in part at settling disputes which continued between Nestorians and 'Chalcedonians'. Thereafter, to belong to the latter group was to belong to one whose loyalties were split between Seleucia-Ctesiphon and Constantinople. The division was sealed even further by the continuation not only of the norm of marriage for the clergy, but by the fact that the Patriarch Babai himself was married.

Apart from the period from AD 540–545 under Khosrau I, the Persian Christians enjoyed considerable toleration throughout the 6th century. They consolidated their position, and Khosrau even included many Christians in his professional bureaucracy. In addition:

'During his reign Mesopotamian Christians, who spoke the same Syriac language as did their neighbours across the frontier, transmitted Byzantine medicine, philosophy and court manners to the Sasanid capital.'[35]

Prominent in leadership was the Patriarch *Mar Aba I* (d. AD 552), who took up his post in AD 540. He was a convert from Zoroastrianism, who visited the west between AD 520 and 525, until the furore about his conversion subsided. Following a treaty between Khosrau I and Justinian I guaranteeing religious toleration, he returned to Nisibis as a teacher in AD 533. In the first months of his patriarchate he settled schisms at Rev-Ardashir and Gondishapur, but then he was under house-arrest and trial for his 'apostasy', at Magian insistence, until AD 543. His safety was secured by house-arrest exile in Azerbaijan for seven years, returning to the capital and to further mild imprisonment until AD 551. Condemning some Christians who supported a rebel prince at Gondishapur, Aba won royal favour from Khosrau I until his death in AD 552. It was during his patriarchate that a council affirmed that

'the Church of Assyria accepts the faith of Nicea, as expounded by Theodore.'[36]

Statements such as this led to some confusion in Antioch and Constantinople over the supposed Nestorianism of the Church in Persia, and this confusion lasted until the time of the Emperor Maurice (d. AD 602).

'A full century and a half after the time of Nestorius Constantinople did not know how to class the Assyrian Church in the controversies of the time',[37] although one would have thought that the condemnation of Theodore, Theodoret and Hiba at the Council of Constantinople in AD 553 would have clarified matters.

The issue was to be put beyond any doubt early in the 7th century through the work of an Abbot of Mt Izala monastery, *Mar Babai the Great* (d. AD 626). Mt Izala had become the leading monastic centre through the work of Abraham of Kaskar (d. AD 588), who set about his reform and reorganisation after a visit to and stay in Egypt. This resulted in the monastery's abbot being ranked next to the patriarch in prestige and authority within the Church. Indeed, during the long enforced vacancy in the patriarchate between AD 608 and AD 628, Babai the Great assumed a leadership role in the Church. The shahs had abrogated the right to nominate the patriarch after AD 552 and Khosrau II (d. AD 626) chose to leave it vacant after the death of Grigor in AD 608, for reasons to be discussed below.

Babai set out to systematise the Nestorian theology, partly in answer to that of the Monophysite Severus (d. AD 538). Not innovative himself he echoed Diodore, Theodore and Nestorius, but did so in a '"Nestorianism" which had absorbed the habit of philosophical analysis into its system.'[38]

Babai denied any doctrine which mixes divine and human properties, and he attacked the Severan use of analogy as misplaced, accusing the Monophysites of Apollinarianism, which they denied. He was prepared to accept the implications of his position for understandings of the Eucharist regarding the presence of Christ and the elements on the altar. Denying the presence of Christ in the elements (as later Calvin was to do), Babai held that

> '"he is one Christ in two natures," just as that body on the altar is one body mystically with the body which is in heaven [that of the ascended and glorified Christ] through virtue and sanctification and in name, though separate from the ascended body of Christ by distance; . . . so "Christ is one person by assumption and participation, not by nature".'[39]

His contribution was incorporated within the liturgy in the statement:

> 'One is Christ the Son of God, worshipped by all in two natures. In his godhead begotten of the Father without beginning before all time: in his manhood born of Mary, in the fullness of time, in a united body. Neither his godhead was of the nature of the mother, nor his manhood of the nature of the Father. The natures are preserved in their *qnume*, in one person of one sonship.'[40]

And consistently with Theodore and Nestorius, the usage of the title *Yāldath Alāhā* ('mother of God' – *Theotokos*) was eschewed in favour of *Yāldath Mšēḥā* ('mother of Christ' – *Christotokos*).

Throughout this 6th century the role of the school at Nisibis had remained very important. Narsai's successor as head of the school had been Elisa Bar Quzbaie (d. AD 522), another exegete who concentrated his attention on the books of the Old Testament in the Peshitta version. He was followed by a relation of Narsai, the head under whom the school reached the peak of its enrolments, over one thousand, – *Abraham de-bet Rabban* (d. ca. AD 569). He had a reputation for asceticism and scholarship which was recognized as far afield as Constantinople. Such was his reputation that Justinian I sought to involve him, or a representative in negotiations aimed at settling Christological differences at Constantinople ca. AD 533. It appears that Abraham sent the scholarly Paulos, whose works were translated into Greek and possibly also into Latin, but the conference was dominated mainly in fruitless discussions between Chalcedonians and Monophysites. In any case Abraham's respect for Diodore and Theodore was inimical to any solution along lines satisfactory to Justinian or Severus. In addition Abraham's efforts took place at a time of upsurge of Monophysite activity in East Syria, under the leadership of John of Tella (d. AD 538). Among his students Abraham was remembered most for his ability to make the Syriac translations of Theodore of Mopsuestia understandable, despite their inherent linguistic difficulty.

The school seems to have suffered a two year enforced closure under Khosrau I in AD 540–541, along with other anti-Christian measures of that shah. Some students went to study at Seleucia-Ctesiphon under Mar Aba, but his days there were numbered, as we have seen above. Nor was Nisibis able to avoid confrontation with the arrogant ex-medico Patriarch Jausep (d. AD 567), in which, along lines pioneered by Bar Sauma, it was one of the centres of episcopal opposition to patriarchal claims.

By this time the school had attained a reputation which occasioned envy and the desire to emulate it as far away as Rome. There Cassiodorus (d. ca. AD 570) hoped to establish a similar institution with the help of Pope Agapetus (d. AD 536). That the hope was not realised does nothing to lessen the lustre of Nisibis. Back in Persia it continued to be

'a centre which attracted all the influential persons who were to play an important role in the East Syrian society as instructors at the school, after having studied there, teachers in other places, founders of the new schools, missionaries, leaders of monastic communities and members of the hierarchy.'[41]

But Nisibis went through considerable upheavals under the directorship of *Henana* (d. ca. AD 610), who broke with the exegetical model of Theodore out of admiration for the modified allegorical approaches of Philo Judaeus (d. AD 45), Origen (d. AD 254) and John Chrysostom (d. AD 407). He departed also from Theodore's voluntary-moral-union

Christology, being attracted to the one hypostasis emphasis of Monophysitism. He accepted and used the title *Theotokos* for the Virgin Mary and further scandalised the Nestorians by carrying the idea of suffering into the divinity. In his views about humanity and sin Henana disagreed with the emphases of Aphrahat, Ephrem and Theodore, which had previously prevailed at Nisibis and had led to the rejection of any concept of original sin.

These views, which led to considerable discord, arose over an extended period of time. Up until AD 590 he had the support of the Bishop of Nisibis, but when in AD 596 a new bishop, Grigor, was elected, and brought with him a reputation for evangelistic, paedagogic and thaumaturgic activism, Henana's opponents gathered. Censures by the bishop failed to move Henana, nor did they when Grigor became Patriarch in AD 605. The somewhat favourable attitude of Khosrau II towards the Monophysite cause was of assistance to Henana. However, rebellion erupted in the school itself, which was the beginning of the end of the glory of the institution, as numbers of students left in AD 609–610.

> 'They departed from the school, and distributed their belongings; they took with them the gospels and the crosses in black veils, and the censers; they departed from the town with prayers and chanting the hymns of supplications; they were about 300 souls; the inhabitants of the town wept, and sighed about their exodus while the shameless chiefs rejoiced that they had chased out Grigor.'

At the gate of the city, the community of this famous centre of learning was assembled for the last time:

> 'When these departing ones arrived at the gate of the town, they completed the prayer and after having said farewell to one another, they separated from each other.'[42]

Henana and his disciples continued for several years, and according to the *Chronicle of Seert*

> 'the adherents and disciples of Henana were spreading and were increasing their activities'[43]

much to the chagrin of Mar Babai the Great, who, sometime after AD 615 deplored the results thus:

> 'Behold, for some time this entire poor town has been corrupted through this wicked error, and only a small seed of the truth has remained through the providence of grace.'[44]

Whereas once Nisibis had been the only and then still the pre-eminent theological school, there were alternatives emerging which received that full approval of the Nestorians, which Nisibis had clearly forfeited. The first and foremost of the alternative schools was that at Seleucia-Ctesiphon which flourished in the 6th and 7th centuries, dwindled somewhat and then was revived under the Patriarch Petion (d. AD 730). In time it was to be overshadowed somewhat by that at the later capital of Baghdad, where the founder was the Patriarch Sabr-ishu II (d. ca. AD 835). Another 6th century foundation had been the school at Gondishapur, which was modelled on that of Antioch and focussed on medical and philosophical studies. It was to be the source of a line of private physicians to Abbasid caliphs. Nisibis itself was but one school among many, as foci of education and theology among the Nestorians.

The line pursued by Henana had emphases which smacked of Monophysitism to Nestorian Persians. By the time he was in full flight the Nestorians were feeling the pressure of Monophysites from Syria within Persia itself. The work of Jacob Baradai from AD 542–578 bore fruit in Persian soil as elsewhere, while a Monophysite physician, Jibrail, was instrumental in converting Shirin, the mistress and de facto queen of Khosrau II, from Nestorian to Jacobite Christianity. Her influence was strong upon the shah, and the Jacobites gathered confidence. Their numbers swelled greatly when, out of his early 7th century conquests in Egypt, Syria and Asia Minor (AD 609–619) Khosrau II brought many captive Christians back to Persia, and most of these were Monophysites. These later 'exiles' joined those whose stay in Persia dated back to campaigns in AD 540 and 573 under Khosrau I (d. AD 579). It was in part due to Jacobite pressure that the Nestorian patriarchate was kept unfilled from AD 609 to 628.

The Nestorians petitioned in AD 612 that a patriarch be appointed, to be opposed by Jibrail with the plea that the appointment be left in his Jacobite hands. The latter request was not granted, for Khosrau realised that such a step would outrage the large majority of the Christian *millet*. Nor was the Nestorian petition successful, but we do glimpse a statement of their creed, in a statement presented to the shah at that time:

> 'This is the doctrine of the orthodox Faith confided to the Catholic Church by the Holy Apostles. In the land of the Persians, from the time of the Apostles to the present day, no heresy has appeared and aroused schisms or divisions. On the other hand, in the land of the Romans . . . there have been numerous and varied heresies; they contaminated many people; when they were chased out of there, and fled, their shadows reached to here. Such are the Manichaeans, the Marcionites . . . the Severians . . .
>
> Now it is our hope and belief that, since the land of the Romans has been submitted to your admirable authority, in an Empire new and astonishing in the number of its lands and cities, your Majesty will direct it, by the authority of useful laws, in such a way that they

shall be established with us in that Apostolic Faith which we have received from the beginning.'[45]

Under their Patriarch Athanasius I (d. AD 631), the Jacobites began to order themselves in Persia. They had their main centre at Takrit, a mountain monastic fastness at Mar Mattai, and an important scientific and medical school at Singar, with their preponderant numbers being thus to the north. While being reasonably widespread throughout Persia, the Jacobites were destined never to reach the numbers of the Nestorians there. However, at Takrit

'Marut, a monk who had been a zealous missionary ruled over twelve suffragans in Persia. Then he made three more sees.'[46]

By AD 628 the Nestorians were allowed a new patriarch and the Jacobites were recognized as a distinct *millet*, under the titular Patriarch of Antioch, with the senior metropolitan in Persia being called the Mafrian. As to the substance of the differences between Nestorians and Jacobites, J. Labourt says:

'Monophysitism in the sixth century was singularly refined, so much so that it is difficult to distinguish it from orthodoxy except by its refusal to admit the Council of Chalcedon and the Tome of Leo. Nestorianism accomplished a similar evolution, and the doctrine of Mar Aba [the great Nestorian Patriarch, AD 540–552] is not far removed from the Byzantine faith.'[47]

Without wanting to leap ahead in time overmuch, a comment from a late 9th century Nestorian, Eliyya Jauhan, is also relevant, regarding the points in common and at variance:

'They agree in observing the Sundays and Christian festivals. With regard to the offering of the Eucharist they are at one in saying that it is the Body and Blood of Christ. They uphold the confession of faith put forward by the 318 Fathers who were gathered together at Nicaea, which is repeated by all at every liturgy. They also agree in the truth of the priesthood in all its ranks, viz. the patriarchate, the episcopate, the presbyterate and the diaconate, and also in the water of baptism. There is no difference between them in blood nor in faith, but only in their party feelings [lit. passions]. . . . And we see that all the Christians agree on the Gospel as the true book of God, and the book of Paul, and the Acts, and the books of the Old Testament, the Torah and the Prophets, and in the creed, and the Eucharist, and baptism, and the festivals and Sundays, and fasting, and the priesthood, and the cross, and belief in the day of resurrection and return and rising again from the dead, in the things that are lawful and unlawful, and in heaven and hell.'

After describing the different doctrines of the three Churches about the person of Christ, he concluded:

> 'So whereas they differ in word they agree in meaning; and although they contradict one another outwardly they agree inwardly. And all of them follow one faith, and believe in one Lord, and serve one Lord. There is no difference between them in that, nor any distinction except from the point of view of party feelings and strife.'[48]

But when Heraclius was at the gates of Seleucia-Ctesiphon early in AD 628, Khosrau II was deposed and murdered. There appears to have been Nestorian complicity in the plot to remove Khosrau, and the appointment of Ishu-Yab II (d. AD 643) as patriarch followed, with him also being sent as ambassador to Rome.

While Ishu-Yab II was also the patriarch who initiated the mission to China, other events were about to overtake the Nestorians and the Sasanian dynasty, as the Arabs swept out of the Arabian peninsula. In AD 632 the Sasanian army was soundly defeated by the Arabs and by the end of that year the whole of the Mesopotamian plain was in their hands. The heartlands of Iran suffered next and in AD 642 the final battle occurred at Nihavand. It was but a few more years before the last Sasanian ruler, Yazdgard II, was assassinated by one of his own soldiers at Merv in AD 651.

UNDER MUSLIMS AND MONGOLS

Hira had been the first centre of importance to fall to the Arabs, and the Muslim conquest ended with the capture of Merv, Balkh and Herat by AD 652. All told some two decades were taken up in this process, so that between actual periods of hostility the invaders and the invaded began to develop a modus vivendi. As had been the case in Syria the Arabs, for all their success on the battlefield, were initially very aware of their inexperience in matters of large scale civil administration. Averse to dualistic Zoroastrians they were consequently the more ready to avail themselves of the services and gifts of their monotheistic Jewish and Christian subjects. The Umayyad dynasty was centred in Damascus, and the oversight of Persia was delegated to local governors, whose attitude towards Christians was, on the whole, a reflection of that of their superiors, the caliphs. The emergence of the Shi'ite Muslims after AD 679 and the resurgence of the Byzantines under Leo III the Isaurian (d. AD 741) kept the caliphs well occupied with more than ways of dealing with Jews and Christians.

In any case the Arabs had inherited from the Sasanians a system of relating to religious minorities which seemed to be working reasonably well, so why make unnecessary work? As elsewhere, as long as the Christians in Persia, as a *millet*, paid their land and poll taxes, the latter in lieu of military service, all would be well. Monks, and on occasions patriarchs, were exempted from poll tax, and the clergy were given appropriate respect. As a *dhimmi,* or protected community, the Christians, like the Jews, had their own residential sectors, and, under the general suzerainty of Muslim law, were left to order their own affairs, not only ecclesiastical but also, to a considerable degree, their own legal system. They appointed their own officials, with the superior ones, like the patriarch, requiring official confirmation as had prevailed previously.

As one Muslim, Abu Yusuf, described the conditions imposed at the time of the Arab conquest:

'As to thy question, O Commander of the Faithful, concerning the *dhimmis,* how it is that their synagogues and churches in the important towns or other places of the Muslim conquest have been left to them without being destroyed, and how it is that they have been allowed to continue to display their crosses at the time of their festivals, the reason thereof is that the arrangement made between the Muslims and the *dhimmis* only took place on condition that neither their churches nor their synagogues, whether within or without the walls, should be destroyed, that their lives should be respected, and that they should be allowed liberty to fight against and repel their enemies. Such are the conditions following the payment of the *jizya* [i.e. tax], and under which the peace was concluded, and the written agreements demanded the non-erection of new churches or synagogues. It is thus that the whole of Syria and the great part of Ḥīra was conquered, which explains why the churches and synagogues have been respected.'[49]

Or, in summary, as a modern writer has it:

'Under the Muslim rule, the *millet* system, whereby a non-Muslim community was ruled through the intermediacy of its religious hierarchy, was consolidated. Under Islam, the system was found necessary for religious, political and economic reasons; the law of the Koran, which was civil as well as religious, could not be applied integrally to Christian and Jewish communities. Like true theocracies, the non-Muslim sects were put under the jurisdiction of the religious heads of their respective creeds and were designated as "millets", or nationalities distinguished by their religious profession. The various churches were thus transformed into a kind of ecclesiastical state whose jurisdiction extended not merely to matters of personal status, such as marriage and inheritance, but also to most of the disputes occurring among the community.'[50]

By the time of Muslim control the Nestorians had built up a considerable minority place within Persian society, being particularly significant in the north-west. With the help of Thomas of Marga's *Book of Governors*, of about AD 840, we are able to develop a reliable account of events in what was called 'the Church of the East' up to AD 800. As a former secretary to the Patriarch Abraham (d. AD 850), Thomas was in a position to give us a quite realistic picture, 'warts and all'.

As to the Christian reactions, initially they mirrored those of their co-religionists in Syria. References to divine retribution and resorts to Danielic apocalypticism abound. So, e.g. the

> 'Nestorians saw in the hardships they endured divine punishment for the Monophysite successes in northern Mesopotamia, or, alterna-tively, moving to a wider viewpoint, the Arab conquest of the Sasanids was understood as a punishment for Zoroastrianism.'[51]

The Patriarch *Ishu-Yab III* (d. AD 660), in the light of the Danielic framework, took a positive attitude towards the events of his day. He called the Arabs 'commenders of our faith who honour the clergy, the churches and the monasteries.'[52] Faced with the 'apostasy' of Christians in Oman, who preferred Islam to giving up no less than half of their possessions to the Arabs, Ishu-Yab did not upbraid the Arabs but the laxity of his own clergy. He used a similar line to take to task those who bemoaned the conversion of some Nestorians in the north to Jacobitism, whom he cleared of the charge that they are favoured by the Muslims.

No less stringent was his criticism of clergy in the province of Fars, where he was faced not only with conversions to Islam but also with repudiation of his authority by the Metropolitan Shimun of Rev-Ardashir. At first Shimun and his 18 bishops, from Fars, down the Gulf to Socotra, and east to Kerman and south-east to India, opted for defiance in the hope that the Arabs would support the schism. Such hopes were denied, for the Arabs appear to have backed the patriarch, who went in person to depose Shimun and split the province into three, with new metropolitans for Tatar and India.

Amidst all of this Ishu-Yab III was able to rejoice in the eastward expansion of the Church of the East beyond the Oxus to Turks in AD 644 and in China in AD 635, a fact which he used in correspondence in AD 651 in which he appealed to the monks at Qatar to abide by his rulings:

> 'Lo, there are more than twenty bishops and two metropolitans in the East, who have received in the past, and receive in the present, episcopal ordination from the Church of God (i.e. the Patriarch), and none of them have come to us for many years, nor did we ask them to come, but we know that in spite of the long distance that separates them from us they fulfil the obligations of their episcopacy in strict conformity with the Church of God, while the rights of their

episcopal jurisdiction are duly received from us. We write to them and they write to us.'[53]

The patriarch's overall positive attitude towards the Arabs is echoed some decades later by John of Phenek, writing in the 690's, following plagues in AD 686–687. With a heightened eschatological expectancy, John is still able to uphold the idea that the Arabs were divinely called:

'We should not think of their advent as something ordinary, but as due to divine working. Before calling them, God had prepared them beforehand to hold Christians in honor; thus they also had a special commandment from God concerning our monastic station, that they should hold it in honor. . . . How otherwise, apart from God's help, could naked men, riding without armor or shield, have been able to win; God called them from the ends of the earth in order to destroy, through them, a sinful kingdom (Amos 9:8), and to humiliate, through them, the proud spirit of the Persians.'[54]

The Arabs encouraged Nestorian educational centres at Nisibis, Gondishapur and Merv, for from them came accountants, scribes, physicians, teachers and interpreters to assist the new rulers, with a good deal of responsibility for finances and local administration left in the hands of local authorities. As the Caliph Sulayman (d. AD 717) is reported to have commented:

'I admire these Persians; they reigned for one thousand years and never, not for one hour, did they stand in need of us; we ruled for 100 years and not for one hour could we do without them.'[55]

Even when intra-Christian bickerings or local outrage led to outbreaks of persecution, as between AD 717 and 720, the stringency was limited by the dependence the Arabs had on Christian bureaucrats. Indeed it is reported that virtually every patriarch approved in the 8th century, was so because of the influence at court of Christian physicians or scribes. So even the order of 'Umar II in AD 720 that all recently constructed churches were to be destroyed, was not seen as a threat to the long term future of Christianity.

When the Abbasid dynasty replaced that of the Umayyads in AD 750, not only did the capital move from Damascus to Kufa and thence in AD 762, to Baghdad, but the new rulers favoured orthodox Islam, and were less prone to advance Arabs ahead of other Muslims. They also set out to give greater attention to the Islamicisation of law and the bureaucracy, not that they were able to dispense forthwith with the services of non-Muslims. Such a step had to await the 9th century, being fired in part by resentment among some Muslims at the ways in which Christians had secured many of the best appointments. It was under them too that Muslim canon law, the *sharia*, was codified and clearly established as superior in authority to all other legal codes. In addition it was only with this dynasty that real inroads were made into the religious loyalties of the population in the north and north-west, the latter being the Christian heartland. Even so, it was going to take the Abbasid Muslims some 100 years of effort to secure firm foundations for Islam in Transoxania.

In a number of ways Nestorians seemed to reach the peak of their influence towards the end of the 8th century, marked as this apogee was by the patriarchate of *Timothy I* (AD 780–823), to whom we shall return below. From AD 775 the patriarch's seat was at Baghdad, rather than at Seleucia-Ctesiphon, so constant contact with the court of the caliphate could be maintained. Another source of Nestorian influence began in AD 765 when the second Abbasid caliph, Mansur (d. AD 775), summoned Jurjis b. Bakhtishu from the medical school at Gondishapur to be his personal physician. This began a six generation dynasty of such personal physicians to the caliphs, and a most useful avenue of Nestorian influence.

These years towards the end of the 8th century also saw considerable dialogue between Muslims and Christians, not least between the Patriarch Timothy I and the third Abbasid caliph, Mahdi (d. AD 785). The patriarch was able to win the respect of the caliph, which was as well in that Mahdi had suffered defeats in AD 777–778 at the hands of the Emperor Leo IV (d. AD 780), which experience had soured his attitude towards Christians for a time. After some six visits to the caliph and assurances of Nestorian hostility towards the Byzantines, permission was obtained to rebuild a number of destroyed churches. Through the good offices of a court counsellor, another Jibrail, further concessions were given to the Patriarch, who recorded his gratitude thus:

> 'May God have mercy on the soul of Rabban Jibrail, who is a shield both for the community, and for us. Indeed, he has obtained an edict from the King, according to which no prince may act against me in matters concerning the laws of the Church.'[56]

In the course of visits to the caliph, in AD 781, Timothy engaged in dialogue on the claims of Christianity and Islam. With a background of apologetics and polemic with respect to Judaism, the Patriarch had considerable material on which to draw, and of course no little common ground to which to refer. A. Mingana has provided us with an account of the dialogue[57] from which the following issues emerge:

> '. . . both accept the Torah: both accept the Gospel (only the Caliph puts in a caveat against possible corruptions, either of Torah or Gospel, in a sense that would be unfavourable to Islam); and what is more strange, both accept in some sense the Quran, or at least the

Christian debater is willing to use the Quran in cases where its testimony coincides with that of the Law and the Prophets.'[58]

They agreed, where they could,

> 'as on the Virgin Birth of Jesus and the sinlessness of his character, (which the caliph holds it is blasphemy to deny), and differing where they must on the unity or trinity of God, and on the question whether either God or Christ really died on the cross.'[59]

Timothy denied that there was any prophecy about Muhammad in the Law, the Prophets or the Gospels, and also set out to refute Mahdi's claim that Muhammad was the promised Paraclete.

> 'If Muhammad were the Paraclete, since the Paraclete is the Spirit of God, Muhammad would therefore be the Spirit of God; and the Spirit of God, being uncircumscribed like God, Muhammad would also be uncircumscribed like God; and he who is uncircumscribed being invisible, Muhammad would also be invisible and without a human body; and he who is without a human body being uncomposed, Muhammad would also be uncomposed . . . etc. etc.'[60]

The caliph responded with a charge that Christians had removed all references to Muhammad from their scriptures, and that they persisted in regarding Muhammad as the Jews did Jesus. Timothy demanded to be shown the uncorrupted texts of the scriptures, and claimed that

> 'To tell the truth, if I found in the Gospel a prophecy concerning the coming of Muhammad, I would have left the Gospel for the Quran, as I left the Torah and the Prophets for the Gospel.'[61]

Mahdi shrank from any claim that Jesus actually died, holding only that 'he made a similitude for them in this way.'[62] Timothy responded by referring the Caliph to the words ascribed to Jesus in Sura 19:33 of the Quran, viz.

> 'Peace on me the day I was born, and the day I die, and the day I shall be raised alive!'[63]

He went on to declare that it was unfitting for God to deceive with a similitude, which would also, in consistency, have to be applied to the resurrection and the ascension. Instead the patriarch while agreeing that the Jews killed the prophets, held that

> 'So far as Jesus Christ is concerned we say that the Jews crucified only the Christ in the flesh which he delivered to them voluntarily, and his murder was not imposed forcibly upon him by them.'[64]

In no way excusing the Jews for their part in the death of Jesus, Timothy (like Athanasius of Alexandria before him in *On the Incarnation of the Word*, section 23) stressed the significance of the public death, so

'that his death should have been first witnessed by all, as his resurrection was witnessed by all.'[65]

The debate returned to the contention that Christians have edited out of their scriptures prophecies which refer to Muhammad, and again the patriarch denied this, pointing, inter alia, to the evidence of the Jewish scriptures. So he claimed that

'The Christians never have had and never will have such deadly enemies as the Jews; if the Jews had tampered with their Book how could we Christians induce ourselves to accept a text which had been corrupted and changed, a text which would have shaken the very foundations of the truth of our religion? No, the truth is that neither we nor the Jews ever tampered with the Books. Our mutual hostility is the best guarantee to our statement.'[66]

Timothy contrasted the Muslims with the Jews, in that while the latter rejected Jesus, the former 'forsook idolatry and polytheism and worshipped and honoured one God.'[67] Further, when pressed he claimed that Muhammad was to be honoured as one of the prophets and added:

'Who will not praise, honour and exalt the one who not only fought for God in words, but showed his zeal for Him in the sword.'[68]

The Patriarch had recourse to 'royal plural' usages in the scriptures in defence of his trinitarianism and rejected Mahdi's complaint that these are but literary devices. In turn he claimed that the enigmatic three-letter references at the outsets of Suras 2, 10, 11, 12, 14, 15, 26 and 28, for example, were themselves mystic references to the Trinity, which contention cut little ice with the caliph. Nor did the references to human 'trinitarian' analogies like 'soul, reason and intellect', which Timothy had to admit, have but limited application.

'I made use of such similes solely for the purpose of uplifting my mind from the created things to God. All the things that we have with us compare very imperfectly with the things of God.'[69]

On ground somewhat more congenial to the Caliph, the Patriarch inveighed against the Byzantines as rebellious and tyrannical, and the dialogue concluded with Timothy's reference to the simile of the pearl of great value in a dark room, which pearl each of several occupants of the room believed was his exclusively. Mahdi responded:

'"We have hope in God that we are the possessors of this pearl and that we hold it in our hands." And I replied "Amen, O King." But may God grant us that we too may share it with you, and rejoice in the shining and beaming lustre of the pearl.'[70]

While one may see in Timothy a staunch defender of his faith, the impression is left of one who is out to stress common ground and to promote acceptance. Given the injunctions against conversion of Muslims this may well be understandable. Recognition of the distinctive novelty of Islam as a new religion had to await the 9th century in Persia as much as elsewhere.

In the interim, Christians felt the fury of the mob, of the outrage of the caliphs in the face of defeat, or what they saw as treachery by Christians. So, after the depredations of Mahdi between AD 775 and AD 785, his younger son, the famous Harun-ar-Rashid (d. AD 809), made life difficult for his Christian subjects after what he saw as Byzantine duplicity over border treaties. This action, which included the destruction of all borderland churches and the enforcement of rules re distinctive dress, led some Christians to emigrate, a pattern to be emulated by others who went to Sinope on the Black Sea during the reign of Mamun (d. AD 833). The caliph's brother caused the destruction of Jacobite and Melkite Churches in Edessa in AD 825, only to be rebuked by the caliph for his action. Christians were involved with Jews in a rebellion in AD 855 against the Caliph Mutawakkil (d. AD 861), which revolt was suppressed vigorously. Many were executed, and churches and synagogues were demolished. However, such episodes of persecution were clearly the exception rather than the rule. They were not infrequently precipitated by Christian presumption, or by Muslim resentment about the appointment of a Christian to a position of eminence, like that by the Caliph Mutadid (d. AD 902) of a Nestorian as governor of Anbar, near Baghdad in AD 892. Similarly offensive to Muslims were the actions of Christians, contrary to the strict letter of the law, in building new churches, which they did from the 7th to the 12th centuries. The most celebrated, and offensive, of these was one at Nisibis reputed to have cost 56,000 gold dinars built near the end of the Abbasid period.

In general the provisions of the Covenant of 'Umar prevailed. The overall legal situation was summed up by a Muslim lawyer, Mawardi, thus:

'In the poll-tax contract there are two clauses, one of which is indispensable and the other commendable. The former includes six articles:

1 they must not attack nor pervert the sacred book [i.e. the Koran],
2 nor accuse the Prophet [Muhammad] of falsehood, nor refer to him with contempt,

3 nor speak of the religion of Islam to blame or contravert it,
4 nor approach a Muslim woman with a view either to illicit relations or to marriage,
5 nor turn a Muslim from the faith, nor harm him in person or possessions,
6 nor help the enemies or receive any of their spies.

These are the duties which are strictly obligatory on them, and to which they must conform.

The second clause, which is only commendable, also deals with six points:

1 change of external appearance by wearing a distinctive mark, the *ghiyar*, and the special waistbelt, *zunnar*,
2 prohibition of erecting buildings higher than those of the Muslims; they must only be of equal height or less,
3 prohibition of offending the ears of Muslims by the sound of the bell, *naqus*, by reading their books, and by their claims concerning Uzair [Ezra] and the Messiah,
4 prohibition of drinking wine publicly and of displaying their crosses and swine,
5 the obligation to proceed secretly to the burial of their dead without a display of tears and lamentations,
6 prohibition of riding on horses, whether pure-bred or mixed, though they are allowed to use mules and asses.

These six commendable prescriptions are not necessarily included in the contract of protection, unless they have been expressly stipulated, in which case they are strictly obligatory. The fact of contravening them when they have been stipulated does not entail breach of the contract, but the unbelievers are compelled by force to respect them, and are punished for having violated them. They do not incur punishment when nothing has been stipulated about it.'[71]

It is instructive to look somewhat further at the work of *Timothy I* (d. AD 823). The office of Patriarch was reported to be open to a considerable use of simony, and it appears that Timothy was no exception in the promises he made to those who supported his election. His refusal to make the undertaken payments fuelled other jealousies, especially those of Ephraim of Gondishapur and Yusuf of Merv. Timothy succeeded in imposing his authority on Ephraim, with the support of the caliphate, but Yusuf pleased the latter rather more by becoming a Muslim in AD 791. As Barhebraeus some 500 years later described the situation which had developed in the south:

'. . . the bishops of the province of Fars were wearing white garments like secular priests, eating meat, and marrying, and were not under the jurisdiction of the Catholicos of Seleucia. They used to say: "We have been evangelised by the Apostle Thomas, and we have no share with the See of Mar." Timothy, however, united them and joined them to him. He ordained for them as Metropolitan a man named Shim'un, and he ordered them not to eat meat, or marry, and to wear white garments made only of wool. He further permitted them to confirm the bishops whom he would ordain, without coming for such confirmation to the Catholicos.'[72]

The latter concession was one indeed, for Timothy made a general rule of demanding the observance of tactile ordination from patriarch to metropolitan to bishop to priest, holding that, in theory a patriarch is consecrated by other patriarchs, in absentia. As we have seen he would brook neither disobedience nor revolt. He stressed the role of education, and also sought to reform abuses in the monasteries, from which came the bishops for the Church of the East. On the issue of the primacy of his patriarchate, not only over all provinces of his Church but all others, he was in no doubt at all, as one of his letters shows:

'Just as the fountain, which went forth from Eden to water the garden was afterwards divided into four heads (Gen. 2:10), . . . so, when the Fountain of life has appeared among us Easterns – for from us Christ appeared in the flesh, who is God over all (Rom. 9:5) – it has irrigated the whole garden of the world, when it irrigates the four thrones and seats of the patriarchs. . . .

In the flesh, Christ came of David, but David was descended from Abraham, and Abraham was one of us Easterns, and belonged to the East. . . . Therefore it was from the Easterns that the Fountain of Christian life arose and spread, and going from us, was divided into four heads, which irrigate the whole garden of the Catholic Church with divine drink and the spiritual Kingdom of Heaven.

And just as priority and logical claim are due to the original fountain, . . . so our Eastern throne . . . ought to be reserved the first and highest rank, but the four other . . . a secondary and derivative rank. If Rome is accorded the first and principal rank on account of Peter the Apostle, how much more should Seleucia and Ctesiphon on account of Peter's Lord!'[73]

While Timothy did what he could to conciliate monothelites, cooperating with the Melkite leader on translation projects, he was adamant in his opposition to the Jacobites who had spread as far east as Herat, and to their supporters among the followers of Henana (d. AD 610). Those Monophysite Yemenis who had been exiled from Najran to near Hira were won over to the Church of the East. Under his rule six new provinces were established, at Rai (Tehran), Merv, Samarkand, Kashgar, Tangut and Chang-an, each with at least three bishops under the metropolitan's supervision. The principality of Kashgar had become Christian at about that time, and when Muslim troops pushed along that Silk Road branch in the 12th century they were opposed by Christian soldiers from Khotan. The metropolitan at Tangut had responsibility for work in Tibet, and that at Chang-an for the work in China. Those metropolitans were, of necessity, granted a good measure of autonomy, since it was impossible to take part at the synodal teachings regularly that were hold at the seat of the Patriarch. The same applied to the bishops of the Church in South-West India, to which he sent episcopal reinforcements, viz. Peroz and Sabr-ishu, in AD 823. Prevented by Muslim law from evangelising among the followers of Islam, Timothy stressed the missionary opportunity beyond Muslim jurisdiction. It was also a way of diverting attention from domestic problems which arose from time to time.

While the Church of the East clearly continued to grow under the Muslim rule it did not do so at the same pace as under the Sasanians, as the following table shows:

YEAR – AD	410	650	820	1000	14th cent.
Catholicos Patriarch	1	1	1	1	1
No. of Metropolitans	6	9	19	20	25
No. of Bishops	38	96	85	75	200 (?)
Total	45	106	105	96	226

As W. G. Young comments:

'After admitting that there is a great deal of uncertainty with regard to the figures of bishops (that of 650 may be too high, that of 820 too low), we are left with the impression that, in spite of losses in Arabia and the Persian Gulf, the Church did expand considerably its area of operation, and improve its organisation, and carried out much real missionary work. The expansion is less marked than in the Sassanid period, but geographically it is just as impressive.

We may come to a tentative conclusion, therefore, that under both the Sassanid Shahs and the early Caliphs, the relations between Church and State did not altogether prevent the Church from exercising its missionary vocation, though at times they may well have hindered it. At the same time, we must record the impression that under the Sassanids the progress of the Church was a much more steady and striking growth than it was under the Muslims.'[74]

For all the increasing Islamicisation of the bureaucracy under the Abbasids there was no lessening of Muslim regard for Christian learning.

The Caliph Mamun (d. AD 833) founded an institution of higher learning at Baghdad, known as the 'House of Knowledge', the most famous head of which was the Nestorian Hunain ibn Isḥaq (d. AD 873). He is reputed to have translated some 100 books from Greek and Syriac into Arabic. Along with others engaged in the same task, he played a significant role in transplanting Greek thought into Arabic minds. Even among Christians, Arabic began to displace Syriac from AD 1000, but the reputation of the Nestorians remained high in Muslim eyes. So early in the 11th century, Albiruni of Khiva mentioned 'the Nestorians' as the most civilized of the Christian communities under the caliph.[75] He added that

'there are three sects of Christians, Melkites, Nestorians and Jacobites. "The most numerous of them are the Melkites and Nestorians; because Greece and the adjacent countries are all inhabited by Melkites, whilst the majority of the inhabitants of Syria, Irak and Mesopotamia and Khurasan are Nestorians. The Jacobites mostly live in Egypt and around it." The Nestorian Catholicos "is appointed by the Caliph on the presentation of the Nestorian community."'[76]

Indeed the appointment of the Patriarch-Catholicos had become seen increasingly as a political act from AD 987 and the holders of the office as civil servants as much as spiritual shepherds, to the detriment of the health of the Church of the East. The governmental implications were clear also in the actions in AD 1062–1072 when

'Jacobite and Melkite bishops (were) placed under the Catholicos of the Nestorians, and commanded . . . to obey his edicts.'[77]

Or as a diploma of patriarchal appointment from early in the 13th century put it:

'The Sublime Authority empowers thee to be installed at Baghdad as Catholicos of the Nestorians, as also for the other Christians in Muslim lands, as representative in these lands of the Rum, Jacobites, and Melkites.'[78]

By that time the Seljuk Turks had made their presence felt, rescuing the Caliph Kaim from a Shi'ite governor in AD 1055 and providing some renewal of Persian Arab culture under such scholars as Omar Khayyam (d. AD 1130) and Ghazzali (d. AD 1111), and with the foundations of Nizamiyah universities at Baghdad and Nishapur. While much given to Muslim orthodoxy the Seljuk Turks' energies were diverted more against the Byzantines, whom they defeated soundly at Manzikert in AD 1071, and later against the crusaders. The Christians in Persia do not appear to have suffered particularly from them, perhaps not least because the Seljuks relied on Persian bureaucrats like the famous vizier Nizam al-Mulk to oversee administration. However, as the Seljuk dynasty disintegrated after AD 1156, the Abbasid power lacked a source of unity and strength, and the way was prepared via a system of principalities for the triumph of the Mongols.

The rise of the Mongol power and Christian associations with it are covered elsewhere, and here we need note only that in AD 1251 Jinghis Khan's youngest son, Hulagu (d. AD 1265), was assigned Persia as his realm. He was ordered

> 'to occupy all the territories between the Oxus and the extreme limits of Egypt. He was to chastise all the elements who were expected to oppose him. If the Caliph of Baghdad submitted, Hulagu was not to do him any harm, but if he showed himself too proud or insincere, no exceptional treatment was to be meted out to him.'[79]

He crossed the Oxus River in AD 1256, and on the way to Baghdad he destroyed the stronghold of the Assassins, with the assistance of Christian Georgians. The latter participated also in the capture and sack of Baghdad in AD 1258, the last Caliph, Mutasim, being executed. The capital was moved to Tabriz, which Hulagu left in September AD 1259 to take Aleppo in January AD 1260 and, soon after that, Damascus. Some difficulties in Central Asia led to some Mongol troops being diverted thither and this, together with the strict neutrality of the crusaders, who in no way impeded the passage of Mamluk troops from Egypt, led to the defeat of the Mongols at Ain Jalut in September AD 1260.

On one hand the Mongols turned to Christians for the bureaucracy of their Il-Khanate of Persia, as no Muslim was anxious to serve these shamanistic conquerors who had extinguished the caliphate. Indeed Hulagu's son, Abaqa (d. AD 1282), went so far as to order that all clerks were to be either Jews or Christians. Nestorian hopes rose accordingly and not a few of them revelled in the opportunity to settle old scores, as was recorded by the Muslim historian Maqrizi, when he described Christian behaviour at the fall of Damascus:

> 'They produced a diploma of Hulagu guaranteeing them express protection and the free exercise of their religion. They drank wine freely in the month of Ramadan, and spilt it in the open streets, on the clothes of the Mussalmans and the doors of the mosques. When they traversed the streets, bearing the cross, they compelled the merchants to rise, and ill-treated those who refused. They carried the cross in the streets, and went to the Church of St. Mary, where they preached sermons in praise of their faith, and said openly: "The true faith, the faith of the Messiah, is today triumphant." When the Mussalmans complained they were treated with indignity by the

governor appointed by Hulagu and several of them were by his orders bastinadoed. He visited the Christian churches, and paid deference to their clergy. The governor here meant was no doubt Kitübuka, who was a Kerait and a Christian.'[80]

Nor were 'apostate' Christians safe from reprisal for the Patriarch Denha I (d. AD 1281) had a number of them drowned in the Tigris in AD 1268, amid general uproar and riot. As a consequence the patriarch was forced to leave Baghdad.

Meanwhile Abaqa, whose wife was an illegitimate daughter of the Byzantine emperor, pursued the possibility of an alliance with western European rulers against the Muslims. Embassies were despatched westwards in AD 1267, 1269, 1274, and 1276, to no avail and Abaqa's forces, along with their Georgian allies, suffered two more defeats at the hands of the Mamluks in AD 1277 and 1280. By AD 1284 Arghun (d. AD 1291) had succeeded as Il-Khan. However, Christians at Takrit learned, from Hulagu's punitive reaction that they did not have carte blanche to plunder their Muslim neighbours. Ever ready, when it suited, to cite his Christian mother, Arghun reinstated the old heathenism of the Mongols while still pursuing the possibility of an alliance with such kings as Philip IV of France and Edward I of England. In fact the only Christian allies with military experience on whom the Mongols could rely were the Georgians and Armenians and their numbers were too few for long-term planning. In the year of Arghun's death, the last crusader stronghold of Acre fell and with it hopes of a useful alliance in Palestine and Syria.

Arghun had persisted with his endeavours to secure an alliance sending a letter to Pope Honorius IV (d. AD 1287) in AD 1285. Then in AD 1287 he despatched as an envoy a Christian bishop, Rabban Sauma (d. AD 1294), a close friend and associate of the Patriarch Yaballaha III (d. AD 1317), an Onghut from the Ordos area. The two Eastern Turks had been frustrated in their attempts to reach Jerusalem, from their homeland, and then after their consecration as bishops for China in AD 1278 were equally frustrated in reaching the area of their new responsibilities. The death of the Patriarch Denha in AD 1281 had led to the election to the office of Yaballaha, which election was confirmed by the Great Khan. It was reported that he was elected

'not because of his learning or piety, but because he knew the manners and customs of the Mongol kings, who were at that time governors of the world' and 'in spite of his protest that he did not know the Syriac language.'[81]

Of course there was something political about this election. For it was the aim of the clerics to establish a good relationship with the Mongol Il-Khan of Persia, which they managed to do by that election. Indicative of the success is the fact that Yaballaha III received a seal from Il-Khan Abaqa (AD 1265–1282) at his consecration. The seal had been in the possession of former patriarchs, and it had originally been given to the then officiating patriarch by the Mongol ruler Mangu.[82] The seal (see pl. 8), affixed to a letter to Pope Boniface VII in AD 1302 and to one to Pope Benedict XI in AD 1304, contains an instructive Turkish inscription which reads:

'[This is] our, Mangu Khan's, command, by the power of the eternal Heaven. In order that vigils might be held for us and in order that praises (to God) be sung, so that benefit arises (therefrom) for our descendants from generation to generation, we have given (this) cross-shaped seal to His Grace, the Patriarch. May he be the sole keeper of this seal. May . . . the bishops, the priests and (other) notables not come (here) at their own initiative and without a letter sealed with this seal . . .'[83]

It is obvious that the special connection between the Mongol Khan and the patriarch, obtaining at Mangu's time, was to be renewed by Abaqa in view of the newly elected patriarch from China.

Barely surviving a plot to assassinate him, on the orders of the Il-Khan Ahmad, Yaballaha enjoyed good relations with his successor Arghun, and the next ruler Kaikato (d. AD 1295), the latter according the patriarch near to royal status. Some disorder and another narrow escape for Yaballaha amidst Muslim reactions to the favouring of Christians followed until Gazan succeeded as Il-Khan until AD 1304. By that time the patriarch had followed up the contacts made with the papacy by his friend Rabban Sauma and then proffered a statement of his faith to Benedict XI in 1304, the year of that pope's death. This statement[84] seems to indicate a desire to be accepted within the Roman Church, but as Budge commented

'we have no right to assume that his views represented those of the Nestorian Church in India, Mesopotamia, Armenia or Syria.'[85]

Indeed to judge from the experience of Rabban Sauma at Rome differences of belief remained and not only concerning the procession of the Holy Spirit, between that Church and the Church of the East.[86] As the ambassador put it:

'I have come from remote countries neither to discuss, nor to instruct [men] in matter of the Faith, but I came that I might receive a blessing from Mar Papa, and from the shrines of the saints and to make known the words of King [Arghun] and the Catholicus. If it be pleasing in your eyes, let us set aside discussion, and do ye give attention and direct someone to show us the churches here and the shrines of the saints.'[87]

Such approaches to the West produced no useful military alliance and the defeats suffered by the Mongols convinced them that Islam was a more successful religion with which to be associated than was Christianity. So whatever may have been indicated by Il-Khans and believed in Europe, after Arghun the Il-Khanate moved towards Islam, becoming explicitly Muslim under Ghazan and Uljaito (d. AD 1316), and de facto so previously. Uljaito treated the patriarch with no special favour, but with respect.

However, Arabs and Kurds alike did not hesitate to exact vengeance for the presumptuous actions of Christians. A massacre of Christians and enslavement of those who escaped death occurred at Arbela in AD 1310, and even the patriarch was forced to flee for a time. Marageh itself came under attack by anti-Christian Muslims and the Il-Khan was disinclined to intervene. The patriarch was not reconciled to him in any way until AD 1312. The disillusionment was mutual. Christians in Amida suffered massacre in AD 1317 and despair mounted. As for the Christians themselves, somewhat like Eusebius' assessment of the causes of the last great persecution under Diocletian,[88] they put it down to divine punishment of their envy, neglect and cliques.

Throughout the century which preceded the wholesale destruction wrought by Timur Leng (d. AD 1405) the Nestorian cause was in decline. Such centres as Susa and Socotra disappeared from the records by AD 1282, and even Gondishapur ceased to figure after AD 1318. In short, decline continued during the reign of Abu Said (d. AD 1335) and in the period of disorder which followed his death. As Budge summarised the situation:

'Before the end of the 14th century Nestorianism had practically ceased to be in Persia, Central Asia and China; but patriarchs of the East were still consecrated at Seleucia-Ctesiphon, and there were many Nestorians in Baghdad and in the districts near Baghdad.'[89]

These groups along with so much else, including monasteries, were destroyed by Timur from AD 1394. So horrific was the path of destruction wrought by Timur that his name is ranked with the Assyrians of old and with the 'Holocaust' of this century for terror and horror. Those Muslims who opposed him suffered as severely as did Christians of all persuasions. The result was that only scattered remnants of the Church of the East remained in the mountain refuges to continue, albeit fitfully, a tradition which had achieved so much, and presumed overmuch.

Two other aspects of this Mongol period require attention also. While the advances to the West in the 13th–14th century achieved nothing in the way of military alliances, they did open up channels of contact. Out of this Catholic missionary work via the Dominicans and Franciscans began in North Persia, Armenia and Georgia. Within Persia itself by AD 1300 there were three main centres at Tabriz, Marageh and Dehikerkan, to which were to be added Sivas and Sultanieh. The last was created as a metropolitan's seat in May 1318, with Francis of Perugia as the first incumbent, and William Adam the second in AD 1323. But by AD 1328 Barthelemy of Bologna was the only Catholic bishop left in Persia, with his see at Marageh. Hopes for progress rose for a while and the visiting Dominican Jordanus Catalani reported that in AD 1330, at Tabriz

> 'we have a fine-enough church and about a thousand of the schismatics converted to our faith, and about as many also in Ur of the Chaldees. . . . Likewise also at Sultanieh we have 500 or 550 . . . and we have a very fine church there.'[90]

However, soon after that Barthelemy departed, leaving but a few isolated friars in Persia, who were overtaken by the plague in AD 1348, and the disorders which preceded Timur. Along the way the Il-Khan, Abu Said, had made a treaty with Egypt in AD 1323, which left Lesser Armenia exposed to the Mamluks, despite the request of the pope for Mongol aid for that kingdom.

While our attention has been focussed on the Church of the East, we must note that the Jacobites also expected much of the Mongols, after the conquest of Hulagu, and down to the reign of Ghazan. Their hopes were as much disappointed as were those of the Nestorians. However, the period saw the work of one of the most notable Jacobite leaders and authors, *Grigor Abu l-Faraj*, better known as *Barhebraeus* (d. AD 1286). He had been born at Melitene in AD 1226, and by AD 1243 was studying at Antioch, where he became a monk. At Tripolis he had a 'Nestorian teacher', and there and in Antioch he studied medicine, rhetoric and philosophy. Consecrated as a bishop, he eventually became Mafrian of the Jacobites in AD 1264.

He wrote widely, and most usefully in his *Universal History*, which remains a prime source for the history of Christianity in Persia down to the 13th century. To this he added works on medicine, a Syriac grammar, commentaries on books of the Bible and a collection of Jacobite canons. Not as much given to anti-Nestorianism as one might have expected, he was respected by all, being buried at Mar Mattai in AD 1286.

The last significant literary figure among the Nestorians was Abdiso bar Berikka (d. AD 1310). In a number of ways he paralleled the contributions of Barhebraeus. But this was a final flowering of Christian scholarship before the decline of the 14th century.

EMPHASES, CONCERNS AND DOMESTIC ORGANISATION OF 'THE CHURCH OF THE EAST'

Given their minority status throughout history, Christians in Persia found in their religion their primary symbol of identity, over against Zoroastrians,

Jews, Manichaeans and Muslims. Their distinctiveness was abetted by their reliance for the first five centuries at least on the Syriac language, which reliance lessened in later centuries in favour of first Persian and then Arabic. Like the Jews, the Christians referred to themselves as a 'People' or a 'Nation', adding the distinction that they were 'the new Bride', in face of 'the old Bride's' (i.e. Israel's) rejection of the Bridegroom.

Aphrahat had used the 'People of God' imagery in the fourth century, and it is used explicitly by the Synod of AD 410 where it was

> 'laid down that anyone who disregards its canons is to be anathematised by the "People of God".'[91]

Parallel expressions such as 'People and Church of God', 'People of the Christians', 'People of the believers' and 'People of Christendom' are also encountered.

> 'The world is divided, not between Phomaye and Persaye, but between the "People of God" and those outside, barraye (or less frequently, "pagans"-hanpe).'[92]

As to the 'Bride' image this was applied to individuals as well as to the community, in a way entirely consistent with early Syrian Christianity. It also found its way into synodical writings in that at the Synod of AD 554

> 'the transfer of bishops from one see to another is forbidden on the grounds that this is a form of adultery; each bishop's see being "a pure spiritual wife who has been given to him".'[93]

While the Syrian ascetic influence remained strong in this way, and is mirrored for example in Thomas of Marga's 9th century *Book of Governors*, related to the monastic life, other forces were at work. Not the least of these was the approach of that Zoroastrianism which set the majority religious context for early Christians in Persia. The Zoroastrians set themselves against Christian asceticism as much as against Manichaean fanaticism. They did so, in principle seeing 'asceticism as . . . a blasphemy against life.'[94]

This was not because Zoroastrianism was in anyway wedded to hedonism. But it saw no reason why the good life should not also be a pleasurable one. So

> 'material pleasure, if divorced from spiritual stirring, is merely an excess; it is a departure from the mean and therefore of the Devil. But to suppress the pleasure principle or even to curb it unduly is to fall into the other extreme, one of deficiency, and thus is the folly and the blasphemy of the Manichees and Christians.'[95]

It would appear that Christians in the old Persian area of Fars responded positively to this emphasis, and developed a specifically Iranian

Christianity which was clearly anti that excessive asceticism which had its roots in Jewish Christianity. One of the evidences of this was the way in which Persian Christians acted to permit the marriage, not only of priests but also of bishops – the latter distinguishing them from Christians elsewhere. Clergy were allowed to remarry as well, and this further distinguished them from those within the Roman Empire. Episcopal celibacy was not to be reimposed until after the 12th century.

Whatever such differences re the attitude to clerical celibacy the Church of the East had, in addition to its Nestorian Christology after AD 497, a number of other differences from Christians elsewhere, especially Latin Christians. It did not accept as sacraments, marriage, unction or confirmation, and had no belief in Purgatory. It maintained reception of both the elements in the Eucharist and the belief that, in some way through the leaven, each Eucharist was linked to the Last Supper.

Even before the AD 725 iconoclastic measures of Leo the Isaurian, Yazdgard II had, in AD 448, persecuted Christians in Persia for the use of images. The latter continued to offend Muslims, and as late as the 13th century, Christian apologists were still appealing to the distinction between adoration and veneration. One such apologia from Ishu-Yab, Bishop of Nisibis (d. AD 1258), shows

'that the Nestorians not only had crosses and images of Christ, but also images and pictures of the saints. These images of the saints were kissed by the people, and incense was offered before them, and before relics of the saints.'

And

'we can trace the use of ikons in the Nestorian Church well on into the Mongol period. In modern times the Nestorians alone of all the Eastern Churches have abandoned the use of images, only using the cross to which they pay the greatest reverence. The use of the plain cross without the figure of Christ on it goes back at least as far as the middle of the thirteenth century, for William of Rubruck, in his journey across Asia from Southern Russia as far as the town of Karakorum, mentions several times that the Armenians and Nestorians whom he met used the cross but not the crucifix. In response to Rubruck's questions they could only reply that it was their custom.'[96]

Lest it be thought that the Church of the East was overly maverick, compared to other Christians, as we have seen, one of their 9th century writers, Eliyya Jauhari, offered some corrective, thus:

'They agree in observing the Sundays and Christian festivals. With regard to the offering of the Eucharist they are at one in saying that it is the Body and Blood of Christ. They uphold the confession of faith put forward by the 318 Fathers who were gathered together at Nicaea, which is repeated by all at every liturgy.'[97]

For all their distinctive emphases the Persian Christians had to come to terms with the environment within which they found themselves. We have noted already how Nestorians and Monophysites both had positions of influence at times, near to the thrones of shahs and caliphs. Both groups had a status of legality which they were denied in Byzantine lands and the Monophysites in particular, while maintaining their religious loyalty, were open to

'social integration within the greater order of all citizens, irrespective of religious difference.'[98]

Those Nestorians, who as accountants, doctors, philosophers and astrologers had positions of influence,

'formed a kind of guild or corporate society, the "learned men" who had the Caliph's ear.'[99]

While such 'learned men' acted as intermediaries by which Greek learning was passed on to Arabs, they also took up and used Persian dating systems and seasonal names in their civil, and even in some of their religious writings. So there was a degree of cultural interchange in which the Nestorians participated as both givers and receivers.

As to the organisation of the Church of the East, it is clear that there were developments in centralising authority after Ishu-Yab III (d. AD 660) had set up an

'organised hierarchy in the distant eastern provinces of the Church, and [gave] it at the same time a reasonable and practical measure of self-government.'[100]

The tendency was, however, to build up the authority of the patriarch. As early as AD 410, and confirmed in AD 424, the Bishop of Seleucia-Ctesiphon had the right to convoke synods and to compel universal or selective attendance. The presence of the Catholicos-Patriarch was needed to legitimate the actions of synods. He had the authority to establish new provinces, to combine sees, to name and appoint and consecrate bishops and metropolitans and to oversee monasteries and doctrine. He could also suspend erring clerics, and his confirmation was needed of suspension of such a cleric by a metropolitan. As Ishu-Yab III wrote:

'Just as the Christians living among you cannot be Christians without priests, and your priests cannot be priests without bishops, so your bishops cannot be bishops without metropolitans, and so again metropolitans cannot be metropolitans without the Patriarch. . . .

To be disobedient to the Patriarch was to abjure the Christian religion, to deny the faith, to revolt against God. To take a quarrel to a secular tribunal was to cut yourself off completely from the hope of Church life.'[101]

Or, as W. F. Macomber put it, almost the only papal prerogatives missing

'are the canonization of saints and the granting of marriage dispensations and indulgences, which seem to have been simply unknown in the ancient Chaldean Church.'[102]

Patriarchal control was increased by the device of having bishops visit the patriarch in order to be confirmed in office. However, this measure led to problems in distant dioceses, like those in China. In that case suitable appointees were consecrated and sent from Baghdad, whither they returned should they discover that they were surplus to local needs when they reached their designated see. Such dependency on the patriarch meant that vacancies in the office could and did lead to disruption of administration. (Vacancies did occur, but most were due more to disputes among Christians rather than to the actions of their rulers.)

For all their authority, wise patriarchs continued to act with and through synods. The autocratic example of Jausep (d. AD 567), and the strong reaction to him warned his successors against over-much unilateral action. Nisibis and Fars always were centres of potential protest, and there is some evidence of the right of appeal from the bishops against the Patriarch to the shah or caliph. The very authority of the patriarchate made it desirable to many who had a craving for power. Just as the Christian *millet* had a constant concern for its rights and privileges, and many a Nestorian was to be found among the wealthy merchant class, there were always those who coveted the patriarchal office, and were ready to take steps to secure it – including simony. L. E. Browne has much to support him when he says:

'Many of the troubles of the Christians were caused by their own leaders, who sought power by any means, giving and receiving bribes. Most of the appointments of patriarchs were the occasion for violent quarrels between the supporters of the rival candidates. For instance, the election of Timothy (Catholicus, AD 780–819) was largely influenced by his offering money to certain people, and pointing to some sacks full of stones as if they were full of money. When, after the consecration, they asked for the money, he showed them what the sacks contained, and said: "The priesthood is not sold for money."'[103]

The Church of the East, given the situation in which it found itself under both Sasanians and Muslims was given to stressing the forbearance of

Christ. It had little real alternative. In addition it sought evidence of divine favour in its worldly success. When the latter was apparent all was well with the world. When it fell away so did faith and confidence in God for most. Their use of worldly power and intrigue was a

'condemnation of their Christianity, and probably more than anything else the cause of its downfall.'[104]

MONKS AND MISSIONARIES

Monasticism played a key role in the Church of the East as it did in that of Syria. The major monastic pioneer in Persia was seen to be Mar Awgin (d. AD 370) who brought from Egypt the ideas of Pachomian coenobitic monasticism. With some 70 brothers he settled at Mt Izala, within the triangle formed by Edessa, Amida and Nisibis. There the monastic community grew to number 350 and to accrue a reputation for good works, and the healing skills and miracles of its leader. The latter's gifts placed Shapur II in his debt and gained for him royal approval to establish further monasteries and convents.

The reputation for asceticism acquired by such monks, made them prime candidates for episcopal office and eventually for appointments as Catholicoi and Patriarchs. Indeed the Catholicos Mar Ahai (d. AD 415) had been a leading monk and is said to have continued his monastic life style while he was head of the Church. His successor Yaballaha I (d. AD 420) was also drawn from monastic circles, and this set a pattern often to be followed.

Monasteries were of such clear importance that some of the canons of the first major synod of AD 410 were directed at their oversight and control. In particular a chorepiskopos (or auxiliary bishop) was appointed in each diocese to supervise the monasteries and the ascetics, and bind them more securely into the regular life of the Church. Some such oversight was needed for the monks displayed an aggressive spirit directed against the centres of Zoroastrian worship. The consequence was that members of the nobility and the Magians complained to Yazdgard II (d. AD 457)

'that the clergy and the monks do not only mock the godheads but also use violence, destroying the fire temples.'[105]

In due course that spirit of aggression was to be channelled into more constructive evangelistic efforts, but before we survey these, we need to learn something more of the type of monasticism nurtured within the Church of the East. Given to asceticism no less than were those in Jacobite monasteries the Nestorians used the example of the essentially human Jesus of Nazareth as a model to inspire them in desert solitariness or sustained fasting. Above all it was a sense of companionship with Jesus which strengthened them in their endeavours.

As to their lifestyle etc.:

'The monks wore tunic, belt, cloak, hood, and sandals, and carried a cross and stick. Their tonsure was distinctive, being cruciform. At first they met for common prayer seven times a day, but later this was reduced to four times. They were vegetarians, and ate only once a day, at noon. Celibacy, of course was rigidly enforced. Those who were more capable engaged in study and the copying of books, while others worked on the land. After three years a monk could, if the abbot agreed, retire to absolute solitude as a hermit. The connexion between the monasteries and the bishops was closer than was usual in the West, the control of monastic property being in the hands of the nearest bishop. This no doubt both strengthened and enriched the hierarchy.'[106]

The situation in which Christians found themselves in Persia was one, both under non-Muslims and Muslims, in which the conversion of those who held to the 'state religion' was forbidden. The penalty applied to one who left Zoroastrianism for Christianity was loss of property and social ostracism, not to mention the possibility of the death of all involved. As a consequence not a few converts to Christianity sought refuge and community support in monasteries, thus swelling the numbers of their inhabitants. Similar difficulties confronted any converts from Islam. As a consequence of this, and with western areas denied them until after Muslim triumphs, the Church of the East had its evangelistic eyes turned to the east, the north-east and the south – to areas outside direct Persian rule. When the Arabs triumphed by AD 652 the Zoroastrian inhabitants were open to evangelisation by Christians, but then they were in competition with the Muslims for the religious loyalties of the adherents of the old religion.

With Seleucia-Ctesiphon at the crossing point of a number of caravan routes, and with many Nestorians involved in the trade along such routes, the Church of the East was well placed to take its faith into Central Asia and China, and to India and South East Asia. Indeed it is

'no exaggeration . . . that in the early Middle Ages the Nestorian Church was the most widespread in the whole world.'[107]

Providing support and consequent leadership for congregations of converts were monks whose energies were diverted to such activities, quite deliberately, by patriarchs such as Timothy I (d. AD 823). Well before that there were Christians across the Oxus River by AD 650, where their chief rivals were Manichaeans until the 9th century, when Muslim impact was experienced. Indeed Turkish Christians had a metropolitan consecrated by

Timothy in AD 781. Wherever the Nestorian monks went they took with them also their medical skills and commitment to education. So each Nestorian bishopric had associated with it a school, a library and hospital services, all of which made great impact.

It was from the monasteries that the needed committed and trained manpower was obtained. One prime source was Bet Abe, the monastic home of Thomas of Marga from whom we learn that not only four or five patriarchs were drawn from it, but between AD 595 and 850

> 'at least 100 of its sons became bishops, metropolitans and governors of Nestorian dioceses in Mesopotamia, Arabia, Persia, Armenia, Kurdistan and China.'[108]

Mention of Arabia reminds us of Nestorian efforts among the Himyarites, probably mounted from Hira. Attention is given below to Central Asia and China elsewhere, as to India. However, we should note that as far as India was concerned Nestorian relationships date back at least to the 5th century and in AD 650 the Patriarch Ishu-Yab III declared it to be a separate province. The route from Persia to India was dotted with Nestorian monasteries which provided lines of communication and facilitated contact and support to congregations as far away as Ceylon (or Sri Lanka).

Somewhat less expected, and therefore surprising, was Nestorian missionary efforts in Syria, Palestine, Cyprus, Egypt and Asia Minor. Made possible by Muslim conquests of former Byzantine territories, and the consequent abrogation of anti-Nestorian laws there,

> 'in Egypt there were Nestorian congregations in the very home of Monophysitism. Under the Patriarch Mar Aba II (d. AD 752) the Nestorians of Egypt had a bishop under the (Nestorian) Metropolitan of Damascus.'[109]

Jerusalem had been designated as the seat of a Nestorian bishop in AD 835 and was raised to metropolitan status in AD 1065. However, the advent of the Crusades led to radical changes and

> 'by the end of the 12th century only the bishopric of Tarsus remained, which lasted until the middle of the 15th century.'[110]

That missionary commitment remained even after the wholesale depredations of Timur Leng towards the end of the 14th century is clear from the report that

> 'Simeon, the Nestorian Patriarch, sent a Metropolitan into southern China in 1490, that about this time India and China were united into one metropolitan see, that in 1502 the Patriarch Elias sent four bishops, Thomas, Jaballaha, Denba and James into India and China, and that James was living in 1510.'[111]

These latter bishops were still drawn from the ranks of the monks, as depleted in numbers as they were by that time.

RETROSPECT

Given the Asia-wide achievements of the Christians of Persia it appears doubly tragic that after Timur Leng's spoilments around the turn of the 14th and 15th centuries, the Church of the East was reduced to refugees in the mountainous areas between Lake Van and Lake Urmiah. Of course it is clear that decline had been in evidence throughout the 14th century so that Timur's blows were more in the nature of a coup de grace than of destruction of a church in its prime.

It is clear that in the declining days of the Mongol Il-Khanate

> 'numerous churches were closed, episcopal sees fell vacant and new bishops were not appointed. Christians in Persia became a small and insignificant minority of little importance in the political and diplomatic life of the country.'[112]

This is not to say that many Nestorians did not convert to the Sunni Islam of Timur out of understandable fear of one who seemed to delight in the destruction not only of non-Muslims but also of Shi'ite Muslims.

When we seek reasons for such decline it does not seem that persecution suddenly became so fierce that the Nestorian spirit of resistance, nurtured since the 3rd century, suddenly evaporated. They had been accused of too ready compromise with Buddhism in areas outside of Persia, but the evidence of this seems flimsy, and snacks more of finding relevant ways in which to explain and proclaim the faith. This endeavour was engaged in far too little by later Western missionaries, or where it was, by people like Matteo Ricci in China or Robert de Nobili in India, ran into entrenched condemnation. It is as tempting to argue, from certain discernible parallels, such as those on p. 320, n. 7 and ibidem, n. 12, that Nestorianism had an influence on the development of Pure Land Buddhism. This remains, for the present, only in the realm of speculation, but see also n. 3 on p. 361 below.

It does appear that Nestorians were lulled into presumption and over dependence on the 'secular' power – which tendencies left them prey to violent reactions from Muslims and others from time to time. Such attitudes may also have fostered a fatal degree of negligence in matters spiritual in the period when hopes were high of Mongol adherence to Christianity. It may also be the case that an over-centralised administration and insufficient attendance to the training of clergy in areas remote from Baghdad, made the Church of the East unable to respond adequately to changing circumstances.

And perhaps Waterfield is right in his assessment that:

'Ultimately the failure of the Church was due to internal weaknesses. It had not grown intellectually; indeed, Professor Burkitt described it as "intellectually timid". It also relied heavily on monasticism and presented asceticism and retreat from the world as the normal Christian way of life. It also failed in other ways to appeal to the mass of the people; its theology was too complicated and, as far as we know, it insisted on using Syriac for its language of worship. In addition to all this, the simplicity of Islam and its identification in the national mind with being a Persian, all contributed to the failure of Christianity at this time.'[113]

Be that as it may, and even when we allow for the mid-16th century division of the remnant Church of the East between the Uniate 'Chaldeans' and those who clung to the old autonomy, there is no gainsaying its achievements. Those of us in the Western tradition are well to be reminded that in the year when St. Aidan was setting out to evangelise pagan Northumbria the Nestorian Al-o-pen was arriving in Chang-an and founding a Christian community in China. No amount of subsequent decline can eliminate the record of tremendous far-flung achievement over a decade of centuries.

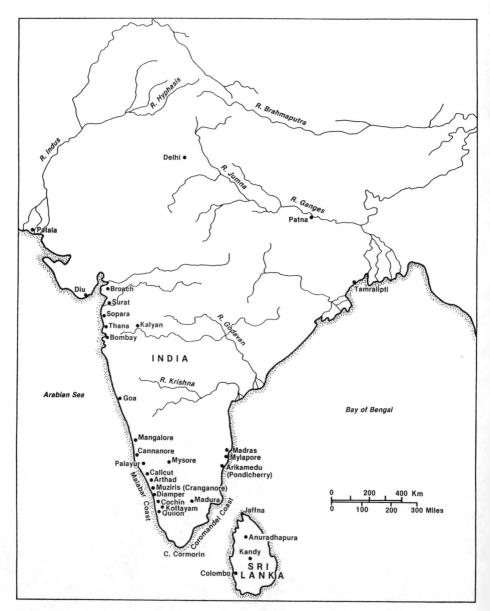

Map 5 India and Sri Lanka

Chapter 8

Christians in India

EARLY LINKS BETWEEN INDIA AND 'THE WEST'

There would be few among those whose cultural roots are in Western Europe who would be aware that links between India and 'the West' antedate the Christian era. Those acquainted with the Asian expedition of Alexander the Great, between 336 and 323 BC, realise that it took him as far as the Hyphasis River in North-West India, where a mutiny among his soldiers put a stop to the push to the east. However, there seems little interest in what happened to those of Alexander's army who, for one reason or another, elected to remain and establish kingdoms in Afghanistan and North-West India. Nor has there been much interest in those who followed the Indus River to its mouth and settled there.

Those Greeks who settled at this river mouth controlled the coast east and west of the outlet for decades. Numbers of their compatriots were busy inland, e.g. with the Indo-Bactrian kingdom which persisted in Afghanistan until it was destroyed by Central Asian nomads ca. 130 BC. A high-point had been reached in such inland endeavours in 150 BC with the king named Menander, who, as Milinda, figures in Buddhist literature as a prominent convert to that faith. For all their achievements, and the continuation of some small kingdoms down to ca. 30 BC, the Indo-Greeks failed to dominate the Indian Maurya kingdom which was established in North India in 186 BC.

However, contact was retained by overland and sea routes between India and the Seleucid kings who had made Antioch in Syria their capital in 300 BC. Not only was it maintained with the Indo-Greeks, who technically at first came under the Seleucid suzerainty, but also with Indian rulers. So Seleucus Nicator (d. 280 BC) sent Megasthenes as ambassador to King Candragupta, at his court in Patna. While by 232 BC Ashoka had extended the Mauryan realm, across North and Central India and as far south as Arikamedu, contact was kept with Syria. This was evidenced at a triumph in Daphne in 166 BC by Seleucus Antiochus IV, who displayed trophies and objects in plenty from India. Indeed such contact was maintained until the collapse of the Seleucid dynasty in 65 BC.

Throughout this period 'European' knowledge of 'India' depended largely on the four volume work of Megasthenes, which indeed was the basis of almost all that was known about India until the 16th century AD. Lacking detailed knowledge of the south of the country Megasthenes believed that Ceylon lay some 20 days sailing south of the Indus mouth, and that the southern tip of India was Cape Cori. His work was taken up and included with information on the Red Sea and Persian Gulf by Eratosthenes (d. 194 BC), the chief librarian at Alexandria.

Even before the time of Alexander the Great, Indian vessels had been coasting from the Indus to the Persian Gulf and to Arabia. In the latter the inhabitants acted as the middle-men on trade between India and the Occident. The 'Greek' settlers on the Indus gathered information about the south of India and by 170 BC were aware of pearl fishing south of Bombay and of the considerable Chola kingdom in the south. Between their voyages to the south and as far to the south east as Thailand, the Straits of Malacca and Vietnam (by one Alexandros in ca. 100 BC) they had come to know that Ceylon was not part of India and much about the extent and surrounds of the Arabian Sea and the Bay of Bengal. In conjunction with the explorations and colonies of their 'cousins' the Ptolemies of Egypt, they knew of the island of Socotra, the horn of Africa, and of the east coast of that continent.

Most significant was the discovery between 120 & 110 BC by a captain named Eudoxos, probably with the aid of an Indian pilot, of the reliable monsoon winds which enabled ships to by-pass the avaricious middle-men of southern Arabia. It was soon established that it was practicable, e.g. to leave Egypt in July and reach India by the end of September. Cargoes could be sold and bought in India, which would be left at the end of November, so as to be back in Egypt by February. The two main ports in India were Barygaza in the north, and Muziris in the south, while on the Red Sea end they were Myros Hormos and Arsinoe, Socotra being the staging port. By the birth of Jesus some 120 ships per annum plied this route, and the way was clear for Roman participation, which certainly interested Augustus. Indeed this Red Sea and Arabian Sea route was the only practicable one given the attitudes which prevailed in Persia at the time.

Nor was interest one-sided, in that Indian embassies were despatched to Augustus in 26 BC, to Claudius in AD 73, and to Trajan in AD 107. Trajan actually saw ships leave the mouth of the Euphrates for India, and hoped to continue control of the route through the Persian Gulf. Retaining an interest in Mediterranean developments, such embassies continued in the reigns of Antoninus Pius (d. AD 161), Elagabalus (d. AD 222), Aurelian (d. AD 275) and Constantine (d. AD 337). The last on record is one of AD 530 to Constantinople.

With this continuing interest and contact[1] what was the situation in South India, at the outset of the Christian era? It

'was divided into three principal kingdoms: the Chera, the Pandyan and the Chola. The Chera kingdom corresponded to present Kerala excluding the extreme south, the Chola territory lay on the east coast from the mouth of the Krishna to the present Rammad district, and between the two was the powerful Pandyan kingdom with its capital at Madura.'[2]

The most relevant area for our concerns was that of the Chera kingdom, the ruler of which was known as the Perumal, or 'Great One'. With his powers limited by assemblies of Nambudiri and Nayar nobles, the Perumal was nevertheless liberal in religious matters, as far as the explicit objects of worship were concerned. Far more of a force to be reckoned with were the Nambudiris, who dictated policy on religious and social matters. In particular they policed the observance of caste differences to the point where 'Malabar. . . was the most caste-ridden country in India.'[3] As long as no caste rules were violated, there was considerable freedom of practice available to Buddhists, Jains, Jews and Christians. But the importance attached to caste in this region was bound to have its influence on Christians once they had established themselves there.

Trade between 'Rome' and 'India' boomed from the early years of Claudius, i.e. from ca. AD 45, up until the time of Hadrian (d. AD 138). This is shown by such evidence as hoards of Roman coins, particularly from the reign of Nero (d. AD 68), found in the south of India, and the 1945 discovery of evidence of a Roman settlement at Arikamedu which was dated to the days of Nero.[4] As this latter settlement was on the east coast it was clear that the Romans had found the Palghat Gap through the mountains, about 190 kilometres north of Cape Cormorin, and were exploiting it for the transport of goods overland. Certainly the three major routes, to the mouth of the Indus, to Barygaza and to Muziris were all known to Pliny (d. AD 79).

Roman maritime police protected the 200 ships per annum involved in the passage of the Red Sea, but unsettled conditions in the 3rd century and the concurrent debasement of Roman coinage conspired to choke the trade from Egypt to India. Emperors visiting Alexandria came under pressure to resume the trade, but could offer no effective guarantees of that protection without which none would sail. This was increasingly the case in the light of militant Jewish influence in southern Arabia which had its own interests to serve and was to be locked into conflict with Ethiopia. This reached the stage where fighting in the Yemen at the end of the 3rd century put an end to the trade with South India. The situation was in no way eased by the actions of the Sasanian dynasty after AD 224, which built up a navy to further disrupt Roman endeavours. Even the reforming of

Roman coinage under Diocletian and Constantine could not restore trade to anything like its old levels,[5] and the last western Roman coins found in India are from AD 395.[6]

As for the trade at its height, full use was made of the discoveries made and the routes pioneered by Indians and Greeks. From the south of India the Romans sought pearls and spices, not least pepper among the latter, while from the north they drew cotton goods. In addition from India came silk, and ivory, while to it the Roman traders brought tin, lead, gold and silver coins, wine, coral, beryl and glass, all of which were under demand – i.e. as long as debasement was not to be found among the coins. A further commodity under demand was the Roman soldier, prepared to act as mercenary bodyguards of Indian rulers. Such trade was extended via coastal shipping and via Cape Cormorin to Ceylon, and there is even evidence of a Caesar-cult in South-West India.[7]

Further ventures resulted from Roman-Parthian problems in the middle of the 2nd century AD. Overland trade with China was disrupted as a result. This caused one trader at the urging of interested parties in both Antioch and Alexandria,[8] to follow the route established by Alexandros, and in AD 166 to push through the Straits of Malacca to make contact with China via Annam. This achievement is attested in Chinese chronicles as dating from the reign of Marcus Aurelius (AD 161–180).[9] Remains of such a Graeco-Roman settlement have been unearthed in the Mekong Delta to give further support to the reputed venture.[10] Such contacts could not be maintained, however, in view of upheavals within the Roman Empire and pressure from Parthia, but they foreshadowed developments in the 16th and subsequent centuries.

Throughout all of this the use of the term 'India' varied considerably. As much associated with the River Indus as was Egypt with the Nile the term has been argued by some to have been applied to South Arabia, Ethiopia, India as we understand it now, and South-East Asia. Along with some others Dihle believes that the confusion between South Arabia and the Indian peninsula has been overdone, and that, e.g.

> 'Pantaenus, the teacher of Clement (of Alexandria), actually did go to South India and there met with the Bartholomew Christians in the middle of the 2nd century.'[11]

By the 4th or 5th century AD, a history of the Apostle Bartholomew, the *Passio Bartholomaei*, described India in a threefold way – one bordering Ethiopia, one bordering Media and 'the third lies at the end of the world.'[12] The second of these would refer to the Kushan kingdom in North-West India, and the first to that 'India' directly accessible across the Arabian Sea from Ethiopia. The 'end of the world' reference applies to the area across the Bay of Bengal, i.e. to Burma and South-East Asia, which areas are described by Claudius Ptolemaeus in his second century AD

Geographia. In summary, while for many the term 'India' would have immediate connotations with the Indus-Ganges region, it would also include South India and thus the peninsula as a whole.

It remains for us here to give some attention to the practicability of specific Christian contacts with India. There are claims of Jewish settlements in South India by AD 100, which some associate with the aftermath of the fall and destruction of Jerusalem in AD 70.[13] Whatever the date of Christian beginnings in the area they were hardly the sole representatives of that tradition which both Jews and Christians share. Clearly the existence and popularity of the trade routes to and from India in the apostolic age meant that there was no technical difficulty in the way of Christianity reaching India in that period. At the likelihood of and evidence for this we shall look in the next segment of this study. So there is no inherent difficulty in accepting Bardaisan's claim in his *Book of the Laws of the Lands* that there were Christians by that time in India, by which he meant the Kushan kingdom of Bactria, Punjab and the Gangetic plain. With the withdrawal of Egyptian based traders from the same level of involvement towards the end of the 3rd century, the Church in Persia seems to have assumed some responsibility for Christians in India. This appeared when in AD 296–297 Bishop David of Basra followed the traditional Persian route to visit the Churches in India and relate them thereafter to the Church in Persia.[14] So it is quite likely that the John, who attended the council of Nicea in AD 325 as Bishop of India/Persia, may have seen his oversight responsibilities extending at least to those Christian merchants from Persia who were resident in India.

APOSTOLIC FOUNDATIONS?[15]

As vehemently as do the Churches of Rome and Antioch point to their associations with the Apostles Peter and Paul, so too do Christians in South India claim association with the Apostle Thomas – and to a lesser extent with Bartholomew. If extant material evidence from the apostolic age is not available to support the Indian claim, it is no more lacking than parallel evidence in Rome or Antioch. Given the situation which has prevailed amongst Indian Christians for centuries, and the possibilities of contact which we have just explored, it may be rather a case in which the historian is challenged to prove that Thomas (and/or Bartholomew) did *not* act as founders instead of being satisfied by irrefutable evidence that they did.

Along the paths of historiography held dear by 'Westerners' there are considerable problems with the case for an apostolic foundation of Christianity in India – be it in the north-west or the south. The earliest authenticated epigraphical and archaeological evidence, in the form of copper plate charters and inscribed stone crosses, dates from the 7th and

8th centuries AD,[16] and we shall return to these below. This lack leaves us with documentary references, the earliest of which, the Syriac *Doctrine of the Apostles* and the *Acts of Thomas* from Edessa date from the late 2nd to the mid-3rd century.[17] As the second of these documents purports to give a detailed account of the mission of Thomas in India it would be as well to provide a summary of it:

'The scene opens in Jerusalem with the apostles assembled to apportion the sections of the world in which each is to labour. India falls to the lot of Thomas. He refuses, but is forced by none other than Christ himself to go, for the latter sells him to a merchant who chances to be in Jerusalem in search of a carpenter to work for his king, Gundaphorus. Forthwith they depart (somewhat surprisingly) by ship (!) for India. En route they stop at Andrapolis, where a wedding is under way. At the feast to which all must go, Thomas abstains, in a manner not unreminiscent of Daniel, from all the dainties; when approached by a Hebrew girl, he averts his eyes and sings a mystic bridal hymn, reminiscent of the Song of Songs, and apparently intended to suggest that the only proper marriage for a Christian is of the soul to Christ. After Thomas has departed from the bridal pair, the wedding is subsequently broken off by Christ, who appears in the form of "his twin brother Thomas".

Having arrived at the court of Gundaphorus, Thomas is directed to build for the king a palace. Instead, he spends the lavish funds on the poor and tells the angered king that a palace has been built and awaits him in heaven. The king's brother, Gad, enraged at Thomas' effrontery, dies that night, sees the palace in heaven, is so enamored of it that he contrives to be restored to life, and returns to tell his brother. Then follows the episode of the serpent who has slain, out of jealousy, a woman's lover. The serpent is forced to confess this and his other, earlier evil deeds (from the days of Adam and Eve on) and dies. Later Thomas meets the colt of a she ass who, able to talk, identifies herself as of direct descent from Balaam's ass. At her bidding Thomas mounts her and rides to the city gate. As he humbly dismounts to enter the city on foot, the ass drops dead. A lustful demon, who has long tormented a woman is exorcised and departs in a cloud of fire and smoke. A young man, impressed by Thomas' preaching, murders his mistress because she will not agree to live in perfect continence. Later, as he eats the Eucharist, his hands wither. Thomas heals him and restores to life the murdered woman. After recounting her experiences while dead – . . . she, with many others, is converted and baptized.

Next a pious captain asks Thomas' help in curing his wife and daughter, long possessed by devils. Thomas sets out with the captain.

Their horses fail. Four wild asses are summoned to draw the chariot on their stead. One of them, upon arrival at the captain's house, is endowed with speech and summons the devils, who are speedily banished and flee. Then the scene changes to another part of India, where the final event, replete with many details and ending with Thomas' martyrdom, takes place. It is in essence the same story, so common in all these apocryphal Acts. Mygdonia, the wife of a wealthy courtier, is converted to celibacy, despite the pathetic and moving pleas and finally the threats of her husband, who at last enlists the aid of the king, Misdaeus. But all, of course, to no avail. Not only is Mygdonia obdurate, but others, including the king's wife and son, are similarly converted. Finally, after Thomas has been several times warned and imprisoned, only to leave the prison whenever he desires through self-opening doors (all highly reminiscent of stories in the canonical Acts), the king attempts to torture him with plates of red-hot metal placed at his feet, only to find a flood rising from the plates, a flood which, had it not been for Thomas' gracious intervention, would actually have drowned him.

Finally Thomas is taken on to a mountain, is pierced by four spears, dies, and is nobly buried by his converts. Eventually the king too is converted, after his demon-ridden son has been cured by dust from Thomas' grave.'[18]

While the account contains at least one historical reference which can be corroborated, viz. that to a king in North India named Gundaphorus,[19] its prime purpose does not seem to be an historical one.

The other early document, the *Doctrine of the Apostles*, adds little but two references to the 'mission' of Thomas in India, correspondence from 'Judas Thomas from India' and that,

'India, and all the countries belonging to it and round about it, even to the farthest sea, received the apostles' ordination to the priesthood from Judas Thomas.'[20]

By the 4th century writers in the Latin and Greek and Syriac Churches seem to have accepted the relationship of Thomas to the Church in India. The writers who express this are surveyed usefully by W. R. Philipps[21], who summarized his findings thus:

1	2nd cent.?	Syriac "Doctrine of the Apostles"	St Thomas wrote letters from "India". He evangelised "India" and countries bordering on it.
2	c. 170	Heracleon	St Thomas died a natural death.
3	c. 210?	Clementine Recognitions	St Thomas evangelised the Parthians.
4	220	Clement of Alexandria	St Thomas died a natural death.
5	251	Origen	St Thomas evangelised the Parthians.

6	340	Eusebius	Do. Do. Do.
7	378	St. Ephraem	St Thomas was martyred in "India". His relics were part at Edessa, part in India.
8	389	St Gregory of Nazianzus	St Thomas evangelised India.
9	394	St Gregory of Nyssa	St Thomas evangelised Mesopotamia.
10	397	St Ambrose	St Thomas was martyred.
11	400	St Asterius	St Thomas was martyred.
12	407	St John Chrysostom	The locality of the grave of St. Thomas was known to him.
13	410	Rufinus	St Thomas evangelised Parthia. His relics were at Edessa.
14	410	St Gaudentius	St Thomas was martyred in India. Some of his relics were at Brescia.
15	420	St Jerome	St Thomas was in India.
16	431	St Paulinus of Nola	St Thomas was allotted India.
17	443	Sozomen	He mentions the famous church of St Thomas at Edessa, and perhaps implies that his relics were there.
18	c. 445	Socrates	Do. Do. Do.
19	594	St Gregory of Tours	St Thomas was martyred in India; his relics were translated to Edessa, and there was then existing a famous church in India, at the place where the body of the apostle was first buried.

The early evidence is, then, that St. Thomas evangelised Parthia; and, apart from the Syriac *Doctrine of the Apostles*, there does not seem to be any mention of 'India' in connection with St. Thomas till we get to St. Ephraem AD 378 and St. Gregory Nazianzen AD 389, the two living in adjacent countries. The *Doctrine of the Apostles* would be more important if we could fix its date; from expressions used in it, it is thought to be of the 2nd century; but Lipsius says 'towards the end of the 4th cent.', which would bring it to the time of St. Ephraem.[22]

Having looked at subsequent authors Philipps reached the considered conclusion that

> '1 There is good early evidence that St. Thomas was the apostle of the Parthian empire; and also evidence that he was the apostle of "India" in some limited sense, – probably of an "India" which included the Indus valley, but nothing to the east or south of it.
> 2 According to the Acts, the scene of the martyrdom of St. Thomas was in the territory of a king named, according to the Syriac version, Mazdai, to which he had proceeded after a visit to the city of a king named, according to the same version, Gudnaphar or Gundaphar.

3 There is no evidence at all that the place where St. Thomas was martyred was in Southern India; and all the indications point to another direction.

4 We have no indication whatever, earlier than that given by Marco Polo, who died 1324, that there ever was even a tradition that St. Thomas was buried in Southern India.'[23]

Other Western scholars have concurred with Philipps' conclusions,[24] and regard the 6th century reports of Cosmas Indicopleustes as the first reliable first-hand evidence about Christianity in India. At most what can be said on the basis of this approach to the question is that an apostolic foundation for the Church in India is 'not proven.'

But that has in no way reduced the adherence of other scholars to such a foundation, and in South India subsequent to North India. In fact, Western scepticism may well have prompted Indians to adopt an even more intransigent stand on the issue. Before we turn to the details of the case they seek to make, we need to note that the Western near-obsession with historicity and associated documentation has never been shared by Indians, of virtually any religious persuasion. They do not have the archival mentality, or at least did not prior to the arrival of Europeans in the modern era. Hindus rely on traditions and legends, and the 'historicity' of Buddhist sutras is a matter of no concern.

> 'If this is the case as regards Hindu India, it is all the more true of Christians in India, whose number was negligible and limited to a few pockets. . . . The so-called details available are mostly the fruit of fertile imaginations, generously employed to fill gaps and provide facile interpretations.'[25]

To demand that they produce the sort of evidence which 'Westerners' accept is one of those pieces of intellectual imperialism to which reference was made in the Introduction. In addition the fact must be faced that the climate in South India is not conducive to the preservation of documents, which fact is doubtless one of the reasons for inscribing charters on copper plates. In any case, if there had been relevant early Syriac documents they may well have been among those burned at the insistence of Roman Catholic authorities at the Synod of Diamper in AD 1599. J.N. Farquhar went so far along this line as to suggest that significant Indian evidence was destroyed in the great flood of AD 201 at Edessa – but clearly this is pure supposition, unlike the reference to Diamper.[26]

In the place of such documentation, emphasis is put upon oral traditions which emerge in poems and songs, such as the 'Thomas Ramban Song' and the 'Margam Kali Puttu' ('Song of the Way'). The fact that such songs did not exist in a written form before the 17th and 18th centuries is no ground upon which to dismiss their antiquity. Nor can we disregard lightly the claims of some families which trace their involvement in the priesthood of the Church in South India over 40, 48 and even 80 generations.[27] (To one of these families, the Pakalomattams, the Malabar Christians turned for bishops after the schism with Roman Catholics following the Koonen Cross incident in AD 1653.)[28]

To such traditions are added those related to the 'tomb of Thomas' at Mylapore. Certainly these latter traditions interested the Portuguese on their arrival, almost as much as others were discounted by them. These 'tomb traditions' were known also among authors such as Amr ibn Matta (AD 1340) and Mafazzal ibn Abil Fazail (AD 1358). While local traditions reject those of Edessa that the 'saint's bones' were transported thither, the point which has wide acceptance is that

> '"the holy man" who for the East Syrians, the St. Thomas Christians, and the Portuguese, was undoubtedly St. Thomas the Apostle, died near the town of Mylapore and his body was buried in the right hand chapel of their house, and this the Portuguese visited in 1517.'[29]

On this claim Stephen Neill commented as follows:

> 'It is certain that the Portuguese excavated a tomb, that all the evidence suggests that this was a genuinely ancient tomb of a rather unusually elaborate kind, and that in the tomb they found human bones in an advanced state of decay (but not a complete skeleton). But whether these were Christian bones, and if so, who was the Christian whose bones they were, there is no evidence of any kind to show.'[30]

Those who support the case for apostolic foundation understandably make much of the established possibilities re travel etc., which possibilities have been detailed in the first section of this chapter. To these they add the claim that the existing Jewish communities in South India provided an audience for Thomas parallel to those used by Paul on his journeys.[31] Use is made also of the fact that the seven churches supposedly founded by Thomas in the Malabar area are situated in and near the reputed Jewish colonies.[32] This is in spite of the doubts cast on the existence of such Jewish colonies in the first century AD (see note 13 above), not least because the earliest copper plate charter for such a group dates from ca. AD 700. It is also in spite of the clear declaration of G. M. Rae that

> 'in the second century there were neither Jews, Christians nor Brahmins in Malabar.'[33]

Even the contentions that out of necessity and wishful thinking the Christians of South India have confused a merchant, Thomas of Cana (variously dated at AD 345 and AD 754)[34] with Thomas the Apostle, which confusion occurs also among Hindu authorities,[35] does not shake convictions of apostolic foundation. Associations with East Syria and later Nestorians, for whom Thomas had the status of Peter among Roman Catholics, are not seen as sufficient to account for the apostolic tradition.[36] So we find Mundadan holding that the overall evidence, both from within and outside of India, confirms that

'St Thomas the Apostle preached, died and was buried in South India. None of the arguments so far advanced seem to be strong enough to erode the validity of this.'[37]

Somewhat more guarded is the judgment accepted by the historian V. A. Smith, that

'St Thomas preached the Gospel in India is a certainty; that he laboured in the Punjab in the territories of King Gondaphares is extremely probable, that South India was a later field of his labour and the scene of his martyrdom is a tradition unverified, and now in all likelihood unverifiable, though not beyond the bounds of possibility.'[38]

As for the association with the Apostle Bartholomew the evidence may be regarded as even more tenuous. Certainly he is the apostle referred to in the reference from Eusebius, e.g.,

'Pantaenus was at that time especially conspicuous, as he had been educated in the philosophical system of those called Stoics. They say that he displayed such zeal for the divine Word, that he was appointed as a herald of the Gospel of Christ to the nations in the East, and was sent as far as India. For indeed there were still many evangelists of the Word who sought earnestly to use their inspired zeal, after the examples of the apostles, for the increase and building up of the Divine Word. Pantaenus was one of these, and is said to have gone to India. It is reported that among persons there who knew of Christ, he found the Gospel according to Matthew, which had anticipated his own arrival. For Bartholomew, one of the apostles, had preached to them, and left with them the writing of Matthew in the Hebrew language, which they had preserved till that time.'[39]

Dihle, for all his scepticism about the role of Thomas in South India, is prepared to accept the association of Bartholomew's name with Christians there. Indeed he goes on to argue that the Thomas tradition would have greater probability if related to North India and its proximity to Persia, while that related to Bartholomew might similarly have probability re the south of India.[40] This he sees as due in large part to the fact that references to Bartholomew fit into the historico-geographical setting of Rome and Alexandria, but 'not the Thomas tradition which has a foundation in a Syrian not a Roman setting.'[41]

The decline in the South Indian-Egyptian trade, in his view led to increased dependence on the Persian Syrian connections by the Christians of South India, cut off as they were from the guidance to which they had become accustomed. Indeed, one of the consistent features of the South Indian Christian community was its dependence on communities abroad for episcopal leadership and liturgical forms – such communities may be in Egypt, in Persia or in Syria, orthodox Chalcedonian, Nestorian or Jacobite.[42] Such relative isolation may well have added fuel to the desire to have apostolic credentials to which to cling.

Our problem here is exacerbated by the fact that,

'no early Indian has ever written the history of the Church of India, and all our information concerning even the mere existence of a Christian community is almost exclusively derived from Syriac and Greek authors. Now, these authors, having no particular interest in India, refer to the Church questions that affect it in a very casual way.'[43]

It may also be increased by our double standards in that Western historians demand documentation from the apostolic era. In the same time they seem ready to accept the 'tradition' of Peter's visit to and death in Rome,[44] but, even more to the point, are ready to overlook the fact that the earliest life we have of Patrick of Ireland dates from the late 8th century – i.e. some 300 years after his death.[45] Are we guilty of demanding from the Indians what we are prepared to concede to the Irish?

While the probability of a Thomas connection is not to be summarily dismissed, as Rae contended:

'The question is one of fact and not of mere probability.'[46]

On the issue of fact, the only reasonable verdict seems to be that beloved of the Scots – 'not proven'.

THE INDIAN CHRISTIAN COMMUNITY UNTIL AD 1520

Whatever the outcome of discussions about apostolic foundation for the Church in India the probabilities are that the Christian community was in existence there at least towards the end of the second century AD, although others would argue for the middle of the 3rd century as a more defensible starting date.[47] What is clear in both camps, and indeed among those who argue for apostolic foundations, is that the earliest Christian communities were to be found in the south east as well as in the south west of India. However, it would appear that for political reasons the communities in the Chola and Pandya kingdoms came under heavy pressure late in the 3rd century,[48] and that numbers of these Christians migrated to the Chera kingdom of Malabar, others reverting to their former faiths. Hambye suggests that it may have been this development which triggered the action of David, Bishop of Basra, who in AD 296–297 is reported to have visited Kerala.[49] However, we have no details of the work of David, although it is highly probable that links with the Church in Persia were a result of his labours there.[50] Such religious/political pressure against non-Hindu faiths (although directed particularly against Buddhism) also occurred in South Travancore between the 6th and 9th centuries, occasioning more migrations of Christians.[51]

The Persian connection receives widespread support from the 4th century onwards,[52] even while there are no references to the Christians there in extant Chaldean documents before AD 425.[53]

Associated with that century are three further visits from abroad, one which seems definite, one contested and the final one under serious doubt. The definite one is that of Joseph of Edessa in AD 345, who is recorded as the third bishop in India and as being sent there by the Catholicos of Persia.[54] The contested visit is that in AD 354 by Theophilus, the Arian despatched to Arabia in the reign of Constantius. While his work in Arabia and Socotra is accepted, that in the Maldives and India is questioned by some.[55] It does appear that the Christian community in India, attested to by the references, was somewhat out of touch with general Church practice elsewhere. As the report of Theophilus had it:

'Thence he sailed to other parts of India, and reformed many things which were not rightly done among them, for they heard the reading of the Gospel in a sitting posture and did other things which were repugnant to the divine law; and having reformed everything according to the holy usage, as was most acceptable to God, he also confirmed the dogma of the Church.'[56]

The final significant visitor, whose dating is more commonly referred to the 8th century, was the merchant Thomas of Cana. There are those writers who assign him to the mid-4th century and relate him and those who accompanied him to Christians who fled Persia during the persecutions of Shapur II (d. AD 379) which began in AD 339.[57] Certainly the significance of Thomas of Cana's arrival is fully recognized but the balance of scholarly opinion and associated archaeological remains tends to favour an 8th century date, to which we will return below.

However, the links with Persia were consolidated by whatever means, and through whatever personal contacts. They were to remain unbroken until the Church in Persia was virtually exterminated by Timur Leng, and even then persisted down into the 16th century. One means of maintaining the link in the 5th century was through the sending of men from India to be educated for the priesthood in East Syria.[58] Then in AD 470, the *Chronicle of Seert* reports, Bishop Mana of Edessa translated the works of Diodore of Tarsus and Theodore of Mopsuestia from the Greek with the help of an Indian priest called Daniel, and, along with religious discourses, canticles and hymns, these were sent to India.[59] So the links were maintained.

Even those historians who retain doubts about the evidence prior to the 6th century are ready to ascribe credibility to the reported existence of Christians in India and Ceylon, if not to all the details, in the writings of Cosmas Indicopleustes, the one time Alexandrian merchant and traveller.[60] His *Christian Topography* was published in AD 535 and, inter alia reported thus on a visit to these areas between AD 522 and AD 525:

> 'Even in Taprobane, an island in Further India, where the Indian sea is, there is a Church of Christians, with clergy and a body of believers, but I know not whether there be any Christians in the parts beyond it. In the country called Male, where the pepper grows, there is also a church, and at another place called Calliana there is moreover a bishop, who is appointed from Persia. In the island, again, called the Island of Dioscorides, which is situated in the same Indian sea, and where the inhabitants speak Greek, having been originally colonists sent thither by the Ptolemies who succeeded Alexander the Macedonian, there are clergy who receive their ordination in Persia, and are sent on to the island, and there is also a multitude of Christians. I sailed along the coast of this island, but did not land upon it.' [61]

Subsequently he referred further to the situation in Ceylon thus:

> 'The island has also a church of Persian Christians who have settled there, and a Presbyter who is appointed from Persia, and a Deacon and a complete ecclesiastical ritual. But the natives and their kings are heathens.'[62]

From these comments G. M. Rae has deduced that

> 'the constituency as well as the constitution of the Church both in Ceylon and on the west coast of Southern India was Persian; as neither, it would appear, had yet begun to associate the natives of the country in Church fellowship. In fact the Church of Ceylon would seem never to have done so, and probably for that reason had but a short-lived tenure in the island; whereas on the other hand, the Church of the Malabar coast largely cultivated the fellowship of the natives.'[63]

To have been closely tied to Persia by the time of Cosmas' visit was to mean that the Church in India would have been Nestorian as was the Church in

Persia by that time. This is not to say that the Indian Christians were necessarily enthusiasts in areas of theological dispute, but that they would have taken on the doctrinal line of that Church on which they had come to depend. As it was, Cosmas was the last visitor from the west of whom we have a record for centuries, as thereafter the old sea route connections between the Middle East and India were dominated by Islam, virtually until the end of the 15th century. However, as we shall see, traditions associating St. Thomas and his tomb with India remained in the consciousness of many to the west of the Persian Gulf.

The next clear contact is seen by most to be that of Thomas of Cana in Syria who is reputed to have arrived in Malabar in AD 754.[64] With this Thomas came a considerable group of Persian immigrants who filled a gap in the local scene in that,

> 'in the absence of the Vaishya or trader caste in the Hindu caste hierarchy of Kerala, the Christians found it easy to step into the breach, and they were welcomed by every ruling family in Kerala.'[65]

The arrival of this group, and of another some 40 years later, led by two bishops, Mar Sabr-ishu or Subhl-ishu and Mar Peroz or Aprot, greatly strengthened the Christian communities, not least at Cranganore and Quilon. As Mundadan sums it up:

> 'All the documents regarding this tradition agree on the great importance of the arrival of this Syrian merchant. His arrival was a turning point in the history of the community as it brought to them both material and spiritual prosperity.'[66]

To such groups, as also to Jewish groups at about the same time, the local rulers granted charters of rights and responsibilities engraved on copper plates. The earliest of these charters, from the eighth century, have been lost, but those which survive from the ninth century provide indications of what was involved (see pl. 9). Such charters gave the Christians considerable status in the local highly significant caste system, not least because it is clear from them that the Christians formed not only a mercantile but also a military group on which local rulers could call for assistance in emergencies.[67] In fact, from later descriptions relating to their carrying of arms and their consciousness of their rank, the Christians seem to have paralleled in some ways the samurai class of Japan, with the very significant addition of involvement in trade.

Beside the charters preserved, which are written in old Tamil, there are inscriptions written in Pahlavi. They are found on stone crosses which date from the 9th century and were discovered at Mylapore, Kottayam, Katamarran, Muttichura and Alangad. The cross from Mylapore was found in AD 1547, and is believed to have provided the model for the others, the Pahlavi inscription reading:

'My Lord Christ, have mercy upon Afras, son of Chaharbukht, the Syrian, who cut this.'[68]

As to the contents of the surviving charters, the following summary and comments upon one from AD 880 will serve to illustrate the sort of privileges granted to the Church at Quilon by King Ayyan of Venat:

'The king gave some low-caste people to be servants of the Church and exempted them from paying certain specified rates and taxes, and gave them the right of entry to the market (denied before because they were not caste Hindus). Any crime committed by these people was to be tried by the Christians. The Church was given also the administration of customs in Quilon, that is, the steelyard and weights and the *kappan* [official seal]. . . . When Marignolli came in 1348 he found that the Christians were "masters of the public weighing office". By Alfonso d'Albuquerque's time (AD 1504) they had lost the privilege of "keeping the seal and the standard weight of the city". It is evident from these privileges that the Christian community had a reputation for integrity, as well as a recognized position in society. Even if the community consisted mostly of immigrants who had settled only some sixty years before, they had settled permanently and were recognized as playing a valuable part in the community life. Probably the slaves they were given would be baptized and absorbed into the community; we know that this practice was common until towards the end of last century.

The second set of plates were also given by King Ayyan and are of about the same date. The plates contain details of grants to the Tarisa Church, to the Jews, and to the Manigrammam. The Church was given land let out under certain conditions to four families of agriculturists and two of carpenters, so as to ensure a perpetual income to the Church. The boundaries of the land given to the Christian community were also marked out in the ancient way, by marking "the course taken by a female elephant let free". The Christians had the sole right of administering justice in this territory and of receiving the bride price, and were entitled to receive protection, if they needed it, from the Venat militia called the Six Hundred, and the Jewish and Manigrammam leaders.'[69]

All of this points to the fact that Christians were treated very much as were high caste Hindus. Indeed permission to convert to Christianity, in this period, was granted only to those from the higher levels of society, which did nothing to lessen the status or self-consciousness of this among Christians.

If the Christians in India saw themselves as clearly related to the Church in Persia, what references are extant from the latter about the situation in

India? Clearly the patriarch at Seleucia, and later Babylon, could exercise very limited oversight, but quite definitely the concern expressed by David of Basra was to remain among the Persian Church leaders for a millennium at least. In part this concern was related to the rivalry which existed between the metropolitans of Rev-Ardashir and the patriarchs. The former assumed special responsibility, or rather claims of oversight at first. This can be traced back at least to the time shortly after the visit of Cosmas Indicopleustes, when a priest called Bodh, related to Rev-Ardashir, was sent to India as an official visitor or 'periodeutes',[70] thus linking India to a see which rivalled Seleucia in its claims to status.

That this did not preclude contact with the patriarchal seat is clear from the report that the Patriarch Sabr-ishu I (d. AD 604) gave to the ambassador from Constantinople

'perfumes and gifts sent to the patriarch from India.'[71]

But something of a crisis emerged in the patriarchate of Ishu-Yab III (d. AD 660) in his contest with the Metropolitan of Rev-Ardashir, Shimun. It was clear that Shimun was anxious to muster support from his region and beyond in an attempt to undercut the authority of the patriarch. As Mingana has pointed out, it is not unlikely that the Thomas tradition was appealed to in order to provide an apostolic credential, proof against patriarchal 'pretension'.[72] If so the metropolitan was unsuccessful, and his province was divided into three, with a metropolitan being named for India itself for the first time – the patriarch being responsible for consecration – an arrangement repeated by the Patriarch Salibazacha (d. AD 728). Thus was established a tradition which came down until at least AD 1504, being further confirmed en route by Timothy I (d. AD 820) following another conflict with the provincial clergy of Fars.

Further bonding of Indian Christians to Seleucia and the patriarch followed the work of Thomas of Cana and Sabr-ishu over this 8th–9th century period. A letter of Timothy I recognized the significance of the local Indian archdeacon as 'head of the faithful in India',[73] under the regular episcopal oversight. In this there was acknowledgment of the fact that while Seleucia might supply the holders of the episcopal offices and that of the metropolitan dignity, such men were most unlikely to have the command of the vernacular language needed for immediate administration and authority.

At the same time the importance of Quilon as a major port was growing. By AD 851 it had become the most considerable port in South-West India and the only one touched by the large Chinese junks on their way home from Persia.[74] In that port community, the Christians, as we have seen, had a considerable part to play. It may be that this played a part in the readiness of the Patriarch Theodosius (d. AD 858) to permit metropolitans as far away as India to make full reports at six year intervals rather than more frequently.[75]

Thereupon the extant records of Persian Christianity are silent about Christianity in India for some four centuries. But this is not to say that we do not have references from elsewhere. The first of these may be founded on legend as related to Thomas and Bartholomew, but it is of interest in that it comes from the England of Alfred the Great (d. AD 899) which was almost as far removed from India as it was possible to be at that time. The entry numbered 883 in the Anglo-Saxon Chronicle, recounting Alfred's struggles against the Danes, tells us that

> 'Sigehelm and Aethelstand took alms to Rome, and also to St. Thomas and St. Bartholomew in India, that King Alfred had promised when they besieged the force in London; and there, by the grace of God, their prayers were granted in accordance with those promises.'[76]

Similar convictions about the location of the tomb of St. Thomas were held by pilgrims like St. Bernard the penitent, who is reported to have visited it between AD 1170–1177. He was to be followed some 20 years later by Henry Morungen, a Saxon king.[77]

References appear again from Nestorian records of AD 1301 when Yaqob is listed as the Metropolitan of India under the Patriarch Yaballaha III (d. AD 1317).[78] And from the 14th century also comes an Armenian account in Arabic by Abu Salih which refers to Nestorians in Quilon (and in Fashur in Sumatra).[79]

By this time other contacts were possible once more as Mongol conquests re-opened the land routes across Asia to non-Muslim traders and adventurers from the West. The first to visit India, en route to his work in China, was John of Montecorvino (d. AD 1328) in AD 1291. He spent some 13 months in India, probably landing at Quilon, including Mylapore in his itinerary, and remarking on the comparatively small numbers of Christians and Jews he met, none of whom struck him as of significance.[80] The next European whose observations we have was the famous Marco Polo (d. AD 1324) who came in AD 1293. He made no mention of Christians in Ceylon (Book 3:19 and 23) but does mention their presence in South India, particularly in connection with the tomb of St. Thomas at Mylapore, where he wrote was

> 'the body of the glorious martyr, Saint Thomas the Apostle, who there suffered martyrdom. It rests in a small city, not frequented by many merchants, because unsuited to the purposes of their commerce; but, from devout motives, a vast number both of Christians and Saracens resort thither. The latter regard him as a great prophet, and name him Ananias, signifying a holy personage. The Christians who perform this pilgrimage collect earth from the spot where he was slain, which is of a red colour, and reverentially

carry it away with them; often employing it afterwards in the performance of miracles, and giving it, when diluted with water, to the sick, by which many disorders are cured. The Christians who have the care of the church possess groves of those trees which produce the Indian nuts, and from thence derive their means of subsistence, paying, as a tax to one of the royal brothers, a groat monthly for each tree.'[81]

He made reference also to the many Christians and Jews, retaining 'their proper language', to be found in Kerala.[82]

It was at this time that Rome was initiating its missions in Persia and beyond through Dominicans and Franciscans under its Societas Peregrinantium pro Christo. One such who visited India ca. AD 1320 was Jordanus Catalani whom we met in relation to his later references to work at Tabriz in Persia. Jordanus visited Thana, near Bombay, and followed up with contacts at nearby Sopara and Broach, as well as more distant Quilon. Of those Christians in the north he reported:

'In this India there is a scattered people, one here, one there, who call themselves Christians but are not so, nor have they baptism nor do they know anything about the faith. Nay, they believe St. Thomas the great to be Christ! There in the India I speak of, I baptized and brought into the faith about three hundred souls.'[83]

He stayed on, having buried four Franciscans at Thana whose derogatory remarks about Islam had led to their executions, and sought reinforcements for the work to continue in this region. As an advocate he was nothing if not enthusiastic, claiming that

'while I was among those schismatic unbelievers, I believe that more than 10,000, or thereabouts, were converted to our faith.'[84]

Consequently he claimed that the same number of conversions could be made each year by 200–300 friars!

However, Muslim antagonism forced him south to Quilon, where he was secure under the Hindu ruler Ravi Varma of Venad (d. AD 1325), who had checked the advance of Islam. Jordanus tells us nothing about the Church at Quilon, but in August 1329 he was back in Avignon where Pope John XXII (d. AD 1334) appointed him Bishop of Quilon. He was given a letter to the head of the Christian community at Quilon, the 'Dominus Nascarinorum' (Lord of the Nazarenes), inviting them to forsake their schism and come under the Roman umbrella. As Juhanon remarks this was the first recorded case of a claim to papal authority over the Christians of Malabar.[85] It was not to be the last. With that the information ceases, and we do not know whether he ever returned to Quilon, nor when he died.

Like John of Montecorvino, en route to China was Odoric of Pordenone (d. AD 1325). He called at India in AD 1321, visiting Quilon and Mylapore. In the latter he found fifteen Nestorian families he regarded as disreputable heretics, but he did remark about those around Quilon that they were the proprietors of the pepper tree orchards and that they also controlled the office of customs.[86]

In AD 1347–1348 another friar, John of Marignolli (d. AD 1357), visited the Christian community in Malabar on his way home from the court of the Great Khan, which he had reached in AD 1342. From him we have confirmation of what had been reported by Odoric, viz.:

'On Palm Sunday, 1348, we arrived at a very noble city of India called Quilon where the whole world's pepper is produced. Now this pepper grows on a kind of vines which are planted just as in our vineyards. . . . These are things that I have seen with my eyes and handled with my hands during the fourteen months that I have stayed there. And there is no roasting of the pepper as authors have falsely asserted, nor does it grow in forests but in regular gardens, nor are the Saracens the proprietors but the St. Thomas Christians. And these latter are the masters of the public weighing office (qui habent stateram ponderis totius mundi), from which I derived, as a perquisite of my office as Pope's legate, every month a hundred gold fanams, and a thousand when I left. There is a church of St. George there, of the Latin communion, at which I dwelt, and I adorned it with fine paintings and taught there the holy law. And after I had been there some time I went beyond the glory of Alexander the Great, when he set up his column. For I erected a stone as my landmark and memorial and anointed it with oil. In sooth, it was a marble pillar with a stone cross on it, intended to last until the world's end. And it had the Pope's arms and my own upon it, with inscriptions both in Indian and in Latin characters. I consecrated and blessed it in the presence of an infinite multitude of people and I was carried on the shoulders of the chiefs in a litter or palanquin like Solomon's. So after a year and four months I took leave of the brethren.'[87]

The origins of a Church 'of the Latin communion' remain a mystery, although it has been suggested that it may have been erected by traders from Genoa or Pisa, or, perhaps less likely, from Venice.[88] This was to provide a model for later enclaves to be established by the English East India Company, for example.

John of Marignolli reported further of that Latin rite Church, that

'the Jews, Muslims, and even some of the Christians, regarded the Latins as the worst of idolaters, because they used statues and images in their churches.'[89]

Before leaving for Europe in September AD 1348 he ensured that he included a visit to Mylapore. Out of all these contacts by the friars the belief grew in Europe that there was a Christian ruler in South-West India and this prompted Pope Eugenius IV (d. AD 1447) to forward a letter thither addressed:

'To my most beloved Son in Christ, Thomas, the illustrious Emperor of the Indians, health and the apostolic benediction. There often has reached us a constant rumour that your Serenity and also all who are subject of your kingdom are true Christians.'[90]

It is not known if the envoys ever reached India, nor to whom, if they did, they delivered the papal letter.

At about the same time we have the reports of the Italian traveller Nicolo Conti (d. AD 1469) who wrote that at Mylapore

'the body of St. Thomas lies honourably buried in a very large and beautiful church; it is worshipped by heretics who are called Nestorians, and inhabit this city to the number of a thousand. These Nestorians are scattered over all India, in like manner as are the Jews among us.'[91]

Conti also commented on another aspect of Nestorian life in India, when noting the prevalence of polygamy there he added

'excepting among those Christians who have adopted the Nestorian heresy, who are spread over the whole of India and confine themselves to one solitary mate.'[92]

That the Nestorians were so widespread, and not infrequently in positions of importance, is shown by the fact that

'Abd-ev-Razzak, who visited India in 1443, said that the vizier of Vijayanagar in the Deccan was a Christian, his name being Nimehpezir.'[93]

Finally two visitors from the early 16th century provide first hand accounts of the situation of the Malabar Christians during the first decades of contact with the Portuguese. The Italian Ludovico di Varthema (d. AD 1517) wrote of the Christians he met just north of Quilon in AD 1505:

'In this city we found some Christians of those of St. Thomas, some of whom are merchants and believe in Christ, as we do. These say that every three years a priest comes there to baptize and that he comes from Babylon. These Christians keep Lent longer than we do: but they keep Easter like ourselves and they all observe the same solemnities that we do. But they say Mass like the Greeks. They use four names, John, James, Matthew and Thomas.' [94]

And by AD 1520 Duarte Barbosa (d. AD 1521) had commented that

'. . . Christians remained in the kingdom of Coulam (Quilon), with
the before mentioned church which St. Thomas built, and with
others about the country. This church was endowed by the King of
Coulam with the revenue from the pepper, which remains to it to this
day. These Christians had not any Christian doctrine amongst them,
nor were they baptised, only they held and believed the faith of
Christ in a gross manner. And at a certain period they held a council
amongst them and sent men about the world to study the Christian
doctrine and manner of baptism; these men reached Armenia,
where they found many Greek Christians and a patriarch who
governed them, who seeing their good intentions sent with them a
bishop and six priests to baptise them and administer the sacraments
and perform divine service, and indoctrinate them in the Christian
faith. And these remain there for five or six years, and then are
released for an equal period of time, and so on. And in this manner
they improved themselves somewhat.'[95]

Barbosa was aware that their attitudes towards the eucharistic elements
differed from that of the Latin Church, and accused the priests of
enriching themselves through the charges made for baptisms.[96] He wrote
also of a church at Cape Cormorin, and described the church at the tomb
in Mylapore thus:

'And the house and church are ordered in our fashion, with crosses
on the altar and at the top of the vault, and a great wooden cross,
and peacocks for a device: the church is much deteriorated. . . . The
Christians of India still go there as pilgrims, and carry away thence as
relics some little pellets of earth of the tomb of this blessed apostle.'[97]

The reference of Barbosa to the church at Mylapore being 'much
deteriorated' seems to have been the impression formed by the
Portuguese about the Indian Christians as a whole. The extent to which
that assessment was justified is debatable, but it is clear that the Portuguese
themselves had no way of coming to grips immediately with a Christian
community which had lived for some 1300 years amidst the emphases of
Hindu religion and culture.

Indeed:

'On the eve of the arrival of the Portuguese, Christian society in
Kerala . . . presented the picture of a community that was Christian
in religion, Syro-Oriental in worship and Indian in culture.'[98]

They seem to have numbered some 200,000 in 1400 churches or as the
Chaldean bishops reported in AD 1504 some 30,000 families. As to
occupations they were involved primarily in farming (not least in pepper

culture) but also in trade and in military service, one report having it that they supplied 50,000 musketeers to the Raja of Cochin![99] The strong social caste structure of society put limits on evangelism, but:

'To say the least, the Malabar Church had a basic missionary orientation, or missionary-mindedness. But it was not sufficiently deep or strong enough to launch a missionary venture into the heart of Hindu land. It was not strong enough to produce great Christian personalities who could influence the socio-cultural milieu so as to facilitate missionary activity. One should also say that there was a lack of that Christian fortitude and theological vision which could go beyond the caste barriers bringing faith even to the humblest and lowest ones.'[100]

While there is evidence of Muslim 'persecution' from time to time,[101] it appears that, in Kerala

'Hindus, Jains, Buddhists, Christians, Jews, and later Muslims, both Indian and foreign, lived in harmony',[102]

out of awareness of mutual interest in commerce. (Parallels with the situation in the Netherlands after the 16th century Reformation spring to mind – commercial interest is everywhere a powerful incentive to more than private enterprise.)

As for the centuries-long tradition of connections with the Nestorians of Persia, there remained evidence that this had not disappeared. In line with what had become quite usual the Malabar Christianity community approached the patriarch in Persia in AD 1490 and secured two bishops, Mar John and Mar Thomas. The latter reported back to Persia in AD 1500, and the Patriarch Elijah V in AD 1503 consecrated three metropolitans and sent them to India, China and Java.[103] We are without information about the successful attainment of their goals by those designated for China and Java, but we do know that in AD 1504 a warm welcome was extended to Mar Thomas and to the new Indian Metropolitan, Mar Jaballaha, by the Malabar Christians.[104] That such prelates were to be an embarrassment to the Portuguese is clear, and an issue to be explored later.

SOUTH INDIAN CHRISTIANS – THEIR LIVES, STATUS AND RELATIONSHIP TO INDIAN CULTURE

Several paragraphs heretofore the contention of C. V. Cheriyan was noted that when the Portuguese arrived the Christians of Malabar were, inter alia, 'Indian in culture'.[105] Given the exposure of some thirteen centuries to such a culture and the relative remoteness of the Christian community there from other cultural influences this is hardly surprising. What is of interest is to sample some of the ways in which this Indian acculturation was expressed. Podipara lists a series of customs in which Indian influences are apparent, and among these are the feeding of a new born babe; early school lessons; aspects of marriage ceremonies such as 'the tying of the marriage thread round the bride's neck by her husband and the investing with the marriage cloth'[106]; the first confinement; modes of dress; the architecture of houses and churches; male inheritance practices, and rites for the dead.[107] L. W. Brown adds further detail to flesh out such cultural interchange and assimilation.

> 'It often happened in such places that Christians were trustees of the temple and Hindus of the church. They often shared things used in festivals. All the paraphernalia of Hindu religious processions were used also by Syrians – various kinds of ceremonial umbrellas, drums, musical instruments, fly whisks, and bombs. A flagstaff was a prominent feature of both church and temple. The Kuravilanat church formerly had elephants for its festivals which were lent to the Ettumanur temple. The Christians at Palayur still follow the Brahmin custom of bathing in the sea on their chief festival day and some of the old Christian families there share house names with the Brahmins or Nayars. . . . In many ceremonies the senior woman of the house would bring a lighted lamp which was a relic of "agni" worship, and there is a special word, *tavikkuga*, used by Christians, which means to extinguish a lamp with a small ladle. Christians, like Nayars, would never blow out a flame with their breath, as this would be an insult to the fire god. For centuries the popular belief in the power of omens to determine good or ill fortune and the belief in auspicious days, prevailed among the Christians too, and is not extinct. The acceptance of Hindu beliefs led to Christians adopting many conventions, such as sleeping with the head to the east and the feet to the west, and never north-south. . . .
>
> At three or four years of age the education of the child started. The teacher of the local village school (*Kalari*), who might be a Christian but was probably a Hindu, was called and sat down beside the child with a large brass plate full of paddy in front of them. A lamp was lit and the members of the family stood round while the teacher took the child's forefinger and traced with it in the rice the words "Hari śrī Gaṇapatē Namā", the name of the Hindu god Ganapathi who was believed to guide education and remove obstacles to success. The teacher was, of course, given a present before he left. From this time he was considered to be in a special relation to the child and had to come to bless him on special occasions such as marriage.'[108]

At the same time the Christians in the main held to their own interpretations of many of these customs. So, e.g. the fire which signified

178

'agni' for the Hindu, symbolised Christ, the light of the world, for the Christian. The customs were fixed and related to the social structure, but the interpretations placed on them were not fixed, and so the Indians welcomed Christians keeping the customs, whatever their own interpretations of them, a fact not recognized by the Portuguese at the end of the 16th century.[109]

On the other hand it may well be that developing Indian, and particularly Hindu customs had at least limiting affects on Christian witness, and not only through the caste system. So J. Stewart contended that

'the introduction of the Krishna cult, combined with the development of the caste system, in the centuries subsequent to AD 600, must be included among the factors that contributed to the decay in the virility of Nestorian Missions.'[110]

In short, the life of the Thomas Christians 'was strikingly similar to that of their Hindu brethren. . . . Christianity in Kerala developed as an essentially Indian religion, while the votaries of that religion zealously guarded the fundamentals of their faith as the most treasured of their possessions.'[111]

Be that as it may, clearly the Christians saw themselves as part of the developed caste system. This was an inescapable given. A prime consideration was to obtain a suitable rung on the caste ladder, and, as we have seen above this they achieved. As a *yogan* or corporation, accepted by the local ruler(s) they were seen as useful members of society and were ranked with the Nayars and so just below the Brahmins. The stiffening of the caste system, as the essentially Dravidian South Indians were increasingly Aryanised, introduced strict limits on proselytising, while it gave the Christian 'caste' a place and security. There appear to have been three successive strata of converts, the earliest being some from the higher castes including some Brahmins, and only a small number from lower castes. The next stratum was represented by immigrants from Persia and Syria, and from Coromandel, which group merged eventually with older elements. The final influx came from lower caste converts made by pre-Portuguese Latin missionaries, which converts found their homes also among the established community.[112]

If the lower castes occasionally were represented amongst the Christians of Kerala, what was their attitude towards the 'Untouchables' of the caste system? They could not be part of the latter and adopt an open attitude towards the former whatever the force of the claim of Aerthayil that:

'If they had any contempt for the low-caste people they would not have assumed the responsibility of protecting the people of 17 low-castes.'[113]

However:

> 'A further consequence of acceptance as a caste was that untouch-
> ability was observed by Christians as by Hindus. Their tradition
> required that some functions at a wedding be performed by converts
> (menial offices like bringing the large pan required for preparing
> certain foods) and it seems that outcaste people were baptized for
> this purpose, but not incorporated in the community. Gouvea
> explains the Christian attitude as follows: they followed the custom of
> the rest of the people of Malabar; if they touched any low-caste
> person they immediately bathed themselves; not that they thought,
> as the heathen do, that they were polluted by such contact, but
> because the Nayars, who are forbidden by the Brahmins to touch the
> lower castes, would not have any communication with them unless
> they purified themselves. The reason given for Christian observance
> of untouchability is thus pure expediency, so that the caste people
> would trade with and give or rent land to the Christians. Other
> evidence suggests that the attitude was more fundamental. Christians
> thought that the value of a fast was lost if they happened to touch an
> outcaste. Respectable landowners used to change their clothes and
> bathe in a special shed on returning from the fields, where they had
> inevitably had contact with outcaste labour, before entering the
> house.'[114]

(It is of interest to note that as late as AD 1956 Brown felt constrained to
add:

> 'The writer was once strongly rebuked by Syrian Christians for having
> outcaste Christian parishioners in his house, on the ground that it
> made it hard for the Syrians to have social contact with him
> afterwards. It is right to add that the Jacobites have had a mission to
> the outcastes since the twenties, the Servants of the Cross Society,
> and the Mar Thomas Evangelistic Association has worked among
> them with great success. I do not think that the converts are fully
> integrated into the life of the Church as yet. Certainly there are no
> clergy from among their number.'[115])

Culturally Indian in so much, the Thomas Christians maintained their
identity not least through the expressions of their religion in worship,
piety and ethical conduct. Not unlike Welsh farmers in Patagonia, to
borrow Stephen Neill's illustration,[116] they used language as a mark of
distinction, in that they retained the use of Syriac for liturgical purposes.
In like manner the Scriptures were in the same language, which meant
that linguistic distinction cut many of the community off from understanding the words used in worship and sacred texts. (It was not until the
19th century that the Bible was available in the vernacular Malayalam

tongue.) At the same time this linguistic device meant that the liturgy was fixed and can be readily explored through any thorough exposition of Syrian liturgical forms,[117] having its probable roots in the 7th century AD work of Patriarch Ishu-Yab III (d. AD 657).

Like Eastern liturgies as a whole, considerable and proper emphasis was placed on the Resurrection, not least via the empty cross found on the altar; the understanding of the body and blood of the Eucharistic elements as being that of the risen Christ; and the 'Jesus prayer' ('Lord Jesus Christ, Son of God, have mercy on me') signifying the aim of present union with the risen Lord. Also embodied was a stress on expectation, contained in the prayer 'Maranatha' ('Even so, come Lord Jesus').[118]

The seasons followed in order were

Annunciation:	4 weeks
Epiphany:	7 weeks
Great Fast (Lent):	51 days
Resurrection:	7 weeks (to Pentecost)
Apostles:	7 weeks (after Pentecost)
Summer:	7 weeks
Elias & the Cross:	5–7 weeks (with a stress on Last Judgment)
Moses:	length varies with date of Easter
Dedication of the Church:	last 4 weeks of the liturgical year.

Fasting played a significant role also and was focussed on a 25 day fast in the season of Annunciation, the Great Fast (of Lent), a 50 day fast in Apostles and 7 weeks in Elias and the Cross. Such a regimen of fasting,

'continued prayer in the church, abstinence from conjugal life, and chewing betel etc. on fast days seem to be the result of Hindu influence.'[119]

At the same time, in common with Syrian Christianity elsewhere, the Thomas Christians kept a place for the monastic life, both coenobitic and eremitic in their midst. Monasteries existed at Angamali, Kuravilangad, Edapalle and Mylapore. In addition there are references to hermits who lived in the vicinity of important sanctuaries.[120]

For all the sense of common Christian identity in the midst of a predominantly Hindu population, the Christians had their own intra-faith divisions even before the arrival of the Portuguese and English and subsequent multiplication of denominations. The division was into two largely mutually exclusive groups called the 'Northists' and the 'Southists'. Rarely if ever inter-marrying, they carried also some differences in complexion, one from the other. It is said that the groups had their origins in the descendants of the two 'wives' of Thomas of Cana. One family lived on the north side of a street in Cranganore and the other on the south side – thus the names adopted.

The 'Southist' group claim descent from a Syrian 'wife', and the 'Northist' from an Indian 'wife', each group regarding the other as of illegitimate origins. At the same time the 'Southists' claim that they have kept pure the Syrian bloodline, never marrying with native Indians. One attractive possibility is that the 'Northists' are the descendants of converts and were ever the more ready of the two groups to welcome later converts, while the 'Southists' are the mainly pure descendants of immigrants. What is clear is that these traditional attitudes have made themselves apparent for centuries (and are to be found also in the late 20th century).[121]

Now while, for all these internal divisions, the cultus and piety contributed in the main to the preservation of a distinctive Christian identity, the Christians of Kerala lived in a region in which the Hindu rulers had a deserved reputation for religious tolerance. The mountainous barrier of the Western Ghats delivered them from the dangers of Muslim invasion, and from their Persian connections they may well have learned more of what was needed in dealing with rulers who did not share the religious views of a minority. The results of this may be seen not least in the ways in which concessions granted to the Christians in the 8th century were still in place in the early 16th century. And they seem never to have had the purging, if not always reinvigorating, experience of persecution, such as was the lot of their co-religionists in Persia.[122]

There was also the tradition of a Christian dynasty of rulers or kings in the area. Some make much of this with references to the palace of such a ruler being in existence in AD 1500, even though there was no such ruler in place in AD 1502. This is supported by references to the belief in Europe that such a ruler existed and could be addressed in correspondence.[123] It is claimed also that a decorated staff presented to da Gama was in fact the sceptre of such a ruler, and that in the presentation the Christians were seeking acknowledgment of their special status from the Portuguese.[124] It is conjectured also that the tradition arose in the confusion which attended the death of the last Perumalil king,[125] while a sort of de facto royal power is associated with the Christians, who, in combining with the Nayar caste could limit the prerogatives of the rajahs.[126]

On the other hand there are those who deny that there ever was a ruling dynasty as such. As Juhanon put it, the idea 'might have arisen because the Rajah of Udayamperur (Diamper) came to be known as the king of the Christians.'[127] Or as Mundadan, following Roz, postulates:

'. . . there never was a Christian kingly family nor a Christian kingdom, but only the tradition that some of the Christians were descendants of kings converted by the Apostle Thomas.'[128]

The origins of the tradition are as difficult to substantiate incontrovertibly as is the case for the apostolic foundation. At least we can appreciate that such a claim was likely to impress da Gama and to contribute to the Indians' desire for Portuguese protection against Muslim incursions. It also suited the aims of the Portuguese themselves, as Brown makes clear:

'Vasco da Gama arrived in India for the second time in 1502. This time he came to Cochin and was visited by a deputation of Christians living near Cranganore who said they wanted protection against Muslims and heathen so that the remnants of Christianity left there by St. Thomas might not entirely disappear. They submitted themselves to the admiral as representative of the King of Portugal and handed over a staff of authority. This was a red-coloured stick decorated with silver, with three silver bells on top. Da Gama seems to have accepted it as of far more significance than it actually was, as do Couto tells us he received it with great pomp, dressing his ships and saluting with all his guns. The Portuguese connected the incident with the Christian dynasty the Pope thought was extant in 1439, and considered they had thus taken over suzerainty of the Christians.'[129]

As for the overall status of the Christians, there is general agreement that this was high in Indian society. They were politically, socially and economically important, and they had a high reputation as skilled soldiers. As K. J. Mathew described them:

'They were considered aristocrats and equal to the Brahmins. They also held patronage over the lower castes like the Kammalas. The Raja and his prime minister alone had authority over them. They had the right to maintain a bodyguard and a standing army of their own.'[130]

He added that they also had the right to use some of the insignia which belonged to the nobility. It may be that Stewart sums them up as well as anybody, thus:

'They were noted for their industry, natural ability, the elegance of their diction and their respect for parents, elders and clergy. The men were always armed, but quarrels were few and murders never heard of. As a general rule, they were rich and possessed a considerable number of slaves whom they treated with the utmost kindness and consideration. They were much employed as merchants and their honour and liberality were acknowledged by all. They were very abstemious, seldom tasting either meat or wine, and lived almost entirely on rice and milk. They did not use images but held the cross in great veneration. They were particular and devout in their Sabbath attendance and at Communion, but not as a matter of obligation. The priests were allowed to marry, and their wives were distinguished by a silver or golden cross worn round the neck.'[131]

THE ORGANISATION AND THEOLOGY OF THE CHURCH

The long-standing links between the Christians of South India and those of Persia have been detailed already. The role of the Patriarch of the Church of the East, whether at Seleucia-Ctesiphon until AD 762, at Baghdad until AD 1258, at Mosul until AD 1400 and thereafter at Qudshanis in the mountains of Kurdistan, was valued. Thence came the episcopal consecrations which tied those remote in India to the Church at large. This sense of connection with, and place in the whole, was strengthened by the practice of making of India a staging post for some bishops destined for South East Asia or China if in the latter case the overland routes were disrupted.[132]

As we have seen the bishops despatched to India were drawn from those of the Nestorian, and much later from the Jacobite Church, the latter in the 17th century. They came without knowledge of the local language, and seeing that the liturgy and sacred texts were in the Syriac with which they were familiar, they were liturgical and pedagogical figures in the main. They never assumed the administrative or evangelistic roles associated at times with the bishops in the Latin West.

In the absence of an Augustinian doctrine of original sin, baptism would generally be reserved for the bishop, with which was also associated chrism, in lieu of a separate rite of confirmation as in the West. From the somewhat scanty evidence we have available it would appear that substantial charges were made for baptisms, on the basis of one third each for the bishop, the other clergy involved, and the Church.[133] It may well have been that such charges were beyond the means of some, despite the claims that the Christian community as a whole was relatively affluent.

The Nicene Creed was used in worship, and at the Eucharist communicants received both bread and wine by intincture. As in the Eastern Orthodox Church general confession rather than private confession was usually employed, and there was no sacramental use of unction for the sick nor of extreme unction for those at the point of death. Instead there was a ceremony of blessing for the sick. The churches contained crosses, but beyond indigenous peacock devices, no images, and the introduction of statues, after the arrival of the Portuguese, was resisted.

The bishops consecrated altars and ordained priests (referred to as *cathenas*) and deacons (*samasas*). The metropolitan dignity seems to date back to the 8th century and the Patriarch Salibazacha (d. AD 728) and carried with it the title of 'The Metropolitan and Gate of All India'.[134] The metropolitan had oversight over the area, variously described as from Cape Cormorin to the River Indus, and/or the regions which made up the three old kingdoms of the south. There was a number of sees, but the actual number is unclear. There is some evidence that Angamali was the senior see and that it was the training centre for priests, most of whom were content with mastering the Syriac needed in the various liturgies. The more adept among them were trained in the Fathers and the theologians and taught to preach – the sermons sometimes extending to 2–3 hours in length. It appears also that Cranganore was the site of the metropolitan cathedral.[135] While it may be that there were as many as five or six such bishops present in India in AD 1504, there does not appear to have been a native-born Indian in the episcopacy until after the Koonen Cross rupture with Rome in AD 1653. He was Mar Thomas I,

'formally ordained after 12 years of independent rule by Mar Gregory (Jacobite) from Antioch, with whose name . . . Jacobitism in Malabar is associated. Mar Thomas . . . belonged to the family, held in high respect and great veneration as one of the Brahmin families, the members of which are supposed to have been consecrated and ordained as priests by the apostle himself.'[136]

The seniors among the *cathenas* were held in high esteem as the firsts among equals, but a special dignity attached to the office of archdeacon or *arkn*. Always native-born, and drawn from a family like that in the last citation, the archdeacon was referred to by Patriarch Timothy I as 'head of the faithful in India'.[137] The *arkn* was the chief assistant to the bishop and indeed responsible for day to day administration of the Church, which gave him far greater authority than archdeacons elsewhere.

'The archdeacon is considered the chief of priests and figuratively called the hand, tongue, glory, light and son of the bishop. The East-Syrian tradition presents him as the head of the ministry, superintendent of the whole ministry, the superior of every ecclesiastical order, spiritual father and teacher of the faithful, director, visitor and governor of the churches, ecclesiastical judge, the confidential vicar of the pontiff etc. The office is permanent and is conferred for a life-term. His office must be considered higher than that of the vicar general in the Latin Church. But after the sixteenth century, certain modifications in the East-Syrian tradition were gradually introduced under the influence of the Latin tradition.'[138]

There is a tradition that the archdiaconal dignity goes back to the days of Thomas of Cana, and that it was related to the Pakalomattan family, but documentary evidence is lacking.[139] What is clear is that the *arkn* had responsibilities and authority in the civil and social spheres, as well as in that of ecclesiastical administration.[140]

As for the laity they played a significant role in many ways. In the matter of the government of Church affairs, the authority lay with

'a general assembly of the clergy and the laity to deal with matters concerning the whole community.'[141]

While various authorities differ as to detail, it appears also that laymen participated in the reciting of the divine office. In particular,

'on Saturday evenings and Sunday mornings, as also on feast days, all the people gathered in the church to join the priests in the recital of the office; on other days a few attended; the custom might have been different in different localities.'[142]

Somewhat to the chagrin of the Portuguese, the Malabar Christians had no knowledge of, or particular interest in the Roman Church beyond the awareness that the Pope lived in Rome.[143] But apart from the appearance for a short time of some Latin churches in their midst, they had had the field entirely to themselves and were remote from the contentions which marked Christians elsewhere as between Chalcedonians and non-Chalcedonians, between Nestorians and Monophysites, and between Rome and Constantinople. In no way did they regard themselves as schismatics

'because they . . . constantly retained their (apostolic) succession and for centuries had no branch of the true Church co-existent with them in their territories. In all the wide territories occupied by Nestorians there was but "one altar".'[144]

A number of factors point to the fact that the Thomas Christians of India were not concerned much, if at all, by the Christological controversies, which divided their co-religionists to the West.[145] Theological works, along with the Scriptures and liturgy, were in Syriac, a language unknown by more than a few in their ranks (cf. Latin for many in the medieval and later Western Church). In addition they did not include in their heritage the Greek philosophical tradition, so important in the framing of the disputes over Christology. They moved, without hesitation it seems, from relationships with the pre-Nestorian Church in Persia to a long history of such with the Church of the East, which was Nestorian by AD 500. When pressed to conform to post-Tridentine Catholicism by the Synod of Diamper in AD 1599, those who rejected this imposition seem to have had no difficulty in relating themselves to the Jacobite Patriarch of Antioch. Throughout what was crucial was the maintenance of the episcopal succession, and orthopraxy more than doctrinal orthodoxy.

Plate 1 An 18th cent. engraving of Antioch across the Orontes.

Downey, R. E. G.: *A History of Antioch in Syria from Seleucus to the Arab Conquest*, Princeton 1961, fig. 18.

Plate 2 Edessa – looking north from the citadel mount.

Segal, J. B.: *Edessa, 'the Blessed City'*, Oxford 1970, pl. 32a.

Plate 3 Edessa – looking east with the citadel mount to the right.

Segal 1970, pl. 36.

Plate 4 Remains of the pilgrimage site where Simeon Stylites sat on his column.

Meer, F. van der & Mohrmann, Chr.: *Atlas of the Early Christian World*, trans. & ed. by M. F. Hedlund & H. H. Rowley, London 1958, p. 102, pl. 244.

Plate 5 10th cent. monastery in north of present-day Armenia.

Museum Haus Völker und Kulturen, St. Augustin (ed.): *Armenien. Geschichte, sakrale Kunst*, St. Augustin 1983, p. 15, pl. 19.

Plate 6 Remains of the 7th cent. palace church of Catholicos Nerses III of Armenia.

Museum Haus Völker und Kulturen, St. Augustin 1983, p. 12, pl. 6.

Plate 7 Reconstruction of the 7th cent. palace church of Catholicos Nerses III of Armenia.

Museum Haus Völker und Kulturen,
St. Augustin 1983, p. 12, pl. 7.

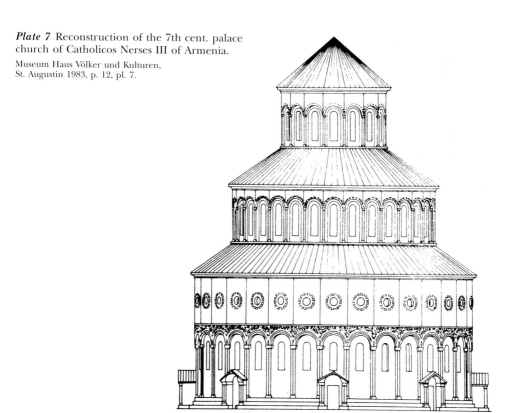

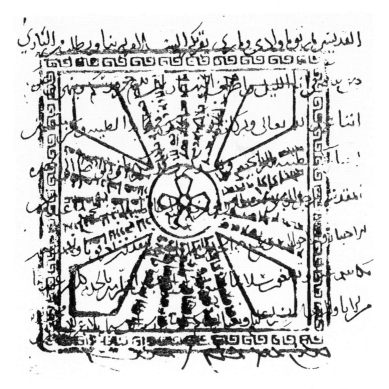

Plate 8 Impression of Seal given by the Mongol Khan Möngke to the Nestorian Patriarch.

Hamilton, J.: 'Le texte turc en caractères syriaques du grand sceau cruciforme de Mār Yahballāhā III', in: *Journal Asiatique* 260 (1972), pp. 155–170, pl. III.

Plate 9 Copper plate charter for Christians in Kerala (South India).

Pothan, S. G.: *The Syrian Christians of Kerala*, London & Bombay 1963, pl. I, opp. p. 32.

Plate 10 Oldest Persian cross with Pahlavi inscriptions at Kottayam.

Frontispiece ex Tisserant, E.: *Eastern Christianity in India. A History of the Syro-Malabar Church from the Earliest Time to the Present Day [. . .]*, authorized adaptation from the French by E. R. Hambye, London 1957.

Plate 11 Cross on altar at Valiyapalli Church, Kottayam (note also peacocks).

Pothan 1963, p. 28, fig. 3.

Plate 12 Carved archway with crosses and peacocks at Kottayam.

Tisserant 1957, pl. IV:1, opp. p. 61.

Plate 15 Pre-Portuguese church in South India, looking toward the east.
Tisserant 1957, pl. II:2, opp. p. 13.

Plate 16 A Syrian church showing a Portuguese facade, near Kottayam.
Pothan 1963, pl. XI, opp. p. 80.

Plate 17 Reverse of a Christian coin from the vicinity of Tashkent, 6th/8th cent. The Nestorian cross is set within a Sasanian ring of pearls.

The State Hermitage Museum, St. Petersburg.

Plate 18 Ostracon with Syriac writing (parts of Psalm 1 & 2) from Pendjikent.

The State Hermitage Museum, St. Petersburg. Cf. Paykova, A. V.: 'The Syrian Ostracon from Panjikant', in: *Le Muséon* 92 (1979), pp. 159–169.

Plate 19 A Sogdian Christian silver vessel, an example of toreutic art, partly gilded, showing the siege of Jericho (Joshua 6). The city is represented by a Sogdian citadel (7th/8th cent.).

The State Hermitage Museum, St. Petersburg.

Plate 20 Sogdian cloth design, showing (in mirror images) Abraham's attempted offering of Isaac (Gen. 22). From the Mosheva Gorge, 6th/8th cent.

The State Hermitage Museum, St. Petersburg.

Plate 21 Sogdian silver vessel with Syrian inscriptions, showing crucifixion, burial and ascension of Christ. 9th/10th cent. copy of a 6th/7th cent. Sasanian silver dish.

The State Hermitage Museum, St. Petersburg.

Plate 22 Sogdian incense burner, with a scene of Christ and the apostles at the Last Supper. From Semiriče, 7th/8th cent.

The State Hermitage Museum, St. Petersburg.

Plate 23 Portion of a Christian (or Manichaean?) relief, with three donors beside a cross surrounded by a border of pearls (Sasanian). Semiriče, 7th/8th cent.

The State Hermitage Museum, St. Petersburg.

Plate 24 Christ with the pose and dress of a Bodhisattva, or a Bodhisattva with a cross ornament? Damaged painting from Tunhuang, 10th cent.

From the Stein Collection, The British Museum, London. Frontispiece ex Saeki, P.Y.: *The Nestorian Documents and Relics in China*, 2nd ed., Tokyo 1951. Cf. also Whitfield, R.: *The Art of Central Asia*, vol. 1: *Paintings from Dunhuang*, Tokyo 1982, pl. 25.

Plate 25 Reconstruction of the above scene by Mr. Furuyama.

Saeki 1951, sketch between pp. 408 & 409.

Plate 26 Nestorian crosses engraved by a Christian traveller on a boulder at Tankse, Ladakh. The Sogdian inscription is dated AD 841/842. The Tibetan inscriptions above and below were added later

Photo by the courtesy of Rev. Yonathan Paljor, Srinagar (Kashmir).

Plate 27 One of the Nestorian crosses at Tankse, beside which is a Sogdian inscription independent the cross. It reads (N. Sims-Williams, 'The Sogdian Inscriptions of Ladakh', in: Jettmar, K. et al. (eds *Antiquities of Northern Pakistan. Reports and Studies*, vol. 2, Mainz 1993, p. 155): 'In the year 210 (i.e. 84 842 A.D.) we (were?) sent – (we, namely) Caitra the Samarkandian together with the monk Nōsh-fa (as) messenger(s) to the Tibetan Qaghan.' On the same boulder, there is an undoubtedly Sogdia Christian inscription that reads: '[I], Uri Tarxan, have come (here) in the name of God.' Cf. Sim Williams, N.: 'Sogdian and Turkish Christians in the Turfan and Tun-huang Manuscripts', in: Cadonna, A. (ed.), *Turfan and Tun-huang. The Texts. Encounter of Civilizations on the Silk Route*, Floren 1992 (Orientalia Venetiana 4), p. 45.

Photo by Rev. Yonathan Paljor, Srinagar (Kashmir).

Plate 28 Sketch by A. Grünwedel of a scene on a mural of the Nestorian church at Kocho, Turfan oasis (9th/10th cent.). Depicted is a Nestorian missionary riding his horse.

Grünwedel, A.: *Altbuddhistische Kultstätten in Chinesisch-Turkistan [. . .]*, Berlin 1912, p. 339, fig. 677.

Plate 29 Scene from a mural painting in the Nestorian church at Kocho, Turfan oasis. A Persian (or Sogdian) priest, with a chalice in his hand, addresses an assembly of two Turks and a Chinese lady.

Le Coq, A. von: *Chotscho [. . .]*, (1913), repr., Graz 1979, pl. 7.

Plate 30 Crosses on bricks at the Buddhist center of Taxila, Gandhara (now Pakistan). The shape of the cross corresponds to one at St. Thomas' Church in Mylapore; cf. pl. 14.

Photo by Prof. Dr. R. Bielmeier, Bern.

Plate 31 Gravestone with Syrian inscription from Semiriče; cross on a lotus set on an altar, flanked by angels in flowing robes. The inscription reads (trans. Wassilios Klein): 'In the year 1613 of Alexander [i.e. AD 1301/1302] the Interpreter-Exegete Nestorius, son of the blessed Karia, went away and departed from this world.'

The State Hermitage Museum, St. Petersburg.

Plate 32 Gravestone with Turkish inscription in Syriac letters, from Semiriče. The inscription reads (trans. Wassilios Klein): 'In the year 167? of Alexander Khan, i.e. the year of the monke [AD 1368/1369]. The blessed lady Constantia . . . departed from this world. May her name b remembered. Amen.'

The State Hermitage Museum, St. Petersburg.

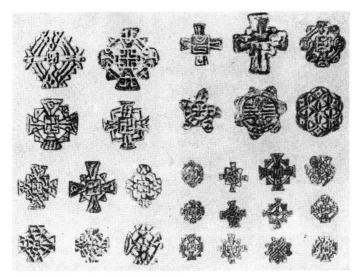

Plate 33 'Ordos crosses', i.e. crosses from the Ordos area in Inner Mongolia (probably Nestorian, from the Yuan Period: 13/14th cent.)
Saeki 1951, p. 424, fig. 11.

Plate 34a Nestorian stone at Sian-fu.
Meer & Mohrmann 1958, p. 162, pl. 611.

Plate 34b Cross on lotus over inscription on Nestorian stone of Sian-fu.

Plate 35 Cross on a lotos throne, based on an altar.

Saeki 1951, p. 436, fig. 21.

Plate 36 Cross on a stylized mountain range (or ocean waves?).

Saeki 1951, p. 437, fig. 23.

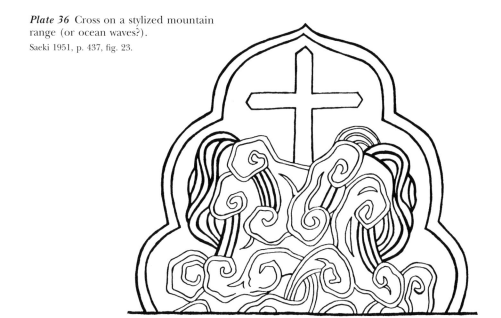

As for classical Nestorianism they imbibed it with the liturgy and via the bishops who came to them. As Tisserant commented:

'Their Nestorianism remained a dead letter in practice, even if their liturgical books contained objectionable formulas.'[146]

While Barbosa may well have exaggerated, in his claim that

'these Christians had not any Christian doctrine amongst them, nor were they baptised, only they held and believed the faith of Christ in a gross manner',[147]

the Portuguese could find no understanding of classical Nestorianism among the Indian Christians. They were more concerned with maintaining age-hallowed customs and simple witness to the incarnate Christ.

'"We", said they, "are of the true faith, whatever you from the West may be, for we come from the place where the followers of Christ were first called Christians."'[148]

So as late as AD 1624, the Archdeacon George, while being ready to admit to errors, is adamant that there was no heresy in their traditional beliefs, thus:

'Errors, perhaps, there might have been, but heresies which have to be confirmed with pertinacity, no.'[149]

If doctrinal heresy as such was not obvious, and the Malabar Christians were oblivious of it anyway, those with heightened theological sensitivity claimed to be able to detect it in liturgical or doxological statements. Mar Aprem provides us with an example in the colophon of a manuscript which dates from AD 1562, viz:

'It was written in the blessed and royal town of Angamalke, in the holy Church of our lady, the blessed Mary, mother of light and life.'[150]

It is clear that the last phrase may well be seen as Nestorian if it is taken to mean that Mary is *Christotokos* (the mother or bearer of Christ who is the life and light of the world) rather than *Theotokos* (the bearer of God). That the dogmaticians may be clear about this is one thing – that the subtleties involved would be clear to the generality of Thomas Christians, both clerical and lay, is by no means apparent.

Due no doubt, in large part, to the relative disinterest in theology in India, Adeney's assessment is probably correct, that the Malabar Christians

'never developed any intellectual energy (sic) or made any contribution to theology'[151] in so far as it relates to dogmatics. On the other hand, as Podipara noted, while

'Thomas Christians have not contributed anything towards the formulation of an Indian Christian theology, they . . . contributed very much in terms of way of life and mode of worship.'[152]

THE IMPACT OF THE PORTUGUESE

On May 27, 1498, Vasco da Gama (d. AD 1524), guided by the Gujerati pilot, Ahmed ibn Majid, reached Calicut. He had made use of the pioneering voyage of Bartholomew Diaz to the Cape of Good Hope in AD 1488, and was well served by his pilot in reaching India from Malindi on the east coast of Africa. There is of course a sense of this arrival being the terminus ad quem of this study, but, as we have discovered already, it is impossible to cut off the history of the Christians in Kerala with the arrival of the Portuguese at Calicut. So, over the 16th century, we will explore a number of the aspects of inter-relationships between these Christians with their long history and the first of those Western Europeans with whom they were destined to be involved for centuries to come.

Of course contact with the Portuguese after da Gama was not the first experience of Europeans by the Thomas Christians – see e.g. pp. 167ff. above. But da Gama arrived under a somewhat different set of circumstances and with different presuppositions. He was a representative of the enterprise begun by the famous Prince Henry the Navigator (d. AD 1460), through which the crusade against Islam was to be continued with sail, cannon and trade. Instrumental in this was to be the work of the Order of Christ, a Portuguese parallel to the Knights Templar, along with improvements to sailing vessels, and the desire to further humble the Muslims, the last of which in Spain, at Granada, had been conquered by Ferdinand and Isabella in AD 1492.

Following his acquisition of the Azores in AD 1440 and attaining the Cape Verde Islands in the next year, Prince Henry received in AD 1454 from Pope Nicholas V (d. AD 1455) a Bull, 'Romanus Pontifex', which granted to the ruler of Portugal the right to rule over all discoveries up to India. This was to be confirmed in AD 1456 in a second Bull, 'Inter Caetera', issued by Pope Calixtus III (d. AD 1458), neither pope having any problem about determining the status of untold numbers of Africans, Asians and Indians. As far as the Portuguese were concerned these documents were of divine authority, coming as they did from succeeding Vicars of Christ on earth. That of AD 1454 ran as follows:

'Our joy is immense to know that our dear son, Henry, Prince of Portugal, following the footsteps of his father of illustrious memory,

King John, inspired with a zeal for souls like an intrepid soldier of Christ, has carried into the most distant and unknown countries the name of God and has brought into the Catholic fold the perfidious enemies of God and of Christ, such as the Saracens and the Infidels.

After having established Christian families in some of the unoccupied islands of the Ocean and having consecrated churches there for the celebration of Holy Mysteries the Prince, remembering that never within the memory of man had anyone been known to navigate the sea to the distant shores of the Orient, believed that he could give God the best evidence of his submission, if by his effort the Ocean can be made navigable as far as India, which, it is said, is already subject to Christ. If he enters into relations with these people, he will induce them to come to the help of the Christians of the West against the enemies of the faith. At the same time, he will bring under submission, with the King's permission, the pagans of the countries not yet afflicted with the plague of Islam and give them knowledge of the name of Christ.

It is thus that during the last twenty-five years that without the support of the armies of Portugal, but in the midst of the greatest perils and faced by the greatest trials, he in his fast caravels, searched without repose the meridianal regions to the Antarctic pole across the oceans, and after having traversed numerous seas reached at last the province of Guinea and from there pushed further to the mouth of the river commonly known as the Nile (sic).

We, after careful deliberation, and having considered that we have by our apostolic letters conceded to King Affonso, the right, total and absolute, to invade, conquer and subject all the countries which are under rule of the enemies of Christ, Saracen or pagan, by our apostolic letter we wish the same King Affonso, the Prince, and all their successors, occupy and possess in exclusive rights the said islands, ports and seas undermentioned, and all faithful Christians are prohibited without the permission of the said Affonso and his successors to encroach on their sovereignty. Of the conquests already made, or to be made, all the conquests which extend to Cape Bajador and Cape Non to the coast of Guinea and all the Orient is perpetually and for the future the sovereignty of King Affonso.'[153]

To these bulls was added the Treaty of Tordesilhas, of June 9, 1494, signed between Spain and Portugal and foreshadowed by Pope Alexander VI (d. AD 1503). In effect it divided the world into spheres of influence and control along a line drawn north and south 370 leagues west of the Cape Verde Islands (and correspondingly through the yet to be entered Pacific Ocean). Areas to the east of the Atlantic line were to come under Portugal, and those to the west under Spain – following the discoveries of Columbus.[154]

The Bull of AD 1454 indicated the pope's belief that . . . 'India . . . is already subject to Christ.' Here we have a reflection of the belief that there was a great Christian ruler in India (see pp. 182f. above), usually identified with the fabled 'Prester John'. So da Gama took with him a letter to 'Prester John' and one to the Raja of Calicut, the latter being the only likely recipient as matters turned out. We do not know what da Gama's expectations were about the Christians he anticipated meeting in India, beyond that they were believed to be numerous indeed. In this he was to be disappointed, as he was about finding 'the illustrious Emperor of the Indians – the beloved Son of Christ'. However, he must have been ready to accept that Christian ways were different from those in Portugal, when he visited a Hindu temple and took it to be a Christian Church in which he could readily say his prayers.[155]

That these ideas about the potential of an anti-Muslim alliance between the Kings of Portugal and India persisted is shown in the letters entrusted to Pedro Cabral (d. AD 1526), who led the second fleet to India in AD 1500 and stayed on the Malabar coast until AD 1501. It seems that because the Muslims regarded the Hindus of Calicut as 'infidels', the Portuguese thought that the epithet, so frequently applied to Christians in their experience, indicated that they and the Hindus shared the same faith. Following hostilities with the Muslims at Calicut, Cabral sailed south to Cochin where he did meet some Thomas Christians and came to recognise the previous misapprehensions.

'After the return of Cabral to Portugal we do not hear anything about the Christians of Calicut or elsewhere, but we do have accounts of the Christians of the Malabar coast, south of Calicut.'[156]

Whatever the religious and crusading motivations there were others of immediate concern and lasting influence. Carlo Cipolla summed up the situation thus:

'When Vasco da Gama dropped anchor in the harbour of Calicut, a native asked what the Portuguese were looking for in Asia. The answer of da Gama allegedly was "Christians and spices". Bernal Diaz speculating about the motives that had driven him and his like to the Indies, wrote that they had left Europe "to serve God and his Majesty, to give light to those who were in the darkness and to grow rich as all men desire to do". Through the idea of mission and crusade the conquistadors succeeded where the medieval merchants failed and were able to reconcile the antithesis between business and religion that had plagued the conscience of medieval Europe. One has no reason to doubt the sincerity of their statements, but one may wonder about their realism and the validity of their rationalizations. That the Europeans were more often than not imbued with religious zeal and intolerance is a fact that does not need to be proven. But it is doubtful whether the religious element was as relevant among the motives that drove people overseas as it was among the forces that helped them once they were there. Religious convictions nourished boldness in battle, endurance through ordeals, truculence after victory. But, missionaries apart, when the Europeans undertook the perilous journey, they were dreaming more about Mammon than about lost souls to enlighten. Ogier Ghiselin de Busbecq, the sixteenth century diplomat, was an inveterate pessimist, but he cannot have been far from the truth when he wrote that for the "expeditions [to the Indies and the Antipodes] religion supplies the pretext and gold the motive".'[157]

Or as C. R. Boxer pointed out there is no gainsaying the force of the attraction of the wealth from spices in keeping the Portuguese involved, whatever the impetus provided initially by religious fervour.[158]

So, on one hand, the Portuguese expectations about probable Christian allies in India needed considerable modification once they were established there, along with their presuppositions that those under their suzerainty would or should behave as Christians did in Portugal. On the other hand religious issues tended to be left aside as commercial prospects beckoned – and in any case the Thomas Christians could call on up to 25,000 soldiers, and needed to be handled with care, in the early decades. No more than they were interested in dialogue with Hindus or Buddhists on the basis of study of their sacred texts – all of which could be seen as works of the devil – were the Portuguese overly concerned with evangelism or the peculiarities, from their viewpoint, of the Thomas Christians.

From the side of the latter there were also presuppositions. Secure in their long tenure within the Christian faith in India, they did not feel threatened at first by the Portuguese. In fact they welcomed them as co-religionists whose aid might well be important in protecting them against Muslim pressure and in securing for them their age long status and rights in Hindu society. So in November 1502 a delegation approached da Gama, during his second expedition, having brought from Cranganore the staff which he took to be a royal sceptre (see p. 182 above). From the report of the incident it would appear that they were ready to accept Portuguese overlordship in return for guarantees of their rights and a fortress in their midst. In due course they may have had good cause to wonder about this, as the Muslims reacted violently to the Portuguese disruption of their monopoly of the spice trade. So by AD 1505 the Muslims attacked Quilon, and, inter alia, burnt the church of the Thomas Christians, within which some 400 of that group had taken refuge, only to perish.

However, initially the hopes of the Indian Christians remained that they would have Portuguese support and maintain their own ecclesiastical identity, including their relationship with the Church of the East. These hopes are revealed in a letter to Persia from the bishops who arrived there in India in AD 1503–1504.

> 'May you also know, Fathers, that from the Occident powerful ships have been sent to these countries of India by the king of the Christians, who are our brethren, the Franks. Their voyage took them a whole year, and they sailed first towards the south and circumnavigated Kush, which is called Habesh. From there they came to this country of India, purchased pepper and other merchandise and returned to their land. By this way thus explored the said king (whom may God preserve in safety) sent six other huge ships, with which they crossed the sea in a half year and came to the town of Calicut, people extremely well-versed in nautical science.'[159]

The letter followed with an account of how the Muslims at Calicut prevailed upon the ruler to deal with the threat represented by Cabral, thus:

> 'The pagan king believed the words of the Ismaelites and followed their advice and went out like a madman and killed all the said Franks, whom they found in the town, seventy men and five worthy priests, who accompanied them, for they are not wont to travel or to go to any place without priests.'

We gain further insights into the attitudes towards the Portuguese from the bishops' account of their meeting with the latter at Cannanore.

> 'Of his people [of the Christian leader from Portugal] there are about 20 living in the town of Cannanore. When we started from the town of Hormizda [Ormuz] and came to this town of the Indians, Cannanore, we made them understand, that we were Christians and indicated to them our condition. We were received by them with the greatest joy and they gave us beautiful vestments and 20 gold drachmas and honoured our pilgrimage exceedingly for Christ's sake. We remained with them two and half months and they told us, we also should on a certain day celebrate the holy mysteries, that is to say, offer the Holy Sacrifice. And they destined for it a beautiful place fit for prayer, wherein there was a kind of oratory. Their priests offer daily the Holy Sacrifice, for this is their custom and rite.
>
> Therefore on Sunday Nosardel [the seventh day after Pentecost] after their priests had celebrated we also were admitted and celebrated the Holy Sacrifice, and it was pleasing in their eyes.

Sailing from there we went to our Christians, who are distant from there an eight days' voyage. The number of the said Franks is estimated at about 400 men. And the fear and dread of them fell on all infidels and Ismaelites of these countries. The country of these Franks is called Portkal, one of the countries of the Franks, and their king is called Emmanuel. We beseech Emmanuel that he may conserve him.'[160]

This section may be concluded with the words of Mar Jacob, one of these four bishops, who was to guide destinies of the Christians of St. Thomas during the first 50 years of their new era. He wrote a booklet containing a small calendar of feasts in the colophon of which he says:

'. . . in the above mentioned year (1504) we arrived in these Indian countries at the town called Cannanore in which we found our Christian brethren in truth, the Franks called the Portuguese . . . .'[161]

There is nothing here which may be taken even to imply that there was any perceived danger of imposed Catholic uniformity on the Thomas Christians, led, as they were, by their own bishops. The leader who emerged here was Mar Jacob, while a prominent early Indian priest was Joseph, the priest in charge of the Church at Cranganore. He had journeyed to Babylon in AD 1490, and sailed to Europe with Cabral in AD 1501. There he spent months in Portugal, Rome and Venice, before returning to India.

In the first two decades of contact, relations between the Portuguese and the Thomas Christians were cordial. In part this was due to problems of communication and to the very 'busyness' of the Portuguese, who had not come prepared for evangelism or proselytising. In addition there was no co-ordination of Portuguese religious work until the arrival of the first vicar-general in AD 1514, and even then the office changed hands six times in the subsequent 28 years, the second being described

'as more a trader than a priest; about another, John Pacheco, the Bishop of Dume remarks that he had "poisoned the entire christianity by his vile life and example". Sebastião Pires, who is otherwise well-known for his pious zeal, was not completely blameless. A number of misappropriations by him came to light in the course of judicial inquiry.'[162]

On the other hand while the records are silent about Mar John and Mar Jaballaha after AD 1505, they do testify to the continued leadership of Mar Jacob, assisted by the younger Mar Denha, among the Indians.

If the Portuguese had begun to detect what they regarded as imperfections in the liturgies of the Indians, there seems to have been no awareness of such among the latter in these first decades. At the same time there was no lack of awareness of their own failings among the Portuguese.

Gonçalo Fernandes, a high official, wrote to the king:

> "'I do not know where else can be found such a vile clergy and friars as come here. I say this on account of the wicked deeds which they commit, their ignorance of their duties, their knavery in the confessional, and the contaminated, beastly, filthy and dissolute life of many of them ... which is scandal alike to the faithful, catechumens and non-Christians."

The above statement appears to be far too pessimistic and exaggerated to be believed. But the Bishop of Dume seems to be much closer to the truth when after his visit to India in 1523 he reported:

> "As to the clergy and friars, who reside outside the monasteries, they are for the most part very corrupt, and their bad example is the cause of the loss of devotion among the native Christians."'[163]

One common concern for Portuguese and Thomas Christians was the reputed tomb of the Apostle Thomas at Mylapore. The interest of the Portuguese king had been aroused as early as AD 1505, possibly through the visit to Portugal of the priest Joseph from Cranganore. Various Portuguese visited the tomb between AD 1507 and 1514 and it was clear by AD 1516 that urgent repairs were needed. Further visits followed in 1517 and 1521, including a joint party of Portuguese and Indians, but it was AD 1523, despite royal interest, before work began on a church and the tomb. Some Portuguese settled there in AD 1519 and by the time of Francis Xavier's visit in AD 1545 their numbers had reached 100. But it is significant, while hardly surprising, that they had named the site, San Thome.[164] This use of a Portuguese rendering of the name of Saint Thomas was symbolic of the developing attitude of the Europeans to the Indian Christians.

One of the first to make this obvious, and indeed the first of whom we know that he called the Thomas Christians, Nestorians, was Father Alvaro Penteado, who reached Goa in AD 1511, and began a career in India marked with zeal but marred by tactlessness. Coming to India of his own accord, he worked in Goa and Hormuz at first, and from AD 1516 at Cranganore for several months. In the absence of the regular priest on a visit to Mylapore, Penteado won some local support for a while. However:

> 'It is beyond doubt that Penteado did all this without any regard for the rights of the local clergy and hierarchy. It was a sort of usurpation which had the approval of the Portuguese authorities. Here we observe that these authorities treated the St. Thomas Christians as if the latter were already subjects of the King of Portugal. Perhaps they

thought they were justified in doing so because of the incident of AD 1503 when these Christians manifested their Christian solidarity with the Portuguese and made certain commitments to Vasco da Gama. But . . . the St. Thomas Christians had never meant that the incident should be interpreted and used in that way.'[165]

Such moves led to guarded actions by the Thomas Christians, and to some extent they succeeded in keeping the Portuguese at arm's length. It was becoming increasingly clear that uniformity, along Roman Catholic lines, was the aim of the Portuguese, and that would involve severing the link with the Church of the East. Both uniformity and such severance were opposed by many among the Thomas Christians. While Mar Jacob could see a number of advantages to be gained by association with the Portuguese, his younger colleague, Mar Denha, was far less enthusiastic.

Mar Jacob seems to have been targetted by Father Penteado who persuaded the Portuguese King Manuel I to use a subsidy to wean the Indian metropolitan away from Babylon. He pointed to problems in having only Portuguese priests conduct all baptisms and gave it as his considered opinion that:

> 'In the mean time the task of the Latin priests would be to instruct the Christians in matters concerning faith. Thus they, after having become acquainted with those priests, would receive them to work in the place of Mar Jacob. That would remedy everything and it would be of the greatest service to God, to Whom the bishop commended the king. . . . He felt they should deal with the St. Thomas Christians tactfully by not interfering with their way of life, their ecclesiastical and social customs and practices, their way of administering the sacraments and their form of liturgy etc. All the necessary reforms could be effected and abuses corrected, but gradually and tactfully.'[166]

In his approach Mar Jacob was supported by the Dominican João Caro, who persuaded the metropolitan to have the Thomas Christians trade their pepper crop directly with the Portuguese after AD 1522, in place of the traditional Muslim agents – a step which was not always to the growers' financial advantage as it turned out. It also led to further punitive Muslim incursions against Christians and their churches and homes in AD 1524, but it was an earnest aspect of Mar Jacob's desire for good relations.

This was not enough for Penteado whose aim of uniformity had still to be achieved. He returned as priest-in-charge at Mylapore in AD 1524, but aroused opposition from among the Portuguese laity there, as well as among the Indian Christians. He switched his focus to Cochin, and, while he found Mar Jacob co-operative to a degree, he made no headway with Mar Denha. The younger bishop was held in high esteem by his people who grew so to detest Penteado that Mar Jacob was unable to take him along as a companion on his visitations. Unpopular also with many of the Portuguese officers and with a reputation for 'a hard head and a very hot temper',[167] Penteado was back in Portugal in AD 1533. He had succeeded only in sowing seeds of suspicion about and antipathy towards the Portuguese ecclesiastics, which some like Father Caro had to attempt to overcome.

Mar Jacob was not without support among his people, and had the backing of the Franciscans as he baptised and married with Latin rites. These he saw as an improvement but the situation was uneasy, and conformity was found in the main in coastal centres open to Portuguese pressure. The metropolitan's position was not made any more palatable to his flock by the attitude of King John III in regarding him as a subject bishop and giving

> 'the charge of the St. Thomas Christians to the East Syrian bishop, as if they were his subjects in some way or other. Further, he orders the bishop to give an account of his ministry to his representative'[168] – the governor!

Mar Denha's fears that he would be exiled grew during a year's confinement with the Franciscans in Goa in AD 1534, when it seemed the aim was to transfer him to Hormuz. He escaped and found refuge among his people in the interior of Kerala beyond the reach of the Portuguese. However, by AD 1536 he had a change of heart, and, if handled sensitively, became co-operative, and this over a considerable period for as a letter to the king in AD 1550 from Matthew Dias had it:

> 'The two Babylonians . . . now . . . no longer do anything after the Babylonian custom, and they are very honest.'[169]

In part this new co-operation was due to a number of developments in the situation. In AD 1538 the first Catholic Bishop of Goa, João de Albuquerque arrived, and in AD 1542 Francis Xavier and the Jesuits came to bring a new seriousness and earnestness into Portuguese efforts. Then too between AD 1538 and AD 1552 the Turks tried to break the Portuguese maritime control over the Arabian Sea, and failed. However,

> 'the Turkish advance in Mesopotamia, Arabia, Egypt and Abyssinia cut off the communications between the Eastern Churches and that of Europe. . . . Mar Jacob saw no other way of providing his Christians, than to put them under the protection of the Portuguese and their bishop in Goa, and his Latin missionaries, to take care of them after his and his companion's death.'[170]

Within Kerala itself the most important development was the foundation in AD 1541 of the College of Santiago (sic) in Cranganore, under

Vincente de Lagos F.M. (d. AD 1552). The College set out comprehensively to Latinise its pupils, much to the resentment of a number of the parents who resented the disparagement of the old ways. Highly regarded by both Jesuits and Franciscans the graduates of the college were more generally acceptable to the Portuguese than to Indians, so that in AD 1604 Roz could report

'that not even one trained in it had worked . . . among the St. Thomas Christians as long as he was there.'

In short, as Mundadan concludes:

'The college was a success in the sense that it produced many well-trained and good Latin priests from the community of St. Thomas Christians. But it failed miserably in its ultimate purpose, namely, of influencing the community of St. Thomas Christians through these latinized priests and of "converting" them to the acceptance of Latin customs, jurisdiction and Rite.'[171]

Completely ignored by the College, Mar Jacob retired to Cochin in AD 1542, dying in AD 1552, much esteemed by all, including Francis Xavier who died in Macao in the same year. The fate of Mar Denha is unknown, but it was clear that he became the butt of attacks on Nestorianism among the Indian Christians.[172] In any case a report of AD 1547 declared that there had been no Syrian bishops in Malabar for four years. Portuguese hopes of complete uniformity arose in consequence.

They suffered something of a set back when there arrived in Goa in AD 1555, (accompanied by two Dominicans) two bishops, Mar Elias and Mar Joseph, who had been consecrated by the Chaldean (Uniate) Patriarch Abdiso. To say the least they were not welcomed with open arms, and were denied entry into the Malabar region for more than a year. In part this resulted from one of those disputes between religious orders and the nations represented over jurisdictional authority in key locations, which were to hinder Catholic endeavours in India as in Japan. While Mar Joseph is reputed to have introduced auricular confession, confirmation and extreme unction into the Indian Churches he was regarded as suspect, and as a threat to their unfettered control by the Portuguese. So no less than twice he was despatched to Rome for examination, but was acquitted of heresy on each occasion, returning to his disputed ministry in India.

During the first of these absences in Europe the Malabar Christians resorted to the old methods of filling a vacancy in the episcopate and approached the Nestorian Patriarch of the Church of the East, Mar Simon bar Denha. He consecrated and sent to them Mar Abraham in AD 1557. The reaction of the Portuguese was hardly sympathetic. As Nunes Barreto put it, in AD 1558 he met 'two "Armenian" bishops, one of whom was in many ways Catholic (in all probability Mar Joseph), who desired to keep the Catholic faith, and the other was of the Nestorian sect (most probably Mar Abraham who entered Kerala before Mar Joseph). Both needed instruction and belief "in the principal articles of our holy faith": the first because he was in "Syria" and brought up among heretics, and although obedient to the Roman Church yet needed understanding of what to hold and what to reject; the second, because he was still in his "errors".'[173]

Mar Abraham was arrested and, like Mar Joseph before him, sent to Rome for examination. Thence he returned in AD 1565 with papal authority to divide the jurisdiction with Mar Joseph. By then, i.e. from AD 1560, the Inquisition was established at Goa at the request of Francis Xavier and in addition Goa itself had become a metropolitan Latin see in AD 1558. On top of that the Roman Church was about to adopt Tridentine attitudes, following the conclusion of the Council of Trent in AD 1563.

Faced with such scrutiny, not least from the Jesuits, Mar Abraham had to tread warily. Catholic sensitivities had been sharpened by the challenge of Protestantism, and the Jesuits were at the forefront of the Catholic Reformation and the Counter Reformation. After AD 1567 Tridentine attitudes were felt increasingly and three major policies were adopted:

'1 All religions other than the orthodox Roman Catholic faith as defined at the Council of Trent were intrinsically wrong and harmful in themselves.

2 The Crown of Portugal had the inescapable duty of spreading the Roman Catholic faith, and the secular power of the State could be used to support the spiritual power of the Church.

3 Conversion must not be made by force, "for nobody comes to Christ by faith unless he is drawn by the heavenly Father with voluntary love and prevenient grace."'[174]

'Heathen' temples in Portuguese enclaves were closed or destroyed, and difficulties placed in the way of non-Christian pilgrims and the celebration of non-Christian marriages. While the Thomas Christians were spared these indignities, they were acutely aware of the intransigent attitudes of those convinced that they had all the truth, and the responsibility to ensure its recognition by others. That those not of the Tridentine outlook, who considered themselves well and truly part of the Holy, Catholic and Apostolic Church, might be tempted to describe the approach as little more than 'Latin arrogance', was understandable.

However, in Kerala and Goa it was part and parcel of the conditions of life within which Mar Abraham continued his ministry. In AD 1572 he wrote to Pope Gregory XIII (d. AD 1585) professing the orthodoxy of his beliefs, a move he apparently thought necessary in the year of the accession of that pope. He held his own synod in AD 1583 and would only attend that at Goa in AD 1585 if his freedom was guaranteed. In return, the Jesuit Francis Roz (d. AD 1624) was assigned to him as counsellor, 'supervisor' and successor. While he clearly repudiated Nestorianism, Mar Abraham wished

> 'to preserve his oriental identity and his Chaldean rite, liturgy and canon law; in AD 1590 he refused to ordain the seminarians of the Jesuit seminary of Vaipicotta in the Latin rite.'[175]

Under suspicion for Nestorianism he was facing further examination when he died in AD 1597, leaving administration in the hands of Archdeacon George. His 'colleague', Roz, recorded his impressions of Mar Abraham, suspecting him of heresy, while recognizing that, unlike some others, the bishop was aware of both orthodox and Nestorian doctrines. He regarded the Syriac New Testament used by Mar Abraham and the Thomas Christians as corrupt in a number of places when put alongside the Vulgate as approved by Trent. The bishop was accused of cleaving to Nestorianism's christological texts as expounded by Theodore of Mopsuestia, Diodore of Tarsus, Nestorius and others. The absence of the sacraments of confirmation and unction was deplored, along with clerical marriage and the consumption by the clergy of too much palm wine. As for Mar Abraham himself he was further accused of dishonesty and of temporising about the correction of abuses.

> 'He pretends to be holy and just, Roz continued, but one should look at his works, he should be removed from his office because of heresy.'[176]

In the year of Mar Abraham's death there arrived a new Archbishop of Goa, Alexis de Menezes, an Augustinian. He resolved to bring matters to a head and to complete the Latinisation of the Malabar Christian Church. To this end, inter alia, the new archbishop overrode the objections of the archdeacon and ordained priests to serve among the Indian congregations. As well as that the caste structure was to be assailed and replaced, and a more critical attitude adopted towards Hinduism – ignoring the centuries-long experience of the Indian Christians in this matter. A consequence of action in this area was that Christianity was untenable for the higher castes, and became increasingly identified with lower castes.

> 'The new converts were never reckoned equal to the Thomas Christians. They were not permitted to have free social contact with the Thomas Christians.'[177]

The problem of Christianity and caste was exacerbated.

A synod was convoked for Diamper (Udayamperur) in June AD 1599, the proceedings of which were to be conducted in Portuguese. In a synod of more than 800 members, with four laymen to each cleric, over six days a comprehensive series of measures were enacted (albeit never confirmed in Rome), among which were the institution of the sacraments of confirmation, penance, extreme unction and marriage; the acceptance of transubstantiation and communion in one kind only; the doctrine of purgatory; the practice of clerical celibacy; the acknowledgment of papal supremacy and the according to the Virgin Mary of the veneration due to her as 'Theotokos'. Suspect documents, suspect because of their Nestorian content, were to be destroyed or purged of what was offensive to Rome, the last provision applying also to the Syriac Scriptures.[178] By June 26, AD 1599 the Church of the Thomas Christians, related to the patriarch of the Church of the East for over a millennium, had ostensibly ceased to exist as a discrete group. Their old traditions of spontaneous adaptability were also undercut.

That the issue was not settled at the grass roots level is clear from the actions of Francis Roz, who in AD 1599 was appointed Bishop of Angamali. This diocese was viewed by the Portuguese as a suffragan see to the Latin metropolitan see of Goa. While this broke the connection to the patriarch of the Church of the East, with respect to the consecration of bishops for the Malabar Christians, Bishop Roz thought it unwise to live at Angamali. He resided at Cranganore under the protection of Portuguese cannon, deeming the latter as necessary for his safety. It is significant also that at Cranganore he was on the coast and remote from those of the interior who remained true to the old ways.

Resentment against imposed Latin uniformity continued as is clear from the events of AD 1652–1654, with the arrival of a monk named Gabriel from the Middle East, his arrest by the Portuguese at Mylapore and his eventual execution at Goa in AD 1654. Also in AD 1652 there was the report that a bishop named Ahatalla had been sent to them by the Jacobite Patriarch, but had been intercepted and arrested by the Portuguese. This incident precipitated disruption within the Church, described in this way by Stephen Neill:

> 'A great gathering was held before the Koonen cross at Mattancerri; the Thomas Christians swore to expel the Jesuits, and to submit to no ecclesiastical authority other than that of the archdeacon until they should receive a bishop from an Eastern Church. At a later meeting on May 22, 1653, the archdeacon was consecrated as bishop by the laying on of the hands of twelve priests, the best form of consecration they could devise in the absence of a bishop.'[179]

The schism thus sealed was the consequence of the insensitive presumptions of the Portuguese, who must bear the primary responsibility. It involved some 50% of the Indian Christians, has never been healed, and indeed more divisions were to follow. These take us well beyond the time limits we have set ourselves in this study, but it is clear that one consequence of the arrival of Western Christians was the division of a group which had had at least 1200 years of single existence. It is a prime example of what may be produced by that sense of superior orthodoxy which the Portuguese imposed on fellow Christians, whose lineage in the faith was at least as long as their own.

RETROSPECT

We have traced in some detail the story of the Christians in India to AD 1653. In looking back over this remarkable story of a staunch minority faith in a culture noted for its ability to absorb newcomers, we could do worse than note with W. W. Hunter, that it

> 'had its origins in the period when Buddhism was still triumphant; it witnessed the birth of the Hinduism which superseded the doctrine and natural polity of Buddha; it saw the arrival of the Muslims, who ousted the Hindu dynasties; it suffered cruelly from the Roman Catholic inquisitors of the Portuguese; but it . . . survived its persecutors.'[180]

That on the whole they enjoyed considerable freedom of religion is clear, and overall they were free from Muslim depredations of the sort which destroyed their mother Church in Persia. This bred a sort of quiescence, which jars somewhat with the values of activistic Westerners, but was very much in the spirit of the society of which they were a respected part for centuries.

> 'The Christians were satisfied with their decorous ritual, respect-ability in the eyes of the people of the land, and occasional contacts with the Churches of Eastern Christendom. The social status which this Church had acquired . . . had the effect of giving it something of the character of a caste. The Church had no experience of persecution which might have taught it the need of qualities that were deeper and more vital.'[181]

That judgment by an Indian may be balanced with that of a European who served the Church in India:

> 'They were Christians of Mesopotamia in faith and worship and ethic; they were Indians in all else. In church they professed belief in one Almighty God, out of church they observed omens and propitious days and were content to recognize the existence of Hindu gods, though they did not worship them.

Perhaps two chief factors contributed to this modus vivendi. On the one hand the Syrians had an intense pride of race and tradition, summed up in their claim to St. Thomas as their apostle, which made them exclusive. On the other hand, the unit in Hindu society was the caste, and the Christian desire to continue as a separate closed community was to the non-Christians not only acceptable but inevitable. Hindus expected the Christians to conform to the general conventions which governed caste society and would not have understood it at all if the Christians had practised evangelism, a means of adding to one's own community entirely unknown among Hindus. Western Christians, beginning with Menezes, could not accept this compromise, and tried to arouse an evangelistic spirit in the Christians. ... Although the cultus was foreign and in an unknown tongue it did keep the community, all down the ages, authentically and deeply Christian. The centre of community life was the parish church, where Sunday by Sunday all the people gathered to see the drama of redemption and Christ's reign in glory shown forth even if they could not understand the words of the service. The people lived through the events of Christ's life as the special ceremonies of the Christian year were observed in cycle, and all the great occasions of their lives were pointed with purpose in the Church. But the cult had an ethical fruit. There are many European witnesses, from Gouvea onwards, to the very high moral standard of the St. Thomas Christians in business dealings and in family relationships. The history of the community points to the freedom with which a culture can be accepted by Christians, provided that the dominant factor in their lives is the worship of God through the Incarnate Son. The importance of a liturgy expressing and impressing the facts and meaning of God's acts in Christ and bringing every time of life to its hallowing by God cannot be over-emphasized. It is a matter for speculation how much vitality would have been added had the Indian Church received at an early stage the Scriptures in its own tongue, as its Syrian mother had done.

There seems no doubt that it was the cultus which enabled the St. Thomas Christians to remain authentically Christian down the ages.'[182]

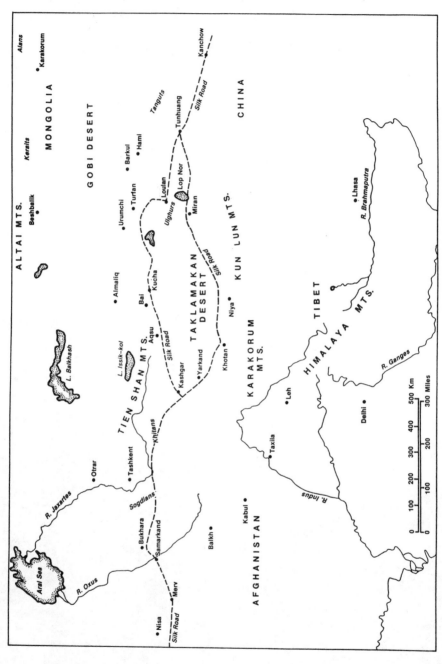

Map 6 Central Asia

Chapter 9

Christians in Central Asia

CENTRAL ASIA AS THE SCENE OF NESTORIAN EXPANSION

As it has no current national boundaries, it may be helpful to describe Central Asia as the wide expanse of land between East Iran and China, a vast area of steppes, mountains and deserts, interspersed with lush river valleys and green oases on the edge of or in the midst of vast wastelands. Through these valleys and oasis towns led paths and tracks in a wide system of interlaced routes. The more important ones led from west to east, this being the direction of the main mountain ranges, but there were also paths connecting these west-east routes at various points, and running from south to north. Since the first centuries AD, trade was conducted along these routes, which were referred to overall as the 'Silk Route'. This was because of the importance of the Chinese silk that was transported along these paths from the 'Middle Kingdom' of China to India, Persia, Western Asia (the Near East) and even Rome.

In the West, it was Byzantium that had contact with areas as remote as the Mongolian steppes, where the Turks made their appearance in history in the 6th century. The Old Turkish inscriptions from the Orkhon river valley, dating from the 7th–9th centuries, testify to the far-reaching contacts of that remote area with various foreign peoples. In one text we hear that at a memorial service for a Turkish Prince, Kül, not only other Central Asian leaders, but also Chinese, Tibetan, Sogdian, Persian and even Byzantine dignitaries were present.[1] In contrast to Tibet, which due to its geographical situation lived in relative isolation (although there were strong contacts with India and China), Central Asia north of the Tibetan highlands was always open to influences from the east and the west.

Certainly trade and commerce played a decisive role in establishing and maintaining such contacts, but together with traders and merchants, political envoys and soldiers, monks and missionaries of the great world religions (Buddhism, Manichaeism and Christianity) also trod the paths of the Silk Route. They spread their teachings from India, Persia and Syria to peoples in Central Asia and China. Hence those engaged in propagating the Christian message were in contact with the promoters of these other religions, of which Buddhism turned out to be the most successful prior to the appearance of Islam. One could almost speak of a Christian-Buddhist dialogue being conducted in Central Asia 1000 years ago, Christians and Buddhists not only living together, but being in constant interaction. Islam, the great rival to Christianity, made considerable advances in West Turkestan in the 7th and 8th centuries and spread into East Turkestan from the 10th to the 15th centuries. Yet Christianity, mainly in its Nestorian form, remained alive up to the 14th century.

In the eastern part of Central Asia, in the Mongolian steppes and the Kansu corridor, Buddhism proved to be a dominating force. In its midst as well as in the midst of shamanistic areas, Christian communities flourished at times when contact with the Patriarch in Baghdad could be upheld. However, in times when such contact was not possible, they were left to themselves, and this isolated situation endangered their existence repeatedly, up to the point where they dwindled in the wake of Islamic self-assertion at the time of Timur the Lame (AD 1370–1405).

Hence the geographical region traversed by Christian messengers of the faith was vast. It included various cultural areas. There was first the East Iranian plateau, giving way to the rugged mountainous area of Afghanistan in the east. This was the region south and north of the Hindukush range and its outskirts. This great divide between the southern and the northern part, of what was long known as Bactria to the Greeks, was not only a barrier but also a bridge between the southern and the northern portion of that country. There were important routes leading over the mountain passes and connecting the cities south of the range with those to its north. We notice that major centres of Christianity spreading to the east lay on both sides of the range, for instance in Herat to the south, and Balkh, the ancient capital of Bactria, to the north.

The area north of the East Iranian plateau, the Turanian lowlands, was accessible from points in eastern Iran like Abarshar. This was one of the major centres from which routes led to cities in those lowlands as well as in Bactria. A city of major importance in those plains was Merv, present Mary in Turkmenistan, a significant cultural centre of the East Iranian Parthians even in Sasanian times (AD 224–650). Beside Merv, there was Nisa, likewise a Parthian city. Yet Merv, due to its central geographical position, attracted the envoys of the world religions in a special manner, for from here routes led to the cities south and north of the Oxus as well as to towns west of the Pamirs and their western extensions.

The area north of the Oxus (Amu Darya), Transoxania, extending to the valley of the Yaxartes (Syr Darya), was, at the time of Christian expansion, populated by diverse peoples. Major cities like Bukhara and Samarkand were inhabited by Sogdians, an East Iranian race that took advantage of its strategic position between Iran and areas further east by wide-reaching commerce. Sogdian traders had a string of settlements on the Central Asian routes leading to China and Mongolia. The old Turkish inscriptions referred to above tell of Sogdian colonies amongst the Turks in the Mongolian steppes, and Sogdian inscriptions have been found not only there but also in areas as far apart as Mongolia, the upper reaches of the Indus valley, and the Southern Gobi desert. Sogdians, originally Zoroastrians, turned to Christianity, Manichaeism and Buddhism when living outside their homeland. They were the great disseminators of cultural and religious traditions from India, Persia and Syria. In turning to Nestorian Christianity, they spread Syriac literature to the east, often translating these texts very closely into their own language.

The homeland of the Sogdians was repeatedly overrun by nomadic tribes migrating from areas further east. Thus in the 5th century AD, the Hephthalites or White Huns who had settled in the towns and rural areas of Sogdia and Bactria, were open to western, i.e. Christian influence, and some of them asked the Metropolitan of Merv for religious instruction. Increasingly, Turks migrated to Transoxania, the area later called West Turkestan. The conversion of such tribes to Christianity must have begun even before the 8th century, when Patriarch Timothy I tells us of a Turkish king and his tribe that had adopted the Christian religion. Nestorianized Turkish tribes between the Oxus and Lake Balkash were to uphold the Christian faith beyond the time of Islamic dominance in the 7th, 8th and subsequent centuries, retaining it to the 14th century.

From Transoxania, various routes led further east. From the upper reaches of the Yaxartes, i.e. from the Fergana valley, a path led over high mountain passes to Kashgar, the westernmost city on the edge of the Tarim Basin, south of the Tien-Shan. There were also more northern routes, leading from the Sogdian cities to the Chu river valley, thence to Lake Issik Köl and to points further east, or to the Ili valley and from there toward the east. These routes continued on to the Dzungarian Basin and to the Mongolian steppes. In the whole area north of the Great Divide, Turks gained an increasingly important role prior to Mongol times (13th–14th century).

From Kashgar, there were two routes circumventing the Tarim Basin with its deadly Taklamakan Desert. One route led through the oasis towns north of the Karakorum, the Tibetan Highlands and the Altyntag range. The most important of these towns were, as one proceeded east, Yarkand, Khotan, Niya, Miran, and Lou-lan, north of Lake Lob Nor. From there a desert path led further east to Tunhuang, the gateway to China proper, which could be reached by following routes through the Kansu corridor between the Richthofen mountain range and the Gobi desert. Another route also led from Kashgar to Tunhuang, passing through the oases south of the Tien-Shan range. The main cities along the route were Aqsu, Bai, Kucha, Turfan and Hami (Komul). Thence there was a connection to

Tunhuang. This was a major Buddhist centre even before the first of the 'Thousand Buddha-Caves' were hewn out of a cliff in the 4th century AD. Tunhuang with its impressive tradition of Buddhist art and learning has preserved valuable documents from the period before the beginning of the 11th century. At this time the Tanguts (Hsi-hsia), a people of Tibetan origin, seized the city and established a Tangut rule between the Tibetan highlands and the Gobi desert. This kingdom was to last for two centuries. In the face of the advance of the Tanguts, a great number of manuscripts and pieces of art were collected and walled up, only to be rediscovered in the beginning of this century. The manuscripts were not only in Chinese, but in various Central Asian languages, this bearing witness to the plurality of peoples determining the cultural fabric of life along the Silk Route. Interestingly enough, these texts were not only Buddhist in content. Important Christian and Manichaean documents, written in Chinese, were discovered; and many texts of a secular nature were also found.

The rise of the Mongols in the 13th century ushered in a period when Nestorian Christianity flourished, for the Mongols, though ruthless in their conquests, were tolerant in areas once subdued. Nestorians played an important role in the Mongol state as soldiers, officials, physicians etc. Furthermore, mothers and wives of some Mongol rulers were Nestorian. The Mongol rule even encompassed China in Yuan times (AD 1279–1368), capitals being Karakorum (AD 1235–1267), Khan Baliq (present Beijing: AD 1267–1368: winter residence) and Shang-tu (AD 1267–1368: summer residence).

Hence Christianity in Central Asia in the Mongol period is interwoven with its appearance in China so that a certain redundancy will be inevitable when we come to the next chapter.

The split of the Mongol realm into separate Khanates in the 13th–14th century, the increasing influence of Islam in western areas and the rise of Muslim states like that of the Timurids created a political situation that made it increasingly difficult for Christian communities to survive. On the other hand, in eastern areas of the once united Mongol realm, Buddhism gained ground. By the end of the 14th century, Christianity was virtually extinct in Central Asia.

CHORASAN AND ADJACENT AREAS

Nestorian Christianity spread from Persia to Central Asia,[2] first being carried to eastern Iranian areas and then further east. The oldest indication of Christians living in Central Asia is a statement by Bardaisan of Edessa, made around AD 196. He mentioned fellow-believers in Gilan, the area south-west of the Caspian Sea, and in Bactria, then part of the Kushan realm. In passing, he remarked: 'Nor do our (Christian) sisters among the Gilanians and Bactrians [i.e. Kushanas] have any intercourse with strangers.'[3] The Kushan Empire, spreading over an area from north of the Oxus to North-West India in its heyday, was founded in the 1st or 2nd century AD by Kujula Kadphises, and it continued to exist up to the 4th century, even after a major portion of it had been incorporated into the Sasanian Empire in the 3rd century. The Kushan Empire had strong contacts with Western Asia and with the Roman Empire, much trade being conducted between these countries east and west of the Iranian realm. Syrian glassware and Roman and Hellenistic coins and objects of art have been found in the former Kushan area in present-day Afghanistan.[4] It is therefore not impossible that there was a number of Syrian traders, even of Christian conviction, in that area in the 2nd century, as in later centuries. This also seems probable in light of the Syrian *Acts of Thomas*, written in the 3rd century, where the Kushan realm is mentioned in a hymn ascribed to St. Thomas, the 'Hymn of the Pearl'. This he is said to have sung when imprisoned in India, in the realm of the Indo-Parthian king Gundaphorus.[5] The *Doctrine of the Apostles*, another Syrian work stemming from the 3rd century, written not much later than AD 250, also referred to Christians in the land of the Gilanians and in that of Gog and Magog. It says that Christian leaders received ordination from a missionary called Aggai, a disciple of a well-known early Christian missionary by the name of Addai.[6] The Biblical terms Gog and Magog refer, according to Mingana, to the Turks and the Tatars. The Turks, however, did not make their appearance in history before the 6th century. So other Central Asian peoples, maybe Prototurks of Altaic stock, living beyond the Caspian Sea, might be meant by these terms. However, we have no further evidence of Christians in western Central Asia at this time.

One of the most reliable sources we have, the records of the synods of the East Syrian Church, the *Synodicon Orientale*,[7] which was compiled at the end of the 8th century, sheds light on the area from the 4th century on. It is supplemented by other Syriac and by Arabic sources. The picture we gain from these documents is, however, fragmentary.

It is only from the middle of the 4th century, around AD 360, that there are conclusive indications of Christians in Merv, the Iranian outpost in the Turanic plains, north of the eastern Iranian plateau. Merv, the gateway to Central Asia proper, was an East Iranian, originally Parthian city, the religious scene of which was determined by a local form of Zoroastrianism. However, there was also a Buddhist presence there, as remains of a Buddhist sanctuary with a large stupa, stemming from the 2nd century, would indicate.[8]

Merv and the whole Parthian east as well as North-West India was the starting point for many Buddhist missions to China, Parthians being among the early Buddhist translators of Indian scriptures into Chinese. From the 3rd century on, Merv was also a centre of Manichaeism, the Gnostic world religion founded by Mani (AD 216–276). It was Mani's disciple Mar Ammo who spread the teaching of the master to East Iran and the Kushan realm. Merv is explicitly mentioned as one of the places where he was highly successful.[9]

Merv had an equal significance for Nestorian Christians in the 4th and the following centuries. It is mentioned in connection with the synod of AD 424 as the seat of a bishop. Its importance for the Nestorian 'Church of the East' is demonstrated by the fact that in the 6th century, specifically by AD 544, its ecclesiastical status was raised to that of a metropolitanate, ranking seventh in seniority after other cities located mainly in Mesopotamia.[10] Prior to this time, a certain Bishop Bar Shabba was active there and in adjacent areas in the 5th century. His name is mentioned in the report about the synod that convened in AD 424.[11] Names of other bishops in the area in the 5th and 6th centuries are also known to us. Furthermore, together with Merv, a number of other Christian centres west of the Oxus are mentioned in the official acts of the East Syrian Church. Mingana, who has collected the evidence, enumerates over 20 centres.[12] For each centre, a number of bishops and archbishops are known by name. The main cities of historical importance for the Church were Abarshar, a cultural and political centre in Chorasan near modern Nishapur, focus of a province of the same name. Bishops here are listed in the synods of the 5th century. It seems that the sees of Abarshar and Tus [i.e. Meshed] were united into a single bishopric by the end of the 5th century.[13] From Abarshar, there was a direct route to Sistan in the south-west corner of present Afghanistan, which was the seat of various bishops in the 5th and 6th centuries. Further to the east was Herat, a town in the north-west of present Afghanistan. It is mentioned as the seat of a bishop in AD 424 and it became the seat of a metropolitan in the 6th century, being responsible for various Christian centres in the vicinity. From here, there were with little doubt connections to North-West India as well as Central Asia. West of the Oxus was also the area known as Gurgan. Nestorians seem to have come to this region in the 5th and 6th centuries, since bishops of that region are listed as being present at synods in that time. In the *Book of Governors* by Thomas of Marga, written in AD 840, there is a description of the work of Mar Subhl-ishu (or Subhalishu) as the Metropolitan of Gilan and Dailam. Here it says:

'He taught and baptised many towns and numerous villages, and brought them to the teaching of the divine life. He built churches, and set up in them priests and deacons, and singled out some brethren who were missionaries with him to teach them psalms and canticles of the Spirit. And he himself went deep inland to the farthest end of the East, in the work of the great evangelisation that he was doing among pagans, Marcionites, Manichaeans, and other kinds of beliefs and abominations, and he sowed the sublime light of the teaching of the Gospel, the source of life and peace.'[14]

One text found in Turfan, the so-called 'Bar Shabba-Fragment', is the Sogdian version of a Syrian document later translated, in abbreviated form, into Arabic.[15] The editor of that text, E. Sachau, calls it 'the legend of the Christianization of Merv'.[16] A fragment of the original Syrian version was also found in Turfan, proving it to be popular throughout Nestorian Central Asia. The preserved Sogdian text contains an account of the Christianization of the provinces north-east of Fars, the core of the Sasanian Empire, by Bishop Bar Shabba and his disciples. In the account, which must have a historical basis, it says:

'He [i.e. Bishop Bar Shabba] bought land and water and built citadels, hostels and houses and laid out gardens . . . and he settled serving brothers and sisters there, in the area of Fars up to Gurgan [i.e. bishopric Hyrcania], in the area of Tus [i.e. one of the three bishoprics of Parthia], in Abarshar, in Serachs [a place at the border of Margiana], in Mervrod [i.e. Merv], in Balkh [ancient capital of Bactria] and in Herat and Sistan. He built churches there and built everything necessary [i.e. for the Christian community]. And he also had presbyters and deacons settle there. And they began to teach and to baptise, by the grace of the Holy Spirit, and by the authority and power which they had received from the pious Lord Bar Shabba. . . . And the proclamation of Christ the Vivifier became great in all areas. They [i.e. the ones engaged in this work] became priests, and Christianity was strengthened. And they praised his name in all the areas up to many distant realms. To the Lord Bar Shabba, the pious Bishop, power and might was given . . . over the unclean spirits . . .'[17]

The text then mentions a great king who was apparently converted to Christianity and who had presbyters and deacons care for the people and hold services.

Although the text has been called the 'legend' of the Christianisation of Merv, we can infer from it that the spread of Christianity in eastern Iran up to the Oxus was greatly promoted by Bar Shabba, whose work was to continue in the following centuries, as the names of bishops of that area, collected by Mingana, would suggest.

Merv then was, as has been noted, the point from which missionary activity was carried further east and eventually beyond the Oxus. Thus in the 6th century, the Hephthalites or White Huns, inhabiting the region of Bactria and the area north of the Oxus, asked for the ordination of a bishop for their realm, having probably come into contact with Christians from Merv or other Christian centres in the area. In AD 549, the Nestorian

Patriarch Mar Aba I sent them a bishop at their request. In the *History of Mar Aba* it says:

'After a short time Haphtar [i.e. the Hephthalite] Khudai sent a priest as a messenger to the King of Kings [i.e. Khosrau I, Anushirvan, reigned AD 531–579] and the Haphtraye [i.e. the Hephthalites], who were Christians, wrote also a letter to the holy Patriarch (Mar Aba I), requesting him to ordain as bishop to all the kingdom of the Haphtraye the priest who was sent from their country. When the priest saw the King of Kings, and the latter learned the nature of the mission on which he was sent, he was astonished to hear it, and amazed at the power of Jesus, and at the fact that even the Christian Haphtraye counted the Patriarch as their head and administrator. He therefore ordered him to go and adorn the Church as was customary on such occasions, and to ordain bishop the man whom the Haphtar Khudai had sent to him. On the following day the Church was adorned, and the Haphtrian priest was ordained bishop for the Haphtrians, and joy increased with the people of the Lord.'[18]

TRANSOXANIA/WEST TURKESTAN

Sogdian texts found in East Turkestan/Sinkiang attest to the fact that Sogdians in that area were active in translating Syrian Christian texts into their language.[19] We even have examples of Syrian-Sogdian bilingual texts.[20]

Whereas it is a well-known fact that Sogdians, living outside their homeland further east, were instrumental in spreading Nestorian Christianity to Turkic peoples in Central Asia, and maybe even to China, it is not clear to what extent Christianity had spread in their actual homeland, the main cities of which were Samarkand, Bukhara, Tashkent and adjoining centers, especially Pendjikent and Paikend. It is clear that Samarkand was a metropolitan see of the Nestorian Church. But it is difficult to date its beginnings. As E. C. D. Hunter points out:

'Several traditions have emerged regarding the date of its creation; ranging from AD 5C under the patriarchate of Ahai (AD 410–415) to AD 8C under the Patriarch Sliba-Zkiha (AD 712–728). Intermediate dates place its founding either to the patriarchate of Shila (AD 505–523) or to Patriarch Ishu-yab. Despite this disparity, the see of *Samarkand* was, notably from its inception, attributed with a status senior to a bishopric.

Certainly by AD 9C *Samarkand* had become a metropolitan see, since Patriarch Theodose (AD 852–858) included the city amongst "les métropoles de l'extérieur". That role was epitomised by the news which the metropolitan sent in AD 1060 to the Catholicos and the Caliphate, giving notice of the Mongol advance as far as *Kashgar*. The see was, however, still in existence in AD 13C, for the metropolitan was listed as amongst those Nestorian ecclesiastical dignitaries present at the consecration of Patriarch Yabhallaha III in AD 1281. Indeed, the contemporary report of Marco Polo, that there was a fine, round church to St. John the Baptist, records the prosperity of Samarkand.'[21]

With respect to the neighbouring Semiriče region, the 'Land of the Seven Rivers' south of Lake Balkash, inhabited as of the 8th cent. by Turks, Hunter points out that

'there do appear to have been longstanding Christian communities in this region, as evidenced by the two Nestorian cemeteries near Tokmak and Pishpek, whose gravestones may be dated between AD 9C – AD 14C. Furthermore their number, approximately 630 inscriptions, suggests that the settlements were sizeable.'[22]

In so far as the cities of Sogdiana are concerned, archaeological work has brought to light various proofs of the existence of Christians in the 6th–8th cent. The most weighty evidence is probably a coin, issued by a Christian authority, showing on the reverse a Nestorian cross set in a ring of pearls – an old Sasanian motif. Only a king, or a city, could have issued such a coin (cf. pl. 17). Furthermore, in the ruins of the ancient Sogdian city of Pendjikent, an ostracon (a pot-sherd) was found, on which is written a Syriac text – portions of Psalm 1 and 2 in the Syriac Peshitta version (cf. pl. 18). A. V. Paykova dates it to the 7th/8th cent. As she points out,

'the character of certain grammatical and orthograpic errors indicates that the inscription was not written by a Syrian, but rather by a Sogdian.'[23]

In placing the find in its setting, Paykova points to various other pieces of evidence for a Christian presence in Sogdiana and neighbouring areas. She refers to a large number of Syro-Nestorian inscriptions found in and around Kirghizia, in the region of Frunze, Togmak and Alamliq, most, to be sure, of late dates (13th–14th cent.). But there are also 'earlier signs of Christian settlements in Kirghizia: the inscription on a brick, deciphered by A. Ja. Borisov, who dated it to the 11th–12th centuries, and a Christian church of the 8th century, excavated in 1954 by L. R. Kyzlasov in the village of Aq-Beshim.'[24]

Paykova further points to a small Syrian inscription on a clay vessel originating from Djambulin in Kazakhstan, dated by A. N. Bernstam, on the basis of archaeological evidence, to the 5th–6th centuries.[25] To the documents testifying the spread of Christianity in Sogdiana, O. Hansen counted a fragment of what he thought was a Church historical work. However, W. Sundermann has shown that this is, rather, the Sogdian version of a Syrian saint's legend.[26] A. V. Paykova, though wrongly basing her observations on Hansen, does correctly point out that a Christian monastery is mentioned by Ibn Ḥaukal (10th century),

> 'situated to the northwest of the present Urghut, about 35 km from Samarkand. When Ibn Ḥaukal visited this monastery, he saw Mesopotamian Christians who had come there, according to his word, in search of solitude, and a healthy climate.'[26]

In and around Urghut further indications of a Christian presence were found. In a gorge of the river Gulbogh, south-west of Urghut, about 25 Syrian Christan rock inscriptions were discovered 'which cover the rock wall from the very bottom to above a man's height.'[28]

In addition, a few interesting examples of Christian Sogdian silver vessels were found, though in remoter places, but stemming, apparently, from Sogdian centres. First to be mentioned is a silver dish, in the form of a disc, showing the siege of a Sogdian castle (cf. pl. 19). It was found near the village of Malaya Anikova in the Ural mountains, having probably been taken here on account of trade relationships. An analysis of the piece reveals that this is the copy of an older piece, our disc having been made with the help of a gypsum copy of the original piece.[29] The main portions, appearing in relief, i.e. the besieged castle, etc., are characteristic of 8th cent. Sogdian art, whereas the details, engraved into the copied silverware, show stylistic elements of the 9th/10th cent. The engraved figures, especially the battle dress of the warriors, show a combination of Sogdian and East Turkestanic elements. This points to an area like Semiriče, south of Lake Balkash, as the place of origin of the silver dish. It was in this area that the regent of the Turkic Karluks, moving in from East Turkestan, converted to Nestorian Christianity at the end of the 8th cent. Quite in accordance with Buddhist art of both India and the Silk Road, various consecutive scenes of a narrative are composed into one picture. The scenes are taken from the book of Joshua. The scenes united in our picture are:

1 Joshua 2:1–16: The siege of Jericho with the prostitute Rahab, in whose home the Israelite spies had hid (v. 1–6), looking out of her window, 'for her house was on the outside of the city wall and she resided within the city wall itself' (v. 15, cf. v. 18 & 21).

2 Joshua 6:4 & 15: The carrying of the ark, 'with seven priests bearing seven trumpets of rams' horns before the ark' (v. 4). On the seventh day, they are to march around the city seven times, 'the priests blowing the trumpets' (cf. v. 15f.). The priests with their trumpets are clearly to be seen. The taking of Jericho (6:15ff.) is implied in this depiction.

3 Joshua 10:12–14: Sun and moon stand still 'on the day when the Lord gave the Amorits over to the Israelites' (v. 12), which is indicated by the depiction of the two celestial bodies on the top of the picture. This motif, as well as the commander of the siege lifting up his hands to heaven, has analogies in Syriac miniature paintings, on the manuscripts of the 6th–8th cent.

It has been pointed out that this specific combination of scenes with warriors approaching from the left and the right (in order to take the Sogdian castle representing the city of Jericho) is reminiscent of a scene occuring repeatedly in the Buddhist art of Kucha, i.e. the siege of Kushinagara, the city which kept the relics of the Buddha after his death, by various Indian kings.[30] However one may judge this analogy, the combination of various scenes of a narrative in one picture is certainly a typical Buddhist mode of artistic representation.[31]

A second interesting depiction of an Old Testament theme which is of Sogdian Christian origin has to do with Gen. 22:1–14 (cf. pl. 20). This is the narrative about Abraham wanting to sacrifice Isaac. We find the scene depicted in a manner typical of designs of Sogdian cloths of the 6th–8th cent., the scene being depicted together with a mirror image on both sides of an axis of symmetry. The double scene is set within a medaillon, as it is typical of such Sogdian cloth illustrations. The cloth, stemming from the Mosheva Gorge, is kept at the State Hermitage Museum of St. Petersburg.[32] Depicted is the climax of the story when Abraham 'reached out his hand and took the knife to kill his son' (v. 10).

A third remarkable piece of Sogdian Christan art which testifies to the influence of Christians in the cultural life of Sogdiana is a silver dish (pl. 21), also kept in the Hermitage Museum of St. Petersburg and found in 1897 in the village of Grigorovskoe in the area of Perm. (It was bought by the Hermitage Museum in 1899.) The relatively flat disc with a soldered circular stand depicts three scenes related to the death and resurrection of Christ. In the triangular fields between the three medaillons, in which the scenes are set, i.e. crucifixion, burial and resurrection, we see, on the left, three soldiers guarding the grave of Christ. On the right is Peter's denial of his Lord, and below Daniel in the lion's den. The various scenes are explained by Syriac inscriptions in Estrangelo script (i.e. from top to bottom): 'Ascension of Christ', 'Simon Peter at the denial of Christ, before the cock crowed three times', 'warriors guarding the grave', furthermore: 'crucifixion of Christ', 'the robber whom he forgave his sin', 'the robber on his left', 'Mary Magdalene', 'Mary', 'angels', 'resurrection', and finally 'lion' and 'Daniel'. The iconography of the resurrection scene is interesting in that Mary, 'the mother of God', often associated with this scene, is not depicted. This early feature, which corresponds to the text of Acts 1:9, was apparently retained in Nestorian circles, as the inclusion of 'the mother of God' was regarded as an addition to the ascension iconography, made by the Western Church in the 5th cent. It has been shown by J. I. Smirnov that many details of the bowl are of Iranian origin. It was probably originally made by Nestorians in Persia. Smirnov dates that art to the 6th/7th cent. In so far as Sasanian Christians are concerned, Peter's denial of Christ would certainly have been a theme of specific significance to Christians under non-Christan rulers. Our disc is such a copy of a Sasanian piece of art, stemming, perhaps, from the Semiriče of the 9th/10th cent.

Finally there is a scene with a Nestorian cross, beside which stand, probably, three donors, as we have them in the art of other religions. They are depicted smaller than the figures above, of which only the feet are preserved (cf. pl. 23).

When Turks, coming from Central Asia and moving westward into 'West Turkestan', broke the power of the Hephthalites, the Metropolitan of Merv, Elijah, won converts among them, too, large communities of Turks turning to Christianity.[33] In a source relating to AD 644, the *Chronica Minora*, a collection of anonymous writings completed in about AD 680, it says:

> 'And Elijah [Elias], Metropolitan of Merv, converted a large number of Turks. . . . About this Elijah . . . it is related that when travelling in the countries situated beyond the border line (of the river Oxus) he was met by a king who was going to fight another king. Elijah endeavoured with a long speech to dissuade him from the fight, but the king said to him, "If thou showest to me a sign similar to those shown by the priests of my gods, I shall believe in thy God." And the king ordered the priests of the demons who were accompanying him, and they invoked the demons whom they were worshipping, and immediately the sky was covered with clouds, and a hurricane of wind, thunder, and lightning followed. Elijah was then moved by divine power, and he made the sign of the heavenly cross, and rebuked the unreal thing that the rebellious demons had set up, and it forthwith disappeared completely. When the king saw what Saint Elijah did, he fell down and worshipped him, and he was converted with all his army. The saint took them to a stream, baptised all of them, ordained for them priests and deacons, and returned to his country.'[34]

As E. C. D. Hunter points out, the *Chronica Minora* claims that the Metropolitan of Merv converted 'Turks and other nations', which he was visiting in remote areas of his jurisdiction, 'in the lands in which the borders were distant'. Here he met the king who was actually a petty ruler, 'the chieftain of a nomadic, bellicose tribe'. The ethnic identity of the ruler remains 'somewhat ambiguous', but the account suggests that the tribe belonged to the Turkic groups moving south of the Syr Darya river in mid-7th century AD[35]. That the ruler was a Turk is also suggested by the fact that his conversion was occasioned by a sign overpowering the shamanistic practice, known as *yat* or *yad*, of attracting wind, rain and snow. As Hunter puts it:

'The immediate and dramatic results produced by the sign of the cross probably convinced the ruler that the Metropolitan was a potent shaman.'[36]

It can safely be assumed that the priests and deacons ordained from among the retinue, maybe the warriors of the king, 'formed the core of a Church somehow related jurisdictionally to the see of Merv. This was the case in the conversion of nomadic peoples in the vicinity of the Caspian Sea, of the Dailamites and Gilanians.'[37] It is hardly probable, however, that the people converted relinquished all shamanistic practices completely. In the later Mongol period, we have reports of Nestorians adhering to shamanistic patterns generations after the acceptance of Christianity. The case would have been similar here.

Christianity must have penetrated to quite an extent among the Western Turks, for we hear that in AD 581, those Turks who were taken prisoner by Byzantine Greeks bore crosses on their foreheads, pricked in black dots. This, they said, had been suggested to them by Nestorians to avert disasters. The later use of the cross among the Eastern Turks and Mongols is attested by various Western travellers of the 13th and 14th centuries.

The conversion of Western Turks to Christianity was not a short-term matter, for Turkic tribes in the western part of Central Asia were to continue to play a significant role in the history of Christianity. In AD 781, Timothy I, Nestorian Patriarch (d. AD 823), wrote in a letter to the Maronites, the monks of the monastery of Mar Maron:

'The king of the Turks, with nearly all (the inhabitants of) his country, has left his ancient idolatry, and has become Christian, and he has requested us in his letters to create a Metropolitan for his country; and this we have done.'[38]

Hunter points out:

'The creation of a metropolitanate at the behest of the "King of the Turks" implies the Christianization of this major ethnic group, or a sizable part of it. The significance of this development is perhaps conveyed by the later comment of Mari ibn Suleiman that, "Henceforth, Timothy led into faith the *Khaqan*, the King of the Turks and other kings." The qualification of the title, King of the Turks by the appellation, *Khaqan*, may indicate later Mongol influence in *The Book of the Tower.* However, the seniority of his title suggests that a supreme monarch, and his people, had undergone conversion.'[39]

It has been thought that the 'King of the Turks' converted to Christianity with his realm around AD 782 was the Uighur ruler Alp Qutlugh Bilgä Qaghan who came to power in AD 779, following a coup d'etat against Bögü Qaghan, who made Manichaeism the state religion in the country of the Uighur Turks.[40] Probably, however, he was one of various Turkish rulers in what was later West Turkestan. There are various instances of the fact that Turkish tribes, once dislocated from their homeland, gave up their indigenous religion and turned to a world religion like Christianity, which gave a more encompassing answer to the problems of life in the new social and political situation.

Patriarch Timothy I was a considerable driving force in the eastern spread of Nestorianism. We hear in one letter of his, written to Mar Sergius, Metropolitan of Elam, that he ordained a bishop for the Turks and that he was even going to ordain one for Tibet. In it, he says: 'In these days the Holy Spirit has anointed a Metropolitan for the Turks, and we are preparing to consecrate another one for the Tibetans.'[41] In another letter, the Patriarch states that in his time 'many monks crossed the sea and went to the Indians and Chinese', and he notifies his correspondent of the death of the Metropolitan of China.[42]

So there were links between the patriarchal seat in Baghdad and Christian communities in remote areas of Asia in the 8th century. We must assume that beyond the monks mentioned, who went to their respective points of destination by sea, there must also have been many who travelled by land to Central and East Asia. Other sources also tell us about the indefatigable Timothy I and his role in the conversion of Central Asian peoples. One of the main sources is Thomas of Marga, who was contemporary with the events he writes about, i.e. around AD 840. In his *Book of Governors* (*Liber Superiorum*), he tells us that Timothy chose more than four score monks for missionary purposes, some of whom he ordained as bishops. He sent them to the Dailamites and Gilanians, south-east of the Caspian Sea, and to people beyond that area. Thomas writes:

'(These bishops) were ordained by the holy Catholicos Timothy the Patriarch to the countries of the savage peoples, who were devoid of every understanding and civilization. No missionaries and sowers of truth had till then gone to their regions, and the teaching of the Gospel of our Saviour had not yet been preached to them; but why should I say the teaching of the Christ, our Lord, while they had not even received, like the Jews and the rest of the Gentiles (i.e. the Muslims), the knowledge of God, Creator and Administrator of the worlds, but were worshipping trees, graven wood, beasts, fish, reptiles, birds and the such like, along with the worship of fire and stars. These were the Bishops who preached the teaching of Christ in those countries of the Dailamites and Gilanians, and the rest of the savage peoples beyond them, and planted in them the light of the truth of the Gospel of our Lord. . . . They evangelised them and they baptised them, worked miracles and showed prodigies, and the news of their exploits reached the farthest points of the East. You may learn all these clearly from the letter which some merchants and secretaries of the kings, who had penetrated as far as there for the sake of commerce and of affairs of State, wrote to (the Patriarch) Mar Timothy.'[43]

It is interesting to note that at the time of Timothy, persons were sent out who by their training were especially fitted for their missionary task, being in good command of various languages. Thus we hear from Thomas of Marga that Bishop Mar Subhl-ishu, Metropolitan of the Dailamites, ordained by Timothy, was versed in Syriac, Arabic and Persian.[44] Similar qualities must have applied to the Christian envoys and Church leaders in other parts of Central Asia.

The areas beyond the Oxus were so far from the seat of the Patriarch that the acts of the Synods of the Nestorian Church shed little light on their history. In terms of distance it was impossible for the bishops of Central and East Asia to attend the general Church assemblies at the patriarchal seat. We hear from Abdiso in his *Synodical Canons*, that the Metropolitans of Samarkand, India and China were exempt from attending the General Synod of the Church, but that each had to write a letter of submission to the patriarch every six years, informing him of the situation in his diocese. These circumstances, the geographical distance and the sparse contact was, as Mingana points out,

> 'the cause of the slight divergences in the religious outlook, and even in some minor points of dogma, that separate the official Christianity of the Eastern Church from that which one finds in the Christian monuments [of Central and East Asia]. . . . By force of circumstances, those far-off Bishops were left more or less to themselves; and cast off from the rest of their religious brethren of the West they had to manage their spiritual and ecclesiastical affairs to the best of their ability.'[45]

On the other hand, the Syrian Christians in the western part of the Sasanian Empire only had vague ideas of areas and peoples beyond the Oxus, later called by Muslim writers the lands 'on the other side of the river'. Everything beyond the Oxus 'is generally referred by Syrian historians to less remote Turks and Huns with whom they had more intimate intercourse.'[46] In the early chronicles of the Synods, Transoxania is often simply called 'the Metropolitan of the Turks'.

The oldest reference in Syriac literature to the existence of bishoprics in Turkestan is recorded in the *History of Mar Aba*, which goes back to AD 549. There is talk of a newly ordained bishop in that area, but there is no mention of where he resided.[47] Another later source of information is a semi-official list of the Metropolitans of the Nestorian Church beyond the Oxus which was compiled by Amr ibn Matta in the 14th century. Amr lists the bishops according to rank of precedence. In his list, the Metropolitan of the Turks is the 22nd, after the Metropolitan of China, India and Samarkand, and before the Metropolitans of Khan Baliq (i.e. Beshbaliq north of Turfan rather than Beijing), of the Tanguts and of Kashgar and Navekath. Amr states that each of these metropolitans had either six or seven suffragan bishops under his jurisdiction.[48] This reflects the scene in Mongol times (13th century), yet it is noteworthy that the Western Turks continued the Christian tradition up to that period, i.e. even at the time when Christianity had died out in China in the 10th century.

Among the other Syriac documents shedding light on Christian Turks in Central Asia is a letter attributed to Akhsnaya, the well-known Monophysite Philoxenus, Bishop of Mabbug, to Abu 'Afr, military Governor of Hirta [i.e. Hirah] of Nu'man. Philoxenus, who died in AD 523, was an eminent Syriac writer. He is known as the author of the Philoxenian version of the Bible. This text, thought not actually written by him, makes use of his authority in first dealing with certain 'heresies', including that of Nestorius, and then describes the introduction of Christianity to the Turks. The writer was a zealous Jacobite, writing probably in the second half of the 8th century. In his historical account, he 'was eager to show that his Church also, and especially his Patriarchate of Antioch, had some share in the conversion of the Turks, and (that) while the Christian peoples beyond the Oxus swore allegiance to the Nestorian Patriarch of Ctesiphon, and technically belonged to his Nestorian community, they did so bona fide and by force of circumstances, ultimately due to the long distance that separated them from the monophysite Patriarch of Antioch.'[49]

Historically the document is important because it sheds light on the situation of the Church among the Turks in the 8th century, although speaking about events among the Eastern Turks. Four Christian kings are mentioned, in addition to the ruler of a border town, Karakor [i.e. Karakorum?]. His name is given as 'Idiqut' [i.e. Iduqqut]. This was actually the title of Turkish rulers, meaning 'Holy Charisma', and being employed by Turkish kings at the time of the Uighur realm in the 8th and 9th centuries. Later (9th–13th century), the title was retained by rulers of the kingdom of Kocho in Turfan.

The description of Turkish life and Turkish customs in the letter applies to a nomadic people living in northern climes, where neither wheat nor vine grew. Hence, though the text purports to describe events at the time of Philoxenus, it actually highlights the Christianity of the Eastern Uighur Turks before the time of their migration to the oasis towns at the fringe of the Tarim Basin. Much of what it says proves to be correct for these Turks in the 8th/9th centuries.[50] Even though it is not absolutely clear that the 'King of the Turks' mentioned by Timothy I was an East Turkish ruler, it is probable that the Christian mission fanned out into the area of the Eastern Turks living in the Mongolian steppes and the region north of the Tien-Shan.

In close contact with the Turks in Transoxania were the Sogdians, that eastern Iranian people living south and north of the Yaxartes, in cities like Bukhara and Samarkand as pointed out above. There were considerable Christian communities in both of these two cities by the 8th century. Probably in the beginning of the 8th century, Samarkand became an archbishopric, becoming a metropolitan see at the time of Patriarch Theodosius (d. AD 858) according to Mingana.[51] Just when it became an important Christian centre, i.e. at the beginning of the 5th century or later, is not clear from the sources, which diverge on this issue. The advance of Islam did affect the Christian community, churches in the area being turned into mosques, as in Western Asia. Yet there seems to have been a degree of understanding between both communities. It was the Metropolitan of Samarkand who in 1260 notified the Patriarch and the Caliph in Baghdad of the advance of the Mongols as far as Kashgar. After the Mongol onslaught, the see of Samarkand was re-established in the 13th century, the Metropolitan of that city being present at the consecration of Patriarch Yaballaha III in AD 1281.[52] In the time of Marco Polo (d. AD 1324) who reported seeing a fine round church to St. John the Baptist, the Christian community was still flourishing.[53]

In the 8th and 9th centuries, there was also an advance of Nestorianism into the delta of the Oxus, i.e. to Chorasmia, the area south of the Aral Sea, where, apparently, an older Christian tradition was lingering on. William of Rubruk, in the 13th century, tells us of Nestorian communities here that had books in their own language and script, using them in their services.[54]

On their way to the east, Nestorian missionaries had, by the 8th century, gained access to Chang-an, the principal city of China. It was the Pax Sinica of the T'ang Period (AD 618–907) that allowed for travel and trade in Central Asia. Hence it is not surprising to hear that a missionary of the Eastern Syrian Church, called by the Chinese A-lo-pen, arrived in Chang-an in AD 635 and laid the foundation of a monastic type of Christianity. This is noteworthy in that there were two basic tendencies in the 'Church of the East', one being inspired by West Syrian monasticism, the other by

Persian Christianity, which gave to laymen a greater responsibility in religious affairs, and at times even required the clergymen to be married. One of the reasons for the spread of Nestorianism to Central Asia was certainly the fact that Nestorians engaging in missionary activity could live by the work of their hands and were thus not dependent upon monastic settlements along the way.

Whereas in Central Asia both attitudes can be met, it was the monastic type of religiosity that gained roots in China in the 8th and 9th century. But whereas in China the monks were to the greatest extent non-Chinese, considerable numbers of indigenous peoples converted to Christianity in Central Asia without entering a monastic type of life and even marrying, the monks being indigenous or Iranians and Syrians. The difference from China is highlighted by the fact that whereas in China family ties and traditions remained firm, many Central Asian family and kinship ties lost their meaning when these groups were displaced by political or economic pressure and hence lost their original coherence. As a consequence, the indigenous religions were more readily given up in favour of a world religion with its new religious fellowship.

It was both from the west and the east, from Persia and China, that Christianity percolated to Central Asia. As noted, Timothy I was largely instrumental in furthering the cause of the Christians in China up to the 8th century. It was probably on account of his activity that groups belonging to the Turkish Qarluqs embraced Nestorianism in that period. Qarluqs living in the city of Taraz, north-east of the Yaxartes, were faced with the Muslim invasion in AD 893 when their church was also turned into a mosque. But here, again, this did not spell the end of a Christian presence. We hear of Turkish Christians in the area of Tashkent and in Otrar on the Yaxartes in the 10th century without knowing exactly of their tribal affiliations. As pointed out, West Turkish groups, even in the vicissitudes of tribal migrations, were to be the most significant supporters of Nestorianism up to the Mongol period.

THE SOUTHERN SILK ROUTE

From Transoxania, later called West Turkestan, Christianity was introduced to East Turkestan, especially to the oasis towns at the fringe of the Taklamakan desert. In the 8th century, Kashgar became the seat of a Nestorian Metropolitan. In the beginning of that century, a Christian king also ruled over the oasis.[55] Probably this was a short-term episode, for there are no archaeological documents or relics here pointing to the presence of Christians for an extended period. However, we know from Syrian sources, that Patriarch Elijah III (d. AD 1190) nominated two metropolitans for the city in that period,[56] thus reviving an older tradition. Some forty years later, however, when the monks Bar Sauma and Mark passed through Kashgar on their way to Jerusalem, they found the whole city empty on account of famine and war.

East of Kashgar, on the southern Silk Route, was Khotan, where Christians may well have been present also in the 8th century. In the 9th century, Christians had a church in the centre of Khotan as well as in one of its suburbs. In this period, there are also indications of a Christian presence in Miran and in the vicinity of Lake Lob Nor. Some personal names in documents from these places may well be those of Christians.[57]

In so far as Tunhuang is concerned, a major centre of Buddhism, a Christian presence among Chinese and Tibetans can be traced, a number of significant Chinese Christian documents being found at that site, dating from the time before the 11th century. They stem from the famous walled-up library in what today is called cave 17. It is probably from this library that there stems a short but remarkable Syriac document, part of a Nestorian Easter liturgy of an early date. This would indicate the presence of Christian monks versed in Syriac at Tunhuang.[58] Among the Turkish texts from Tunhuang there are letters stemming from the 9th/10th cent. containing Christian names like David and Sergius. There are Sogdian/ Turkish letters beginning 'In the name of God', which could also have been written by Turkish or Sogdian Christians.[59] The author of one such letter is a Christian priest named Mar Sargis (Sergius).[60] Beside Christian documents, a damaged painting on silk was also found by Sir Aurel Stein (d. AD 1943) in the walled-up library, representing either, as has been suggested, Jesus as Good Shepherd, or a Christian saint (see pls. 24 and 25). He is depicted in a manner reminiscent of a Bodhisattva. On the silk banner, the figure raises the right hand in *vitarka* mudra, the posture of instruction (lit. 'argument'), as we find it in many Buddhist paintings. However, this figure has a cross in its head gear, and one attached to a necklace hanging around its neck. It is highly probable that Christianity came to Tunhuang from China, in its Chinese version. Tunhuang leads us to the question of Christianity among Tibetans and Tanguts.

Apparently Nestorians were known to Tibetans in Tunhuang in the 8th century and in subsequent times. A Tibetan book from Tunhuang, a book of divination from the time between the 8th and the 10th century, contains the title 'Jesus, the Messiah', and mentions 'the judge at the right hand of God.'[61] G. Uray has shown that even Tibet itself, not only Tibetans in that oasis, had contact with Nestorians and Manichaeans between the 9th and the 10th century. These indications show that the references of Timothy I to Tibet are to be taken seriously. A further indication of this matter is the fact that in Tankse, Ladakh (West Tibet), various inscriptions were found beside rock carvings of Nestorian crosses, dating from the 8th century (see pls. 26 and 27). As N. Sims-Williams has shown, the texts are sometimes to be seen as being independent of the crosses,[62] although there are undoubtedly Christian as well as Manichaean inscriptions.[63]

Though the crosses and inscriptions testify only to the fact that Christian travellers would have passed through the area, it does make us aware of links between Tibet and Nestorians in Central Asia. G. Uray is correct in pointing out that the inscriptions of Tankse, some of which are Christian, are evidence of the fact that the interior of Tibet stood open to Nestorian merchants and travellers.[64]

Finally, as evidence of Tibet's connection with Manichaeism, as close as it is to Christianity, there is a Buddhist philosophical treatise, written in the last quarter of the 7th century by the Tibetan king Khri Sroṅ lde btsan, under the guidance of Shantarakshita, a well-known Indian Buddhist teacher. The work is called the 'Summary of the Proofs of the Right Revelation'. As Uray points out, it justifies the introduction of Buddhism as the state religion and it condemns, at the same time, the 'Persian heretic' Mani and his teaching.[65]

Tibet, finally, is also mentioned in a Chinese Christian inscription, a stone tablet set up in memory of Prince A-lo-han (Abraham?) of Persia in AD 710. Here it says:

> 'This is the Stone-tablet erected in memory of A-lo-han, a Persian Prince by birth and the most illustrious of the whole tribe. During the period of Hsien-ch'ing (656–661 AD), the then reigning Emperor Kao-tsung the Great, hearing of the meritorious service and illustrious deeds of this Persian prince, sent a special messenger to invite him to his own Palace. . . .
>
> As soon as the Prince arrived at the capital, the Emperor appointed him Generalissimo, and charged him with the responsibility of defending the Northern Gate . . . and sent him as the Imperial Envoy to the tribes of Tibet, Ephraim, and other countries.'[66]

Beside Tibetans, a people affiliated with that race and coming from the Tibetan plateau before spreading into the Kansu corridor in the 11th century were the Tanguts or Hsi-hsia. It was perhaps due to their advance that the Tunhuang library mentioned above was walled up. The Tanguts established, in AD 1004, a kingdom that was to extend from the fringe of the Tibetan highlands to the Mongolian steppes. The realm was to last up to the appearance of the Mongols upon the scene in the 13th century, the empire being conquered by Jinghis Khan in AD 1227. The number of Christians in the Tangut realm, which was bounded by the Sung Empire of China in the east and the realm of the Turkish Uighurs in the west, must have been considerable. A Russian geographical expedition, in 1908, found in the 'dead city' of Kara Khoto, one of the centres of the Tangut kingdom, beside Buddhist books, manuscripts in the Persian language and three Christian fragments in Syriac script, two being in Syriac and one in Turkish. One of the Syriac texts is a prayer for rain, which is also symbolically meant as a request for God's mercy and grace. Thus it says here:

> 'The water – thy symbol – let it fall down at thy command on our fields, . . . and our earth, chose (this) our desert (for your rain) through thy grace and have mercy upon us.'

The second Syriac text is a hymn to the crucified and risen Lord, stemming, probably, from a liturgy. The fragmentary Turkish text is on the passion of Christ which is prefigured by Jonah in the belly of the whale and (as on our silver dish) by Daniel in the lion's den, – associations often to be found in Syriac literature.[67]

In Syrian sources, there is mention of a Tangut archbishopric and a Metropolitan of the Tanguts.[68] The monks Rabban Sauma and Mark who travelled through Tangut area in the 13th century testify to the religious zeal of the Tanguts. In the history of Yaballaha III it says:

> 'They went from there to the town of Tangut. When the inhabitants heard that Fathers Sauma and Mark came there on their way to Jerusalem, they went with diligence to meet them, men and women, young men and children, because the faith of the Tangutians was very staunch and their heart pure.'[69]

It is conceivable that Christianity among the Tanguts, though inspired by missionary activity from Christian centres to the east or to the west, did have a root in a Christian tradition in and around Tunhuang. The question of the historical sources of Tangut Christianity calls for further research.

THE NORTHERN SILK ROUTE

On the northern branch of the Silk Route circumventing the Taklamakan desert, Christians were probably present at various points. There was a Christian presence in Bai and Aksu west of Kucha. The most important centre, however, was the Turfan oasis. In the village of Bulayiq north of the town of Turfan, German expeditions, before World War I, found a considerable number of Christian manuscripts in what must have been a monastery. 400–500 of these texts were written in Syriac, only a few being hitherto published. Besides, there were Sogdian translations, Syrian-Sogdian bilinguals and about a dozen fragmentary Turkish texts. We shall turn to this literature at a later point. Apart from the monastic centre mentioned, there was also a Nestorian church in the ancient Uighur capital of Kocho (Kao-chang) in the oasis of Turfan. Although partially destroyed, some paintings were discovered there. One such painting depicts a priest, apparently of Iranian origin, holding a chalice in his hand and preaching to an assembly (see pl. 29). The scene confirms the picture we gain from the texts. Leading members of the Church were Iranians, including Sogdians, while Turks, probably from a lower stratum of society, comprised part of the congregation.

It is not unimportant for our theme that Turfan was also a centre of Manichaeism in the time of the Uighur realm of Kocho (ca. AD 850–1250), and perhaps even before that period. The Manichaeans considered themselves as true Christians, though they integrated Zoroastrian, and increasingly Buddhist concepts into their religion. But they did make use of portions of the New Testament, especially the Gospels (including Mt. 24 & 25) and the Pauline letters. Furthermore they read and copied Christian apocryphal literature, parts of which were discovered in the ruins of Manichaean sites. In particular, texts that lent themselves to a dualistic interpretation of the world, in terms of Good and Evil, Light and Darkness, were cherished by them. Though only fragments of this literature have been found, but in considerable number, they do give us a picture of the range of Christian works used by the Manichaeans.

Further east of Turfan, there surely were Christians as well as Manichaeans in Hami (Komul) and perhaps other oasis towns west of Tunhuang. Whereas Manichaean texts refer to brethren in the faith in that area, Syrian literary evidence points to Nestorians in that region. We know from Amr that the town of Hami sent its Bishop John to the consecration of Patriarch Denha in AD 1265. Probably there had been a Christian presence there from earlier times.

NORTH OF THE TIEN-SHAN MOUNTAINS

How many Christian communities remained alive in wake of the first missionary effort, we do not know. As indicated, a number of Turkish, especially West Turkish tribes were true to the religion for centuries. It was in the 11th century that Christian merchants, and probably also monks, won further Turkish tribes north-east of the great divide, the Tien-Shan range. At this time the Keraits, living in the area between Lake Baikal and the eastern Mongolian steppes, converted to Nestorianism together with their Khan. They were to retain their Christian faith for two centuries, until the appearance of the Mongols in the 13th century. In spite of all military tensions and wars with surrounding neighbours and with inhabitants of the realm of Kin, the power ruling over Manchuria and northern China at this time, they were to spread their faith to those neighbours. The origins of Kerait Christianity are documented in Syrian sources. In one text, a letter written in about AD 1009 by Abdiso, Metropolitan of Merv, to the Nestorian Patriarch John in Baghdad, we hear that 200,000 'Turks', i.e. Turkish Keraits, embraced Christianity. The Metropolitan asks the Patriarch about the food they should eat at Lent, no suitable edibles being available for that time in their country. Barhebraeus, in his *Ecclesiastical Chronicle* (*Chronicon Ecclesiasticum*), who tells us about the matter, says:

'In that time 'Abdishō, Metropolitan of Merw, ... wrote and informed the Catholicos (i.e. the Patriarch) that while the king of a people called Keraits ... was hunting in one of the high mountains of his country, he was overcome by a violent snow-storm, and wandered hopelessly out of the way. When he lost all hope of salvation, a saint appeared to him in vision and said to him, "If you believe in Christ, I will lead you to the right direction, and you will not die here." When he promised him that he would become a lamb in the Christian sheepfold, he directed him and led him to salvation; and when he reached his tents in safety, he summoned the Christian merchants who were there, and discussed with them the question of faith, and they answered him that this could not be accomplished except through baptism. He took a Gospel from them, and lo he is worshipping it every day; and now he has summoned me to repair to him, or to send him a priest to baptise him. He also made enquiries from me concerning fasting, and said to me, "Apart from meat and milk, we have no other food; how could we then fast"; he also told me that the number of those who were converted with him reached two hundred thousand. The Catholicos wrote then to the Metropolitan, and told him to send two persons, a priest and a deacon, with all the requisites of an altar, to go and baptise all those who were converted, and to teach them Christian habits. As to the Fast of Lent, they should abstain in it from meat, but they should be given permission to drink milk, if, as they say, Lent food is not found in their country.'[70]

In his *Syrian Chronicle* (*Chronicon Syriacum*), Barhebraeus also refers to the event, dating it as 398 A.H., i.e. AD 1009.[71] Here he says:

'In this very year a nation from the nations of the Turks inhabiting the interior of the country towards the East, called Kerit, believed in Christ, and were instructed in the faith and baptised through a miracle that happened to their king.'[72]

The legend about 'Prester John', which was widely diffused in Europe in the Middle Ages because help was expected from him against the common foe, the Muslims,[73] is connected with the Keraits. The name of their king is given as John. Barhebraeus, for one, in his *Syrian Chronicle*, clearly identifies the legendary John with the king whose name was Ung-Khan, which might have been a variation of the Syriac 'Yohannan', i.e. John.[74]

The conversion of the Keraits is also referred to in the *Book of the Tower* of Mari ibn Suleiman, a Nestorian chronicler who wrote in Arabic in the 12th century. Here we read a similar conversion legend with respect to the king.

The name of the Christian saint he met is given as Mar Sergius, who, as we know, hailed from Samarkand and who became a very popular saint in Central and East Asia, various monasteries being dedicated to him. Of the king, having turned to Christianity, Mari's account says:

> 'The King had set up a pavilion to take the place of an altar, in which was a cross and a Gospel. . . . The Metropolitan inquired from (the Patriarch) what was to be done with them as they had no wheat, and the latter answered that he was to endeavour to find them wheat and wine for Easter; as to abstinence, they should abstain at Lent from meat, and be satisfied with milk. If their habit was to take sour milk, they should take sweet milk as a change to their habit.'[75]

In comparing the accounts in the writings of Barhebraeus, who skilfully also used the *Chronicle* of the Jacobite Patriarch Michael, and of Mari ibn Suleiman's *The Book of the Tower,* E. C. D. Hunter points out:

> 'In essence, the accounts of Mari ibn Suleiman and Barhebraeus agree that a Turkic king, together with 200,000 subjects became converted to Christianity. By contrast, the information supplied about the application of Christianity amongst these converts differs dramatically, converging only in the expressed concern over the dietary difficulties which would ensue from a Lenten fast. Whilst the variant traditions offered by the *Kitabu'l Mijdal* [i.e. *The Book of the Tower*] and the *Chronicon Ecclesiasticum* suggest little interdependence, the core of information common to both accounts possibly derived from the original correspondence of the Metropolitan of Marv to the Patriarch, John VI.'[76]

In view of the preceding conversions of Turkic tribes, Hunter comes to this conclusion:

> 'Whilst the *Chronicon Ecclesiasticum* only exhibits a minimal quantity of ethnological material, Barhebraeus undoubtedly was acquainted with Kerait customs due to their presence in the (Persian) Il-Khanate. Given their ethnographic classification amongst the Turkic tribes, the interpolation of their designation into the conversion episode of AD 1007 would have been fitting. Furthermore, in the light of the Christian heritage and a lineage of kings that extended back, with Ung Khan and his predecessors to the mid twelfth century AD, Barhebraeus may have assumed that the event did actually relate their adoption of Christianity – especially since no other tradition is extant.
>
> It would be a convenient solution to correlate the conversion of the Kerait with the event of AD 1007. However, the question remains unanswered. This conversion was the third in a process, albeit

sporadic and unrelated, that was first dated to the mid seventh century AD, soon after the advent of the Oghuz in the regions of Transoxania. That the final event can be ascribed to the early eleventh century AD, suggests that the conversions were linked with the encroaching domination of the Oghuz. At this time, they were poised to expand into Khurasan and beyond, to Baghdad where an Islamic offshoot established the dynasty of the Saljuks.'[77]

The implication is, then, that the conversion of AD 1007 may not have affected the Kerait, who only became known to Syrian writers in Mongol times, as allies of the Mongol rulers of Persia (13th–14th century). Yet by this time they, like other tribes including the Naiman, Merkit and Ongut, were Christians. When their conversion took place must, then, remain a matter of conjecture. But the Keraits do seem to be the first converts in the area.

Once Christianity was established in the land of the Keraits, further missionary activity was apparently carried out without the Metropolitan of Merv being directly involved. Christianity was passed on to neighbouring tribes in the wake of direct contacts.

One powerful Turkish confederacy inspired by the Christian faith of the Keraits was that of the Naimans. They comprised nine clans and lived in the mountains of Tarbagatai, the upper Irtish valley and adjoining regions. Like the Keraits, many were Christians at the time of Mongol rule, when Nestorian Naimans as well as Keraits played a significant role at the Mongol court, as we read in the *Secret History of the Mongols* (13th cent.).

Another people of Turkish stock, the Merkites, living in the area of the lower Selenga, were probably half Christian, as we learn from William of Rubruk, at whose time their ruler had 'rejected the Christian religion and worshipped idols, having pagan priests by him.'[78] Probably there were Christians among the Mongolian Oirats as well.

The Turkish Khitans who established the Liao Dynasty in northern China (AD 907–1218) adopted Christianity to some extent, probably from the other Turkish tribes. The succeeding state, that of the Kara Khitai (AD 1124–1218), was also affected by older and newer Christian traditions. Some of its rulers were Christians. In its heyday, the kingdom of the Kara Khitai extended from the western part of the Tarim Basin, where there were probably still vestiges of Christianity from the first missionary period, to northern China. At the time of the Kara Khitai, we hear of Christians in Khotan again and even of the fact that a Christian king ruled over the oasis town in the middle of the 12th century.[79] Kashgar must also have become a Christian centre for it was raised to metropolitan status in the second half of the 12th century. Furthermore, there were still Christians among the Uighur Turks in the Turfan area.[80] The last ruler of the Kara Khitai, Küčlük (1213–1218), who played a major role in

Transoxania, was of Naiman extraction. He became king by marrying a lady of the ruling house. Originally a Christian, he then embraced Buddhism. This epitomized the fate of Christianity in Eastern Turkestan. It was increasingly pushed into the background by the Indian religion, even before the advance of Islam and the appearance of the Mongols. In AD 1218, Küčlük lost his realm and his life when the Mongol ruler Jinghis Khan conquered his state.

To the east of the Keraits, in what is now Inner Mongolia, and in the Ordos country, the area surrounded by the Huang-ho at its great bend, there were various Turkish groups. Amongst them were the Onguts, among whom Christianity, apparently strongly influenced by shamanistic elements, did play a certain role in leading circles as well as in the lower strata of society. There different types of folk belief allowed for the incorporation of Christian elements. In one of the capitals of the Onguts, in the city of Olon Süme (or Olon Süme-in-tor), which in Mongol times was to become a centre of Buddhist learning, there existed a Nestorian church, built in the Mongol period, but arising from a tradition that probably went back to the Ongut period, Onguts still playing a decisive role in the area after the rise of Jinghis Khan.[81] In Mongol times, a Latin church was built here as well.[82] Furthermore, a number of Nestorian tombstones from the 13th and 14th century, ornamented by crosses and leaves, were found in the Ongut area. K. Grœnbech points out: 'Similar stones have been found elsewhere, too, but nowhere in such numbers.'[83] These tombstones, found in the vicinity of towns, bear inscriptions in Syriac letters, their language being Turkish, however. They usually consist of a single line, reading: 'This tomb is that of N. N.'

A greater number of amulets, combining the symbol of the cross with Buddhist and shamanistic emblems like that of the lotus and the swastika, etc., were also found in the Ordos area[84] (see pl. 33). Such amulets must have been used by people of various Turkish and Mongol tribes, even if they had not been converted to Christianity. The magical power ascribed to the cross would have enabled the incorporation of this sign into the religious symbolism employed to ward off worldly dangers and enhance the positive powers in a life constantly endangered by incalculable outward events. William of Rubruk tells us about the use of the cross, pigmented on the hand, among the Uighurs.[85]

Another Turkish area partly Christianized lay further west to the south of Lake Balkash, in the area of the 'seven rivers', especially in the area of Semiriče. Here, a great number of Christian tombstones, stemming from the 9th to the 14th century, i.e. a period of 500 years, were found at the end of the last century. Many similar stones have been discovered in the region since.[86] The inscriptions are written in Syrian and Turkish, with the use of Syriac letters. In two graveyards more than 600 tombstones with such inscriptions surrounding the sign of the cross were found. N. N.

Pantusov, who was one of the pioneers in that discovery, was of the opinion that in one graveyard near Pishpek alone, measuring 256 × 128 m, about 3000 people must have been buried.[87] Of the 610 inscriptions available to the first decipherer, D. Chwolson, 423, i.e. two thirds, had dates inscribed on them. These are indicated by the use of the Sasanian calendar as well as of the Turkish cycle of 12 years. The oldest date found on the tombstones is AD 825, followed by those of 911 and 1201. The latest is AD 1367/1368. This makes it quite clear that we have here an old Nestorian tradition, continuing up to the second missionary phase and ending with the decline of Mongol power. However, there is also another reason for the end of the Christian tradition here. For the tombstones dated AD 1338 and 1339 refer to the black plague, which must have eliminated most remnants of the Christian community in that area. In addition, Christianity was losing ground simultaneously in neighbouring Mongol dominated Persia, when the Il-Khans turned to Islam at about this time.[88] However, the first examples of Sogdian Christian sepulchral art stem from a later period. Thus one remarkable stone, the gravestone of one 'exegete Nestorius', dated to AD 1301/1302, shows a Nestorian cross on a lotus flower, flanked by two angels in long flowing robes of Chinese appearance, the flower being based on an altar reminiscent of Zoroastrian fire altars[89] (cf. pl. 31). The latest gravestone found hitherto is dated to AD 1367/1368 (i.e. the year of the fall of the Mongol dynasty in China), and commemorates the death of 'the blessed lady Constantina' (cf. pl. 32). The very well executed inscription is surrounded by an ornamental border and crowned by a Nestorian cross.[90]

The contents of the inscriptions from Semiriče, as well as Almaliq, make it quite clear that Nestorian priests, to some extent at least, led married lives.[91]

Yet there are also references to monasteries. Of importance was apparently the office of the periodeut who travelled about to preach in the country-side. Yet other religious persons, especially regular preachers and exegetes, are also mentioned. On one tombstone it says:

> 'In the year 1627 (i.e. AD 1316) which was the year of the Eclipses, and the Turkish Luu (i.e. Dragon). This is the tomb of Shelicha, the famous Exegete and Preacher who enlightened all the Cloisters with Light, being the son of Exegete Peter. He was famous for his wisdom, and when preaching his voice sounded like a trumpet. May our Lord unite his enlightened soul with those of the righteous and of the forefathers so that it may be worthy of participating in all glories.'[92]

Of interest is the fact that the Christians of Semiriče were buried together with the Christians from other areas in Asia, including India and China. Thus one woman is described as 'Tarim the Chinese', a priest is called 'Banus the Uighurian' and a layman 'Sazik the Indian'. Furthermore there are references in the tombstone inscriptions that people were buried here not only from the vicinity, but also from other areas, including East and West Turkestan, Mongolia, Manchuria, Siberia and Persia.[93] The inscriptions, though terse, thus shed light on the Nestorian community of Turks with their international contacts in the area south of Lake Balkash, giving evidence of a varied Christian life in one corner of Central Asia.[94]

Related to the tombstones of Semiriče, among which there is even a bilingual Syrian-Armenian inscription, there are those of Almaliq in the upper Ili valley, on the eastern side of the present Chinese border. Almaliq was the residence of the Turkish Čagatai rulers in the 13th and 14th centuries. The fact that it was at this time an important centre of Nestorianism is borne out by the fact that it then had metropolitan status.[95] Most of the inscriptions on tombstones from Almaliq are Syrian, but Turkish epitaphs have also been found.[96] In recent times, further such gravestones were discovered in the area by Chinese archaeologists.

West of Almaliq, in the region of Lake Issik-Köl, mainly in the city of Navekath, similar gravestones were also discovered. Navekath too was a metropolitan see in the 13th and 14th centuries.[97] Of the tombstones found in this area, now part of Kirgizia, about 15% bear Turkish inscriptions, the rest Syrian ones. The oldest ones are in Syrian alone, then follow, chronologically, those in Syrian and Turkish, and finally those in Turkish only. This indicates a marked tendency toward indigenisation, which becomes more apparent the further we go east. Though Syrian names appear which Turks would also have borne, the names are mainly Turkish. Whereas the shorter inscriptions only indicate the name of the deceased, others mention his age at the time of death and indicate the position he held in respect to his family and tribe. It is noteworthy that not only common people but also Khans and Queens were buried in these graveyards. Thus one Turkish inscription from Kirgizia records:

> 'According to the calendar (based on) Alexander the Great, it was in the year 1647 (i.e. AD 1336), on the 14th of December. At the dawn of the morning, in the year of the mouse, the Khan Changshi sat down on the throne at the topmost position . . ., and he prepared a memorial service for this Queen Alma. She was a new bride (?). . . . That lady departed in the year of the pig. . . . She died at exactly 26. May a memorial stone be erected for her and may she not be forgotten by her friends.'[98]

It is probable that the Christian Turks north of the main range of the Tien-Shan mountains derived the Syrian script with its particular peculiarities from the Christians in the Turfan area with whom they probably had close contact since the 9th century. The fact that they were later integrated into Čagatai country is borne out by the language of the inscriptions which belong to the Qarluq-Čagatai group of Middle Turkish languages.

The rise of the Mongols under Jinghis Khan occurred in the area where Christianity had thrived amongst the Keraits and Naimans for as much as two centuries.[99] Jinghis Khan, whose original name was Temüčin, originally served in the army of the Christian king of the Keraits as his father had done. On his way to power, he rose up against the Kerait ruler in AD 1203, defeated him and subjugated his tribe. In the same manner, he also subjugated the Naiman and other Turkish clans amongst whom there was a considerable number of Christians. Though he gradually gained power, the beginning of his rule is taken to be AD 1206, at which time he had gained decisive influence in the Mongolian steppes. In AD 1220, Mongol power was established as far west as Transoxania, including Sogdia, i.e. the whole area referred to as Western Turkestan. The conquest of Bukhara and Samarkand by the Mongols was so bloody a campaign that in Samarkand alone only one fourth of the population survived. The majority of the citizens of the country, including Christians, was eradicated by the Mongols, even though many Christians served in the Mongol army.

The cities south of the Oxus probably met with the same fate. Merv, still an important Nestorian centre, was devastated to such an extent in AD 1221 that a million or more people are said to have died in the area.[100] The ruthlessness of the Mongols in subjugating new territories is referred to often by Muslim writers. But once Mongol power was established, the new rulers exercised a great amount of tolerance. They could now even promote and protect Christianity which thrived anew in the great realm.

Mongol rule in Central Asia made it possible for trade and commerce to flourish once more, the routes from Persia to China being secure again. Together with commercial activity, other contacts were also re-established. Thus it was now possible for Christians in the most remote areas of Central Asia to revive ties with the Patriarch in Baghdad. A whole chain of Nestorian metropolitan sees and bishoprics stretched from Mesopotamia to China, certainly areas in which the Nestorians were often a dwindling minority. But they were held together by the common faith and the Syrian Church language, used in liturgy and theology.

South of the Oxus, the ecclesiastical centre of Merv flourished anew in the 13th century, beside which Tus became an important episcopal see again. In the area of the upper Oxus, there was, in the 14th century, a metropolitanate responsible for the Kalač, a Turkish people roughly occupying an area formerly held by the Hephthalites.[101] By the end of the 13th century, Samarkand had a flourishing Christian community again. And in the area of the Yaxartes, the old metropolitanate 'Turkestan' was revived. The same ecclesiastical status, enjoyed by Samarkand, was also given to Kashgar again. The city of Yarkand further east also had a Christian population at this time. Turfan must have remained a centre of Christian learning up to Mongol times, the metropolitan see of Almaliq probably being responsible for that oasis.

Marco Polo tells us that he met Buddhists, Muslims and Christians in Turfan,[102] which must have remained a Christian centre of learning up to Mongol times. In the linguistic usage of Syrians in Mesopotamia, 'Christians' and 'Uighurs' were synonymous.[103]

As long as the Pax Mongolica lasted, and as long as the successor states to the great Mongol Empire founded by Jinghis Khan had not adopted Islam or Buddhism as the official religion, Nestorian Christianity in Central Asia could flourish. With the decline of the Mongols, however, and with the spread of Islamic power from West Turkestan to the area of East Turkestan, and with the adoption of Buddhism by the Mongols in the steppes in and after the 14th century, Christianity was pushed more and more into the background.

DECLINE OF CHRISTIANITY

It is difficult to trace the demise of Christianity in Central Asia. One of the reasons for its final death-blow in the middle of the 14th century was the spread of the plague, records of which we find in the Semiriče inscriptions. Thus one inscription reads: 'In the year 1650 (i.e. AD 1339) the hare year. This is the grave of Kutluk (Qutlugh). He died of plague with his wife Mangu Kelka (Mängü Kalqa).'[104] A number of inscriptions make reference to the plague which seems also to have been one of the reasons for the demise of the small Christian community in areas west of Lake Issik-Köl.[105] The plague haunted Central Asia in AD 1337–1339. It was to spread to China, India, the Near East and Europe in the middle of the 14th century.

But the spread of the terrible disease was only one reason for the end of Christian communities. After all, it affected other religious communities as well. So political history also has to be taken into account. A major reason for the demise of Christianity was the spread of an intolerant Islam, which initially had exercised tolerance over against Christians as a people having a holy book.[106]

The successors of Muhammad had appointed Christians to high positions at the court and in the administration. In Abbasid times, the patriarch was allowed to reside in Baghdad, the centre of power, a privilege not granted to other religious groups. In spite of pressure on Christians to convert, which led to conversions to Islam or to emigration, there is evidence of Islamic tolerance toward Christians even in the 12th century. One document, described by Mingana as a 'charter of protection granted to the Nestorian Church in AD 1138, by Muktafi II, Caliph of Baghdad',[107] is really a document confirming and recognizing the election of Patriarch Abdiso III (AD 1138–1147) to his office and reiterating 'statutory prerogatives' to Christians granted by earlier Caliphs.[108] Of course there were intermittent times of persecution, especially in the wake of the Arab conquest of West Turkestan.[109] In particular the Turks, turning to Islam, adopted this new faith with fervour. Among these were the Seljuks, one of the first Turkish tribes of importance to become Islamic. Spreading their rule to the west and capturing Baghdad in AD 1055, their dynasty was to last up to AD 1156, when their realm started to break up. Although among the Seljuk rulers there appear to have been Christians bearing such names as Israel and Michael, a ruler like Alp Arslan (d. AD 1072) violently persecuted adherents of Christianity.

The spread of Islam in Turkestan does not allow us to discern a definite pattern of Muslim attitude toward Christians. Yet with regard to Turks and Mongols, Stewart aptly sums up the change of attitude after the acceptance of Islam. He points out:

'So far as either the Turks or the Mongols were concerned, the fact of a man becoming a Christian did not weaken his sense of nationality. The nation was put first, and Christian and pagan alike were united in common loyalty to their country. When they became Moslems, however, religion was put first, and gradually the Turkish rulers came to look upon the combining of the religious and political elements as one way by which their power might be increased, and acted accordingly.'[110]

The complex history of Turkish Islam in Central Asia and its effect on the Christian community cannot be understood without sketching the disintegration of the Mongol Empire.

AD 1260 is of key importance for that development. The family of the Jinghissides now split up into two parties, the realm of the Golden Horde (Kipčak) and of Čagatai (Transoxania and Turkestan) on the one hand, and the Khanate of China, first ruled by Khubilai Khan (d. AD 1294), and the Il-Khanate of Persia on the other. The next main stage is marked by the secession of Mongol Persia from the Khanate of China in AD 1295. With this step, the great Mongol realm had fallen apart. In China and Persia, the indigenous race and culture now increasingly absorbed that of the nomadic conquerors.

In so far as the Mongol state of the Golden Horde or the Kipčaks was concerned, the first ruler of which was Batu (d. AD 1255), an opponent of Christianity, the realm opened up politically under the fourth ruler Berke (d. AD 1266). With regard to international affairs, religious tolerance was maintained, but in terms of foreign policy, Berke made a treaty with the Islamic state of the Mamluks, forming an alliance with them in AD 1265. Thus the cause of Islam was strengthened. The ruler Tuda Mangu (d. AD 1287) was strongly inspired by Islam. And though the counter-ruler Mogar allowed for Christianity to flourish temporarily, a wave of Islamization went over the realm in the middle of the 14th century, bringing traditional Mongol tolerance and Christian activity to an end.[111]

South-east of the Golden Horde was the Khanate of Čagatai, named after the first ruler of this realm (d. AD 1242). Its two main centres of power were the Persian-Arab Bukhara and the Turkish-Uighur Beshbaliq. Main religions in this realm were Buddhism and Nestorian Christianity, beside indigenous religions of a shamanistic type. In the beginning of the 14th century, under the reign of Tarmaširin (d. AD 1334), the court became and remained Islamic. This led to a persecution of Christians in Almaliq and probably in other places, in the wake of which many turned to the religion of Muhammad. It was probably at this time that Christianity became extinct in the Turfan area.

In so far as the Il-Khanate of Persia was concerned, its roots go back to the establishment of Mongol power in Chorasan, i.e. eastern Iran. The generals of the Great Khans remained there up to AD 1256, keeping the rulers of Western Asia at bay. After Mangu (d. AD 1259) had been elected Great Khan, Hulagu, designated ruler of Mongol Persia, conquered large areas of Western Asia. In 1258, Baghdad and with it the Abbasid Caliphate, fell. It was only in AD 1260 that advancing Mongol power was checked by the Islamic Mamluks of Egypt.

The realm of the Il-Khans, having main centres in Chorasan and Asserbaijan, was limited geographically in the west by the Islamic Mamluk state with its capital in Cairo. In the north-east there was the Golden Horde with its centre at Serai, opening up to Islamic influence at the time of Berke. To the north-west, finally, was the realm of Čagatai,[112] becoming increasingly Islamic.

The main line of events as sketched above indicates the general situation for Christians in Persia and Central Asia in the second half of the 13th century. It is obvious that political changes were the main factors leading to an extinction of Christian communities. Although such communities continued to exist into the 14th century, the demise was epitomized by the bloody conquests and ravages of Timur (d. AD 1405), who established the house of the Timurids which was to exist up to AD 1500.[113] We need not outline the establishment of a Muslim empire by Timur, nor is it necessary to sketch his ruthless campaigns. Suffice it to point out that it was not only his devastating scourge, inspired by fierce anti-Christian sentiments, that resulted in the lapse of Christianity, but also the substitution of the law of Islam for the tolerant legal system established by the Mongols. 'He [i.e. Timur] thus broke entirely with Mongol tradition and drew the Turks of Central Asia out of touch with the East.'[114] The inscriptions of Semiriče throw the last beams of light on the vanishing Christian community. One inscription from the year AD 1333 says: 'This is the grave of the scholar [i.e. student] San-da-jok, the boy Pazak Tekin, and the young girl Marian. These three have died in Muhammadanism.'[115] Whatever the reasons for burying converts to Islam at the Christian cemetery, the fact of the free-willed or forced conversion is obvious. As pointed out, the last Christian tombstone is dated AD 1367/ 1368.

In 1295, the Catholicos-Patriarch left Baghdad, receding to the highlands of Hakkari (in the border area between Turkey, Irak and Iran). Here, as well as in the Mossul area, the contemporary representatives of the Nestorian community still exist as the national 'Assyrian Church', having lost its 'outer metropolitans' further east. Outside their homeland, the Assyrians are to be found in other parts of the world, as far away as in the USA and in Australia.

In the eastern part of the Mongol realm, it was Buddhism, especially in its Tibetan form, that won the day over against the other religions, only Eastern Turkestan becoming Islamic by AD 1500. The first contacts of Mongol rulers with Tibetan Lamaism go back to the 13th century, when Prince Godan, after the election of Kuyuk (d. AD 1248), met with the Tibetan lama Sa-skya Pandita. His nephew 'Phags-pa (d. AD 1280), active diplomatically at the Mongol court of Khubilai Khan, was able to arouse the interest of leading circles in the Tibetan form of Buddhism. Although we do hear of Nestorians and other Christian denominations at the Mongol court in Khan Baliq in the accounts of Western travellers, including Marco Polo, it is apparent that the influence of Tibetans, especially from the monastery of Sa-skya, was a decisive one.[116] But conversions were of a religio-political nature. The actual far-reaching conversion of Mongols to Buddhism was a matter of later centuries. In Yuan times (AD 1279–1368), the increasing influence of the lamas on the Khans had to be of disadvantage to representatives of other religions. However, it was only with the fall of the Mongol Yuan Dynasty in China in AD 1368 that all foreigners were driven out of the land. This also had its effect on Turkish and Mongolian eastern Central Asia, where we have no more definite marks of Christianity after that time.[117]

ORGANISATION OF THE CHURCH IN CENTRAL AND EAST ASIA

In the Persian Church's mission to the east, we see at work both monastic and such ecclesiastical forces as displayed a more positive orientation towards the world. A number of texts found at Turfan reflect monastic and eremitic ideals with an emphasis on fasting, penance, mystic experience and preparation for death and judgement. But beside such documents we also have a great number pertaining not to personal mystic experience but to religious life in the community, the centre of which was the celebration of the liturgy, especially the Eucharist.[118]

Perhaps the main characteristic feature of the 'Church of the East', however, spreading out to Central Asia and China, was the development of a balance between ecclesiastical centralisation and regional autonomy granted to more remote 'outward areas'. The metropolitans had far-reaching freedom in so far as regulating internal affairs was concerned. Yet they owed allegiance to the patriarch, having to inform him of major events in their areas.

In accordance with East Syrian tradition, there were various priestly ranks in the hierarchy of the Nestorian Church.[119] Head of the Church was, of course, the Patriarch, the Metropolitan of Seleucia-Ctesiphon, who resided in Baghdad from Abbasid times on (i.e., after mid-7th century). He was called 'Father of Fathers', 'Supreme Shepherd' and 'Peter of our Days'. Since AD 544 he had called himself 'Catholicos-Patriarch'. He had full jurisdictional powers, always in loyalty to non-Christian rulers. It was the Catholicos who convened and led synods, who consecrated bishops, even for more remote 'outward regions', and who established bishoprics.

In accordance with the hierarchy of the angels, there being nine grades grouped into threes, the hierarchy of the Church was also divided into three triads:[120]

1 the high priestly triad (Catholicos-Patriarch, metropolitans, bishops)
2 the priestly triad (rural assistant bishops, archdeacons and priests)
3 the serving triad (deacons, subdeacons, lectors).

In reality, there were also other offices having a supervising or serving function. Basically, this structure can also be found in Central and East Asia. Under the metropolitans were the archbishops and bishops who could be married. Junior to these were the chorepiscopoi, the 'assistant bishops', who looked after the country districts. Although there was supposed to be only one assistant bishop in a diocese, the vast areas of Central and East Asia sometimes made it necessary to have several. In AD 781, there were three chorepiscopoi under the bishop in Sian-fu. Under the assistant bishop was the periodeut, the visiting superintendent, whose work it was to travel around to members of the far-flung diocese, this being especially important in the case of a nomadic situation. There was no limit to the number of visiting superintendents in a diocese, and we hear of a great number in the congregations around Lake Issik-Köl in the 13th and 14th centuries. Increasingly, the function of the visiting superintendent was accommodated to that of the assistant bishop, whose significance waned as the number of superintendents increased. Next in rank was the archdeacon who was responsible for the daily administration of the diocese and the supervision of the priests, deacons and subdeacons. In the course of time, the rank of the archdeacon, still mentioned after the chorepiscopus in the stele of Sian-fu in AD 781, could be raised to such an extent that he became superior to the latter (cf. also the parallel to be found in the Church in South India).

Below the priest in a stricter sense, to whom the greatest number of clergymen belonged, were the deacons and subdeacons. Their number was much smaller than that of the priests. In the Sian-fu inscription, only two are mentioned beside 24 priests. The most junior members of the clergy, finally, were the sextons or liturgical assistants helping in the Church service. Apparently of a lower order were also the exorcists whose function it was to cast out evil spirits, which would appeal especially to Christians in a shamanistic environment.

Beside the clerics, there were also laymen serving in the Church in different positions. There was a steward, subject to the control of the bishop, to take care of the local property and material wealth of the Church. Similar in function was the office of the Church superviser. According to the Sian-fu inscription, an archdeacon could hold the office of a supervisor, a certain Gabriel being named as such (as 'head of the Church' in some translations) for Sian-fu and Loyang. Finally, we also hear of charity superintendents to supervisor the charitable work of the Church.

The Nestorian Church did not demand celibacy of its priests. At times, marriage was even allowed for bishops, archbishops and the Patriarch himself. Even after being consecrated, priests could take a wife, and clergymen who had lost their wives could marry for a second time. Often enough, the sons of clergymen became priests themselves, as in the case of Mark, son of an archdeacon, who devoted himself to a monastic life and later became Patriarch Yaballaha III. In a family in the Issik-Köl area, not only the grandfather was a periodeut, but in due course also his son and grandson, not that the office was hereditary. Whereas in China the clergy was almost exclusively of foreign extraction, consisting mainly of Syrians and Iranians, even one and a half centuries after the introduction of Christianity, many natives, mainly Turks and Mongols, were consecrated to clerical offices in Central Asia. Yet beside them there were also Syrians and Persians in the far-flung area. Thus we know of a Syrian clergyman at the court of the Mongol ruler Kuyuk. William of Rubruk was critical of a Nestorian practice in the area of Karakorum where he heard that almost all male children baptised received consecration as priests. Maybe this is the reason why men ordained also held other offices, even in the military, as we learn from tombstone inscriptions. Even King George (Giwargis) of the Onguts who was to turn to Catholicism at the urging of John of Montecorvino, was consecrated a Nestorian priest.

The Nestorians in Central Asia had no problems with the recruitment of clergy, but other Christian confessions, more sparsely represented, did. Among the Jacobites there were probably sufficient priests in areas well populated by such Christians, but others like the Alans, coming from the Caucasus, were without spiritual guidance. Like the Chalcedonians (and later the Russian Orthodox) they were dependent on individual priests who would come to Central Asia by themselves or as prisoners of the Mongols. Thus John of Plano Carpini met Russian clerics at the court of Guyuk.

Beside priests of various ranks, Christian monks played a decisive role in the religious life in Central and East Asia.[121] The traveller Cosmas Indicopleustes tells us at the beginning of the 6th century of monks in Bactria living among the Hephthalites as hermits.[122] Many Christian envoys in Central Asia in the following period, including those sent out by Timothy I, were monks. Mar Sergius who is credited with the conversion of the king of the Keraits retired to the remote Altai mountains as a hermit.

A number of Christian monasteries were established in the course of time in the wide area between Iran and China. In the region of Merv, there were several monasteries, the first being founded, according to tradition, by Bar Shabba in the 5th century, others in the 8th and 9th century. We know of a monastic centre in the mountains south of Samarkand, at a place called Wazkarda. Further east, Christians had monasteries in Qurutqa and Bulayiq in the Turfan region. In all probability they were established before the 10th century. In one text from Bulayiq we hear of a 'visiting priest' in the monastery of that town whose presence led to a severe argument.[123] In China, to which we will turn again in the next chapter, the monasteries were also pillars of Christian life before their extinction in the 9th century.

Although the gravestones of the region of Lake Issik-Köl contain no hints as to monks buried here, there must have been a monastery in this region in the 13th and 14th centuries, as there was one in a mountain pass between Lake Issik-Köl and Kashgar; perhaps the monks were buried in monastic cemeteries.

There were also Nestorian monks at the courts of the great Mongol Khans, some being engaged in the education of young princes, others serving in various other positions.[124] According to tradition, 'holy men' from Syria had come previously to Jinghis Khan, the founder of the Mongol Empire. And at the time of Emperor Kuyuk who was favourably disposed towards Christians, there were monks at his court from Asia Minor, Syria, the Caucasian mountains and Russia. William of Rubruk tells us about the respect shown to a Nestorian monk by Kuyuk himself.

Beside monks devoted to a communal life in monasteries, there were also Christian hermits. The Syrian eremitic life-style came to be esteemed in China. We have had occasion to talk about the hermits Rabban Sauma and Mark, who was to become Patriarch Yaballaha III[125], in a previous chapter.

In accord with the Nestorian Synods of the 7th–9th century, the monasteries and hermitages were under the jurisdiction of the regional bishop. In Sian-fu, the bishop even resided in a monastery in T'ang times. The monastic centre in the region of Lake Issik-Köl was subject to administrators under the supervision of the metropolitan of Navekath or Almaliq.[126]

In the Mongol realm, all monasteries including the Christian ones were exempt from taxes according to a decree of Jinghis Khan which was renewed by Ogodai (d. AD 1241) and Mangu (d. AD 1259). In the Yuan-Dynasty, a Ministry of Rites, headed first by a Tibetan lama and then by a Christian of the Ma family, had to supervise the ecclesiastical life of the Christians.[127]

Beside Nestorian monks, other Christian monks also found their way to Central and East Asia.[128] In the 6th century the Armenian Bishop Makarios lived among christianized Turks. In the court of Mangu, a certain Bishop Stephanos, a monk, appeared in the company of the Armenian king Hetum I in AD 1255, and an Armenian monk Sergius, coming from Jerusalem, arrived at the court of Mangu a month before William of Rubruk came. The Franciscan describes him as a man of detestable appearance and character. The presence of Armenians in Central Asia is also attested by an Armenian monastery near Lake Issik-Köl in the 14th century, an apparent head of which, a certain Bishop Jovan, was buried in a Nestorian cemetery there in AD 1323.

Monks of Chalcedonian persuasion, i.e. Melkites, had come to Transoxania in the 6th century. They might have come as far as the oasis of Khotan.

The European monks finally who found their way to Central and East Asia in the 13th and 14th century belonged primarily to the order of the Franciscans. We shall now turn to them and their relationship to other Christians.

THE PLURALITY OF CHRISTIAN DENOMINATIONS IN CENTRAL ASIA AND THE APPEARANCE OF LATIN CHRISTIANS

Hitherto, we have sketched the expansion of Nestorian Christianity in Central Asia, i.e. the eastern branch of Syrian Christianity that had its roots in the autocephalous Persian Church. Its patriarchs resided in Seleucia-Ctesiphon, the winter capital of the Sasanians up to the rise of Islam in the middle of the 7th century.

Beside the Nestorian East Syrian Church, which called itself the 'Church of the East', the monophysite West Syrian Church, also known as the Jacobite ('Syrian Orthodox') Church,[129] was well represented in Persia as well as in areas further west. It, too, had its hierarchy, the head of which was also a patriarch. The West Syrian Church, though never as strong as the Nestorian Church before the 14th century, had communities in eastern Iran, in Chorasan, and in the area west and south of the Oxus. The main source for the history of the eastern expansion of the Jacobites is the *Chronicle of Michael the Syrian*,[130] written by that Jacobite Patriarch around AD 1196 and covering the time between the 8th and 12th centuries. It reports on bishops and metropolitans of the Church. Further sources are

Syriac annals and histories, in particular the chronicles of the great Church leader, theologian and historian Barhebraeus (d. AD 1286), who as head of the Jacobite Church under the Mongol Il-Khans in Persia was well informed about historical and contemporary events. His two main works are the *Chronicon Syriacum* and the *Chronicon Ecclesiasticum*,[131] which do not restrict themselves to Jacobite history. These and other sources[132] make us aware of Jacobite deportees from Edessa who had settled in Chorasan in the 7th century. Herat was one of their main centres, and in the 9th century Patriarch Denys of Tel Mahre (d. AD 845) created a bishopric and then a metropolitan see there. The Jacobite tradition established thereby was to stay alive up to the first half of the 11th century. In the 7th century, Jacobite soldiers were also stationed in Gurgan, south-east of the Caspian Sea. Jacobite bishops were installed here under the Patriarch Philoxenus (d. AD 817) and the above-mentioned Denys of Tel Mahre. They seem to have lapsed permanently in the 9th century.

As far as Transoxania and areas further east are concerned, a Jacobite presence was not marked, but we do hear of not only individual priests of that community in the far-flung area of Central Asia proper, but also of Jacobite colonies.[133] According to Dauvillier, there was such a one in the country of the Uighurs.[134] As E. C. D. Hunter points out:

'The Nestorian preponderance may have dissuaded the Jacobites from establishing anything other than a marginal foothold. But it would be trite to attribute the Jacobite sparseness in Transoxania and Turkestan, solely to Nestorian opposition.

. . . On the other hand, the decline of Nestorian influence, with the disintegration of the Sasanid court in AD 7C, may have enabled the Jacobites to expand into territories that were traditionally Nestorian.'[135]

From Western travellers to the Mongol courts we know that beside Nestorians and Jacobites, other Christian denominations were also present in Central Asia, even before the appearance of Latin envoys on the scene. Thus Armenians[136] are attested at various places and at various times. According to the Catalanian world map of Abraham Cresques of AD 1375, there was an Armenian monastery near Lake Issik-Köl. And in an inscription on a tombstone in Semiriče, written in Syriac and Armenian, we learn that an Armenian bishop was buried here in the first half of the 14th century. Whether he was a bishop of that monastery, we do not know. But the use of both languages is striking. It seems to reflect a harmonious relationship between Syrian and Armenian Christians, in spite of all animosities between both groups in Western Asia.

At this point, the missions of Latin priests to the Mongol courts must be sketched. We shall concentrate here on the diplomatic contacts between

Western Christianity and the Mongol rulers, initiated, mainly, by Pope Innocent IV.

The history of Franciscan monks travelling to Central and East Asia is one that lasted hardly one hundred years. Yet the events of this epoch are important in view of the information those travellers have supplied, which sheds light on religious as well as social and political affairs. Their reports are of great interest since they came into direct contact with an Asian Christianity that had spread independent of Western missionary efforts.[137]

The capitals of the Mongols to which the Latin envoys travelled were Sira Ordu and Karakorum in the Mongol steppes (capitals from AD 1235–1257) and later Khan Baliq in China (capital AD 1267–1368). We shall deal here with the early period.

The beginning of contact between Western Europe and the Mongols was ushered in when the Golden Horde, one of the powers that emerged from the realm of Jinghis Khan, under the nominal command of Batu (d. AD 1241) and the Mongol general Subotai, advanced into Eastern Europe. They entered the plains of Poland and Hungary in AD 1240 and 1242 respectively, after the conquest of north-eastern Russia in AD 1238. Europe itself now seemed threatened. Jinghis Khan's son Ogodai (d. AD 1241) aimed at establishing an empire stretching from China to Europe. Under his rule, a great portion of China had already been incorporated. Persia had been lain waste. When Mongol horsemen appeared on the Hungarian plains, 'the complacency and lassitude of Europe was shaken', as C. Cary-Elwes puts it.[138] Ogodai died in AD 1241 in the Central Asian steppes, and this caused the Golden Horde, under Batu, to retreat as suddenly as it had come. But this fact, the death of the Great Khan, was not known in Europe.

In AD 1245, a great Council of the Catholic Church was held at Lyons, convoked by Pope Innocent IV, in agreement with the Emperor. One of the main issues was to be the consideration of means to avert the Mongol threat. Although the Council did not achieve much, it did make Europe aware of the mighty power further east that was to determine the course of history. In the letter of invitation to the Council, the aim was proclaimed as 'to find a remedy against the Tartars.'[139]

Even before the Council convened, Innocent IV decided to send envoys to the Great Khan, fathoming the possibility of peace, endeavouring to hold him back from the continued ravaging of Christian countries, and even trying to win him for Christianity. He did so in light of the fact that in the winter of AD 1244/1245, a Russian Archbishop by the name of Peter had appeared at the Papal court and had brought news to the effect that the Mongols received foreign diplomats in a friendly manner.[140]

The first envoy selected for a diplomatic mission to the 'Tartars' was Laurence of Portugal. He was to bring a letter to the Khan, to be presented as a Papal Bull, dated Lyons, 5th March, 1245. The Pope began his letter with a summary of christological theology, and admonished the Khan to accept Christianity as it would be explained to him by the friar envoys, i.e. by Laurence and his companions,

> 'so that following their salutary instructions you may acknowledge Jesus Christ the very son of God and worship His glorious name by practising the Christian religion.'[141]

The letter concluded with the request

> 'to receive these Friars kindly and to treat them in considerate fashion out of reverence for God and for us, indeed as if receiving us in their persons.'[142]

Laurence never embarked on his trip. Yet the document preserved is interesting in that it vividly reveals the Papal attitude towards the Mongols at this time.

About a week later, another letter was written to the Khan, dated Lyons, 13th March, 1245. This letter, also written in the form of a Papal Bull, is like the aforementioned document, but is somewhat different in content. It refers to the order of the universe, sanctioned by God, it reproaches the Mongols for having disturbed this order, and it exhorts them to penitence. The main concern is the demand for political peace. The Pope writes to the Khan:

> 'Make fully known to us through these . . . Friars what moved you to destroy other nations and what your intentions are for the future.'[143]

The envoy to bring this letter to the Great Khan was the Franciscan Friar John of Plano Carpini. John hailed from a little Italian village near Perugia. When he set out from Lyons, he was already 65 years of age. Like his master, St. Francis, it was his wish to win converts for the Christian faith and this was also his aim with respect to the Khan, although his prime task was to act as a Papal envoy. He was neither equipped with the knowledge of any Oriental language nor with material means. But he was endowed with a dauntless spirit. As he wrote in the Prologue of his *History of the Mongols*:

> '. . . we feared that we might be killed by the Tartars or other people, or imprisoned for life, or afflicted with hunger, thirst, cold, heat, injuries and exceeding great trials almost beyond our powers of endurance – all of which, with the exception of death and imprisonment for life, fell to our lot in various ways in a much greater degree than we had conceived beforehand.'[144]

When Friar Plano Carpini left Lyons on April 16th, AD 1245, he was accompanied by another Friar of the Franciscan order, Stephen of Bohemia. From King Wenzeslaus IV of Bohemia he received letters to allow for his journey through Poland and the kingdom of Kiev. In Warsaw, Friar Benedict of Poland joined the group; he was to act as translator. Friar Plano Carpini has left us a narrative about this Polish companion who apparently won closer contact to the court than he himself did.[145]

The party travelled by way of Kiev to the Black Sea, then following a southern route to Mongolia and being taken from one Mongol camp to the other. On the way, Stephen became ill and had to return. On February 4th, AD 1246, they reached the camp of Batu on the Volga. Batu examined the Papal letter and then sent the friars on with his own letters and Tartar guides who took the envoys 'to the son of the Great Emperor . . . in the native land of the Tartars', as we hear in the narrative of Brother Benedict.[146] They reached their destination in Sira Ordu on 2nd July, AD 1246. They were to leave again on 13th November. John finally appeared before the Pope to report in November AD 1247. In accordance with the rule of discipline, he had travelled the whole way on foot, barefoot. On his way back already, Plano Carpini started to write his *History of the Mongols* (*Historia Mongalorum*), in which he described the land and the people of the Tartars (Ch. I-IV), the organisation of their state, as well as political and military affairs (Ch. VI-VIII). In the prologue, he discusses the objective of his trip, pointing out:

'. . . we did not spare ourselves in order to carry out the will of God as laid down in the Lord Pope's mandate, and be of some service to Christians, that, at all events, having learned the truth about the desire and intention of the Tartars, we could make this known to the Christians . . .'[147]

When the truth of the account was questioned, John of Plano Carpini added another chapter relating to personal affairs and to the experiences he made on his trip, including his experiences at the camp of the Khan.

From these personal notes as well as from the account of Friar Benedict we learn that when Plano Carpini arrived at the court of the Khan, Kuyuk was about to be elected as new ruler. Plano Carpini was struck by the great number of representatives of various tribes and nations at the Mongol centre of power at this time. He says:

'There were more than four thousand envoys there, counting those who were carrying tribute, those who were bringing gifts, the Sultans and other chiefs who were coming to submit to them, those summoned by the Tartars and the governors of territories.'[148]

There was present, for instance, a Russian duke, two Christian princes from Georgia (Georgian soldiers serving in the Mongol army), an ambassador from Baghdad, the centre of Abbasid power, and many Chinese dignitaries.

The election of Kuyuk took place a month after Plano Carpini arrived. When he then was finally able to take up contact with the new Khan, always mediated by high officials, his approach seems not to have been too diplomatic, for he tells us that the ruler 'set up a flag of defiance against the countries of the West.'[149] Brother Benedict, the Pole, seems to have been much more circumspect. Both received a letter for the Pope. The letter entrusted to Benedict well reflects the self-understanding of the Khan, who refers to himself as 'the Emperor of all men', pointing out that if God (he probably meant *tengri*, Heaven) had not been on his side, he could not have achieved the military feats he did. He questions the Christian's self-assurance, saying:

> 'But how can you know to whom God deigns to confer His grace? But we worshipping God have destroyed the whole earth from the East to the West in the power of God. And if this were not the power of God, what could men have done? Therefore if you accept peace and are willing to surrender your fortresses to us, you Pope and Christian princes, in no way delay coming to me to conclude peace and then we shall know that you wish to have peace with us. But if you should not believe our letters and the command of God nor harken to our counsel then we shall know for certain that you wish to have war. After that we do not know what will happen, God alone knows.'[150]

The letter entrusted by Kuyuk to Plano Carpini is similar in content. It is preserved in a Latin translation. Here too, Kuyuk, speaking with the same self-assertion, stresses that he is only ready for peace if the Pope and the rulers of Europe appear at the court and subject themselves to his rule. Furthermore he points out that he has no intention to convert to Christianity:

> 'Though thou . . . sayest that I should become a trembling Nestorian Christian, worship God and be an ascetic, how knowest thou whom God absolves, in truth to whom He shows mercy? How dost thou know that such words as thou speakest are with God's sanction? From the rising of the sun to its setting, all the lands have been made subject to me. Who could do this contrary to the command of God?'[151]

The self-esteem of the Khan is finally made visible in the inscription of the seal affixed to the letter which reads:

> 'We, by the power of the eternal Tengri [Heaven], universal Khan of the Great Mongol Ulus [Realm] – our command. If this reaches peoples who have made their submission, let them respect and stand in awe of it.'[152]

On his way back, Plano Carpini visited the Hungarian King Bela IV, 'who had provided him with most valuable information, and for whom up-to-date knowledge about the Mongols was a matter of life and death.'[153]

At the time when John of Plano Carpini went to the capital of the Mongols, a Dominican Friar, Asceline, was sent as Papal envoy to Batu, supreme commander of the Mongol army in Persia. After spending some time in Egypt and Syria, the legate, accompanied by other friars, reached the main camp of the Mongols in Chorasan on May 24, AD 1247. Simon of Quentin OP who talks about the events,[154] informs us that religious and theological questions were also discussed. The Mongols reprimanded the Christians for venerating wood and stone (i.e. the cross) and they expressed doubt about the divine mission of the Pope in view of his helplessness over against the Khan. The behaviour and the answer of the Dominicans was apparently in no way diplomatic so that they could only be saved from the death sentence by the wife of the commander. On July 25, AD 1247, they appeared before the Pope with an answer from the Mongols.

In close contact with Pope Innocent IV was Louis IX of France (d. AD 1270).[155] His crusade plans made it necessary to establish contact with the Mongols. In the winter of AD 1248/1249 the king took up diplomatic contact with envoys of the 'Tartars' from Persia on Cyprus. These contacts included talks between the King of France, the Mongols and the Christian rulers of the Near East. Louis, having heard exaggerated reports about the Christians in Mongol Central Asia, conceived of a plan to join forces with the Mongols against the Islamic Orient. In January AD 1249, the envoys of the French king, being led by Andrew of Longjumeau, met Ilchi-Khatai, the Mongol general in Persia, in Nikosia. Ilchi-Khatai had a high position at the court of the deceased Kuyuk. Through him, the envoys could take up contact with the ruling widow of Kuyuk, Oghul Gaymish. She wrote what was felt to be an arrogant letter to the king. Together with reports of the envoys who returned after AD 1250, this must have had a sobering effect.[156]

The most prominent envoy of Louis IX to the Mongols, however, was the Franciscan Friar William of Rubruk (or Rubruck) (d. AD 1270), who primarily understood himself as a monk and priest (*monachus et sacerdos*) rather than as a political agent (*nuntius*),[157] even though he had letters of recommendation from Louis IX. William was born around AD 1215 in Rubruk in French Flanders. He was active in Paris before accompanying Louis IX to Cyprus in AD 1248. Up to AD 1252 he stayed at Akkon. Having heard that the son of Batu, Sartach, had converted to Christianity, he decided to work as a priest in his area. He reached the camp of Sartach with a letter of Louis IX on July 31, AD 1253. Whether Sartach had actually become a Christian is hard to say. Sartach sent him to his father Batu, who in turn directed him to the great Khan Mangu, whose camp he reached on December 27, AD 1253. At this time the capital city of Karakorum had just been erected. William worked as a priest for the Latin Christians there, but he also had contact with Nestorians and other religious groups.

As the Khan did not allow William to stay in his realm for an extended period, he returned via the camp of Batu, Georgia and Armenia, going to Cyprus where Louis IX still was.

Having remained at Akkon for some time, William sent his itinerary to the king, requesting him, at the same time, for permission to return to France. Having received that permission, he returned to Paris, where he had occasion to report his observations, one of his hearers being Roger Bacon. Friar William died in AD 1270 at the age of fifty-five.

The importance of William of Rubruk's account of his journey to the Mongols lies in the fact that he provides a wealth of information not only on political and social affairs, but also on the very pluralistic situation, including reports on Nestorianism which was starting to dwindle when he took up his work around AD 1250. From William we also hear of people of the most varied background, present at the Mongol court. We read of Tanguts, Tibetans, Chinese, 'Saracenes' (i.e. Muslims), Keraits, Naimans, Alans, Georgians, Armenians, even a Frenchman, an Englishman and a woman from France who had been made prisoner in Hungary. The Frenchman, William Bouchier, was there with his wife. In so far as Christians were concerned, we hear that the Nestorians would not allow men of other denominations to partake of the sacraments except for the Latins.

We read of an encounter between William and the Great Khan Mangu soon after his arrival. Having been searched for weapons, he was allowed into the tent of the ruler. But since both the Khan and William's interpreter were drunk, no important matters were discussed. Later Mangu visited the Nestorian Church and examined William's bible and breviary. At a later point, the Khan criticised the Nestorians, pointing out that they did not follow the rules of their scripture.

To William the Nestorian Church seemed decadent. Commenting on the Chinese Nestorians he met at Karakorum, he decries the fact that they are more concerned about obtaining money than with spreading the faith. Those who educate young noble Mongols teach them the Gospel and the faith, but yet alienate them from the practice of Christian virtue by setting a bad example in their own lives. They are for him usurers and drunkards, given to simony, for they do not administer the sacraments without a fee. The lives of the 'idolaters' seem to him more innocent than their lives.[158]

Beside Nestorians, John and William also met Christians of other confessions in Central Asia. We have already spoken of Armenians, Russians, Georgians, Hungarians and French at the court of the Khans in Karakorum in the middle of the 13th century. Germans, too, are to be mentioned in this connection. Some of them had been sent to dig for gold and to manufacture arms.[159] Others had the positions of slaves.[160] The two Franciscan friars talk vividly of these various groups and the relationships between them.

248

We can use the travel accounts of John of Plano Carpini and William of Rubruk to throw light on the diversity of Christian communities in Central Asia at the time of the Mongols. We can hereby follow a path blazed out by W. Hage who has assembled material on the subject of coexistence of Christian communities.[161]

Turning back to the Nestorians, John and William did not have the best of experiences with them. We have heard of William's criticism. William also tells us that they took his liturgical implements, including vestments, for their own use, and that he was involved, against his will, in intrigues by Nestorian priests against an Armenian.[162] William had no doubts that the Nestorians are heretical; he observed their rituals critically, though he admitted that they baptise in an acceptable manner.[163] He regarded it as superstitious when they claimed that they had oil used by Mary Magdalene to anoint Jesus, and flour used for the bread of the Last Supper. However, there seem to have been no serious dogmatic discussions between him and the Nestorians, for he probably steered clear of the same.[164] When, in a religious discussion between Nestorians, Muslims and Buddhists in the presence of the Khan, the Nestorians gave a general presentation of their theology, he did have various points to criticise and to correct, but he was finally chosen as their speaker. William was also critical of an Armenian priest because of his desire to assert himself and his vice for healing drugs and fortune telling, but he did call the Monophysite his 'brother' and said he honoured him 'almost like my bishop.'[165] At this time Armenians were present in various places in Mongol Central Asia as well as in China,[166] as were also the Christian Melkites.[167]

In spite of all differences and even animosities, there seems to have been a certain degree of tolerance and even mutual help between the Christians of different denominations, these becoming obvious even in small affairs. Thus we hear that a Russian helped the Franciscan when he was in dire need of food, that a king of Lesser Armenia, Hetum I, who happened to be present at the court saved one Latin monk from slavery by his intercession; that Nestorians came to the aid of William when he was abused by a Muslim; that a Frenchman received a healing drink from the aforementioned Armenian; that a Nestorian priest, at the point of death, asked an Armenian for his blessing and that the Franciscan William gives him the last sacraments according to Latin rite, although the Nestorian was not acquainted with this usage.[168] The Nestorians invite William to partake of their Eucharist; he, however, would rather celebrate mass himself and he has Hungarians, Alans, Russians, Georgians and Armenians participate. The Nestorians let him use their church for this occasion. He tells us that he prays and sings in all Christian churches he finds, irrespective of their denominational affiliation. Finally Nestorian priests ask him about his view on various religious issues including reincarnation.

The tolerance displayed by the Nestorians toward others is, of course, to be understood from the position of a minority group, not only in regard to other religions but also other Christian denominations. Such tolerance seems to be typical for the Nestorian Church. Thus the great Patriarch Timothy I wrote to one of his bishops at the turn from the 8th to the 9th century:

> 'We all . . . confess in the same manner our saviour as true God and true man. And not about the union (of the natures) itself is there quarrel and contest between us, but about the manner and kind of that union.'[169]

A few centuries later, the Nestorian Bishop Ishu-Yab b. Malkun of Nisibis (d. AD 1256) said:

> 'The Gospel calls to love. And love includes the believer and the unbeliever, the near and the far, the friend and the enemy. And this love is like unto the love of the Most High Creator in its characteristics, for He makes His sun to rise and sends down His rain upon the good and the wicked. And the Gospel incites both enemies and friends to good works, and urges enemies and friends to love, in the same way.'[170]

If such was the expression of tolerance among Christians in the Near East, even between Nestorians and monophysite Jacobites, it seemed to be all the more marked in distant Central Asia, remote from centres of official Church politics and seats of dogmatic learning.[171] Especially in view of an overwhelming non-Christian majority, William himself restrained from theological controversies. Furthermore, tolerance was the policy and postulate of the Mongol Khans, who had priests of various religions praying for them, keeping representatives of different creeds at their courts. As long as the Khan adhered to hereditary shamanistic beliefs including the belief in a highest being, Heaven, there was no privileged religion.[172] In view of the Christians, a Mongol Khan, before this time, could write to Louis IX that all denominations were respected by him in equal manner: Latins, Greeks, Armenians, Nestorians and Jacobites.[173]

It is only later that this harmony and the tolerance demanded by the Khan gave way to animosities between rival Christian groups. When King George of the Onguts was led to Catholicism by the Franciscan John of Montecorvino, who was to become the first Latin Archbishop of Khan Baliq (Beijing) at the end of the 13th century, the reaction of the Nestorians was vehement. Thus John writes, in AD 1305, almost in resignation:

> 'The Nestorians have grown so powerful in these parts that they have not allowed any Christians of another rite to have however small a chapel, nor to publish any other doctrine than the Nestorian.'[174]

A century after William of Rubruk, the completely new situation amongst Christians in Central Asia is highlighted by the murder of two Franciscans by Nestorian Christians in Turkestan. Commenting on this state of affairs, W. Hage writes:

'Thus the harmonious coexistence and intercommunication of Christian confessions in Central Asia became a hate-filed antipathy a few decades before the Ming dynasty, having arisen in China, became hostile to foreigners, before the Khans of the separate Mongol Empires converted to Islam, and before the bloody military expeditions of Timur destroyed all forms of Christianity in these lands.'[175]

CHRISTIAN LITERATURE IN CENTRAL ASIA

The Christian literature of Central Asia was determined by two tendencies, the wish to retain Syriac as a liturgical and ecclesiastical language, and the simultaneous effort to translate Syrian texts into regional languages (mainly Sogdian, Turkish and Chinese). The bulk of the Syrian literature found by the "Prussian Turfan Expeditions" in the oasis of Turfan, primarily in the Christian centre of Bulayiq, has not yet been edited and translated. These include some 400–500 texts.[176] Hitherto published are mainly portions of New Testament readings especially in so far as they belong to the bilingual (Syrian-Sogdian) texts.[177] A number of Sogdian and Turkish texts preserved stem from Central Asians themselves, to the greatest extent from the Turfan oasis, there also being some Sogdian Christian fragments from Tunhuang.[178] Some of these Christian texts contain Buddhist notions and terms, Buddhism being the most widespread religion in pre-Islamic times. Certainly in popular religions, shamanistic elements did play a major role, as we learn from the reports of Western travellers to the Mongol court at Karakorum. But such elements are hardly reflected in Christian texts found. The greater part of the literature preserved, especially in Turfan, but also in Kara-Khoto, is of more official, i.e. orthodox type, even in its translations.[179] The biblical passages generally follow the Syrian Peshitta version.[180]

The prerequisite for using and transmitting literature, i.e. literacy, was not a prerogative of the monks. In the East Syrian Synods of the 5th–6th century, the requirement was formulated that priests and deacons should have a certain degree of education raising them above the level of 'unknowing laymen'.[181] Yet laymen, too, could be instructed, and we observe that the Christian mission is often accompanied by the effort to teach those newly converted to read and write. Thus in the middle of the 6th century, Bishop Qaradusat (or Kardutsat) of Arran taught the Christianized 'Turcs', i.e. Huns, to write in their own language.[182] Later, we hear of a correspondence between the Turkish Khan converted to Christianity around 800 with Timothy I, and of the king of the Keraits with the Metropolitan of Merv at the beginning of the 11th century. Even if the rulers did not write themselves, there would be scribes at their courts. In the 13th century, we hear from William of Rubruk, that almost all Nestorians he met in Inner Asia knew how to write, using the Uighur-Mongol script. In the 13th and 14th century, the Nestorians near Lake Issik-Köl had a school, perhaps attached to a monastery, where teachers and commentators were active. Apparently the position of a teacher was a highly esteemed one.

Yet education was not widespread everywhere. Thus we hear that Khubilai Khan had Marco Polo ask the Pope for a hundred learned men to instruct the Nestorians, as they seemed uneducated in the view of the non-Christian environment.[183] Yet it was possible to get a good ecclesiastical education in a city like Khan Baliq where the young man later known as Rabban Sauma studied under a capable teacher, being later esteemed as a sage even in the Near East. And the young Ongut Mark, his disciple, may have acquired his education in Olon Süme-in-tor, even though it was restricted to non-Syrian literature, since he hardly knew Syrian when he became Catholicos.

Though Syriac was of great importance for Nestorian Christianity, Syrian texts were translated into regional languages at an early stage. In the 5th century, Syrian liturgical hymns had been rendered into Middle Persian.[184] Among the early Turfan texts, a Pahlavi Psalter, used in services, was found, accompanied by canons ascribed to Patriarch Mar Aba I. Beside it, portions of a Psalter in early New Persian were also discovered.[185]

Although preserved only fragmentarily, there was a rich literature in Sogdian, stemming from the 8th–13th centuries.[186] These documents are usually faithful translations of Syrian texts. Portions of the Peshitta version of the Psalms, as well as of the New Testament, were found, the Gospel Harmony of Tatian, however, also being in use. Biblical passages found in the Christian centre of Bulayik in the Turfan oasis are to some extent bilingual, a Syrian sentence being followed by a Sogdian one. A number of Biblical texts are part of a book of gospel lessons used in the Church service. This also included Sogdian hymns and a creed.[187] The Sogdian creed is interesting in that it is free of Arianism and Docetism, stressing Christ's incarnation, his birth by the Virgin Mary, his death on the cross 'in the days of Pontius Pilate', and his resurrection. In the creed it says:

> (*recto*) 'We believe in one God, the Father, who upholds everything, the Creator of all things that are seen and unseen. [We believe] in one Lord God, and in Jesus [Christ], the only son of God, [the firstborn] of all beings, who . . . in the beginning was not created but begotten by the Father; (*verso*) [true God] of the true God . . . by

whose hand the [aeons] were fashioned and everything was created, he who for the sake of men and for our salvation descended from the heavens and clothed himself in a body by the Holy Spirit, and became man and entered the womb; who was born of Mary, the virgin, and [who] suffered agony and [was] raised on the cross [in] the days of Pontius Pilate; and [was buried] and ascended and sits on the right hand of the Father and is ready to come (again) to judge the dead and the living. And [we believe] in the Spirit of Truth, the Holy Spirit, who went forth from the Father, the Holy Spirit who gives life . . .'

Commenting on the Sogdian creed, my colleague, Dr. Gillman, in a tentative conclusion, pointed out:

'I see no grave possibility of a charge of heresy being tenable concerning the Sogdian text as it stands translated. Those clauses which give cause for surprise by their wording or their absence, when set against the whole, do not have the seriousness they may appear to have in isolation.'[188]

The Sogdian literature preserved in Turfan is translated from a wide spectrum of Syrian texts in use in the 'Church of the East', including OT and NT passages, apocryphal literature, legends, a considerable number of martyr Acts, i.e. Acts of Persian Christian martyrs, the *Apostolic Canons*, the *Verba Seniorum* and the *Apophthegmata Patrum* (a document of Coptic origin), as well as the *Antirrhetikos* of Evagrius Ponticus (d. AD 399), a prolific writer who strongly influenced Syrian monasticism as well as Byzantine mysticism. In the *Antirrhetikos*, passages from the scripture are cited as a means to counter the power of the demons of evil thought. In the more encompassing manuscripts from Turfan, there are texts of the most varied nature. Thus in the manuscript C 2, containing some of the texts mentioned,[189] we find homilies, e.g. 'On the mercy of God', or on solitary life, commentaries to homilies, a commentary on the baptismal and eucharistic liturgies, and a catena of excerpts on the subject of humility, encompassing recollections of the lives of holy fathers. Interesting is the influence of Coptic monasticism on Syrian works translated into Sogdian. Thus there is a commentary on the 15th homily of Abba Isaiah where we hear of St. Anthony's experiences in the Egyptian desert, his fight against demons and his aid through angels. Texts of this type would have appealed to Central Asian monks.[190]

Of interest is the fact that fragments of legends concerning Christian martyrs were found.[191]

Among the legends translated into Sogdian, there is a story concerning St. George, who seems to have occupied a special position in the religiosity of Central Asians. In this text he rebukes the spirit in a Buddhist Mahākāla figure. In the Syrian original as well as in other versions it speaks of the 'corrupter', a reference to Revelation 9:11.[192] Hence we have here an interesting interpretation of that Biblical term (Gr. *apollyon*) within the religious scene of Central Asia, where Mahākāla did indeed have destructive aspects.

A number of Sogdian texts, including introductory words of some hymns, a list of names of saints and a conversation between a teacher and a disciple about Noah and Mary Magdalene still await publication.[193] Among, probably, Sogdian or Chorasmian texts lost are those to which William of Rubruk refers when he speaks about Christians in Chorasmia, in the lower region of the Oxus. Writing in the 13th century, he says: 'That country used to be called Organum [i.e. Urgančě, capital of Chorasmia] and used to have its own language and script, but now it has all been seized by the Turcomans. Also the Nestorians of those parts used to perform their services and write books in that script and language.'[194]

It may be added again that a few fragments of Sogdian Christian literature from Tunhuang also survive.[195] As mentioned, we also have from that oasis a Sogdian letter written by a Christian priest by the name of Sergius to a Turkish *tarxan* (high official).[196]

The Christian literature in Turkish languages was with little doubt much more encompassing than the texts and fragments in Uighur that are known to us today. Among these Uighur texts from Turfan,[197] there is the story of the three Magi who go to Bethlehem to venerate the Christ child. The text rests, ultimately, on a Syriac tradition of the *Protevangelium Jacobi*. As J. P. Asmussen points out: 'In Oriental Christendom, this Childhood Gospel of James was popular.' In the Turkish version, the titles given to the Christ child, and related to the gifts, were readily understandable to Central Asians. He is not only called 'the King Messiah' or 'the God Messiah', but also 'Son of Heaven (or God)' (*tängri oγli*), 'King/Khan' (*ilig khan*) and 'Physician' (*otačï ämči*), both a Christian and a Buddhist epithet of the Saviour. In the second part of the story, the Christ child breaks a piece of stone from his stone crib and gives it to the Magi. They take it but cannot carry it away, it being even too heavy for their horses. Then they throw it into a well, whereupon 'a great radiance of fire' arises from that well. This miracle makes them realise that they, too, had been given a gem, worthy of adoration. An explanation is added: 'This is why the Magi from that time to the present day worship the fire.'[198] Fire worship is then explained as being based on a misunderstanding of the Magi. This is reminiscent of a Sogdian text on St. George where it says: 'And he gave us holy baptism so that we should no longer come (to the fire).'[199] The Arabic polyhistorian Mas'udi (10th century), as well as Marco Polo, knew of a similar story.[200]

Also preserved in Uighur is the last page of St. George's passion which goes back to a Syrian tradition. It contains the last prayer of the saint before his execution, and it declares the effects of calling upon his name in times of need. Hence he had a position parallel to Avalokiteshvara, a helper in need,[201] in Central Asian Buddhism.

A further Christian Uighur text is a collection of sayings of apostles, reminiscent of an oracle book, but not to be addressed as such.[202] In this fragmentary text of uncertain origin, the Apostles Matthew and Zebedee (Zavtai) are mentioned and Luke is quoted as saying:

> 'O son of man, wash your hands pure. Have no fear of the evil one. Keep your thoughts pure. Do everything that the love of God tells you to do . . .'[203]

It is not clear whether this is based on an apocryphal text or not. A. Arlotto says in view of the text that

> 'it is probably merely a collection of apocryphal sayings intended for spiritual readings.'[204]

About 40 fragments of Christian scrolls in Uighur language and script are preserved.[205] In one of these texts, a 'guest priest' or 'visiting priest' tells about his unfriendly treatment in a monastery that retained some of his belongings including a barrel of wine. In a colophon type of ending the Christian priest transfers his merit, for praises sung, to the royal family, quite in accordance with Buddhist custom. Another text contains a type of supplicatory prayer to 'the Lord God', the saviour for those in need and suffering, the physician of the ill and the one granting remission of sins. A similar text is a prayer to 'the only God', asking for blessing 'for all men who stand in the house of God.' Praise is rendered to God for his having averted the people 'from the veneration of the demons.'[206]

A number of Uighur texts are written in Syrian script. Among these, there is a wedding song, written in Uighur (old Turkic), but with Syrian letters, asking God to bless the young bride.[207] Furthermore, a book of prayers in Uighur and Syrian is to be listed, ending with a colophon in which the writer again bestows his merit upon another person, probably his father.[208] A fragmentarily preserved Turkish text in Syriac script from Kara-Khoto is on the passion of Christ.[209]

On the whole, the Nestorian texts in Uighur reflect the spoken language of the people; a few words of Syrian and Indian origin occur. These religious texts are supplemented by a few texts of a more secular nature in Uighur and Syrian, e.g. letters (one written to a dignitary at the Byzantine court) and a medical document.[210]

Like the Uighurs, other Christian peoples in Central Asia were of course also acquainted with the Syrian tradition, both directly and through the medium of their language. As W. Hage has pointed out, the book of selected NT passages and its (Sogdian) translation as well as other texts in regional languages pertaining to the Church service make it clear that there was an attempt to open an understanding for the liturgy, central as it was in the life of the Church.[211] Quite in accordance with this intention is a remark by Timothy I around AD 800 that the 'Trishagion' (Three Holies), a central part of the Eucharist, was being sung in different languages by Persians, Indians, Chinese, Tibetans and Turks.[212]

Once a regional language had advanced to be used in the liturgy beside Syrian, it could become so esteemed that its ecclesiastical use was perpetuated even after it was no longer in general use. Thus the Franciscan Friar William of Rubruk met Turkish Nestorian Christians south of Lake Balkash using a dialect in their services that was no longer in use in everyday life.[213]

Of course Syriac remained in use, not only because there were Syrian traders and priests coming into the most remote areas, but because the Syrian tradition was as sacred to the Nestorians as Sanskrit to the Buddhists. Syrian liturgical texts from Turfan, edited by E. Sachau and others, and more recently by H. Engberding attest to this fact.[214] The Syrian letter found in Turfan,[215] written to a person at the Byzantine court, shows that it had the significance of a lingua franca for Christians of the 10th century. Indicative of the situation is also the fact that a book of 223 preserved leaves, written in Syriac in AD 752, containing passages of the Bible as well as canticles (including the 'Song of Light' ascribed to Theodore of Mopsuestia), portions of the Psalms (*qanonê*) and other pieces of religious literature, and probably used by a missionary as a handbook, found its way to China.[216] The Syrian language of course also influenced the vernacular languages used by Christians.[217]

Before the end of the first millennium, more than 500 titles of books in Syriac are attested in China, amongst them a holy scripture containing 27 books, including probably OT books.[218] They were probably known in Central Asia, too. The same applies to a number of collections of liturgical passages in Syrian, used in the Eucharist and the hourly prayers between the 9th and the 13th century, which survived in China.[219] Their wide dissemination is witness to the fact that they were not only used by Syrian speaking Christians from Western Asia, but also by Central and East Asians wishing to follow the Syrian liturgy which remained central, in spite of all accommodations to regional languages, in the reading of scripture passages and the singing of hymns.[220] Be it mentioned here that various Syriac texts were found in Peking in this century. They probably stem from Yuan times.[221]

It should be noted that the Franciscans also started to produce Christian literature in the Turkish dialects of Central Eurasia. One extant text to be mentioned in this connection is the 'Codex Cumanicus', a text written, or rather translated, for the Turkish Cumans, probably of the Crimea. It contains a hymn to Mary – 'Ave porta paradisi'.[222] The translation must stem from the first half of the 14th century. It is written in a Middle Turkic dialect. Its various portions were collected and in part glossed by German and Italian friars of the Minor Order, working, probably, in the lower Volga area which belonged to the 'Tartar Curacy' of the Franciscans. In AD 1314, there were over 17 Franciscan monasteries here. The Codex contains grammatical paradigms and word lists in Latin, Persian and Turkish, a Turkish-German list of words and several Turkish texts. These are mainly hymns and religious prose texts, translated from Latin. The orthography of the first 110 pages shows that it was written by Germans, whereas Italians wrote the remaining 63 pages. The very well translated hymns show that the Franciscans had acquired a complete mastery of the language.[223]

To be mentioned, also, is a Christian Creed in Middle Turkic, written on a sheet containing similar texts in Latin, Arabic and Armenian.[224] It was found in the Biblioteca Medicea Laurenziana in Florence and is dated AD 1439. It was written at the Council of Florence in that year and reflects the christological discussions of Rome with the Eastern Churches. W. Hage, commenting on the four versions, says:

> 'Whereas the Armenian and Latin version confess Christ as "the one person in two natures", the Turkish version (as well as the Arabic one) speak only of "the one person". . . . This seems to be not without intention in view of the very different positions of the partners with whom Rome was negotiating: "One person in two natures" corresponds to the orthodox christology of the Church of the [Roman] empire which was adopted by the Occident (Latin version); "in two natures" stands in contrast to the monophysite tradition of the Armenians (and can therefore be found in the version meant for them); but this as such legitimate formula is suppressed when every basis for the extreme diophysitism of the Nestorians is eliminated (which is to be seen behind the Turkish and the Arabic version).'[225]

Dr. Gillman, on commenting on the Turkic text and relating it to another Creed, remarked: 'Clearly this is an entirely new reading of the Apostles' Creed, but not heterodox for all that.'[226]

It is interesting to see that the contact of the Franciscans with the Eastern Churches, including that of the Nestorians of Central Asia, led to a reflection on basic theological issues, and a reformulation of such issues.

Before we conclude this chapter it should be pointed out that a wealth of apocryphal texts, as well as various Gospel Harmonies, originally written in Syriac and including Tatian's *Diatessaron*, were transmitted to Central Asia by the Manichaeans who lived in close contact with the Buddhists in the oasis towns of the Silk Road. This was especially true with respect to the Kingdom of Kocho (ca. 850–1250) in the Turfan Basin, a Nestorian Christian community also being present here. Manichaeism had been adopted as the state religion of the Uighur Turks in the steppes of

Mongolia in AD 763. In spite of initial opposition to the new religion, founded by the Persian Mani (d. AD 277), who had been raised in a Jewish-Christian community in Mesopotamia, it prevailed in that 'Kingdom of the Steppes' up to AD 840, when this kingdom was destroyed by the Turkish Kirghiz. Many Uighur Turks fled to the Kansu Corridor, as well as to the oasis towns on the northern fringe of the Taklamakan desert. It was here, in Turfan, that they established the Uighur Kingdom of Kocho, many rulers of which were Manichaeans up to the 11th cent. Kocho had already been the seat of a high Manichaean Church leader in the rank of a "teacher" (*mozak*).

From the time when the Kingdom of Kocho flourished, we have approximately 10,000 Manichaean texts and fragments, written in Middle Persian and early New Persian, Parthian, Sogdian and Uighur (Old Turkic). They reflect the great interest on the part of the Manichaeans in Christian apocryphal literature, both in apocryphal Gospels and in the apocryphal Acts of various apostles. Manichaean documents frequently contain quotations from and references to such, and other, early Christian texts. Thus a Gospel harmony used by them was based upon the *Gospel of Peter*, the *Gospel of Nicodemus* and the *Acts of Pilate*, as well as on the canonical gospels. We know that the Manichaeans transmitted to Central Asia the *Gospel of Thomas*, logion 17 of which is quoted 3 times in hitherto published Manichaean documents, the *Gospel of Philip*, the *Memoria Apostolorum*, probably the *Gospel of the Twelve* (i.e. Apostles), and perhaps also the *Gospel of the Seventy* (i.e. Disciples). They knew of, and probably used, various Infancy Gospels, like the *Infancy Gospel of Thomas* and perhaps the *Genna Mariae*, as well as the *Gospel of Pseudo-Matthew*. Many quotations in Manichaean texts are, of course, from Mani's *Living Gospel*. Furthermore, we have in Manichaean literature a number of apocryphal words (*logia*) of Jesus not attested elsewhere. An early Christian work, the *Shepherd of Hermas*, written in the Rome of the 2nd cent., was known to them in a Middle Persian version, as a fragment from Turfan (M 97) proves. Also a number of fragments of Old Testament apocrypha, belonging originally to the *Book of Giants*, a work of Jewish Enochic literature, and even attested in cave 4 of Qumran, have been found in Turfan in Middle Persian and Uighur. As hitherto only a part of the Manichaean texts from Turfan in the German Turfan collection has been published, information about other categories of early Christian literature is also to be expected. [227]

Finally, a word about the mutual influence of Christians and Buddhists as reflected in Sogdian and Turkic literature seems apt. To be sure, the Christians of Nestorian persuasion remained more aloof from Buddhist learning than did the Manichaeans who adopted Buddhist phrases, concepts and motifs in rich measure. Thus in their literature, the Manichaean Jesus is referred to as 'the Buddha Jesus' or 'the Messiah

Buddha' (*mšixa burxan*). In a Parthian text (M 104), we read that Jesus, after his crucifixion and death, entered the highest state of Nirvana.[228] But we also have occasion to note various instances of Buddhist influence on Christian texts. This influence becomes especially conspicuous in the colophons, i.e. the postscripts to traditional works. Thus the general Buddhist notion of acquiring 'merit' (Skr. *puṇya*) by doing good works like the copying of scriptures and of being able to refer, i.e. pass on, such merit to others, is to be found in Christian texts in Turkish.[229] But in spite of such adaptations, the Nestorians did seek to assert such elements in their faith as were peculiarly Christian. To these belonged, beyond the faith in Christ as the risen Lord, the notion that the world, in spite of its perils and woes, is a good creation of God. Thus in a Turkic text (T III Kurutka/ U330) the Greek 'cosmos' is used as a loan-word for 'world' rather than the Indian *saṃsāra*,[230] which the Manichaeans preferred. In wake of the Persian tradition of the Nestorian Church, the Christians could emphasize that salvation is not only a purely spiritual affair, as the Buddhists and Manichaeans maintained, but ultimately a new creation, and that it implies the resurrection from the dead, with its implicit affirmation of bodily existence.[231] But of course there were also more ascetic and purely spiritually oriented tendencies as expressed in texts of the Syrian tradition.[232]

On the other hand, Christian influence on Buddhist literature is scant, Christians being a small minority in a mainly Buddhist world in pre-Islamic times. Yet there was such an influence, and it, too, becomes obvious mainly in the postscripts of writers and donors, appended to 'official' Buddhist texts copied. Interestingly enough, the earliest Buddhist literature in Old Turkic from Central Asia, being mainly from 8th–10th cent., reveals the strongest traces of such influence. The word 'influence', however, has to be qualified. Nestorian Christianity, as well as Manichaeism, had a *catalytic* effect on Sogdian and Turkish Buddhism in that it served to stress and bring to the fore ideas that were already present in the Buddhist tradition, ideas that corresponded to basic Christian – and Manichaean – notions. This is not surprising in view of the fact that adherents of these religions lived side by side in the oasis towns along the Silk Road, towns which were themselves always open to foreign ideas. Representatives of the various religions even intermarried, as we learn from European travellers in Mongol times (13th–14th cent.), including Marco Polo and the Franciscan friars. The close contacts, then, between members of various religious communities in the relatively small oasis towns inevitably led to a certain convergence of ideas, even with respect to shamanistic notions and practices.[233] But this is also true of Buddhism, the Buddhists then placing emphasis on certain ideas in their own tradition that corresponded to those in Christianity. Thus there was a catalytic influence of Nestorian Christianity as well as state-supported Manichaeism on Turkish Buddhism.

A special case in point is the notion of Buddha's suffering for the sins of all men, or more generally, of all living beings. Of course there are many Jataka stories in which the Bodhisattva, i.e. the Buddha in a former existence, sacrifices himself for others. Thus were illustrated the Buddhist virtues of 'giving' (*dāna*), even giving up one's life for the sake of others, of compassion (*karuṇā*), patience (*kṣanti*) etc. It is striking that the Buddhist idea of self-sacrifice becomes prominent at a time when Christianity makes itself felt further and further to the east of Persia, a process that sets in in about the 5th century. In the 8th and 9th centuries, Nestorian crosses even appear on Old Turkic inscriptional monuments as far north as Mongolia and southern Siberia.[234]

As pointed out, the catalytic effect of Christianity and Manichaeism on Central Asian Buddhism becomes obvious mainly in the colophons. Thus in a Buddhist text, a colophon type of introduction to the *Maitrisimit*, a Turkish Buddhist work on the future Buddha Maitreya, the donor says:

'The first portion of merit that has accrued therefrom (i.e. from having this Sutra copied) do I render (*ävirär m(ä)n*) to the four great (divine) kings, (i.e.) Brahma, Indra, Vishnu and Maheshvara, who guard the jewel of the Law which the divine Buddha bought by giving his life for sale.'[235]

Often Buddhist and Christian (or Manichaean) notions are very intimately connected with one another. As the Turkic texts frequently use hendiadys, i.e. combinations of indigenous and foreign words, to express one notion, we have what could be referred to as 'religious hendiadys', i.e. combinations of Buddhist and Christian terms, or notions, which only become visible as such upon closer philological analysis.[236] Thus the idea of thankfulness to the Buddha, or of love to the enemy, is reminiscent of Christian teachings,[237] though to be sure, there are also Buddhist roots for such notions.

An interesting catalytic influence of Christian theology on Buddhist thinking is to be discerned in passages that speak of Buddha as giving his life as a ransom (*urunčaq*), or receiving living beings as a forfeit. The idea is quite foreign to Indian Buddhism. Evidently not only Christian ideas, but also apocryphal Christian texts which had been brought to Central Asia by the Manichaeans, had their effect on Buddhist thought in this respect. One such text is the *Gospel of Philip*, which we know from the Nag Hammadi finds in the Egyptian desert. Here it says (in logion 9a according to H.-M. Schenke):

'Christ has come to ransom some, to save others, to redeem others. He ransomed those who were strangers and made them his own . . .'[238]

This idea seems to be echoed indirectly with respect to the Buddha in various Turkish Buddhist texts.[239]

Beside the *Gospel of Philip*, it was especially the *Gospel of Thomas* (which we also know from Nag Hammadi) that had its effect on the pluralistic situation of Central Asia. Thus the idea, already conceived of in India, that the 'Buddha-Nature' pervades everything in the world, even the smallest speck of dust, an idea that was to become central for certain East Asian schools of Buddhism, was apparently accentuated under the catalytic influence of early Christian and Gnostic notions about the ubiquitous Saviour. In the *Gospel of Thomas*, this idea of the omnipresence of the Saviour is expressed in logion 77 in these terms:

'Jesus said, "It is I who am the light which is above them all. It is I who am the all. From me did the all come forth, and unto me did the all extend. Split a piece of wood and I am there. Lift up the stone, and you will find me there."'[240]

Very similar notions are to be found in the 'Flower Garland Sutra' (*Avataṃsaka-Sūtra*) and related documents. The core of this text was formulated in India, but as a major sutra, it was compiled in Central Asia. Here it says, inter alia:

'The Buddha manifests his presence in every speck of dust / . . . / He resides in the essence of all things / . . . / Like the atoms, / His manifestations / Are innumerable in each stone / . . . The Power of Buddha is seen / Even in the slightest grain of sand.'[241]

In an Old Turkish fragment apparently indigenous to Central Asia (Turfan text T II D 200), the idea is further elaborated. Here it says with respect to the Buddha Vairocana, the Buddha of the Sun, or the Light visible in the Sun:

'The essence of the Buddha Vairocana is everything: earth, mountains, stones, sand, the water of streams and rivers, all ponds, rivulets and lakes, all plants and trees, all living beings and men. There is absolutely no place which is not filled with the essence of the Buddha Vairocana. If a monk lifts up and stretches out his hand against something, he becomes sinful over against the essence of the Buddha Vairocana.'[242]

This leads us, finally, to the strong consciousness of sin and guilt which we find in Central Asian texts. There are confessions, and confessional formulae, even for laymen, something quite foreign to Indian Buddhism, but common to both the Nestorian and Manichaean traditions.[243]

Noteworthy is the fact that such 'foreign' ideas are often connected with the Buddhas of Life and Light, Amitābha and Amitāyus, whose compassion, benevolence and grace are stressed repeatedly, over against which man is called to faith as a prerequisite for all striving for and attainment of salvation.[244] But such ideas, reminiscent of Christian notions, are also to be found in the theology of Maitreya, the future Buddha. These theologies developed in Central Asia, after having evolved in the first centuries AD in North-West India (Gandhara) and the Kushan Kingdom, where there was, indeed, a strong Hellenistic, i.e. Mediterranean influence, as visible in art. Thus the classical texts about the 'Realm of Light' of the Buddha Amitābha, written probably in the 3rd/4th century in Gandhara, are reminiscent of the descriptions of the Realm of Light as we find them in the Parthian Manichaean Hymn-cycles. The core of these was written by Mani's disciple Mar Ammo, who in the mid-3rd century was active in the Kushan Kingdom and the Indo-Parthian border area.[245]

It was, then, especially the pluralistic milieu of the oasis towns of the Silk Road that had a deep impact on Buddhism as it passed along this route from India to East Asia, where such originally 'foreign' ideas were developed further. The role of Central Asian Christians in this process can only be assessed more precisely by further research, which will call for a three-way discussion among scholars of Mahāyāna, Oriental Christianity, as well as Hindu theism, especially of the Vaishnavite tradition, there being often Vaishnava parallels to Buddhist texts.

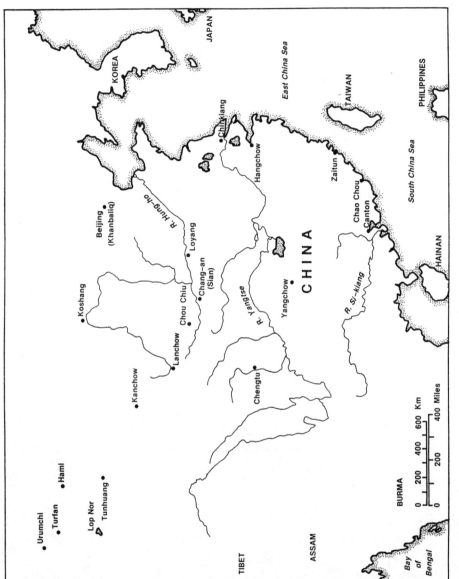

Map 7 China

Chapter 10

Christians in China

CHRISTIANS IN PRE-T'ANG CHINA?

It was in the beginning of the glorious T'ang period (AD 618–907), open as it was to international trade, to diplomatic missions from abroad and to foreign ideas, that Nestorian Christianity made its official appearance on the scene in China. The first reliable news of a Christian presence comes from this time.

Before we review that information, it seems appropriate to consider the reports and rumours about Christians in China in pre-T'ang times.[1] According to one not very early tradition, Christianity was introduced into China by St. Thomas, the Apostle to India. This tradition seems to be based on information gleaned from a breviary of the Syrian Malabar Church. Here it says:

> 'By the means of St. Thomas the Chinesses and Aethiopians were converted to the truth. . . . By the means of St. Thomas the Kingdom of Heaven flew and entered into China. . . . The Chinesses . . . in commemoration of St. Thomas do offer their adoration unto thy most holy name, O God.'[2]

This breviary, however, was composed in or after the 13th century. As Latourette points out,

> '. . . the tradition may have arisen from the reports of envoys of the Malabar Church who visited Cambaluc (Peking) [i.e. Khan Baliq] in AD 1282 and who may have met the Nestorian Christians who resided there under the Mongols.'[3]

Indeed, the South Indian Christians who ascribed the origin of their tradition to St. Thomas could hardly have conceived of Christians further east, with which they had contact by sea even prior to this time, as other than going back to the time of St. Thomas. It is uncertain whether they already had contacts with fellow-believers in China in the T'ang period, but it does seem possible, even probable, that they knew of Christians in

South China, in ports like Zaitun, in Mongol times. For there was an active trade between Zaitun and South Indian ports at that time. The origins of such Christians must have then been projected back (in the breviary) to the time of St. Thomas.

Some would ascribe an indirect Christian influence on pre-T'ang and T'ang China, maintaining that Mahāyāna Buddhism, which developed in India in various regions, mainly in the north-western area of Gandhara in the first centuries AD, was inspired by Christian (perhaps also Gnostic) ideas. Thus the Buddhism that was to spread to China from this area, so it is claimed, had imbibed a Christian spirit and was 'in many respects Christianity in disguise.'[4] Whereas there could have been links between Christians in the Persian realm of the Sasanids (AD 224–650) and a possible Christian community in north-western India, Herat as a Nestorian metropolitanate not being far away, there is no definite proof of a Christian influence on developing Mahāyāna Buddhism. But certain parallels, as discussed by R. Garbe in 1914, and other writers in recent times, are striking.[5] There does seem to be an influence of apocryphal and Gnostic literature on early Mahāyāna Buddhism.[6] Mani, the founder of a Gnostic world religion, established congregations in North-West India in the third century. In fact he was in India in AD 240/241, where, according to Manichaean tradition, he converted Kings like the Turan Shah.[7]

Of course there are remarkable analogous concepts, especially in so far as the altruistic notion of help granted to all in need, as incorporated in the Bodhisattva ideal, is concerned. Yet this could have developed on Indian soil with or without the catalytic influence of Christianity. There remain some striking parallels like the Christian and the Buddhist parables of the lost son, the latter being found in the famous Lotus Sutra, chapter 4. Though its intention deviates from that of the Christian parable in Luke 15, it is quite unusual in Buddhism to represent the Buddha as a loving father, for the idea is hardly in accord with the story of his leaving house and home to find salvation for himself. Later Central Asian Buddhist texts, especially those written in Uighur between the 9th and 14th century, do reveal a Christian or Gnostic, i.e. Manichaean influence, especially in portions not translated from Sanskrit or Chinese.[8] Such influences can be found mainly in the colophons and editorial passages inserted into holy texts, but also in indigenous Turkic Buddhist works. Furthermore, there was contact and even co-operation between individual Christian and Buddhist scholars. Thus we know that the Persian Christian monk Ching-Ching worked together with an Indian Buddhist monk from Kapisha in present-day Afghanistan to translate a Buddhist text from an Iranian language ('*hu*'), possibly Sogdian, into Chinese.[9] This work did not find acceptance at the Chinese court, but the fact shows that there were intimate contacts between Buddhists and Christians in Medieval Central and East Asia.[10]

Western, i.e. Latin, Greek and Syrian sources on an early Christian presence in China are to be viewed with caution. Thus Arnobius the Elder, a rhetorian in Numidia who converted to Christianity after fighting against it, in his seven volume *Adversus nationes*, written AD 304–310, talks about missions to the 'Seres', i.e. 'silk people', but it is doubtful whether this information is reliable.[11] Another link is suggested by the fact that in AD 511, Christian monks who had supposedly resided in China, brought silk-worms to Constantinople.[12] However, it seems more likely that they were in eastern Persia or the western or eastern part of Central Asia. There the art of growing silk-worms and producing silk was known, for instance, in the oasis of Khotan by that time. Of course news of Christianity could have reached China in the 6th century, since that religion was established among various Turkish tribes in Central Asia, as we saw. The Syrian tradition asserts that Archaeus, Archbishop of Seleucia-Ctesiphon from AD 411 to AD 415, and Silas, Nestorian Patriarch from AD 505 to AD 520, created metropolitan sees in China, but this information comes from a later period and seems untrustworthy.[13] When the Portuguese had contact with India, finally, the Metropolitan of the Malabar Church is said to have included China in his title, yet here again this tradition is late.[14] But even if the South Indian Metropolitan claimed jurisdiction over Christians in China, it is not clear how old such a claim would be. It would hardly go back to the pre-T'ang period, in spite of the sea links between India and China since the first centuries AD.

Thus direct or indirect Christian influence on pre-T'ang China remains a matter of conjecture. There are, however, traces of Manichaean and Zoroastrian activities in the China of that period.[15] Since Manichaeans often followed the Christians in their eastern mission, a Christian presence in China in the 6th century cannot be completely ruled out.

THE APPEARANCE OF CHRISTIANS IN T'ANG CHINA

The appearance of Christians on the Chinese scene in the T'ang period is not remarkable in view of the contacts mentioned at the beginning of this chapter. T'ang China maintained diplomatic contacts, trade relations and cultural and religious ties with the most remote areas of Eurasia. It extended its boundaries far west into Central Asia, even though the actual limits of Chinese authority were never clearly demarked for long periods. The form of authority ranged from direct sovereignty to loose suzerainty, or even just the acceptance of tributary gifts, interpreted as acknowledgment of the rule of the Emperor, the 'Son of Heaven'. T'ang China had political influence, then, in a manner not always clearly defined, over Manchuria, North Korea and Mongolia in the north, Tonking and Annam in the south, and Tibet and present Sinkiang in the west. The T'ang Empire in the 7th century was probably the largest and wealthiest of its time, being ruled by strong personalities. Of these, it was the mighty Emperor T'ai-tsung (AD 626–649) who received the first Christian mentioned in the official records. But the account of his reception almost presupposes a knowledge, even vague, of the Christian religion. To gain such a knowledge would not have been difficult in view of the influx of foreigners into China from the West. A prince from the Sasanian court, for instance, is said to have taken refuge in China when Persia was overrun by the Arabs in the middle of the 7th century, and after this time, even the rulers of the Abbasid realm, at whose capital of Baghdad the Patriarch was residing, sought diplomatic contact with China. A large number of non-Chinese, beside diplomats, merchants and men of various trades, also foreign priests and monks, lived in the capital cities like Loyang and Chang-an. The great variety of peoples in the big Chinese cities and especially at the court is not only evidenced by literary sources,[16] but also by archaeological discoveries like figures and paintings of foreigners found in the graves of the great rulers near Chang-an, representing the wide range of men at the court.

The great openness to things foreign was accompanied, in the beginning of the T'ang period, by a remarkable degree of tolerance of other religions, though this gave way to proscriptions, persecutions and the confiscation of churches and monasteries in the middle of the 9th century, specifically in AD 845, when an edict was issued, aiming at the secularisation of foreign religious establishments. But prior to this time, various Western religions, beside Christianity Manichaeism, Zoroastrian-ism and Islam, were represented in the big cities, being mainly the religions of foreigners. These attempted to win Chinese converts, which was only possible to a limited degree.

Of course Buddhism played a major role, having established itself as a recognized foreign religion with an enormous literary and artistic output. The Chinese Buddhist literature consisted not only of translations of Indian texts, but also of significant indigenous works as well. It was in T'ang times that pilgrims like Hsuan-tsang (7th century), following the example of Fa-hsien (around AD 400), would travel abroad, in this case to India, spending many years there and returning with scriptures to be translated and commented upon. One of the major assets of Buddhism, of which the other religions including Nestorianism could not boast, was the fact that in the course of centuries it had developed a terminology acceptable to the high standards of Chinese literati.

Manichaeism, the Gnostic religion founded by Mani (d. AD 276), who had grown up in a Jewish-Christian community in Mesopotamia, gained a certain foothold. We have spoken of Manichaean literature in the last chapter and pointed out that it also included canonical and apocryphal Christian writings. To what extent these were translated into Chinese, we do not know. But there are many references to Biblical images and notions in the Chinese Manichaean texts preserved, even if they give themselves a Buddhist appearance.[17] It was the fate of Manichaeism to be limited to non-Chinese by an Imperial decree of AD 732. The great persecution of AD 845, which aimed at the expulsion of all foreign religions, including Buddhism, uprooted the Manichaean community almost completely. However, it continued to thrive in the small realm of Kocho in Central Asia up to the 13th, and in South China up to the 16th century.[18]

Other foreign religions from Western Asia in T'ang China were Zoroastrianism, Judaism and Islam. Zoroastrianism, which adopted monastic features in China, was almost completely restricted to Iranians (i.e. Persians, Parthians and Sogdians) living in China, Sogdians also turning to other world religions.[19] Likewise, there could have been a small Jewish community in capital cities and in the southern port of Zaitun, which became a stronghold of Judaism, borne mainly by traders, in the Mongol period. Islam, though represented mainly by Western Asians, was winning a growing amount of converts in the cities along the Silk Road as well as in the southern ports.

In so far as Christian communities in T'ang China are concerned, K. S. Latourette sums up the general situation pertinently when he says:

'When it is recalled that at this time there were Christian communities in Southern India and that in Central Asia the Nestorians were widespread and active, it is not surprising to find Christians in China. It would, indeed, be surprising if they had not been there.'[20]

Our main source of information on Nestorianism in China and its introduction by a monk named A-lo-pen is the famous monument of Sian-fu, erected in AD 781. To this we shall return soon. What other early indigenous sources are there beside this monument?

It has been pointed out that references to Christians have been found in Chinese records, viz. in Imperial decrees of AD 638, AD 745 and AD 845,[21] as well as in historical works.[22] In the decree of AD 638, issued by the T'ang Emperor T'ai-tsung (d. AD 649), it says:

'The Way [Tao] has no immutable name, sages have no unchanging method. Teaching is founded to suit the land that all the living may be saved. The Persian monk A-lo-pen bringing scriptures and teaching from far has come to offer them at Shang-ching. The meaning of the teaching has been carefully examined: it is mysterious, wonderful, calm; it fixes the essentials of life and perfection; it is the salvation of living beings, it is the wealth of man. It is right that it should spread through the empire. Therefore let the local officials build a monastery in the I-ning quarter with twenty-one regular monks.'[23]

269

Eichhorn, in quoting a text dating from AD 635 and being basically similar to this one, points out that in that passage, the earliest reference to Christianity in China, the Buddhist term 'Emptiness' (*hsü-k'ung*) is used to denote God.[24] It is not quite clear in what relationship the texts of AD 635 and AD 638 stand to each other.

A historical note for the year AD 732 tells us that 'the king of Persia sent the chief P'an-na-mi with the monk of great virtue, Chi-lieh, as ambassadors with tribute.'[25] The chief was granted a high rank and the monk given a purple robe and fifty pieces of silk before they were sent home.[26] It is not unequivocal, however, that the monk was a Christian, even though Saeki does translate the term 'monk of great virtue' with 'bishop'.

In the decree of AD 745, issued under Emperor Hsüan-tsang (d. AD 755), we hear something about the spread of Nestorianism. Here it says:

'The Persian religion of the scriptures, starting from Ta-ch'in and coming to preach and practise, has long existed in the Middle Kingdom. When they first built monasteries [Persian] was consequently taken for the name. Wishing to show men the necessity of correct knowledge of the original [we decree that] the Persian Monasteries at the two capitals must be changed to Ta-ch'in Monasteries. Those which are founded in the departments and districts of the empire will also observe this.'[27]

The term Ta-ch'in is used to denote a not exactly defined region in Western Asia, more specifically Syria and Palestine. In the text quoted it becomes obvious that beside two Nestorian monasteries in Loyang and Chang-an, there were also a number in various provinces. The renaming of such ecclesiastical establishments was probably done to avoid confusion with Manichaean and Zoroastrian centres. What is not clear here is whether the Christian monasteries were inhabited by foreigners alone or not. The translations of Nestorian texts and the writings of such works in Chinese, of which we will speak later, were certainly meant to be available to Chinese readers. And amongst these there would have been Chinese monks. So it can be surmised that there were Chinese Christian monks in the cities and especially in the monasteries out in the countryside as in Chou-chih, 150 Chinese miles (*li*) north-west of Sian-fu,[28] for such out of the way places would hardly be attractive to non-Chinese if they were not on a commercial route.

It is clear that Nestorianism, or the 'Luminous Religion', as it was called, was sanctioned and even promoted by a number of emperors after its introduction by A-lo-pen in AD 635. Eichhorn surmises that in the age of these Emperors, the introduction of Christianity could have been felt to pacify and assuage the minds of those who were stirred up by outward turmoil – which would also have been true of Buddhism – and that the patronizing of Nestorian establishments could furthermore have served to attract foreign Christian merchants to come to China.[29] As he points out, in AD 744 Nestorian monasteries received from the Emperor tablets which made them officially recognized by the state.[30]

Beside monasteries and churches, there were also Nestorian monuments. There is a reference to one in Cheng-tu in a geographical work of the 9th century.[31] The main monument, however, is that of Sian-fu, to which we shall now turn.

THE MONUMENT AT SIAN-FU

The Sian-fu monument (pls. 34a and b) is the most significant source of information on Christianity in the T'ang period. It was discovered in AD 1623 or 1625 in the course of excavation work.[32] A local official examined the long Chinese inscription, which is accompanied by portions in Syriac, made a copy of it and sent it to a friend in Hanchow. Here it was brought to the notice of Jesuit missionaries. The first translation – into Latin – was made by a Jesuit priest in AD 1625. The Syriac portions were first translated by a Western missionary at the court in Peking, J. Terrenz, in AD 1629. When news about the discovery of the Christian monument was reported to Europe soon after AD 1628, scholars were divided on the question of its authenticity. Whereas some thought it to be genuine, others, and also the French philosopher Voltaire, held it to be a pious fraud of the Jesuits. Now, however, it is quite clear that the monument is genuine, and that it was erected in AD 781, either in the premises of a Nestorian monastery in Chang-an or in a Christian monastery at Wu-chun in the District of Chou-chih, where it was discovered.[33] Today many models of the stone exist in the west, and paper-rubbings are readily available. The document has been studied extensively and translated repeatedly.[34]

The author of the text on the monument was a Persian priest named Adam, whose Chinese name is recorded as Ching-Ching. In the Syrian text he is referred to as 'Adam, priest and country-bishop [i.e. chorepiscopus] and *fapshi* [Spiritual Master] of Zinistan [i.e. China].'[35] According to the Chinese text, he was 'monk of the Ta-ch'in Monastery',[36] probably at Chang-an. Ching-Ching is also known from a Chinese source. As mentioned, he translated a Buddhist scripture from the '*hu*' language into Chinese together with an Indian Buddhist monk.

The Sian-fu monument was erected in honour of a very colourful personality, a married monk with the name of I-ssu who was engaged in religious as well as military activities. He is described, in the monument, as 'a man of harmonious nature and loving to do good, hearing the Way [Tao] and diligently practising it . . .'[37] He is furthermore characterized as being learned, skilled (in teaching) and officially distinguished. It is also said of him that he was made to follow the military expedition of a certain Duke Kuo Tzu-i, Prince of the region of Fen-yang, and that he was 'nails and teeth for the Duke, he was the army's eyes and ears',[38] i.e. he must have engaged in secret service activities. At any rate, he helped to suppress a rebellion, thereby earning the favour of the Emperor. Beside his military skills, his Christian virtues are also stressed. He is referred to as being benevolent and charitable, and he is praised for restoring old Nestorian monasteries and doubling the size of churches. Furthermore, it is pointed out: 'Every year he gathered the monks of the surrounding monasteries together; acting reverently, serving precisely, he provided everything for fifty days.'[39] Finally, it is emphasized that he cared for the sick and needy, in a manner unheard of before.[40] Thus I-ssu was a many-faceted man, having success both in the worldly and the ecclesiastical spheres, as this eulogy would suggest. He was in the military service, as a general, under three Emperors, viz. Su-tsung (AD 756–762), Tai-tsung (AD 762–779) and Te-tsung (AD 779–805).[41] Saeki identifies him with the donor of the monument, 'Lord Yazdbuzid [Izd-buzid according to Moule]' in the Syrian text, who hailed from Balkh in Tokharistan, present-day Afghanistan.[42]

The inscription of the monument, though Christian, is reminiscent of Buddhist texts in that it contains a major prose portion which is then summed up in verse form. In content, it gives us a short history of 'The Luminous Religion of Ta-ch'in' from the arrival of the first Christian monk, A-lo-pen, to the time of the inscription. In the historical portions, various Emperors are mentioned, viz. T'ai-tsung (AD 626–649), Kao-tsung (AD 649–683), Hsüan-tsung (AD 712–755), Su-tsung (AD 756–762) and Tai-tsung (AD 762–779) who are portrayed (probably in an exaggerated manner) as promoting and protecting the religion from the West.

The text itself is often obscure in its expressions and allusions. In spite of good translations, not everything is readily understandable. This applies mainly to the introduction which prefaces the main part. Thus the triune God is referred to in the beginning with these words:

'Behold! The unchanging in perfect repose, before the first and without beginning; the inaccessible in spiritual purity, after the last and wonderfully living; he who holds the mysterious source of life and creates, who in his original majesty imparts his mysterious nature to all the sages; is this not the mysterious Person of our Three in One, the true Lord without beginning . . .?'[43]

There is then an account of the creation of the world, of man's fall from his original state of goodness, of Satan's rule and of ensuing errors. Then follows a life history of the Messiah (*Mi-shih-he*) and a short account of his work which culminates in the fact that 'he disclosed life and abolished death.'[44] The crucifixion is not mentioned, and there are only vague hints at the resurrection.[45] The significance of Christ is then indirectly expressed by the idea that the Way [i.e. Tao, or more generally Truth] requires a prophet, for 'the way without a prophet will not flourish; a prophet without the way will not be great.'[46] There follows a reference to 27 books of Scripture, it being unclear whether books of the Old Testament and New Testament are meant (even though there are 27 books in the Syriac Old Testament), or other books. The text then emphasizes the cleansing power of baptism, the virtue of worship and the value of ritual praise; the sabbath is referred to as a day of offering and of purification. On the whole, monastic virtues are extolled, and even the outward signs of monasticism are interpreted in terms of religious values. The equality of men is emphasized when it says that they (i.e. the monks),

'do not keep male or female slaves, reckoning honourable and mean among men alike; they do not amass goods and wealth, displaying devotion and generosity among themselves.'[47]

Quite in accord with Christian monastic ideals as developed in Syria, it says:

'Purification is made perfect by seclusion and meditation; self-restraint grows strong by silence and watching.'[48]

All this makes it quite obvious that it was a monastic type of Christianity that established itself in T'ang China, laymen playing a minor role, as opposed to the situation in Yuan times.

The historical part of the inscription throws light on the arrival of A-lo-pen in Chang-an in AD 635, i.e. at the time of the great Emperor T'ai-tsung. A-lo-pen was given a grand reception, being escorted into the city, which presupposes that there would have been news about him and his message in the capital beforehand. The sacred Scriptures he had with him were translated into Chinese, their content was then examined by the Emperor himself, who, as it says, 'thoroughly understood their propriety and truth and specially ordered their preaching and transmission.'[49] After recognizing the Nestorian teaching as one in accordance with 'the Way', being 'mysterious, wonderful, full of repose' and being conducive to 'the salvation of living beings', it was, then, deemed right to have it propagated.[50] A practical consequence thereof was the establishment of a 'Ta-ch'in monastery in the I-ning quarter of the capital with twenty-one men as regular monks.'[51] A portrait of the Emperor was then painted on the walls of the monastery, indicating the close connection between the ruler and the newly established religion.

During the reign of the third T'ang Emperor Kao-tsung of whom it says that he 'adorned and glorified the true principle',[52] many monasteries were founded, so we hear, one in every department (*chou*); 'monasteries occupied every city', and this went hand in hand with the blessing and prosperity of the land, as the inscription would suggest.[53] Furthermore, A-lo-pen was promoted to the rank of a 'Great Spiritual Lord, Protector of the Empire'. But we also hear that at this time criticism was voiced by the Buddhists and the gentry, but that eminent Christian monks from the West were able to win the day.

Under the rule of Emperor Hsüan-tsung, Nestorianism, having suffered a further setback, was again promoted by members of the ruling family in accordance with the wish of the ruler. Only hinting at this situation, it says:

'The beam of the religion had been weak for a moment but was raised again; the stone of the Way had been thrown down for a time but stood upright once more.'[54]

In the 'third year' of T'ien-pao (i.e. 744), a second Nestorian mission from Persia, under the leadership of Chi-ho, arrived at Chang-an.[55] The text says:

'It was decreed that the monk Lo-han, the monk P'u-lun, and others, altogether seven men, with Chi-ho of great virtue, should practise meritorious virtue in the Hsing-ch'ing Palace.'[56]

The last paragraphs of the historical portion praise Emperor Tai-tsung for his wise policies and extol the deeds of the donor, 'the monk I-ssu', who 'exerted himself beyond measure for the brilliant school' [i.e. Nestorianism].[57]

In the second portion, consisting of verses, the main ideas are summarised. Here again it is interesting to note that the blossoming of the new religion together with the virtue of the ruler allegedly led to peace, happiness and prosperity in the whole land, a motif also found in Confucian texts. Beyond the Emperors named in the first part, Su-tsung and Tai-tsung are here also mentioned and praised as virtuous and successful rulers, which applied in special manner, of course, to Tai-tsung, the ruler at the time the inscription was made.

At the end of the inscription, there is a reference in Syrian to Adam (i.e. Ching-Ching) and his mission in China. Furthermore, a great number of dignitaries, mainly priests and monks, are named in Syriac and Chinese. They could be the names of those present at the annual meetings organized by Izd-buzid, as Moule suggests.[58]

Of course the Sian-fu inscription presents the history of Christianity since A-lo-pen in a most favourable light. Other sources in this early period are few. But the account of Ching-Ching's criticized co-operation with Prajñā as well as other texts to which we shall turn later shows that the acceptance of Christianity by the court, at least since Ching-Ching's time, was not as unanimous as the inscription would suggest. Yet the inscription does show, as F. S. Drake points out, 'that the monasteries were dependent upon Imperial favour for their existence, and even upon Imperial support.'[59] It may be that this is one reason why Nestorianism could vanish so rapidly in T'ang China.

THE CHINESE NESTORIAN TEXTS OF THE T'ANG PERIOD

In the famous grottoes of Tunhuang, a huge hoard of manuscripts was found at the beginning of this century in a walled up little chapel, now numbered cave 17. Beside secular and Buddhist texts, it also contained Manichaean and Christian documents which must have been written before the beginning of the 11th century when the cave was sealed.[60] The British explorer Sir Aurel Stein, in 1908 and in subsequent years, was able to purchase many of these documents, now kept in the British Museum in London. Likewise, the French Sinologist Paul Pelliot also acquired a large number of texts, now preserved in the Bibliothèque Nationale in Paris.

Amongst the Paris texts is a roll of Christian origin. Although found in Tunhuang by Pelliot in 1908, it was probably written in Chang-an. It contains a hymn to the Trinity, called 'Hymn of the Saved in Praise of the Triune God', identified with the East Syrian form of the *Gloria in excelsis Deo*, translated in T'ang times.[61] This is followed by two addenda, a list of saints and scriptures, called by Saeki the *Book of Praise*, and a historical note written by a later hand. It includes the comment that 'the religious books of this church of Ta-ch'in are in all 530 works.'[62] There follows the notice that

> 'by imperial order the monk of great virtue Ching-Ching [i.e. the author of the Sian-fu inscription] of this church obtained by translation the above thirty and more rolls of books.'[63]

Of these, a number have been found and identified, being ascribed, not always correctly, to Ching-Ching. According to Drake, the date of the latter part of the manuscript is a little later than AD 781, the time of the erection of the Tablet.[64]

Besides the aforementioned *Gloria* and the attached list of saints and books, there are three further texts, also ascribed to Ching-Ching, 'A Nestorian Hymn in Adoration of the Transfiguration of our Lord', 'The Ta-ch'in Luminous Religion Sutra on the Origin of Origins', and the 'Sutra on Mysterious Rest and Joy'. To what extent they can really be regarded as works of Ching-Ching will have to be considered. Most of these texts must have been translated or written in the 8th century, the originals being written 'on patra leaves in the Sanskrit (i.e. Syriac or Persian?) tongue.'[65]

Apart from these documents which will be discussed later, two other documents, also found at Tunhuang, belong to those translated by A-lo-pen about 150 years before Ching-Ching's time. They are also named in the list of books mentioned above. Their titles are 'The Jesus Messiah

Sutra', composed between AD 635 and 638, and a 'Discourse on Monotheism', probably written around AD 641–642. In accordance with the names of those who acquired these documents in 1922 and 1916 respectively, Saeki called the first the 'Takakusu Document', the second the 'Tomeoka Document'. This document consists of three parts, (1) 'The Parable, Part II', (2) 'The Discourse on the One Ruler of the Universe, Part I' and (3) 'The Lord of the Universe's Discourse on Alms-Giving, Part III', as F. S. Drake renders these titles. He points out that

> 'these titles are confusing; for only the second is really appropriate to the contents; and the numbering is out of order. . . . It is not at all clear, therefore, what relation the various parts have with one another, and whether or not there was a larger work of which they formed parts, or what its nature may have been.'[66]

The A-lo-pen texts which stem from the beginning of the Nestorian mission in China, when no terminology adequate for rendering Christian concepts had been found, are not easily understandable. G. Rosenkranz says in view of these texts:

> 'Their style is so clumsy, their content so dark, that for this reason every translation becomes a paraphrase and there can be no doubt that they do not belong to the Ching-Ching literature.'[67]

As P. Y. Saeki points out, the 'Jesus Messiah Sutra' must have been the first work written by A-lo-pen, containing a 'surprisingly complete outline of the fundamental doctrine of Christianity', fit for introducing the Emperor T'ai-tsung to the principles of the Nestorian faith.[68] F. S. Drake observes:

> 'The most striking feature of the manuscript is its extraordinary style, which renders the meaning of a large part of it very obscure, and makes it in part unintelligible. . . . One can imagine it as the work of a foreigner insufficiently versed in Chinese . . .'[69]

The A-lo-pen texts contain several Syriac words in Chinese phonetization, words like 'Jehova', 'Messiah', and names of Biblical persons and geographical places. But also Sanskrit words, probably taken from Buddhist scriptures and written in Chinese phonetization, are used.

Within the group of the A-lo-pen texts a development can be traced in terminology. Thus in the 'Jesus Messiah Sutra', the word 'Buddha' was used for God, whereas in the 'Discourse on Monotheism', the word employed is *I-shen* (lit. one God). Similarly, other central concepts like 'Messiah' and 'Holy Spirit' were first rendered in misleading, even ridiculous forms of transcription (e.g. 'Remove-Rat-Confusing Teacher' or 'Confused-Teacher-Upbraid' for Jesus the Messiah in the Takakusu document, whereas the Tomeoka text has more satisfying renderings like 'Full-Teacher-Upbraid' for Jesus).[70] The 'Jesus Messiah Sutra' falls into two parts. The first part is doctrinal, explicating God's qualities as source of life and listing his commandments, including the charge to obey the Emperor. The second part includes the gospel story from the incarnation to the crucifixion of Jesus.[71]

With respect to doctrinal teachings, a development can be traced. A-lo-pen's first text meant to introduce the Emperor to the Christian faith. It emphasises Chinese virtues like ancestor worship, filial piety and loyalty to the Emperor, even Emperor worship, whereby the Emperors were depicted as being sacred, as gods born in the world, i.e. as 'Sons of Heaven', as those blessed by the Buddhas, and even as the manifestation of the Lord in heaven.[72] These Chinese concepts are of course most intimately connected with Christian precepts for daily life. Thus the ten commandments are explicated in Buddhist and Confucian terms, and the life of Jesus, up to his death, is described in terms understandable to educated Chinese. Unfortunately the text breaks off before the account of the resurrection.[73]

In the other A-lo-pen texts, contained in the Tomeoka manuscript, the concept of Monotheism figures prominently. In the 'Discourse on Monotheism', the first part, 'The Parable, Part II',[74] narrates the story of Adam. His image is contrasted to that of Jesus, whose crucifixion, resurrection and ascension are set forth, the story of Pentecost also being added. Here it is emphasised that God is manifest in all things, both visible and invisible, everything being made by him. The discussion of the qualities of God is linked with the discussion of the nature of the soul, the singularity and all-pervasive character of which is stressed. A further discussion of God's qualities, to which belong the quality of 'non-action' (*wu-wei*), a Taoist ideal, is then exemplified by short parables.

Intimately connected with the text discussed is the 'Discourse of the Oneness of the Ruler of the Universe', as Saeki translates it.[75] It emphasises the creative activity of God, referring again to visible and invisible things. The immortality of the soul and the 'five attributes' of the body are then discussed. They are connected with the five organs of sensation, i.e. the capacities of the physical body. Yet the concept of the 'five qualities' is not quite clear. One is reminded of the five *skandhas,* i.e. groups of dharmic elements constituting the human person in Buddhism. However, the 'five attributes' seem to be characteristic of the body, within which the soul dwells. Thus it says (v. 87): 'A human body seems to consist of both, "the five attributes" and the soul forming one complete being.'

Interesting is the emphasis on doing good and meritorious works, in accordance with the will of God, as a prerequisite for entering the other world. Although it is pointed out in view of Christ's bearing all sins that 'no meritorious deed is necessary (for salvation)' (v. 137), the significance of such deeds is yet emphasised (v. 142ff.), reference being made to the house sturdily built on the rock of good deeds (Matthew 7:24f. and Luke 6:48f.).

The last portion is concerned with evil deeds. It is inspired by Buddhist concepts, including the notion of reincarnation in a lowly state as a consequence of bad actions. However, those who pray to the one God who 'gives people a desire to do good and causes them to do so', 'unceasingly shall be satisfied' (v. 215, 217).

The third text in this connection, entitled 'The Lord of the Universe's Discourse on Alms-Giving',[76] extols a virtue praised in Buddhism, i.e. giving alms to monks (Skr. *dāna*). Yet alms-giving is only referred to in the beginning, and the discourse is quite biblically inspired, pointing out that to seek 'the Lord of Heaven' is more important than to seek worldly wealth. The text contains a number of references to Jesus' sayings as expressed in the Sermon on the Mount and in other New Testament passages. It narrates and comments upon the suffering, death, resurrection and ascension of the Messiah who is again contrasted with Adam as sinful man. There is also a reference to Pentecost when the Messiah 'admitted them (i.e. the disciples) into the secret of the Way [Tao]' and gave them 'the Holy Wind' (v. 165). (It may be added that for spirit and wind the same word is used in Hebrew and also in Greek.) They were then entrusted with the mission to teach all nations and races. After stressing the significance of the future judgement, the text then goes on to talk about the Messiah's followers in Fu-lin (the Roman Empire) and Persia and their persecution at the hands of Jews,[77] Romans and Persian kings. But the people of Fu-lin, and most men in Persia, so we hear, 'now', i.e. in AD 641, have come to 'worship the Lord of the Universe' (v. 218, 220). Connected with this statement is the exhortation of the Chinese reader to avoid the 'perverted Way' (v. 239) and to follow the Christian path, 'the Way of the one God' (v. 240). The author conceives of his time as 'these last days, when the end of the world is drawing near' (v. 249), devils and demons making their influence felt in the world. But the Messiah will come again, exercising his 'reforming and curing influence' for three and a half years (v. 251f.), after which time the living and the dead, raised again to life, will be judged.

The A-lo-pen texts thus endeavour to present to Chinese readers the principles of the Christian faith, employing Taoist and Buddhist terminology. But the literary forms chosen were apparently not very appealing to a larger audience. Time was needed to develop a Christian terminology that would be more in accord with Chinese literary standards.

Over against the A-lo-pen texts, the texts ascribed, rightly or wrongly, to Ching-Ching, written 150 years later, were more satisfying in literary form, although here Christianity could almost appear as a specific form of Taoism. The so-called Ching-Ching texts include, as we have heard, more than 30 books, which he 'obtained by translation', by Imperial order, there still being a great number of scriptures untranslated.[78]

Of the over 30 books, five are known. Closer scrutiny shows that they cannot all, in fact, have been written by Ching-Ching. To be treated first is the already mentioned *Book of Praise* (*Tsun-ching*), containing names of saints and holy books, attached to the Chinese *Gloria*.[79] Saeki identifies this book with the Nestorian *Diptychs*, the purpose of which was to offer praise and thanksgiving to God for the living and the dead. The *Diptychs* contain 22 names of Christian saints and 35 titles of sacred books. On the basis of internal evidence, Saeki comes to the conclusion that the *Book of Praise* was written 150 years after the time of Ching-Ching, i.e. in the early part of the 10th century, at least between AD 906 and AD 1036, when the library of Tunhuang was sealed.[80] Since there were hardly any Christians left in China proper at this time, it was probably written in Tunhuang itself. The works mentioned in the *Book of Praise* must of course have been written before this time.

The *Book of Praise* starts with an invocation of the Trinity, stressing the unity of the three divine persons 'in one body'.[81] The list of saints includes OT figures, writers of NT Scriptures and other holy men of the Church. These were regularly invoked in Nestorian services.

The second text to be discussed here is 'The Nestorian Hymn in Adoration of the Transfiguration of our Lord', as Saeki calls it.[82] In an editorial note it is called (in Saeki's translation) 'The Ta-ch'in Luminous Religion's Eulogy on the Holy One-equal-to-God's leading (people) to the truth and causing (them) to return to (the) Law.'[83] In the hymn, the Saviour is virtually identified with God, the 'Merciful Father'. Thus it says: 'Thou alone art the Holy One who is equal to God Almighty.'[84] This is quite in accordance with all Orthodox theologies that claim that he *is* God, 'true God from true God'. At the end we find liturgical instructions concerning scripture readings which would make it likely that the whole hymn was used in the liturgy. This hymn must have been composed in the beginning of the 8th century. The copy preserved, written by one Su-yuan of the 'Ta-ch'in Temple of Shachow' in Kansu, bears a colophon with the date AD 720. Hence this book must have been written before the time of Ching-Ching. Saeki ascribes it to one Bishop Cyriacus.[85]

Probably also to be ascribed to Cyriacus is the Chinese Gloria, entitled, according to A. C. Moule, 'A Hymn of the Brilliant Teaching of the Three Majesties (i.e. the Trinity) for obtaining salvation'.[86] The text shows that it was not literally translated, but rather freely, using terms familiar to Taoists and Buddhists. This may not be true of the name of God, 'Al-lo-he, the merciful Father of the universe', but with respect to terms like 'man's first true nature' or 'all enlightened natures' etc. the trend to 'Buddhicize' is obvious.[87] It is also in accord with Buddhist imagery when it says: 'Send down the raft to grant escape from tossing on the stream of fire.'[88] The stream of fire is a common image for worldly life in Buddhism, and the image of the raft is a common picture for salvation. Equally Buddhist are the words: 'Clear and strong is the law; beyond thought or dispute.'[89] In Buddhism, the 'law' is a reference to that religion. Here the term is claimed for Christianity, as was done by Manichaeans for their religion.[90]

The fourth text to be mentioned here is entitled (in Saeki's translation) 'The Ta-ch'in Luminous Religion Sutra on the Origin of Origins'.[91] It is also to be ascribed to Bishop Cyriacus. It is strongly tainted by Taoist and Buddhist elements as well. Unfortunately, only a portion at the beginning and the end is extant. According to the colophon, the copy preserved was made in AD 717 by a certain Church member Chang-ku also 'at the Ta-ch'in Temple at Sha-chow' in Kansu. It therefore stems from the same monastery and time as the second hymn discussed. It must therefore be doubted whether Ching-Ching who wrote the inscription on the monument of Sian-fu in AD 781 was the author.

The Sutra presents itself as the Sermon of 'Ching-t'ung, the Patriarch (lit. Law-King)'. As Saeki notes, Ching-t'ung, literally meaning 'all comprehending the luminous', may refer to the Messiah or Saviour here.[92] He sits on 'the throne of Precious Law surrounded by the Holy Clouds', that throne being set up 'at the palace of Peace and Enlightenment, situated in the City of Nazareth in the country of Ta-ch'in' (v. 1). A boundless multitude of people and heavenly beings surround him, including those 'who were known as the men of the Enlightenment and Purity' (v. 3). All complain that their views and ways have not led them to salvation, and therefore they have come to hear his message. Thereupon Ching-t'ung, after praying solemnly, 'was taken up to the Clouds over the Temple Palace, and from on high He spoke solemnly what [He] Himself [had] heard from God, the Father, to the beings and people below' (v. 7). It is quite a Buddhist notion when it says (v. 8): 'Let you who hold the Law of God attain the utmost pure Emptiness.' But then Taoist notions also come to the fore when it says (v. 10): 'If you understand (the meaning of the non-origin or non-creation) your stumbling block of doubt will melt away at once.' (v. 10).

> 'And at the moment when you understand the truthfulness of [the] Mysterious Creator you will attain (the state) of non-creation, non-expression, non-religion and non-connection as well as mysterious existence and mysterious non-existence profound and serene.' (v. 11)

The last part of the document stresses God's and Christ's merciful acceptance of all beings. The teaching of the Christian 'Way', so it says, leads to Enlightenment, if people have their 'true nature' restored, for then they would be

> 'pardoned and saved from the results of the sins – mortal or not – committed since the beginning of the world', (a notion that implies the concept of reincarnation), for 'such is due to the mysterious power of God.'[93]

The final section of the text points out that 'the holy men (of God)' can contribute something to the end that people do their work more assiduously and can promote peace and justice in the land, for such is in conformity with 'the Way of Faith, and the Marvellous Convention (existing between God and man)'.[94] It is quite clear that such utterances were also meant for the ears of the Imperial officials.

The fifth text to be discussed here is the 'Sutra on Mysterious Rest and Joy',[95] ascribed to Ching-Ching. It is not a book translated into but written in Chinese. As in Buddhist scriptures, it is the glorified Master (i.e. Jesus), here called 'the peerless and unique Lord of Eternity', who teaches disciples and a big crowd of people around him.[96] His sermon is elicited by a question of a disciple; in Buddhist texts this is often Ananda, here it is Peter, called 'Simon Samgha'. He asks the Master about the means of obtaining salvation. The Master, after praising the disciple for the well-asked question, then answers with a lengthy explication. It is quite Taoist in essence, stressing values like 'non-action' (*wu-wei*), the form, however, being Buddhist. An example may serve to illustrate the style of the book. The Messiah says to Peter:

'Know you Simon Samgha that if any of you wants to prepare himself for "the Victorious Way", as a rule he must get rid of both "motion" and "desire" before everything else. If he be "of non-motion" and "of non-desire", then he may be "of non-solicitation" and "non-assertation". If he is "of non-desire" and is "of non-action", then he may be pure and serene. If he can be pure and serene, then he may understand and demonstrate (the truth). If he can understand and demonstrate (the truth) then he will be "all illumining" and "all pervading". And to be "all illumining" and "all pervading" is nothing but the concatenation of cause and effect which will lead (people) to the state of Rest and Joy.' (v. 5–9)

The content of the book is not specifically Christian. Rather, it extols Taoist and Buddhist values that can be brought into harmony with Christian teachings and which are then ascribed to the Messiah. Like a Mahāyāna text, the work concludes with the remark:

'Listening to these words all the crowds were filled with happiness and joy. Saluting the Messiah most respectfully, they all retired and acted in accordance with the orders of the Lord.' (v. 105)

This text is strongly reminiscent of the fourth text discussed above. Whether it can really be ascribed to Ching-Ching can only be decided on the basis of a philological comparison with the Sian-fu inscription.

There are various other sources on Nestorianism in T'ang China, including Syriac texts (which might go back to that time, but which probably stem from the Yuan period),[97] and various inscriptions and archaeological relics, mainly from South Chinese ports.[98] These throw a more limited, though interesting light on certain aspects of Christianity in Mongol times. On the whole we can say that the documents we have discussed are examples of a new religious and spiritual synthesis between Christian thought and Chinese tradition, and that they do not merely use conventional Buddhist or Taoist concepts to expound Christian doctrine or morality.

THE DECLINE OF CHRISTIANITY IN T'ANG CHINA

The account of Ching-Ching's co-operation with Prajñā in the translation of the Buddhist *Ṣatpāramitā Sūtra* ('Sutra on the seven perfections [of a Bodhisattva]') voices criticism about the amalgamation of Christian and Buddhist concepts in that translation. Here it says that in AD 786 Prajñā,

> 'with the help of Ching-Ching, a Persian monk of the Ta-ch'in Monastery, . . . translated the *Lu po lo mi ching* (Ṣatpāramitā Sūtra) from a *hu* copy, dividing it into seven chapters. Since at that time Prajñā (Pan-jo) was unfamiliar with the *hu* language and did not yet understand the speech of T'ang, and Ching-Ching did not know Sanskrit nor understand Buddhist doctrine, though they professed to have made a translation they had not caught half the gems. They were seeking for vain glory with no thought of doing good. They composed and presented a memorial with the intention and hope that [their work] would be published. His Majesty, endued with learning and intelligence and reverencing the law of Buddha, examined their translation. The doctrine was obscure, the style indifferent. Since a Buddhist convent (*ch'ieh-lan*) and a monastery of Ta-ch'in monks differ in customs and are wholly opposed to one another in their religious practices, Ching-Ching must preach the teaching of Messiah (Mi-shih-he) and the Buddhist monk (*sha-mên*) make known the *sūtra* of Buddha. We wish to have religious teaching well defined that men may have no uncertainty. Truth and error are not the same; the Ching and the Wei [rivers] are not alike.'[99]

Here a critical attitude is adopted not only over against Ching-Ching but also over against Christianity as such, truth being ascribed to Buddhism, likened to the clear water of the Ching river, and error to Christianity, compared with the muddy water of the Wei river.

The text in which these words are contained stems from AD 800, although the passage is also found in an earlier book of the same author, Yuan-chao, dating to AD 794 or 795.[100] By the end of the 8th century, then, the tide was turning against Christianity.

In our section on Central Asia, we had occasion to refer to the various monastic establishments in T'ang China.[101] In an inscription written soon after AD 824 in the Ch'ung-yen monastery in Yung-hsing hsien (the modern Hsing-kuo chou in Hupei), the great change of events over against the situation described in the Sian-fu inscription, which may certainly have been exaggerated, becomes obvious. Here it says:

'Among the different foreigners who have come there [i.e. to China] are the Mo-ni (Manichees), the Ta-ch'in (Christians), and the Hsien-shên (Zoroastrians). All the monasteries of these three sorts of foreigners in the Empire together are not enough to equal the number of our Buddhist monasteries in one small city.'[102]

The great persecution of foreign religions in AD 845 of course affected the Christians drastically. In a historical passage relating to the decree of AD 845, it says, with respect to Christians:

'For the monks and nuns who came under the charge of the controllers of aliens making known the religions of foreign countries, they compelled the Ta-ch'in (Christians) and Mu-hu-fu (Zoroastrians) to the number of more than three thousand persons to return to lay life and to cease to confound the customs of China (*Chung hua*).'[103]

And in the official history of the T'ang period, the *Chiu t'ang shu*, it says in respect to the Christians and Zoroastrians, in a summary of Moule:

'. . . these heretical religions must not alone be left when the Buddhists have been suppressed; they [i.e. the monks of those religions] must all be compelled to return to lay life and resume their original callings and pay taxes, or if they are foreigners they shall be sent back to their native places.'[104]

How radical the persecution of AD 845 was, is borne out by an account of the results of the persecution of Buddhists. Moule sums it up thus:

'More than 4600 monasteries were destroyed in the empire, 260 500 monks and nuns were secularized, more than 40 000 smaller establishments suppressed, many thousands of myriards of *ch'ing* of land confiscated, more than 150 000 men and women slaves set free.'[105]

Some light is shed on the fate of Christians in China in the second half of the 9th century, after the great persecution, by a Muslim writer, Abu-Zaid, who collected information from travellers to that country without having been there himself. Referring to the story of one Suleyman who had been in China in AD 851, and to more recent news, he talks about the siege, by a rebel group under one Bansu (Huang Ch'ao) of Khanfu (probably Canton) in AD 878–888. Having become lord of the city, Bansu massacred 6000 Moslems, Jews, Christians and Parsis who were in the city to do business. Abu-Zaid adds the interesting remark:

'The exact number of those who perished of these four religions could be known because the Chinese levied a tax on these foreigners according to their number.'[106]

The Nestorians were extinct in China by the end of the 10th century, as documented by an Arab writer, Abu l-Faraj, who wrote in Baghdad at that time. In his *Kitab al Fihrist,* he says:

'In the year 377 (AD 987), in the Christian quarter [i.e. of Baghdad] behind the Church, I met a monk from Najran who seven years before had been sent by the Catholicos to China with five other clergy to set in order the affairs of the Christian Church. . . . I asked him for some information about his journey, and he told me that Christianity was just extinct in China; the native Christians had perished in one way or another; the church which they had used had been destroyed; and there was only one Christian left in the land. The monk having found no one remaining to whom his ministry could be of any use returned more quickly than he went.'[107]

This seems to be the last information on Christians in the aftermath of the T'ang Church. In the period of the Sung Dynasty (AD 960–1279) China had grown extremely introverted, severing ties with foreign forces, both political and religious. The many new influences obtaining in the T'ang period had now to be mastered intellectually, or excluded. Since Christianity was borne mainly by foreigners, and since it was heavily dependent on the monastic centres where they lived, the elimination of these centres spelt out the end of the first Christian period in China.

Yet memories of a Christian tradition lingered on. The reminiscence of a Christian presence, sometimes even tinged with poetic imagination, can be found in later texts. Thus Ts'ai meng-pi, writing at the beginning of the 13th century and quoting the *Shu tu ku shih,* written probably in the Sung period, refers to a 'Ta-ch'in monastery', built 'long ago' by foreigners in Ch'eng-tu, now destroyed, the foundations alone remaining visible. There is almost a romantic reminiscense of T'ang exotics when it says: 'Every time that there is a great rain the people in front and behind pick up many rare things like pearls, shê-shê, gold, and blue jade.'[108]

In a Taoist book dealing with the legendary mission of Lao-tzu to the lands of the West, the *Yu lung ch'uan,* written in the Sung Dynasty, the term 'Messiah' (*Mi-shi-he*) is to be found beside the names of Western deities. The name was probably inspired by T'ang records rather than by contact with contemporary Christians.[109] In so far as other sources in post-T'ang times are concerned, Moule points out:

'The mentions of Christianity in contemporary Chinese authors of the tenth, eleventh, and twelfth centuries are very few, and what

there are are either extremely vague or refer definitely to an already
distant past, and we believe that nothing has yet been found to
suggest that there were Christians surviving in China during the
eleventh and twelfth centuries.'[110]

This dictum remains true today. As pointed out, Syriac texts found in
Peking in 1925 or 1926, containing liturgical passages and mentioning
martyrs in China who were merchants, could go back to the second half of
the ninth century; it is more probable, however, that they stem from Yuan
times.[111]

THE MONGOLS IN CHINA

The Mongol state, founded by Jinghis Khan, was so dynamic that it spread
out in all directions, including China. In AD 1239 the Tanguts who had
established a kingdom between the Tibetan Highlands and the Gobi
Desert, as well as the Kin of Manchuria, were conquered. Mongol armies
then marched further south into Sung China. In AD 1251, the Khan
Mangu gave Khubilai Khan the order to conquer the whole Sung realm.
Khubilai, having been elected as Great Khan in 1260, then started his
invasion. By AD 1278, the last Sung Emperor had died.

The key year of the Mongol occupation of China was AD 1271. At this
time Khubilai consolidated his power in East Asia and gave to his realm,
the Khanate China, the Chinese name *Ta Yuan*, i.e. 'The Great Primal
Beginning'. At this time he also made Khan Baliq, present Beijing, his
winter residence. The city with its good connections with Mongolia was to
become the capital of Yuan, i.e. Mongol China.

Khubilai's role as the founder of the Yuan Dynasty was decisive, for he
paved the way for a religious policy that was to be observed by later Khans.
Being a grandson of Jinghis Khan, he accepted the heritage of the great
founder of the realm, but he transformed the mission he felt he had been
entrusted with by imbibing the spirit of China.[112] This fact becomes
obvious in a regal declaration where he says:

'I, the ruler, wish to establish peace in the ten thousand lands, and
especially wish to cultivate the important duties of goodness. To
Heaven I report the exalted great name [i.e. *Ta Yuan*], and to all of
you (subjects) I declare it with my highest satisfaction.'[113]

As opposed to Sung rule which had great reservations about all foreign
influences, Khubilai Khan, as most of his successors, displayed the
religious tolerance characteristic of Mongol rule in Central Asia, even
though the connections with Tibetan Buddhism grew increasingly
important for him and for subsequent rulers. In the last chapter, we have
spoken of Khubilai's connection with the Tibetan Lama 'Phags-pa

(d. AD 1280), under whose influence a theory of two orders, a religious and a political one, both supporting each other, was formulated.[114]

Of the rulers after Khubilai, some were to become ardent promoters of Buddhism. Thus Jen-tsung (Buyantu: AD 1311–1320) became an earnest student of Lamaism, supporting it where he could. But it is indicative of the whole situation that he became a strong promoter of Confucian education as well. Yet Jen-tsung backed Buddhist monasteries to such a degree that it caused wide dissatisfaction among his people and distrust among the Confucian literati. With Wen-tsung (Togh Temur: AD 1328–1333), finally, the power of the Lamaist monks became so great that bitterness and hate against foreigners became widespread. At this time, the suppression of Christianity set in.

The end of the Yuan Dynasty came when Hung-wu (T'ai-tsu, d. AD 1398), the founder of the Ming Dynasty, subdued the last Mongol Emperor Shun-ti (Toghan Temur: d. AD 1368). Hung's armies conquered Khan Baliq in AD 1368, and this caused the Mongols to flee from Chinese soil. With the Mongols, foreign officials, mercenaries, traders and even monks were expelled from China. And since Christians were to the greatest extent non-Chinese, this marked the end of Christianity in China.

One of the main reasons for the hatred of the Chinese against the Mongols was the ostentatious splendour they displayed, whereas the economic situation of the people grew worse and worse.[115] The reports of Western travellers, including Marco Polo, refer only to the situation of the privileged. The lot of the people was quite a different one.[116] This has to be kept in mind in view of our sources, which throw little light on the Chinese populace.

Mongol rule in China was strongly determined by the political and cultural outlook of Khubilai Khan who laid the foundation for the Yuan Dynasty. O. Franke remarks:

> 'This man, who was to become one of the greatest rulers of world history, not only towered highly above the puffed up world of letters of the Sung, but also above his whole time with respect to intellectual prudence, unprejudicial quality of character and goodness of heart.'[117]

Khubilai was not only open to Buddhist but also to Confucian ideas, developed as they were in the Sung Dynasty. On the one hand this was a matter of necessity, since the civil administration in China, retained in Mongol times, was basically borne by Confucians. On the other hand, the ethical ideals of the Confucians, including the important duties of goodness, appealed to Khubilai personally.

In spite of all affiliations to Buddhism and Confucianism, Khubilai, himself the son of a Nestorian princess, remained open to other religions, and it was this attitude of tolerance, also upheld by later rulers, that allowed Christianity to thrive.[118]

The establishment of Mongol power in Central and East Asia was thus one of the most prominent factors in the spread and blossoming of Nestorian Christianity in the 13th and 14th century. Beside the tolerant attitude of most Mongol rulers, it was the Pax Mongolica, allowing for commercial and other contacts between East and West, even between China and Western Asia, that made possible the strengthening of ties between the Patriarch in Baghdad and the most remote eastern areas of Nestorian Christianity, thus giving it new buoyancy in Asia Major. It was due to the Mongols, then, that Christianity was reintroduced into China after its demise in the 9th–10th century, most Nestorians being of Central Asian, i.e. Turkish or Mongol extraction. But there were also Syrian and Iranian, i.e. Persian and Sogdian merchants and officials, priests and monks, who found their way to China.

NESTORIANS AMONG THE RULING MONGOLS

In sketching the role of Nestorians in China, it is necessary to refer back to the Mongols in Central Asia, the situation there being intimately connected with that in China in Mongol times. We thus return to the description of the Nestorians under the Khans in Central Asia, expanding on such issues as are relevant for China.

We have had occasion to point to the significance of the Kerait and the Naiman Nestorians who were integrated into Jinghis Khan's new state. Prominent figures in early Mongol history were Nestorians from these Turkish tribes. Thus Chinkai, a Kerait born around AD 1171, was companion-in-arms of Jinghis Khan, even warring at his side against his own tribe, until it had been subdued by the Mongols.[119] He rose to such a rank that in northern China no edict could be issued without his signature. He was 'Secretary of the State' under Jinghis as well as Ogadai, and he held the position of a 'Chancellor' under Kuyuk. Another prominent Christian, Qadaq, who had served under Jinghis as an army leader, was made 'Administrator of the Realm' under Kuyuk. Bolghai, the Chancellor of Mangu, the fourth Khan, was also a Christian from the tribe of the Keraits. At the same time another Kerait Nestorian, Kitbugha, was the general commanding the Mongol army in its advance to Western Asia. He vanquished the army of the Abbasids, became governor of Damascus, and finally commanded the Mongol forces that fought against the Egyptian Mamluks. It was in this struggle that he lost his life in AD 1260.

One of the leading military men in Yuan China in the early 14th cent. was a Central Asian Turkish official of Nestorian confession, Sama (chin. Hsin-tu) by name. He hailed from Dadu (Peking) and served as district commander, probably in the south, under Emperor Jen-tsung (Buyantu, reg. 1311–1320). The *Annals of the Yuan Dynasty* shed light on his prowess. The gravestone of his young Christian wife has recently been discovered. It is embellished by a cross on a lotus, flanked by two four-winged angels. The recently published inscription is trilingual, having a Syriac introductory formula, a Turkish text in Syriac script, and an accompanying Chinese text summing up the Turkish lines. The Syriac and Turkic texts read:

> '[Syriac] In the name of Jesus Christ. [Turkic] In the year 1629 of (the era) of Emperor Alexander, in the snake year according to the Turkish calendar, on the 9th day of the 3rd month [i.e. May 20th, 1317 AD], the wife of Samša, District Commander from Dadu [Peking], the lady Elizabeth, died at the age of 33. The body of her excellency was buried in this grave. May her soul rest eternally in Paradise. . . . May she enjoy peace forever, and may her name remain. [Syriac] Amen! Yes and Amen!'[120]

In the portion not translated here, there is a reference to the 'pure charisma' (*arïy qutïlar*, pl.!) of her husband, and the hope is expressed that the country may be at peace for a thousand years. Even if this is the typical hyperbolic language of such grave stone inscriptions, it is interesting to note that the high military official had no inhibitions in expressing his Christian affiliation publicly.

Beside being army leaders, Nestorian Christians of Turkish and Mongol extraction also had high positions in the administration. As W. Hage points out:

> 'They made of Christianity self-evidently a confession a noble Mongol could embrace without loss of honour, because it did not have to be regarded as a foreign religion of peoples conquered in the West.'[121]

This also accords with gravestone inscriptions of other high Turkish officials serving as officers in the southern ports of Yuan China. One gravestone, found in Zaitun, again written in Turkic and Chinese, testifies to the fact that the Christians were headed by a high ecclesiastical authority, who must have been an Ongut Turk, since the language of the inscription is East Turkic. The text reads:

> 'This is the grave of the lord (Mar) priest, the lord *episcopus* Šlimun (= Šilemun) (head of?) the religious congregations (?). On the 15th of the 8th month (i.e. August) of the year of the ox (in the) *kui* (series) [i.e. 1313 AD], Zauma, who had come leading (a delegation?), wrote (this inscription.)'[122]

The accompanying Chinese inscription makes it clear that the *episcopus* concerned was head of Nestorian, Manichaean and other congregations south of the Yangtze. It says of him that he 'administered (the affairs) of the Manichaeans, Nestorians etc. in the area south of the Yangtze River.'[123]

K. Enoki and S. Murayama, who has published both versions of the text, make us aware of a number of further Syriac inscriptions in the southern part of China stemming from this period.[124]

It should be added at this point that the Nestorian Turkish officials in the south Chinese ports must have had contact with European merchants. Some of these would have been well aware of their Christian associations. This is attested by a gravestone inscription in Latin, found at Yangzhou. It is inscribed in Gothic letters and it commemorates a certain Anthony who seems to have come from a Genoese family. The inscription, dated to 1344, translates:

'In the name of the Lord, Amen. Here lies Anthony, son of the deceased Lord Dominicus of Ilionis, who died in the year of the Lord 1344, in the month of November.'[125]

Among the ancient documents of the city of Genoa, one has been found, dating from 1348, which actually names a Dominicus Ilionis, of whom we know that he had been in China. The Ilionis family belonged to the wealthy Genoese merchants at the beginning of the 14th cent. The grave stone mentioned is especially interesting in that it is embellished by a scene of Christ as Judge of the world, a scene in which European and Chinese elements are amalgamated.[126]

Apart from Naimans and Kereits, Uighurs and Onguts, many of whom, then, were Christians, had various positions in the administration of the new realm. The Mongol script was derived from that of the Uighurs who influenced the developing Mongol culture. In a certain sense they had the position of cultural mentors, which is evidenced by the fact that they were often asked to educate the children of Mongol noblemen. The Nestorian Onguts, on the other hand, were administrators of the Mongols in China, also participating in the cultural and intellectual life of the time. Christian physicians, stemming mainly from Syria, also worked for the Mongols in Central Asia, their fame spreading to China. But there were also Nestorians from Central Asia who became recognised physicians. Thus the father and grandfather of Mar Sargis, a Nestorian from Samarkand working in the service of Khubilai Khan, were court physicians.[127] Finally, wives and concubines of ruling Khans and people in authority were not seldom Nestorian ladies. Thus one of the wives of Jinghis Khan, Turakina, as well as the wife of his successor Ogadai, father of Kuyuk, were Nestorian women. Men in the family of the Khans often married Kerait girls, and the rulers of the Christian Onguts were bound to the ruling Mongol house by matrimonial bonds. The most prominent of Christian ladies among the Mongols was Sorghoqtani, mother of the Khans Mangu, Khubilai and Hulagu. She was active politically even after the death of her husband Tului, son of Jinghis. Being honoured also outside the ranks of the Christians, her memory lingered on, and her picture was even honoured in a church in Kanchow 80 years after her death.[128] Although her sons were not Christians, they did have Christian wives and were open to the Christian cause.

KHUBILAI KHAN'S ATTITUDE TO CHRISTIANITY

In view of Khubilai's importance for the religious scene in Yuan China, his attitude to the religions represented at his court and in his realm should be scrutinized. The reports of Western travellers, especially Marco Polo, throw light on that attitude. In spite of his leanings toward Buddhism and his interest in Confucianism, he did have an open attitude to other forms of faith.

According to Marco Polo, Khubilai left the question as to which religion was the true and highest one open, ascribing different religions to different peoples in the world. Thus he is quoted as saying:

'There are four Prophets who are worshipped and to whom all the world does reverence. The Christians say their God is Jesus Christ, the Saracens Mahomet, the Jews Moses, the idolaters [i.e. Buddhists] Sogomoni Borcan [i.e. Shakyamuni Buddha], who was the first God of the idols; and I do honour and reverence to all four, that is to him who is the greater in heaven and more true, to him I pray that he may help me.'[129]

This is probably a dictum of the ruler directed specifically to the Polos as Christians. The basic interest in Buddhism seems relativized here, and one almost has the impression that Khubilai wants to be on the safe side in so far as the greatest and truest God is concerned.

In the same document, the authenticity of which has been questioned, however,[130] we read that Khubilai held the Christian faith 'for the most true and good' because, as Marco Polo puts it, 'he says that it does not command a thing which is not full of all goodness and holiness.'[131] This stands in opposition to Marco Polo's remark that

'these Tartars do not care what God is worshipped in their lands. If only they are faithful to the Lord Khan and quite obedient, and give therefore the appointed tribute, and justice is well kept, thou mayest do what pleaseth thee with the soul.'[132]

Khubilai himself would not convert to Christianity for the sake of the non-Christians attached to his court who would demand an outward sign that the Christian God is stronger than the divine powers of the Buddhists. Yet he expressed interest in Christian learning. When the Venetian merchants Maffeo and Nicolo Polo visited him the first time, he requested them to go to the Pope ('your High Priest') and ask him to send 'a hundred men skilled in your religion who before these idolaters may be able to reprove what they do and may say to them that they know and can do such things but will not, because they are done by diabolical art and through evil spirits, and may so restrain them that they may not have power to do such things in their presence. Then when we shall see this we shall condemn them and their religion; and so I shall be baptized, and when I shall be baptized all my barons and great men will be baptized, and then their subjects will receive baptism, and so there will be more Christians here than there are in your parts.'[133]

According to another passage in Marco Polo's book, the Khan asked the Venetians to bring him 'some of the oil of the lamp which burns above the sepulchre of God in Jerusalem.'[134] Marco Polo tells us that when his father and his uncle returned with him on their second trip, they presented the Khan

'with the privileges and the letters which the Apostle [i.e. the Pope] sends him, in which he had great delight. Next they hand him the holy oil, at which he made great rejoicing and holds it very dear.'[135]

The Polos, arriving with Marco in Khan Baliq in AD 1275, were to stay in China for 17 years, reaching Venice again in 1295. Marco, like his father and uncle, learned to communicate well in Mongolian, and perhaps also Turkish and Chinese. Marco travelled extensively in the eastern Mongol realm, including South China, gaining insight into the political and religious situation in various quarters. Upon his return, he dictated his book, *Description of the World*, to Rustichello (or Rustico) of Pisa when both were imprisoned at Genoa.[136]

The travel account of Marco Polo furnishes us with information on Central Asia as well as China, since he travelled to East Asia along the 'Silk Route'. Thus we hear that there were many Nestorians at Karakhoja, in the Turfan oasis, who freely intermarried with non-Christians. We are told about Christians in Barkul (Ghinghintalas), Sachow (Sacion) near Tunhuang, Kanchow (Canpicion), Yung-ch'an (near modern Liangchow) and other places further east belonging already to China proper. We hear that in these various places mentioned Christians were living beside Buddhists and Moslems.[137] Marco's report about his travel through the Ordos area gave him occasion to speak about the Nestorian king, George of the Onguts, whom he thinks to be a descendant of Prester John.[138] He points out that 'the great Khans have always given of their daughters and of their kindred to the kings who reign who are of the lineage of Prester John. . . . The rule belongs to Christians . . ., but there are idolaters enough and men who worship Mahomet.'[139]

291

In Marco Polo's description of the Khan's court at Khan Baliq, we learn that a certain Nestorian Christian by the name of Naian, an insurgent, had been overcome by the ruler. When non-Christians made fun of the cross which Naian had borne on his banner, the Khan rebuked them comforting the Christians, as their God had not helped a traitor.[140] We hear that the Khan observed the chief feasts of the Christians, i.e. Easter and the Nativity, summoning all Christians to him and revering 'the book in which are the four Gospels.'[141] On the Khan's birthday, so we learn, people of various religions prayed to their gods to give long life, health and joy to the Khan. Especially significant is the note that in the high administration of China, 'Tartars, Saracens, and Christians, who were of his own family and loyal to him and were not of the province of Cathay', played a decisive role,[142] and that there were Christians, including Alans, who were in the military service.[143] The Alans, probably a Scythian tribe from the Caucasus, served in Mongol armies since the time of Jinghis Khan. They were Christians, but they had no priests of their own and therefore depended on other Christians priests for spiritual guidance.

In so far as the areas and cities with Christian inhabitants are concerned, we hear of Nestorians in Khubilai's realm as far away as the southern Province of Yunnan, furthermore in the cities of Yangchow and Chen-chiang on the Yangtze-Kiang river, and in various other cities including the southern port of Zaitun.[144]

Of interest, finally, is the fact that in Fu-Chou (Fugiu) Marco Polo found a group, possessing a church, which he addressed as Christians, although they were in fact probably Manichaeans.[145] In the whole province, so we hear, there were 'more than seven hundred thousand families who followed this rule.'[146] S. N. C. Lieu points out:

> 'The Manichaeans whom the Polos [i.e. Marco and his uncle] met had clearly been deprived of the teaching of their priests. They had little idea of what they believed in except the little they could learn from the few books which had been passed on to them by their ancestors. Thus it was not difficult for the Polos to persuade them to believe that they were Christians. . . . However, although they might have been glad to be classed as a recognized religious group together with the Christians, they did not totally lose their self-identity.'[147]

According to the wish of this group, Christian priests, rather than Buddhist monks, were to administer their affairs.[148]

Such administration was, of course, directed by the court, for in AD 1289 Khubilai established an office to supervise the Christians. So we can surmise that Khubilai, as later Khans, was well informed about Christians, as well as Buddhists, in his realm. In how far his religious tolerance was motivated by political considerations is hard to say. It seems, however, that his personal attitude was an encompassing one, allowing for different faiths to exist beside each other, as long as they did not endanger the stability of the state.

NESTORIANISM IN THE SECULAR LIFE OF YUAN CHINA

The Nestorian communities in China were spread out in various areas from the Ordos region in the north-east to coastal cities in the south. They were all subordinate to a Nestorian metropolitan residing in Khan Baliq, which was raised to metropolitan status some years before AD 1275. The exact juridical relationship between the individual communities and the metropolitanate is, however, unclear.

Significant areas with a Nestorian population were, firstly, the north-eastern regions in the present province of Kansu and in neighbouring areas. There were still Nestorians among the Tanguts, and the Turkish Onguts were to a significant extent Christian. We have already spoken of the Ongut crosses found in the Ordos region and have mentioned the tombstones with Turkish inscriptions discovered in that area. Remains of a Nestorian church as well as a Catholic one were found in Olon Süme, beside the remains of a royal library.[149] The Onguts, in the second half of the 13th century, had a Nestorian king, George by name, as we heard from Marco Polo. When he was converted to Latin Christianity by John of Montecorvino, this caused unrest at the court and amongst his subjects. It must have been at this time that the Catholic church mentioned above was built. After George's death in AD 1299, the royal house reverted to the Nestorian confession, which was bound to have an effect on Christians who had turned to Catholicism. We shall discuss this development when dealing with the activity of John of Montecorvino, the Latin Archbishop of Khan Baliq.

The role of the Nestorians at the court as well as in various cities of China was mentioned, as we saw, by Marco Polo, who travelled extensively in the realm of the Khan. We have pointed to his reference to Christians in Chen-chiang, which we shall have occasion to highlight when we speak of monastic life. There were also Christians in Yangchow, where there were three Nestorian churches, one of which had been founded by a rich merchant named Abraham, as well as in Hanchow (if they were not all Manichaeans) and 'in the cities on the main arteries of trade.'[150]

A city with a small but important Christian minority was the southern port of Zaitun, known in Chinese as Ch'uan-chou. Being an important commercial city with many foreign merchants, including Arabic and non-Arabic Moslems, Jews, Armenians and even Genoese, various religions were represented here. Living in specific areas of the city, they enjoyed a kind of extra-territoriality, but their business was supervised and their goods taxed by trustworthy officials of the Mongols, a considerable number of whom were Turkish Nestorians. The importance of Zaitun as a port from which trade was conducted with South-East Asia, India, and even Western Asia had already led the Sung to levy taxes on all goods that passed through the city. Khubilai and his successors continued this practice, demanding a ten percent revenue.[151] The city did gradually lose its importance as the harbour was silted up, Canton then becoming the most important port for maritime trade on the southern coast. But Western writers of the 14th century still tell us of Christian communities in Zaitun, including Nestorians, Armenians and Latins.

The presence of Nestorians at Zaitun is also documented by indigenous sources, consisting mainly of inscriptions on tombstones, often being decorated with a cross on a lotus flower, these sometimes being flanked by angels in flowing robes. We have already had occasion to refer to some. Most of the tombstone inscriptions found at Zaitun are Arabic, pointing to the significance of the Moslem community, which also had a large mosque in the city. Of the Christian inscriptions, various ones are written in Syriac script, some being in the Syriac language, others in an East Turkish dialect comparable to Ongut. The great number of such tombstones, of which many were later used to repair the city walls, would indicate a sizeable Turkish Nestorian community at Zaitun.[152] It is therefore not surprising to see that some of the inscriptions were written in Uighur script, the script of the Turks of Central Asia. Even the 'Phags-pa script, developed by the Tibetan monk 'Phags-pa at the time of Khubilai Khan, was employed. One bilingual Turkish-Chinese inscription, dated 5th September 1313, is in memory of a Bishop Mar Solomon. It reads:

> 'To the Administrator of the Manichaeans and Nestorians in the Circuit of Chiang-nan, the Most Reverend Christian Bishop Mar Solomon, Timothy Sauma and others have mournfully and respectfully dedicated this tombstone . . .'[153]

It is interesting to note that both the Nestorians and the Manichaeans in South China, south of the Yangtse river, were under the control of this Nestorian bishop, as the Chinese text tells us. He came from Samarkand and was probably a Turk.[154]

Besides Nestorians, there were then Armenians and Latins in Zaitun, this being an important centre of the Franciscan mission, to which we shall return later. Suffice it to mention here that one epitaph is in Latin, written in memory of the Franciscan Andrew of Perugia who died in Zaitun in 1332.[155] We have already made reference to the Latin tombstone inscription, written in Gothic letters, of a Genoese merchant (1344).

The Nestorian community in Zaitun probably continued to thrive up to the middle of the 14th century, when the decline of Mongol rule was foreshadowed by intolerance on the part of the rulers.

Generally speaking, Nestorianism in Yuan China, as in T'ang China, remained basically a foreign religion, and though attempts were made to win people from the Chinese population for this creed, we have no indication of a greater number of Chinese being converted. This was probably also the case in Manchuria where Christianity was now introduced along the coast and further inland between the rivers Sungari and Amur.

Yet the Nestorian Church did thrive in Yuan China. W. Hage, in discussing the situation at that time, points out that the 'Apostolic Church of the East' with its wide network of communities in Central and East Asia 'was at the height of its power, being the most successful missionary Church in the Christendom of the age.'[156] Even then, the Nestorians remained a dwindling minority in view of the whole Chinese population. John of Cora, writing in about 1330, speaks of over 30,000 Christians in the 'empire of Cathay', pointing out that they belonged to the well-to-do.[157] Further he adds:

> 'They have very beautiful and orderly Churches with crosses and images in honour of God and of the saints. They hold many offices under the said Emperor and have great privileges from him; whence it is believed that if they would agree and be quite at one with these Minor Brothers and with these other good Christians who live there in this country, they would convert all this country and this Emperor to the true faith.'[158]

This optimistic view probably suggested itself on account of the power the Nestorians wielded, rather than on account of their numbers.

CHRISTIAN MONKS AND HERMITS IN YUAN CHINA

Having shed light on Nestorian Christianity as upheld mainly by laymen, many of whom were in influential positions, we shall now turn to the monastic and eremitic life of Nestorian clergymen in China. These, too, were to a great extent of foreign extraction. But apparently the Church was not as dependent on a monastic organisation as in the T'ang period, laymen playing an important role in all walks of life, including commerce, administration and even politics, as the case of Nestorians at the court shows. Yet the monasteries were pillars of religious and intellectual life. They were places of learning, and it is clear from documents found that the Nestorians in Yuan China had a literature of their own, in Syriac as well as in Turkish, and perhaps also in Chinese. Of this literature, however, little has been preserved. It is difficult to tell whether the texts from the T'ang period survived and were again in use, or whether Syriac literature was now being introduced completely anew.

The monasteries were scattered over the wide country from Khan Baliq to the southern coast. The monastic centre at Khan Baliq could go back to earlier times. There were also monastic establishments in the lower reaches of the Yangtze-Kiang, especially in Chen-chiang and Yangchow, as well as in Hanchow. We have already had occasion to refer to the seven monasteries founded by Mar Sargis, a Turkish Nestorian from Samarkand who was a high official in the service of Khubilai Khan. Of the monastic centres established by him, six were built in Chen-chiang and one in Hanchow. A Chinese text, *The History of Chen-chiang of the Chihshun Period*, gives us an account of the monasteries in Chen-chiang, a port on the southern bend of the Yangtze-Kiang, about 140 miles from that river's mouth.[159] It also throws light on the untiring efforts of Mar Sargis, who had been active as an official in that city. In spite of all honours bestowed upon him in political life, he was devoted to the propagation of the Nestorian faith. We hear that he was summoned to the task of building the monasteries in a dream, in which he saw seven gates open in heaven. Angels gave him the charge to erect the monasteries. This he then did with great fervour and devotion. The abovementioned work notes:

'These seven monasteries were truly the outcome of his Excellency's zeal. He was loyal to the sovereign and devoted to the empire, not seeking to make himself conspicuous but only making his monasteries so.'[160]

The monasteries built by Mar Sargis around AD 1281 were given Chinese and Turkic names, which indicates that Turkish monks must have lived here, perhaps beside some Chinese brethren. The Turkish names of these establishments are interesting. They are:

1. 'The main monastery', 2. 'The monastery of the stone', 3. 'The monastery of restoration', 4. 'The ocean-like monastery', 5. 'The monastery of the great rock or of the deep ravine', 6. 'The monastery of St. George' and 7. 'The new monastery'. It was this seventh monastery that was erected in Hanchow.[161]

The History of Chen-chiang mentioned above also gives us some insight into the practice of worship. We hear of the importance of worship toward the east which, as the place where the sun and the moon rise, symbolises creative activity and is an allusion to 'the ever-creative God'.[162] The text also tells us something about the significance of the cross, the figure for ten in Chinese script. It had anthropological as well as cosmological connotations. On the one hand it was 'an image of the human body', on the other hand it was considered to be 'an indicator of the four quarters, the zenith and nadir.'[163] The old Chinese idea of a correspondence between man and the cosmos is here interpreted with the help of the central Christian symbol.

Surprisingly, *The History of Chen-chiang*, which speaks so favourably about Mar Sargis and his work, also contains a passage most critical of that work and of Christianity at large, regarding Buddhism as the only true religion.[164] It tells us how 'Monasteries of the Cross', i.e. Christian monasteries, were converted into Buddhist ones. Thus an artist by the name of Liu Kao who had painted and embellished one church, was ordered, in 1311, to repaint the walls with Buddhist motifs. And in the case of other monasteries as well, the Christian paintings and images were replaced by Buddhist ones.[165] This happened on account of an Imperial decree issued by Emperor Jen-tsung (Buyantu: AD 1311–1320) immediately after his accession to the throne.

Beside the monastic institutions, there were also hermitages where individual monks would live a life of seclusion, rather than a coenobitic one. This was quite in accord with the Syrian tradition. Such hermits must have lived in various secluded spots in the wide deserts and wastes of Central Asia as well. Thus we know that the monk Mar Sargis (Sergius) who converted the Kerait king had retreated to the Altai mountains. To balance the picture, however, it must be pointed out that monks were also active in court life, hence appearing on the political scene and having contact with those who wielded power.

Both these aspects are combined in the persons of Rabban Sauma and Mark, who was later to become Patriarch Yaballaha III, whereas his teacher Rabban Sauma was given a high ecclesiastical position as 'Vicar General'. The story of their role in the diplomatic contact between the Il-Khan of Mongol Persia on the one hand and the pope and European rulers on the other has been outlined above. We are here concerned only with their life in China.[166]

Rabban Sauma was the son of a noble, rich and respected Turkish Nestorian in the rank of a 'Visitor', a Periodeut, in Khan Baliq. He was given a religious education by a 'worthy master', the parents also making him 'apply himself with care to religious learning.'[167] He seemed fit for the priesthood, was ordained as a priest and became a sacristan in the church at Khan Baliq. It was his wish, however, to renounce the world, much to the dismay of his wealthy parents. Like St. Anthony in Egypt, he distributed all his property to the poor. Having been tonsured at the hands of the Nestorian Metropolitan of Khan Baliq, Mar Giwargis (George), he shut himself up in a cell for seven years. Since he was increasingly molested by men coming to see him, he then chose as a dwelling a cave in the mountains west of his home town. Though living in such a remote place, his reputation grew and people came to hear him teach. Among these was Mark, the son of a Nestorian Archdeacon in Koshang (also known as Olon Süme) in the Ordos area, whose wish it was to become a monk and live with him as a hermit. Rabban Sauma endeavoured to persuade him to return to his parents, pointing to the rigour demanded of an ascetic life. But in view of the steadfastness of the young man, Rabban Sauma finally allowed him to live with him. Having been taught for three years, Mark received the tonsure at the hands of the metropolitan. Then he returned to his teacher, living an ascetic life with him. It was he who urged Rabban

Sauma to undertake the long pilgrimage to Jerusalem together with him. Though they did not reach that city, they were to play an important ecclesiastical and political role in the Near East where Mark became Patriarch Yaballaha III.

The story of Rabban Sauma and Mark in China throws light on eremitic life amongst Nestorians in the East. Noteworthy is the fact that the hermits Rabban Sauma and Mark retained contact with the Church and its leaders, regarding the tonsure as a necessary prerequisite for their lonely life. The strict asceticism they subscribed to included fasting and other observances. The purport of such a life is expressed in the account of Mark and Rabban Sauma where it says:

> 'They laboured on the mountain at the work of their purification and sanctification, and received comfort from God for whom they were consecrated.'[168]

Hence the purity of the soul, the sanctification of life and the consecration to God were aims of hermetic life. There is also something very ascetic about the long and arduous pilgrimage to the West that Rabban Sauma and Mark undertook, wishing to worship at the tombs of the martyrs and patriarchs, in the hope of obtaining 'plenary indulgence for our sins and absolution for our faults.'[169] The aim of this pilgrimage is aptly summed up by Rabban Sauma when he says: 'We wish for perfection.'[170]

FRANCISCAN ENVOYS, LEGATES AND MISSIONARIES

The mission of the Western Christians to Yuan China was basically one conducted by the Franciscans, the friars of the Minor Order. Their writings give us a relatively clear picture of their activity in Asia.[171] These writings are supplemented by papal and other ecclesiastical letters to the Great Khan as well as by the letters of the friars in China to persons in the West. Of course these writings also throw a side-light on Nestorians in China and on the relationship of the Latins to them. That relationship was not always favourable. In spite of the tolerance and even co-operation between Christians of varying confessions at the Mongol court in Karakorum, William of Rubruk could be very critical of them. His impression of the Nestorians from China whom he met at the court are summed up in very negative terms. Thus he says:

> 'The Nestorians there know nothing. For they say their service and have sacred books in Syriac (a language of which they are ignorant) from which they sing just like uneducated monks amongst ourselves; and in this way they have become wholly corrupt. First they are usurers and drunkards. Some of them also who live with the Tartars have several wives like the Tartars. When they go into Church they

wash their lower limbs like the Saracens. They eat flesh on Friday, and have their feasts on that day in the manner of the Saracens. A bishop comes but rarely in that land – scarcely once perhaps in fifty years. Then they cause all their boys, even in the cradle, to be ordained priests, so that almost all their men are priests, . . . and they commit bigamy, for even the priests marry a second wife when the first is dead. They are also given to simony, administering no sacrament without a fee. They are concerned for their wives and children, and so they strive not for the spread of the faith but for gain. And so it comes to pass that when any of them bring up some of the sons of the Moal [i.e. Mongol] nobles, although they teach them the Gospel and the faith, yet by their evil life and covetousness they still more estrange them from the Christian religion; for the lives of the Moals themselves and even of the *Tuins* [i.e. Turks], that is to say the idolaters, are more innocent than their lives.'[172]

This dictum throws at least as much light on William's attitude to the Nestorians as on these themselves. Of course William had no contact with Nestorians in China itself. John of Montecorvino, on the other hand, who lived in the capital of Yuan China for many years, though also complaining about Nestorian intransigence, was apparently respected and even loved by many outside the ranks of the Latin Christians, as we hear from John of Cora, to whom reference will be made later. The religious situation at the court in Khan Baliq, comparable to that of Karakorum, at least in the time of Khubilai, demanded a certain degree of religious harmony. Khubilai himself was interested in raising the educational standards of the Nestorians. Yet tensions did mount, and this was due to the different role of the Franciscans in China.

The Friars John of Plano Carpini and William of Rubruk were Papal envoys at the Mongol court in Karakorum, having the status of diplomats. William's self-understanding certainly went further than that, but his influence was limited in so far as conversion was concerned. The Franciscans in China, on the other hand, were both envoys, legates of the Pope, and missionaries. Even when they enjoyed diplomatic status, they were keen to spread the Western, Latin version of Christianity, also among Nestorians, which inevitably led to repercussions and tensions. Though the Franciscan mission was marked by some degree of success, probably more amongst Turks and Mongols than amongst Chinese, the price paid was a high one. The death of two Franciscan friars at the hands of Nestorians in Central Asia, referred to in the last chapter, is also indicative of the situation in China toward the end of the Yuan Dynasty. One of these was James of Florence, Archbishop of Zaitun, who was killed in AD 1362. At the beginning of this period, however, stands a man, John of Montecorvino, who, in the midst of Nestorian distrust, combined missionary zeal with a respect for others that led to wide mutual friendships.

JOHN OF MONTECORVINO

Of decisive importance for the Catholic mission in Yuan China was the work of John of Montecorvino, a Franciscan who was born in southern Italy in AD 1247. He was a man of considerable physical energy, intellectual power and of great amiability. He had already been sent with ecclesiastical letters to various regents in the Near East, including Armenia and Persia, where he brought papal messages to Il-Khan Arghun. He returned in AD 1289 with news from Arghun, being sent back immediately by Pope Nicholas IV with further letters.

A papal letter addressed to Khubilai Khan, dated 15th July 1289, asking the Khan to receive John and his fellow-travellers favourably,[173] had to wait for two years before John could proceed to East Asia in AD 1291.

On his journey to China, John was accompanied by Nicholas of Pistoia OP and the Italian merchant Peter of Lucalongo. He travelled by ship via the Persian port of Hormuz to South India, where he disembarked at Quilon in present Kerala. He then spent 13 months in the area of present Madras, at Mylapore, a place where St. Thomas is said to have been buried. Here his companion, Nicholas, died. John preached extensively and baptized 'about a hundred persons in different places'[174] before he left for China. We have no information about this trip, which ultimately led him to Khan Baliq, the seat of the Khan.

John was probably received with all honours, as in the case of other envoys. The papal letter to the Khan, starting with the words 'Gaudeamus in Domini' ('We rejoice in the Lord'), expresses the Pope's joy about Khubilai's request for stronger ties with the head of Latin Christianity. In this letter, the Pope states that he had heard from Arghun 'that your Magnificence bears a feeling of great love towards our person and the Roman Church and also towards the nation or people of the Latins.'[175] Pointing out that the Khan had asked for Latin monks, the Pope expresses the wish that the Khan would accept the Christian faith. Finally he requests him to receive John and his companions with kindness and to allow them to carry out the work entrusted to them.[176]

In his first preserved letter, dated January 8, 1305, John of Montecorvino told the addressee, the Father Vicar of the province of Gazzarie, that his plan to win the Khan and his court for Latin Christianity had failed, although he had received the special favour of the Emperor.[177] John then continues to talk about the Nestorians who guard their rights enviously and do not allow other Christians to have even a small chapel of their own. John complained about their malice and slander, about the fact that they discredit him as a false envoy, 'a spy, magician and deceiver of men.'[178] At the end of a five year period of intrigues, however, the Khan became convinced about his innocence and sent the slanderers into exile.

About his religious activity John tells us that after being alone for 11 years, a German Brother, Arnold of Cologne, had come to be with him. He, John, had built a church with a bell tower in Khan Baliq and had baptized about six thousand people. He had furthermore baptized and trained about 40 boys, whom he had taught the Latin letters and the Latin Church rites. He had written psalms, hymns and breviaries for them; their chanting even delighted the Emperor. Futhermore we hear that he had learned the 'Tartar' script and language well enough to translate the whole New Testament and the Psalms into that language.

One of the great successes of John was the conversion of the Ongut king, George, to Catholicism. He, like Marco Polo, also thought that George was a descendant 'of that great king who was called Prester John.'[179] George, though a Nestorian king, had taken the Lesser Orders of the Latins and had served him with sacred vestments as he celebrated mass. Although accused of apostasy by other Nestorians, George had brought a great number of his subjects to Catholicism. And in his capital he had built a magnificent church.[180]

When King George died in AD 1299, John of Montecorvino's hope of spreading Catholic Christianity further among the Onguts dwindled. For soon a Nestorian opposition built up in the family of the monarch. The brothers of the deceased king started a campaign to lead all converted Catholics back to Nestorianism. John, being bound to the court of the Khan as a papal legate, could only watch and see how the fruit of his work was destroyed. Without the Nestorian opposition, so he wrote in the letter referred to, the Khan himself would have been converted and 30,000 rather than 6,000 would have been baptized.

In his second letter of February 13, 1306,[181] John talks about the purchase of a piece of land for a church and a convent by his merchant friend Peter of Lucalongo. The place was only a stone's throw away from the palace of the Khan, so that he could hear the singing of the liturgy. Soon after receiving the plot in 1305, he had erected a wall around it and built simple houses and an oratory which would hold two hundred persons. John conducted services in the old and the new site every other week, having housed some of the boys in the new buildings. This report about John's religious activity is supplemented by information about his life at the court where he had 'a regular right of entry and of sitting, as legate of the lord Pope.'[182]

John wrote a number of letters to men in Europe and to his colleagues in Persia, but only the two letters mentioned above are preserved.[183] The first was written to the Vicar and the brothers of the Province of Gazzarie. He requested them to make the contents known to the Pope, the

Cardinals and the Procurator of the Order. The second letter was written to the head of his order.

We do not know when the Pope first heard of his activities. Pope Clement V (AD 1305–1314) sent several letters to him, all dated July 23, 1307.[184] In the first of these, John of Montecorvino was appointed Archbishop of Khan Baliq. He and his successors were invested with Apostolic authority.[185] The Pope praised John's work in the past and exhorted him to diligently carry out the charge committed to him.

In a second letter, the Pope appointed the Franciscan Brother Andrew of Perugia to assist the Archbishop and gave him a bishop's rank.[186] The same Bull is directed to five brothers of the Minor Order whom the Pope invests with power to consecrate John. Accompanied by a number of young Franciscans, they travelled to China by the same route John had used, i.e. by sea via South India. Three brothers died on the way, but the remaining two duly consecrated John upon arrival.[187] As Archbishop, John of Montecorvino enjoyed great popularity among Christians as well as non-Christians, in spite of all animosities on the part of the Nestorians. This popularity is highlighted by John of Cora, who writes:

> 'He was a man of very upright life, pleasing to God and men, and stood in high grace with the emperor. The emperor at all times caused him and his people to be furnished with all that they required; and much was he beloved by all, pagans as well as Christians.'[188]

About his burial he writes:

> 'To his obsequies and burial there came a very great multitude of people, both Christians and pagans. And those pagans rent their mourning garments as their manner is; and both Christians and pagans devoutly laid hold of the clothes of the archbishop, and carried them off as relics with great reverence. . . . And they still visit the place of his internment with very great devotion.'[189]

Thus the memory of John of Montecorvino must have lingered on for decades.

LATER FRANCISCANS IN CHINA

In AD 1311, Pope Clement V sent three more Franciscan brothers in the rank of bishops to China. We then learn more about the Latin Church in that country in a letter of Peregrinus of Castello, Bishop of Zaitun, written in AD 1318.[190] At his time, Archbishop John had retired from the establishments he had founded, restricting himself to the care of the Armenians and Alans in Khan Baliq.[191] From here, a bishopric had been established in Zaitun, the southern port. As we saw, it was also a centre of

Nestorian Christianity. Under the leadership of Bishop Peregrinus, a church with a monastery was constructed outside the city, money having been devoted to this cause by a rich Armenian lady. In his letter, the bishop is concerned about the recruitment of young missionaries, but he consoles himself with the fact that a great number of people gather when he preaches in public.[192]

Another letter from Zaitun was written by Bishop Andrew of Perugia in January AD 1326.[193] He had worked at the side of Archbishop John in Khan Baliq, then he became successor to Bishop Peregrinus in Zaitun, having already come to the city in AD 1318. In his letter, Andrew first tells us of his difficult passage to China, then of the glory of the Khan's court and the wide extent of his kingdom. In Khan Baliq as well as in Zaitun he lived on very generous 'royal charity'. With part of this money he established a church and a monastery for twenty brothers outside the city. In so far as the spread of Christianity was concerned, Andrew pointed to the religious tolerance in this religiously pluralistic society. Of course it was an 'indifferent tolerance' (Troll). No Jews or Moslems were converted, and most of the Buddhists ('idolaters') who did accept the new faith soon deviated from the Christian path.

We can also glean important information on the spread of the Latin Church in China from the *Relatio* of the Franciscan Friar Odoric of Pordenone.[194] It was written in 1330, after completion of his journey. Odoric used the sea route to go to China. On his trip to Khan Baliq from Canton he passed through Hanchow and Yangchow. In Hanchow, at that time the largest city of China, he met a number of Minor Brothers, pointing out that there were other Christians here as well. In Yangchow, he saw a whole convent of Franciscan brothers. He stated that there were also three Nestorian churches in the city, indicative of a larger Nestorian community.

In Khan Baliq, where Odoric spent three years, the Franciscans were still esteemed at the court and had the ranks of envoys. At state festivals, they appeared before the Khan, beside Buddhist lamas of great monasteries, and foreign rulers, in order to honour and bless the Emperor. At the court were also prominent men converted to Catholicism. Beside the Bishop of Khan Baliq there were, at this time, a number of other Franciscans.[195] Odoric impressively describes an encounter with the Khan whom he met when travelling outside the city. When the Franciscans approached him, holding a cross on a pole before them and singing 'Veni Creator Spiritus', the Khan did reverence to the cross, allowing the bishop to cense him.[196]

Another report on the Franciscans in China for the year 1330 is John of Cora's *Book of the Estate of the Great Khan*.[197] John of Cora OP had served under John of Montecorvino in Persia. He was sent to Khan Baliq after the death of John of Montecorvino. John of Cora gave a detailed description of China and its inhabitants, its cities and Buddhist monasteries, its transport system and its economy. Then in a fourth part he talked about the Franciscans in China. He first described the personality of Archbishop John of Montecorvino, talked about his burial and pointed out his popularity with the Emperor and the people. He too spoke of the animosities of the Nestorians against the Catholics who, however, were aided by the Khan financially under the provision that they prayed for his well-being.

John of Cora was not to be the successor of John of Montecorvino. Rather, the Pope had named a certain Nicholas Archbishop of Khan Baliq and Papal Nuntius to that city. He was sent out with a company of 24 Minor Brothers. Although the Pope recanted his charge on October 10, 1334, Nicholas had apparently already left for China. We do not know, however, whether he actually ever arrived at Khan Baliq.[198]

The contact between the Mongol court at Khan Baliq and the papal seat (since AD 1309) at Lyons is highlighted by the fact that on May 31, 1338, envoys from China appeared before the Pope, bringing two letters. The first letter, by the Great Khan himself, had as its aim the intensification of diplomatic contacts. The other was written by 'the Chief of the Alans' (*Princeps Alanorum*) at the Court of the Great Khan. In their letter, the Alans thank the Pope for the spiritual guidance they received from John of Montecorvino. They pray for a successor who would be their 'head' (*caput*) and 'consoler' (*consolator*).[199] From the Pope they received answering letters to the Khan and the Alans as well as the Khans of Kipčak and Čagatai. After visiting the French court, they returned by way of Italy, Constantinople and Central Asia. They reached Khan Baliq in AD 1342.[200]

Light on Christianity in China in the middle of the 14th century is finally shed on the scene by John of Marignolli of Florence.[201] In his 'Chronicle' (*Relatio*) we read that he was one of the four papal legates to the Khan's court, sent in response to a mission from the Khan. The whole party consisted of 32 members. He probably arrived in Khan Baliq in AD 1342, staying there for several years, before he returned to Avignon in 1353.

On his way to China, John of Florence passed through Almaliq in Central Asia in AD 1340. As we heard, it had been an important Nestorian centre, but it was also a seat of Franciscans. John found no more Christians there. The monastery the Franciscans had built was destroyed, together with a library. As we know from another source, the whole assembly of monks had been killed in the year previously, when its members refused to turn to Islam. All other Christians in the city had become Moslems.[202] When John of Florence arrived at Khan Baliq in AD 1342, he was received with all honours by the Khan who supported the party for four years. John tells us about discussions with the Jews and Muslims at the court, where Franciscans were still highly esteemed, and the memory of John of

Montecorvino was still vivid. John of Florence returned to Europe by way of Zaitun where he found three great churches and other institutions of the Minor Brothers.

After John's return to Avignon at the end of 1353, Pope Urban V selected William of Prat to the office of the Archbishop of Khan Baliq. William left for China with a great number of Franciscan missionaries in AD 1370. Whether they reached their destination or not is not known.[203] As his successors, various titulary archbishops were selected. But they never left for China. For by this time, viz. in AD 1368, Mongol rule in China came to an end. With its lapse, Nestorians and Latin Christianity ceased to exist in East Asia. Vestiges of the Christian past could have lingered on to the 15th century.[204] Remnants of Nestorianism could still be found among the Mongolian Erkut at the beginning of this century.[205]

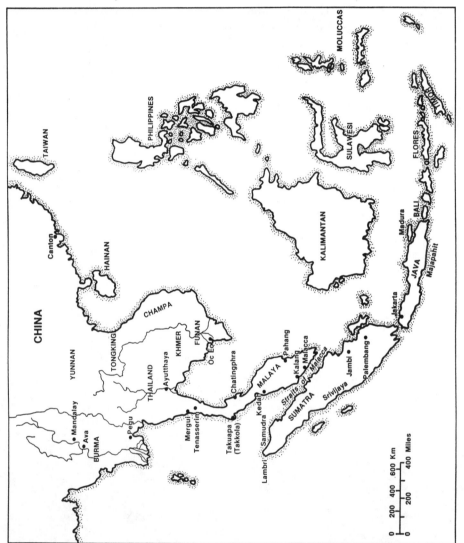

Map 8 South-East Asia

Chapter 11

Christians in South-East Asia

ANCIENT TRADE ROUTES AND CONSEQUENT POSSIBILITIES

When we explored the practicability of Christianity reaching India in the age of the apostles notice was taken of the establishment as early as 100 BC of a route from India through the Straits of Malacca to Vietnam. Likewise the 'embassy', probably commercial more than official, of Roman merchants to the Chinese court at Loyang in ca. AD 166 and the base established in the Mekong Delta have been noted. The Chinese were offered ivory, rhinoceros horn and tortoise shell and the Chinese Annal commented:

'From that time dates the direct intercourse with this country.'[1]

With respect to the time when the Parthians had cut off overland links, M. P. Charlesworth says:

'But from this time onward we have frequent mention in the Chinese records of the country of Ta-tsin (Syria) and an appreciation of the honesty and integrity of the Roman traders, as surprising as it is gratifying.

The discovery of direct intercourse with China was, however, made at a time when trade was beginning to languish, when the Empire itself was suffering from the rule of incompetent or weak princes and from the menace of civil wars, when Parthia and the Middle East were undergoing a series of great and important changes. In consequence the overseas trade with China, which might have developed into a considerable business, and might have brought far-reaching discoveries in geography and general knowledge, which might have led to the "opening-up" of China centuries earlier, and the inter-penetration of two civilisations, never had a chance and died of inanation.'[2]

Chinese voyages to the West have also been noted not least in the period of the T'ang Dynasty (AD 618–907) and the routes and major ports of call were well known and established.

So, e.g.:

'In the early Muslim period in the seventh and eighth centuries there are cases of Persian ships coming and going beyond Ceylon. Thus Vajrabodhi travelled in 717 from Ceylon to Srivijaya in South-East Sumatra with a fleet of thirty-five Persian vessels, while I-Tsing voyaged in 671 from Canton to Srivijaya with a Persian shipmaster.'

To this we may add

'the statement of Hui Ch'ao, a pilgrim who travelled to India in 727, . . . by saying that "the Persians are accustomed to set sail into the Western Sea, and they enter the Southern Sea making for Ceylon to obtain all kinds of precious objects." . . . Hui Ch'ao does not leave us there in Ceylon but takes us right across the Indian Ocean: "Moreover they head for the *K'un-lun* country (Malay and Indonesia) to get gold." This is not the end of their route either: "Furthermore they set sail for the land of Han, going directly to Canton, where they obtain various kinds of silk gauze and wadding."'[3]

Those who made the whole journey by sea travelled south and west from China via Java, Sumatra and the Straits of Malacca, and thence up the coast of Burma to Arakan and on to Tamralipti. If you were more adventurous you might cut across the Bay of Bengal from Quedah (Kedah?) directly for Ceylon. Those who combined sea route and land route may well have used land portage between Takuapa and Pak Phanang in Thailand. To the chain of significant ports, which figure in accounts we must add those of Kalang, Kedah and Kuala Terenggamu in Malaya; Mergui and Pegu in Burma; Lambry, Samudra, Peureulak, Jambi, Telangaipa and Palembang in Sumatra; Djakarta, Tubon, Surabaya and Madura in Java; the old Thai capital of Ayutthaya; Tonking in Vietnam; and Hainan. In all of these places references may be found to Persians and other residents in considerable numbers, which fact at least raised the possibility that among these communities were to be found Christians of various persuasions, e.g. Nestorians from Persia or Monophysites from Armenia. Only in a relatively few cases do we have the probability or the actuality of such resident Christian communities, while the fact that Nestorian and 'Jacobite' traders plied these sea routes is well established.

Prominent in the reputation of the Persian traders was their association with pearls and gems, while Christians in the Syriac tradition made much of the pearl of great price of which Jesus spoke in the parable in Matthew 13:45–46. The 'Pearl' held the same place in the interest of Eastern Churches that the 'Holy Grail' did for Westerners. If the Grail was the

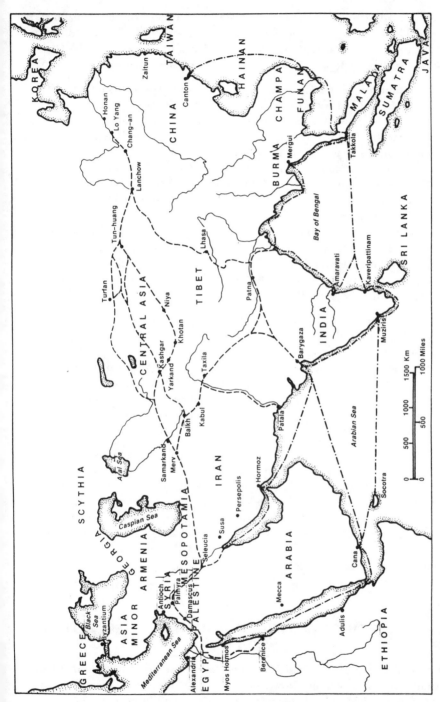

Map 9 Asia and Ancient Trade Routes

chalice used at the Last Supper, the Pearl was a piece of dough from the original loaf used at the same meal.[4] The fixation with the Pearl is found in poetic form in the 'Song of the Pearl' or 'Hymn of the South' to be found in the 'Acts of Thomas'.[5] In brief the poem recounts the story of

> 'a certain prince, who is sent on a mission to Egypt by his father and mother, the King and Queen of the East; his task is to wrest the pearl from the serpent that has entwined itself around it, and to bring it home with him. After many years of setbacks the quest is achieved, and upon his arrival home the prince is rewarded with a suit of robes, which he discovers to be an exact counterpart of himself and to have the image of the Supreme King stamped on them. When he has donned his robes he comes into the presence of the King. In this regard it is interesting to note that above the Chinese and Syriac inscriptions of the famous Nestorian Stone are the figures of two monsters clutching a pearl. This particular instance has been interpreted as a Buddhist symbol adapted for Christian use, but in any case we can see from the "Song of the Pearl" that the treasure is a symbol for the soul caught up in the clutches of sin and death.'[6]

So both commercially and spiritually Persian Christian traders and missionary monks dealt in 'pearls'.

That monks sometimes sailed with merchants to East Asia is clear from several sources. The Nestorian Patriarch Timothy I wrote of monks who crossed the seas to India and China with nought but staff and scrip. And, e.g. we have the case of Bar Sadhe, a 7th century monk of Baith Qatraye near Oman, of whom it was reported that he went to sea in the company of merchants, at least as far as 'India'. Another 7th century monk,

> 'Simon of Taibutheh, in his medico-mystical writings, uses three significant analogies; the merchant going to China and India with goods for trading, the visitor from China or India who is alien to the ways of the country in which he is sojourning, and "the wealthy wise man who wished to possess valuable musk and . . . traversed mountains, sea, and land, and repaired to China." This shows that by the seventh century the Far East was a familiar concept to the minds of Middle Eastern Christians, offering great potential for mercantile and missionary activities.'[7]

EVIDENCE OF CHRISTIANS IN SOUTH-EAST ASIA BEFORE AD 1500

The possibility was there and the potentiality was obvious. The question remains as to if, when and how Christians made their presence felt in this area, and left evidence of that presence. All too often even a scholar like

Colless is left grasping at the slim fact that while there is evidence for Persian traders etc. in this location or that, there is only the possibility that Christians were among them.[8]

So while we have references which date back as far as AD 657–658 to the importance of Qalah (or Kalang) as an entreport in Malaya, and to Takkola (or Takuapa) in Thailand and to the Kedah region near the Malayan-Thai border there is no material evidence of a Christian presence in any one of these places.[9] The same situation applies to the sites we have listed above in Sumatra. At most a Christian presence is not proven.[10] The same situation applies in Funan (Cambodia and the Mekong Delta) and elsewhere in the region called overall 'Indo-China'.[11]

On the more positive side we are on firmer ground at Malacca. There epigraphical evidence of a Christian presence was uncovered, the details of which are as follows:

> 'Writing early in the seventeenth century, the Portuguese chronicler Manuel Godinho de Eredia reported that in the plot of land owned at that time by his mother the ruins of a tiled subterranean building had been uncovered by workmen digging among the mango trees. It was apparently a hermitage or an oratory, wherein lay a patent relic of Christianity in the form of a copper cross, somewhat corroded, set on a square block of marble of the same size ("three palms"). Eredia suggested that this sacred object had belonged to "some Christian from Meliapor, who came to Malacca in company with merchants from Choromandel, and was favourably received into the district under the protection of this Ray Modiliar" (the Malay sultan whose property this piece of land had formerly been). On this interpretation the cross attested to the presence of a Saint Thomas Christian from Mylapore in South India; but it could conceivably have had a West Asian as its owner.'[12]

While the Italian Ludovico di Varthema, who visited Malacca in AD 1510, made no mention of Christians in the town, which according to his Christian companion-guides had a bad reputation,[13] there is more information of a positive or probable nature from Tomé Pires a year or two later. In his *Suma Oriental* he includes in his list of the nationalities represented in the trades of Malacca those from Ormuy, Parsees and Christian Armenians.[14] While the religion of the last is clear, elsewhere Pires associates the 'Parsees' or Persians with Turkomans, as one of their sub-groups, and these are

> 'warlike men and fighters who are highly esteemed . . . and are said to be of Christian birth.'[15]

So it would appear that we can, with a cónfidence not engendered elsewhere, hold to the belief that a Christian presence was to be found in

Malacca well before the Portuguese captured it in AD 1511, even if it did little to increase the acceptability of the place to Varthema's Christian companions.

The evidence for such a presence is at best tenuous in Sumatra and gains no support from the references of Marco Polo, Conti or Varthema. However, an Arabic work of the Armenian Abu Salih, from the turn of the 14th century, offers some further evidence about Sumatra. The work, entitled *Description of Churches and Monasteries of Egypt and Some Neighbouring Countries*, includes reference to 'Fashur', which is most probably Barus, on the west coast of the island.

> 'Here there are several churches and all the Christians are Nestorians. . . . It is from this place that camphor comes. . . . In this town there is one church named after our Lady, the Pure Virgin Mary.'[16]

The evidence is firmer in Java, in the southern 14th century Majapahit kingdom. This is despite the fact that little weight is placed on Nestorian references from as late as AD 1503, to the appointment of a metropolitan for Dabag, the Syriac equivalent of Javaka, as we have no knowledge whether that metropolitan ever proceeded beyond India, which he reached in AD 1504, or whether this was anything more than a titular appointment by that time, whatever may have been the case in earlier times.

While there are no Nestorian crosses or inscriptions in this Hindu-Buddhist Javanese kingdom, and no reference in the writings of Odoric of Pordenone, we do find such in the work of John of Marignolli, the Franciscan friar from Florence who was sent to China as a papal legate in AD 1338. He described a kingdom of Saba which has been identified as that of Majapahit, under the Queen Tribhuwana, who reigned from AD 1329 to 1350. He mentioned the presence of a few Christians there who were in all likelihood Nestorians, when we take into account the traditions to which they clung concerning the Magi and Elijah.[17]

Some ambiguity surrounds the report of a ruined Christian chapel in Pegu in Burma. There, in AD 1496 the Italian trader Hieronimo de Santo Stefano buried a travelling companion, and reported also contact there with Armenian Christians.[18] The ambiguity arises only from the possibility that the ruined chapel may have been a Buddhist edifice. This is countered somewhat by the report of Varthema some 14 years later that the Burmese king numbered among his soldiers more than 1000 Christians from Thailand.[19]

Varthema's travelling companions and guides claimed that they came from a city called Sarnau (or Shahr-i Naw in Persian). This has been identified with the pre-Bangkok capital of Thailand called Ayutthaya.[20] According to Varthema these 'Christian merchants' 'said that in their country there were many lords also Christian, but they are subject to the great Khan of Cathay. . . . These same men are as white as we are, and confess that they are Christians, and believe in the Trinity, and likewise in the Twelve Apostles, in the four Evangelists, and they also have baptism with water. But they write in the contrary way to us, that is, after the manner of Armenia. And they say that they keep the Nativity and the Passion of Christ, and observe our Lent and other vigils in the course of the year.'[21]

It would seem probable that they were Nestorians from Central Asia or Persia, who had been forced out of China when the Mongol dynasty was overthrown in AD 1368. As to their mode of writing, Varthema is wrong about it being Armenian; it was more likely to be Syriac or Arabic. Further details about these merchants emerge in the course of their voyages, thus:

'These Christians were most faithful, we formed a very great friendship with them. . . .

While on our way the said Christians had no other pleasure, night and day, than that of conversing with me upon subjects relating to the Christians and about our faith. And when I told them of the Volto Santo which is in St. Peter's, and of the heads of St. Peter and St. Paul, and many other saints they told me secretly that if I would go with them I should be a very great lord, for having seen these things.'[22]

On their own claim 'many lords in their country . . . are also Christians and possess immense riches',[23] and, even if we discount some of this as exaggeration to impress the Westerner, the picture is one of a substantial Christian community in Thailand.

So it is clear that a group of Christian merchants like those with whom Varthema travelled had trading contacts from India to Burma, Thailand, Malaya, Sumatra and the Moluccas, and that Persians and Armenians were to be found in many places from Canton and Hainan to Java and Burma. What remains somewhat problematical is the determination of how many settled Christian communities, Nestorian or Jacobite, there were or had been in the region before AD 1500. That there were such in Pegu, Ayutthayah, Malacca, and the Majapahit kingdom seems certain, with that at Barus in Sumatra being probable. Equally certain is the fact that a Christian presence in the region was in existence long before the arrival of the Portuguese, not least with the capture of Malacca in AD 1511, and a toehold in the Moluccas in AD 1512.

Chapter 12

Conclusion

Not long after the vessels led by Vasco da Gama reached the south west coast of India on May 27, 1498, Western Christians met the largest group of Christians east of Mesopotamia, and the group which may well have had the longest unbroken tradition of continuity in the faith. The St. Thomas Christians were soon to discover that the Western Christian newcomers brought with them not only superior technology in cannon and ships, and an avid desire for wealth. They brought also an assured sense of European superiority which was fed by technological and naval achievement. Within several decades, urged on by the forces of the Catholic Reformation, the Europeans undertook a definite campaign to require these Indian Christians to replicate the belief-forms and practices of Portugal.

That this policy was pursued vehemently and comprehensively was bad enough; that it was marked by a failure to appreciate how Christianity was to be expressed relevantly and sensitively in an ancient Asian culture was worse. The learning of centuries of experience were disregarded and jettisoned, along with what were seen to be 'fatal compromises'. In contrast European Christians, if conscious at all of their accommodations with Graeco-Roman culture, regarded such accommodations as 'desirable', if not 'God-Given'. Or as the Holy Office put it when condemning Galileo in AD 1633, he and his followers had erred in that they had trodden

> 'underfoot the entire philosophy of Aristotle, which had been of such service to scholastic theology.'

It was not to be expected that Hindu, Buddhist, Taoist or Confucian philosophies could in any way be constructive means for expressing Christianity.

In somewhat similar fashion the ethos of Syrian and Persian Christianity was certain to cause affront to Western Christians, as it did to Franciscans who encountered it in Mongol camps or in Yuan China. Again European certainty of superiority was matched only by that of the Mongol Great Khans themselves. There is little, if any, evidence that European Christians

315

were ready, or even saw any necessity, to sit at the feet of those whose experience of Asian culture was infinitely greater, and whose loyalty to the Christian gospel, albeit differently expressed in matters of detail, was not one whit less.

That Asian Christianity was in some of its features different from that form familiar to Western Christians, both Catholic and Protestant, is no more strange than the same differences those Western Christians would feel when in contact with Eastern Orthodoxy in any of its expressions. For Asian Christianity to be built on assumptions familiar to the Aramean mind and to have Syriac as its primary language for liturgy and theology was as much to be expected as Western Christianity and Eastern Orthodoxy being expressed through Graeco-Roman thought and having Latin and Greek respectively as their primary liturgical and theological languages. Each tradition, Catholic, Protestant, Orthodox, Nestorian and Monophysite is in need of the other if, in the spirit of 1 Corinthans 12:12–27, the body of Christ is to be more clearly evident. That all these traditions are able to hold fully to the 'Nicene' Creed (of AD 381) makes the need all the more urgent in the face of contemporary challenges to Christian belief as a whole, no less virulent than were those of Gnosticism and Manichaeism or were and are those of Buddhism and Islam.

As we look back over the path we have traced we cannot but be struck by certain prominent facts. Among these are:

- the achievements of the community at Edessa, which made its name as honoured in the Roman Empire, as some later Western crusaders were later to dishonour themselves in their dealings with this city;
- the witness of Nestorian Christians across Central Asia to China in the east and to Indonesia in the south-east, whatever may be acknowledged about the ecclesiastical politics which frequently marked the Church in Iran;
- the staunchness of the faith of some of the Arab tribes in the border lands between the Roman and Persian empires, which commands admiration, as do not the ways in which they were treated both by Constantinople and Seleucia-Ctesiphon;
- the equally staunch independent lines pursued by Christians in Armenia and Georgia, both with respect to Christians in the Roman Empire and in Iran, as well as of each other, so that their cultural identities should not be lost;
- the openness of Central Asian Christians to the cultural world in which they lived and their determination, at the same time, to adhere to the faith as it was expressed in the Syriac and Persian tradition;
- the willingness on the part of Christians in China to address their compatriots in forms of language understandable to them, using even Taoist and Buddhist terminology to express the traditional faith;

- the readiness of Chalcedonian Christians to insist on only their understanding of the faith, and to exclude all others, which was to be echoed in the approach of Portuguese Catholics to the Christians of Malabar. Only recently does it appear that second thoughts on such things have prevailed between Chalcedonian Rome and Coptic Alexandria, and in reconsideration by Orthodox theologians of the sufficiency of the formula developed at Chalcedon.

None of this is to claim that Asian Christians before da Gama were paragons, whose example we should follow slavishly. They were as fallible as we are – and their history is as sprinkled with failures as much as is ours. Of course, as always, we are ever more ready to see theirs than we are to acknowledge our own – or even to be conscious of them. But there is no gainsaying their achievements across centuries and great distances and areas.

Today's Asian Christians have a heritage of which to be justly proud. Increasingly, Asian emphases within Christianity will be experienced, along with those from Africa, South America and Oceania, to challenge the often all-too-glib assumptions of those of us whose roots lie in Europe.

Notes

1 INTRODUCTION

1 Lach, D. F. & Flaumenhaft, C. (eds.): *Asia on the Eve of Europe's Expansion*, Englewood Cliffs, N.J. 1965, p. 1.

3 A NECESSARY EXCURSUS INTO THEOLOGY

1 At this point let us note that we are using the term 'logical subject' instead of the traditional term 'person' (from the Latin *persona*). This is because the latter has psychological and individualistic overtones nowadays, which are misleading when applied to this issue in the ancient world. There, *persona* had more the theatrical quality of a role being played (cf. 'Dramatis Personae' in a theatre programme or the text of a play). Greek-speaking Christians came to use the term *hypostasis* instead of *prosopon*, the strict Greek equivalent of *persona*. This also had theatrical associations, as it meant the mask worn by an actor to denote the role being played. However, *prosopon* was discredited by its association with Sabellius. Similarly the Latins' use of *natura* ('nature') has a descriptive functional content, and had no relation to what we mean today by the term 'nature', as used in 'the world of Nature'. The Greek term was *physis*, which you will recognize as behind the word 'Mono-physite' – or one who holds a 'one-nature' view about Jesus Christ. Those who hold that Jesus Christ had two natures, one divine and the other human, are called 'Diophysites'. Please keep in mind constantly that this was an issue debated in relation to logic, rather than to psychology.

4 CHRISTIANS IN SYRIA AND PALESTINE

1 Quispel, G.: 'The Discussion of Judaic Christianity', in: *VigChr* 22 (1968), p. 81.
2 Quispel 1968, pp. 81–82. Note also the references to Christianity as a 'Way' in such passages as John 14:6, Acts 9:2, 19:9 & 22:4, and 1 Corinthians 12:31. Cf. also references to the use of the description on the 8th century Sian-fu monument.
3 Both groups may be distinguished nominally from the Greek speaking converts dubbed 'Christians' at Antioch, in Acts 11:26.
4 Daniélou, J.: *The Theology of Jewish Christianity*, trans. and ed. by J. A. Baker, London & Chicago 1964 (The Development of Christian Doctrine before

319

the Council of Nicea 1), p. 405: 'The axis pinning together their immeasurable sphere of things and events is the Incarnation, the tabernacling in human flesh and season of the concealed glory of the Son.' Cf. also Taylor, J. E.: 'The Phenomenon of Early Jewish-Christianity. Reality or Scholarly Invention?', in: *VigChr* 44 (1990), pp. 313–334; Brown, R. E. & Meier, J. P.: *Antioch and Rome. New Testament Cradles of Catholic Christianity*, New York & Ramsey, N. J. 1983.

5 Traces of this are to be found also in the references of Paul to the descent of Jesus (Ephesians 4:9), of the contest with the principalities of power (Colossians 2:15), and the exaltation of Christ above all heavens (Ephesians 1:21 & 4:10, and Philippians 2:9 & 10).

6 Daniélou 1964, p. 405.

7 Daniélou 1964, p. 407. It is interesting to note how this space and time comprehensiveness of the Cross parallels that assigned to Amida Buddha in Pure Land Buddhism. See also the reference to 'saving knowledge' (*gnosis*) on p. 18.

8 Ibid.

9 O'Leary, De L. E.: *The Syriac Church and Fathers. A Brief Review of the Subject*, London 1909, p. 31. Cf. also Harnack, A. von: *The Expansion of Christianity in the First Three Centuries*, trans. and ed. by J. Moffat, vol. 2, London 1904 & New York, pp. 276 & 286.

10 Brock, S. P.: 'Greek into Syriac and Syriac into Greek', in: *Journal of the Syriac Academy* 3 (1977), p. 1.

11 Burkitt, F. C.: *Early Eastern Christianity*, London 1904, p. 115.

12 It is reminiscent also both in transliteration and content with that example of Mahāyāna Buddhism we have referred to already i.e. the role of Amida Buddha in Pure Land Buddhism. See note (7) above, and note the suggestions of some scholars that Pure Land Buddhism in its origins, may have been influenced by Nestorianism and/or by Gnosticism.

13 Burkitt, F. C.: *Early Christianity outside the Roman Empire*, Cambridge 1899, p. 22.

14 Atiya, A. S.: *A History of Eastern Christianity*, London 1968, p. 179.

15 Wallace-Hadrill, D. S.: *Christian Antioch. A Study of Early Christian Thought in the East*, Cambridge 1982, p. 116.

16 For discussion of this issue see Brown & Meier 1983, chapter 1.

17 See the outline of Apollinarius' views on p. 14 above.

18 Bettenson, H. (ed.): *Documents of the Christian Church*, 2nd ed., Oxford 1963, part II, section I: 1(a).

19 Bettenson 1963, part II, section I: 1(c).

20 The historian Eusebius of Caesarea records that there was a 'Jude, who is said to have been the Lord's brother according to the flesh' (*The Church History* 3:20:1). It is this Jude, or Judas Thomas, who it is believed is referred to in Mark 6:3, Jude 1:1 and possibly also in 1 Corinthians 9:5.

21 It should be noted that both the father and wife of Abgar IX have the same names as those in the Abgar legend set in the time of Jesus' earthly ministry. It seems likely that the conversion of Abgar IX was projected back some 140 years to provide Edessa with a dominical and apostolic foundation.

22 Segal, J. B.: *Edessa, 'the Blessed City'*, Oxford 1970, p. 86.

23 Some discussion as the role and significance of a stylite may be found on p. 55.

24 Segal 1970, p. 109.

25 Barnard, L. W.: 'The Origins and Emergence of the Church in Edessa during the First Two Centuries A.D.', in: *VigChr* 22 (1968), p. 173.

26 Wallace-Hadrill 1982, p. 69.

27 Wallace-Hadrill 1982, p. 73.
28 Ibid.
29 Wallace-Hadrill 1982, p. 87.
30 Wallace-Hadrill 1982, p. 121.
31 Wallace-Hadrill 1982, p. 36.
32 Wallace-Hadrill 1982, p. 124.
33 Wallace-Hadrill 1982, p. 125.
34 Daniélou, J. & Marrou, H.: *The First Six Hundred Years,* trans. by V. Cronin [. . .],
    New York & London 1964 (The Christian Centuries 1), p. 361.
35 Vööbus, A.: *History of Asceticism in the Syrian Orient,* vol. 1, Louvain 1958
    (CSCO.Sub 14) [= 1958a], p. 47.
36 Drijvers, H. J. W.: 'East of Antioch. Forces and Structures in the Development
    of Early Syriac Theology', in: idem, *East of Antioch,* London 1984 (CStS 198),
    pp. 12 & 14 (entry I).
37 Drijvers, H. J. W.: *Bardaisan of Edessa,* Assen 1966 (Studia Semitica Neerlandica
    6), p. 225.
38 'The Christian Church in the East', in: Bury, J. B. et al. (eds.), *The Cambridge
    Ancient History,* vol. 12, Cambridge 1939, p. 497.
39 *Aphrahat and Judaism. The Christian-Jewish Argument in Fourth-Century Iran,*
    Leiden 1971 (Studia Post-Biblica 19), pp. 5–7.
40 Wallace-Hadrill 1982, p. 41.
41 Ibid.
42 Neusner 1971, p. 7.
43 Cited in Smith, M.: *Studies in Early Mysticism in the Near and Middle East [. . .],*
    (1931), repr., Amsterdam 1973, p. 27.
44 See examples in Murray, R.: *Symbols of Church and Kingdom. A Study in Early Syriac
    Tradition,* London & New York 1975, p. 29.
45 An example of this is to be found in the post-communion hymn which appears
    in a number of contemporary hymnals, the first stanza of which runs in *The
    English Hymnal* version: 'Strengthen for service, Lord, the hands that holy
    things have taken, let ears that now have heard your songs to clamour never
    waken.'
46 For the translation of most of this work see Mitchell, C. W. (trans. & ed.): *S.
    Ephraim's Prose Refutations of Mani, Marcion, and Bardaisan [. . .],* 2 vols., London
    1912 & 1921 (The Text and Translation Society).
47 Segal 1970, p. 91.
48 Drijvers, H. J. W.: 'The Persistence of Pagan Cults and Practices in Christian
    Syria', in: Garsoan, N. et al. (eds.), *East of Byzantium. Syria and Armenia in the
    Formative Period [. . .],* Washington, D. C. 1982, p. 40.
49 Cited in Vööbus, A.: *Literary, Critical and Historical Studies in Ephrem the Syrian,*
    Stockholm 1958 (PETSE 10) [= Vööbus 1958b], pp. 104f.
50 Vööbus 1958b, p. 109.
51 Vööbus 1958b, p. 101.
52 Murray 1975, p. 31, citing his own article on Ephrem in: *The Catholic Dictionary
    of Theology,* London 1967.
53 A succinct statement of such rules, for monks, nuns and the Sons and
    Daughters of the Covenant may be found in McCullough, W. S.: *A Short History
    of Syriac Christianity to the Rise of Islam,* Chico, Cal. 1982 (Scholars Press General
    Series 4), pp. 73–77.
54 Atiya 1968, p. 251.
55 See Pelikan, J. J.: *The Spirit of Eastern Christendom (600–1700),* Chicago 1974,
    pp. 57–59.

56 Barnard 1968, p. 163.
57 Vööbus, A.: *History of Asceticism in the Syrian Orient. A Contribution to the History of Culture in the Near East*, vol. 2, Louvain 1960 (CSCO.Sub 17), p. 315.
58 Eusebius: *Church History* 2:23:5 (trans. A. C. McGiffert, NPNF 2nd series 1).
59 Vööbus 1958a, p. 19.
60 Vööbus 1958a, p. 37.
61 Cited by Vööbus 1958a, p. 43.
62 Vööbus 1958, p. 69.
63 Bornkamm, G.: 'The Acts of Thomas', in: Hennecke, E. & Schneemelcher, W. (eds.), *New Testament Apocrypha*, vol. 2, London 1965, p. 449.
64 'Early Syrian Asceticism', in: *Downside Review* 88 (1970) p. 405.
65 Duncan, E. J.: *Baptism in the Demonstrations of Aphraates, the Persian Sage*, Washington, D.C. 1945, p. 85.
66 Brock, S. P.: 'Early Syrian Asceticism', in: *Numen* 20 (1973), p. 17.
67 Smith 1973, p. 93.
68 Cited by Smith, ibid.
69 Smith 1973, p. 94.
70 Smith 1973, p. 102.
71 Colless, B. E.: 'The Place of Syrian Christian Mysticism in Religious History', in: *JRH* 5 (1968–1969), p. 7.
72 Liebeschuetz, J. H. W. G.: *Antioch. City and Imperial Administration in the Later Roman Empire*, Oxford 1972, p. 239.
73 Vööbus 1958a, p. 168.
74 Cited by Vööbus, A.: 'The Origin of Monasticism in Mesopotamia', in: *ChH* 20 (1951), p. 35.
75 Vööbus 1960, p. 139.
76 Cited by Segal 1970, p. 149.
77 Smith 1973, p. 117.
78 See Vööbus 1958a, pp. v–viii.
79 Vööbus 1960, pp. 354f.
80 Vööbus 1960, pp. 359f.
81 Cited in Segal 1970, p. 100.
82 Wallace-Hadrill 1982, p. 143.
83 Murray 1975, p. 238.
84 Meyendorff, J.: 'Byzantine Views of Islam', in: *Dumbarton Oaks Papers* 18 (1964), p. 118.
85 Sahas, D. J.: *John of Damascus on Islam. The 'Heresy of the Ishmaelites'*, Leiden 1972, p. 128.
86 E.g. see Jeffery, A.: 'Ghevond's Text of the Correspondence between 'Umar II and Leo III', in: *Harvard Theological Review* 37 (1944), pp. 269–332.
87 Smith 1973, p. 113.
88 Tritton, A. S.: *The Caliphs and their Non-Muslim Subjects. A Critical Study of the Covenant of 'Umar*, London 1970 (Islam and Muslim World), p. 25.
89 Watt, W. M.: *The Majesty that was Islam. The Islamic World, 661–1100*, London 1974, p. 48.
90 Smith 1973, p. 122.
91 Smith 1973, p. 109.
92 Ibid.
93 Cited by Tritton 1970, pp. 6–8.
94 Cited by Tritton 1970, p. 11.
95 Tritton 1970, p. 233.
96 Smith 1973, p. 124.

97 Browne, L. E. citing Mari, in: *The Eclipse of Christianity in Asia from the Time of Muhammad till the Fourteenth Century*, (1933), repr., New York 1967, pp. 60f.

98 Such actions on the part of the crusaders and the Latin church resulted in multiple claims to authority in particular locations, and especially over the 'holy sites' in Palestine. The problem thus initiated continues to this day.

99 Uniate arrangements allowed the Maronites, whose name came from an ancient monastery dedicated to St. Maron, to maintain the celebration of the Eucharist in both kinds, the marriage of priests, their own fast-days and their own saints.

100 Braccolini, P. & Varthema, L. de: *Travellers in Disguise. Narratives of Eastern Travel*, English trans. by W. W. Jones, revised, with an introduction by L. D. Hammond, Cambridge, Mass. 1963, p. 63.

5 CHRISTIANS IN 'ARABIA'

1 See the discussion of this on p. 158.

2 See Stewart, J.: *Nestorian Missionary Enterprise. The Story of a Church on Fire [. . .]*, (1928), repr., New York 1979, pp. 50f.

3 Bosworth, C. E.: 'Iran and the Arabs before Islam', in: Yarshater, E. (ed.), *The Cambridge History of Iran* 3 (1), Cambridge 1983, p. 607.

4 Smith, M.: *Studies in Early Mysticism in the Near and Middle East [. . .]*, (1931), repr., Amsterdam 1973, reprint from 1931, p. 105. It should be noticed that while Syriac and Arabic are both Semitic languages and have some parallels in vocabulary and structure, it is not possible for an Arabic speaker and reader to understand Syriac in either its spoken or written form.

5 Trimingham, J. S.: *Christianity among the Arabs in Pre-Islamic Times*, London 1979 (Arab Background Series), p. 261, n. 39.

6 Wright, T. (ed.): *The Travels of Marco Polo*, London 1946, p. 390.

7 See Socrates: *Ecclesiastical History* 4:36; cf. also Sozomen: *Ecclesiastical History* 6:38 and Theodoret: *Ecclesiastical History* 4:20.

8 *The Eclipse of Christianity in Asia from the Time of Mohammad till the Fourteenth Century*, (1933), repr., New York 1967, p. 13.

9 Ibid.

10 Cited in Guillaume, A.: *Islam*, Harmondsworth 1954, p. 17.

11 Ibid.

12 Zarrīnkūb, 'Abd Al-.: 'The Arab Conquest of Iran and its Aftermath', in: Frye, R. N. (ed.), *The Cambridge History of Iran* 4, Cambridge 1975, p. 3.

13 Cited by Zarrīnkūb 1975, p. 18.

14 Zarrīnkūb 1975, pp. 18f. A foundation on which experience of the Crusader period was to build among Arabs.

15 See Serjeant, R. B.: *Studies in Arabian History and Civilization*, London 1981 (CStS 145), pp. 570ff.

16 Pickthall, M. M. (trans.): *The Meaning of the Glorious Koran*, New York n. d., p. 104.

17 Pickthall n. d., p. 148.

18 Sura 4:157.

19 Cf. Wensinck, A. J. & Johnstone, P.: 'Maryam', in: *The Encyclopaedia of Islam. New Edition* 6 (1991), p. 630.

20 Wensinck, A. J. & Jomier, J.: 'Ka'ba', in: *The Encyclopaedia of Islam. New Edition* 4 (1990), p. 320.

21 Cited in Browne 1967, p. 34.

22 Browne 1967, p. 34. One has some suspicions about the accuracy of numbers related to 40 because of its generality in ancient records.
23 Smith 1973, p. 109.
24 Smith 1973, p. 111. These two caliph dynasties ruled from AD 661 to AD 945.
25 Watt, W. M.: *The Majesty that was Islam. The Islamic World, 661–1100*, London 1974, p. 90.
26 Tritton, A. S.: *The Caliphs and their Non-Muslim Subjects. A Critical Study of the Covenant of 'Umar*, London 1970 (Islam and the Muslim World 14), pp. 90f.

6 CHRISTIANS IN ARMENIA AND GEORGIA

1 Malan, S. C. (trans. & ed.): *The Life and Times of S. Gregory, the Illuminator [. . .]*, London 1868, p. 8. The basic sources for the early history of Christians in Armenia are the 4th century Faustus Byzantinus, and the life of St. Gregory in Agathangelos in the 5th century. The more renowned Moses of Khoren (late 5th century) is of dubious value re chronology and detail.
2 See e.g. Eusebius: *Church History* 6:46.
3 *Church History* 9:8:2.
4 Echmiadzin, which means 'the descent of the only-begotten', was the new name thus given to the old capital Vagarshapat.
5 Arpee, L.: *A History of Armenian Christianity from the Beginning to our Own Time*, New York 1946, p. 19.
6 Cf. Malan, S. C. (trans. & ed.): *A Short History of the Georgian Church*, trans. from the Russian of P. Iosselian, and ed. with additional notes [. . .], London 1866, pp. 1–16.
7 Malan 1866, pp. 16f.
8 Malan 1866, p. 44.
9 Arpee 1946, p. 28.
10 Toumanoff, C.: 'Armenia and Georgia', in: Hussey, J. M. (ed.), *The Cambridge Medieval History* 4 (1), Cambridge 1966, p. 593.
11 Toumanoff 1966, p. 594.
12 Arpee 1946, p. 23.
13 Cf. e.g. Zaehner, R. C.: *Zurvan. A Zoroastrian Dilemma*, Oxford 1955, pp. 39–47.
14 Cf. Zaehner 1955, pp. 49–52 for an assessment of Khosrau's policy and possibly Christian convictions.
15 Lang, D. M.: 'Iran, Armenia and Georgia', in: Yarshater, E. (ed.), *The Cambridge History of Iran* 3 (1), Cambridge 1983, p. 523.
16 Cited in Runciman, S.: *The Medieval Manichee. A Study of the Christian Dualist Heresy*, (1947), repr., Cambridge 1955, p. 32. See also Conybeare, F. (ed. & trans.): *The Key of Truth. A Manual of the Paulician Church of Armenia*, Oxford 1898, pp. 31–62, and Garsoïan, N. G.: *The Paulician Heresy. A Study of the Origin and Development of Paulicianism in Armenia and the Eastern Provinces of the Byzantine Empire*, The Hague & Paris 1967 (Publications in Near and Middle East Studies, Series A, 6).
17 Conybeare 1898, p. vii.
18 Conybeare 1898, pp. xxxiii–xl. Cf. Runciman 1955, pp. 46ff. Conybeare doubts it but Runciman claims that 'the dualism of the Paulicians is unquestionable', p. 58.
19 *Armenia and the Byzantine Empire. A Brief Study of Armenian Art and Civilisation*, Cambridge, Mass. 1945, pp. 37–38.
20 Toumanoff 1966, p. 604.

21 Segal, J. B.: *Edessa, 'the Blessed City'*, Oxford 1970, p. 208.

22 The ecumenical 'Nicene' Creed, as determined by AD 381, declared that the Spirit 'proceeds from the Father'. Under the influence of St. Augustine's trinitarian theology the Western Church, by ca. AD 1000, had added, unilaterally, words which changed the formula to 'proceeds from the Father *and the Son*' (Lat. *filioque*). This was done despite the long-term opposition of the papacy itself and was and is still rejected by the Eastern Church on the grounds of both theology and conciliar propriety.

23 Allen, W. E. D.: *A History of the Georgian People from the Beginning down to the Russian Conquest in the Nineteenth Century*, (1932), repr., New York 1978, p. 267.

24 Toumanoff 1966, p. 605.

25 Der Nersessian 1945, p. 8.

26 Fortescue, E. F. K.: *The Armenian Church Founded by St. Gregory the Illuminator [. . .]*, London 1872, p. 25.

27 Lang, D. M.: *The Georgians*, London 1966 (Ancient Peoples and Places), p. 113.

28 Malan 1866, p. 130. Cf. also the Armenian experience detailed below.

29 Malan 1866, p. 132.

30 Lang 1966, p. 116.

31 Atiya, A. S.: *A History of Eastern Christianity*, London 1968, p. 333.

32 Toumanoff 1966, p. 632.

33 Catalani, J.: *Mirabilia Descripta. The Wonders of the East [. . .]*, trans. from the Latin original [. . .] by H. Yule, London 1863, pp. 5f.

7 CHRISTIANS IN PERSIA (IRAN)

1 While Iran is a more general title for the whole area concerned it is intended to make greater use of the title, Persia, recognizing that strictly speaking it refers to only one province, as does 'Holland' in the Netherlands or 'England' in Britain.

2 See Flavius Josephus: *The Jewish War* 2:16:4.

3 E.g. see Holme, H.: *The Oldest Christian Church [. . .]*, London 1896, pp. 2f.

4 Young, W. G.: *Patriarch, Shah and Caliph. A Study of the Relationship of the Church of the East with the Sassanid Empire and the Early Caliphates with Special Reference to Available Translated Syriac Sources*, Rawalpindi 1974, pp. 8ff., and Wigram, W. A.: *An Introduction to the History of the Assyrian Church or the Church of the Sassanid Persian Empire 100–640 A.D. [. . .]*, London 1910, p. 30.

5 See e.g. Asmussen, J. P.: 'Christians in Iran', in: Yarshater, E. (ed.), *The Cambridge History of Iran* 3 (2), Cambridge 1983, p. 927.

6 Adeney, W. F.: *The Greek and Eastern Churches*, (1908), repr., New York 1965, pp. 299f. & Browne, L. E.: *The Eclipse of Christianity in Asia from the Time of Muhammad till the Fourteenth Century*, (1933), repr., New York 1967, p. 10.

7 Wigram 1910, p. 37.

8 *The Life of Constantine* 4:8, 11 & 13 (trans. E. C. Richardson, NPNF 2nd series 1).

9 Asmussen 1983, p. 934.

10 For an account of this event see Sozomen: *Ecclesiastical History* 2:9–14. Cf. also Zaehner, R. C.: *Zurvan. A Zoroastrian Dilemma*, Oxford 1955, pp. 39ff.

11 Cited by Young 1974, p. 6.

12 Cited by Vööbus, A.: *A History of Asceticism in the Syrian Orient. A Contribution to the History of Culture in the Near East*, vol. 1, Louvain 1958 (CSCO.Sub 14), p. 274.

13 Browne 1967, p. 5.

14 Cited by Brock, S. P.: 'Christians in the Sasanid Empire: A Case of Divided Loyalties', in: Mews, S. (ed.), *Religion and National Identity*, Oxford 1982 (Studies

in Church History 18) [= Brock 1982a], p. 11. Cf. also the comments of Boyce, M.: *Zoroastrians. Their Religious Beliefs and Practices*, London 1979, pp. 100–128, and Zaehner 1955, p. 39.

15 Cited by Young 1974, p. 51.

16 Cited by Young 1974, p. 7.

17 Adeney 1965, p. 483.

18 Barthold, V. V.: *Iran*, trans. by G. K. Nariman, Bombay 1935, pp. 124f.

19 See e.g. Wigram 1910.

20 Vööbus, A.: *The Statutes of the School of Nisibis*, Stockholm 1961 (PETSE 12), p. 14.

21 'On the Exposition of the Mysteries', 'On the Mysteries of the Church and on Baptism', and 'On Baptism'.

22 Vööbus 1961, p. 3.

23 Cited by Vööbus, A.: *A History of the School of Nisibis*, Louvain 1965 (CSCO.Sub 26), p. 106.

24 See e.g. the canons of Narsai numbered 3, 4, 5, 6 & 21 on pp. 75–78 & 84 of Vööbus 1961.

25 Vööbus 1965, p. 109.

26 See Gero, S.: *Barsauma of Nisibis and Persian Christianity in the Fifth Century*, Louvain 1981 (CSCO.Sub 63), passim.

27 Asmussen 1983, p. 943 & cf. Sellers, R. N.: *The Council of Chalcedon. A Historical and Doctrinal Survey*, London 1953, pp. 49 & 77, and Jackson, B. (trans.): 'The Ecclesiastical History, Dialogues, and Letters of Theodoret', in: Theordoret et al., *Historical Writings*, (1892), repr., Grand Rapids 1953 (NPNF 2nd series 3), p. 323, n. 4.

28 Gero 1981, p. 84.

29 See pp. 30 and 110 above.

30 See Gero 1981, p. 107.

31 While it was, and is, canonically possible for a married man to be ordained as a deacon and a priest it was not possible for one already ordained to marry. This applied generally throughout the East, including the Byzantine realm. So it was possible, before the restriction of the episcopacy to single men, for a married man to become patriarch. For a patriarch to marry would cause outrage.

32 Gero 1981, pp. 73f.

33 Gero 1981, p. 45.

34 Cited in Vine, A. R.: *The Nestorian Churches. A Concise History of Nestorian Christianity in Asia from the Persian Schism to the Modern Assyrians [. . .]*, (1937), repr., New York 1980, p. 54.

35 Young 1974, p. 59. Cf. also Zaehner 1955, pp. 49–51.

36 Wigram 1910, p. 191.

37 Wigram 1910, p. 216.

38 Wallace-Hadrill, D. S.: *Christian Antioch. A Study of Early Christian Thought in the East*, Cambridge 1982, p. 149.

39 Wallace-Hadrill 1982, p. 147.

40 Cited by Atiya, A. S.: *A History of Eastern Christianity*, London 1968, p. 254. Note that *qnume* (sing. *qnōmē*) is the Syriac term meaning nature or description of a person.

41 Vööbus 1965, p. 209.

42 Vööbus 1965, p. 309.

43 Vööbus 1965, p. 314.

44 Ibid.

45 Cited by Young 1974, p. 75.

46 Fortescue, A.: *The Lesser Eastern Churches [. . .]*, London 1913, p. 329.

47 Cited by Browne 1967, p. 8, from: *Le Christianisme dans l'Empire Perse*, Paris 1904, p. 266.
48 Browne 1967, pp. 7f.
49 Cited by Browne 1967, pp. 38f. (Cf. the 'Covenant of 'Umar' on pp. 69ff. above).
50 Joseph, J.: *The Nestorians and their Muslim Neighbours. A Study of Western Influence on their Relations*, Princeton, N. J. 1961 (Princeton Oriental Studies 20), p. 27.
51 Brock, S. P. : 'Syriac Views of Emergent Islam', in: Juynboll, G. H. A. (ed.), *Studies on the First Century of Islamic Society*, Carbondale 1982 (Papers on Islamic History 5) [= Brock 1982b], p. 20.
52 Brock 1984, p. 15.
53 Cited by Young 1974, p. 91.
54 Cited by Brock 1982b, p. 16.
55 Cited by Barthold 1935, p. 136.
56 Cited by Young 1974, p. 139.
57 'The Apology of Timothy the Patriarch before the Caliph Mahdi', in: *BJRL* 12 (1928), pp. 137–227. A summary of the dialogue is provided by Young 1974, pp. 197–205.
58 Mingana 1928, pp. 141f.
59 Mingana 1928, p. 145.
60 Mingana 1928, pp. 169f.
61 Mingana 1928, p. 172.
62 Mingana 1928, pp. 176f.
63 Pickthall, M. M. (trans.): *The Meaning of the Glorious Koran*, New York n. d., p. 223.
64 Mingana 1928, p. 178.
65 Mingana 1928, p. 182.
66 Mingana 1928, p. 193.
67 Mingana 1928, p. 195.
68 Mingana 1928, p. 197.
69 Mingana 1928, p. 207.
70 Mingana 1928, pp. 225f. See also references to the pearl of great value in the section on South East Asia below.
71 Vine 1980, pp. 99f.
72 Cited by Young 1974, p. 148.
73 Cited by Young 1974, pp. 139f.
74 Young 1974, p. 49.
75 Fortescue 1913, p. 96.
76 Ibid.
77 Latourette, K. S.: *A History of the Expansion of Christianity*, vol. 2, London 1938, p. 267.
78 Cited in Vine 1980, p. 106.
79 Minorsky, V. F.: *The Middle East in Western Politics in the 13th, 14th and 15th Centuries*, repr. from the *JRAS* [. . .], London 1940, p. 431.
80 Browne 1967, p. 150.
81 Budge, E. A. W. (trans.): *The Monks of Ḳûblâi Khân, Emperor of China, or the History of the Life and Travels of Rabban Ṣâwmâ [. . .] and Marḳôs [. . .]*, London 1928, p. 58.
82 For this seal inscription cf. Hamilton, J.: 'Le texte turc en charactères syriaques du grand sceau cruciforme de Mr Yahballāhā III', in: *Journal Asiatique* 260 (1972), pp. 155–170.
83 Hamilton 1972, p. 160.

84 Budge 1928, pp. 96–100.
85 Budge 1928, p. 100.
86 Budge 1928, pp. 175–177.
87 Budge 1928, p. 177.
88 Eusebius: *Church History* 8:1.
89 Budge 1928, p. 92; cf. also the comments of Vine 1980, pp. 156ff.
90 Catalani, J.: *Mirabilia descripta. The Wonders of the East [. . .]*, trans. from the Latin original [. . .] by H. Yule, London 1863, pp. 8f.
91 Brock 1982a, p. 13.
92 Ibid.
93 Brock 1982a, p. 15. Such an attitude was to be found also among Byzantine bishops.
94 Zaehner, R. C.: *The Dawn and Twilight of Zoroastrianism*, (1961), repr., London 1975, p. 279.
95 Zaehner 1975, p. 300.
96 Browne 1967, pp. 78f.
97 Browne 1967, p. 7.
98 Atiya 1968, p. 211.
99 Fortescue 1913, p. 93.
100 Young 1974, p. 92.
101 Cited by Young 1974, p. 97.
102 'The Authority of the Catholicos Patriarch of Seleucia-Ctesiphon', in: *I patriarchati orientali nel primo millennio [. . .]*, Rome 1968 (OCA 181), p. 189.
103 Browne 1967, p. 57.
104 Browne 1967, p. 92.
105 Vööbus 1958, p. 265.
106 Vine 1980, p. 74.
107 Atiya 1968, p. 240.
108 Young 1974, p. 109.
109 Fortescue 1913, p. 104.
110 Vine 1980, p. 126.
111 Holme, H.: *The Oldest Christian Church [. . .]*, London 1896, p. 34.
112 Waterfield, R. E.: *Christians in Persia. Assyrians, Armenians, Roman Catholics and Protestants*, London 1973, p. 14.
113 Waterfield 1973, p. 54.

8 CHRISTIANS IN INDIA

1 For further information on such early contacts consult works such as Charlesworth, M. P.: *Trade-Routes and Commerce of the Roman Empire*, 2nd ed., rev., Cambridge 1926; Tarn, W. W.: *The Greeks in Bactria and India*, (1926), 2nd ed., Cambridge 1951, and Dihle, A.: *Der Seeweg nach Indien*, Innsbruck 1974 (Innsbrucker Beiträge zur Kulturwissenschaft. Dies philologici Aenipontani 4). Cf. also Pollet, G. (ed.): *India and the Ancient World. History, Trade and Culture before A. D. 650 [. . .]*, Louvain 1987 (OLA 25).
2 Thomas, P.: *Christians and Christianity in India and Pakistan. A General Survey of the Progress of Christianity in India from Apostolic Times to the Present Day*, London 1954, p. 3.
3 Thomas 1954, p. 9.
4 See Wheeler, R. E. M. et al.: 'Arikamedu: An Indo-Roman Trading Station on the East Coast of India', in: *Ancient India* 2 (1946), pp. 17–124.
5 See Dihle, A.: 'Neues zur Thomas-Tradition', in: *JAC* 6 (1963), pp. 54–70.

6 Rawlinson, H. G.: *Intercourse between India and the Western World from the Earliest Times to the Fall of Rome*, Cambridge 1916, p. 151.
7 Dihle 1963, p. 62.
8 Rawlinson 1916, p. 130.
9 Charlesworth 1926, p. 73.
10 Dihle 1963, p. 63.
11 Ibid. p. 62, referring to a reference by Eusebius in his *Church History* 5:10, and by Jerome in his *Epistle* 70.
12 Dihle 1963, p. 62.
13 Brown, L. W.: *The Indian Christians of St Thomas*, London 1956, pp. 62f. But this was called in question by Garbe, R.: *Indien und das Christentum. Eine Untersuchung der religionsgeschichtlichen Zusammenhänge*, Tübingen 1914, p. 149, and Mundadan, A. M.: *History of Christianity in India*, vol. I: *From the Beginning up to the Middle of the Sixteenth Century (up to 1542)*, Bangalore 1984, pp. 20f. See also the discussion by J. H. Lord on 'Jews in Cochin', in: *Encyclopedia of Religion and Ethics* 7 (1914), pp. 557–559.
14 Dihle 1963, p. 66.
15 A good bibliography of sources, published and unpublished and of secondary works is available on pp. 523–544 of Mundadan 1984.
16 This is despite the case made by Schurhammer for the contemporaneity of bricks from the reputed tomb of Thomas at Mylapore with those from the Roman settlement at Arikamedu, in the foreword to Mundadan, A. M.: *Sixteenth Century Traditions of St. Thomas Christians*, Bangalore 1970 (Dharmaram College Studies 5).
17 An English text of both these works is to be found, e.g. in Roberts, A. & Donaldson, J. (eds.): *The Twelve Patriarchs [. . .]*, (1886), repr., Grand Rapids 1951 (ANFa 8), pp. 535–549 & 667–672. The Acts of Thomas text is also in James, M. R. (ed.): *The Apocryphal New Testament*, Oxford 1924, pp. 364–438, and in Bornkamm, G.: 'The Acts of Thomas', in: Hennecke, E. & Schneemelcher, W. (eds.), *New Testament Apocrypha*, vol. 2, London 1965, pp. 425–531.
18 The summary is that of Enslin, M. S.: *The Interpreter's Dictionary of the Bible*, Buttrick, G. A. et al. (eds.), vol. IV, New York 1962, p. 633.
19 For a detailed discussion of the numistatical and other evidence for Gundaphorus, see e.g. Dar, S. R.: 'Gondophares and Taxila', in: Rooney, J. (ed.), *St. Thomas and Taxila*, Rawalpindi 1988 (Pakistan Christian History Study 1), pp. 16–30. Note that the name of the king concerned here is spelled in various ways, as is apparent above and in the passage cited in footnote 23 below.
20 See e.g. Roberts & Donaldson 1951, p. 671.
21 'The Connection of St. Thomas the Apostle with India', in: *IndAnt* 32 (1903), pp. 1–15 & 145–160.
22 Cited in Philipps 1903, p. 15.
23 Philipps 1903, p. 151.
24 E.g. Burnell, A. C.: 'On Some Pahlavi Inscriptions in South India', in: *IndAnt* 3 (1874), pp. 308–316; Garbe 1914; Hunter, W. W.: *The Indian Empire*, new & rev. ed., London 1893; Rae, G. M.: *The Syrian Church in India*, Edinburgh & London 1892; Hough, J.: *History of Christianity in India from the Commencement of the Christian Era*, 5 vols., London 1839–1860; and Dihle 1963.
25 Mundadan 1984, p. 3.
26 'The Apostle Thomas in South India', in: *BJRL* 11 (1927), p. 43.
27 Podipara, P.: 'The South Indian Apostolate of St. Thomas', in: *OCP* 18 (1952), pp. 234–236, and Hambye, E. R.: 'Saint Thomas and India', and 'The Syrian Church in India', in: *CleM* 16 (1952), pp. 363–375 and 376–389.

28 Thomas 1954, p. 15. See p. 220 for details of the Koonen Cross incident.
29 Mundadan 1984, p. 49.
30 Neill, S.: *A History of Christianity in India. The Beginnings to AD 1707*, Cambridge 1984, p. 35.
31 E.g. see Cheriyan, C. V.: *A History of Christianity in Kerala from the Mission of St. Thomas to the Arrival of Vasco da Gama (A. D. 52–1498)*, Kottayam 1973, pp. 32f.
32 Puthiakunnel, Th.: 'Jewish Colonies of India Paved the Way for St. Thomas', in: Vellian, J. (ed.), *The Malabar Church [. . .]*, Rome 1970 (OCA 186), p. 189.
33 Rae 1892, p. 69.
34 E.g. Stewart, J.: *Nestorian Missionary Enterprise. The Story of a Church on Fire [. . .]*, (1928), repr., New York 1979, p. 107; Keay, F. E.: *A History of the Syrian Church of India*, London 1938, p. 22; Garbe 1914, p. 145.
35 E.g. Podipara 1952, p. 237.
36 Rae 1892, pp. 59ff.
37 Mundadan 1984, p. 64. In this he is supported by such authors as Thomas 1954; Farquhar 1927; Tisserant, E.: *Eastern Christianity in India. A History of the Syro-Malabar Curch from the Earliest Time to the Present Day [. . .]*, authorized adaptation from the French by E. R. Hambye, London 1957; Keay 1938; Podipara 1952, and idem: *The Thomas Christians*, London 1970; Stewart 1979, p. 104; Medlycott, A. E.: *India and the Apostle Thomas. An Inquiry. With a Critical Analysis of the Acta Thomae*, London 1905.
38 *The Early History of India*, 4th ed., Oxford 1924, pp. 249f.
39 *Church History* 5:10:1–3 ((trans. A. C. McGiffert, NPNF 2nd series 1). Note also the case made out by Perumalil, H. C.: 'The Apostles of Kalyana (Bombay)', in: *Journal of Indian History* 22 (1943), pp. 76ff., where he opts for AD 55 as the date of Bartholomew's arrival at Kalyana; and the support for Pantaenus' visit from Cheriyan 1973, pp. 60ff.
40 Dihle 1963, p. 62. However, Mundadan 1984, pp. 65ff., points out that there are no Indian traditions about Bartholomew, whom the Persians see as related to Armenia.
41 Dihle 1963, p. 64.
42 See Mingana, A.: 'The Early Spread of Christianity in India', in: *BJRL* 10 (1926), pp. 440f.; Thurston, E.: *Castes and Tribes of Southern India*, vol. 6, Madras 1909, pp. 422f.
43 Mingana 1926, p. 437.
44 On the use of the parallel with Peter see e.g. Juhanon Mar Thoma: *Christianity in India*, Madras 1954, p. 5. and cf. also Buchanan, C.: *Christian Researches in Asia [. . .]*, Cambridge & London 1811, p. 113.
45 This parallel was drawn by Richards, W. J.: *The Indian Christians of St. Thomas [. . .]*, London & Derby 1908. For discussions of the historicity of Patrick and his mission in Ireland see, e.g. Hanson, P. R. C.: *Saint Patrick. His Origins and Career*, Oxford 1968, and idem: *The Life and Writings of the Historical Saint Patrick*, New York 1983; Hood, A. B. E. (trans. & ed.), *St. Patrick: His Writings and Muirchu's 'Life'*, London 1978 (History from Sources).
46 Rae 1892, pp. 22f.
47 See, e.g. the statements of Hunter 1893, pp. 280f.; Garbe 1914, pp. 143f.
48 Thomas 1954, p. 29.
49 Hambye 1952, p. 377.
50 Cheriyan 1973, p. 72.
51 Richter, J.: *A History of Missions in India*, trans. by S. H. Moore, Edinburgh 1908, p. 37.
52 E.g., see Brown 1956, pp. 65ff.; Dihle 1963, p. 69; Garbe 1914, p. 152.

53 Tisserant 1957, pp. 7f.
54 Mingana 1926, p. 496.
55 Mingana 1926, p. 459. Cf. Agur, C. M.: *Church History of Travancore*, Madras 1903, p. 10.
56 Cited by Brown 1956, p. 67.
57 E.g. Hambye 1952, pp. 377f.; Brown 1956, p. 71; Keay 1938, p. 22; Stewart 1979, pp. 107ff.; Thomas 1954, p. 30.
58 Mingana 1926, p. 459. It has been suggested also that through such contacts the Thomas tradition associated with Edessa may have come into South India – see Dihle 1963, p. 70.
59 See Hambye 1952, p. 378; Mar Aprem (G. Mooken): 'The Nestorian Church in India from the Fifth to the Sixteenth Century', in: John, K. J. (ed.), *Christian Heritage of India [. . .]*, Cochin 1981 p. 37; Joseph, T. K.: *Malabar Christians and their Ancient Documents*, Trivandrum 1929, p. 31.
60 E.g. Rae 1892, p. 117.
61 McCrindle, J. W. (trans. & ed.): *The Christian Topography of Cosmas [. . .]*, London 1897, pp. 118f. Note that Taprobane = Ceylon; Male = Malabar; Calliana = Kalyana; Dioscorides = Socotra.
62 McCrindle 1897, p. 365. It is unclear how long this Sri Lankan Christian enclave persisted, but it has left evidence of its existence in a sunken relief stone cross discovered in AD 1912 at Anuradhapura. (Once the capital of the Sinhalese kingdom, it had ceased to be so in the 10th century and fell into ruins in the 13th.) The cross is of similar design to a number found in South India and probably dates from the time of Cosmas, i.e. from the 6th century. See Somaratne, G. P. V.: 'Pre-Portuguese Christianity in Sri Lanka', in: *Indian Church History Review* 23 (1989), pp. 144–155.
63 Rae 1892, p. 117. This assessment is supported by Keay 1938, p. 22.
64 This mid 8th century date has the support of such as Adeney, W. F.: *The Greek and Eastern Churches*, (1908), repr., New York 1965, p. 520; Agur 1903, p. 12; Garbe 1914, p. 145; Hambye 1952, p. 379, the last holding for dates of AD 774 or 795.
65 Cheriyan 1973, p. 83.
66 Mundadan 1984, p. 95.
67 Agur 1903, p. 34.
68 From Winckworth, C. P. T.: 'A New Interpretation of the Pahlavī Cross-Inscriptions of Southern India', in: *Journal of Theological Studies* 30 (1929), pp. 237–244.
69 From Brown 1956, p. 75. The Manigrammam were a community, believed to be made up of lapsed Christians, who still had some relationship to their former co-religionists.
70 Hambye 1952, p. 379.
71 Mar Aprem 1981, p. 38.
72 Mingana 1926, pp. 462ff., and Cheriyan 1973, p. 102, who cites the claim from Barhebraeus: 'We are disciples of the Apostle Thomas; we have no relation with the see of Mari.'
73 Mundadan 1984, p. 102.
74 Mundadan 1984, p. 125.
75 Hambye 1952, p. 380.
76 Savage, A. (trans. & ed.): *The Anglo-Saxon Chronicles*, London 1982, p. 97.
77 Mundadan 1984, p. 120.
78 Mar Aprem 1981, p. 40.
79 Mundadan 1984, p. 108.

80 Yule, H. (trans. & ed.): *Cathay and the Way Thither [. . .]*, new ed. by H. Cordier, London 1913–1916, vol. 3, p. 45.
81 Marco Polo: *Travels*, London 1908 (Everyman's Library), bk. III: xx, pp. 363–365. Cf. idem: *The Book of Ser Marco Polo, the Venetian, Concerning the Kingdoms and Marvels of the East*, trans. and ed. with notes by H. Yule, 3rd ed., revised, vol. 2, London 1929, pp. 353ff.
82 Marco Polo 1908, bk. III:xxv., p. 377.
83 Catalani, J.: *Mirabilia Descripta. The Wonders of the East [. . .]*, trans. from the Latin original [. . .] by H. Yule, London 1863, p. 23.
84 Catalani 1863, p. 35.
85 Juhanon 1954, p. 15.
86 Yule 1913–1916, vol. 2, pp. 141f.
87 Yule 1913–1916, vol. 3, pp. 216–218.
88 Neill, S.: *The Story of the Christian Church in India and Pakistan*, Grand Rapids 1970 (Christian World Mission Books), p. 24.
89 Mundadan 1984, p. 139. In this we have a foretaste of Nestorian attitudes towards the Portuguese, in the 16th century.
90 Cited by Brown 1956, p. 84.
91 Major, R. H.: *India in the Fifteenth Century. Being a Collection of Narratives of Voyages to India*, vol. 2, London 1857, p. 7.
92 Major 1857, p. 23.
93 Stewart 1979, p. 92.
94 Bracciolini, P. & Varthema, L. de: *Travelers in Disguise. Narratives of Eastern Travel*, Engl. trans. by J. W. Jones, revised, with an introduction, by L. D. Hammond, Cambridge, Mass. 1963, p. 180.
95 Barbosa, D.: *A Description of the Coasts of East Africa and Malabar in the Beginning of the Sixteenth Century*, trans. [. . .] by H. E. J. Stanley, London 1866 (WHS 35), p. 162. It is likely that he confused Armenians and Nestorians.
96 Barbosa 1866, p. 163.
97 Barbosa 1866, p. 176. While peacocks are venerated in a number of cultures, and are to be found frequently represented on the iconostasis (icon screen) in Orthodox churches, the blue peacock is native to and prolific in South India. That they were used as a device would have immediate relevance for people there (see pls. 11 and 12 for evidence of this use). The reference to relics of earth parallels that of Marco Polo some 230 years earlier – see note 81 above.
98 Cheriyan 1973, p. 136.
99 Aerthayil, J.: *The Spiritual Heritage of the St. Thomas Christians*, Bangalore 1982, pp. 209ff.
100 Aerthayil 1982, p. 215.
101 E.g. Latourette, K. S.: *A History of the Expansion of Christianity*, vol. 2, New York & London 1938, p. 284.
102 Mundadan 1984, p. 153.
103 Mundadan 1984, pp. 258f. & 273.
104 Mundadan 1984, pp. 175f. & 272f.
105 See note 98 above. Note also the support to this assessment by such as Podipara, P.: 'The Social and Socio-Economic Customs of the Syrian Christians of India', in: *Eastern Churches Quarterly* 7 (1947), pp. 235f.; Matthew, K. J.: 'The Role of the Kerala Church in Indian Culture', in: Vellian, J. (ed.), *The Malabar Church [. . .]*, Rome 1970 (OCA 186), pp. 119–121.
106 Brown 1956, p. 4.
107 Podipara 1947, pp. 223–235.

108 Brown 1956, pp. 172f., 186.
109 See Cherukarakunnel, A.: 'The Hindu Christians of India', in: Vellian, J. (ed.), *The Malabar Church [. . .]*, Rome 1970 (OCA 186), pp. 204f.; Aerthayil 1982, p. 51.
110 Stewart 1979, p. 248.
111 Cheriyan 1973, p. 153.
112 See Hambye 1952, pp. 386f.
113 Aerthayil 1982, p. 208.
114 Brown 1956, pp. 173f.
115 Brown 1956, p. 174, note 2.
116 Neill 1984, p. 30. Cf. also his statements, *op. cit.* 1970, p. 19.
117 See e.g. Codrington, H. W.: *Studies of the Syrian Liturgies*, London 1952. See also Brown 1956, chapters VIII-XI.
118 See discussion in Aerthayil 1982, p. 99.
119 Aerthayil 1982, p. 200.
120 See Hambye 1952, p. 387.
121 E.g., see the comments of Brown 1956, pp. 174–178; cf. Mundadan 1984, pp. 95–98.
122 Cheriyan 1973, p. 154.
123 See Joseph, T. K.: 'A Christian Dynasty in Malabar', in: *IndAnt* 52 (1923), pp. 157–159, and idem: *The Malabar Christians and their Ancient Documents*, Trivandrum 1929, p. 7.
124 See Brown 1956, pp. 13f. and 14, n. 5.
125 Rae 1892, p. 179.
126 Thurston 1909, vol. 6, p. 408.
127 Juhanon 1954, p. 12.
128 Mundadan 1984, p. 165. Not that Roz had any desire to promote claims to distinction by the Thomas Christians.
129 Brown 1956, p. 13.
130 Mathew 1970, p. 119. Cf. also Mundadan 1984, pp. 231–233.
131 Stewart 1979, pp. 123f.
132 Mundadan 1984, p. 175, and see, e.g. p. 177 above for response to the continuation of this practice in AD 1503–1504.
133 Mundadan 1970, p. 173.
134 Cheriyan 1973, p. 137. It should be noted that 'The Gate' is a reference, common in the 'East', to supreme authority. Cf. the designation of the Ottoman Government at Constantinople as 'The Sublime Porte'.
135 Mundadan 1984, pp. 177ff.
136 Thurston 1909, vol 6., pp. 434f.
137 Mundadan 1984, p. 102.
138 Mundadan 1984, p. 181.
139 Mundadan 1984, pp. 181ff.
140 Podipara 1947, p. 225.
141 Hambye 1952, p. 388.
142 Mundadan 1984, pp. 197f.
143 Cheriyan 1973, p. 144.
144 Rae 1892, p. 112.
145 Thurston 1909, vol. 6, pp. 422f.
146 Tisserant 1957, p. 18.
147 Barbosa 1866, p. 162.
148 Buchanan 1811, p. 89.
149 Cited by Mundadan 1984, p. 511.

150 Mar Aprem 1981, p. 43.
151 Adeney, W. F.: *The Greek and Eastern Churches*, (1908), repr., New York 1965, p. 521.
152 Podipara 1970, p. 171.
153 Cited by Panikkar, K. M.: *Asia and Western Dominance. A Survey of the Vasco da Gama Epoch of Asian History 1498–1945*, 5th impr., London 1961, pp. 26f. Note here that the reference to Affonso is actually to Alfonso V (d. 1481). See also Boxer, C. R.: *The Portuguese Seaborne Empire, 1415–1825*, New York 1969, pp. 20–23.
154 See the 1493 bull 'Inter Caetera Divinae', a translation of which appears in Fremantle, A. (ed.): *The Papal Encyclicals in their Historical Context*, New York 1956, pp. 77–80.
155 See Mundadan 1984, pp. 249f.
156 Mundadan 1984, p. 252.
157 Cipolla, C. M.: *European Culture and Overseas Expansion*, Harmondsworth 1970, pp. 99f.
158 Boxer 1969, p. 37., also cf. his comments in 'The Portuguese and the East', in: Livermore, H. V. (ed.), *Portugal and Brazil. An Introduction*, Oxford 1953, pp. 192 & 214.
159 Cited by Mundadan 1984, p. 270. 'Franks' of course was a generic term in the Middle East for all Western Europeans.
160 Mundadan 1984, pp. 270f.
161 Mundadan 1984, p. 271.
162 Mundadan 1984, p. 515.
163 Mundadan 1984, p. 514.
164 For details, including diagrams of the layout of the church and tombs see Mundadan 1970, the chapter headed 'Tomb at Mylapore', especially pp. 18ff.
165 Mundadan 1984, p. 292.
166 Mundadan 1984, p. 297.
167 Mundadan 1984, p. 306.
168 Mundadan 1984, p. 311. Cf. also Schurhammer, G.: *The Malabar Church and Rome during the Early Portuguese Period and Before*, Trichinopoly 1934, pp. 20ff.
169 Cited by Mundadan 1984, p. 314.
170 Schurhammer 1934, p. 38.
171 Mundadan 1984, p. 341.
172 Mundadan 1984, pp. 505ff.
173 Mundadan 1984, p. 508.
174 Boxer 1969, p. 67.
175 Ploeg, J. P. M. van der: *The Christians of St. Thomas in South India and their Syriac Manuscripts*, Bangalore 1983 (Placid Lectures Series), p. 13.
176 Ploeg 1983, p. 268.
177 Cherukarakunnel 1970, p. 208.
178 See Buchanan 1811, p. 117.
179 Neill 1970, p. 36.
180 Hunter 1893, p. 280.
181 Cheriyan 1973, p. 154.
182 Brown 1956, pp. 4f.

9 CHRISTIANS IN CENTRAL ASIA

1 Tekin, T.: *A Grammar of Orkhon Turkic*, The Hague 1968 (Indiana University Publications. Uralic and Altaic Series 69), pp. 264 & 271f.

2 This expansion of Christianity to the east as evidenced in Syrian materials was first sketched by Sachau, E.: *Zur Ausbreitung des Christentums in Asien*, Berlin 1919 (APAW 1919, 1). Cf. also Barthold, W.: *Zur Geschichte des Christentums in Mittel-Asien bis zur mongolischen Eroberung [. . .]*, ed. by R. Stübe, Tübingen & Leipzig 1901.

3 Mingana, A.: 'The Early Spread of Christianity in Central Asia and the Far East: A New Document', in: *BJRL* 9 (1925), p. 301. Cf. also Drijvers, H. J. W. (trans. & ed.): *The Book of the Laws of Countries. Dialogue on Fate of Bardaisan of Edessa*, Assen 1965 (Semitic Texts with Translation 3), p. 61.

4 Rosenfield, J. M.: *The Dynastic Arts of the Kushans*, Berkeley & Los Angeles 1967 (California Studies in the History of Art 6), pp. 20, 284.

5 Bornkamm, G.: 'The Acts of Thomas', in: Hennecke, E. & Schneemelcher, W. (eds.), *New Testament Apocrypha*, vol. 2, London 1965, pp. 498–504. Cf. also Drijvers, H. J. W.: 'Thomasakten', in: Schneemelcher, W. (ed.), *Neutestamentliche Apokryphen in deutscher Übersetzung*, vol. 2, 5th ed., Tübingen 1990, pp. 289–367. Cf. the reference to the "Song of the Pearl" in p. 368.

6 Mingana 1925, p. 302. Cf. Pratten, B. P. (trans.): 'Ancient Syrian Documents', in: Roberts, A. & Donaldson, J. (eds.), *The Twelve Patriarchs [. . .]*, (1886), repr., Grand Rapids 1951 (ANFa 8), pp. 671f. ("The Teaching of the Apostles", § 10).

7 Chabot, J.-B. (ed.): *Synodicon orientale ou receuil des synodes nestoriens*, Paris 1902 (NEMBN 37). This material is well evaluated in Hunter, E. C. D.: 'Syriac Christianity in Central Asia', in: *ZRGG* 44 (1992), pp. 362–368.

8 Cf. Frye, R. N.: *The History of Ancient Iran*, Munich 1983 (Handbuch der Altertumswissenschaft 3, 7), p. 18; Koshelenko, G.: 'The Beginnings of Buddhism in Margiana', in: *AA* 14 (1960), pp. 175–183.

9 Lieu, S. N. C.: *Manichaeism in the Later Roman Empire and Medieval China. A Historical Survey*, 2nd. ed., Tübingen 1992 (Wissenschaftliche Untersuchungen zum Neuen Testament 63), pp. 220ff.; Sundermann, W.: *Mitteliranische manichäische Texte kirchengeschichtlichen Inhalts*, Berlin 1981 (BT 11), pp. 27, 39–41; Klimkeit, H.-J.: *Gnosis on the Silk Road. Gnostic Texts from Central Asia*, San Francisco 1993, pp. 203ff.

10 Hunter, E. C. D.: 'The Conversion of the Kerait to Christianity in A.D. 1007', in: *ZAS* 22 (1989–1991), pp. 142–163. Cf. also Hunter 1992.

11 Mingana 1925, p. 320.

12 Mingana 1925, pp. 318ff. Cf. also Sachau 1905, pp. 64ff.

13 Cf. sources quoted in Hunter 1992.

14 Mingana 1925, pp. 307f.

15 Cf. Müller, F. W. K. & Lentz, W.: 'Soghdische Texte II', in: *SPAW* 1934, pp. 522–528.

16 Sachau, E.: 'Die Christianisierungs-Legende von Merw', in: Frankenberg, W. & Küchler, F. (eds.), *Abhandlungen zur semitischen Religionskunde und Sprachwissenschaft* , Giessen 1918, pp. 399–409.

17 Müller & Lentz 1934, p. 524. It should be pointed out that according to E. Sachau the Bishop Bar Shabba of Merv was probably identified with the legendary founder of Christianity in that city at the time of Shapur II (309–379). Sachau 1918, p. 407.

18 Mingana 1925, pp. 304f.

19 For the Sogdian Christian literature of the Turfan area cf. Sims-Williams, N.: 'Sogdian and Turkish Christians in the Turfan and Tun-huang Manuscripts', in: Cadonna, A. (ed.), *Turfan and Tun-huang. The Texts. Encounter of Civilizations on the Silk Road*, Florence 1992 (Orientalia Venetiana 4), pp. 43–61.

20 Cf., for instance, Müller, F. W. K.: 'Neutestamentliche Bruchstücke in soghdischer Sprache', in: *SPAW* 1907, pp. 260–270; Müller, F. W. K. & Lentz, W.: 'Soghdische Texte II', in: *SPAW* 1934, pp. 504—607.

21 Hunter 1992, pp. 366f. For Christians in the Samarkand area cf. also Colless, B. E.: 'The Nestorian Province of Samarqand', in: *Abr-Nahrain* 24 (1986), pp. 51–57.

22 Hunter 1992, p. 367. It seems, however, that these tombstone inscriptions from the cemeteries named stem mainly from the 13th and 14th cent.

23 Paykova, A. V.: 'The Syrian Ostracon from Panjikant', in: *Le Muséon* 92 (1979), p. 165.

24 Paykova 1979, p. 161. For the Christan Church at Aq-Beshim where there was also a Buddhist monastery, cf. Clauson, G.: 'Ak Beshim – Suyab', in: *JRAS* 1961, pp. 1–13.

25 Paykova 1979, p. 161.

26 Hansen, O.: 'Die buddhistische und christliche Literatur', in: Gershevitch, I. et al., *Literatur*, Leiden, Cologne 1968 (Handbuch der Orientalistik I,4,2,1), pp. 98f. Cf. Sundermann, W.: 'Ein Bruchstück einer soghdischen Kirchengeschichte aus Zentralasien?', in: *AA* 24 (1976), pp. 95–101.

27 Paykova 1979, p. 162.

28 Paykova 1979, p. 162.

29 This and the following information is gleaned from a catalogue of silverware in the Hermitage Museum, St. Petersburg: Effenberger, A. et al.: *Spätantike und frühbyzantinische Silbergefäße aus der Staatlichen Eremitage Leningrad*, Berlin 1978 (Staatliche Museen zu Berlin. Ausstellungskataloge der Frühchristlich-byzantinischen Sammlung 2), pp. 129–131.

30 Effenberger et al. 1978, p. 131.

31 Cf. Schlingloff, D.: 'Traditions of Indian Narrative Painting in Central Asia', in: *Akṣayanīvī. Essays Presented to Dr. Debala Mitra*, Delhi 1991, pp. 163–169, and other works of Schlingloff on Buddhist art in India and Central Asia.

32 Publication of a sketch of that scene in Stawiskij, B. J.: *Die Völker Mittelasiens im Lichte ihrer Kunstdenkmäler. Archäologische Reise durch die Geschichte Alt-Mittelasiens [. . .]*, Bonn 1982, fig. 68.

33 For the conversion of the Turks we refer to Hunter 1989–1991 and Hunter 1992.

34 Mingana 1925, pp. 305f.

35 Hunter E. C. D.: 'Conversions of the Turkic Tribes to Christianity', unpublished MS 1988, publication forthcoming, p. 2. I am thankful to Dr. Hunter for making this MS available to me. Cf. also Hunter 1989–1991, pp. 157–160.

36 Hunter 1988 (MS), p. 2.

37 Ibid.

38 Mingana 1925, p. 306.

39 Hunter 1988 (MS), p. 3.

40 Hunter 1988 (MS), p. 4.

41 Mingana 1925, p. 306.

42 Ibid.

43 Mingana 1925, p. 307.

44 Ibid.

45 Mingana 1925, p. 321, also Hunter 1989–1991, pp. 142ff., who suggests that the Turks converted at the time of Timothy I belonged to the Turkic Oghuz tribes.
46 Mingana 1925, p. 322.
47 Mingana 1925, pp. 322f.
48 Mingana 1925, p. 323.
49 Mingana 1925, pp. 346f.
50 Mingana 1925, p. 350.
51 Mingana 1925, p. 323.
52 Budge, E. A. W. (trans.): *The Monks of Ḳûblâi Khân, Emperor of China, or the History of the Life and Travels of Rabban Ṣâwmâ [. . .] and Marḳos [. . .]*, London 1928, p. 156.
53 Moule, A. C. & Pelliot, P. (eds.): *Marco Polo, Description of the World*, vol. 1, London 1938, pp. 143f.
54 Dawson, C. (ed.): *The Mongol Mission. Narratives and Letters of the Franciscan Missionaries in Mongolia and China in the Thirteenth and Fourteenth Centuries*, London & New York 1955, p. 137 (The Makers of Christendom); reprint under the title: *Mission to Asia [. . .]*, London 1980 (Spiritual Masters).
55 Hage, W.: 'Der Weg nach Asien: Die ostsyrische Missionskirche', in: Schäferdiek, K. (ed.), *Die Kirchen des frühen Mittelalters*, Munich 1978 (Kirchengeschichte als Missionsgeschichte II,1) [= Hage 1978a], p. 365.
56 Mingana 1925, p. 325.
57 Mingana 1925, p. 325
58 Klein, W. & Tubach, J.: 'Ein syrisch-christliches Fragment aus Dunhuang / China', in: *ZDMG* 144 (1994), pp. 1–13 & 446.
59 Sims-Williams, N. & Hamilton, J.: *Documents turco-sogdiens du IXe–Xe siècle de Touen-houang*, London 1990 (Corpus Inscriptionum Iranicarum, Part II, 3), pp. 23f.
60 Sims-Williams & Hamilton 1990, pp. 51f. Cf. also Sims-Williams 1992, pp. 54f.
61 Uray, G.: 'Tibet's Connection with Nestorianism and Manichaeism in the 8th – 10th Centuries', in: Steinkellner, E. & Tauscher, H. (eds.), *Contributions on Tibetan Language, History and Culture*, vol. 1, Vienna 1983, p. 413; also idem: 'Zu den Spuren des Nestorianismus und des Manichäismus im alten Tibet (8. – 10. Jh.)', in: Heissig, W. & Klimkeit, H.-J. (eds.), *Synkretismus in den Religionen Zentralasiens [. . .]*, Wiesbaden 1987 (StOR 13), pp. 197–206.
62 Sims-Williams, N.: 'The Sogdian Inscriptions of Ladakh', in: Jettmar, K. et al. (eds.), *Antiquities of Northern Pakistan. Reports and Studies*, vol. 2, Mainz 1993, pp. 151–163. The text alongside the cross in pl. 27 has been translated by Sims-Williams (p. 155) thus: 'In the year 210 (i.e. 841/842 A.D.) we (were?) sent – (we, namely) Caitra the Samarkandian together with the monk Nošfarn (as) messenger(s) to the Tibetan Qaghan.' Sims-Williams sees these messengers, a Samarkandian and a Buddhist monk, as being sent to Tibet by the Uighur Turkish Khan after the invasion of his empire by the Kirghiz in AD 840.
63 We are indebted to Pastor Yonathan Paljor, Srinagar (Kashmir), for new photographs of these inscriptions.
64 Uray 1983, p. 407.
65 Uray 1983, pp. 408ff.
66 Saeki, P. Y.: *The Nestorian Documents and Relics in China*, 2nd ed., Tokyo 1951, pp. 453f. For Ephr(a)im = Fu-lin cf. pp. 109f.
67 Pigoulewsky, N.: 'Fragments Syriaques et Syro-Turcs de Hara-Hoto et de Tourfan', in: *Revue de l'Orient Chrétien* 30 (1935–1936), pp. 3–46.
68 Mingana 1925, pp. 324f.; Hage 1978a, p. 372.
69 Mingana 1925, p. 324.

70 Mingana 1925, pp. 308f.
71 E. C. D. Hunter, in discussing the various dates suggested, opts for the date AD 1007. Hunter 1989–1991, pp. 157ff.
72 Mingana 1925, p. 309. For a complete English translation of this work cf. Budge, E. A. W. (trans.): *The Chronography of Gregory Ab'l Faraj [. . .]. Being the First Part of his Political History of the World [. . .]*, 2 vols., Oxford 1932.
73 For the legends about Prester John cf. Rachewiltz, I. de: *Papal Envoys to the Great Khans*, London 1971 (Great Travellers), pp. 19–40.
74 Mingana 1925, p. 310.
75 Mingana 1925, pp. 310f. It should be pointed out here that the name of the son of the Nestorian King George who flourished in the Ordos area in the 13th cent. was John, he being named after John of Montecorvino. However, he seems to have died young. Cf. Ch'en Yüan: 'On the Damaged Tablets Discovered by Mr. D. Martin in Inner Mongolia', in: *MSer* 3 (1938), pp. 250–256.
76 Hunter 1989–1991, pp. 156f.
77 Hunter 1989–1991, pp. 161f.
78 Dawson 1980, p. 122.
79 Hage 1978a, p. 379.
80 Hage 1978a, p. 370.
81 Enoki, K.: 'The Nestorian Christianism in China in Medieval Time According to Recent Historical and Archaeological Researches', in: *Atti del Convegno Internazionale sul Tema: l'Oriente cristiano nella storia della civiltà [. . .]*, Rome 1984 (Problemi attuali di scienza e di cultura 62), pp. 45ff. Cf. also Ch'en Yüan 1938.
82 Murayama, S.: 'Über die nestorianischen Grabinschriften in der inneren Mongolei und in Südchina', in: *op. cit.* n. 81, pp. 77–81.
83 Grœnbech, K.: 'Turkish Inscriptions from Inner Mongolia', in: *MSer* 4 (1939–1940), p. 305.
84 Cf. Saeki 1951, pp. 423ff. For the use of the cross in Central and East Asia cf. Moule, A. C.: 'The Use of the Cross among the Nestorians in China', in: *TP* 28 (1931), pp. 78–86; Klimkeit, H.-J.: 'Das Kreuzessymbol in der zentralasiatischen Religionsbegegnung', in: *ZRGG* 31 (1979), pp. 99–116.
85 Dawson 1955, p. 137.
86 Cf. Chwolson, D.: *Syrische Grabinschriften aus Semirjetschie*, St. Petersburg 1886 (MAIS, 7e série, 34,4); idem: *Syrisch-nestorianische Grabinschriften aus Semirjetschie. Nebst einer Beilage [. . .]*, St. Petersburg 1890 (MAIS, 7e série, 37,8); idem: *Syrisch-nestorianische Grabinschriften aus Semirjetschie. Neue Folge*, St. Petersburg 1897. Cf. also Hjelt, A.: *Drei syrisch-nestorianische Grabinschriften*, Helsinki 1909 (Annales Academiae Scientiarum Fennicae, Series B, 1, 2); Nau, F.: 'Les pierres tombales nestoriennes en Asie', in: *Annales du Musée Guimet. Bibliothèque de vulgarisation*, vol. 40: *Conférences faites en 1913*, Paris 1914, pp. 193–388. Cf. also Thacker, T. W.: 'A Nestorian Gravestone from Central Asia in the Gulbenkian Museum, Durham University', in: *The Durham University Journal* 59, N. S. 28 (1966–1967), pp. 94–107; Džumagulov, Č.: 'Die syrisch-türkischen (nestorianischen) Denkmäler in Kirgisien', in: *MIO* 14 (1968), pp. 470–480.
87 Džumagulov 1968, p. 472.
88 Cf. Spuler, B.: 'Die Mongolen und das Christentum. Die letzte Blütezeit der morgenländischen Kirchen', in: *Internationale Kirchliche Zeitschrift* 28 (1938), pp. 156–175; Saunders, J. J.: 'The Decline and Fall of Christianity in Medieval Asia', in: *JRH* 5 (1968–1969), pp. 93–104.
89 Cf. Klein, W.: 'Christliche Reliefgrabsteine des 14. Jahrhunderts von der Seidenstrasse. Ergänzungen zu einer alttürkischen und zwei syrischen

Inschriften sowie eine bildliche Darstellung', in: Lavenant, R. (ed.), *VI Symposium Syriacum 1992 [. . .]*, Rome 1994 (OCA 247), pp. 419–442.

90 Published in Džumagulov, Č.: *Jazyk siro-tjurkskich (nestorianskich) pamjanikov Kirgizii*, Frunze 1971, pp. 120–123. For a new German translation see Klein 1994, p. 432.

91 Cf. Stewart, J.: *Nestorian Missionary Enterprise. The Story of a Church on Fire [. . .]*, (1928), repr., New York 1979, p. 206.

92 Saeki 1951, p. 414.

93 Cf. Mingana 1925, p. 335; Stewart 1979, pp. 206f.

94 For a more comprehensive evaluation of the Semiriče inscriptions cf. Stewart 1979, pp. 198–213.

95 Hage 1978a, p. 372.

96 Džumagulov 1968, p. 473.

97 Hage 1978a, p. 372; Džumagulov 1968, p. 474.

98 Džumagulov 1968, p. 478.

99 They played a major role in the early history of the Mongol Empire, as recorded in the *Secret History of the Mongols* which was written in 1241. Cf. Cleaves, Fr. W. (ed. & trans.): *Secret History of the Mongols*, Cambridge, Mass. 1982 (Harvard-Yenching Institute Publications); Taube, M.: *Geheime Geschichte der Mongolen. Herkunft, Leben und Aufstieg Činggis Qans*, Munich 1989 (Orientalische Bibliothek).

100 Vine, A. R.: *The Nestorian Churches. A Concise History of Nestorian Christianity in Asia from the Persian Schism to the Modern Assyrians [. . .]*, (1937), repr., New York 1980, p. 130.

101 Hage 1978a, p. 372.

102 Moule & Pelliot 1938, vol. 1, p. 156.

103 Hage 1978a, p. 372.

104 Quoted in Stewart 1979, p. 213. For the many gravestones of Christians who died in this year of the plague cf. Chwolson 1897, pp. 33–36.

105 Cf. Hage 1978a, pp. 391f., n. 166.

106 For the situation of Christians under Persian Shahs and Abbasid Caliphs up to 820 in the light of Syrian sources, cf. Young, W. G.: *Patriarch, Shah and Caliph. A Study of the Relationship of the Church of the East with the Sassanid Empire and the Early Caliphates with Special Reference to Available Translated Syriac Sources*, Rawalpindi 1974, and pp. 127–143 above. Cf. also Spuler 1968 and Saunders 1968/69.

107 Mingana, A.: 'A Charter of Protection Granted to the Nestorian Church in A. D. 1138 by Muktafi II, Caliph of Bagdad', in: *BJRL* 10 (1926), pp. 127–133.

108 Cf. Stewart 1979, pp. 217ff.

109 Cf. Stewart 1979, pp. 218ff.

110 Cf. Stewart 1979, p. 228.

111 Cf. Troll, Chr. W.: 'Die Chinamission im Mittelalter', in: *Franziskanische Studien* 48 (1966), p. 116.

112 For this and the following cf. Troll 1966, p. 117.

113 Golzio, K.-H.: *Regents in Central Asia since the Mongol Empire*, Cologne 1985 (AR 12), p. 35.

114 Cf. Stewart 1979, p. 285.

115 Cf. Stewart 1979, p. 209.

116 Heissig, W.: *The Religions of the Mongols*, trans. [. . .] by G. Samuel, Berkeley & London 1980, p. 24.

117 It should be pointed out, however, that Christian traces are visible in the tradition of the Mongol Erkut. Cf. Mostaert, A.: 'Ordosica: I. Les Erkut,

descendants des chrétiens médiévaux, chez les Mongols Ordos', in: *Bulletin de l'Université Catholique de Pékin* 9 (1934), pp. 1–20; Ramstedt, G. J.: 'Reste des Nestorianismus unter den Mongolen', in: *JSFO* 55 (1951), pp. 40–46.

118 Cf. Hage, W.: 'Apostolische Kirche des Ostens (Nestorianer)', in: Heyer, F. (ed.), *Konfessionskunde*, Berlin & New York 1977 (De-Gruyter-Lehrbuch), pp. 208ff. and Bibliography, pp. 211–214.

119 Cf. Hage, W.: *Untersuchungen zum Leben der Christen Zentralasiens im Mittelalter*, 'Habilitationsschrift', unpublished, Marburg [1970], pp. 12ff. Prof. Hage kindly made available the MS of his thesis, to be published in due course. Source references to the following can be found here (chap. 1, 'Priesterstand').

120 Cf. Hage 1977, p. 206.

121 The following presentation is indebted to Hage 1970, pp. 20ff. (chap. 2, 'Mönchtum').

122 Cf. Dieterich, K.: *Byzantinische Quellen zur Länder- und Völkerkunde (5. – 15. Jh.)*, vol. 1, Leipzig 1912 (Quellen und Forschungen zur Erd- und Kulturkunde 5), p. 19.

123 Zieme, P.: 'Zu den nestorianisch-türkischen Turfantexten', in: Hazai, G. & Zieme, P. (eds.), *Sprache, Geschichte und Kultur der altaischen Völker [. . .]*, Berlin 1974 (SGKAO 5), pp. 662f.

124 Hage has collected material on this aspect in chap. 4 ('Christen in staatlichen Diensten') of his *Untersuchungen* (Hage 1970).

125 Cf. Budge 1928, pp. 127ff.

126 Hage 1970, p. 23.

127 Ibid. Cf. also p. 9.

128 References to the following are given in Hage 1970, pp. 23ff.

129 A survey of the history of this church is given by Hage, W.: 'Jakobitische Kirche', in: *TRE* 16 (1987), pp. 474–485.

130 Chabot, J.-B.: 'Les évêques Jacobites du VIIIe au XIIIe siècle, d'aprés la Chronique de Michel le Syrien', in: *Revue de l'Orient Chrétien* 4 (1899), pp. 444–451, 495–511; 5 (1900), pp. 605–636; 6 (1901), pp. 189–220.

131 Bedjan, P. (ed.): *Gregorii Barhebraei Chronicon Syriacum [. . .]*, Paris 1890; Abbeloos, J. B. & Lamy, T. J. (eds.): *Gregorii Barhebraei Chronicon Ecclesiasticum [. . .]*, 3 vols., Louvain 1872–1877.

132 This material is evaluated in Hunter 1989–1991.

133 For Jacobites in Central Asia see Hunter 1992, pp. 365–368.

134 Dauvillier, J.: 'L'expansion de l'Église syrienne en Asie Centrale et en Extrême-Orient', in: *L'Orient Syrien* 1 (1956), pp. 76–87.

135 Hunter 1992, p. 368.

136 Hage, W.: 'Das Nebeneinander der christlichen Konfessionen im mittelalterlichen Zentralasien', in: Vogt, W. (ed.), *17. Deutscher Orientalistentag vom 21. –27. Juli 1968 in Würzburg. Vorträge*, Part 2, Wiesbaden 1969 (ZDMG Supplementa 1,2), pp. 517ff.

137 For these reports cf. Dawson 1955, pp. 3–72, 89–220. The reports of the Franciscan travellers to Central and East Asia are summed up in Rachewiltz 1971. Cf. also Cary-Elwes, C.: *China and the Cross. Studies in Missionary History*, London et al. 1957.

138 Cary-Elwes 1957, p. 39.

139 Cf. Troll 1966, p. 121.

140 Troll 1966, pp. 120f.

141 Dawson 1955, p. 75. Cf. Troll 1966, p. 121.

142 Ibid.

143 Dawson 1955, p. 76.
144 Dawson 1955, p. 3.
145 Dawson 1955, pp. 79–84.
146 Dawson 1955, p. 80.
147 Dawson 1955, p. 3.
148 Dawson 1955, p. 62.
149 Komroff, M.: *Contemporaries of Marco Polo [. . .]*, London 1929, pp. 46f.
150 Dawson 1955, pp. 83f.
151 Dawson 1955, pp. 85f.
152 Dawson 1955, p. 86.
153 Sinor, D.: 'John of Plano Carpini's Return from the Mongols. New Light from a Luxemburg Manuscript', in: *JRAS* 1957, p. 206.
154 Cf. Troll 1966, p. 122.
155 Cf. Troll 1966, pp. 123f.
156 Cf. Troll 1966, p. 124.
157 Cf. Troll 1966, p. 124.
158 Moule, A. C.: *Christians in China before the Year AD 1550*, London et al. 1930, p. 104, n. 17.
159 Dawson 1955, pp. 135f.
160 Dawson 1955, pp. 200f.
161 Hage 1969, pp. 515–523. Cf. also Hage, W.: 'Religiöse Toleranz in der nestorianischen Asienmission', in: Rendtorff, T. (ed.), *Glaube und Toleranz. Das theologische Erbe der Aufklärung*, Gütersloh 1982, pp. 99–110.
162 Hage 1969, p. 519.
163 Ibid.
164 Ibid.
165 Hage 1969, p. 520.
166 For the spread of Armenians cf. Dauvillier, J.: 'Les Arméniens en Chine et en Asie Centrale au Moyen Age', in: *Mélanges de Sinologie offerts à Monsieur Paul Demiéville* II, Paris 1974 (Bibliothèque de l'Institut des hautes études chinoises 20), pp. 1–17.
167 For the spread of the Melkites in Central Asia cf. Sims-Williams 1992, pp. 46ff. See also Klein, W.: 'Zentralasien', in: Müller, K. & Ustorf, W. (eds.), *Einleitung in die Missionsgeschichte. Tradition, Situation und Dynamik des Christentums*, Stuttgart 1995 (Theologische Wissenschaft 18), pp. 121–130.
168 For this and the following cf. Hage 1969, pp. 520f.
169 Quoted in Hage 1969, p. 521.
170 Quoted in Browne, L. E.: *The Eclipse of Christianity in Asia from the Time of Muhammad till the Fourteenth Century*, (1933), repr., New York 1967, p. 66.
171 Hage 1969, p. 522.
172 Cf. Hage 1982, pp. 101ff.
173 Cf. Barthold 1901, p. 25, n. 1.
174 Moule 1930, p. 172.
175 Hage 1969, p. 525.
176 Thus according to information by Dr. W. Sundermann of the Turfan Project of the Berlin-Brandenburg Academy of Sciences of Berlin.
177 Cf. Müller, F. W. K.: 'Neutestamentliche Bruchstücke in soghdischer Sprache', in: *SPAW* 1907, pp. 260–270; idem: *Soghdische Texte I*, Berlin 1913 (APAW 1912, 2); Sundermann, W.: 'Nachlese zu F. W. K. Müller's "Soghdischen Texten I"', in: *AoF* 1 (1974), pp. 217–255; 3 (1975), pp. 55–90; 8 (1981), pp. 169–225.
178 An excellent survey of Christian literature from Turfan and Tunhuang is given in Sims-Williams 1992, pp. 43–61.

179 Hage, W.: 'Das Christentum in der Turfan-Oase. Zur Begegnung der Religionen in Zentralasien', in: Heissig, W. & Klimkeit, H.-J. (eds.), *Synkretismus in den Religionen Zentralasiens [. . .]*, Wiesbaden 1987 (StOR 13) [= Hage 1987a], p. 55. For Shamanistic influences in Christianity and vice versa in Mongolia cf. idem: 'Christentum und Schamanismus. Zur Krise des Nestorianertums in Zentralasien', in: Jaspert, B. & Mohr, R. (eds.), *Traditio – Krisis – Renovatio aus theologischer Sicht.* Festschrift W. Zeller zum 65. Geburtstag, Marburg 1976, pp. 114–124.
180 Peters, C.: 'Der Text der soghdischen Evangelienbruchstücke und das Problem der Pešiṭta', in: *Oriens Christianus* III, 11 (1936), pp. 153–162.
181 Cf. Hage 1970, p. 25. For the following observations cf. also Hage 1970, pp. 25ff.
182 Cf. Thompson, E. A.: 'Christian Missionaries among the Huns', in: *Hermathena* 67 (1946), pp. 73–79.
183 Moule 1930, p. 136.
184 Baumstark, A.: *Geschichte der syrischen Literatur*, (1922), repr., Berlin 1968, pp. 107ff.
185 Cf. Hansen 1968, p. 92. Cf. also Schwartz, M.: 'Sogdian Fragments of the *Book of Psalms*', in: *AoF* 1 (1974), pp. 257–261; Sundermann, W.: 'Einige Bemerkungen zum syrisch-neupersischen Psalmenbruchstück aus Chinesisch-Turkistan', in: Gignoux, G. & Tafazzoli, A. (eds.), *Mémorial Jean de Menasce*, Louvain 1974, pp. 441–492. Cf. also Sims-Williams 1992.
186 For Sogdian Christian literature cf. Hansen, O.: 'Die christliche Literatur der Soghdier, eine Übersicht', in: *Akademie der Wissenschaften und der Literatur. Jahrbuch 1951*, Wiesbaden 1951, pp. 296–302; idem: 'Der Anteil der Iranier an der Ausbreitung des Christentums nach Zentralasien', in: Vogt, W. (ed.), *17. Deutscher Orientalistentag vom 21. – 27. Juli 1968 in Würzburg. Vorträge*, Part 3, Wiesbaden 1969 (ZDMG Supplementa 1,3), pp. 1032–1035; Asmussen, J. P.: 'Iranische neutestamentliche Zitate und Texte und ihre textkritische Bedeutung', in: *AoF* 2 (1975), pp. 79–92; idem: 'The Sogdian and Uighur-Turkish Christian Literature in Central Asia before the Real Rise of Islam. A Survey', in: Hercus, L. A. et al. (eds.), *Indological and Buddhist Studies*. Volume in Honour of Professor J. W. de Jong on his Sixtieth Birthday, Canberra 1982, pp. 11–29; Schwartz, M.: *Studies in the Texts of Sogdian Christians*, [PhD thesis, University of California], Berkeley 1967. See also Sims-Williams 1992.
187 Text and German trans. in Müller 1913, pp. 85ff.
188 Note to the author in September 1987.
189 Cf. Sims-Williams, N.: *The Christian Sogdian Manuscript C 2*, Berlin 1983 (BT 12).
190 Cf. Sims-Williams, N.: 'A Sogdian Fragment of the Work of Dadišoʻ Qaraya', in: *Asia Major* 18 (1973), pp. 88–205; Sims-Williams 1985, pp. 78–86.
191 E.g. Sundermann, W.: 'Ein Bruchstück einer soghdischen Kirchengeschichte aus Zentralasien?', in: *AA* 14 (1976), pp. 95–101.
192 Hansen 1968, cf. p. 13 and pp. 26ff. Hansen comes to the conclusion that the term 'corrupter' (Gr. *apollyon*) is not to be mistaken for Apollon, the Greek God.
193 Cf. Asmussen 1982, pp. 19f. Another discussion between a teacher and his student is published in Sundermann, W.: 'Der Schüler fragt den Lehrer. Eine Sammlung biblischer Rätsel in soghdischer Sprache', in: *A Green Leaf.* Papers in Honour of Professor Jes P. Asmussen, Leiden 1988 (Acta Iranica 28), pp. 173–186. The text is made up of a series of riddles on Biblical questions.
194 Dawson 1955, p. 137.
195 Sims-Williams 1992, pp. 54ff.

196 Sims-Williams 1992, pp. 50ff.
197 Cf. Asmussen 1982, pp. 20ff.
198 Asmussen 1982, p. 21. Cf. Müller, F. W. K.: *Uigurica [I]*, Berlin 1908 (APAW 1908, 2), p. 9.
199 Hansen, O.: *Berliner soghdische Texte I. Bruchstücke einer soghdischen Version der Georgspassion (C 2)*, Berlin 1941 (APAW 1941, 10), p. 9.
200 Cf. Asmussen 1982, p. 22.
201 Cf. Asmussen 1982, p. 23. Cf. Bang, W.: 'Türkische Bruchstücke einer nestorianischen Georgspassion', in: *Le Muséon* 39 (1926), pp. 41–75.
202 Arlotto, A.: 'Old Turkic Oracle Books', in: *MSer* 29 (1970–1971), pp. 693–696, 'Appendix: The So-Called Christian Oracle-Book'; Zieme, P.: 'Zwei Ergänzungen zu der christlich-türkischen Handschrift T II B 1', in: *AoF* 5 (1977), p. 271f.
203 Asmussen 1982, p. 22.
204 Arlotto 1970–1971, p. 695. A fragment from a similar text, belonging to the British Museum (Or. 8212/182), is regarded by N. Sims-Williams as belonging to an oracular book, 'such as is known in many languages' in Central Asia. Sims-Williams, N.: 'The Sogdian Fragments of the British Library', in: *Indo-Iranian Journal* 18 (1976), pp. 63f. Here Sims-Williams points out that the Turkish text quoted above was recognized by F. C. Burkitt as 'a version of what has been known in the West as the *Sortes Apostolorum*' (p. 64).
205 Zieme, P.: 'Zu den nestorianisch-türkischen Turfantexten', in: Hazai, G. & Zieme, P. (eds.), *Sprache, Geschichte und Kultur der altaischen Völker [. . .]*, Berlin 1974 (SGKAO 5), pp. 661–668.
206 Cf. Zieme 1974, pp. 662–665.
207 Zieme, P.: 'Ein Hochzeitssegen uigurischer Christen', in: Röhrborn, K. & Brands, H. W. (eds.), *Scholia. Beiträge zur Turkologie und Zentralasienkunde [. . .]*, Wiesbaden 1981 (Veröffentlichungen der Societas Uralo-Altaica 74) [= Zieme 1981a], pp. 221–232.
208 Zieme 1974, p. 666.
209 Pigoulewsky 1935–1936, pp. 29–31.
210 Syriac texts from Turfan have been edited by Maróth, M.: 'Ein Fragment eines syrischen pharmazeutischen Rezeptbuches aus Turfan', in: *AoF* 11 (1984), pp. 115–125; idem: 'Ein Brief aus Turfan', in: *AoF* 12 (1985), pp. 283–287.
211 Hage, W.: 'Einheimische Volkssprachen und syrische Kirchensprache in der nestorianischen Asienmission', in: Wiessner, G. (ed.), *Erkenntnisse und Meinungen* II, Wiesbaden 1978 (Göttinger Orientforschungen I. Reihe: Syriaca 17) [= Hage, 1978b], p. 131.
212 Cf. Hage 1978b, p. 136.
213 Hage 1978b, pp. 137f.
214 Sachau, E.: 'Litteratur-Bruchstücke aus Chinesisch-Turkistan', in: *SPAW* 1905, pp. 964–977. For an English translation cf. Saeki 1951, pp. 337–347. Engberding, H: 'Fünf Blätter eines alten ostsyrischen Bitt- und Bussgottesdienstes aus Innerasien', in: *Ostkirchliche Studien* 14 (1965), pp. 121–148.
215 Maróth 1985, pp. 283–287.
216 Hage 1978b, pp. 137f. Cf. Mingana 1925, pp. 336f. A copy of this text has found its way into the John Rylands Library, Manchester, where it is preserved as *Ryland Syr. 4*. I thank Dr. J. F. Coakley of Lancaster University, who is finishing a catalogue of the Syrian mss. (to be published in the Library's *Bulletin*), for information on this text.
217 Cf. e.g. Sims-Williams, N.: 'Syro-Sogdica III: Syriac Elements in Sogdian', in: *A Green Leaf. Papers in Honour of Professor J. P. Asmussen*, Leiden 1988 (Acta Iranica 26), pp. 145–156.

218 Hage 1978b, p. 138; Saeki 1951, p. 254.
219 Hage 1978b, p. 138; Saeki 1951, pp. 315–333, 337–347.
220 Hage 1978b, p. 139. For further examples of Syrian being used in Central and East Asia cf. Hage 1978b, pp. 139ff.
221 Taylor, W. R.: 'Syriac MSS Found in Peking, ca. 1925', in: *JAOS* 61 (1941), pp. 91–97.
222 For the 'Codex Cumanicus' cf. Bang, W.: 'Der Komanische Marienpsalter', in: *Abhandlungen der Königlichen Gesellschaft der Wissenschaften zu Göttingen*, Phil.-hist. Kl., N.F. 13 (1914), pp. 241–276; and for the Christian mission to the Cumans cf. Vásáry, I.: 'Orthodox Christian Qumans and Tatars of the Crimea in the 13th – 14th Centuries', in: *CAJ* 32 (1988), pp. 260–271.
223 Cf. Gabain, A. von: 'Die Sprache des Codex Cumanicus', in: Deny, J. et al. (eds.), *Philologiae Turcicae Fundamenta*, vol. 1, Wiesbaden 1959, pp. 46–49.
224 Poppe, N.: 'A Middle Turkic Text of the Apostles' Creed', in: *MSer* 24 (1965), pp. 273–306.
225 Hage 1987a, pp. 54f.
226 Note to the author of September 1987.
227 For a survey of Christian apocryphal literature used by the Manicheans cf. Puech, H.-Ch.: 'Gnostic Gospels and Related Documents', in: Hennecke, E. & Schneemelcher, W. (eds.), *New Testament Apocrypha*, vol. 1, London 1963, pp. 231–362; Sundermann, W.: 'Christliche Evangelientexte in der Überlieferung der iranisch-manichäischen Literatur', in: *MIO* 14 (1968), pp. 386–405; Klimkeit, H.-J.: 'Die Kenntnis apokrypher Evangelien in Zentral- und Ostasien', in: Tongerloo, A. van & Giversen, S. (eds.), *Manichaica Selecta*. Studies presented to Professor J. Ries on the Occasion of his Seventieth Birthday, Louvain 1991 (Manichaean Studies 1), pp. 149–175. For Enochic literature in Central Asia cf. Milik, J. T. (ed.): *The Books of Enoch. Aramaic Fragments of Qumrān Cave 4*, Oxford 1976, pp. 298ff.; Klimkeit, H.-J.: 'Der Buddha Henoch: Qumran und Turfan', in: *ZRGG* 32 (1980), pp. 367–376; Sundermann, W.: 'Ein weiteres Fragment aus Manis Gigantenbuch', in: *Orientalia J. Duchesne-Guillemin Oblata*, Leiden 1984 (Acta Iranica 23), pp. 491–505. Reeves, J. C.: *Jewish Lore in Manichaean Cosmogony. Studies in the Book of the Giants Traditions*, Cincinnati 1992 (Monographs of the Hebrew Union College). For the Manichean version of the *Shepherd of Hermas* cf. Müller, F. W. K.: 'Eine Hermas-Stelle in manichäischer Version', in: *SPAW* 1905, pp. 1077–1083; Cirillo, L.: '"Hermae Pastor" and "Revelatio Manichaica". Some Remarks', in: Wiessner, G. & Klimkeit, H.-J. (eds.), *Studia Manichaica [. . .]*, Wiesbaden 1992 (StOR 23), pp. 189–197.
228 Cf. Klimkeit, H.-J.: 'Jesus' Entry into Parinirvāṇa: Manichaean Identity in Buddhist Central Asia', in: *Numen* 33 (1986), pp. 225–240.
229 Cf. Zieme 1974, pp. 661–668; Zieme 1981a, pp. 221–232.
230 Zieme 1974, pp. 666f.
231 Cf. Klimkeit, H.-J.: 'Christentum und Buddhismus in der innerasiatischen Religionsbegegnung', in: *ZRGG* 33 (1981), pp. 208–220.
232 Thus in the texts published in Sims-Williams 1985. For Buddhist-Christian and Buddhist-Manichaean interrelations cf. also Klimkeit, H.-J.: 'Das Kreuzessymbol in der zentralasiatischen Religionsbegegnung', in: *ZRGG* 31 (1979), pp. 99–116; idem: 'Gottes- und Selbsterfahrung in der gnostisch-buddhistischen Religionsbegegnung Zentralasiens', in: *ZRGG* 35 (1983), pp. 236–247; idem: 'Christian-Buddhist Encounter in Medieval Central Asia', in: Houston, G. W. (ed.), *The Cross and the Lotus*, Delhi 1985, pp. 9–24.

233 Cf. Hage 1976, pp. 114–124; idem: 'Kulturelle Kontakte des ostsyrischen Christentums in Zentralasien', in: Lavenant, R. (ed.), *Les contacts du monde syriaque avec les autres cultures [. . .]*, Rome 1983 (OCA 221), pp. 143–154.

234 Cf. Granö, J. G.: 'Archäologische Beobachtungen von meinen Reisen in den nördlichen Grenzgegenden Chinas in den Jahren 1906 und 1907', in: *JSFO* 26 (1909), plates III & XI.

235 Tekin, Ş.: *Maitrisimit nom bitig. Die uigurische Übersetzung eines Werkes der buddhistischen Vaibhāṣika-Schule*, vol. 1, Berlin 1983 (BT 9), pp. 25f.

236 Cf. Klimkeit, H.-J.: 'Religion in a Pluralistic Society: The Case of Central Asia', in: Bianchi, U. (ed.), *The Notion of 'Religion' in Comparative Research. Selected Proceedings of the XVIth Congress of the International Association for the History of Religions [. . .]*, Rome 1994 (Storia delle religioni 8), pp. 89–96.

237 Cf., for instance, Zieme, P.: *Buddhistische Stabreimdichtungen der Uiguren*, Berlin 1985 (BT 13), pp. 73f., 164, 167 (blessing on the enemy).

238 Quoted after Robinson, J. M. (ed.): *The Nag Hammadi Library in English*, 3rd ed., Leiden 1988, p. 142. Cf. Schneemelcher, W. (ed.): *Neutestamentliche Apokryphen*, vol. 1, 6th ed., Tübingen 1990, p. 155.

239 Usually it says that living beings give themselves to the Buddha as a pawn, or forfeit, or that he accepts them as such. Thus in the *Maitrisimit*, the historical Buddha Shakyamuni says to his successsor Maitreya, the future Buddha: 'I have received all living beings from the (former) Buddha Kashyapa as a ransom (or a forfeit: *urunčaq*); thus also accept them from me as a ransom.' Geng Shimin & Klimkeit, H.-J.: *Das Zusammentreffen mit Maitreya. Die ersten fünf Kapitel der Hami-Version der Maitrisimit [. . .]*, part 1, Wiesbaden 1988 (AsF 103), pp. 260f. The peculiar use of the word *urunčaq* in Turkish Buddhist texts needs further investigation.

240 Quoted after Robinson 1988, p. 135.

241 Quoted after Steinilber-Oberlin, É.: *The Buddhist Sects of Japan. Their History, Philosophical Doctrines and Sanctuaries*, (1938), repr., Westport, Conn. 1976, pp. 67f. Cf. also Cook, F. H.: *Hua-yen Buddhism. The Jewel Net of Indra*, University Park & London 1977, pp. 90ff.

242 Turkish text and German transl. in Zieme, P.: 'Uigurische Steuerbefreiungs-urkunden für buddhistische Klöster', in: *AoF* 8 (1981), p. 242, n. 46.

243 Cf. Klimkeit, H.-J.: 'Manichäische und buddhistische Beichtformeln aus Turfan. Beobachtungen zur Beziehung zwischen Gnosis und Mahāyāna', in: *ZRGG* 29 (1977), pp. 193–228. For confessional practices in the Nestorian Church cf. Hage 1977, pp. 210f.

244 For the strong emphasis on faith, and grace, found in Amitābha theology, but also in Central Asian and Chinese commentaries on basic sutras, cf. Zieme, P. & Kudara, K.: *Guanwuliangshoujing in Uigur*, Kyoto 1985; Bang, W. & Gabain, A. von: 'Türkische Turfan-Texte V. Aus buddhistischen Schriften', in: *SPAW* 1931, pp. 340–349 (Text B: 'Die zehnfache Auslegung des Glaubens').

245 Cf. Boyce, M.: *The Manichaean Hymn-Cycles in Parthian*, London 1954 (London Oriental Series 3); Sundermann, W.: *The Manichaean Hymn Cycles Huyadagmān and Angad Rōšnān in Parthian and Sogdian*, London 1990 (Corpus Inscriptio-num Iranicarum, Supplementary Series 2). For the Buddhist *Sukhāvatī* texts, the classical documents on Amitābha's Realm of Light, cf. Cowell, E. B. et al. (trans.): *Buddhist Mahāyāna Texts [. . .]*, (1894), repr., Delhi 1965 (Sacred Books of the East 49).

10 CHRISTIANS IN CHINA

1 Here and in the following we sum up and supplement the information collected by Latourette, K. S.: *A History of Christian Missions in China*, (1929), repr., Taipei 1966, pp. 48–51. Cf. also Gensichen, H.-W.: 'Asien, Christliche Kirchen in', in: *TRE* 4 (1979), pp. 177–180 & 194.

2 Quoted in Latourette 1966, p. 48, n. 11. Cf. Yule, H. (trans. & ed.): *Cathay and the Way thither [. . .]*, new ed. by H. Cordier, vol. 1, London 1913, p. 101.

3 Latourette 1966, p. 49.

4 Cf. ibid. See discussion above and his Appendix B, n. 3.

5 Garbe, R.: *Indien und das Christentum. Eine Untersuchung der religionsgeschichtlichen Zusammenhänge*, Tübingen 1914. Critical of this is Klatt, N.: *Literarkritische Beiträge zum Problem christlich-buddhistischer Parallelen*, Cologne 1982 (AR 8). Derrett, J. D. M.: 'Der Wasserwandel in christlicher und buddhistischer Perspektive', in: *ZRGG* 41 (1989), pp. 193–214; Klatt, N.: *Jesu und Buddhas Wasserwandel [. . .]*, Göttingen 1990.

6 Cf. Conze, E.: 'Buddhism and Gnosis', in: Bianchi, U. (ed.), *Le origini dello gnosticismo [. . .]*, Leiden 1967 (SHR 12), pp. 651–667. Cf. also Cowell, E. B.: 'The Northern Buddhist Legend of Avalokiteśwara's Descent into the Hell Avîchi', in: *IndAnt* 8 (1879), pp. 249–353 (influence of the *Gospel of Nicodemus* on the *Kāraṇḍavyūha*); Hoffmann, H.: *Die Religionen Tibets. Bon und Lamaismus in ihrer geschichtlichen Entwicklung*, Freiburg & Munich 1956, pp. 40ff. (Gnosticism and Manichaeism and their influence on developing Mahāyāna, referring to G. Tucci); idem: 'Kālacakra Studies I: Manichaeism, Christianity, and Islam in the "Kālacakra Tantra"', in: *CAJ* 13 (1969), pp. 52–73; Conze, E.: 'Buddhist *prajñā* and Greek *sophia*', in: *Religion* 5 (1975), pp. 160–167.

7 Cf. Sundermann, W.: 'Zur frühen missionarischen Wirksamkeit Manis', in: *AOH* 24 (1971), pp. 79–125; idem, *Mitteliranische manichäische Texte kirchengeschichtlichen Inhalts*, Berlin 1981 (BT 11), pp. 18ff.

8 Cf. Klimkeit, H.-J.: *Die Begegnung von Christentum, Gnosis und Buddhismus an der Seidenstrasse*, Opladen 1986 (RhWAW.G 283); idem: 'Buddha als Vater', in: Waldenfels, H. & Immoos, T. (eds.), *Fernöstliche Weisheit und christlicher Glaube. Festgabe für H. Dumoulin zur Vollendung des 80. Lebensjahres*, Mainz 1985, pp. 235–259.

9 Cf. Moule 1930, p. 68f. We shall return to this remarkable co-operation at a later point.

10 For the Medieval Christian encounter with Buddhism cf. Almond, P. C.: 'The Medieval West and Buddhism', in: *The Eastern Buddhist* N.S. 19 (1986), pp. 85–101.

11 Latourette 1966, p. 49f. Cf. Dihle, A.: 'Serer und Chinesen', in: idem, *Antike und Orient. Gesammelte Aufsätze [. . .]*, Heidelberg 1984 (Supplemente zu den Sitzungsberichten der Heidelberger Akademie der Wissenschaften, Phil.-hist. Kl., Jg. 1983, 2), pp. 201–215.

12 Evidence in Latourette 1966, p. 50.

13 Ibid.

14 Ibid.

15 Liu Ts'un-yan: *Selected Papers from the Hall of Harmonious Winds*, Leiden 1976, p. 55.

16 Cf. Bauer, W. (ed.): *China und die Fremden. 3000 Jahre Auseinandersetzung in Krieg und Frieden*, Munich 1980.

17 Cf. Tsui Chi: 'Mo Ni Chiao Hsia Pu Tsan. "The Lower (Second?) Section of the Manichaean Hymns"', in: *BSOAS* 11 (1943–1946), pp. 174–219; Lieu, S. N. C.:

Manichaeism in the Later Roman Empire and Medieval China. A Historical Survey, 2nd ed., Tübingen 1992 (Wissenschaftliche Untersuchungen zum Neuen Testament 63), pp. 243–255; Bryder, P.: *The Chinese Transformation of Manichaeism. A Study of Chinese Manichaean Terminology*, Löberöd 1985; Schmidt-Glintzer, H. (ed.): *Chinesische Manichaica. Mit textkritischen Anmerkungen und einem Glossar*, Wiesbaden 1987 (StOR 14); idem: 'Das buddhistische Gewand des Manichäismus. Zur buddhistischen Terminologie in den chinesischen Manichaica', in: Heissig, W. & Klimkeit, H.-J. (eds.), *Synkretismus in den Religionen Zentralasiens [. . .]*, Wiesbaden 1987 (StOR 13), pp. 76–90.

18 Cf. Lieu 1992, pp. 240–242 & 263–304.

19 Cf. Hansen, O.: 'Die Literatur der Sogdier', in: Einsiedel, W. von (ed.), *Die Literaturen der Welt in ihrer mündlichen und schriftlichen Überlieferung*, Zürich 1965, pp. 929–932.

20 Latourette 1966, p. 52.

21 Havret, H.: *La stèle chrétienne de Si-ngan-fou*, part 2: *Histoire du monument*, Shanghai 1897 (Variétés sinologiques 12), p. 247.

22 Moule 1930, pp. 65–77; cf. also Drake, F. S.: 'Nestorian Monasteries of the T'ang Dynasty', in: *MSer* 2 (1936–1937), pp. 293–340.

23 Moule 1930, p. 65.

24 Eichhorn, W.: *Die Religionen Chinas*, Stuttgart 1973 (RM 21), p. 256.

25 Moule 1930, p. 66; cf. Saeki 1951, p. 459.

26 Ibid.

27 Moule 1930, p. 67.

28 Cf. on this monastery, Saeki 1951, pp. 390–399.

29 Eichhorn 1973, p. 256.

30 Ibid.

31 Pelliot, P.: 'Chrétiens d'Asie Centrale et d' Extrême-Orient', in: *TP* 28 (1931), pp. 623–644. Cf. Moule 1930, p. 72, n. 86.

32 For reports on the discovery and the subsequent discussion about the monument's authenticity cf. Moule 1930, pp. 27–33 and Saeki 1951, pp. 11–25.

33 For the discussion on the place of its erection cf. Moule, A. C.: 'The Nestorians in China', in: *JRAS* 1933, pp. 118–120; idem: *Nestorians in China. Some Corrections and Additions*, London 1940 (Sinological Series 1), pp. 7–12; Drake 1936–1937, pp. 293ff.; Saeki 1951, pp. 33–37 and Hsü, C. Y.: 'Nestorianism and the Nestorian Monument in China', in: *Asian Culture Quarterly* 14 (1986), pp. 41–81, especially pp. 48–52. A succinct summary of the contents of the Nestorian tablet of Sian-fu is given by Drake, F. S.: 'Nestorian Literature of the T'ang Dynasty', in: *ChinRec* 66 (1935) [= Drake 1935a], pp. 609–614.

34 We refer in the following mainly to the translation of Moule 1930, pp. 34–51, also taking Saeki's rendering into account. Cf. Saeki 1951, pp. 53–77. A new translation is by Hsü 1986, pp. 41–81, where further references on the subject can be found. A good critical discussion of its content is to be found in: Mehlhorn, R.: 'Nestorianische Texte aus China', in: Vogt, W. (ed.), *17. Deutscher Orientalistentag vom 21. – 27. Juli 1968 in Würzburg. Vorträge*, Part 2, Wiesbaden 1969 (ZDMG Supplementa 1,2), pp. 443–449.

35 Moule 1930, p. 35.

36 Ibid.

37 Moule 1930, p. 43.

38 Moule, 1930, p. 44.

39 Moule 1930, pp. 44f.

40 Moule 1930, p. 45.

41 Saeki 1951, p. 37.

42 Ibid.; Moule 1931, p. 48.
43 Moule 1930, p. 35.
44 Moule 1930, p. 37.
45 The crucifixion, and the post-Anselmic interpretations placed upon it by European Christians, remains a stumbling block for some Asians to this day. It may be that the early Nestorians had already divined this.
46 Moule 1930, p. 38.
47 Ibid.
48 Ibid.
49 Moule 1930, pp. 38f.
50 Moule 1930, p. 39.
51 Ibid.
52 Moule 1930, p. 40.
53 Ibid.
54 Moule 1930, p. 41.
55 Cf. Drake 1936–1937, p. 306.
56 Moule 1930, p. 41.
57 Moule 1930, pp. 43f.
58 Moule 1930, p. 52, n. 51.
59 Drake 1935a, p. 614.
60 For the sealing of the library, either because of the advance of the Tanguts, as P. Pelliot surmised, or because it was a 'deposit of sacred waste', as M. A. Stein thought, cf. Fujieda, A.: 'The Tunhuang Manuscripts. A General Description, Part I', in: *Zinbun* 9 (1966), p. 15.
61 Cf. Moule 1930, p. 57. Cf. also Drake, F. S.: 'The Nestorian "Gloria in Excelsis Deo"', in: *ChinRec* 66 (1935), pp. 291–300. There is also a hitherto unedited Sogdian version of the *Gloria*. Cf. Sims-Williams 1992, p. 49.
62 Moule 1930, p. 57.
63 Moule 1930, p. 57.
64 Drake 1935a, p. 614.
65 Ibid.
66 Drake 1935a, p. 682.
67 Rosenkranz, G.: 'Die älteste Christenheit in China in den nestorianischen Quellenzeugnissen der Tang-Zeit', in: *ZMR* 52 (1937), p. 194.
68 Saeki 1951, pp. 116f. Cf. Drake 1935a, p. 679.
69 Drake 1935a, p. 678.
70 Saeki 1951, pp. 119f.
71 Cf. literary analysis in Drake 1935a, pp. 680f.
72 Saeki 1951, pp. 121–124.
73 Cf. Moule 1930, pp. 59–64 and Saeki 1951, pp. 125–146.
74 Cf. Saeki 1951, pp. 161–168.
75 Saeki 1951, pp. 174–193. Cf. Drake 1935a, pp. 683–685.
76 Saeki 1951, pp. 206–230. Cf. Drake 1935a, pp. 685–687.
77 For persecution by the Jews see the chapter on Christians in Arabia.
78 Cf. Moule 1930, p. 57; Saeki 1951, p. 276.
79 Moule 1930, pp. 55–57; Saeki 1951, pp. 273–276.
80 Saeki 1951, pp. 252f.
81 Moule 1930, p. 55.
82 Saeki 1951, pp. 314A – 314C.
83 Ibid., p. 314C.
84 Ibid., p. 314A.
85 Saeki 1951, p. 265.

86 Moule 1930, p. 53. Saeki 1951, p. 266, translates the title as 'A Nestorian Motwa Hymn in Adoration of the Holy Trinity'. Cf. Drake 1935a, p. 614.
87 Moule 1930, p. 53.
88 Moule 1930, p. 54.
89 Moule 1930, p. 55.
90 Cf. Tsui Chi 1943–1946, pp. 176ff.
91 Saeki 1951, pp. 312–313D.
92 Saeki 1951, p. 314.
93 Saeki 1951, p. 313C.
94 Saeki 1951, p. 313D.
95 Saeki 1951, pp. 281–302.
96 Saeki 1951, p. 281.
97 Cf. Taylor 1941; Saeki 1951, pp. 315–333, 419–422, 429–450. Cf. also his Appendices I–VII, pp. 453–470. See our discussion of this material within the scope of Christian literature in the chapter on Central Asia.
98 Cf. Goodrich, L. C.: 'Recent Discoveries at Zayton', in: *JAOS* 77 (1957), pp. 161–165; Enoki, K.: 'The Nestorian Christianism in China in Medieval Time according to Recent Historical and Archaeological Researches', in: *Atti del Convegno Internazionale sul tema: L'Oriente cristiano nella storia della civiltà [. . .],* Rome 1964 (Problemi attuali di scienza e di cultura 62), pp. 47–77; Murayama, S.: 'Über die nestorianischen Grabinschriften in der Inneren Mongolei und in Südchina', in: *ibid.* [= Murayama 1964a], pp. 77–81; idem: 'Eine nestorianische Grabinschrift in türkischer Sprache aus Zaiton', in: *UAJb* 35 (1964) [= Murayama 1964b], pp. 394–396); Peintinger, F. X.: 'Fund eines christlichen Grabsteins in Yangzhou (1344)', in: Mittag, A. (ed.), *In memoriam Achim Hildebrand. Gesammelte Aufsätze,* Munich 1991 (Chinablätter 18), pp. 65–72.
99 Moule 1930, pp. 68f.
100 Moule 1930, p. 69, n. 82.
101 For the further information on this matter cf. Drake 1936–1937, pp. 293–340.
102 Moule 1930, pp. 69f.
103 Moule 1930, p. 70.
104 Moule 1930, pp. 70f., n. 84.
105 Moule 1930, p. 71, n. 84. Cf. the claim in the Sian-fu inscription that the Christians kept no slaves p. 273.
106 Moule 1930, p. 76.
107 Moule 1930, pp. 75f.
108 Moule 1930, pp. 71f.
109 Moule 1930, pp. 72f.
110 Moule 1930, p. 73.
111 Saeki 1951, pp. 315–333.
112 Troll 1966, p. 126.
113 Franke, O.: *Geschichte des chinesischen Reiches,* vol. 4, Berlin 1948, pp. 431f.
114 Cf. Franke 1948, pp. 431ff.; Sagaster, K.: *Die weisse Geschichte (Čaγan teüke). Eine mongolische Quelle zur Lehre von den Beiden Ordnungen Religion und Staat in Tibet und in der Mongolei,* Wiesbaden 1976 (AsF 41), pp. 9–49.
115 Franke 1948, pp. 510ff.
116 Troll 1966, p. 129 (refering to W. Eberhard).
117 Franke 1948, p. 311.
118 For a well documented, succinct summary of Christianity in China under the Mongols cf. Latourette 1966, pp. 61–73.
119 For this and the following cf. Hage, W.: 'Der Weg nach Asien: Die ostsyrische Missionskirche', in: Schäferdiek, K. (ed.), *Die Kirchen des frühen Mittelalters,*

Munich 1978 (Kirchengeschichte als Missionsgeschichte II, 1) [= Hage 1978a], pp. 377–380.
120 Geng Shimin, Klimkeit, H.-J. & Laut, J. P.: 'Eine neue nestorianische Grabinschrift aus China', in: *UAJb* N. F. 14 (1996), p. 170.
121 Hage 1978a, p. 378.
122 Murayama 1964b, p. 395.
123 Murayama 1964b, p. 394.
124 Enoki 1964; Murayama 1964a and 1964b.
125 Peintinger 1991, p. 67.
126 Peintinger 1991, pp. 65ff.
127 Ligeti, L.: 'Les sept monastères Nestoriens de Mar Sargis', in: *AOH* 26 (1972), p. 170.
128 Hage 1978a, p. 379.
129 Moule 1930, p. 135.
130 Cf. Troll 1966, p. 132, n. 6.
131 Moule 1930, pp. 135f.
132 Quoted according to the translation of Lieu, S. N. C.: 'Nestorians and Manichaeans on the South China Coast', in: *VigChr* 34 (1980), p. 76.
133 Moule 1930, pp. 136f.
134 Moule 1930, p. 129.
135 Moule 1930, p. 131.
136 For the manuscript situation cf. Moule 1930, p. 128, and Lieu 1980, p. 85, n. 26 and n. 30. Marco's book became known under the title *Il Milione.*
137 Moule 1930, pp. 131f.
138 Moule 1930, p. 133. King George is mentioned not only by Marco Polo, but also in letters of the Franciscan Brother John of Montecorvino, in the Syrian story of Mar Yaballaha and in Chinese sources. Cf. Moule 1930, pp. 234–240.
139 Moule 1930, pp. 133f.
140 Moule 1930, p. 134.
141 Moule 1930, p. 135.
142 Cf. Moule 1930, p. 138.
143 Cf. Moule 1930, p. 140.
144 Cf. Moule 1930, p. 81 and pp. 138–143.
145 Moule 1930, p. 130 and pp. 141–143. Cf. also Lieu 1980, p. 79.
146 Moule 1930, p. 143.
147 Lieu 1980, p. 83.
148 Ibid.
149 Enoki 1964, pp. 48f.
150 Latourette 1966, p. 65.
151 Cf. Lieu 1980, pp. 71ff.
152 For the inscriptions and other materials from Zaitun cf. Enoki 1964, pp. 52ff., and Murayama 1964a and 1964b.
153 Quoted in Lieu 1980, p. 73. For the identical East Turkish version cf. Murayama 1964b, pp. 394–396. Murayama also translates the Chinese text.
154 Cf. Lieu 1980, pp. 73f., and Murayama 1964b, p. 396.
155 Enoki 1964, p. 63.
156 Hage 1978a, p. 373.
157 Moule 1930, p. 251.
158 Ibid.
159 Moule 1930, pp. 145–155.
160 Moule 1930, p. 149.
161 Cf. Ligeti 1972, pp. 171–177.

162 Moule 1930, p. 147.
163 Ibid.
164 Moule 1930, pp. 152–155.
165 Moule 1930, pp. 152f.
166 Cf. Moule 1930, pp. 94–127 for the account of their experiences. Cf. also Budge, E. A. W. (trans.): *The Monks of Ḵūblâi Khân, Emperor of China, or the History of the Life and Travels of Rabban Ṣâwmâ [. . .] and Marḵôs [. . .]*, London 1928, and Pelliot, P.: 'Màr Ya(h)bhallàhâ, Rabban Ṣàumâ et les princes Öngüt chrétiens', in: idem, *Recherches sur les Chrétiens d'Asie Centrale et d'Extrême-Orient*, Paris 1973 (Œuvres Posthumes de Paul Pelliot), pp. 239–288.
167 Moule 1930, p. 95.
168 Moule 1930, p. 97.
169 Moule 1930, p. 98.
170 Moule 1930, p. 99.
171 We shall here summarise the findings of W. Troll, based on the sources in Moule 1930, supplementing them with other observations. Cf. Troll 1966, pp. 135–150. Cf. for this chapter also Elia, P. M. d': *The Catholic Missions in China. A Short Sketch of the History of the Catholic Church in China from the Earliest Records to our own Day*, (1934), repr., Shanghai 1941, and Rachewiltz, I. de: *Papal Envoys to the Great Khans*, London 1971 (Great Travellers).
172 Moule 1930, p. 104, n. 17.
173 Cf. Moule 1930, p. 167.
174 Moule 1930, p. 171.
175 Moule 1930, p. 168.
176 Moule 1930, p. 169.
177 Moule 1930, pp. 171f.
178 Moule 1930, p. 172.
179 Moule 1930, p. 173.
180 The remains of a Catholic and a Nestorian church as well as other archaeological material of Christian origin were found in Olon Süme. Cf. Enoki 1964, pp. 46–51.
181 Moule 1930, pp. 177–181.
182 Moule 1930, p. 180.
183 Troll 1966, p. 140.
184 Cf. Moule 1930, pp. 183–188.
185 Moule 1930, pp. 185f.
186 Moule 1930, pp. 189f.
187 Troll 1966, p. 141.
188 Quoted in Troll 1966, p. 144.
189 Quoted in Troll 1966, pp. 144f.
190 Moule 1930, pp. 207–210.
191 Troll 1966, p. 142.
192 Troll 1966, p. 142.
193 Moule 1930, pp. 191–195.
194 Moule 1930, pp. 241–249.
195 Troll 1966, pp. 143f.
196 Moule 1930, pp. 249–251; Troll 1966, pp. 144f.
197 Moule 1930, pp. 249–251; Troll 1966, pp. 144f.
198 Troll 1966, p. 145.
199 Troll 1966, p. 146.

200 Troll 1966, pp. 146f.
201 Cf. Moule 1930, pp. 252–264; Troll 1966, pp. 147ff.
202 Cf. Troll 1966, p. 147.
203 Troll 1966, pp. 149f.
204 Troll 1966, p. 150; Willeke, B. H.: 'Did Catholicism in the Yuan Dynasty Survive until the Present?', in: *Tripod* 47 (1988), pp. 64–69, does, however, point to indications for a survival.
205 Cf. Mostaert, A.: 'Ordosiaca: I. Les Erkut, descendants des chrétiens médiévaux, chez les Mongols Ordos', in: *Bulletin de l'Université Catholique de Pékin* 9 (1934), pp. 1–20, and Ramstedt, G. J.: 'Reste des Nestorianismus unter den Mongolen', in: *JSFO* 55 (1951), pp. 40–46.

11 CHRISTIANS IN SOUTH-EAST ASIA

1 Charlesworth, M. P.: *Trade Routes and Commerce of the Roman Empire*, 2nd ed., rev., Cambridge 1926, p. 73. Cf. also Warmington, E. H.: *The Commerce between the Roman Empire and India*, (1928), repr., London 1974, and Puskás, I.: 'Trade Contacts between India and the Roman Empire', in: Pollet, G. (ed.), *India and the Ancient World. History, Trade and Culture before A. D. 650*, Louvain 1987 (OLA 25), pp. 141–156.
2 Charlesworth 1926, p. 73.
3 Colless B. E.: 'The Traders of the Pearl. The Mercantile and Missionary Activities of Persian and Armenian Christians in South-East Asia', in: *Abr-Nahrain* 9 (1969–1970), pp. 22f. Under the same title and in the same periodical note also vol. 10 (1970–1971), pp. 102–121; 11 (1971), pp. 1–21; 13 (1972–1973), pp. 115–135; 14 (1973–1974), pp. 1–16; 15 (1974–1975), pp. 6–17; 18 (1978–1979), pp. 1–18.
4 In Orthodox tradition the term 'pearl' is also used to refer to those portions of the eucharistic bread retained for use with the sick, and could be even more widely applied, as it was in ca. AD 631 by the Nestorian patriarch, Ishu-Yab III, to religious relics.
5 See Bornkamm, G.: 'The Acts of Thomas', in: Hennecke, E. & Schneemelcher, W. (eds.), *New Testament Apocrypha*, vol. 2, London 1965, pp. 498–504. It may be pointed out that in T'ang times the literary motif of the Persian trader seeking for pearls occurs repeatedly in Chinese literature. Cf. Thilo, T.: 'Ausländer und Kostbarkeiten. Zu einem Motiv der Erzählungsliteratur der Tang-Zeit', in: *AoF* 11 (1984), pp. 149–173, especially p. 171.
6 Colless 1969–1970, p. 28 (see pl. 34a).
7 Colless 1969–1970, p. 32.
8 See e.g. Colless 1969–1970, pp. 34f. Cf. also England, J.: 'The Earliest Christian Communities in Southeast and Northeast Asia. An Outline of the Evidence Available in Seven Countries before 1500 AD', in: *Asia Journal of Theology* 4 (1990), pp. 174–185.
9 See Colless 1970–1971. There is an inference that a Nestorian presence was in Qalah, but no firm evidence beyond a reference by the Patriarch Ishu-Yab III (d. AD 660). See Colless 1978–1979, p. 1.
10 See Colless 1971.
11 See Colless 1972–1973.
12 Colless 1978–1979, p. 2.
13 Bracciolini, P. & Varthema, L. de: *Travellers in Disguise. Narratives of Eastern Travel*, English trans. by J. W. Jones, revised, with an introduction, by L. D. Hammond, Cambridge, Mass. 1963, p. 184.

14 Cortesão, A. (trans. & ed.): *The Suma Oriental of Tomé Pires. An Account of the East, from the Red Sea to Japan [. . .], and The Book of Francisco Rodrigues [. . .]*, 2 vols., London 1944, vol. 2, p. 268.
15 Cortesão 1944, vol. 1, p. 22.
16 Mundadan, A. M.: *History of Christianity in India*, vol. 1, Bangalore 1984, p. 108.
17 See Colless 1971, pp. 11–13.
18 Major, R. H. (ed.): *India in the Fifteenth Century. Being a Collection of Narratives of Voyages to India*, vol. 2, London 1857, p. 9.
19 Bracciolini & Varthema 1963, p. 179.
20 See Colless 1972–1973, pp. 121–123 & 125.
21 Bracciolini & Varthema 1963, p. 177.
22 Bracciolini & Varthema 1963, pp. 177f.
23 Bracciolini & Varthema 1963, p. 198.

Appendices

WESTERN CHRISTENDOM	EASTERN CHRISTENDOM	ARMENIA & GEORGIA	SYRIA (& 'ARABIA')	PERSIA	KEY PERSONS AND EVENTS	Dates A.D.
WESTERN ROMAN EMPIRE		ARMENIA and GEORGIA know independence and division and rule by Rome and Persia		ARSACID DYNASTY	Ignatius of Antioch	100
					Tatian of Edessa	
				224	Pantaenus Mani	200
Christianity established as State religion AD 380		301. Armenia adopts Christianity 330. Georgia accepts Christianity	SYRIA part of Eastern Roman Empire	SASANIAN DYNASTY	Bardaisan Origen Gregory the Illuminator	300
					Constantine converted Council of Nicea	
Rome sacked 410					Ephrem Syrus Augustantine Nestorius	400
TURMOIL AS GOTHIC PEOPLES INVADE AND SETTLE	EASTERN ROMAN EMPIRE	Armenian Church becomes Monophysite			Council of Chalcedon	500
					Jacob Baradai Mar Babai Mar Aba I	
				651	Augustine of Canterbury	600
			UMAYYAD CALIPHATE		Muhammad Ishu Yahb III	700
HOLY ROMAN EMPIRE BEGUN			749		John of Damascus	
					Charlemagne	800
					Timothy I	
		885				900
VIKINGS RENEW TURMOIL		BAGRATID DYNASTY IN ARMENIA	ABBASID CALIPHATE		First Crusade	1000
		1045				
		1080				1100
MEDIEVAL WESTERN CHRISTENDOM AND EMERGING NATIONAL STATES	1204	LESSER ARMENIA ESTABLISHED			St Francis St Dominic	1200
	LATIN RULE OVER CONSTANTINOPLE			1258	Pope Innocent III Fourth Crusade	
				IL-KHAN MONGUL RULE	Mar Yaballaha III	1300
				1335		
	Constantinople falls 1453				Timur the Lame	1400
	OTTOMAN TURKS				Columbus to America	1500
					Luther Calvin Ignatius Loyola	
						1600

356

Dates A.D.	KEY PERSONS AND EVENTS	INDIA	CENTRAL ASIA	CHINA	JAPAN & S.E. ASIA
	Thomas in India?				
100				HAN DYNASTY	YAMATO ERA (Age of the Clans)
200		KUSHAN DYNASTY		220	
300		300	279	THREE KINGDOMS PERIOD	
400	Thomas Cana in India	GUPTA DYNASTY	HSIUNGA-NU KMS		MONS KMS in BURMA 7th–16th centuries
500	Cosmas visits India	500	CITY STATE		
600	Buddhism to Japan Alopen in China Nestorian metropolitans for Samarkland, India and China	REALM OF HARSHA RULERS	PRE-ISLAMIC TURKISH RULE Uighurs etc.	618	SRIVI-JAYAN EMPIRE in Sumatra and Malaysia 7th–13th centuries
700	Nestorian physician visits Japan	647		T'ANG DYNASTY	710 NARA PERIOD
800	Nestorian movement at Sian-fu	ISLAMIC RULE	ISLAMIC RULE IN WEST CENTRAL ASIA		784
900		HINDU STATES		906	HEIAN ERA and FUJI-WARA REGENTS (857–1192)
1000	Keraits converted to Christianity	962	5 DYNASTIES	960	KHMER EMPIRE 9th–14th centuries
1100		GHAZHA-VIDES	CITY STATES	SUNG DYNASTY	THAI KM 12th century onwards
1200	Jinghiz Khan John de P. Carpini William Rubruk Marco Polo	1186		1260	1192 MINA-MOTO and HOJO SHOGUNS
1300	John of Montecorvino John de Marignolli Christianity banned in China	SULTAN-ATE OF DELHI	MONGOL RULE	YUAN (Mongol) DYNASTY	MAJAPAHIT EMPIRE in Java 13th–15th centuries
1400	Timur the Lame			1368	1333 ASHI-KAGA SHOGUNS
1500	Diaz rounds the Cape Da Gama reaches India	1525		MING DYNASTY	
1600	Francis Xavier	MOGUL DYNASTY			1573 CIVIL UNREST

CHRONOLOGICAL TABLE FOR THE 'CHURCH OF THE EAST' IN IRAN

Drawn from Young, W. G.: *Patriarch, Shah and Caliph*, Rawalpindi 1974, pp. 206f.

Date (AD)	Head, Catholicos, Patriarch	Shah
399	Izhaq I, 399 – end 410	Yazdgard I, 399–420
411	Mar Ahai, 411 – end 414	
415	Yab-alaha I, 415 – beginning 420	
420	(Ma'na, 420)	Bahram V, 420–438
	(Fara-bakht, 420)	
421	Dad-ishu' I, 421/2–456	
438		Yazdgard II, 438–457
457	Babowai, May 457 – June 484	
459		Firoz, 459–486
485	Aqaq, 485–495/6	
486		Walgash, 486–488
		Qubad, 488–531
497	Babai, 497–502/3	
505	Shila, 505–521/2	
524	"The Duality", 524–538/9	
538		Khusrau I, 531–579
539	Paul I, d. Palm Sunday 539	
540	Mar Aba I the Great, Jan. 540 – 29 Feb. 552	
552	Yusuf, May 552–566/7 (d. 576)	
567	Hizqiel elected	
570	Hizqiel consecrated, d. 581	
579		Hurmizd IV, 579–590
582	Ishu-Yab I, 582–595	
590		Khusrau II, 590–628
595	Sabr Ishu' I, 595–604	
605	Gregory I, Apr. 605–609	
609	Vacancy, 609–628	
628	Ishu-Yab II, between 11 May and 30 Aug. 628–646	Shiruya, 628–629
630		Queen Buran, 630–631
632		Yazdgard III, 632–651

Note: The names of a few Shahs of the period 629–632 have been omitted as unimportant.

Date (AD)	Patriarch	Caliph
628	Ishu-Yab II, between 11 May and 30 Aug. 628–646	
632		Abu Bakr, 632–634
634		'Umr, 634–644
644		'Uthman, 644–656
647	Mar-amma, or Maran-amma, 647–650	
650	Ishu-Yab III, 650–658	
656		'Ali, 656–661
660		Mu'awiya, 660–680*
661	George I, 661–680/1	
680	John I, 680/1–683	Yazid I, 680–683
684		Marwan I, 684–685
685	Hanan-ishu' I, 685/6–699/700	'Abd-al-Malik, 685–705
691	John "the Leper", 691–692/3	
700	Vacancy, 700–714	
705		Walid I, 705–715
714	Saliba-zakha, 714–728	
715		Suleman, 715–717
717		'Umr II, 717–720
720		Yazid II, 720–724
724		Hisham, 724–743
728	Vacancy, 728–731	
738	Phethion, 731–740	
740	Mar Aba II, 740–751	
743		Walid II, 743–744
744		Marwan II, 744–750
750		Abu'l-Abbas, 750–754**
754	(Surin, 12 Apr. – 26 May 751) Ya'qub II, 754–773	al-Mansur, 754–775
775	Hanan-ishu' II, 775–780	al-Mahdi, 775–785
780	Timothy I, 1 May 780 – Jan. 823	
785		al-Hadi, 785–786
786		Harun-al-Rashid, 786–809
809		al-Amin, 809–813
813		al-Mamun, 813–833

* Here begin the 'Umayyads. A few less important 'Umayyad Caliphs are omitted.
** Here begin the Abbasids.

CHRISTIANS IN JAPAN

While with the arrival of Francis Xavier at Kagoshima in Kyushu in AD 1549 the history of Christianity in that country becomes clear, there are those who make reference to contacts prior to this date. At most it is possible that some Nestorians accompanied a high Japanese official who returned to Japan in AD 739. The official was Dosen, the founder of the Kegon school, and one Nestorian in his entourage was a physician of Persian nationality. Given the Japanese name of Rimitsu he was granted official court rank and was involved with the hospital plans of the Emperor Shomu (d. AD 748).[1] Certainly some Nestorians would have been among the troops of Khubilai Khan's attempted invasions of Japan in AD 1274 and 1281. It is even probable that the Uighur secretary of the ill-fated envoys of Khubilai Khan in AD 1280 was a Nestorian. If so, he and numbers of other Nestorians paid very brief visits indeed to Japan as they faced execution and military disaster at the hands of the Japanese and the Kamikaze winds.[2]

In neither case was any continuing Christian community a result of such contacts. Nor, despite surface similarities in a number of areas has it proved to be possible yet to trace uncontrovertibly direct or even indirect Nestorian influence on the genesis and development of Pure Land Buddhism, the most popular form of that faith in Japan.[3]

There the matter may be allowed to rest, except for some correspondence from Sakae Ikeda in 1949–1951 issues of the Nestorian periodical *Light from the East*. In the June–July 1949 issue he claimed that there were Nestorian chapels in the vicinity of Kyoto in Japan more than 1000 years prior to 1949. The October–November 1949 number included an extract of an article in the *Osaka Shimbun* in which Ikeda claimed that the 'Church of the East' was brought to Japan from China at the same time as Buddhism.

In the issue of June–July 1950 the publication of Ikeda's book *Nestorianism and Japanese Culture by Sanma Shoko* is noted, as is the contribution of Rimitsu, or Timi, a Nestorian Physician from Balkh. Finally, in June–July 1951 it was claimed that

> 'a likeness of Mar Thoma, Assyrian missionary of the Church of the East to Japan, who died in AD 601, is now venerated in a large Buddhist temple near Kyoto. When Mar Thoma died, Prince Shotoku, regent of Japan, a Buddhist, who had nursed Mar Thoma personally, had him buried with the greatest reverence.'[4]

Ikeda went on to claim that since then the likeness has been confused with that of Daruma (or Bodhidharma).

All of this is intriguing, but even the author admitted the need of confirmation, and his book has not been located. As a result, and, as with some other issues in our study, we must content ourselves with pointing to a Nestorian presence from time to time, but no continuing witness over generations before AD 1549.

NOTES

1 Lloyd, A.: *The Creed of Half Japan. Historical Sketches of Japanese Buddhism,* London 1911, pp. 222f.
2 See Saeki, P. Y.: *The Nestorian Documents and Relics in China,* 2nd ed., Tokyo 1951, pp. 444–447.
3 See above and the discussions of this in Eilert, H.: *Boundlessness. Studies in Karl Ludwig Reichelt's Missionary Theology with Special Regard to the Buddhist-Christian Encounter,* Copenhagen 1974 (Studia Missionalia Upsaliensia 24), pp. 40f.; Corless, R. J.: 'Monotheistic Elements in Early Pure Land Buddhism', in: *Religion* 6 (1976), p. 177; Dumoulin, H.: *Christianity Meets Buddhism,* trans. by J. C. Maraldo, La Salle, Ill. 1974 (Religious Encounter East and West), p. 64, and Eliot, C.: *Japanese Buddhism [. . .],* (1935), repr., London 1959, pp. 301 & 393–395.
4 No page numbers in journal.

Bibliography

Abbeloos, J. B. & Lamy, T. J. (eds.): *Gregorii Barhebraei Chronicon Ecclesiasticum [. . .]*, 3 vols., Louvain 1872–1877.

Adeney, W. F.: *The Greek and Eastern Churches*, (1908), repr., New York 1965.

Aerthayil, J.: *The Spiritual Heritage of the St. Thomas Christians*, Bangalore 1982.

Agur, C. M.: *Church History of Travancore*, Madras 1903.

Allen, W. E. D.: *A History of the Georgian People from the Beginning down to the Russian Conquest in the Nineteenth Century*, (1932), repr., New York 1978.

Almond, P. C.: 'The Medieval West and Buddhism', in: *The Eastern Buddhist* N. S. 19 (1986), pp. 85–101.

Aprem, Mar (G. Mooken): 'The Nestorian Church in India from the Fifth to the Sixteenth Century', in: John, K. J. (ed.), *Christian Heritage of India [. . .]*, Cochin 1981, pp. 37–47.

Arlotto, A.: 'Old Turkic Oracle Books', in: *MSer* 29 (1970–1971), pp. 685–696 [pp. 693–696: 'Appendix: The So-Called Christian Oracle-Book'].

Arpee, L.: *A History of Armenian Christianity from the Beginning to our Own Time*, New York 1946.

Asmussen, J. P.: 'Iranische neutestamentliche Zitate und Texte und ihre textkritische Bedeutung', in: *AoF* 2 (1975), pp. 79–92.

—— (ed.): *Manichaean Literature. Representative Texts Chiefly from Middle Persian and Parthian Writings*, Delmar, N. Y. 1975 (Persian Heritage Series 22).

—— 'The Sogdian and Uighur-Turkish Christian Literature in Central Asia before the Real Rise of Islam. A Survey', in: Hercus, L. A. et al. (eds.), *Indological and Buddhist Studies*. Volume in Honour of Professor J. W. de Jong on his Sixtieth Birthday, Canberra 1982, pp. 11–29.

—— 'Christians in Iran', in: Yarshater, E. (ed.): *The Cambridge History of Iran* 3 (2), Cambridge 1983, pp. 924–948.

Atiya, A. S.: *A History of Eastern Christianity*, London 1968.

Baker, A.: 'Early Syriac Asceticism', in: *Downside Review* 88 (1970), pp. 393–409.

Bang, W.: 'Der Komanische Marienpsalter', in: *Abhandlungen der Königlichen Gesellschaft der Wissenschaften zu Göttingen*, Phil.-hist. Kl., N. F. 13 (1914), pp. 241–276.

—— 'Türkische Bruchstücke einer nestorianischen Georgspassion', in: *Le Muséon* 39 (1926), pp. 41–75.

—— & Gabain, A. von: 'Türkische Turfantexte V. Aus buddhistischen Schriften', in: *SPAW* 1931, pp. 323–349.

Barbosa, D.: *A Description of the Coasts of East Africa and Malabar in the Beginning of the Sixteenth Century*, trans. [. . .] by H. E. J. Stanley, London 1866 (WHS 35).

Barnard, L. W.: 'The Origins and Emergence of the Church in Edessa during the First Two Centuries A. D.', in: *VigChr* 22 (1968), pp. 161–175.

Barthold, W. [= Bartol'd, V. V.]: *Zur Geschichte des Christentums in Mittel-Asien bis zur mongolischen Eroberung [. . .]*, ed. by R. Stübe, Tübingen & Leipzig 1901.
—— *Iran*, trans. [. . .] by G. K. Nariman, ed. by M. E. Dadrawala, Bombay 1935.
Bauer, W. (ed.): *China und die Fremden. 3000 Jahre Auseinandersetzung in Krieg und Frieden*, Munich 1980.
Baumstark, A.: *Geschichte der syrischen Literatur mit Ausschluss der christlich-palästinensischen Texte*, (1922), repr., Berlin 1968.
Beck, E.: *Ephräms Polemik gegen Mani und die Manichäer im Rahmen der zeitgenössischen Polemik und der des Augustinus*, Louvain 1978 (CSCO.Sub 55).
Bedjan, P. (ed.): *Gregorii Barhebraei Chronicon Syriacum [. . .]*, Paris 1890.
Bettenson, H. (ed.): *Documents of the Christian Church*, 2nd ed., London 1963.
Bianchi, U. (ed.): *Le origini dello gnosticismo [. . .]*, Leiden 1967 (SHR 12).
Bornkamm, G.: 'The Acts of Thomas', in: Hennecke, E. & Schneemelcher, W. (eds.), *New Testament Apocrypha*, vol. 2, London 1965, pp. 425–531.
Bosworth, C. E.: 'Iran and the Arabs before Islam', in: Yarshater, E. (ed.), *The Cambridge History of Iran* 3 (1), Cambridge 1983, pp. 593–612.
Boxer, C. R.: 'The Portuguese and the East', in: Livermore, H. V. (ed.), *Portugal and Brazil. An Introduction*, Oxford 1953, pp. 185–241.
—— *The Portuguese Seaborne Empire, 1415–1825*, New York 1969.
Boyce, M.: *The Manichaean Hymn-Cycles in Parthian*, London 1954 (London Oriental Series 3).
—— *Zoroastrians. Their Religious Beliefs and Practices*, London 1979.
Bracciolini, P. & Varthema, L. de: *Travelers in Disguise. Narratives of Eastern Travel*, English trans. by J. W. Jones, revised, with an introduction, by L. D. Hammond, Cambridge, Mass. 1963.
Brincken, A.-D. von den: *Die 'Nationes Christianorum Orientalium' im Verständnis der lateinischen Historiographie von der Mitte des 12. bis in die 2. Hälfte des 14. Jahrhunderts*, Cologne & Vienna 1973 (Kölner Historische Abhandlungen 22).
Brock, S. P.: 'Early Syrian Asceticism', in: *Numen* 20 (1973), 1–19.
—— 'Greek into Syriac and Syriac into Greek', in: *Journal of the Syriac Academy* 3 (1977), pp. 1–7 [= 422–406].
—— 'Christians in the Sasanid Empire: A Case of Divided Loyalties', in: Mews, S. (ed.), *Religion and National Identity*, Oxford 1982 (Studies in Church History 18), pp. 1–19.
—— 'Syriac Views of Emergent Islam', in: Juynboll, G. H. A. (ed.), *Studies on the First Century of Islamic Society*, Carbondale 1982 (Papers on Islamic History 5), pp. 9–21, 199–203.
—— *Syriac Perspectives on Late Antiquity*, London 1984 (CStS 199).
Brown, L. W.: *The Indian Christians of St Thomas*, London 1956.
Brown, R. E. & Meier, J. P.: *Antioch and Rome. New Testament Cradles of Catholic Christianity*, New York & Ramsey, N. J. 1983.
Browne, L. E.: *The Eclipse of Christianity in Asia from the Time of Muhammad till the Fourteenth Century*, (1933), repr., New York 1967.
Browning, R.: *The Twelve Apostles*, New York 1974.
Bryder, P.: *The Chinese Transformation of Manichaeism. A Study of Chinese Manichaean Terminology*, Löberöd 1985.
Buchanan, C.: *Christian Researches in Asia [. . .]*, Cambridge & London 1811.
Budge, E. A. W. (ed.): *The Book of Governors. The Historia Monastica of Thomas, Bishop of Margâ, A.D. 840 [. . .]*, 2 vols., London 1893.
—— (trans.): *The Monks of Ḳûblâi Khân, Emperor of China, or the History of the Life and Travels of Rabban Ṣâwmâ [. . .] and Marḳôs [. . .]*, London 1928.

—— (trans.): *The Chronography of Gregory Ab'l Faraj [. . .]. Being the First Part of his Political History of the World [. . .]*, 2 vols., Oxford 1932.

Burkitt, F. C.: *Early Christianity outside the Roman Empire*, Cambridge 1899.

—— *Early Eastern Christianity [. . .]*, London 1904.

—— 'The Christian Church in the East', in: Bury, J, B. et al. (eds.), *The Cambridge Ancient History* 12, Cambridge 1939, pp. 476–514.

Burnell, A. C.: 'On Some Pahlavi Inscriptions in South India', in: *IndAnt* 3 (1874), pp. 308–316.

Buttrick, G. A. et al. (eds.): *The Interpreter's Dictionary of the Bible*, 4 vols., New York 1962.

Cary-Elwes, C.: *China and the Cross. Studies in Missionary History*, London et al. 1957.

Catalani, J.: *Mirabilia descripta. The Wonders of the East [. . .]*, trans. from the Latin original [. . .] by H. Yule, London 1863.

Chabot, J.-B.: 'Les évêques Jacobites du VIIIe au XIIIe siècle, d' après la Chronique de Michel le Syrien', in: *Revue de l'Orient Chrétien* 4 (1899), pp. 444–451, 495–511; 5 (1900), pp. 605–636; 6 (1901), pp. 189–220.

—— (ed. & trans.): *Synodicon orientale ou receuil des synodes nestoriens [. . .]*, Paris 1902 (NEMBN 37).

Charlesworth, M. P.: *Trade Routes and Commerce of the Roman Empire*, 2nd ed., rev., Cambridge 1926.

Ch'en Yüan: 'On the Damaged Tablets Discovered by Mr. D. Martin in Inner Mongolia', in: *MSer* 3 (1938), pp. 250–256.

Cheriyan, C. V.: *A History of Christianity in Kerala from the Mission of St. Thomas to the Arrival of Vasco Da Gama (A. D. 52–1498)*, Kottayam 1973.

Cherukarakunnel, A.: 'The Hindu Christians of India', in: Vellian, J. (ed.), *The Malabar Church [. . .]*, Rome 1970 (OCA 186), pp. 203–208.

Chwolson, D.: *Syrische Grabschriften aus Semirjetschie*, St. Petersburg 1886 (MAIS, 7e série, 34,4).

—— *Syrisch-nestorianische Grabinschriften aus Semirjetschie. Nebst einer Beilage [. . .]*, St. Petersburg 1890 (MAIS, 7e série, 37,8).

—— *Syrisch-nestorianische Grabinschriften aus Semirjetschie. Neue Folge*, St. Petersburg 1897.

Cipolla, C. M.: *European Culture and Overseas Expansion*, Harmondsworth 1970.

Cirillo, L.: '"Hermae Pastor" and "Revelatio Manichaica". Some Remarks', in: Wiessner, G. & Klimkeit, H.-J. (eds.), *Studia Manichaica [. . .]*, Wiesbaden 1992 (StOR 23), pp. 189–197.

Clauson, G.: 'Ak Beshim – Suyab', in: *JRAS* 1961, pp. 1–13.

Cleaves, Fr. W. (ed. & trans.): *Secret History of the Mongols*, Cambridge, Mass. 1982 (Harvard-Yenching Institute Publications).

Codrington, H. W.: *Studies of the Syrian Liturgies*, London 1952.

Colless, B. E.: 'The Place of Syrian Christian Mysticism in Religious History', in: *JRH* 5 (1968–1969), pp. 1–15.

—— 'The Traders of the Pearl. The Mercantile and Missionary Activities of Persian and Armenian Christians in South-East Asia', in: *Abr-Nahrain* 9 (1969–1970), pp. 17–38; 10 (1970–1971), pp. 102–121; 11 (1971), pp. 1–21; 13 (1972–1973), pp. 115–135; 14 (1973–1974), pp. 1–16; 15 (1974–1975), pp. 6–17; 18 (1978–1979), pp. 1–18.

—— 'The Nestorian Province of Samarqand', in: *Abr-Nahrain* 24 (1986), pp. 51–57.

Conybeare, F. C. (ed. & trans.): *The Key of Truth. A Manual of the Paulician Church of Armenia*, Oxford 1898.

Conze, E.: 'Buddhism and Gnosis', in: Bianchi, U. (ed.), *Le origini dello gnosticismo [. . .]*, Leiden 1967 (SHR 12), pp. 651–667.

—— 'Buddhist *prajñā* and Greek *sophia*', in: *Religion* 5 (1975), pp. 160–167.

Cook, F. H.: *Hua-yen Buddhism. The Jewel Net of Indra*, University Park & London 1977.

Corless, R. J.: 'Monotheistic Elements in Early Pure Land Buddhism', in: *Religion* 6 (1976), pp. 176–189.

Cortesão, A. (trans. & ed.): *The Suma Oriental of Tomé Pires. An Account of the East, from the Red Sea to Japan [. . .], and The Book of Francisco Rodrigues [. . .]*, 2 vols., London 1944 (WHS 2nd Series 89).

Cowell, E. B.: 'The Northern Buddhist Legend of Avalokiteśwara's Descent into the Hell Avîchi', in: *IndAnt* 8 (1879), pp. 249–253.

—— et al. (trans.), *Buddhist Mahāyāna Texts [. . .]*, (1894), repr., Delhi 1965 (Sacred Books of the East 49).

Cross, F. L. & Livingstone, E. A. (eds.): *The Oxford Dictionary of the Christian Church [. . .]*, 2nd ed., London 1974.

Daniélou, J.: *The Theology of Jewish Christianity*, trans. and ed. by J. A. Baker, London & Chicago 1964 (The Development of Christian Doctrine before the Council of Nicaea 1).

—— & Marrou, H.: *The First Six Hundred Years*, trans. by V. Cronin [. . .], New York 1964 (The Christian Centuries 1).

Dar, S. R.: 'Gondopharnes and Taxila', in: Rooney, J. (ed.), *St. Thomas and Taxila*, Rawalpindi 1988 (Pakistan Christian History Study 1), pp. 16–30.

Dauvillier, J.: 'L'expansion de l'Église syrienne en Asie Centrale et en Extrême-Orient', in: *L'Orient Syrien* 1 (1956), pp. 76–87.

—— 'Les Arméniens en Chine et en Asie Centrale au Moyen Age', in: *Mélanges de Sinologie offerts à Monsieur Paul Demiéville* II, Paris 1974 (Bibliothèque de l'Institut des hautes études chinoises 20), pp. 1–17.

—— *Histoire et institutions des Églises orientales au moyen âge*, London 1983 (CStS 173).

Dawson, Chr. (ed.): *The Mongol Mission. Narratives and Letters of the Franciscan Missionaries in Mongolia and China in the Thirteenth and Fourteenth Centuries*, London & New York 1955 (The Makers of Christendom); repr.: *Mission to Asia [. . .]*, London 1980 (Spiritual Masters).

Der Nersessian, S.: *Armenia and the Byzantine Empire. A Brief Study of Armenian Art and Civilisation*, Cambridge, Mass. 1945.

Derrett, J. D. M.: 'Der Wasserwandel in christlicher und buddhistischer Perspektive', in: *ZRGG* 41 (1989), pp. 193–214.

Dieterich, K.: *Byzantinische Quellen zur Länder- und Völkerkunde (5. – 15. Jh.)*, 2 parts, Leipzig 1912 (Quellen und Forschungen zur Erd- und Kulturkunde 5).

Dihle, A.: 'Neues zur Thomas-Tradition', in: *JAC* 6 (1963), pp. 54–70.

—— *Der Seeweg nach Indien*. Innsbruck 1974 (Innsbrucker Beiträge zur Kulturwissenschaft. Dies philologici Aenipontani 4).

—— 'Serer und Chinesen', in: idem, *Antike und Orient. Gesammelte Aufsätze [. . .]*, Heidelberg 1984 (Supplemente zu den Sitzungsberichten der Heidelberger Akademie der Wissenschaften, Phil.-hist. Kl., Jg. 1983, 2), pp. 201–215.

Downey, R. E. G.: *A History of Antioch in Syria from Seleucus to the Arab Conquest*, Princeton, N. J. 1961.

Drake, F. S.: 'The Nestorian "Gloria in Excelsis Deo"', in: *ChinRec* 66 (1935), pp. 291–300.

—— 'Nestorian Literature of the T'ang Dynasty', in: *ChinRec* 66 (1935), pp. 608–617, 677–687, 738–742.

—— 'Nestorian Monasteries of the T'ang Dynastie and the Site of the Discovery of the Nestorian Tablet', in: *MSer* 2 (1936–1937), pp. 293–340.

Drijvers, H. J. W. (trans. & ed.): *The Book of the Laws of Countries. Dialogue on Fate of Bardaiṣan of Edessa*, Assen 1965 (Semitic Texts with Translation 3).

—— *Bardaisan of Edessa*, Assen 1966 (Studia Semitica Neerlandica 6).

—— *The Religion of Palmyra*, Leiden 1976 (Iconography of Religions 15, 15).

—— *Cults and Beliefs at Edessa*, Leiden 1980 (Études préliminaires aux religions orientales dans l'Empire Romain 82).

—— 'The Persistence of Pagan Cults and Practices in Christian Syria', in: Garsoïan, N. et al. (eds.), *East of Byzantium. Syria and Armenia in the Formative Period [. . .]*, Washington, D. C. 1982, pp. 35–43.

—— *East of Antioch. Studies in Early Syriac Christianity*, London 1984 (CStS 198).

—— 'Thomasakten', in: Schneemelcher, W. (ed.), *Neutestamentliche Apokryphen in deutscher Übersetzung*, vol. 2, 5th ed., Tübingen 1990, pp. 289–367.

Dumoulin, H.: *Christianity Meets Buddhism*, trans. by J. C. Maraldo, La Salle, Ill. 1974 (Religious Encounter East and West).

Duncan, E. J.: *Baptism in the Demonstrations of Aphraates, the Persian Sage*, Washington, D.C. 1945.

Džumagulov, Č.: 'Die syrisch-türkischen (nestorianischen) Denkmäler in Kirgisien', in: *MIO* 14 (1968), pp. 470–480.

—— *Jazyk siro-tjurkskich (nestorianskich) pamjanikov Kirgizii*, Frunze 1971.

Effenberger, A. et al.: *Spätantike und frühbyzantinische Silbergefäße aus der Staatlichen Eremitage Leningrad*, Berlin 1978 (Staatliche Museen zu Berlin. Ausstellungskataloge der Frühchristlich-byzantinischen Sammlung 2).

Eichhorn, W.: *Die Religionen Chinas*, Stuttgart 1973 (RM 21).

Eilert, H.: *Boundlessness. Studies in Karl Ludwig Reichelt's Missionary Thinking with Special Regard to the Buddhist-Christian Encounter*, Copenhagen 1974 (Studia Missionalia Upsaliensia 24).

Elia, P. M. d': *The Catholic Missions in China. A Short Sketch of the History of the Catholic Church in China from the Earliest Records to our own Day*, (1934), repr., Shanghai 1941.

Eliot, C.: *Japanese Buddhism [. . .]*, (1935), repr., London 1959.

Engberding, H.: 'Fünf Blätter eines alten ostsyrischen Bitt- und Bussgottesdienstes aus Innerasien', in: *Ostkirchliche Studien* 14 (1965), pp. 121–148.

England, J.: 'The Earliest Christian Communities in Southeast and Northeast Asia. An Outline of the Evidence Available in Seven Countries before AD 1500', in: *Asia Journal of Theology* 4 (1990), pp. 174–185.

Enoki, K.: 'The Nestorian Christianism in China in Medieval Time according to Recent Historical and Archaeological Researches', in: *Atti del Convegno Internazionale sul tema: L'Oriente cristiano nella storia della civiltà [. . .]*, Rome 1964 (Problemi attuali di scienza e di cultura 62), pp. 44–81.

Farquhar, J. N.: 'The Apostle Thomas in North India', in: *BJRL* 10 (1926), pp. 80–111.

—— 'The Apostle Thomas in South India', in: *BJRL* 11 (1927), pp. 20–50.

Fortescue, A.: *The Lesser Eastern Churches [. . .]*, London 1913.

Fortescue, E. F. K.: *The Armenian Church Founded by St. Gregory the Illuminator [. . .]*, London 1872.

Foster, J.: *The Church of the T'ang Dynasty*, London 1939.

Franke, O.: *Geschichte des chinesischen Reichs*, 5 vols. [vol. 1: 2nd ed.], Berlin 1930–1965.

Fremantle, A. (ed.): *The Papal Encyclicals in their Historical Context*, New York 1956.

Frye, R. N.: *The History of Ancient Iran*, Munich 1983 (Handbuch der Altertumswissenschaft 3, 7).

Fujieda, A.: 'The Tunhuang Manuscripts. A General Description', in: *Zinbun* 9 (1966), pp. 1–32; 10 (1969), pp. 17–39.

Gabain, A. von: 'Die Sprache des Codex Cumanicus', in: Deny, J. et al. (eds.), *Philologiae Turcicae Fundamenta*, vol. 1, Wiesbaden 1959, pp. 46–73.

Garbe, R.: *Indien und das Christentum. Eine Untersuchung der religionsgeschichtlichen Zusammenhänge*, Tübingen 1914.

Garsoïan, N. G.: *The Paulician Heresy. A Study of the Origin and Development of Paulicianism in Armenia and the Eastern Provinces of the Byzantine Empire*, The Hague & Paris 1967 (Publications in Near and Middle East Studies, Series A, 6).

—— et al. (eds.): *East of Byzantium. Syria and Armenia in the Formative Period [. . .]*, Washington, D. C. 1982.

Geng Shimin & Klimkeit, H.-J.: *Das Zusammentreffen mit Maitreya. Die ersten fünf Kapitel der Hami-Version der Maitrisimit [. . .]*, 2 parts, Wiesbaden 1988 (AsF 103).

——, Klimkeit, H.-J. & Laut, J. P.: 'Eine neue nestorianische Grabinschrift aus China', in: *UAJb* N. F. 14 (1996), pp. 164–175.

Gensichen, H.-W.: 'Asien, Christliche Kirchen in', in: *TRE* 4 (1979), pp. 173–195.

Gero, S.: *Barsauma of Nisibis and Persian Christianity in the Fifth Century*, Louvain 1981 (CSCO.Sub 63).

Goodrich, L. C.: 'Recent Discoveries at Zayton', in: *JAOS* 77 (1957), pp. 161–165.

Golzio, K. H.: *Rulers and Dynasties of East Asia. China, Japan, Korea*, Cologne 1983 (AR 10).

—— *Kings, Khans and Other Rulers of Early Central Asia*, Cologne 1984 (AR 11).

—— *Regents in Central Asia since the Mongol Empire*, Cologne 1985 (AR 12).

Granö, J. G.: 'Archäologische Beobachtungen von meinen Reisen in den nördlichen Grenzgegenden Chinas in den Jahren 1906 und 1907', in: *JSFO* 26 (1909), pp. 1–54 & 16 plates.

Grœnbech, K.: 'Turkish Inscriptions from Inner Mongolia', in: *MSer* 4 (1939–1940), pp. 305–308.

Gropp, G.: 'Die Pahlavi-Inschrift auf dem Thomaskreuz in Madras', in: *Archäologische Mitteilungen aus Iran* N. F. 3 (1970), pp. 267–271.

Grünwedel, A.: *Altbuddhistische Kultstätten in Chinesisch-Turkistan [. . .]*, Berlin 1912.

Guillaume, A.: *Islam*, Harmondsworth 1954 (Pelican Books A 311).

Hage, W.: 'Das Nebeneinander christlicher Konfessionen im mittelalterlichen Zentralasien', in: Vogt, W. (ed.), *17. Deutscher Orientalistentag vom 21. – 27. Juli 1968 in Würzburg. Vorträge*, Part 2, Wiesbaden 1969 (ZDMG Supplementa 1,2), pp. 517–525.

—— *Untersuchungen zum Leben der Christen Zentralasiens im Mittelalter*, 'Habilitationsschrift', unpublished, Marburg 1970.

—— 'Die oströmische Staatskirche und die Christenheit des Perserreiches', in: *ZKG* 84 (1973), pp. 174–187.

—— 'Christentum und Schamanismus. Zur Krise des Nestorianertums in Zentralasien', in: Jaspert, B. & Mohr, R. (eds.), *Traditio – Krisis – Renovatio aus theologischer Sicht. Festschrift W. Zeller zum 65. Geburtstag*, Marburg 1976, pp. 114–124.

—— 'Apostolische Kirche des Ostens (Nestorianer)', in: Heyer, F. (ed.), *Konfessionskunde*, Berlin & New York 1977 (De-Gruyter-Lehrbuch), pp. 202–214.

—— 'Einheimische Volkssprachen und syrische Kirchensprache in der nestorianischen Asienmission', in: Wiessner, G. (ed.), *Erkenntnisse und Meinungen* II, Wiesbaden 1978 (Göttinger Orientforschungen I. Reihe: Syriaca 17), pp. 131–160.

—— 'Der Weg nach Asien: Die ostsyrische Missionskirche', in: Schäferdiek, K. (ed.), *Die Kirchen des frühen Mittelalters*, Munich 1978 (Kirchengeschichte als Missionsgeschichte II, 1), pp. 360–393.

—— 'Religiöse Toleranz in der nestorianischen Asienmission', in: Rendtorff, T. (ed.), *Glaube und Toleranz. Das theologische Erbe der Aufklärung*, Gütersloh 1982, pp. 99–110.

—— 'Kulturelle Kontakte des ostsyrischen Christentums in Zentralasien', in: Lavenant, R. (ed.), *Les contacts du monde syriaque avec les autres cultures [. . .]*, Rome 1983 (OCA 221), pp. 143–159.

—— 'Yahballaha III.', in: Greschat, M. (ed.), *Mittelalter* II, Stuttgart 1983 (Gestalten der Kirchengeschichte 4), pp. 92–101.

—— 'Das Christentum in der Turfan-Oase. Zur Begegnung der Religionen in Zentralasien', in: Heissig, W. & Klimkeit, H.-J. (eds.), *Synkretismus in den Religionen Zentralasiens [. . .]*, Wiesbaden 1987 (StOR 13), pp. 46–57.

—— 'Jakobitische Kirche', in: *TRE* 16 (1987), pp. 474–485.

—— *Syriac Christianity in the East*, Kottayam 1988 (Mōrān 'Eth'o Series 1).

—— 'Nestorianische Kirche', in: *TRE* 24 (1994), pp. 264–276.

Hambye, E. R.: 'Saint Thomas and India', in: *CleM* 16 (1952), pp. 363–375.

—— 'The Syrian Church in India', in: *CleM* 16 (1952), pp. 376–389.

—— 'The Eastern Church (in Medieval India)', in: Perumalil, H. C. & Hambye, E. R. (eds.), *Christianity in India. A History in Ecumenical Perspective*, Alleppey 1972, pp. 30–37.

Hamilton, J.: 'Le texte turc en caractères syriaques du grand sceau cruciforme de Mār Yahballāhā III', in: *Journal Asiatique* 260 (1972), pp. 155–170.

Hansen, O.: *Berliner soghdische Texte I. Bruchstücke einer soghdischen Version der Georgspassion (C 1)*, Berlin 1941 (APAW 1941, 10).

—— 'Die christliche Literatur der Soghdier, eine Übersicht', in: *Akademie der Wissenschaften und der Literatur. Jahrbuch 1951*, Wiesbaden 1951, pp. 296–302.

—— 'Die Literatur der Sogdier', in: Einsiedel, W. von (ed.), *Die Literaturen der Welt in ihrer mündlichen und schriftlichen Überlieferung*, Zürich 1965, pp. 929–932.

—— 'Über die verschiedenen Quellen der christlichen Literatur der Sogder', in: Asmussen, J. P. & Læssøe, J. (eds.), *Iranian Studies Presented to Kaj Barr on His Seventieth Birthday*, Copenhagen 1966, pp. 95–102.

—— 'Die buddhistische und christliche Literatur', in: Gershevitch, I. et al., *Literatur*, Leiden & Cologne 1968 (Handbuch der Orientalistik I,4,2,1), pp. 77–99.

—— 'Der Anteil der Iranier an der Ausbreitung des Christentums nach Zentralasien', in: Vogt, W. (ed.), *17. Deutscher Orientalistentag vom 21. – 27. Juli 1968 in Würzburg. Vorträge*, Part 3, Wiesbaden 1969 (ZDMG Supplementa 1,3), pp. 1032–1035.

Hanson, P. R. C.: *Saint Patrick. His Origins and Career*, Oxford 1968.

—— *The Life and Writings of the Historical Saint Patrick*, New York 1983.

Harnack, A. von: *The Expansion of Christianity in the First Three Centuries*, trans. and ed. by J. Moffat, 2 vols., London & New York 1904.

Havret, H.: *La stèle chrétienne de Si-ngan-fou*, part 2: *Histoire du momument*, Shanghai 1897 (Variétés sinologiques 12).

Heissig, W.: *The Religions of the Mongols*, trans. [. . .] by G. Samuel, Berkeley & London 1980.

—— & Klimkeit, H.-J. (eds.): *Synkretismus in den Religionen Zentralasiens [. . .]*, Wiesbaden 1987 (StOR 13).

Hjelt, A.: *Drei syrisch-nestorianische Grabinschriften*, Helsinki 1909 (Annales Academiae Scientiarum Fennicae, Series B, 1, 2).

Hoffmann, H.: *Die Religionen Tibets. Bon und Lamaismus in ihrer geschichtlichen Entwicklung*, Freiburg & Munich 1956.

—— 'Kālacakra Studies I: Manichaeism, Christianity, and Islam in the "Kālacakra Tantra"', in: *CAJ* 13 (1969), pp. 52–73.

Holme, H.: *The Oldest Christian Church [. . .]*, London 1896.

Hood, A. B. E. (trans. & ed.): *St. Patrick: His Writings and Muirchu's 'Life'*, London 1978 (History from the Sources).

Hough, J.: *History of Christianity in India from the Commencement of the Christian Era*, 5 vols., London 1839–1860.

Hsü, C. Y.: 'Nestorianism and the Nestorian Monument in China', in: *Asian Culture Quarterly* 14 (1986), pp. 41–81.

Hunter, E. C. D.: 'The Conversion of the Kerait to Christianity in A.D. 1007', in: *ZAS* 22 (1989–1991), pp. 142–163.

—— 'Syriac Christianity in Central Asia', in: *ZRGG* 44 (1992), pp. 362–368.

Hunter, W. W.: *The Indian Empire*, new & rev. ed., London 1893.

James, M. R. (ed.): *The Apocryphal New Testament*, Oxford 1924.

Jeffery, A.: 'Ghevond's Text of the Correspondence between 'Umar II and Leo III', in: *Harvard Theological Review* 37 (1944), pp. 269–332.

John, K. J. (ed.): *Christian Heritage of India [. . .]*, Cochin 1981.

Jonas, H.: *The Gnostic Religion. The Message of the Alien God and the Beginnings of Christianity*, 2nd ed., Boston 1963.

—— *Gnosis und spätantiker Geist*, I: *Die mythologische Gnosis*, 3rd ed., Göttingen 1964 (Forschungen zur Religion und Literatur des Alten und Neuen Testaments 51).

Joseph, J.: *The Nestorians and their Muslim Neighbours. A Study of Western Influence on their Relations*, Princeton, N. J. 1961 (Princeton Oriental Studies 20).

Joseph, T. K.: 'A Christian Dynasty in Malabar', in: *IndAnt* 52 (1923), pp. 157–159.

—— *Malabar Christians and their Ancient Documents*, Trivandrum 1929.

Juhanon Mar Thoma: *Christianity in India*, Madras 1954.

Kawerau, P.: *Ostkirchengeschichte*, I: *Das Christentum in Asien und Afrika bis zum Auftreten der Portugiesen im Indischen Ozean*, Louvain 1983 (CSCO.Sub 70).

Keay, F. E.: *A History of the Syrian Church of India*, London 1938.

Kidd, B. J.: *The Churches of Eastern Christendom from A.D. 451 to the Present Time*, London 1927.

Klatt, N.: *Literarkritische Beiträge zum Problem christlich-buddhistischer Parallelen*, Cologne 1982 (AR 8).

—— *Jesu und Buddhas Wasserwandel [. . .]*, Göttingen 1990.

Klein, W.: 'Christliche Reliefgrabsteine des 14. Jahrhunderts von der Seidenstrasse. Ergänzungen zu einer alttürkischen und zwei syrischen Inschriften sowie eine bildliche Darstellung', in: Lavenant, R. (ed.), *VI Symposium Syriacum 1992 [. . .]*, Rome 1994 (OCA 247), pp. 419–442.

—— 'Zentralasien', in: Müller, K. & Usdorf, W. (eds.), *Einleitung in die Missionsgeschichte. Tradition, Situation und Dynamik des Christentums*, Stuttgart 1995 (Theologische Wissenschaft 18), pp. 121–130.

—— & Tubach, J.: 'Ein syrisch-christliches Fragment aus Dunhuang / China', in: *ZDMG* 144 (1994), pp. 1–13 & 446.

Klimkeit, H.-J.: 'Manichäische und buddhistische Beichtformeln aus Turfan. Beobachtungen zur Beziehung zwischen Gnosis und Mahāyāna', in: *ZRGG* 29 (1977), pp. 193–228.

—— 'Das Kreuzessymbol in der zentralasiatischen Religionsbegegnung', in: *ZRGG* 31 (1979), pp. 99–116.

—— 'Der Buddha Henoch: Qumran und Turfan', in: *ZRGG* 32 (1980), pp. 367–376.

—— 'Christentum und Buddhismus in der innerasiatischen Religionsbegegnung', in: *ZRGG* 33 (1981), pp. 208–220.

—— 'Christians, Buddhists and Manichaeans in Central Asia', in: *Buddhist-Christian Studies* 1 (1981), pp. 46–50.

—— 'Gottes- und Selbsterfahrung in der gnostisch-buddhistischen Religionsbegegnung Zentralasiens', in: *ZRGG* 35 (1983), pp. 236–247.

—— 'Buddha als Vater', in: Waldenfels, H. & Immoos, T. (eds.), *Fernöstliche Weisheit und christlicher Glaube*. Festgabe für H. Dumoulin zur Vollendung des 80. Lebensjahres, Mainz 1985, pp. 235–259.

—— 'Christian-Buddhist Encounter in Medieval Central Asia', in: Houston, G. W. (ed.), *The Cross and the Lotus*, Delhi 1985, pp. 9–24.

—— *Die Begegnung von Christentum, Gnosis und Buddhismus an der Seidenstrasse*, Opladen 1986 (RhWAW.G 283).

—— 'Jesus' Entry into Parinirvāṇa: Manichaean Identity in Buddhist Central Asia', in: *Numen* 33 (1986), pp. 225–240.

—— *Hymnen und Gebete der Religion des Lichts. Iranische und türkische liturgische Texte der Manichäer Zentralasiens [. . .]*, Opladen 1989 (ARWAW 79).

—— 'Die Kenntnis apokrypher Evangelien in Zentral- und Ostasien', in: Tongerloo, A. van & Giversen, S. (eds.), *Manichaica Selecta*. Studies Presented to Professor J. Ries on the Occasion of his Seventieth Birthday, Louvain 1991 (Manichaean Studies 1), pp. 149–175.

—— *Gnosis on the Silk Road. Gnostic Texts from Central Asia*, San Francisco 1993.

—— 'Religion in a Pluralistic Society: The Case of Central Asia', in: Bianchi, U. (ed.), *The Notion of 'Religion' in Comparative Research. Selected Proceedings of the XVIth Congress of the International Association for the History of Religions [. . .]*, Rome 1994 (Storia delle religioni 8), pp. 89–96.

Komroff, M.: *Contemporaries of Marco Polo [. . .]*, London 1929.

Koshelenko, G.: 'The Beginnings of Buddhism in Margiana', in: *AA* 14 (1960), pp. 175–183.

Labourt, J.: *Le Christianisme dans l'Empire Perse sous la dynastie Sassanide (224–632)*, Paris 1904.

Lach, D. F.: *Asia in the Making of Europe*, vol. 1, 2nd ed., Chicago 1971.

—— & Flaumenhaft, C. (eds.): *Asia on the Eve of Europe's Expansion*, Englewood Cliffs, N. J. 1965.

Lang, D. M.: *The Georgians*, London 1966 (Ancient Peoples and Places).

—— 'Iran, Armenia and Georgia', in: Yarshater, E. (ed.), *The Cambridge History of Iran* 3 (1), Cambridge 1983, pp. 505–536.

Latourette, K. S.: *A History of Christian Missions in China*, (1929), repr., Taipei 1966.

—— *A History of the Expansion of Christianity*, vol. 1: *The First Five Centuries*; vol. 2: *The Thousand Years of Uncertainty, A. D. 500 – A. D. 1500*, New York & London 1937–1938.

Le Coq, A. von: *Chotscho [. . .]*, (1913), repr., Graz 1979.

Liebeschuetz, J. H. W. G.: *Antioch. City and Imperial Administration in the Later Roman Empire*, Oxford 1972.

Lieu, S. N. C.: 'Nestorians and Manichaeans on the South China Coast', in: *VigChr* 34 (1980), pp. 71–88.

—— *Manichaeism in the Later Roman Empire and Medieval China. A Historical Survey*, 2nd ed., Tübingen 1992 (Wissenschaftliche Untersuchungen zum Neuen Testament 63).

Ligeti, L.: 'Les sept monastères de Mar Sargis', in: *AOH* 26 (1972), pp. 169–178.

Liu Ts'un-yan: *Selected Papers from the Hall of Harmonious Winds*, Leiden 1976.

Lloyd, A.: *The Creed of Half Japan. Historical Sketches of Japanese Buddhism*, London 1911.

Lord, J. H.: 'Jews in Cochin', in: *Encyclopedia of Religion and Ethics* 7 (1914), pp. 557–559.

Macomber, W. F.: 'The Authority of the Catholicos Patriarch of Seleucia-Ctesiphon', in: *I patriarchati orientali nel primo millennio [. . .]*, Rome 1968 (OCA 181), pp. 179–200.

Major, R. H. (ed.): *India in the Fifteenth Century. Beeing a Collection of Narratives of Voyages to India*, London 1857.

Malan, S. C. (trans. & ed.): *A Short History of the Georgian Church*, trans. from the Russian of P. Iosselian, and ed. with additional notes [. . .], London 1866.

—— (trans. & ed.): *The Life and Times of S. Gregory, the Illuminator [. . .]*, London 1868.

Maróth, M.: 'Ein Fragment eines syrischen pharmazeutischen Rezeptbuches aus Turfan', in: *AoF* 11 (1984), pp. 115–125.

—— 'Ein Brief aus Turfan', in: *AoF* 12 (1985), pp. 283–287.

—— 'Die syrischen Handschriften in der Turfan-Sammlung', in: Klengel, H. & Sundermann, W. (eds.), *Ägypten, Vorderasien, Turfan. Probleme der Edition und Bearbeitung altorientalischer Handschriften [. . .]*, Berlin 1991 (SGKAO 23), pp. 126–128.

—— 'Eine unbekannte Version der Georgios-Legende aus Turfan', in: *AoF* 18 (1991), pp. 86–108.

Mathew, K. J.: 'The Role of the Kerala Church in Indian Culture', in: Vellian, J. (ed.), *The Malabar Church [. . .]*, Rome 1970 (OCA 186), pp. 119–121.

McCrindle, J. W. (trans. & ed.): *The Christian Topography of Cosmas [. . .]*, London 1897.

McCullough, W. S.: *A Short History of Syriac Christianity to the Rise of Islam*, Chico, Cal. 1982 (Scholars Press General Series 4).

Medlycott, A. E.: *India and the Apostle Thomas. An Inquiry. With a Critical Analysis of the Acta Thomae*, London 1905.

Meer, F. van der & Mohrmann, Chr.: *Atlas of the Early Christian World*, trans. & ed. by M. F. Hedlund & H. H. Rowley, London 1958.

Mehlhose, R.: 'Der Niedergang der nestorianischen Kirche in China', in: Göttinger Arbeitskreis für syrische Kirchengeschichte (ed.), *Paul de Lagarde und die syrische Kirchengeschichte*, Göttingen: Lagarde-Haus 1968, pp.135–149

—— 'Nestorianische Texte aus China', in: Vogt, W. (ed.), *17. Deutscher Orientalistentag vom 21. – 27. Juli 1968 in Würzburg. Vorträge*, Part 2, Wiesbaden 1969 (ZDMG Supplementa 1,2), pp. 443–449.

Meyendorff, J.: 'Byzantine Views of Islam', in: *Dumbarton Oaks Papers* 18 (1964), pp. 115–132.

Milik, J. T. (ed.): *The Books of Enoch. Aramaic Fragments of Qumrān Cave 4*, Oxford 1976.

Mingana, A.: 'The Early Spread of Christianity in Central Asia and the Far East: A New Document', in: *BJRL* 9 (1925), pp. 297–371.

—— 'A Charter of Protection Granted to the Nestorian Church in A. D. 1138 by Muktafi II, Caliph of Bagdad', in: *BJRL* 10 (1926), pp. 127–133.

—— 'The Early Spread of Christianity in India', in: *BJRL* 10 (1926), pp. 435–514.

—— 'The Apology of Timothy the Patriarch before the Caliph Mahdi', in: *BJRL* 12 (1928), pp. 137–227.

Minorsky, V. F.: *The Middle East in Western Politics in the 13th, 14th and 15th Centuries*, repr. from the *JRAS* [. . .], London 1940.

Mirbt, C. & Aland, K. (eds.): *Quellen zur Geschichte des Papsttums und des römischen Katholizismus*, 6th ed., Tübingen 1967.

Mitchell, C. W. (trans. & ed.): *S. Ephraim's Prose Refutations of Mani, Marcion, and Bardaisan [. . .]*, 2 vols., London 1912 & 1921 (The Text and Translation Society).

Moberg, A. (ed. & trans.), *The Book of the Himyarites. Fragments of a hitherto Unknown Syriac Work*, Lund 1924.

Moffett, S. H.: *A History of Christianity in Asia*, vol. 1: *Beginnings to 1500*, San Francisco 1992.

Montgomery, J. A. (ed. & trans.): *The History of Yaballaha III, Nestorian Patriarch, and of his Vicar, Bar Sauma [. . .]*, New York 1927.

Mostaert, A.: 'Ordosica: I. Les Erkut, descendants des chrétiens médiévaux, chez les Mongols Ordos', in: *Bulletin de l'Université Catholique de Pékin* 9 (1934), pp. 1–20.

Moule, A. C.: 'The Christian Monument at Hsi-an Fu', in: *JNCB* 41 (1910), pp. 76–115.

—— *Christians in China before the Year AD 1550*, London et al. 1930.

—— 'The Use of the Cross among the Nestorians in China', in: *TP* 28 (1931), pp. 78–86.

—— 'The Nestorians in China', in: *JRAS* 1933, pp. 116–120.

—— *Nestorians in China. Some Corrections and Additions*, London 1940 (Sinological Series 1).

—— & Giles, P.: 'Christians at Chên-Chiang Fu', in: *TP* 16 (1915), pp. 627–686.

—— & Pelliot, P. (eds.): *Marco Polo, Description of the World*, 2 vols., London 1938.

Müller, F. W. K.: 'Eine Hermas-Stelle in manichäischer Version', in: *SPAW* 1905, pp. 1077–1083.

—— 'Neutestamentliche Bruchstücke in soghdischer Sprache', in: *SPAW* 1907, pp. 260–270.

—— *Uigurica [I]*, Berlin 1908 (APAW 1908, 2).

—— *Soghdische Texte I*, Berlin 1913 (APAW 1912, 2).

—— & Lentz, W.: 'Soghdische Texte II', in: *SPAW* 1934, pp. 504–607.

Mundadan, A. M.: *Sixteenth Century Traditions of St. Thomas Christians*, Bangalore 1970 (Dharmaram College Studies 5).

—— *History of Christianity in India*, vol. I: *From the Beginning up to the Middle of the Sixteenth Century (up to 1542)*, Bangalore 1984.

Murayama, S.: 'Eine nestorianische Grabinschrift in türkischer Sprache aus Zaiton', in: *UAJb* 35 (1964), pp. 394–396.

—— 'Über die nestorianischen Grabinschriften in der inneren Mongolei und in Südchina', in: *Atti del Convegno Internazionale sul tema: L'Oriente cristiano nella storia della civiltà [. . .]*, Rome 1964 (Problemi attuali di scienza e di cultura 62), pp. 77–81.

Murray, R.: *Symbols of Church and Kingdom. A Study in Early Syriac Tradition*, London & New York 1975.

Museum Haus Völker und Kulturen, St. Augustin (ed.): *Armenien. Geschichte, sakrale Kunst*, St. Augustin 1983.

Nakamura, H.: *Ways of Thinking of Eastern Peoples. India, China, Tibet, Japan*, rev. Engl. trans., ed. by Ph. P. Wiener, Honolulu 1964.

Nau, F.: 'Les pierres tombales nestoriennes en Asie', in: *Annales du Musée Guimet. Bibliothèque de vulgarisation*, vol. 40: *Conférences faites en 1913*, Paris 1914, pp. 193–388.

Neill, S.: *The Story of the Christian Church in India and Pakistan*, Grand Rapids 1970 (Christian World Mission Books).

—— *A History of Christianity in India. The Beginnings to AD 1707*, Cambridge 1984.

Neusner, J.: *Aphrahat and Judaism. The Christian-Jewish Argument in Fourth-Century Iran*, Leiden 1971 (Studia Post-Biblica 19).

O'Leary, De L. E.: *The Syriac Church and Fathers. A Brief Review of the Subject*, London 1909.

—— *Arabia before Muhammad [. . .]*, London 1927.

Panikkar, K. M.: *Asia and Western Dominance. A Survey of the Vasco da Gama Epoch of Asian History 1498–1945*, 5th impr., London 1961.

Paykova, A. V.: 'The Syrian Ostracon from Panjikant', in: *Le Muséon* 92 (1979), pp. 159–169.

Peintinger, F. X.: 'Fund eines christlichen Grabsteins in Yangzhou (1344)', in: Mittag, A. (ed.), *In memoriam Achim Hildebrand. Gesammelte Aufsätze*, Munich 1991 (Chinablätter 18), pp. 65–72.

Pelikan, J. J.: *The Spirit of Eastern Christendom (600 – 1700)*, Chicago 1974.

Pelliot, P.: 'Chrétiens d'Asie Centrale et d'Extrême-Orient', in: *TP* 15 (1914), pp. 623–644

—— 'Christianity in Central Asia in the Middle Ages', in: *JRCAS* 17 (1930), pp. 301–312.

—— *Recherches sur les Chrétiens d'Asie Centrale et d'Extrême-Orient*, Paris 1973 (Œuvres Posthumes de Paul Pelliot).

Perumalil, H. C.: 'The Apostles of Kalyana (Bombay)', in: *Journal of Indian History* 22 (1943), pp. 71–92.

—— & Hambye, E. R. (eds.): *Christianity in India. A History in Ecumenical Perspective*, Alleppey 1973.

Peters, C.: 'Der Text der soghdischen Evangelienbruchstücke und das Problem der Pešiṭta', in: *Oriens Christianus* III, 11 (1936), pp. 153–162.

Philipps, W. R.: 'The Connection of St. Thomas the Apostle with India', in: *IndAnt* 32 (1903), pp. 1–15 & 145–160.

Pigoulewsky, N.: 'Fragments Syriaques et Syro-Turcs de Hara-Hoto et de Tourfan', in: *Revue de l'Orient Chrétien* 30 (1935–1936), pp. 3–46.

Ploeg, J. P. M. van der: *The Christians of St. Thomas in South India and their Syriac Manuscripts*, Bangalore 1983 (Placid Lectures Series).

Podipara, P.: 'The Social and Socio-Economic Customs of the Syrian Christians of India', in: *Eastern Churches Quarterly* 7 (1947), pp. 223–235.

—— 'The South Indian Apostolate of St. Thomas', in: *OCP* 18 (1952), pp. 234–236.

—— *The Thomas Christians*, London 1970.

Pollet, G. (ed.): *India and the Ancient World. History, Trade and Culture before A. D. 650 [. . .]*, Louvain 1987 (OLA 25).

Polo, M.: *The Book of Ser Marco Polo, the Venetian, Concerning the Kingdoms and Marvels of the East*, trans. and ed. with notes by H. Yule, 3rd ed., revised, vol. 2, London 1903.

—— *Travels*, with an introduction by J. Masefield, London 1908 (Everyman's Library).

Poppe, N.: 'A Middle Turkic Text of the Apostles' Creed', in: *MSer* 24 (1965), pp. 273–306.

Pothan, S. G.: *The Syrian Christians of Kerala*, London & Bombay 1963.

Puech, H.-Ch.: 'Gnostic Gospels and Related Documents', in: Hennecke, E. & Schneemelcher, W. (eds.), *New Testament Apocrypha*, vol. 1, London 1963, pp. 231–362.

Puskás, I.: 'Trade Contacts between India and the Roman Empire', in: Pollet, G. (ed.), *India and the Ancient World. History, Trade and Culture before A. D. 650 [. . .]*, Louvain 1987 (OLA 25), pp. 141–156.

Puthiakunnel, Th.: 'Jewish Colonies of India Paved the Way for St. Thomas', in: Vellian, J. (ed.), *The Malabar Church [. . .]*, Rome 1970 (OCA 186), pp. 187–191.

Quispel, G.: 'The Discussion of Judaic Christianity', in: *VigChr* 22 (1968), pp. 81–93.

Rachewiltz, I. de: *Papal Envoys to the Great Khans*, London 1971 (Great Travellers).

Rae, G. M.: *The Syrian Church in India*, Edinburgh & London 1892.

Ramstedt, G. J.: 'Zwei uigurische Runeninschriften in der Nord-Mongolei', in: *JSFO* 30 (1913–1918), pp. 3–5.

—— 'Reste des Nestorianismus unter den Mongolen', in: *JSFO* 55 (1951), pp. 40–46.

Rawlinson, H. G.: *Intercourse between India and the Western World from the Earliest Times to the Fall of Rome*, Cambridge 1916.

Reeves, J. C.: *Jewish Lore in Manichaean Cosmogony. Studies in the Book of Giants Traditions*, Cincinnati 1992 (Monographs of the Hebrew Union College 14).

Richard, J.: 'Le christianisme dans l'Asie centrale', in: *JAH* 16 (1982), pp. 101–124.

Richards, W. J.: *The Indian Christians of St. Thomas [. . .]*, London & Derby 1908.

Richter, J.: *A History of Missions in India*, trans. by S. H. Moore, Edinburgh 1908.

Robinson, J. M. (ed.): *The Nag Hammadi Library in English*, 3rd ed., Leiden 1988.

Rockhill, W. W. (trans. & ed.): *The Journey of William of Rubruck to the Eastern Part of the World, 1253–55, as Narrated by Himself [. . .]*, (1900), repr., London 1941.

Rosenfield, J. M.: *The Dynastic Arts of the Kushans*, Berkeley & Los Angeles 1967 (California studies in the history of art 6).

Rosenkranz, G.: 'Die älteste Christenheit in China in den nestorianischen Quellenzeugnissen der Tang-Zeit', in: *ZMR* 52 (1937), pp. 193–226; 241–280.

—— *Die älteste Christenheit in China in den Quellenzeugnissen der Nestorianer-Texte der Tang-Dynastie*, Berlin 1938 (Schriftenreihe der Ostasien-Mission 3/4).

Runciman, S.: *The Medieval Manichee. A Study of the Christian Dualist Heresy*, (1947), repr., Cambridge 1955.

Sachau, E.: 'Litteratur-Bruchstücke aus Chinesisch-Turkistan', in: *SPAW* 1905, pp. 964–978.

—— 'Die Christianisierungs-Legende von Merw', in: Frankenberg, W. & Küchler, F. (eds.), *Abhandlungen zur semitischen Religionskunde und Sprachwissenschaft [. . .]*, Giessen 1918, pp. 399–409.

—— *Zur Ausbreitung des Christentums in Asien*, Berlin 1919 (APAW 1919, 1).

Saeki, P. Y.: *The Nestorian Documents and Relics in China*, 2nd ed., Tokyo 1951.

Sagaster, K.: *Die weisse Geschichte (Čaɣan teüke). Eine mongolische Quelle zur Lehre von den Beiden Ordnungen Religion und Staat in Tibet und der Mongolei*, Wiesbaden 1976 (AsF 41).

Sahas, D. J.: *John of Damascus on Islam. The 'Heresy of the Ishmaelites'*, Leiden 1972.

Saunders, J. J.: 'The Decline and Fall of Christianity in Medieval Asia', in: *JRH* 5 (1968–1969), pp. 93–104.

Savage, A. (trans. & ed.): *The Anglo-Saxon Chronicles*, London 1982.

Schlingloff, D.: 'Traditions of Indian Narrative Painting in Central Asia', in: *Akṣayanīvī. Essays Presented to Dr. Debala Mitra*, Delhi 1991, pp. 163–169.

Schmidt-Glintzer, H.: 'Das buddhistische Gewand des Manichäismus. Zur buddhistischen Terminologie in den chinesischen Manichaica', in: Heissig, W. & Klimkeit, H.-J. (eds.), *Synkretismus in den Religionen Zentralasiens [. . .]*, Wiesbaden 1987 (StOR 13), pp. 76–90.

—— (ed.): *Chinesische Manichaica. Mit textkritischen Anmerkungen und einem Glossar*, Wiesbaden 1987 (StOR 14).

Schneemelcher, W. (ed.): *Neutestamentliche Apokryphen in deutscher Übersetzung*, vol. 1: *Evangelien*, 6th ed., Tübingen 1990; vol. 2: *Apostolisches, Apokalypsen und Verwandtes*, 5th ed., Tübingen 1989.

Schoeps, H.-J.: *Das Judenchristentum. Untersuchungen über Gruppenbildungen und Parteikämpfe in der frühen Christenheit*, Bern & Munich 1964 (Dalp-Taschenbücher 376).

Schurhammer, G.: *The Malabar Church and Rome during the Early Portuguese Period and Before*, Trichinopoly 1934.

Schwaigert, W.: *Das Christentum in Ḥūzistān im Rahmen der frühen Kirchengeschichte Persiens bis zur Synode von Seleukia-Ktesiphon im Jahre 410*, [Dr. theol. thesis, Philipps-Universität], Marburg 1989.

Schwartz, M.: 'Sogdian Fragments of the *Book of Psalms*', in: *AoF* 1 (1974), pp. 257–261.

—— *Studies in the Texts of Sogdian Christians*, [PhD thesis, University of California], Berkeley 1967.

Segal, J. B.: *Edessa, 'the Blessed City'*, Oxford 1970.

Sellers, R. V.: *The Council of Chalcedon. A Historical and Doctrinal Survey*, London 1953.

—— *Two Ancient Christologies. A Study in the Christological Thought of the Schools of Alexandria and Antioch in the Early History of Christian Doctrine*, (1940), repr., London 1954 (Church Historical Society. Publications. N. S. 39).

Semenov, G. L.: 'Zum Christentum in Mittelasien. Archäologische Funde in Sogdien', in: Semenov, G. L.: *Studien zur sogdischen Kultur an der Seidenstrasse*, Wiesbaden 1996 (StOR 36), pp. 57–68.

Serjeant , R. B.: *Studies in Arabian History and Civilization*, London 1981 (CStS 145).

Sims-Williams, N.: 'A Sogdian Fragment of a Work of Dadišoʻ Qaṭraya', in: *Asia Major* 18 (1973), pp. 88–105.

—— 'The Sogdian Fragments of the British Library', in: *Indo-Iranian Journal* 18 (1976), pp. 43–74.

—— 'Syro-Sogdica I: An Anonymous Homily on the Three Periods of the Solitary Life', in: *OCP* 47 (1981), pp. 441–446.

—— 'Syro-Sogdica II: A Metrical Homily by Bābay bar Nṣibnāye «On the Final Evil Hour»', in: *OCP* 48 (1982), pp. 171–176.

—— *The Christian Sogdian Manuscript C 2*, Berlin 1985 (BT 12).

—— 'Syro-Sogdica III: Syriac Elements in Sogdian', in: *A Green Leaf*. Papers in Honour of Professor Jes P. Asmussen, Leiden 1988 (Acta Iranica 26), pp. 145–156.

—— 'Die christlich-sogdischen Handschriften von Bulayïq', in: Klengel, H. & Sundermann, W. (eds.), *Ägypten, Vorderasien, Turfan. Probleme der Edition und Bearbeitung altorientalischer Handschriften [. . .]*, Berlin 1991 (SGKAO 23), pp. 119–125.

—— 'Sogdian and Turkish Christians in the Turfan and Tun-huang Manuscripts', in: Cadonna, A. (ed.), *Turfan and Tun-huang. The Texts. Encounter of Civilizations on the Silk Route*, Florence 1992 (Orientalia Venetiana 4), pp. 43–61.

—— 'The Sogdian Inscriptions of Ladakh', in: Jettmar, K. et al. (eds.), *Antiquities of Northern Pakistan. Reports and Studies*, vol. 2, Mainz 1993, pp. 151–163.

—— 'Dādišoʻ Qaṭrāyā's Commentary on the *Paradiese of the Fathers*', in: *Analecta Bollandiana* 112 (1994), pp. 33–64.

—— 'Christian Sogdian Texts from the Nachlass of Olaf Hansen I: Fragments of the Life of Serapion', in: *BSOAS* 63 (1995), pp. 50–68.

—— & Hamilton, J.: *Documents turco-sogdiens du IXᵉ – Xᵉ siècle de Touen-houang*, London 1990 (Corpus Inscriptionum Iranicarum, Part II, 3).

Sinor, D.: 'John of Plano Carpini's Return from the Mongols. New Light from a Luxemburg Manuscript', in: *JRAS* 1957, pp. 193–206.

Smith, M.: *Studies in Early Mysticism in the Near and Middle East [. . .]*, (1931), repr., Amsterdam 1973.

Smith, V. A.: *The Early History of India*, 4th ed., Oxford 1924.

Somaratne, G. P. V.: 'Pre-Portuguese Christianity in Sri Lanka', in: *Indian Church History Review* 23 (1989), pp. 144–155.

Spuler, B.: 'Die Mongolen und das Christentum. Die letzte Blütezeit der morgenländischen Kirchen', in: *Internationale Kirchliche Zeitschrift* 28 (1938), pp. 156–175.

—— *Die Mongolen in Iran. Politik, Verwaltung und Kultur der Ilchanzeit 1220–1350,* 2nd ed., Berlin 1955

—— *Iran in früh-islamischer Zeit. Politik, Kultur, Verwaltung und öffentliches Leben zwischen der arabischen und der seldschukischen Eroberung 633 bis 1055,* Wiesbaden 1952 (Akademie der Wissenschaften und der Literatur. Veröffentlichungen der orientalischen Kommission 2).

—— *Die morgenländischen Kirchen,* offprint from Handbuch der Orientalistik I, 8, 2, Leiden & Cologne 1964.

—— 'Die armenische Kirche', in: *Monumentum H. S. Nyberg* II, Leiden 1975 (Acta Iranica 5), pp. 251–263.

—— 'Syrisches Christentum in Vorderasien und Südindien', in: *Saeculum* 32 (1981), pp. 242–254.

Stawiskij, B. J.: *Die Völker Mittelasiens im Lichte ihrer Kunstdenkmäler. Archäologische Reise durch die Geschichte Alt-Mittelasiens [. . .],* Bonn 1982.

Steinilber-Oberlin, É.: *The Buddhist Sects of Japan. Their History, Philosophical Doctrines and Sanctuaries,* (1938), repr., Westport, Conn. 1976.

Stewart, J.: *Nestorian Missionary Enterprise. The Story of a Church on Fire [. . .],* (1928), repr., New York 1979.

Sundermann, W.: 'Christliche Evangelientexte in der Überlieferung der iranisch-manichäischen Literatur', in: *MIO* 14 (1968), pp. 386–405.

—— 'Zur frühen missionarischen Wirksamkeit Manis', in: *AOH* 24 (1971), pp. 79–125.

—— 'Einige Bemerkungen zum syrisch-neupersischen Psalmenbruchstück aus Chinesisch-Turkistan', in: Gignoux, G. & Tafazzoli, A. (eds.), *Mémorial Jean de Menasce,* Louvain 1974, pp. 441–452.

—— 'Nachlese zu F. W. K. Müllers "Sogdischen Texten I"', in: *AoF* 1 (1974), pp. 217–255; 3 (1975), 55–90; 8 (1981), 169–225.

—— 'Ein Bruchstück einer soghdischen Kirchengeschichte aus Zentralasien?', in: *AA* 14 (1976), pp. 95–101.

—— *Mitteliranische manichäische Texte kirchengeschichtlichen Inhalts,* Berlin 1981 (BT 11).

—— 'Ein weiteres Fragment aus Manis Gigantenbuch', in: *Orientalia J. Duchesne-Guillemin oblata,* Leiden 1984 (Acta Iranica 23), pp. 491–505.

—— 'Der Schüler fragt den Lehrer. Eine Sammlung biblischer Rätsel in soghdischer Sprache', in: *A Green Leaf.* Papers in Honour of Professor Jes P. Asmussen, Leiden 1988 (Acta Iranica 28), pp. 173–186.

—— *The Manicaean Hymn Cycles Huyadagmān and Angad Rōšnān in Parthian and Sogdian,* London 1990 (Corpus Inscriptionum Iranicarum, Supplementary Series 2).

—— 'Byzanz und Bulayïq', in: Vavroušek, P. (ed.), *Iranian and Indo-European Studies.* Memorial Volume of O. Klíma, Prague 1994, pp. 255–264.

Tarn, W. W.: *The Greeks in Bactria and India,* (1926), 2nd ed., Cambridge 1951.

Taube, M.: *Geheime Geschichte der Mongolen. Herkunft, Leben und Aufstieg Cinggis Qans,* Munich 1989 (Orientalische Bibliothek).

Taylor, J. E.: 'The Phenomenon of Early Jewish-Christianity. Reality or Scholarly Invention', in: *VigChr* 44 (1990), pp. 313–334.

Taylor, W. R.: 'Syriac MSS Found in Peking, ca. 1925', in: *JAOS* 61 (1941), pp. 91–97.

Tekin, Ş.: *Maitrisimit nom bitig. Die uigurische Übersetzung eines Werkes der buddhistischen Vaibhāṣika-Schule,* 2 vols., Berlin 1983 (BT 9).

Tekin, T.: *A Grammar of Orkhon Turkic*, The Hague 1968 (Indiana University Publications. Uralic and Altaic Series 69).

Thacker, T. W.: 'A Nestorian Gravestone from Central Asia in the Gulbenkian Museum, Durham University', in: *The Durham University Journal* 59, N. S. 28 (1966–1967), pp. 94–107.

Thilo, T.: 'Ausländer und Kostbarkeiten. Zu einem Motiv der Erzählungsliteratur der Tang-Zeit', in: *AoF* 11 (1984), pp. 149–173.

Thomas, P.: *Christians and Christianity in India and Pakistan. A General Survey of the Progress of Christianity in India from Apostolic Times to the Present Day*, London 1954.

Thompson, E. A.: 'Christian Missionaries among the Huns', in: *Hermathena* 67 (1946), pp. 73–79.

Thurston, E.: *Castes and Tribes of Southern India*, vol. 6, Madras 1909.

Tisserant, E. *Eastern Christianity in India. A History of the Syro-Malabar Church from the Earliest Time to the Present Day [. . .]*, authorized adaptation from the French by E. R. Hambye, London 1957.

Toumanoff, C.: 'Armenia and Georgia', in: Hussey, J. M. (ed.), *The Cambridge Medieval History* 4 (1), Cambridge 1966, pp. 593–637 & 983–1009.

Trimingham, J. S.: *Christianity among the Arabs in Pre-Islamic Times*, London 1979 (Arab Background Series).

Tritton, A. S.: *The Caliphs and their Non-Muslim Subjects. A Critical Study of the Covenant of 'Umar*, London 1970 (Islam and the Muslim World 14).

Troll, Chr. W.: 'Die Chinamission im Mittelalter', in: *Franziskanische Studien* 48 (1966), pp. 109–150; 49 (1967), pp. 22–79.

Tsui Chi: 'Mo Ni Chiao Hsia Pu Tsan. "The Lower (Second?) Section of the Manichaean Hymns"', in: *BSOAS* 11 (1943–1946), pp. 174–219 [pp. 216–219: W. B. Henning, 'Annotations to Mr. Tsui's Translation'].

Uray, G., 'Tibet's Connection with Nestorianism and Manichaeism in the 8th–10th Centuries', in: Steinkellner, E. & Tauscher, H. (eds.), *Contributions on Tibetan Language, History and Culture*, vol. 1, Vienna 1983, pp. 399–429.

—— 'Zu den Spuren des Nestorianismus und des Manichäismus im alten Tibet (8. – 10. Jh.)', in: Heissig, W. & Klimkeit, H.-J. (eds.), *Synkretismus in den Religionen Zentralasiens [. . .]*, Wiesbaden 1987 (StOR 13), pp. 197–206.

Vásáry, I.: 'Orthodox Christian Qumans and Tatars of the Crimea in the 13th–14th Centuries', in: *CAJ* 32 (1988), pp. 260–271.

Vine, A. R.: *The Nestorian Churches. A Concise History of Nestorian Christianity in Asia from the Persian Schism to the Modern Assyrians [. . .]*, (1937), repr., New York 1980.

Vööbus, A.: *Celibacy: A Requirement for Admission to Baptism in the Early Syrian Church*, Stockholm 1951 (PETSE 1).

—— 'The Origin of Monasticism in Mesopotamia', in: *ChH* 20 (1951), pp. 27–37.

—— *Literary, Critical and Historical Studies in Ephrem the Syrian*, Stockholm 1958 (PETSE 10).

—— *History of Asceticism in the Syrian Orient. A Contribution to the History of Culture in the Near East*, 2 vols., Louvain 1958 & 1960 (CSCO.Sub 14 & 17).

—— (ed. & trans.): *Syriac and Arabic Documents Regarding Legislation Relative to Syrian Asceticism*, Stockholm 1960.

—— *The Statutes of the School of Nisibis*, Stockholm 1961 (PETSE 12).

—— *A History of the School of Nisibis*, Louvain 1965 (CSCO.Sub 26).

—— 'The Origin of the Monophysite Church in Syria and Mesopotamia', in: *ChH* 42 (1973), pp. 17–26.

Wallace-Hadrill, D. S.: *Christian Antioch. A Study of Early Christian Thought in the East*, Cambridge 1982.

Wand, J. W. C.: *The Four Great Heresies*, London 1955.

Warmington, E. H.: *The Commerce between the Roman Empire and India*, (1928), repr., London 1974.

Waterfield, R. E.: *Christians in Persia. Assyrians, Armenians, Roman Catholics and Protestants*, London 1973.

Watt, W. M.: *The Majesty that was Islam. The Islamic World, 661 – 1100*, London 1974.

Wensinck, A. J. & Johnstone, P.: 'Maryam', in: *The Encyclopaedia of Islam. New Edition* 6 (1991), pp. 628–632.

Wensinck, A. J. & Jomier, J.: 'Ka'ba', in: *The Encyclopaedia of Islam. New Edition* 4 (1990), pp. 316–322.

Wheeler, R. E. M. et al.: 'Arikamedu: An Indo-Roman Trading Station on the East Coast of India', in: *Ancient India* 2 (1946), pp. 17–124.

Whitfield, R.: *The Art of Central Asia. The Stein Collection in the British Museum*, vol. 1: *Paintings from Dunhuang*, Tokyo 1982.

Widengren, G.: *Mani and Manichaeism*, trans. by Ch. Kessler. London 1965.

—— *Die Religionen Irans*, Stuttgart 1965 (RM 14).

—— 'The Nestorian Church in Sasanian and Early Post-Sasanian Iran', in: Lanciotti, L. (ed.), *Incontro di religioni in Asia tra il III e il X secolo d.C.*, Florence 1984, pp. 1–30.

Wiesehofer, J.: 'Geteilte Loyalitäten. Religiöse Minderheiten des 3. und 4. Jh. n. Chr. im Spannungsfeld zwischen Rom und dem sasanidischen Iran', in: *Klio* 75 (1993), pp. 362–382.

Wiessner, G. & Klimkeit, H.-J. (eds.), *Studia Manichaica. II. Internationaler Kongress zum Manichäismus [. . .]*, Wiesbaden 1992 (StOR 23).

Wigram, W. A.: *An Introduction to the History of the Assyrian Church or the Church of the Sassanid Persian Empire 100–640 A. D. [. . .]*, London 1910.

Willeke, B. H.: 'Did Catholicism in the Yuan Dynasty Survive until the Present?', in: *Tripod* 47 (1988), pp. 64–69.

Williams, H. A.: *Some Day I'll Find You. An Autobiography*, London 1984.

Wilson, R. McL.: 'Gnosis, Gnosticism and the New Testament', in: Bianchi, U. (ed.), *Le origini dello gnosticismo [. . .]*, Leiden 1967 (SHR 12), pp. 511–527.

Winckworth, C. P. T.: 'A New Interpretation of the Pahlavī Cross-Inscriptions of Southern India', in: *Journal of Theological Studies* 30 (1929), pp. 237–244.

Young, W. G.: *Handbook of Source Materials for Students of Church History up to 650 A. D.*, Madras 1969 (Indian Theological Library 2).

—— *Patriarch, Shah and Caliph. A Study of the Relationships of the Church of the East with the Sassanid Empire and the Early Caliphates with Special Reference to Available Translated Syriac Sources*, Rawalpindi 1974.

Yule, H. (trans. & ed.): *Cathay and the Way thither [. . .]*, new ed. by H. Cordier, 4 vols., London 1913–1916.

Zaehner, R. C.: *Zurvan. A Zoroastrian Dilemma*, Oxford 1955.

—— *The Dawn and Twilight of Zoroastrianism*, (1961), repr., London 1975.

Zarrīnkūb, 'Abd Al-Ḥ.: 'The Arab Conquest of Iran and its Aftermath', in: R. N. Frye (ed.), *The Cambridge History of Iran* 4, Cambridge 1975, pp. 1–56.

Zieme, P.: 'Zu den nestorianisch-türkischen Turfantexten', in: Hazai, G. & Zieme, P. (eds.), *Sprache, Geschichte und Kultur der altaischen Völker [. . .]*, Berlin 1974 (SGKAO 5), pp. 661–668.

—— 'Zwei Ergänzungen zu der christlich-türkischen Handschrift T II B 1', in: *AoF* 5 (1977), pp. 271f.

—— 'Ein Hochzeitssegen uigurischer Christen', in: Röhrborn, K. & Brands, H. W. (eds.), *Scholia. Beiträge zur Turkologie und Zentralasienkunde [. . .]*, Wiesbaden 1981 (Veröffentlichungen der Societas Uralo-Altaica 74), pp. 221–232.

—— 'Uigurische Steuerbefreiungsurkunden für buddhistische Klöster', in: *AoF* 8 (1981), pp. 237–263.

—— *Buddhistische Stabreimdichtungen der Uiguren*, Berlin 1985 (BT 13).

—— & Kudara, K.: *Guanwuliangshoujing in Uigur*, Kyoto 1985.

Index